HANDFULS
ON PURPOSE

HANDFULS ON PURPOSE

for Christian Workers and
Bible Students

SERIES VII-IX

by

James Smith

WILLIAM B. EERDMANS PUBLISHING COMPANY
Grand Rapids, Michigan

Guide to Series 1 to 12

SERIES 1 to 10 .. By Pastor JAMES SMITH
SERIES 11 and 12, .. By ROBERT LEE
SERIES 13, .. COMPLETE INDEX TO SERIES

PREFACE.

IT is with deep thankfulness to the Giver of every good gift that we send forth this SEVENTH Series of "Handfuls on Purpose." It is very gratifying to us that the interest taken in them has been steadily growing since the first; and as they have been the means of leading many Christian workers into a closer study of the Word for themselves, we rejoice, as this was one of the chief objects of their publication.

We hoped at first to publish, perhaps, *four* volumes of these Outlines Studies, thinking that they might be quite sufficient to cover the whole Bible in the manner in which we had purposed to deal with it. But this is now Volume *Seven*, and we have only managed to get about half through the Book. Although we have made some gallant attempts to get over the ground more quickly, yet, somehow, the further we go, the attractions to linger becomes growingly powerful.

We should like, if the Lord will, to issue other three volumes, and so complete the blessed task that has been on our heart to do unto His Name. But perhaps this will depend on whether our many friends, who have hitherto received them gladly, will care to continue their favour to such an extent. For the many grateful expressions that reach us of the helpfulness of these books, we seek to praise Him, from whom all blessings flow.

JAMES SMITH.

INDEX OF SUBJECTS.

INDEX OF SUBJECTS—Continued.

INDEX OF TEXTS.

INDEX OF TEXTS—Continued.

Handfuls on Purpose

SERIES VII

Old Testament Outlines

STUDIES IN JOB

JOB'S CHARACTER

JOB 1. 1-10

"My strength is as the strength of ten
Because my heart is pure."—TENNYSON

THIS book, supposed to have been first committed to
writing by Moses, is regarded by many as the
oldest in the world. Its object is to set before us the trial
of an "upright man." Job himself is quite unconscious of
the fact that he is being used by God as an object-lesson to
all generations; he knows nothing at all about the conference that has taken place concerning him, recorded in
verses 7 to 12. The days of Job were probably about the
time of Abraham, as in the book there is no mention of
Israel, the Tabernacle, the Temple, or the Law. The
book is of great value as a revelation of the forces that are
at work against the life of the righteous. All the characters
are representative: Job, the servant of God; Satan, the
adversary; the three Friends, the wisdom of the world;
Elihu, the wisdom of God; God, the Judge of all. That

Job was no mythical character is clearly proven in Ezekiel
14. 14 and 20, when his name is mentioned by Jehovah
Himself. As the teaching of this book is centred in the
person of Job, we shall try and grasp its leading principles
through this *man*, that they may, if possible, become more
interesting and powerful in our own individual lives.

I. **He was Perfect.** "Perfect and upright, one that
feared God, and eschewed evil" (v. 1). "There is none
like him in the earth" (v. 8). As a man, he was all that
a man in those days could be in holiness of character.
That there was "none like him in the earth" is not his own
testimony, but the statement of Him who knows what is in
man. "The Lord knoweth them that trust in Him"
(Nahum 1. 7). He was perfect, not in the sense of being
sinless, but in the sense of being *plainly* (Heb.) devoted to
God and to righteousness. He was transparently upright,
according to his knowledge and ability. He walked in the
light, although that light may have been but twilight.
Like an honest man, Job straightened himself up, morally,
before God and men. His character is in strong contrast to
the multitude of men who, like the woman in the Gospel,
are so "bowed down" with the love of the world, and the
fear of man, that they can in no wise lift themselves up.
Love and lust are fetters that bind the souls of men as
with iron bands.

II. **He was Rich.** "His substance was 7000 sheep,
3000 camels, 500 yoke of oxen," etc.; "so that he was the
greatest of all the men of the east" (v. 3). Good men
are not always rich; but God had surely put a premium on
the goodness and faithfulness of Job, by allowing *him* to
become the wealthiest man in the country. The *best* man
will always be the richest, if not in material goods, certainly in the more enduring treasures that are spiritual and
Divine. Although there was a gulf of agony between Job's

present and future life, yet he found that it paid to be
righteous. The *perfect* man will be upright, will fear God
and hate evil, if all his worldly possessions should need to
be sacrificed for this end. If his riches increase—even
spiritual riches—he sets not his heart on *them*.

III. **He was Wise.** "Job rose up early in the morning
and offered burnt-offerings for all his family, for he said,
It may be that my sons have sinned and cursed God in
their hearts. This did Job *continually*" (v. 5). These
family gatherings, for social enjoyment, were in themselves
a good testimony to their upright and priestly father.
Those seven sons must have been well brought up, when
they sought so often the fellowship of one another, and did
not fail to give their three sisters a special invitation to
their parties. Job did not forbid such festivities, but he
knew human nature too well to suppose that there was no
moral danger connected with such seasons. "It may be
that my sons have sinned." When it is a question of
pleasure-seeking it is so easy to forget God, and to act in
such a way as to dishonour His holy Name. So Job, as
priest in his own family, offers a sacrifice for each of his
sons. As a wise father, he is most concerned that his sons
should be kept right with God. It is not enough for the
"perfect man" that his family should be healthy and happy
and prosperous in the world; he longs intensely, and spares
no sacrifice, that they might *each one* live and walk in the
fear and favour of God. *Sin* against God is that one thing
which his upright soul has learned to hate.

IV. **He was Protected.** "Hast Thou not made an
hedge about *him*, and about his *house*, and about *all that he
hath* on every side?" (v. 10). His person, his family,
and his property, were hedged about by the special care of
God. Three circles of defences had been raised about him.
He and his were as the vineyard of the Lord (Isa. 5. 1, 2).

Satan seems to have known more about the impregnable position of Job than Job himself. His fear of God had made him safer than he thought. The God of yesterday is the same God to-day. We cannot see that "angel of the Lord that *encampeth round about* them that fear Him," but the Devil does. Hedges of the Lord's making are too thick even for the cunning hand of Satan. Satan's testimony to the security of God's children is of great value. Without God's permission his great power is utterly useless against the man that is hiding in the bulwarks of his God. "God is our refuge...therefore will not we fear."

V. He was Marked. "The Lord said unto Satan, Hast thou *considered* My servant Job...Then Satan answered, Doth Job fear God for nought?" (vv. 8, 9). Job, being a perfect and upright man, was an object of special consideration to the Lord and to Satan. He was a marked man for the favour of the Lord, and for the envy and hate of Satan. Both God and the Devil marks the perfect man (Psa. 37. 37). The divine consideration is all for our safety and usefulness—the Satanic consideration is how to disturb and destroy. Is it not true in a sense, of every "perfect man in Christ Jesus," that they become the special objects of assault by the powers of darkness? When Joshua, the high priest, was seen "standing before the angel of the Lord," Satan was seen "standing at his right hand to *resist* him" (Zech. 3. 1). Why was Satan so desirous to have Simon Peter that he might sift him as wheat? Did he dread lest that warm impetuous nature should be wholly yielded to the cause of Jesus Christ? Those whom Satan and his host takes no trouble at must be accomplishing very little for God. Heaven and Hell marks the holy man. Put on the whole armour of God, that ye may be able to stand against the wiles of the Devil.

JOB'S ADVERSARY.

JOB 1. 6-22; 2. 1-10.

"When the fight begins within himself
A man's worth something."—BROWNING.

JOB'S case was typical. Ye have *heard* of his patience, as ye have *seen* the faith of Abraham, and the meekness of Moses. Job's desperate struggle is allowed to take place in the open arena, that we might learn the secret of resistance. It is a battle between the best of men and the worst of enemies. Satan does his best to crush and overthrow the integrity of this "perfect man" who has been incased with the special providence of God, and who can offer but a passive resistance. Although God's environments were everything that could be desired, he was not proof against the powerful temptations of the Devil. The environments of Christ Himself did not save Him from Satanic assaults. Job had a good house, and a good income, but houses and wages are not everything that men need, if they would stand firm against all the deadly wiles of the Devil. About this enemy of all righteousness, let us not forget—

I. **His Personality.** According to the teaching of Scripture there is but one Devil, but many demons. The apostles and evangelists in referring to him always speak in the singular, and this they do about thirty times. "Get behind Me Satan" could never be said of a mere impersonal influence. He is a *liar* from the beginning, an influence cannot lie. Only men and devils can lie. All lying is devilish, and devilishness proves there is a Devil.

II. **His Origin.** "The Lord said unto Satan, *Whence comest thou?* Then Satan answered, From going to and fro in the earth, and from walking up and down in it" (v. 7). The same mystery that hangs over the fact of sin, hangs over the origin of Satan. When our Lord says that he was a murderer, and a liar, *from the beginning*, it is difficult to believe that he has ever béen anything better. According to his own confession, his sphere of work is "going to and fro in the earth." His domain is the world, and his condition is one of eternal restlessness. That Satan and his demon host are the disembodied spirits of a pre-Adamic race, that brought the condemnation of God upon them because of sin, is a theory not without some attractions.

III. **His Object.** His unwavering purpose is to set God and man at variance (v. 11). In his devilish business he is, alas, too often successful. Before he attempted the separation of Job from his God, he had succeeded with Adam and with Cain, and afterwards with Saul and with Judas, and a multitude of others. There is no man in all the earth that annoys Satan so much as the "perfect man." He directs all his energy against the praying, sacrificing man. While Jesus Christ was on the earth, the forces of Hell were continually meeting Him in one form or another. The names given to Satan in the Scriptures are strongly indicative of his character and purpose. He is the *Adversary*; the *Accuser* of the brethren; the *Murderer*; the Prince of *darkness*; the Prince of *this world*; the roaring *lion*. He is the god of this lost world; the ruler of its darkness. He is the opposer and the accuser of the brethren; the liar against the truth, and the murderer of souls. "*Resist* the Devil, and he will flee from you" (James 4. 7).

IV. **His Power.** That Satan is capable of great power as well as great wrath is unquestionable. But he is utterly powerless to touch a child of God, or anything that he has, without His permission. Satan was allowed to send his messengers, one after another, to buffet Job, just as he was afterwards permitted to do with the Apostle Paul (2 Cor.

12. 7), and blessed be God, with much the same result. Although the Devil may be allowed at times to sift, he is not allowed to devour the wheat: "Behold all that he hath is in thy power; only upon himself put not forth thine hand" (v. 12). So far, but no farther. Then when this adversary made his second challenge, the Lord said, "Behold *he* is in thine hand, but save his life" (chap. 2. 6). It was a long rope this roaring lion got, and he used every inch of it. He had got access to everything but the spirit of this evil-hating man, and having received liberty to exercise his fiendish art, we soon discover where the secret of his power lies. He finds his mighty weapons in the Sabeans, the Chaldeans, the lightning, and the wind (vv. 15-19). That he should be able to commandeer such forces is a revelation of his wonderful power and resources. The Devil has two arsenals, one in the heavens, and the other in the earth, namely, the *elements*, and the *hearts* of ungodly men. Such an enemy is not to be trifled with.

V. **His Manner of Working.** His first act is, to get himself away out of the presence of God. "So Satan went forth from the presence of the Lord" (v. 12). Satan, and all his host, seen and unseen, whether they be men or demons, love the darkness rather than the light, because their deeds are evil. He has a great task before him— to break down a perfect man's confidence in his God— so he waits for the best time to make the attack. That opportune day arrived when Job's "sons and daughters were eating and drinking in their eldest brother's house" (v. 13). To get at Job, the Devil had to break down the outside fences first; this he did by prevailing upon *men* to steal his oxen, his asses, his camels, and to kill his servants. Little, perhaps, did these men think that when they were helping themselves to the property of Job, they were the

agents of the Devil carrying out his diabolical ends. The
same spirit is *now working* in the children of disobedience
(Eph. 2. 2). Ungodly men are tools lying ready at hand
for the work of Satan. He entered Judas just because he
was a fit person for the accomplishment of his 'fiendish
purposes against the Son of God. He sent *fire from the
heavens*, and burned up the sheep, to make Job believe that
it was a judgment from God. Satan surely thought this
was a master-stroke, when the servant whom he had spared
to carry the tidings went and said, "The *fire of God* is fallen
from Heaven, and hath burned up the sheep" (v. 16).
If Satan can only get God's people to believe when the
time of affliction and testing comes, that God is against
them, he has gained a victory. He was very careful to
spare one, who might run to Job, saying, "I *only* am
escaped *alone* to tell thee." The *I*'s here are most emphatic. The *method* he adopted in breaking the news to
Job was in itself devilish. The Devil's wheat is all bran.
King Canute promised to make the man who would kill
King Edmund, his rival, the highest man in England; he
fulfilled his promise by hanging him on the *highest* tower
in London. We fight not against flesh and blood, but against
"*wicked spirits*," which use flesh and blood as their instruments in seeking to overthrow our faith in God. We are
not ignorant of his devices; give no place to the Devil.

JOB'S TRIALS.
JOB 1. 13-22; 2. 1-10.

"Satan desires us, great and small,
　　As wheat to sift us, and we all are tempted.
Not one, however, rich or great,
　　Is by his station or estate exempted."
　　　　　　　　　　　　　　　　—LONGFELLOW.

THE very name of Job means persecuted. In his unique
trials he is the prototype of Christ. Every perfect man

will have his Eden to enjoy, his Isaac to sacrifice, and his wilderness of severe and prolonged testing. It is through much tribulation that we enter into the kingdom of God's greater fullness and power. No affliction for the present is joyous, but grievous, but, nevertheless, *afterward* it yieldeth the peaceable fruits of righteousness to them that are exercised thereby. Was there ever a man more exercised about his troubles than Job? But meanwhile we shall look at—

I. **Their Purpose**. Two cross-purposes find their centre in Job. The one was Divine, the other was Satanic. Satan said, "Doth Job fear God for nought?...Put forth Thine hand now, and touch all that he hath, and he will curse Thee to Thy face" (vv. 9-11). Satan did not believe that any man would remain true to God if bereft of all material and earthly enjoyment. If Job staggered under such a test, Jesus Christ did not. He had not where to lay His head. He was *"the* Man of Sorrows," yet He always did those things which were pleasing to His Father. Job, being utterly unconscious that he was being used in this fashion as a test case, must have felt it as a severe trial of his *faith*. Well the Devil knows, that if men are going to overcome the world by *faith*, his power is broken, and his kingdom lost. It has been so since the beginning; those who would fear God, and eschew evil, must fight the good fight of faith.

II. **Their Nature**. The character of Job's troubles was of the worst kind. There were no half measures. Every separate trial was a complete catastrophe. There was the—

1. LOSS OF PROPERTY. His "seven thousand sheep, three thousand camels, five hundred yoke of oxen, and five hundred asses," were all suddenly stolen, or burned up with fire from Heaven. The richest man in the east had in

one day become a bankrupt. That in itself would have driven many a one into absolute despair.

2. Loss of Family. Seven sons and three daughters all killed by one terrific stroke (v. 19). This judgment must have been "a great deep" to the upright, sensitive soul of Job (Psa. 36. 6). There is no natural law by which such workings of the providence of God can be understood. The dominion of faith, for the spirit of man, is beyond nature.

3. Loss of Health. "Satan went forth and smote Job with sore boils from the sole of his foot unto his crown" (chap. 2. 7). He was covered with a loathsome disease; there was no soundness in his flesh. Like Lazarus, he was "full of sores." This bodily affliction, like the others, came suddenly. He had no premonition of the approach of this fearful malady—no time to fortify himself even by prayer against the assault. Satan had permission to touch his flesh, and he touched every inch of it. With the exception of the Lord Jesus Christ—for in all things He has the pre-eminence—it is questionable if ever any other mortal was so sorely tried. If there was not something supernatural about faith in God, it could not possibly survive such a shock.

4. Loss of Position. The *greatest* man in the east" has now become the most loathsome object in the east. He who sat among princes is now sitting "among ashes" (chap. 2. 8). He has been stripped of everything but his life.

5. Loss of Sympathy. "Then said his wife unto him, Dost thou still retain thine integrity? Curse God and die" (v. 9). His wife, the only comfort left him, turns out to be a canker. She cannot understand faith in God in circumstances like these. Fair-weather Christians always get ship-wrecked in a storm like this. This taunt

through his wife was the Devil's last weight to break the back of Job's integrity. It was the poisoning of his last earthly spring of consolation. Job has at last sounded the abyss of his sufferings; he has found the bottom of this great deep. His is now "a lifeless life," a finished monument to that great master of the malignant art. And this is the master many take pleasure in serving. To serve sin is to be the slave of the Devil.

III. Their Effect. The immediate result of those awful trials which stripped Job naked of every earthly comfort was a clearer revelation of the inward, spiritual man. "He fell upon the ground, and *worshipped*, and said, The Lord gave, and the Lord hath taken away: blessed be the Name of the Lord" (chap. 1. 20, 21). These words, spoken by this pre-eminent sufferer, have come down as a legacy to the bereaved in every generation since then; on many tombstones they may be read as the language of deep, heart-felt sorrow and submission. "The *Lord* hath taken away." Job saw the Lord behind the Sabeans and the Chaldeans who fell upon his flocks. "In all this did not Job sin with his lips" (chap. 2. 10). That no murmur escaped those burning lips in such a furnace proves how completely he had given himself and all that he had to God. "What! shall we receive good at the hand of God, and shall we not receive evil?" Has the Giver of all good not the right to withhold that good or His own pleasure? What have we that we have not received? Job may not be a prophet, but he has "spoken in the Name of the Lord, for an example of suffering affliction, and of patience" (James 5. 10). There is a life that does not consist of the *things* which we possess; it is infinitely superior to them and independent of them. After getting a glimpse behind the scenes of the purpose of Job's trials, let us by faith count it all joy when we fall into divers temptations (trials), knowing that the *testing* of your faith leads to power of endurance (James 1. 2, 3).

JOB'S COMFORTERS—ELIPHAZ.

JOB 4-7.

"How that to comfort those that mourn
   Is a thing for saints to try;
Yet, haply, God might have done less
   Had a saint been there—not I.

"Alas! we have so little grace,
   With love so little burn,
That the hardest of our works for God
   Is to comfort those that mourn."—FABER.

THE beauty and meaning of some pictures are best seen and understood at a distance. We can see deeper into the meaning of Job's sufferings than either Job or his comforters could see. From our sun-lit mountain top, we look down upon these friends as all working in the darkness, just as, perhaps, some of the angels of God may look down upon us in pity as they see us vainly striving to find out the reason why God in His providence so deals with us. The great fundamental lesson of the book of Job is "Have faith in God." These comforters cannot be charged with hardness of heart, or of having impure motives. Men that could "lift up their voice and weep" at the sight of Job's condition, and sit in company with him for "seven days and seven nights" were surely not void of real sympathy and compassion. Their weakness and their sin lay in their self-confidence. Each seemed sure that he was laying his finger on the cause of Job's downfall, although his experience was a *new thing* in the providence of God. To us, their eloquent reasonings is a powerful evidence of the utter inability of the "wisdom of this world" to explain or to understand the mysteries of Christian experience.

Job began this great wordy warfare by opening his mouth and "cursing the day wherein he was born" (chap. 3. 1-3). Satan had said, "Touch his bone and his flesh, and he will *curse Thee* to Thy face." Job went perilously near the fulfilling of the Devil's prediction, when he "cursed his day," but yet he did not curse his God. Many a one has been constrained, through sin and suffering, to curse the day of their first birth, but history has never told us of one who had any desire to curse the day of their *second* birth. Man that is born in sin is born to trouble as the sparks fly upward, but the man that is born again is born into the kingdom of peace. During those long, weary, seven days the gold of Job's character seemed to become dim, and the most fine gold changed, for he did speak unadvisedly with his *lips* (chap. 2. 10). In the day of darkness and trial let us beware of that "unruly evil," the tongue. This opening speech of the suffering patriarch betrays a soul overwhelmed with bewilderment. It has many questions. Yet this outburst of agony has taught many to be still under the mighty hand of God. It is no mere hyperbole to say that the sufferings of Job, like the sufferings of Jesus Christ, were for the good of others. The Bible would have been much poorer if there never had been the conflict and the patience of Job. It will be impossible in these brief notes to grasp anything like the full meaning of those great torrent speeches. We shall only attempt to catch a word here and there that might help us to understand the book, and to enter into a deeper experience of the things of God.

I. The Speech of Eliphaz (chaps. 4, 5).

1. "IF WE ASSAY TO COMMUNE WITH THEE, WILT THOU BE GRIEVED" (chap. 4. 2). Eliphaz begins very tenderly; he feels that the wound to be dressed is very deep and painful. One needs the tongue that is learned by experience to speak a word in season to him that is so weary and heavy-laden. It is a solemn and gracious work to commune with the sorrowing, but let such missionaries see that their own hearts are at the same time in communion with God, or they may but aggravate the anguish.

**2. "Thy words have upholden him that was falling
...but now...thou faintest"** (vv. 3-5).   This friend
knew Job's past life, and ventures to remind him of how he
had been a means of blessing to others in their time of
need.   This was but a small spark of light for Job's great
darkness, but still there was a glimmer in it.   To tell a
man that he once was rich will not console him much now
that he is bankrupt.   It is easier to speak cheering words
to the tempted than to bear the temptation.   The comforters of others need at times to be comforted.   "They
that wait on the Lord shall...not *faint."*

"Remember, I pray thee, who ever perished, being
innocent?" (v. 7).   This saying is like a double-edged
sword, it cuts both ways.   It may mean, if you were
innocent, as you profess to be, you would not have been
perishing in this fashion; or, because you are innocent, it is
impossible for you to perish.   The Lord knoweth them that
are His, and how to deliver them out of temptation
(2 Peter 2. 9).   The Lord could do nothing with the guilty
Sodomites until the righteous were taken out (Gen. 19. 22).
The facts of history are well worth *remembering.*

**3. "Affliction cometh not forth of the dust...As
for me, I would seek unto God"** (chap. 5. 6-8, r.v.).
Affliction doth not spring up by chance; it is not the
sudden outcome of spontaneous generation.   The law of
microbes is included here, and if I were you, "I would seek
unto God, and unto Him would I commit my cause."
What could be better than this?   But Eliphaz was not in
Job's position, and so it was comparatively easy for him
to say what he would do.   Still, it is the best thing to do.
To whom can we go but unto Him.   The Lord alone knew
all the reasons why this dark and cloudy day had come.
In the day of adversity consider, yes, consider Him who
endured contradictions for us.

4. "BEHOLD, HAPPY IS THE MAN WHOM GOD CORREC-
TETH" (v. 17). To be reproved of God is a comforting
evidence of His love and carefulness. Every true child of
God desires to have their thoughts, feelings, and ways
corrected by their heavenly Father. We ought to count
it a great privilege to be put right by either His word or
His rod.

5. "HE SHALL DELIVER THEE IN SIX TROUBLES; YEA, IN
SEVEN" (v. 19). "HEAR IT, AND KNOW IT FOR THY GOOD"
(v. 27). Solomon says that "a just man falleth seven
times, and riseth up again" (Prov. 24. 16). Six troubles
had overtaken Job, and he had not yet been delivered out of
any of them; but God is the God of deliverances. Let not
the *number* of our troubles or our difficulties limit the
Holy One. "Hear it." Let not the voices of the world,
or an evil heart, so dull the ear that you cannot hear the
still small voice of promise (Psa. 34. 19).

II. Job's Reply (chaps. 6, 7). The wonderful words
of Eliphaz had little effect. Job begins by saying:

1. "OH, THAT MY GRIEF WERE THOROUGHLY WEIGHED."
What is more heavy and more difficult to weigh than grief?
But what benefit would it bring the distracted sufferer
even could he know the full weight and measure of it. His
grief, like the grief of Him who agonised in Gethsemane,
was both terrible and mysterious.

2. "THE ARROWS OF THE ALMIGHTY ARE WITHIN ME"
(chap. 6. 4). A week ago he said, "The *Lord* gave and the
Lord hath taken away," but now his soul is pierced with
the arrows of the *Almighty*. Still, he does not say with
"the fiery darts of the Devil." The arrows have been many
and sharp, but they have come from the finger of God
(Psa. 38. 2). The arrows of the Almighty never miss the
mark (Lam. 3. 12), and when they are *within* us, only He
who sent them can remove them (2 Cor. 5. 11).

3. "Is my flesh brass?" (chap. 6. 12). God could easily have made our flesh to be as hard, as endurable, and as insensible as brass, and our strength as "the strength of stones," if it had not been good for us to be afflicted. The rod of correction would be useless on a brazen body. He knows the frailty of our frame, and will not lay upon us more than we are able to bear.

4. "Cause me to understand wherein I have erred" (chap. 5. 24). If this calamity has come upon me because of my sin—as Eliphaz seemed to think (chap. 6. 8)—then, show me, says Job, where the sin is. Suffering is not always a chastisement or correction, it may be but a narrow gate or a rough road into a place of larger blessing, the Jordan, through which we go into a new land of promise. Job was not conscious of having sinned. The last thing we see him doing, is offering sacrifices for his sons, lest they may have sinned. If in our affliction there is no consciousness of sin, we may be sure God has something new to reveal to us. Wait patiently on the Lord.

5. "I will speak...I will complain" (chap. 7. 11). This is the language of a spirit in anguish, and a soul in bitterness. We would much rather have heard him say, "I will trust....I will pray." There is a silence and a dimness that savours of unbelief more than submission, but why should a believer in God make up his mind to complain? When the Man Christ Jesus was in an agony He prayed more earnestly. The "perfect man" in the Old Testament comes far short of the perfect Man in the New. "*Call* upon Me in the day of trouble." It is just as easy to call as to complain.

6. "Let me alone" (chap. 7. 16). It may at times be hard to bear the weight of the heavy hand of God, but it is infinitely worse to be let alone. What becomes of the branch that is let alone by the tree? What would happen

to the child that was left alone by its mother? Ephraim
is joined to his idols—let him alone. There is a painless
disease that speaks of certain death. As saints or as sinners we know not what we do when we ask God to let us
alone. It is of the glory of His grace in His kindness
towards us in Christ Jesus that He does not let us alone.
There are prayers God graciously refuses to answer.

JOB'S COMFORTERS—BILDAD.

JOB 8-10.

I. The Speech of Bildad (chap. 8). His manner is
abrupt to begin with, and seems less sympathetic than
Eliphaz. His argument amounts to this, that unless God
sends deliverance speedily we must conclude that both you
and your family have been guilty of sinning against God,
and that this dire calamity is the just reward of your works.
Like Eliphaz, he is in total ignorance of the purpose of
Job's trials, but speaks with all the confidence of an oracle.
Mark some of his key-notes—

1. "DOTH THE ALMIGHTY PERVERT JUSTICE?" (chap.
8. 3). Is it possible for God to be unjust? Can He who
sits upon a Great *White* Throne be unrighteous in His
dealings with any one? No. But what comfort can an
aching, bleeding heart find in this? That the *Law* is holy,
just, and good, is not much of a consolation to a soul
smitten with profoundest anguish. The troubled heart
yearns for love, and grace, and pity.

2. "IF THOU WERT PURE AND UPRIGHT, SURELY NOW HE
WOULD AWAKE FOR THEE" (v. 6). If you are all that you
profess to be, surely *now*, when you have got into such a
depth of misery, God would arise to your help. The
glitter of the cold steel is easily seen in this merciless
thrust. How the tender soul of Job must have felt it.
It is the silver not dross that the refiner puts into the fire.

"Every *branch in me* that beareth fruit He purgeth *it.*"
Joseph was fruitful in the land of affliction (Gen. 41. 52).
Yet there is truth in Bildad's statement, for "Whatsoever
we ask, we receive of Him, because we keep His commandments, and do those things that are pleasing in His sight"
(1 John 3. 22).

3. "Prepare thyself to the search" (v. 8). There
is much to be learned from the past, and from God's
dealings with the fathers, but that all things are to continue
as they were is not the teaching of the Holy Ghost (1 Peter
3. 4). Job would "prepare himself" in vain to search for
the cause of his sorrows in the teaching of a "former age."
Man by *searching* cannot find out God; it is by *trusting*
that we learn to know Him. The life of faith is on
altogether a different plane from the life of reason and of
sight. Believe and thou shalt see.

4. "Can the rush grow up without mire?" (v. 11).
The Shuhite now says some plain things about hypocrisy.
As the rush cannot grow up without mire, neither can a
"hypocrite's hope" flourish without being nourished with
that which is suitable to it. If Job has still hope, it is
because of the mire of his hypocrisy. If "he is still green
before the sun's" withering rays it is because he has within
him the waters of deceit (v. 16). Although "the hope
of the hypocrite shall perish" that does not prove that
because, through excessive trial, a man's hope has fainted
that he is perishing without hope. God pity the man
whose trust is only in "a spider's web" (v. 14). Hope
thou in God.

5. "Behold, God will not cast away a perfect man"
(v. 20). This, like many others of their sayings, is capable
of a double interpretation. If you had been a "perfect
man" God would not have cast you away like this; or, if
you are in reality a perfect man, God will not cast you

away although you have been brought so low. It is a mercy to know that when others are misjudging you, that God looketh upon the heart. He knoweth them that are His. "He will not forsake His inheritance" (Psa. 94. 14). To Bildad's credit let us say, that he closes his address with a word of hope (vv. 21, 22). They that sow in tears shall reap in joy.

II. Job's Reply (chaps. 9, 10). Job begins his answer to Bildad by asking a very searching question.

1. "How shall man be just with God?" (v. 2). It is easy to tell a man what he should be, but how is this thing to be done? A *man* should be just with *God*, but in what way is this to be accomplished? How is man's iniquity to be put away, and the guilt of his sin cleansed? Who shall make the key that shall fit this lock? On what ground shall a sinner stand righteous *before* God (R.V.). There is no use of "contending with Him" (v. 3). It is a question of how shall we escape. But this question has been fully answered by God Himself who doeth wonders without number (v. 10) in the gift and sufferings of Jesus Christ His Son.

2. "How shall I . . . reason with Him" (v. 14). He is not a man as I am. What arguments can an unholy man use with a holy God? If it is a question of sin and judgment then there is absolutely no room for man's reasonings. He cannot justify himself (v. 20). Although he should wash himself with snow water, yet will he find himself plunged into a filthy ditch, and his own clothes an abhorrence to him (vv. 30, 31). But God's own backsliding *children* are asked to "Come and reason" with Him, (Isa. 1. 18) and a precious promise is herewith given to such. What God asks for those smarting for their sins is, not to come and reason, but to confess, and forsake their sins.

3. "Neither is there any daysman betwixt us"

(v. 33). These well-known words truthfully express the deepest need of a sinful suffering spirit. O for one capable to act as umpire between a mighty God and a miserable soul. One who is Divine and human, one able to lay his hand on both and meet the need of each, satisfying the just claims of God and speaking peace to a troubled heart. This great need has been perfectly met in Jesus Christ for, "If any man sin, we have an advocate *with the Father*, Jesus Christ the *righteous*, and He is the *propitiation* for our sins" (1 John 2. 1, 2). "No man cometh unto the Father but by Me" (John 14. 6).

4. "I WILL SAY UNTO GOD . . . IS IT GOOD UNTO THEE?" (chap. 10. 2, 3). Yes, say it unto God. Let the thoughts of the heart come up before Him. There is nothing hid from His eyes, and as a gracious Father He will even listen to our complaints. Many things may seem bad to us which are "good unto Him." If Job could have but known all the meaning of his sufferings, he no doubt would have said, "Good is the will of the Lord." He had said this before (chap. 1. 21).

5. "THOU KNOWEST THAT I AM NOT WICKED" (v. 7). If our hearts condemn us not then have we confidence toward God. Negative purity is not everything, but it is something. This is not the language of the Pharisee, "I thank God that I am not as other men," it is the honest confession of one who is not conscious of having, through sin, merited such terrible judgments. This is not a boast, but a protest against the idea of *punishment*, being an explanation of the mystery of his afflictions. We should surely bow with holy reverence, submission, and faith, when His hand is heavy upon us, if our hearts are clean. "The pure in heart shall see God."

6. "REMEMBER . . . THOU HAST MADE ME AS THE CLAY" (v. 9). Then it is not for the clay to resist the wonder

working hand of the Divine Potter. He will not reduce the clay to dust; the potter cannot fashion dry dust into a useful vessel. When we have been brought low by the weight of affliction, so low that we feel as if we had been brought back to that condition of soul in which we were at first, when God, by His Spirit, began to operate upon us. Let us believe that His purpose is to make us into "another vessel" more meet for His service; or in other words, when God's vessels are reduced again to *clay* it is that they might be refashioned for higher and more honourable work. Job's latter days is an evidence of this.

7. "I AM FULL OF CONFUSION, THEREFORE SEE THOU MINE AFFLICTION" (v. 15). This is an honest confession: he cannot understand the meaning of this terrible tragedy. He is covered with shame, yet his conscience is clear, but he makes his appeal to the eye of the Omniscient, "See Thou mine affliction." My light is turned into darkness, I cannot see, but see Thou. There is no confusion in the mind of God, no matter how perplexing and inexplicable His providence toward us may be. In the realm of spiritual things, human *reasonings* can only end in confession. Saul was full of confusion when he said, "What wilt Thou have me to do?" (Acts 9. 6). So were many on the Day of Pentecost, when they cried, "Men and brethren, what shall we do?" God who commanded light to shine out of darkness, can still bring order out of confusion. Commit thy way unto Him.

JOB'S COMFORTERS—ZOPHAR.
JOB 11-14.

The Speech of Zophar. Like the others, he is fully convinced that Job is suffering because of his sins, and like Bildad, he opens his address with some biting questions. He cannot bear to hear Job justifying his "doctrine as

pure" and his life as being "clean in thine eyes" (chap.
11. 4). So he says, as in an agony of soul, *"Oh that God
would speak!"* He is sure that if God would but speak, he
and his friends would be justified in all that they said, and
Job's secret sins revealed, and all his arguments confounded and put to shame. They found it otherwise
when God did speak (chap. 42. 7). We may know much,
but let us remember that we don't know everything. He
that exalteth himself shall be abased. But Zohpar goes
on to say, "Canst thou by searching find out God? Canst
thou find out the Almighty unto perfection?" A perfection that is "high as Heaven," "deeper than Hell," "longer
than the earth and broader than the sea." The soul makes a
great find when it finds God, although it may never be able
to search out the fathomless depths of His infinite per-
fections. This is eternal life, to know Him and Jesus
Christ whom He hath sent. The closing part of his speech
contains wonderful words and might be called—

A HOMILY ON THE WAY OF LIFE.

I. **The Needed Work.** He mentions three things that
are essential to salvation:

1. "PREPARE THINE HEART" (v. 13). The heart needs
preparation, for it is deceitful above all things. The one
good thing found in Jehoshaphat was that he "prepared
his heart to seek God" (2 Chron. 19. 3). The best way
to get the heart prepared is to yield it unto the Lord
(Prov. 16. 1).

2. "STRETCH OUT THINE HANDS." Let the hands of
prayer and supplication be stretched toward God. He only
can bring about the great deliverance so much needed.
He is able to save to the uttermost. Stretch out thine
empty, helpless hands to Him, whose mighty hands are
outstretched in mercy for the uplifting of the poor and the
needy.

3. "PUT AWAY INIQUITY" (v. 14). Let the wicked forsake his wicked ways, and his unrighteous thoughts about God, and let him *turn*, and the Lord will have mercy upon him. "He that covereth his sins shall not prosper." Those who would draw nigh to God must confess and forsake their sins. Then, what follows?

II. **The Blessed Result.** Such heart preparation, and stretching out of hands, will certainly be answered in a copious, soul-satisfying measure. Zophar mentions eight privileges that will be enjoyed.

1. "Thou shalt LIFT UP THY FACE without spot" (v. 15). Thou shalt have *confidence* before God, and a clean countenance. All the boil spots of sin and suffering will be taken away (1 John 3. 19).

2. "Thou shalt be STEDFAST." Established as a house built upon the rock. Taken from the fearful pit, and the feet established in the ways of truth and righteousness.

3. "Thou shalt FORGET THY MISERY" (v. 16). Like Joseph, in the day of his exaltation and glory, thou shalt forget all the toil of the past (Gen. 41. 51). In the joy of the new life in Christ, the wretchedness of the old life of sin is forgotten.

4. "Thou shalt SHINE FORTH...as the morning" (v. 17). Thou shalt not only be illumined, but shall also become a guiding light to others. This new light is not of thine own kindling, but, like the dawning of the day, it is the gift of God—the brightest and the best.

5. "Thou shalt be SECURE, because there is hope" (v. 18). Thou shalt have such a hope as will make you and all your higher interests perfectly secure—a hope that maketh not ashamed.

6. "Thou shalt take thy REST IN SAFETY." Thou shalt have such a rest as cannot be disturbed by the turmoils of earth—a God-given rest (Matt. 11. 28).

7. "Thou shalt lie down, and NONE SHALL MAKE THEE
AFRAID" (v. 19).   Thy salvation will be so perfect that
thou shalt be fearless in the face of men or of devils.   This
is the blessing wherewith the Lord shall bless all those who
put their trust in Him.

8. "MANY WILL ENTREAT THY FACE" (v. 19, *margin*).
The face that has been lifted up to God, and cleansed and
brightened, is always attractive.

Job's Reply.   His answer to Zophar occupies three
chapters, and has reference to the unanimity of his three
friends in condemning him through a false judgment of his
case.   "No doubt but ye are the people, and wisdom will
die with you" (chap. 12. 2).   Perhaps if they had prayed
more and argued less, they all would have come sooner to a
better understanding of the whole case.   As long as they
trusted their own wisdom, and depended on the skill and
force of their own reasonings, they were all "physicians of
no value" (chap. 13. 4).   Their prescriptions were worthless, because their diagnosis was wrong.   In this world of
mysteries we cannot judge moral principles by physical
symptoms.   Job's well-known saying in chapter 13, verse
15, expresses the true attitude of the soul in the midst of
such a storm of bewildered suffering, "Though He slay
me—or is slaying me—yet will I trust—or wait for Him."
Knowing as we do the Divine purpose in Job's calamities,
it makes it much easier for us to say, like the Psalmist,
"Yea, though I walk in the shadow of death, I will fear
no evil" (Psa. 23. 4), or with the apostle, "I am persuaded
that neither death...*nor any other creature* shall be able to
separate me from the love of God" (Rom. 8. 38, 39).   In
the last part of his speech the patriarch deals with *man* in
general (chap. 14).   This portion might be fitly entitled—

WHAT IS MAN?

It has been said that "man was made to mourn."   This

chapter begins with "man" and ends with "mourn." But hear the voice of this man of sorrows.

1. Man! he "is FULL OF TROUBLE" (v. 1). His troubles are so numerous that he is brimful of them. "He is as a rotten thing" (chap. 13. 28). Who can bring a clean thing out of this? (v. 4). Who is able to prescribe for such a complication of troubles as man's? What a bundle of miseries God has to deal with in saving man.

2. Man! HE "FLEETH ALSO LIKE A SHADOW" (v. 2). As the cloud shadows rush along the hillside like breathless spectres, so man hurries on from the mystery of birth to the mystery of death. Here he has no continuing city. He cometh forth like a flower, to be seen and felt by a few, and cut down.

3. Man! HIS DAYS AND MONTHS ARE NUMBERED (v. 5). The limit of his life has been fixed by God. He knoweth not when the end will be. He has not even authority for saying, "I will do so and so *to-morrow.*"

4. Man! HE "DIETH AND WASTETH AWAY" (v. 10). He soon becomes insensible to the pains or pleasures of earth, his mental and physical powers speedily waste away. He has scarcely attained maturity when the wasting process begins.

5. Man! HE "GIVETH UP THE GHOST, AND WHERE IS HE?" (v. 10). He yieldeth up his spirit as one who cannot keep it longer, but where has he gone? Where is he? He must be somewhere. The *where* depends on the character of that spirit (see Luke 16. 22, 23).

6. Man! HE "LIETH DOWN, AND RISETH NOT TILL THE HEAVENS BE NO MORE" (v. 12). When he lieth down it is till the dawning of the new heavens (Isa. 65. 17). This seemed a long way off to Job, but it is not so far away now (1 Thess. 4. 14-16).

7. Man! "IF HE DIE, SHALL HE LIVE AGAIN?" (v. 14).

"There is hope of a tree, if it be cut down, that it will sprout again" (v. 7), and how much better is a man than a tree? Job was not without the hope of immortality; he knew that after his body had been destroyed by worms, that he would yet—in another body—see God (chap. 19. 25, 26). This question finds its perfect answer in Rev. 20. 12: "I saw the *dead*, small and great, stand before God."

_____

THE WORK OF THE DEVIL.
JOB 16. 7-14.

IN this book we see much more than "the patience of Job;" we are face to face with the dreadful deeds of the Devil; for just now Job is in the hand of Satan, but with this Divine limitation, "Save his life" (chap. 2. 6). The upright patriarch would fain see the hand of God in it all, and this constrains him to say something about God, that coming from other lips would be sheer blasphemy; but God graciously overlooks it all. He knows that His servant is entirely in the dark as to the purpose and cause of his sufferings. By the Lord's permission, Satan was the cause of all his sorrows. Job, in the midst of his hopeless misery, is a finished specimen of the Devil's workmanship. His purpose and business is to kill and to destroy. It is a terrible thing to fall into the hands of the living Devil. The "god of this world" is also a "consuming fire." Our God consumes the chaff and the dross, but this god would burn up the wheat and the silver. The Lord delights to *give*, but Satan glories in *taking away*. Note here some of his devices—

I. **He Separates from the Best Company.** "Thou hast made desolate all my company" (v. 7). His family was cut off, and even his wife became strange to him. The fellowships in which he formerly delighted had all been broken up by the hand of the enemy, and his new friends were all miserable comforters. This is what happens when any child of God falls into the condemnation of the Devil through yielding to sin. Christian fellowship is made desolate, and the company that he keeps, in his back-sliding state, are miserable helpers in his time of need. Satan is a professional schismatic. Beware of him in the church and in the family.

II. **He Disfigures the Face.** "Thou hast filled me with wrinkles" (v. 8). The joy and peacefulness that used to beam in the countenance of Job has now given place to gloom and discontent. Those who walk in fellowship with the Lord have their faces transfigured with the heavenly light, but those in the power of the Devil have often his own dark image stamped upon their faces. The Devil will so mar and blacken the face that the man is ashamed to lift it up unto God. This satanic change has often been observed in the countenance of backsliders. The wrinkles of sullen despair and God-defiance are easily seen. That face that should be illumined with the glory of God, becomes an index of the darkness of death.

III. **He Brings Leanness into the Life.** "My leanness beareth witness to my face." No wonder the face gets wrinkled and disfigured when the soul is being starved to death. When the Devil gets a man out of touch with God he will soon get him out of touch with His Word. The Devil's corn is all bran, and his wheat nothing but chaff. His dupes mistake quantity for quality; they may eat much, but still *leanness* "riseth up in them." No servant of sin can know anything of the soul-satisfying fullness of the Lord Jesus Christ.

IV. **He Takes Advantage of the Helpless.** "He teareth me in his wrath; he hateth me; he gnasheth upon me with his teeth" (v. 9). This language is highly figurative, but most terribly expressive. Satan can show no mercy, the weaker we are the better for him. Job has been, for the time, handed over to him to be tested, and he makes it his business to pile on sorrow upon sorrow and agony after agony. If he gets possession of a boy he will tear him and cast him into the fire and into the waters (Mark 9. 22), he hath no compassion on the helpless lad. If he even gets hold of the helpless swine, he will hurl them out into the sea. To be without Christ is to be without power and without a defence against the wiles and wrath of the Devil. Tears have no effect on him (v. 16).

V. He Breaks Asunder, and Shakes to Pieces (v. 12). Job "was at ease" in his prosperity, like a ship at sea with a fair wind, but suddenly the ship was overtaken with a crushing tempest, and driven furiously on the rocks, and broken asunder, and shaken to pieces by the violence of the waves. Whenever Satan gets hold of the helm of the life he seeks to make a shipwreck of the faith. He will break the soul asunder, separating all he can get of it from God and spiritual things, and shake in pieces the future prospects of his victims.

VI. He has Many Helpers. "His archers compass me round about" (v. 13). The Devil has many angels, or demons, waiting his bidding to surround the soul, guarding every way of escape, and ready to shoot their fiery darts at every attempt made for liberty and salvation. It is no easy matter for some to escape out of the hands of this Giant Despair. His archers are sharp-eyed, and have had long practice in dealing with fugitives. They know when and where to hit to be most effective. Men and women that are likely to do damage to his kingdom are specially watched. His most zealous servants usually prove, when delivered, his bitterest enemies. No garrison of demons can hinder a soul for a moment when the overcoming blood of Christ is trusted.

VII. He Uses Powerful Tactics. "He runneth upon me like a giant" (v. 14). He does not trifle with his opportunities. When he sees a chance of overcoming any upright man, he *runneth* like one in haste to catch a felon, and grips at once with a giant hand. He lingers about the gates of the soul, with luring temptation and bewitching enticement, until he gets a gate open, then he rushes in like a giant, to overthrow the citadel. He is a strong one, and seeks to get possession of the goods of man's soul, and then make peace, a peace that means certain death and destruction. But a stronger than he has come to spoil him of his goods, establish a new order of things, making peace and inaugurating the Kingdom of Heaven. "Resist the Devil and he will flee from you." Job longed for "One that might plead for a man with God." To us, Jesus Christ is that One (v. 21).

————

TERRIBLE PROSPECTS.
Job 18. 5-18.

BILDAD begins his second speech, if anything, more exasperated than the others at the reasonings of Job. His wickedness must be very great he thinks, when he still persists in justifying himself in their eyes, and maintaining his integrity in the sight of God. The Shuhite's description of the dreadful calamities that are sure to come upon the wicked, and those that "knoweth not God" (v. 21), is most graphic and appalling in its fullness and truthfulness, but utterly wasted on the innocent patriarch. Still, we feel thankful to Bildad for these burning words. As a description of the condition and prospects of those who are living in lawlessness toward God, it is one of the most powerful within the compass of the Bible. The key-note of this terrible speech is found in the last sentence of it: "And this is the place (portion) of him that knoweth not God" (v. 21). See what this portion is. It implies—

I. **Darkness.** "The light of the *lawless* shall be put out, and the spark of his fire shall not shine" (v. 5). The light of the ungodly is of their own making; it is but the sparks of the fire which they themselves have kindled, and which *shall not shine* when abiding light is needed (Isa. 50. 10, 11). This light is in their own eyes, and when their eyes grow dim, and faint, and blind, their candle is put out, and darkness settles down in the tabernacle of the soul. How different it is with the man of faith! He can say, "The Lord my God who hath lit my candle, He will enlighten my darkness" (Psa. 18. 28).

II. **Disappointment.** "The steps of his *strength* shall be straitened, and his own *counsel* shall cast him down" (v. 7). The confidence of the self-righteous and the ungodly is in their strength and their wisdom, but both shall utterly fail to bring them into their desired haven. The *steps* of *his strength* shall be suddenly shortened and hindered, so that he will be compelled to give up the objects of his pursuit, and sink down like a weary exhausted traveller who has lost his way and finds it impossible for him to reach his home. "His own counsel shall cost him dear." His boasted wisdom shall turn out to be his confusion. The counsel he has given to others shall cover his own face with shame, when he staggers and falls under the burden of his own folly and failure. "He that trusteth in his own heart is a fool." By the wisdom of this world God is not known.

III. **Danger.** The position of the ungodly is so fraught with dangers that the fowler's vocabulary is exhausted in describing them. "His feet in a *net*...the *gin* shall take him by the heel...the *noose* (R.V.) shall prevail against him...the *snare* is laid for him...a *trap* set for him in the way" (vv. 8-10). Satan uses every possible means to prevent that man who "knoweth not God" from escaping out of his hands. But it is with "his own feet" that a man walks into the Devil's net. It is when he yields to temptation that the noose "prevails against him." He falls into the snare of the Devil, because he walks in the Devil's territory. If he neglects the salvation of Jesus Christ, there is no escape for him; but by trusting Him the snare will be broken, and his soul shall escape like a bird.

IV. **Dread.** "Terrors shall make him afraid on *every side*" (v. 11). He may say peace, peace, but the time will come when terrors shall break in upon him from every side. Terrors behind him, and terrors in front of him; the past, the present, and the future, all full of dread. Terrors crowding in upon him, and "chasing him at his heels," like so many beasts of prey (v. 11, R.V.). What an awful experience, to go into eternity and up to the Judgment Throne of God, chased by the sins and iniquities of a God-neglected life. The terrors of the Lord must follow close upon the "heels" of the sinner. The guilty man's feet are never swift enough to outrun the pursuing justice of God.

V. **Desolation.** "The firstborn of DEATH shall devour his strength, root up his confidence, and bring him to the king of terrors" (vv. 13, 14). What a sorrowful plight to be in: strength devoured, confidence rooted up, and face to face with the king of terrors. The *firstborn* of death is like that disease, or physical disorder, which is the forerunner of death, and is gradually eating up the strength, and tearing the hope of health up by the roots, and bringing the life under the dominion of temporal death. Spiritually the *firstborn* of death is *unbelief*, that forerunner of eternal separation from God and Heaven, which devours all strength for the service of Christ, roots up all real confidence before God, and brings the soul into the bondage and dread of the king of terrors (Mark 16. 16). After death the judgment. The Lord, the righteous Judge, upon the great White Throne will be the King of Terrors to all who have rejected His redeeming grace (Rev. 6. 15-17).

VI. Despair. "His roots shall be dried up:.., his remembrance shall perish:...he shall be driven from light into darkness, and chased out of the world" (vv. 16-18). Could words present a more dismal picture than this? The "place of him that knoweth not God" is indeed the place of dispair. His *roots* shall be dried up, because they are not in God, but in the barren wastes of self and the world (Mal. 4. 1). His *remembrance* shall perish, because his name is not written in the Lamb's book of life. He shall be *driven* from the light of the Gospel into the darkness of hopeless despair. He shall be *chased* out of the world as unworthy to live in it, as one unfit for the Kingdom of Heaven, and as one who is as loath to leave this world as Lot's wife was to leave Sodom.

VII. Destruction. "Destruction shall be ready for his halting" (v. 12, R.V.). All that destruction means is here personified as a powerful enemy. Keeping step with the man that knows not God, watching, and waiting for that moment when death shall cause him to halt, that he might have the opportunity of accomplishing his dreadful work. To the ungodly, death means destruction. It is the destruction of all his coveted fellowships, of all his boasted possessions, of his joy, of that false peace with which he comforted himself, of his hope for time and eternity. It is the destruction of all the faculties of his soul for the seeing or enjoying of those pleasures which are at God's right hand. His god was his belly, his glory was his shame, and his end is destruction.

LIGHT IN DARKNESS.

JOB 19. 25-27.

JOB'S soul was sorely vexed with the words of his would-be comforters. "These ten times have ye reproached me," he says. Anybody with enough hardness of heart can easily reproach another in the day of their downfall. "If ye will magnify yourselves against me," he continues then, "know now that God hath overthrown me" (vv. 5, 6). The overthrowing was the work of the Devil, and it was complete, permitted by God, as was the crucifixion of Christ, yet the work of "wicked hands." It is most interesting to notice that it was after Job had experienced the weakness and deceitfulness of *all earthly kinships*, that the vision of the kinsman-Redeemer came upon his desolate spirit. Surely this is the work of the Spirit of God, it is absolutely true to the manner of the Holy Spirit in New Testament times. The unsatisfactory nature, the insufficiency and inability of all earthly friendship to meet the needs of a sinful, sorrowful soul, must be fully realised, ere the glories of the kinsman-Redeemer can be fully appreciated. "I know that my Redeemer liveth" (v. 25). Who but the Lord Jesus Christ was ever able to record such a melancholy list of broken friendships as Job does in this chapter. Hear what he says about them: "My *brethren* are far from me...mine *acquaintance* are estranged from me...my *kinsfolk* have failed, my *familiar friends* have forgotten me...my *maids* count me a stranger...my *servant* gave me no answer...my breath was strange to my *wife*...all my *inward friends* abhorred me" (vv. 13-19). There was not one arm of flesh left on which he could lean, when this new light dawned upon him constraining him to say, "I know that my *kinsman-Redeemer* liveth," and that apart from my flesh I shall have God on my side (R.V.). We are cautioned by some commentators not to read

too much into these words, but we are bound to take
them as they stand, and believe they mean all that they
say   The teaching of the Spirit of God is not limited to
the conditions and circumstances of men.   The language
of Job here is full of prophetic meaning, and is rich in
spiritual consolation.   *We* can at least easily read into
these words—

I. The Fact of Redemption.   "My Redeemer liveth. "
What a relief for the oppressed and bewildered soul to
turn from the failing kinships of earth to the unfailing
Kinsman above, who ever liveth to make intercession for
us.   Yes, Job, out of all your troubles this Kinsman-
Redeemer will yet deliver you.   He shall redeem thy life
from destruction, and crown thee with lovingkindness and
tender mercies.   He *vindicates* the cause of all who put
their trust in Him.   He who redeems and purchases the
soul by His own blood lives for the salvation and vindication of His own.   That HE, the eternal Son of God,
should condescend to be our Goel (kinsman) is the mystery
and marvel of infinite grace.

II. The Joy of Personal Assurance.   "I know. "   He
knew that all his earthly friends had forsaken him, but he
also knew that his Kinsman in Heaven, the living One
would ultimately prove Himself to be good and faithful.
There were some things Job did not know.   He knew not
the reason why he had been so suddenly stripped of every
earthly comfort, and crushed down to the dust with a load
of sorrow, but he knew and believed that *"my* Redeemer
liveth, " and liveth to make all things work together for
good to them that love Him.   He could scarcely talk now
of *my* brethren, *my* kinsfolk, *my* friends, *my* servant, for
they had all forsaken him, but he could say "MY
REDEEMER. "   When heart and flesh fail, God will be the
portion of the believing soul.   It will still be sweet to say,

"my Redeemer," when all the joys and friendships of this world have to be left behind.

III. **The Prospect of His Appearing.** "I know... that He shall stand at the latter day upon the earth." All that this meant to Job we cannot say, but he surely believed in the personal appearing of his great Kinsman-Redeemer on the earth. Now we know that this prophecy hath been fulfilled, and that the Redeemer hath come, and by the sacrifice of Himself has put away sin—the seed of the woman hath bruised the serpent's head—and by His own blood hath provided a ransom price for the souls of men. The earth needed Him, and He hath identified Himself with its sins and sorrows by standing on it and dying for it. To us these words are still prophetic, and we look for the appearing of our great God and Saviour Jesus Christ, who shall yet as King of kings stand in the latter day upon the earth.

IV. **The Hope of a Beatific Vision.** "Though worms destroy this body, yet without my flesh shall I see God" (R.V., *margin*). The flesh is the veil that hides the vision of God from the spirit of man. Even the Redeemer's flesh had to be rent asunder as a veil, ere the new way of entrance could be made for us (Heb. 10. 20). Paul's way of putting it is, "*Absent* from the body, *present* with the Lord" (2 Cor. 5. 8). When He shall appear we shall be like Him, for we shall see Him as He is. "The pure in *heart* shall see God." If there be no God to see, why should the purest of hearts have this longing and hope strongest within them? It surely does not follow, that because a man is good and upright, he is in greater danger of being deluded and deceived in the most important of all questions—that of future hope.

V. **The Confidence of Final Satisfaction.** "Whom I shall see on my side...and not as a stranger" (v. 27, R.V.,

margin). God's present dealings with Job are to him full of
mystery and contradictions. All things seem to be against
him, but when apart from his flesh he sees God, he knows
that he will find that God all along has been on His side,
making all things work together for his good. He will not
see Him as a *stranger*, but as a faithful *Kinsman*-
Redeemer. Here "we see through a glass darkly, but then
face to face." What we know not now we shall know
hereafter. Our present circumstances may be as perplexing
to human reason as Job's was to him; but with the vision
of our Divine Kinsman before us, we are assured that in
love He is doing all things well. "I shall be satisfied
when I awake" (Psa. 17. 15) in the presence of His likeness.

THE WICKED MAN'S PORTION.

JOB 20. 29.

ZOPHAR winds up this speech, which is full of the horrors
which belong to a life of ungodliness, with these words:
"This is the portion of a wicked man from God" (v. 29).
It is interesting to find that this is the view of wickedness
held by these wisest of men, away back in times before the
law was given. The word "wicked" here is *lawless*, and
refers to those who are not restrained in any way through
the knowledge or fear of God. The description still holds
good of the man that *obeys not* the Gospel of Jesus Christ.

I. **His Triumph shall be Short** (vv. 5-7). He does
triumph in a way; he has "joy," he has "excellency,"
and his head seems to "reach unto the clouds." His
success is of such a nature that failure and ruin looks
like an impossibility. But his triumph is short, his
joy is but for a moment, his excellency shall perish like
his own dung. Like the Egyptians, these lawless ones say,
"*I will* pursue, *I will* overtake, *I will* divide, *my lust* shall

be satisfied; but God shall blow upon them, and they shall sink like lead in the mighty waters of death and destruction" (Exod. 15. 9, 10). Permanent victory only belongs to those who "Overcome by the blood of the Lamb. "

II. His Sin shall Abide with Him. "His bones are full of the sin of his youth, which shall lie down with him in the dust" (v. 11). David dreaded this terrible experience when he prayed, "Remember not the sins of my youth" (Psa. 25. 7). Sin is a most uncomfortable bedfellow to lie down with in the grave. No human power can shake it off. It seeks to cling to the soul in death, in resurrection, in judgment, and in eternity. To die in sin is to die out of Christ, and to meet Him with a sin-stained resurrection body.

III. His Moral Appetite shall be Vitiated. "Wickedness sweet in his mouth...yet the gall of asps within him" (vv. 12-14). He finds that sweet to his taste which he knows shall prove bitter to his conscience. Through practice and force of habit he now clings to the things which, in his innermost nature he condemns. His moral senses are so blunted and perverted that he calls bitter sweet, and sweet bitter. The lie of Satan is more pleasant to him than the truth of God. He loves darkness rather than light, and prefers the broken cisterns to the Fountain of living water.

IV. His Precious Things shall all be Disgorged. "He hath swallowed down riches, and he shall vomit them up again" (v. 15). Many a valuable thing he hath swallowed for the satisfaction of his own lust and passion. Much goods have been laid up for the future, as a gourmand would stuff his stomach against coming want, but he shall vomit them up again, as one who is sickened by them, and finds himself unable longer to keep them. The things which formerly delighted him, and in which he trusted for future strength and succour, will suddenly become soul-sickening and turned into a vomit. The riches of Christ will never be so parted with.

V. His Abundance shall not Satisfy. "In the fullness of his sufficiency he shall be in straits" (v. 22). No matter how much a man may have of the world's riches and honours, *he* shall still be in straits if the "one thing needful" is lacking—personal acquaintance with God. Sufficiency of perishing things cannot meet all the needs of an imperishable spirit. The rich man mentioned in Luke 12 was in straits when he said: "What shall I do?" But he was in a greater strait when God said unto him: "This night thy soul shall be required of thee; then whose shall these things be?"

VI. His Treasures shall be Found to be Darkness. "All darkness is laid up for his treasures" (v. 26, R.V.). What an inheritance this is, reserved for those who die rebels against the grace of God. Darkness laid up for him—*all* darkness, nothing but darkness—as the reward of his earthly life and labours. Complete disaster is secretly lurking in the future for him. His treasures are not in Heaven, and outside the light of God's presence there is nothing but the blackness of darkness. He loved the darkness of a godless life rather than the light of a godly life. Now all is darkness! The seed sown has brought forth its harvest of blackness.

VII. His Iniquity shall be Revealed. "The Heavens shall reveal his iniquity" (v. 27). Even "the earth shall rise up against him." The heavens and the earth shall combine to carry out the unerring word of God. "The Lord will bring to light the hidden things of darkness, and will make manifest the counsels of the hearts" (1 Cor. 4. 5). "There is nothing *covered* that shall not be revealed" (Luke 12. 2). Every unforgiven sin and crooked thing shall be made manifest by the searchlight of Heaven; then who that have died without Christ shall be able to stand when He appeareth as the Judge of the quick and the dead? No Achan will ever be able to bury his sins deep enough that the eye of God will not see them. The portion of the wicked (lawless) is indeed a miserable portion, but, thank God, it may be exchanged for a better portion, if, like Mary, he will choose now the "better part" (Luke 10. 42).

THE PRAYER OF THE WICKED.
Job 21. 14, 15.

In Job's reply to Zophar's last speech, he shows that material prosperity is not sufficient evidence that a man is morally righteous, for the wicked "become old and are mighty in power." But in these verses he lays bare the secret thoughts of the ungodly and lawless soul by putting this prayer into their mouth. The godless man of the world would not perhaps audibly dare to use these words, but nevertheless they are practically the sentiments of his every-day life. Look at—

I. **The Meaning of It.** It reveals a—

1. Dread of God's Presence. "They say unto God, Depart from us." Their carnal mind is enmity against God. They fear His presence as the owl does the approach of the sun, or as the thief dreads the daylight. As a gracious Saviour, they may say to Him, "Depart," and He may leave their coast, but, as a Judge, they will yet hear Him say, "Depart from Me."

2. Dislike at God's Ways. "We desire not the knowledge of Thy ways." They are wedded to their own ways, and are not willing to forsake them (Isa. 55. 7). The knowledge of God's ways would make them more miserable in their own sinful ways. They cover their heads with the mantle of ignorance, and say darkness is better than light.

Though His ways are pleasantness and His paths peace,
their minds are so blinded by the god of this world, and
their spiritual appetite so vitiated, that they have no *desire*
for them.

3. DENIAL OF GOD'S CLAIMS. "What is the Almighty,
that we should serve Him?" They do not even say,
"Who," as Pharaoh did, but "What," as if He were a
creation of man, instead of the Creator of all. The
Almightiness in their estimation is in the *"we."* What is
He that *we* should serve Him. This exalting of self above
all that is called God is the essence of Satanic opposition.
Those who make it their business to serve themselves are
morally unfit for the service of God. "Ye cannot serve two
masters."

4. DISBELIEF IN GOD'S LOVE. "What profit shall we
have if we pray unto Him?" They have no faith in God
as a loving Father ready and willing to answer the cry of
the needy. They have no consciousness of real need, and
so have no faith in prayer. Like the Laodiceans, they
have "need of nothing," not even of Him who stands
knocking outside their door. They also said in their own
way, "Depart from us, for we desire not the knowledge of
Thy ways," by keeping the door closed against His
entrance. "Ye have not because ye ask not." Men
ought always to pray and not to faint.

II. **The Cause of It**. *"Therefore* they say unto God,"
etc. The occasion of it is found in the foregoing verses.
In their worldly prosperity they had many marks of the
goodness of God, *yet* they said unto God, "Depart from us,"
etc. (R. V.). This lawless spirit manifests itself in the
grossest ingratitude and thanklessness. The prosperity of
the wicked is a mystery to those who know not that "the
wicked have their portion in this life." Observe the nature
of that prosperity as it appeared to the afflicted patriarch.

1. THEIR INFLUENCE IS GREAT. "The wicked become old, yea, are mighty in power" (v. 7). Long years after this the Psalmist said the same thing, "I have seen the wicked in great power, and spreading *himself* like a green bay tree" (Psa. 37 35). The godly man seeks to spread the knowledge of God, but the godless, selfish worldling spreads himself. The world loves its own, and admires the man who is able to spread himself like a green bay tree, although he should starve to death all the lesser plants that seek an existence beneath his shade.

2. THEIR AFFLICTIONS ARE FEW. "Their houses are safe from fear, neither is the rod of God upon them" (v. 9). They don't seem to be afflicted as other men. Grey hairs don't seem to come so quickly upon their heads. They are quite unaccustomed to the yoke of discipline. The rod of Divine chastisement does not visit them because they are not harnessed to the will of God, but are, like the wild asses, doing their own pleasure. They have a liberty, but it is the liberty of the *lawless*, the freedom of the rebel. The rod and staff of the Great Shepherd does not guide them, so they rush on comfortably to destruction. "Whom the Lord loveth He chasteneth."

3. THEIR POSSESSIONS ARE MULTIPLIED. "Their bull gendereth, and faileth not; their cow calveth, and casteth not her calf" (v. 10). "Behold the ungodly...they increase in riches" (Psa. 73. 12). They add house to house, and land to land, and offer sacrifices to their own genius (Hab. 1. 16). The rich *fool* had not where to bestow his goods. The meek shall yet *inherit* the earth, but meanwhile it seems to be largely the portion of the godless.

4. THEIR CHILDREN ARE HAPPY. "Their children dance ...and rejoice at the sound of the organ" (vv. 11, 12). Well, God bless the "little ones," why should they not be happy? They have not yet become positively lawless by

actual transgression. They are in ignorance of the enmity that lurks in the heart of that father to the being and grace of God. But they are in great danger of following in the steps of their world-deluded parents, by setting their affections on the things of earth and neglecting the eternal treasure. This picture of the ungodly is very attractive to many. No wonder the Psalmist said, "I was *envious* at the foolish, when I saw the prosperity of the wicked (they are not in trouble as other men...their eyes stand out with fatness; they have more than heart could wish)...UNTIL *I went into the sanctuary of God* and saw them in the light of His presence; then understood I their end" (Psa. 73. 3-17). They who said, "Who is the Almighty, that we should serve Him!" "shall drink of the wrath of the Almighty" (v. 20). What an awful cup awaits those who refuse the cup of salvation. The rich man died, and in Hell he *lifted up* his eyes. Better far to lift them up now.

ACQUAINTANCE WITH GOD.
JOB. 22. 21-30.

IN closing his third speech, Eliphaz talks like a New Testament prophet. The phraseology is, of course, old, but the teaching is up-to-date, and the moral order in which the truths are presented are almost apostolic. His words suggest—.

I. **A Great Need.** "Acquaint now thyself with Him, and be at peace" (v. 21). Acquaintanceship with God is the first step toward peace. A theoretical knowledge of God cannot satisfy the heart. *Acquaintanceship* implies a personal intimacy. After Adam, through sin, had separated himself from God, a new acquaintanceship had to be formed. Divine friendship had to be set up on a new basis (Gen. 3. 15). Sin implies separation and enmity;

acquaintanceship implies reconciliation and peace. No man now can be said to be acquainted with God who is a stranger to the Lord Jesus Christ, who bore the combined image of God and of man. He who was God manifest in the flesh, hath made peace by the blood of His cross. Kiss the Son lest He be angry with thee, and ye perish in the way. "This is life eternal that they might know Thee, the only true God, and Jesus Christ whom Thou hast sent" (John 17. 3).

II. **A Plain Way.** The way back into the favour and fellowship of God is very simple and easy to the willing heart. It is stated here in two words: "Receive!" "Return!" "Receive the law from His mouth,...and return to the Almighty" (vv. 22, 23). Receive into thine heart the word that has come from His mouth, believe what He hath said about sin and salvation, and return to God by yielding your will to Him, and resting your soul upon His finished redemption. We can now read into the words of Eliphaz a much deeper meaning than he could at that time understand. Receive the word of the Gospel and return, not to a creed or a church, but to the living God.

III. **A Manifold Result.** To be closely acquainted with any great personality will certainly affect our manner of thinking and acting; how much more when we are acquainted with GOD. There will be—

1. A RENEWAL OF THE NATURE. "Thou shalt be built up" (v. 23). The spiritual nature of man has been so broken down by sin that it is a complete ruin. Apart from the knowledge and grace of God, he can never build himself up as a temple of God. It is when we come into the light of His presence that we get rebuilt, and made new creatures. "If any man be in Christ he is a new creature." "We are His workmanship, created (anew) in Christ Jesus." Return unto Him just as you are, and He shall build thee up.

2. GREAT RICHES. "The Almighty shall be thy treasure" (v. 25, R.V.). The gold of Ophir is but the dust of the
earth compared with the riches that are in Him. Material
things cannot meet the needs of an immaterial spirit. Our
eternal spirits need the adorning of the eternal God. Your
little life shall be filled up out of His infinite fullness.
When you get truly acquainted with Him, you will find
that Himself is sufficient for thee. To know God is to be a
spiritual millionaire. "My God shall supply all your
need, " (Phil. 4. 19), not only with His gifts, but with
Himself. We have this treasure in the earthen vessel
when we are filled with the Holy Spirit.

3. UNFAILING JOY. "Then shalt thou have thy delight
in the Almighty" (v. 26). Only the pure in heart who see
God can find their delight in Him. The unrenewed in
nature will still seek after the world's broken cisterns,
which cannot hold water enough to quench the thirst of the
soul. Those who find their delight in God have the purest
of all pleasures from a source which can never fail. "We joy
in God through our Lord Jesus Christ, by whom we have
received the reconciliation. "

4. BOLDNESS OF ACCESS. "And shalt lift up thy face
unto God. " When we become the *children* of God through
faith in Jesus Christ, it is but natural that we should lift up
our faces unto our Father. The consciousness of unforgiven
sin hinders many from lifting up their faces unto God
(Luke 18. 13). Those who see no beauty in Him who
was the Man of Sorrows, hide, as it were, their faces
from Him. The open face turned to God is the evidence
of a soul at peace with Him. "Our fellowship is with
the Father. "

5. ANSWERED PRAYER. "Thou shalt make thy prayer
unto Him, and He shall hear thee" (v. 27). What a
privilege! The ear of the Almighty God always at your

lips to hear thee when thou speakest unto Him. Speak out the desires of thy soul, and wait patiently on Him. "If we know that He hear us, whatsoever we ask, we know that we have the petitions that we desired of Him" (1 John 5. 15).

6. FRUITFUL TESTIMONY. "Thou shalt also decree a thing, and it shall be established unto thee" (v. 28). The word of thy testimony in His Name shall be made to stand firm. His word shall not return unto Him void. New eyes will be given thee to see wondrous things, and thy tongue shall speak forth things which God will make to come to pass (Jer. 23. 28).

7. WALKING IN THE LIGHT. "The light shall shine upon thy ways." Thou shalt not walk in darkness, for the guiding light of His presence shall be with thee. His Holy Spirit will guide thee into the truth, which always illumines the heart and mind. Just now Job was enveloped in thick darkness, but, by yielding Himself unreservedly to God, light would arise, and he would yet walk with a light step in the sunny paths of peace.

8. ABILITY TO HELP OTHERS. "When men are cast down, then *thou* shalt say, There is lifting up" (v. 29). We must be lifted up ourselves before we attempt to lift up others. There be many who are "cast down" through sin and shortcoming, disappointment and failure, many who need this cheering message, "There is lifting up." When crushed and broken spirits are saying, "Who will show us any good?" it is the privilege of those whose faces have been lifted up to God to carry the uplifting Gospel of Jesus Christ, who was "lifted up," that He might draw men to Himself. The man of God is the only man that has the real message of hope for fallen humanity.

THE OUTSKIRTS OF GOD'S WAYS.

JOB 26. 6-14.

JOB'S three comforters said much, and did the best they could, but their remedies never touched the disease. They were as blind men seeking to lead a blind man. In the previous chapter, Bildad, whose great arguments have all been already spent in vain, has his last little say which closes the whole case for him and his friends. Now when they have exhausted themselves, Job begins his great and final oration, which occupies the following six chapters. These wonderful words bear ample proof that although Satan had brought such ruin and desolation upon Job, he had no power to touch his living spirit within. His mind remained clear, which doubtless made his anguish all the more keen. In brief but striking language we have here parts of His ways set before us. If these are but the "outskirts" (R.V.)—the ripple on the shore of the Divine doings, what must it be to get into the centre of the operations of God. What, then, are these merely outlying acts of the great Creator of all? Here they are—

I. **"Hell is naked before Him"** (v. 6). Sheol, or the shady world of spirits, lies uncovered before His gaze. His eyes pierce the gloom of that awful abyss called "the bottomless pit." If I make my bed in Hell (Sheol) Thou art there—there in justice and judgment. No darkness, no matter how dense, can cover a human soul from the holy eye of God (Psa. 139. 8-11). If Hell is naked before Him, so is your heart and mine. There is many a human heart that is little else than a miniature Hell, yet it, with all other things, is naked and opened unto the eyes of Him with whom we have to do (Heb. 4. 13).

II. **"He Hangeth the Earth upon Nothing"** (v. 7). Some seem to be afraid lest we should read into these words more than was meant by the afflicted patriarch, lest we credit Job with knowing more about astronomy than he really did. He surely meant what he said when he said, "He hangeth the earth upon *nothing*." He could not mean that He hangeth the earth on *something*. The statement is scientifically accurate, although made thousands of years before the fact was discovered by science. But the point is, this wonderful balancing of worlds in space is but one of the outworks of this wonder-working God. Job may not know anything about the law of gravitation, but, if moved by the Spirit of God, he speaks worthy of God. The Spirit of truth is always in advance of the discoveries of men.

III. **"He Bindeth up the Waters in His Thick Clouds"** (v. 8). The seemingly fickle clouds are God's. He binds them together with invisible bands so that they cannot be rent to pour out their treasures until He unties them. How often have we seen those great water-carriers rolling along the heavens, and piled up at times like huge bales of wool. "Great and marvellous are Thy works, O Lord."

IV. **"He Closeth in the Face of His Throne"** (v. 9. R. V.). Behind all the laws and forces of nature, Job sees the throne of God. The whole visible creation is as a veil spread over the face of His eternal throne, but the glory and majesty of the Divine Personality, who ruleth over all, shines through this cloudy covering. The material world is like the pillar of cloud in the wilderness. God is in the midst of it. Clouds and darkness are round about Him (Psa. 97. 2).

V. **"He Describeth a Boundary upon the Face of the Waters"** (v. 10, R. V.). The waters of the great deep are in the hollow of His hand, and by His infinite wisdom He has marked out that line which we call the horizon, where the sea and sky seem to meet and kiss each other. God sets His limitations to every earthly thing. So far, but no farther; but the Spirit-taught soul looks beyond to the things which are eternal and lie hidden in the depths of eternity.

VI. **"He Stirreth up the Sea with His Power"** (v. 12, R.V.). The same mighty hand that pushed back the rolling flood and made "dry land" that the Israelites might pass over, still controls the restless billows (Psa. 74. 13).

VII. **"He Smiteth through Rahab"** (v. 12, R.V.). Rahab stands for pride and arrogance. By His understanding is human pride smitten through. The wisdom and power of God, even as seen in the visible creation, ought to pierce the arrogance of man. But how much more ought the wisdom and love of God, as seen in the Cross of Christ, stay the enmity of the carnal mind. Rahab is condemned already.

VIII. **"He hath Garnished the Heavens by His Spirit"** (v. 13). The same Spirit who beautified the heavens now beautifies the soul in whom He dwells. "The Spirit of God *moved* upon the face of the waters." His *moving* is always for the glory of God, whether it be in the heart or in the heavens. Bildad said, "Yea, the stars are not pure in His sight." But Job takes a different view of that work which at the beginning was pronounced "good." When the beauty of the Lord our God is put upon us, we are clean and beautiful in His sight. The Spirit of God is a wonderful artist. He who beautified the heavens can beautify thy life.

IX. **He hath Subdued the Swift Serpent** (v. 13, R.V.). Whether this swift fleeing serpent is the Devil, or the forked lightning-flash, it matters not, both are under His control. Neither of them can fly so fast that God cannot at any time pierce them through with His arrow. The forked lightning is an apt emblem of the movements and terrible character of Satan, but he is a conquered foe.

What a mighty God our God is, when THESE are but the

outskirts of His ways, part of the fringe of the great garment of His works. In these parts of His ways, Job adds, we hear but *"a small whisper of Him"* (v. 14, R.V.). From the visible creation there comes an unmistakable "whisper of Him," which any attentive ear may hear. The voice may be "small," but it is the voice of God. In creation, we hear the small whisper of the goodness of God; but in Christ, the loud cry of an agonising heart of love. This God who in times past whispered into the dull ears of men, through the marvellous works of His hands, now speaks with a loud voice through the death of His Son. "God in these last days hath spoken unto us by His Son" (Heb. 1. 2). "To-day, if ye will hear His voice, harden not your hearts." Consider the two *cries* of Christ: John 7. 37; Matthew 27. 46.

PRICELESS WISDOM.
JOB 28. 12-28.

IN this chapter Job continues his wonderful parable. He has just been showing that there is a *place* where gold and silver and precious stones can be found (vv. 1-6), and how that men by searching and digging and overturning (vv. 9, 10) bring these hidden treasures to light, but as these can never meet all the needs of a human heart, he goes on to ask this great question of world-wide interest, "But where shall WISDOM be found?" (v. 12). A man may be loaded with the treasures of earth and yet be a fool (Luke 12. 19, 20). The soul of man cannot find its perfect satisfaction even in the very best that this world can yield it. Wisdom is the chief thing; with all thy getting, get wisdom.

I. **Its Nature.** Wisdom is not something we can put on like a garment. Wisdom is character; it is the quality of *being wise*; it is a condition of heart, and has to do with

our relationship to God. It *begins* with fearing the Lord
(v. 28), and grows as the knowledge of God increases.
If Job had not "Christ, the wisdom of God" in his mind
when he spoke these beautiful and far-reaching words,
doubtless the guiding Spirit of God had, for they are
brimful of New Testament meaning to all who are wise
in Christ. Men have no difficulty in finding the wisdom
of this world, which is foolishness with God, but a man
is not truly wise until he becomes a partaker of the
wisdom of God.

II. **Its Unearthliness.**   "Where is wisdom to be
found? and where is the place of understanding?" Where
is this knowledge of God to be got? this wisdom of heart
that enables a man so to act before God and men that it
will bring satisfaction to his own soul, good to his fellows,
and glory to God. Where? It is not found "in the land of
the living" (v. 13). This barren wilderness of human
beings cannot produce it. "The depth saith, It is not in
me; and the sea saith, It is not with me" (v. 14). No
created thing, or one, can offer to a thirsty soul this
satisfying gift. Out of the *land*, and the *depths*, and the
sea, men have brought multitudes of valuable things, but
the wisdom that maketh wise unto eternal life has never yet
been found there, although generation after generation
have followed in diligent search. These are all as broken
cisterns which cannot hold this heavenly water. Is there
no answer to this cry of Job, "Where is the place?" Yes,
that place is called Calvary, where Christ the wisdom of
God is offered to a world perishing for lack of knowledge.

III. **Its Preciousness.** The language here concerning
wisdom is sublimely graphic, if we read it with our eye on
Him who is the wisdom of God.

1. IT CANNOT BE PRICED. "Man knoweth not the price
thereof" (v. 13). What man on earth would dare to

attempt to reckon up the value of the Lord Jesus Christ? "In Him are hid all the treasures of wisdom and knowledge" (Col. 2. 3)—"unsearchable riches. "

2. It Cannot be Bought. "It cannot be gotten for gold" (v. 15). All the wealth of the world could never purchase the wisdom of God. It would be an insult to God, even if man had the power, to offer Him a whole world of gold as a price for His Son. Even the gold of man's *righteousness* is as filthy rags when offered as a recompense to God.

3. It Cannot be Equalled. "The gold and the crystal cannot equal it" (v. 17). "The price of wisdom is above rubies; the topaz of Ethiopia shall not equal it" (vv. 18, 19). The world's best cannot be compared with this gift of God. The joy of finding rubies and diamonds cannot equal the joy of finding the wisdom of God in Christ Jesus.

4. It Cannot be Exchanged. "The exchange of it shall not be for jewels of fine gold" (v. 17). Nothing can take its place. There is no substitute or equivalent for heavenly wisdom. Nothing will ever stand in Christ's stead.

5. Its Power Cannot be Doubted. "Destruction and death say, We have heard the fame thereof" (v. 22). We have here the testimony of wisdom's enemies. The *fame* of this wisdom is that it saves from "destruction and death. " They have heard the tidings to their cost.

IV. **Its Discovery.** Another question is asked, "Whence then cometh wisdom?" (v. 20), and the answer is, "God understandeth the *way* thereof, and He knoweth the *place*" (v. 23). The *way* is the way of love and mercy, the *place* is the place where Christ was crucified. Only God could understand how the deep eternal need of man can be fully met. He only could unveil the secret of everlasting bliss. He alone knew where this soul-satisfying treasure could be found. Deliver from going down to the pit, I have found the Ransom. It will put a new meaning into verse 27 if you read "Him" instead of "it." "He did see *Him*, and declare *Him*; He prepared *Him*, yea, He searched Him out." Then "unto man He said, Behold, the fear of the Lord, that is wisdom; and to depart from evil is understanding" (v. 28). To be made a recipient of this wisdom, we must so *fear* the Lord that we shall submit ourselves entirely to Him, and so hate evil that we shall depart from it. Foolishness and evil go together; wisdom and holiness are twin sisters. "Whence then cometh wisdom?" Christ is made of God unto us wisdom, which is accompanied with righteousness, sanctification, and redemption. "With all thy getting, get wisdom" (Prov. 4. 7).

THE MAN IN GOD'S STEAD.
Job 33.

AFTER the words of Job were ended, and the **three men** had ceased to answer him, Elihu—God is He—broke forth in holy wrath at the manner, or spirit, in which the great controversy had been carried on. Job had been more inclined to justify himself than God, and his three friends had condemned him without discovering a cause (chap. 32. 1-3). Elihu had evidently been a silent listener during the whole debate; but now, though young, he would unburden his soul before them all. This young man was not one of the "three friends" who came to comfort Job; he is an independent witness—an outsider, so to speak—specially fitted by God to throw fresh light upon the mystery of the whole case, or, at least, to put a new emphasis into some of the phrases commonly used. This is what the "man of God" always does. He does not speak a new language; he does not coin ear-tickling sentences, he speaks plain words with a new power. Elihu, then, comes before us as a typical Spirit-filled man, and as such we shall look at—

I. **His Character**. This apostle of the Old Testament will compare favourably in many ways with the great apostle of the New Testament. Of course, in judging Elihu by the light of New Testament teaching, we must never lose sight of the fact that we are putting a meaning into his words that perhaps Job or his friends or himself could not understand. But it is a wonderful evidence of the consistency of the Holy Spirit's work and words all down through the ages. He never contradicts Himself. If the Spirit of God fashioned and taught Elihu, He must, in some measure, reveal the same features of a Spirit-filled life to-day. Light is light, although it is 3000 years old. What are some of these features?

1. HE IS A SPIRIT-MADE MAN. "The Spirit of God hath made me" (v. 4). This may be true, in a general sense, of all men, but it is true, in a very special and unique sense, of the real "man of God." He is born by the Spirit—quickened by the Spirit into a new life. He is a new creation after the image of God by the Holy Ghost. God needs *new* vessels for the new wine of His Gospel.

2. HE IS A SPIRIT-INSPIRED MAN. "The breath of the Almighty hath given me life." This also may be true, in a measure, of every man, but it is a marvellous description of the new life in God. Those dead in sin need the breath of God to put new life into them (Ezek. 37. 9). Those quickened by the Spirit of God are possessed by Him and inspired, as by the very warmth of the breath of the living God dwelling in them. They can say: "I live, yet not I, but Christ, who is the life of God, liveth in me; the breath that I now breathe is the breath of the Almighty; the spirit that I now have is animated by the Spirit of God."

Christ *breathed* on them and said: "Receive ye the Holy
Ghost."

II. **His Position.** Job longed for a "Daysman"
(9. 33). Elihu is bold enough to say: "I am according to
thy wish *in God's stead*" (v. 6). It was a great statement
to make, but the man who is appointed by God to stand in
His stead ought surely to know it, and should not be
ashamed to confess it before men. Did not the Apostle of
the Gentiles say: "*We* are ambassadors for Christ, as
though God did beseech you *by us*: we pray you *in Christ's
stead*, be ye reconciled unto God?" The man in God's
stead is "an *interpreter*, one among a thousand, to shew
unto man what is right for him" (v. 23 R.V.). He himself
is an example and interpretation of the invisible God. His
business is to seek first the Kingdom of God and His
righteousness, and to exhort others to seek these first. He
knows nothing about flattering men with self-pleasing titles
(chap. 32. 22), the claims and character of Him whose he is
and whom he serves are ever before him. An interpreter
of God's mind and will must first be a partaker of that mind
and will. We must drink deeply of this water of life, if
we would become springs of living water for others. Every
spirit-possessed man is an interpreter for God, and such
interpreters are needed, for "the things of God knoweth no
man, but the Spirit of God" (1 Cor. 2. 11). A man may
have all the wisdom of the world, and yet be unable to
interpret the things of God. "The natural man receiveth
not the things of the Spirit of God" (1 Cor. 2. 14).

III. **His Message.** He it is who can say with the
utmost confidence, "God speaketh" (v. 14). He knows
in his own soul that God hath spoken to him, and that He
can still speak in divers ways to the slumbering spirits of
men, that He may draw man away from his evil and
delusive purpose (vv. 15-17). This is a comforting truth

to those who seek the salvation of others, that God in answer to prayer can speak to men "in dreams and visions of the night. " Even then He can open the ear, and seal instruction in their hearts. So, the man of God is a man of faith and hope. But he has also a very definite message to deliver. What is that message? There is in it—

1. REDEMPTION. "Deliver him from going down to the pit: I have found a ransom" (v. 24). God hath found the ransom—the atoning sacrifice in the Man Christ Jesus (1 Tim. 2. 5, 6), so He calls upon all those who stand in His stead to say to that man going down to the pit of darkness and death, "There is *deliverance.*" He, as it were, commands His servant and interpreter to "deliver him" who is on the way to the pit, on the ground that He hath found and provided the Ransom. Apart from the power and virtue of the Cross of Christ, there is no message of salvation from the pit to give. "The Son of Man came... to give His life a ransom for many" (Matt. 20. 28).

2. REGENERATION. "His flesh shall be fresher than a child's (v. 25). This may be figurative language, but it expresses most forcibly the radical change which is wrought by God's redeeming power. Like Naaman—after he had dipped himself seven times in Jordan—he was made a new creature. What the waters did for the famous Syrian captain, the atoning blood of Christ now does for those who believe Him—makes *clean*. The redemption that is in Christ Jesus not only "*satisfies* thy mouth with good," but also "thy youth is *renewed* like the eagle's" (Psa. 103. 5).

3. FELLOWSHIP. "He shall pray unto God, and He shall be favourable unto him; and he shall see His face with joy" (v. 26). After redemption and regeneration comes the privilege of praying and *rejoicing* in the *favour* of God. Yes, the pure in heart shall see God's face and rejoice— that face of love and mercy which has been unveiled to us

in Jesus. "We joy in God through our Lord Jesus
Christ, by whom we have now received the atonement."
"Our fellowship is with the Father and with His Son"
(1 John 1. 3).

4. TESTIMONY. They who would preach redemption to
others should themselves be examples of its regenerating
power. The words here are full of evangelical fervour and
personal experience. "He *singeth* before men, and *saith*,
I have sinned and perverted that which was right, and it
profited me not; He hath redeemed my soul from going
into the pit, and my life shall behold the light" (vv.
27, 28, R.V.). His past life was *profitless*, because it was
one of *perversion*; but now, being *redeemed*, he lives in the
light of the truth. This man who is as one in "God's
stead" was once a sinner like others, but by grace was he
saved. "Such were some of you, but ye are washed." The
personal element must have a place in the preaching of
the Gospel.

THE LORD ANSWERED.
JOB 38. 1; 40. 1-5.

"MAN'S extremity is God's opportunity." It was when
the words of Job and his friends were ended that the Lord
answered Job out of the whirlwind. God's answer is
always final. There is no appeal. The book of Job, like
the books of the Old Testament, closes with the Theophany
—the *appearance* of God. Here, as when He sent His Son,
God's last plea was the manifestation of His own character.
Although God answered Job *out of* the whirlwind, we need
not infer that the *voice* was like a roaring, uprooting
tempest, but that the arguments used had a whirlwind
effect upon the spirit of Job, completely lifting him out of
his present condition of mind into a better way of thinking.

I. Job's Prayer. "Answer Thou me. How many are

mine iniquities and sins? Make me to know my transgression" (chap. 13. 22, 23). He was set on maintaining
his own way. He had lived, no doubt, in all good
conscience before God, but there was now a tendency to
boast of his integrity, as if it were something independent
of the grace of God. If I have sinned, he says, make
me to know the number and nature of my transgressions. God's answer to Job reveals the fact that his
iniquities lay in a different direction than what he
supposed. He is not charged with actual transgression,
but he is overwhelmed with a sense of his own ignorance
and impotency. His *self-confidence* has been rebuked
and withered up.

II. God's Answer. "Then the Lord answered Job"
(chap. 38. 1). God's answer comes in the form of an
avalanche of questions. There are fifty-seven in chapters
38 and 39 alone. Every question seems to bring with
it a flash of self-blinding light. Each interrogation is
in itself a revelation and an education to the wavering
patriarch. All His "hast thous" and "canst thous" are
evidences of what HE *has done* and *can do*. These questions
are so many revelations of God's wisdom and power—of
His perfect control of "the ordinances of Heaven" (chap.
38. 33), or of what we call natural phenomena. Those who
would find fault with the providence of God should study
this divine declaration. The Lord's first question is
enough to take Job's breath away: "Where wast *thou* when
I laid the foundations of the earth?" (v. 4). His word is
truly as a "hammer and a fire." Think of these burning
inquiries: "Hast *thou* commanded the morning?" "Hast
thou entered into the springs of the sea?" "Hast *thou*
walked in the secret of the depth?" "Hast *thou* entered
into the treasures of the snow?" "Canst *thou* bind the sweet
influences of Pleiades?" "Knowest *thou* the ordinances of

Heaven?" "Canst *thou* lift up *thy* voice to the clouds?"
"Canst *thou* send lightnings, that they may go and say unto
thee, Here we are?" The wisdom of man is but foolishness
with God, as the brightest of earth's lights is but a black
spot in the face of the sun. So man at his best is but a
vile speck in the presence of the glory of God.

III. **Job's Confession.** "Behold, I am vile: what
shall I answer Thee? I will lay mine hand upon my mouth
Once have I spoken; yea, twice; but I will proceed no
further" (chap. 40. 4, 5). Job's boasted greatness, like the
tower of Babel, ended in utter confusion when God
appeared. As long as we compare ourselves with men like
ourselves there may be occasion for glorying, but let God
speak, then the hand is laid upon the mouth. "Behold, I
am vile," for this mouth of mine has been speaking the
God-dishonouring thoughts of my mind, but I will "proceed no further" along this way of self-confidence and self-
assertiveness. I will lay mine hand upon my mouth, and
bow in silent submission to the word and will of the Lord
my God. The Lord is in nature as in a holy temple; let all
the earth keep silence before Him. God who at sundry
times, and in divers manners, spake unto the fathers by the
prophets, and to Job through the whirlwind of natural
phenomena, has in these last days spoken unto us by His
Son. The voice is the same, but the revelation is vastly
different. What have we to say for ourselves in the
presence of the Cross of Christ? Here every boastful
mouth must be stopped. Although in self justification,
I have spoken once, yea, fifty times, "but I will proceed
no further" when I see sin in the light of the sufferings and
death of the only begotten Son of God. "Behold, I am
vile;" my righteousness, in the glare of His light, has
turned out to be but "filthy rags." "God be merciful to
me a sinner."

THE BLISSFUL END.
Job 42.

THE storm-tossed soul of Job has got anchored at last in the harbour of God's manifest goodness. As a traveller he has been passing through a dark and dreary desert, hearing anon the howling of ravenous beasts, but is now entered into the light and joys of home. Through much tribulation he entered into this new kingdom of honour and blessing. All great spiritual attainments are reached through suffering. It was so with Moses, Abraham, Joseph, David, Daniel, and Christ. The disciple is not greater here than his Master. "If we suffer, we shall also reign." Now the great climax of Job's history has been reached, but there is about it more of the quietness of a birth than the shock of a revolution. The storm of words is over; the calm of His "Peace be still" has settled upon the troubled waters. In the closing act of this powerful drama there is—

I. **Confession**. Job began his brief answer to the Divine appeal by saying, "I know that Thou canst do everything, and that no thought can be withholden from Thee." Thou canst *do* everything, and Thou dost *see* everything. Thou art omnipotent and omniscient. The whole universe, visible and invisible, is under Thy control, and naked and bare before the eyes of Him with whom we have to do. As man is to be judged by his works, so may the Lord be judged by His. By *His works* ye shall know Him. "The heavens declare His glory, and the firmament showeth forth His handiwork" (Psa. 19. 1). But what does the Cross of His Christ declare? What handiwork does the firmament of His infinite love and mercy shew forth? In the matter of salvation, as well as creation and government, "I know that Thou canst do everything."

II. **Revelation**. "I have heard of Thee by the hearing of the ear, but now mine eye seeth Thee" (v. 5). It is one thing to hear another speak about God; it is a very different thing to see Him by the revelation of His own word, spoken personally to the heart, as Job had now seen Him. The sum of the LORD's answer to Job was a *manifestation of Himself* through His word. The voice of God brought the vision of God to the patriarch's faith. He saw God by the hearing of faith. "Believe, and thou shalt see" (John 11. 40). "The Word of God is quick and powerful,...and is a *discerner* of the thoughts and intents of the heart" of man, and is also a *revealer* of the thoughts and intents of the heart of God. This is the mystery of the incarnation. "The *Word* which was God was made flesh and dwelt among us,...full of grace and truth." Christ, the Word of God, was to a suffering world the revelation of God. You may have often heard of Him, but has your eye yet seen Him?

III. **Humiliation.** "Wherefore I abhor myself, and repent in dust and ashes" (v. 6). Self-abhorrence is the natural consequence of coming face to face with God. When Isaiah saw the Lord upon a throne high and lifted up, he also abhorred himself, saying, "Woe is me!... because I am a man of unclean lips" (Isa. 6. 5). Oh, these *lips!* It was Job's lips that had been acting as traitors in the cause of God. But the lips are only the instruments of the heart and will. Where is boasting when the truth of God comes home to the heart? It is excluded. Saul of Tarsus found this out when the light of the exalted Son of God fell upon him on the way to Damascus. Then he abhorred himself and *repented.*

IV. **Intercession.** "My servant Job shall pray for you; for him will I accept" (v. 8). Job's friends did all that human wisdom and eloquence could do for a man overwhelmed by the power of the Devil, and that was *nothing.* This kind goeth not out but by prayer and sacrifice. *"My servant,"* sweet words to the perplexed and bruised sufferer. It is easy for us to thrash others with our scourge of words, whose prayers we need to save us from our sins. What a privilege and responsibility rests upon the servant of the Lord: *"Him* will I accept." What an encouragement to those who have found favour with God, to plead for others. This ministry belongs to every one who has been reconciled to God. In this Job is a type of our Lord Jesus Christ, who maketh intercession for us, and whom God heareth always, and in whom we are accepted (Heb. 10. 10-14).

V. Emancipation. "The Lord turned the captivity of Job when he prayed for his friends" (v. 10). To Job's "miserable comforters," and to himself, *praying* was much more effectual than arguing. Is it not always so? His friends had misjudged him, but he had all the more need to pray for them. In so doing, the Lord loosed him from the bondage and power of Satan, and made him once more a free man. The Devil had him chained as with iron bands, but God honoured prayer as the means of deliverance. Praying for his friends implied a willingness to forgive them and a readiness to return blessing for cursing. Such an attitude of soul, and such a work of grace, cannot but bring greater liberty and blessing into the life of the suppliant. "First be reconciled to thy brother, and then come and offer thy gift" (Matt. 5. 24).

VI. Satisfaction. "The Lord gave Job twice as much as he had before...The Lord blessed the latter end of Job more than his beginning" (vv. 10-17). Satan has been defeated, and the mercy and truth of God hath triumphed. James said, "Ye have heard of the patience of Job, and have seen the end of the Lord, that the Lord is very pitiful and of tender mercy" (James 5. 11). Yes, the the *end* of all God's dealings with us is *mercy*. While the number of Job's sheep, camels, oxen, and asses was doubled, it was not so with his sons and daughters. He had but the same number that he had before, perhaps implying that his former family were not lost, but only "gone before"—still his, although on the other side of the Jordan of death. If Job was *seventy* years old when he lost all, his years were also doubled, for he lived after this "an hundred and forty years" (v. 16). The Lord's measure is always "heaped up and running over." Those to whom He shows His salvation will be satisfied with long life, yea, eternal life (Psa. 91. 16). No one would covet Job's sufferings. but who would not say, "Let my last end be like his." Judge not before the time. If God hath begun a good work in you, He will carry it on till the day of perfection. Comfort one another with these words.

READY.

1. Some are Ready to Perish (Isa. 27. 13).
2. God is Ready to Pardon (Neh. 9. 17).
3. Be not Ready to Halt (Psa. 38. 17).
4. Be Ready to Speak (Isa. 32. 4).
5. Be Ready to Go (Luke 22. 33).
6. Be Ready to Work (Titus 3. 1).
7. Be Ready to Testify (1 Peter 3. 15).
8. Be Ready to Suffer (Acts 21. 13).
9. Be Ready for His Appearing (Matt. 25. 10).

GREAT NEEDS.
PSALM 80. 18, 19.

1. Life, ...   "Quicken us."
2. Faith, ...   "We will call upon Thy Name.
3. Consecration, ..   "Turn us again, O Lord."
4. Fellowship,   ..   "Cause Thy face to shine."
5. Full Salvation,   "We shall be saved."

STUDIES IN THE PSALMS.

THE HAPPY MAN.
PSALM 1.

THIS First Psalm is a fitting introduction to the sacred Psalter. It constitutes almost a perfect epitome of the whole book. Like the sermon on the mount, it begins with the word "Blessed." The word is in the plural, and has been rendered, "O the happinesses of the man," etc. He is not only blessed, but blessed with all spiritual blessings. This happy man comes before us in a twofold aspect:—

I. **His Negative Character.** There are some things that he will not do; not because law and judgment dares him to do them, but because he has got something better to enjoy, and a positive hatred in his heart for ways and things that are at enmity with the mind and will of God.

1. HE DOES NOT WALK IN THE COUNSEL OF THE UN-GODLY. He knows that "the way of the ungodly shall perish," and he keeps out of it. The *counsel* of the ungodly is to walk in the broad way that leadeth to destruction. His manner of life is not directed by the wisdom of this world, but by that wisdom which cometh from above.

2. HE DOES NOT STAND IN THE WAY OF SINNERS. The *ungodly* may mean those who live in ignorance of God, but *sinners* are those who deliberately transgress against the light. To abide in their way of doing things is to show an attitude that is more at home with the way of sinners than merely walking in the counsel of the ungodly.

3. HE DOES NOT SIT IN THE SEAT OF THE SCORNFUL. Those who begin to walk in the counsel of the ungodly are

in danger of ending in the seat of the scornful.   This seat is the chief seat in the kingdom of Satan.   There is no promotion beyond this.   In a few hours, the Apostle Peter ran through all this experience, from walking in the counsel of the ungodly to the seat of the scornful.   He sat by the fire and denied the Lord with oaths and curses, but when he was converted he strengthened his brethren. Those who scorn at the things of God and His Christ walk after *their own lusts* (2 Peter **3.** 3).

.II. **His Positive Character.**   He is—

1. JOYFUL.   He has many blessings, but "his *delight* is in the law of the Lord" (v. 2).   The Christian life is not one merely of giving up this or that, but it is entering into a new and happy inheritance in the Word of God. True, the prodigal had to give up some things ere he could possess the best robe and enter into the joys of a happy home.   But what were they?   The swine troughs and his rags.   The Word of the Lord is a land flowing with milk and honey.   "Here everlasting streams abide, and never withering flowers."   It is indeed a *"delightsome* land." All who love the Lord will find delight in His Word.

2. THOUGHTFUL.   "In His law doth he meditate day and night."   In the day of prosperity, and in the night of adversity, he makes the Word of God the man of his counsel. *Meditation* on the word of truth is as needful to our spiritual health and strength as mastication is for the physical. Like Elijah's servant, we may need to look again and again before we see the cloud like a man's hand.   "What *think* ye of Christ?"   The Lord expects us to think deeply into these things which He hath caused to be written for our learning. There is no book in all the world that yields such a harvest of blessing to the humble student as the Bible.   The testimony of Thomas à Kempis was, "I have no rest, but in a nook, with the *Book.*"

3. HOPEFUL. "He shall be like a tree planted by the streams of water" (v. 3, R.V.). He is full of expectation, because his circumstances are so very favourable. He is "like a tree that spreadeth out her roots by the river." While other trees are being starved and stunted by drought, his roots are being fully satisfied; buried in the streams of God's truth, and mercy, and grace. He has a meat to eat that others know not of. All whose delight is in the law of the Lord are as trees planted by streams of living waters. The roots of faith and love feed in these life-giving streams.

4. FRUITFUL. "That bringeth forth its fruit in its season." The fruit is according to the character of the tree, and is always in season. Men do not gather grapes of thorns. His roots being in the rivers of God, he has abundance of life, so that fruit-bearing is the natural and simple result. Being *filled* with the Spirit, the fruit of the Spirit is manifested (Gal. 5. 22, 23). The man who is ready, as opportunity offers, to bear testimony for Christ, will bring forth fruit in his *season*. Being filled out of the river of life, he will be filled with the fruits of righteousness (Phil. 1. 11).

5. BEAUTIFUL. "Whose leaf also doth not wither." There is a vital connection between the root and the leaf. Dry roots soon bring the dry rot into the leaf. Men cannot see the roots of the Christian character, but they can see the leaf, and the hidden condition of the roots may be judged by the outward appearance of the leaf. The outward life will be fresh and green when the inward life is pure and full. Withered leaves are signs of a withered life. When our testimony for Christ and His truth loses its freshness and power, we may be sure that there is something wrong with the *roots*, for the streams never run dry. It is the Spirit's purpose to put the beauty of the Lord our God upon us.

6. SUCCESSFUL. "Whatsoever he doeth shall prosper;"
or, whatsoever the tree produceth shall come to maturity.
The bud, and the blossom, produced by the Spirit of
life, will come to perfect fruition. "All cry and no
wool," does not belong to the sheep of His pasture. The
purposes of God begotten in the heart of Joseph, ripened
into perfection, for the Lord was with him and made it to
prosper (Gen. 39. 23). Our Lord could say, "I have
finished the work Thou gavest me to do." And He has left
us an example that we should follow His steps. If it be
God who worketh in us both to will and to do, then what
soever we do shall prosper, for He who hath begun the
good work will carry it on, until the day in which it is
perfected.

III. **The Contrast.** "The ungodly are not so" (v. 4).
No, they are far from it. The ungodly are the *lawless ones*
who have no delight, or reverence for the law of the Lord;
They are a law unto themselves, and the fruits of their own
character and deeds shall be reaped by them. They are
not likened to a tree planted, but to chaff driven. They
have neither root, nor life in themselves. Chaff had once
a close connection with the wheat, and may, in its outward
aspect resemble it, but it is a dead worthless thing, to be
burned with unquenchable fire (Matt. 3. 12). "The way of
the ungodly shall perish" (v. 6). The chaff has no power
to resist either the wind or the fire. The lawless, like
chaff, are driven about with every wind of doctrine,
popular opinion, or worldly success; they have no connection with, or capacity for receiving of those streams of life,
that flow so copiously in the hidden Kingdom of God. They
shall not stand accepted in the judgment nor be numbered
with the congregation of the righteous (v. 5). Only "he that
doeth the will of God abideth for ever" (1 John 2. 17).
How helpless the empty chaff is before the driving force of

the wind. There is no refuge for it. "The wicked is driven
away in his wickedness; but the righteous hath hope in his
death." "Every plant which My heavenly Father hath not
planted shall be rooted up" (Matt. 15. 13). The way of
the ungodly must perish, because it is the way of pride,
pleasure, unbelief, and Christ rejection. It is the way
that seemeth right unto a man, but the end is death. "He
that believeth not the Son shall not see life, but the wrath
of God abideth on him."

THE TRIUNE TESTIMONY.
Psalm 2.

In the book of the Acts, Peter and Paul both quote this
Psalm as having reference to David, and also to the Lord
Jesus Christ as the exalted Son of God. Paul refers to it
as the *Second* Psalm (Acts 4. 25; 13. 33). Undoubtedly
a greater than David is here. This Psalm is separated into
three divisions, and these different sections contain the
testimony of Father, Son, and Holy Spirit; the declaration
of God the Ruler, God the Mediator, and God the
Comforter. Let us hear them—

I. **The Voice of God the Sovereign.** In verses
1 to 6 it is God who speaks. His words reveal the attitude
of the nations toward Himself, and His attitude toward
them as rebels against His law and His Son. These words
of the Lord contain an exhibition of—

1 Human Enmity and Folly. Why do the nations
rage, and their representatives—kings and rulers—take
counsel together against the Lord and His Anointed?
There can be no denial of this, for the charge is made by
Jehovah Himself, who judgeth not by the outward appearance, but who looketh upon the heart. Man, in all his
madness and folly, never imagined a more "vain thing"
than when he thought by breaking the *bands* of His law and

casting away the cords of His love, he could enjoy liberty
and prosperity. To cast off His yoke which is easy, and
His burden which is light, is to put on the iron shackles of
diabolical rule and eternal despair. God anointed Jesus
of Nazareth with the Holy Ghost and with power, that He
might deliver us from all our enemies. Why *rage* against
the Lord and His Anointed? Because the carnal mind is
enmity against God. They will not have this *Anointed*
One to reign over them. These words also reveal—

2. DIVINE DERISION AND DEFIANCE. "He that sitteth
in the Heavens shall laugh: the Lord shall have them in
derision." Jehovah, as the Ruler of the world, is at rest
in the highest Heaven. The rage of a tumultuous people
can no more hinder Him in the fulfilment of His purpose
than the howling of dogs can arrest the progress of the
moon. "*Yet*," despite all their wrath and rebellion, He
has set His King upon His holy hill of Zion. With wicked
hands men crucified the Lord's Anointed, but God raised
Him from the dead and enthroned Him at His own right
hand in the Heavens. The resurrection of Christ is God's
derisive answer to the rage and hatred of men against His
Son. As the waves of the sea put to defiance the silly
mandate of King Canute, so shall the irresistible purposes
of God roll over the proud purposes of men, and "vex them
in His sore displeasure" (v. 5). It is a fearful thing
to fall into the hands of the living God, as Pharaoh's host
fell into the Red Sea. In derision He shall *laugh* at them;
in wrath He shall *speak* to them; and in His sore displeasure
He shall *vex* them. Who shall comfort those whom God
hath purposely vexed? The policy of Mr. Blatchford was
"to fight and defeat the churches," but He that sitteth in
the Heavens shall laugh, and have all such in derision; for
until He is defeated the gates of Hell shall not prevail
against His Church.

II. **The Voice of God the Son** (vv. 7-9). Hear now the language of the Anointed One who shall reign until all His enemies are put under His feet. In David, these words were not fulfilled in their literal and complete sense, but in David's Lord they shall be perfectly accomplished. This statement from the lips of Him who is the Mediator between God and man is full of deep significance. The meaning may be summed up under these four words.

1. REVELATION. "I will declare the decree." The *decree* may here stand for the covenant, or the purpose of God in His Son, with relation to the ungodly nations. In Christ the Word of God was made flesh and dwelt among us; the Only Begotten of the Father hath declared His mind and will, for the law of God was written in His heart.

2. SONSHIP. "The Lord hath said unto Me, Thou art My Son." Sonship, in a very unique sense, is emphatically taught, but there is no attempt to explain the mystery. Jehovah never said to any of the angels, "Thou art My Son, *this day* have I begotten Thee" (Heb. 1. 5). What "this day" may mean is difficult to understand. But it surely points to the fact that this relationship of Fatherhood and Sonship was entered into for the definite purpose of redemption. These words are referred to by Paul, as being fulfilled when God raised up Jesus from the dead (Acts 13. 33). Spoken as they are in this Psalm by the Son, they may be prophetic of that notable day when He would be begotten from the dead, declaring Him to be the Son of God with power (Rom. 1. 3, 4).

3. TRIUMPH. "I shall give Thee the heathen for Thine inheritance, and the uttermost parts of the earth for Thy possession." The Son of God did not come into this world on a matter of speculation. He had the promise of God the Father that a people would be given Him, and finally, as King of the nations, He would have dominion from sea

to sea, and "from the river unto the ends of the earth"
(Psa. 72. 8). The prophet Daniel saw the ANCIENT of
Days giving Him dominion, and glory, and a kingdom,
that all people, nations, and languages should serve Him.
"The pleasure of the Lord shall prosper in *His hand*."
Surely our interests also are safe enough in His hands.

4. JUDGMENT. "Thou shalt break them—lawless
nations—with a rod of iron; Thou shalt dash them in pieces
like a potter's vessel" (v. 9). When He comes, whose *right*
it is to reign, He shall put down all ungodly rule and
authority. In judgment will He establish righteousness
in the earth. The kings and rulers of the earth take counsel
together against the Lord and against *His Anointed*. But
the Lord shall have them in derision, for "the kingdoms of
this world shall become the Kingdom of our Lord and His
Christ" (Rev. 11. 15). Christ is the Man Child brought
forth to rule all nations with a *rod of iron* (not in grace, but
in unyielding righteousness), and has now been caught up
unto God, and to His throne (Rev. 12. 5). This same
Jesus shall come again.

III. **The Voice of God the Spirit.** In verses 10 to
12 we have a different tone. It is more like the voice of
wounded love and entreaty. It is the Holy Spirit's work
to convince of sin, and to guide into all truth. "To-day, if
ye will hear His voice, harden not your hearts." He says—

1. BE WISE. "Be wise now therefore, O ye kings"
(v. 10). Seeing that the Son of God will bring you into
judgment, be wise *now*, while the day of your trial lasts.
"Behold, now is the accepted time." Submission to God
and His Son is the highest wisdom. They are wise who
build on this rock.

2. BE INSTRUCTED. "Be instructed, ye judges of the
earth." The wisdom of this world is foolishness with God.
Don't be so puffed up with pride as to refuse Him who

speaketh from Heaven. Be willing as a child to sit at the feet of the Son of God and learn of Him. Receive the word at His lips. "Search the Scriptures." Gregory the Great said, "The Bible is God's heart in God's words."

3. BE RECONCILED. "Kiss the Son, lest He be angry." To *kiss* the Son is to *lay hold* of Him in an act of love and devotion. He who so kisses the Son kisses the Father also (John 5. 23). The Holy Spirit does not speak of Himself, but pleads with foolish, ignorant men to be reconciled to God lest they "perish in the way" (R.V.). Be reconciled to God, for God hath made Him (Christ) to be sin for us... that we might be made the righteousness of God in Him.

4. BE HUMBLE. "Serve the Lord with fear, and rejoice with trembling" (v. 11). Having given the Son the kiss of confession, and received from Him the kiss of forgiveness, we should serve the Lord with holy fear all the days of our life (Heb. 12. 28). Rejoice in His forgiving grace, but tremble at the thought of falling back into the lawlessness of the self-life. Serve the Lord with that holy reverence which fears lest it should offend Him in any way. Be obedient to His word, ready to do whatever your Lord may appoint. "Grieve not the Holy Spirit" (Eph. 4. 30).

A SONG OF SALVATION.

PSALM 3.

THE historical ground-work of this Psalm is found in the fifteenth chapter of Second Samuel. David's beloved son, Absalom, steals the hearts of the men of Israel, and then rebels against his father. It is a most humbling and distressing experience to discover that your own flesh, whom you had nourished and cherished, has become your most deadly enemy. What Absalom became to David, *self*, or the carnal mind, will sooner or later become to us, if, like him, we fall into temptation and sin. The flesh warreth against the Spirit. This Psalm may profitably be read with the Seventh of Romans. The Psalmist here suffers the agonies and joys of a soul passing from death into life; or from the power of the enemy into the liberty and gladness of God's salvation. Several things may be noted :—

I. **His Enemy.** They were numerous. "*Many* are they that rise up against me" (v. 1). They were exultant. They said, "There is no help for him in God" (v. 2). That soul is in a sad plight indeed, that is shut out from the "help of God." But sin-blinded men are incapable of forming a right judgment of such a case as this. They threw the same taunt in the teeth of our Lord while He hung helpless upon the Cross. "He trusted in God: let Him deliver Him now, if He will have Him." What looks like failure and defeat, in the eyes of our enemies, may be but God's method of leading us into a larger experience of the riches of His grace.

II. **His Faith**. "But Thou O Lord art a shield about me; my glory, and the lifter up of mine head" (v. 3, R.V.). While the unbelievers are saying, "There is no help for him *in* God," the believer is rejoicing in the consciousness that God is *round about* him as a shield of defence, and that he is even now *in* God. Being in God, God becomes his glory, and the *Lifter* up of his head. My Shield, my Glory, my Lifter. He endures, like Moses, by seeing Him who is invisible. The heart that trusteth in Him will be *helped* (Psa. 28. 7).

III. **His Testimony.** "I cried unto the Lord, and He heard me; I laid me down and slept; the Lord sustained me" (vv. 4, 5). Selah. This is a comforting word. He prayed, the Lord heard him, and so delivered him from all his fears and anxieties, that he was able to lie down and sleep peacefully, because the Lord sustained him. The prayer of faith shall save the fearful as well as the sick. The apostle James says, "Is any among you afflicted? let him pray" (5. 13). He shall be kept in perfect peace whose mind is stayed on the Lord (Isa. 26. 3). This "Selah" at the end of verse 4 is most significant, when contrasted with the one at the end of verse 2. The word is supposed to be a musical sign, a *pause*, and used here to arrest attention. The word occurs in the Psalms 73 times. The language of verse 4 contradicts and belies the statement in verse 2. So these "Selahs" should be solemnly emphasised. Christian experience gives the lie to infidelity.

IV. **His Courage.** "I will not be afraid of ten thousands of people that have set themselves against me round about" (v. 6). Why should he fear the forces of evil which surrounded him, while he knew that Jehovah was about him as a *shield*. The man of holy vision is a man of courage. The servant of Elisha was full of fear when he saw the Syrian host encamped round about them, so he cried, "Alas my master, how shall we do?" But confidence and courage came into his heart after his eyes were opened (2 Kings 6). Joshua "feared not" after the "Captain of the Host" revealed Himself to him. As an old writer has said: "It makes no matter what our enemies may be, though for number, legions; for power, principalities; for subtilty, serpents; for cruelty, dragons; for vantage of place, a prince of the air; for maliciousness, spiritual wickedness. In Christ Jesus our Lord, we shall be more than conquerors." "If God be for us, who can be against us?" (Rom. 8. 31).

V. **His Victory.** "Thou hast smitten all mine enemies upon the cheek bone; Thou hast broken the teeth of the ungodly" (v. 7). The Lord never smites a man behind his back. The cheek that was burning with pride and arrogance, will be made to burn with shame and dishonour.

The teeth of the ungodly are often sharp and merciless,
seeking to tear the character of the godly man to pieces:
but the Lord can break their teeth, so that they become
perfectly harmless. The salvation of God's people
belongeth unto the Lord (v. 8). We are ready to forget
this, and to cease to work out in our daily life, that which
God the Spirit hath wrought in us. It is ours to trust, it
is His to smite. Vengeance belongeth unto Him. The
enemy may count us, as they counted Christ, sheep for
their slaughter; and though for His sake we are killed
all the day long, yet are we "more than conquerors through
Him that loved us" (Rom. 8. 37). Thanks be to
God who giveth us the victory through our Lord Jesus
Christ

WHOLESOME WORDS.

Psalm 4.

This psalm is dedicated to the leader of those who use
stringed instruments. It is indeed a psalm of life. There
are in it notes that speak of sadness, gladness, and madness.
The various conditions, or seasons, of the life year are here,
in a way, represented. We shall try and gather up the
truth taught as having reference to three classes of
individuals.

I. Words of Encouragement to the Believing.
This testimony of the psalmist should be an inspiration to
every child of God. What God did for him He can still
do for those who put their trust in Him. What was that?

1. He made him free. "Thou hast set me at large
when I was in distress" (v. 1, R.V.). Through fear and
distress, he had been like one in a prison, but the Lord
set him at liberty. It is when men are at their wit's end,
that they are made to see the salvation of God. We are

shut up to *faith* that we might be brought out into a *large* place. To be set at large by the saving grace of God is a great deliverance.

2. HE MADE HIM GLAD. "Thou hast put gladness in my heart" (v. 7). The gladness of a harvest time is not to be compared with the gladness of a great spiritual deliverance. "Corn and wine," the richest of earth's blessings, come far short of the "joy of the Lord." God put gladness in the heart, by the manifestation of His grace and power on our behalf. Although we see Him not, yet believing, we rejoice, with joy unspeakable and full of glory.

3. HE MADE HIM SAFE. "Thou Lord makest me dwell in safety" (v. 8). He could lie down, and sleep the sleep of peace; for the Lord gave him that sweet assurance of His protecting care, that all fear fled. "The beloved of the Lord shall dwell in safety by Him" (Deut. 33. 12). Free, Glad, and Safe, is the condition of all, who by faith have received the Gospel of the Lord Jesus Christ. They are set apart by the Lord as His own peculiar, personal treasure (v. 3).

II. **Words of Rebuke to the Unbelieving**. There are three things those "Sons of men" were guilty of, and for which the psalmist rebukes them. Three sins which many of the unbelieving "sons of men" in our own day are guilty of.

1. PRACTISING RIDICULE. "How long will ye turn my glory into dishonour?" (v. 2, R.V.). The glory of David was in that he trusted and hoped in the Lord (Psa. 3. 3). Any fool may mock at faith, as he may mock at sin. The man must be morally mad who would attempt to make confidence in God appear to be a dishonourable thing. Yet some do it.

2. LOVING VANITY. "How long will ye love vanity?"
They love vanity who love that which is worthless to
satisfy, that which is uncertain, that which has the
appearance of being what it is not—the world. The
experience of Solomon stands as a warning and a rebuke
to all who set their hearts on earthly things. Anything
and everything that occupies the place Christ should have,
is vanity (1 John 2. 15).

3. SEEKING FALSEHOOD. "How long will ye...seek
after falsehood" (v. 2, R. V.). One does not need to go
far in search of falsehood. He will find it in his own
heart. To seek falsehood, for its own sake instead of
the truth, is a positive proof of a mind at enmity with
God. The false and deceitful heart seeks food convenient
for it. Christ is the truth; true and honest hearts will
seek Him. "Without are dogs...and every one that loveth
a lie" (Rev. 22. 15, R. V.).

III. **Words of Entreaty to the Anxious**. Let us
now hear as with trumpet tone, a call to—

1. STAND. "Stand in awe, and sin not" (v. 4). Stop,
before you go any further in sinful unbelief, and consider
where, and what you are. Stand in awe at the thought of
disobeying God's Word (Psa. 119. 161). Stand in awe at
the thought of the wages of sin (Rom. 6. 23). Stand in
awe at the thought of opportunities lost, the uncertainty of
life, and the certainty of judgment. Stand in awe as you
think of the infinite love and mercy of God towards sinners,
in the sufferings and death of His Son. Stand in awe, lest
ye should resist the gracious stirrings of His Holy Spirit
and die in your sin.

2. COMMUNE. "Commune with your heart upon your
bed, and be still." Have a quiet time with your own heart.
Examine *yourself*. "If we would judge ourselves, we should

not be judged" (1 Cor. 11. 31). The heart is deceitful. Commune with it, find out its motives, search into its desires, and cross-question its purposes. In the solitude of the bed-chamber, and in the stillness of the night, there is a favourable opportunity of finding out the true character of our own hearts. "Prove your own selves" (2 Cor. 13. 5). The bed and the heart are fields in which many startling discoveries have been made, many great battles fought, and many victories lost and won—bloodless battles, whose issues reach away into the depths of eternity.

3. SACRIFICE. "Offer the sacrifices of righteousness" (v. 5). As the result of standing and communing, there are sure to be revelations. Things to be given up, or offered unto God as sacrifices. Then let the sacrifice be *righteous*. Let there be a willing and whole-hearted surrender to the will of God. There are sacrifices, like Absalom's which are not righteous, but only a hypocritical performance, to blind the eyes of the God-fearing, and secure some personal advantage (2 Sam. 15. 12). Your reasonable service is to present *yourselves* unto God, "for ye are not your own, ye are bought with a price." Let us not forget Him, who did offer unto God the sacrifice of righteousness, when He offered Himself without spot. He hath left us "an example that we should follow His steps."

4. TRUST. "Trust in the Lord." Trust and obey, there is no other way. The standing in awe, and the communing with the heart should lead to *faith* or it will end in failure. *Trust* is a very simple and sweet word, associated as it is with the greatest of all names, JEHOVAH, and the most precious of all privileges and blessings. Any child can understand it, but does any man, or angel in Heaven, understand to the full all the possibilities that lie within it, as the link that binds the soul to the Eternal God?

PRAYERFUL PURPOSES.

Psalm 5. 1-8.

THOSE who believe in set forms of prayer can find no justification for such a practice in the Book of Psalms. There is throughout the whole book a blessed disregard for all such mechanical and stultifying conventionalities, because the prayers of the psalmists are the utterances of burning, agonising hearts. Every variety of form is adopted, according to the varied needs of the soul. We shall note—

I. **His Requests.** There are four definite petitions. He prays—

1. That his WORDS may be attended to. "Give ear to my words, O Lord." We don't always wish the Lord to mark our words, they are at times such poor vehicles of our soul's desires. But the psalmist *meant* every word that he uttered in the Divine ear. Beware of vain words. We are not heard for our much speaking.

2. That his MEDITATION may be considered. "O Lord, consider my meditation." There may be abundance of eloquent words where there is no real exercise of soul, no true spirit of prayer. The Lord hath said, "Come, let us *reason* together." Surely to reason out a matter implies serious and deliberate thinking. Our prayer-words should be the outcome of solemn meditation on the whole inner condition and circumstances of the soul. God not only heareth the words, but He looketh upon the heart. It has been said that "Prayer without fervency is like hunting with a dead dog."

3. That his CRY may be heard. "Hearken unto the voice of my cry, my King and my God" (v. 2). These are three expressive "Mys." "My Cry, My King, My God." The meditation is the *source*, the words are the *channel*, but the cry is the *force* with which the stream of prayer rushes

on. It is possible to have correct words, and deep thinking, and yet no real intensity of heart, no agony of soul. It was when God heard the *"Cry* of the Israelites" that He sent deliverance (Exod. 3. 7). The cry is unto Jehovah, as his King and God, as his Ruler and Creator. As He who fashioned his being, and governs his life. This consciousness of subjection and ownership gives intensity and hopefulness to the cry of need. It was with kindred, but deeper feelings, that Christ cried on the Cross, "My God, My God."

4. That in RIGHTEOUSNESS he might be *led*. "Lead me, O Lord, in Thy righteousness, because of mine enemies" (v. 8). Newberry reads it, "because of mine *observers.*" We need leading into the righteousness of God because of those who are watching our words and our ways, that they, seeing our good works, may glorify our Father in Heaven. This He is willing to do for His Name's sake (Psa. 23. 3). "In all thy ways acknowledge Him, and He shall direct thy paths" (Prov. 3. 6).

II. His Resolutions. Earnest praying will lead to earnest acting. Our Lord said, "He that heareth and *doeth* these sayings of Mine, I will liken him unto a wise man" (Matt. 7. 24).

The psalmist resolves that—

1. IN THE MORNING HE WOULD PRAY. "My voice shalt Thou hear in the morning" (v. 3). Let each opening day be met with an open heart. God hears the voice of the bird in the morning, why not thine? Morning by morning let the keys of your life be put into the hands of your Lord and Master. The morning voice must be specially sweet to Him, who, "in the morning, rising up a great while before day, went into a solitary place, and there prayed."

2. IN EXPECTATION HE WOULD LOOK. "In the morning

will I order my prayer unto Thee, and will keep watch"
(v. 3, R.V.). Like Daniel, he would open his window and
look toward the Holy City. He would order his prayer, as
Elijah ordered the sacrifice upon the altar on Carmel, and
kept watch for the coming fire; or as when he prayed
for the rain, and told his servant to go again and watch
for the cloud like a "man's hand." We direct our letters
to our friends at a distance, and "keep watch" for the
postman. In the well-doing of praying and watching be
not weary, "for in due season ye shall reap if you
faint not."

3. IN GRACE HE WOULD COME. "But as for me, in the
multitude of Thy lovingkindness I will come into Thy
house" (v. 7, R.V.). The praying spirit longs for closer
fellowship with God. He believes, that through the great
lovingkindness of God, he would yet have the joy of
fellowship and service in His house. He does not look upon
this privilege as being the result of any merit of his own,
but all according to the goodness of God. The house of
God not made with hands, can only be entered through the
mercy and grace of Him who is the Way, the Truth, and
the Life (John 14. 1-6).

4. IN FEAR HE WOULD WORSHIP. "In Thy fear will I
worship toward Thy holy temple." The earthly temple
had not yet been built, but David would worship toward
the throne of His Holiness. *Worship* is the highest
possible form of service. Praying, serving, worshipping.
We first pray in the outer court, at the altar of sacrifice.
We serve in the holy place, but in the holiest of all we
worship. The voice of testimony should frequently give
place for the silence of adoration. In His strength we
serve, in His fear we worship. What Satan asked of
Christ, Christ expects from us. "Worship Him" (Matt.
4. 9) and the Kingdom shall be thine.

POWERFUL PLEAS.

Psalm 6.

The chief reason why the Psalms are so full of praise is because they are so full of prayers. In this Psalm we have a troubled soul using some powerful arguments with God, giving us an example of prevailing importunity. He mentions—

I. **The Anger of the Lord.** "O Lord, rebuke me not in Thine anger." His sensitive soul is deeply alarmed at the thought of the awfulness of God's anger, and the hotness of His displeasure (v. 1). He is terrified at the possibility of deserving his chastening in wrath. Serve the Lord with fear.

II. **His Own Weakness.** "Have mercy upon me, O Lord, for I am weak" (v. 2). A real consciousness of our own impotency will give urgency and point to our pleadings.

III. **His Own Sorrowfulness.** "My soul is sore vexed, but Thou, O Lord, how long?" (v. 3). His was no mere lip-praying; the depths of his soul were stirred up; there was agony in his cry.

IV. **The Mercies of God.** "Oh save me for Thy mercies' sake" (v. 4). This is a mighty plea in the eyes of Him whose Name is the Lord God "Merciful." He who "delighteth in mercy" will not be deaf to this cry.

V. **The Profitlessness of Death.** "In death there is no remembrance of Thee," etc. (v. 5). This is true of those spiritually dead. Plead for quickening that ye might be saved from a God-forgetting state of soul.

VI. **The Significance of Tears.** "I water my couch with my tears" (v. 6). Jesus also wept, and God can never forget the value of such pure heart-drops of grief and silent witnesses of love.

VII. **His Own Hatred of Iniquity.** "Depart from me all ye workers of iniquity" (v. 8). He further pleads his separateness in spirit from the ways and methods of the ungodly.

VIII. **His Own Faith in God**. "The Lord hath heard... the Lord will receive my prayer" (vv. 8-10). The answer had come into his heart; he believed the message, and rested on the faithfulness of God. "Go thou and do likewise."

IN THE FACE OF THE FOE.

Psalm 7.

LEARN from this Psalm how to behave when face to face with wicked men, and the principles and forces of unrighteousness.

I. **Trust**. "O Lord my God, in Thee do I put my trust" (v. 1). Keep the shield of faith ever bright with constant use. "Happy is He who hath the God of (wayward) Jacob for his help" (Psa. 146. 5).

II. **Pray**. "Save me from all them that persecute me" (v. 1). Call upon God to arise, and to lift Himself up for your defence (v. 6). It is His prerogative to execute righteousness and judgment for the oppressed (Psa. 103. 6).

III. **Search**. Search yourself and your ways, lest this trial may have come upon you because of iniquity (vv. 3, 4) Let God also search your heart and your hands, lest there may be some hidden hindrance to His help (Psa. 66. 18).

IV. **Testify**. "The Lord shall judge the people" (v. 8). Don't be afraid to speak out and declare His righteousness, even when His providence seems most against thee, for the Lord doth reward us according to the cleanness of our hands (Psa. 18. 20).

V. **Confess**. "My defence is of God, which saveth the upright in heart" (v. 10). Although the enemy may say, "There is no help for Him in God," make full confession of Him as your present and all-sufficient Saviour.

VI. **Warn**. "God is angry with the wicked every day, if he turn not He will whet His sword" (vv. 11, 12). Don't be intimidated by their threatenings or scorn. Warn them that the axe is laid at the root of all fruitless trees (Matt. 3. 10). The sword of the Lord is never sharpened in vain.

VII. **Praise**. "I will praise the Lord according to His righteousness, and will sing praise to the Name of the Lord Most High" (v. 17). Fearless trust is sure to end in fullness of praise. "Blessed are all they that put their trust in Him."

THE EXCELLENT NAME.
PSALM 8.

"How excellent is Thy Name in all the earth." These are the first and last words of this Psalm, and may be taken as the keynote. His NAME stands for all the riches and glory of His character. The glory of it is "above the Heavens," although the Heavens are a reflection of it (Psa. 19. 1). This wondrous glory, the glory of infinite grace, can also manifest itself through such weak things as "babes and sucklings" (v. 2; Matt. 11. 25). God hath been pleased so to choose weak things that the might of the worldling might be confounded (1 Cor. 1. 27). But the glory of this Name, which is seen in the "moon and the stars"—the work of His fingers (v. 3)—finds its chief manifestation in "man," insignificant as he is, when contrasted with the greatness of the material heavens. "What is man that Thou art mindful of him?" (v. 4). See how the excellency of His Name is revealed in His dealings with man. It is seen—

I. **In the Character of Man**. "Thou hast made him a little lower than God" (v. 5, R.V.). Made after His image, but a "little lower." How near God has come to man in imprinting His own likeness in Him. What

ravages sin hath wrought that this holy temple should become the workshop of the Devil.   Grace restores to sonship.

II. **In His Mindfulness of Him.**   "What is man that
Thou art mindful of Him?"   The mindfulness of God is
another manifestation of the excellency of His character.
He is mindful of man in all the arrangements of His
material creation and providence.   This gracious mindfulness began before the foundation of the world, when in His
purpose the Lamb was slain.   What is man that his highest
interests are for ever in the mind of God?

III. **In the Honour given Him.**   "Thou hast crowned
him with glory and honour; Thou madest him to have
dominion over the works of Thy hands" (vv. 5, 6).   All
things were put under him, till sin entered, then the crown
fell from his head, and had to be given to another, even
Jesus, who was made for a little while lower than the
angels; who, after the sufferings of a substitutionary death,
was crowned with glory and honour (Heb. 2. 8, 9).   How
excellent is the Name of Him who sought to put such glory
on the head of man!

> "How poor, how rich, how abject, how august,
> How complicate, how wonderful is man."

IV. **In His Sacrifice for Man**   "What is man... that
Thou visitest him?"   In a very deep and real sense, God
hath visited man in the Person of His only beloved Son.
Man, in his sin and shame, could not visit God in peace,
but in the excellency of His Name, and at an awful cost,
He hath visited man.   Visited him in his hopeless distress,
bringing with Him and offering to him a perfect remedy
for all his sins and sorrows.   "Lord, what is man that Thou
shouldest *set Thine heart upon Him?*" (Job 7. 17).

"WHAT IS MAN?" (vv. 4, 5).

1. "That Thou art *mindful of him?*" Merciful CON-
  SIDERATION.

2. "That Thou *visitest* him?" INCARNATION.

3. "That Thou hast *made him* a little lower than God?" REGENERATION.

4. "That Thou hast *crowned him with glory*?" GLORIFICATION.

_____

I WILL, FOR THOU HAST.

PSALM 9. 1-10.

IT is good when *our* "I wills" find their motive power in the "Thou hasts" of God. In this Psalm there is—

I. **A Joyful Purpose,** This purpose was—

1. To PRAISE GOD. "I will praise Thee, O Lord" (v. 1). Praise is surely the expression of a full and satisfied heart. The salvation accomplished for us by Jesus Christ is such as demands continual praise (Heb. 13. 15).

2. To TESTIFY FOR GOD. "I will shew forth all Thy marvellous works." His wonderful works of grace are well worthy of being shown forth by the lips and lives of all who have experienced the power and riches of them.

3. To REJOICE IN GOD. "I will be glad and rejoice in Thee" (v. 2). This gladness is something deeper than that produced by the mere increase of corn and wine (Psa. 4. 7). It is the joy of the Lord, because it is joy in God (Phil 4. 4).

II. **A Powerful Reason.** This reason, like the purpose, is threefold.

1. Because of His FAITHFULNESS. "Thou hast maintained my cause" (v. 4). It is His to maintain the cause of the afflicted and the poor in spirit (Psa. 140. 12). When our cause is the cause of God, it will be stoutly maintained by Him.

2. Because of His POWER. "Thou hast rebuked the heathen" (v. 5). All the pride and possessions of the ungodly "shall flow away in the day of His wrath" (Job. 20. 28).

Heathenish thoughts and practices are rebuked in the presence of the Lord.

3. Because of His MERCY.   "Thou Lord hast not forsaken them that seek Thee" (v. 10).   God, in all the riches of His grace and power is ever within the reach of the whole-hearted seeker (Jer. 29. 13).   The great Deliverer of the past, is the same Deliverer for the present and the future.

III. **An Inspiring Hope.**   This is—

1. The Hope of ENDURANCE.   "The Lord shall endure for ever" (v. 7).   The blessings of God's grace are as lasting as God Himself.   As long as HE endures, His redeemed ones will be enriched with the Divine life and fullness.   "Ye are Christ's, and Christ is God's."

2. The Hope of RIGHTEOUSNESS.   "He shall judge the world in righteousness" (v. 8).   Unrighteousness, the fruit of the mystery of sin, is ever with us, but "He hath appointed a day, in the which He will judge the *world* in righteousness, by that Man whom He hath ordained" for this purpose (Acts 17. 31).   "Shall not the Judge of all the earth do right?"

3. The Hope of SALVATION.   "The Lord shall be a refuge for the oppressed" (v. 9).   For those oppressed with inward sin or outward trouble.   "God is our refuge and strength, a *very present* help in time of trouble."   They are safely kept whose life is hid with Christ in God.

CHARACTERISTICS OF THE WICKED.

PSALM 10.

WHEN God, as the light of His people, hides Himself (v. 1), the ungodly owls of darkness are sure to manifest themselves.   They are—

I. **Boastful.**   "The wicked boasteth of his heart's

desire" (v. 3); although that desire is for things forbidden of God and destructive to his own soul. Even the man that boasted in his lawful riches was branded by God as a fool (Luke 12. 20). "The desire of the wicked shall perish" (Psa. 112. 10).

II. **Perverse.** "He blesseth the covetous, whom the Lord abhorreth" (v. 3). They honour men according to the amount of their possessions, instead of the pureness of their lives. They call light darkness, and darkness light. Like Balaam, they love the wages of unrighteousness.

III. **Proud.** "The wicked, through the pride of his countenance, will not seek after God"—will not require it (R. V., v. 4). In his pride and self-confidence, he has no sense of his need of God. The natural man receiveth not the things of the Spirit of God.

IV. **Godless.** "God is not in all his thoughts" (v. 4). Every day he plays the fool, by practically saying, "There is no God." No matter how much God in His providence may be doing for him, in his own soul and character he is utterly godless, guilty, and hopeless.

V. **Blind.** "Thy judgments are far above out of his sight" (v. 5). He is so short sighted, that he cannot see the marvellous workings of God in nature or in grace. Like the man with the muck rake, the crown of glory is out of his sight, because he is blinded by the love of this world.

VI. **Self-confident.** "He saith in his heart, I shall not be moved" (v. 6). Because sentence against unbelief and evil workers is not executed speedily, they imagine themselves secure. But while they say, Peace and safety, sudden destruction cometh upon them. In wrath God shall move them—move them out of their very graves, into a hopeless eternity (Rev. 20. 12, 13).

VII. **Deceitful.** "Under his tongue is mischief...he lieth in wait as a lion to catch the poor...he humbleth himself that the helpless may fall" (vv. 7-10, R.V.). The principle of righteousness is not in him. His smooth words have under them the poison of sinful lust. If he croucheth in lowliness, it is that he might devour as a lion. His *heart* is deceitful, and his life can be nothing else.

VIII. **Deceived.** "He hath said in his heart, God hath forgotten; He will never see it" (v. 11). But "God hath seen it, for He beholdeth mischief and spite, to requite it with His hand" (v. 14). In deceiving others, he deceives himself. "Be not deceived, God is not mocked, whatsoever a man soweth, that shall he also reap" (Gal. 6. 7).

_____

A BLESSED AND SORROWFUL CONDITION.

Psalm 11.

THE state of the righteous and the wicked are set before us here in striking contrast.

I. The Condition of the Righteous. They are—

1. TRUSTFUL. "In the Lord put I my trust" (v. 1). Their confidence is not in themselves, but in the Lord, and, though He slay them, yet will they trust in Him. They knew the NAME of the Lord as a strong tower, they ran into it, and are safe (Prov. 18. 10).

2. DESPISED. The ungodly deride them, saying, "Flee as a bird to your mountain" (v. 1, Psa. 9. 9). Yes, thank God, they have a mountain to flee to; but where will *they* flee to when the wrath of God is revealed from Heaven against all ungodliness? They may bend their bow now and "shoot at the upright in heart" (v. 2), but where shall they flee when God whets His sword and bends His bow? (Psa. 7. 12).

3. TRIED. "The Lord trieth the righteous" (v. 5). It is because that He is righteous that He trieth the hearts of men (Psa. 7. 9). He tried Abraham, and the blessedness of the man that endureth temptation came upon him (James 1. 12). Wood, hay, and stubble are never put into the fiery furnace of trial (Dan. 6. 23).

4. LOVED. "The righteous Lord loveth the righteous" (v. 7). The compassionate eyes of the Lord are ever over the righteous, and His ears open unto their prayers (1 Peter 3. 12). Loved with an everlasting love, a love that is stronger than death, and that the many waters of this world's sins and sorrows cannot quench.

II. The Condition of the Wicked.

1. THEY SECRETLY OPPOSE THE RIGHTEOUS. "They make ready their arrow upon the string, that they may *privily* shoot at the upright in heart" (v. 2). "They shoot their arrows, even bitter words, that they may shoot in secret at the perfect" (Psa. 64. 3, 4). Their carnal minds are at enmity against God, and all that is Godlike in His people. But every hidden thing shall be revealed.

2. THEIR ACTS ARE SEEN BY THE LORD. "His eyes behold, His eyelids try the children of men" (v. 4). Their secret purposes are naked before Him with whom they *have to do*. Even now they suffer for their evil-doing, for "the face of the Lord is against them" (Psa. 34. 16). All that the "face of the Lord" stands for is set against their principles of life.

3. THEIR MANNER OF LIFE IS HATED BY THE LORD. "The wicked and him that loveth violence, His soul hateth" (v. 5). God loved a world of sinners, but the Cross of Christ is the expression of His infinite hatred of sin. To love wickedness and hate righteousness is to be in league with the Devil, and become a fit subject

for the wrath of God.   God is angry with the wicked
every day.

4. THEIR FINAL PORTION IS FEARFUL.   "Upon the
wicked He shall rain snares, fire and brimstone, and an
horrible tempest: this shall be the portion of their cup"
(v.6).   The wider the cup of iniquity, the greater the
portion of curse.   This rain of *snares* will entrap every
guilty foot, and this fire and tempest will search out
every hidden thing (Psa. 75. 8).

HELP, LORD.
PSALM 12.

IN this psalm we have a loud cry to the Lord for help in
backsliding times.   To whom can we go, when the tongues
of pride and vanity are clamouring so loudly that the testimony of God's people can scarcely be heard.   Our help
cometh from the Lord, He giveth power to the faint.   The
psalmist gives us many reasons for thus calling upon the
help of the Lord.   "Help, Lord—

I. **For the Godly Man Ceaseth"** (v. 1).   Godliness
has never been popular amongst men.   In proportion to
the fewness of their number, and the weakness of their
character, will wicked men and the powers of darkness
prosper.   "Ye are the salt of the earth; if the salt lose His
savour, wherewith shall it be salted?"

II. **"For the Faithful Fail."**   In such times of testing
and general backsliding, the faithful are in great danger
of letting go their grip of God and drifting down with the
polluting stream.   To fail in our faithfulness to God and
men, in such adverse circumstances, is always a great
temptation.   Then is the time to cry "Help, Lord."

III. **For Vanity, Flattery, and Deceit are Pre-
valent** (v. 2).   This is a threefold cord that can only be

broken by the help of God. In the absence of godliness, vanity, flattery, and deceit, are the natural outcome of the unrenewed heart (Rom. 5. 9).

IV. For Men's Confidence is in Themselves. They say, "With our tongue we will prevail; our lips are our own; who is lord over us?" (v. 4). *Confidence*, was never put to a baser use than this. The tongue is a mighty weapon, but when ungodly men hope to *prevail* by it, it is but an "unruly evil, full of deadly poison." "He that trusteth in his own heart is a fool." Such self-confidence is sure to lead to the denial of the Lordship of Christ.

V. For Thou hast Promised. "For the sighing of the needy, now will I arise, saith the Lord" (v. 5). The promises of God are always a powerful plea for help. The ungodly are "strangers to the covenant of promise," but let us see that we don't act as if we were strangers to them. His promises are given that they might be claimed.

VI. For Thy Words are Pure (v. 6). There is no possibility of corruption and deceit in them. His words are "as silver tried in a furnace *on the earth*, purified seven times" (R.V.). The words of the Lord are pure, *enlightening* the eyes (Psa. 19. 8). The eye-sparkling power of the Word of God is being constantly proven. Every answered prayer, every promise received, has an eye-enlightening effect. "He is faithful that has promised."

VII. For without Thy Help, Wickedness shall Prevail. "The wicked walk on every side, when vileness is exalted among the sons of men" (v. 8, R.V.). The world loves its own. The power of the presence of God, in His people, and with them, is a standing rebuke to all vileness. All our efforts, apart from this, will be utterly useless. "Not by might nor by power, but by My Spirit, saith the Lord." "Help, Lord!"

HOW LONG, LORD?
Psalm 13.

THE preceding psalm is a cry for help: to the psalmist this help seems long in coming.   One has to learn to wait as well as pray.   Such varied experiences are needed for the discipline of the soul.   The language of this psalm is—

I. **The Language of Anxiety.**   He is concerned about—

1. THE DIVINE FORGETFULNESS.   "How long wilt Thou forget me, O Lord?" (v. 1).   God is mindful of His people, but sometimes His dealings with us may seem as if He had forgotten.   Prayers are long in being answered, and the supernatural may for a time have disappeared from our lives.

2. THE FELT WANT OF HIS PRESENCE.   "How long wilt Thou hide Thy face from me?"   Those who *never* miss the absence of the face of God are more to be pitied.   It may be our own iniquities and sins that hide him from us (Isa. 59. 2); but, if not, though He hide His face for a moment, we are still assured of His everlasting kindness (Isa. 54. 7, 8).

3. HIS OWN IMPOTENCY.   "How long shall I take counsel in my soul?" (v. 2).   Cast upon his own resources, he finds them altogether unavailing.   Even the best and wisest of men, when left to themselves, are poor indeed.   He longs to get out of himself into the wisdom and strength of God.   To be fruitful, we must abide in Him.

4. THE POWER OF HIS ENEMY.   "How long shall mine enemy be exalted over me?"   The absence of the power of God, implies the presence of the power of the enemy.   How long shall mine enemy triumph?   Just so long as the

face of God is unseen. Thy face Lord will we seek; that face revealed to us, in the face of Jesus Christ.

II. **The Language of Intercession.** He now pleads for—

1. THE CONSIDERATION OF HIS CASE. "Consider and hear me, O Lord my God" (v. 3). There is a holy familiarity about this request. He who said, "Come, let us reason together," condescends to deal with us as a man. The case that is stated *fully* will by Him be considered carefully.

2. ENLIGHTENED EYES. "Lighten mine eyes, lest I sleep the sleep of death" (v. 3). The influence of Divine light is to awaken from death (Eph. 5. 14). The absence of spiritual light, like the natural, means barrenness and death. The eyes of our understanding need to be enlightened ere we can know what is the *hope* of His calling, the *riches* of His inheritance, or the exceeding greatness of His *power* (Eph. 1. 18, 19).

III. **The Language of Confession.** He makes confession of his—

1. FAITH. "I have trusted in Thy mercy" (v. 5). What else can any needy soul trust. Having trusted *His mercy* in the past, we will trust it still. It is a mercy that *His* mercy is available.

2. HOPE. "My heart shall rejoice in Thy salvation." "Weeping may endure for a night, but joy cometh in the morning." He rejoices in hope, at the remembrance of His past mercies, saying, "I will sing unto the Lord, *because He hath* dealt bountifully with me" (v. 6). The God who hath delivered will yet deliver, so faith may sing, even while it seems, in the providence of God, as if He had forgotten. Yet, how long, Lord?

GENERAL CORRUPTION.
PSALM 14.

ALTHOUGH this Psalm is by no means the most popular, it has the unique honour of appearing twice in this book (Compare Psa. 53). The utter failure of man, in the sight of God, needs to be emphasised. See here—

I. **Human Folly.** "The fool hath said in his heart, there is no God." Humanity as a whole is that fool; it is practically atheistic. The word "fool," it is said, comes from a term which means the act of *withering*. The sin-withered deceitful heart of unbelief departs from a living God, and would seek to justify self by saying, "No God."

II. **Divine Scrutiny.** "The Lord looked down from Heaven," etc. What for? To see if there were any seeking the advancement of science, art, or philosophy? No, to see if there were any that did understand their true condition, and *seek God* (v. 2). The chief concern of God about man is, that he seeks not Himself. "Seek ye the Lord while He may be found."

III. **Universal Failure.** "They are all gone aside (all grown sour), all together become filthy: none that doeth good, no, not one" (v. 3). Sour and filthy; like savourless salt, good for nothing. This is a terribly sweeping indictment, but it is a Divine one. God here speaks of what He saw; we may pretend to see something different, but His judgment will stand (Rom. 3. 10-12).

IV. **Practical Ungodliness.** "Have all the workers of iniquity no knowledge? who eat of My people, and call not upon the Lord" (v. 4). Even in the midst of general, moral corruption, God has never been without a witness. The characteristics of the workers of iniquity are the same to-day as of old: ignorance of God; hatred of His people; unbelief—"they call not upon the Lord." To reject the knowledge of God is to be rejected by Him (Hosea 4. 6).

V. Salvation Needed. "O that the salvation of Israel were come out of Zion," etc. (v. 7). Backsliding Israel, like the sinners of to-day, needed to be "*redeemed* out of all his troubles" (Psa. 25. 22). The Deliverer, who is able to turn away ungodliness, must come out of Zion (Rom. 11. 26)—out from the presence of God, and the place where His eternal honour dwelleth. "God so loved the world that He gave His only begotten Son." "Grace and truth *came* by Jesus Christ."

———

THE HEAVENLY CITIZEN.

PSALM 15.

THIS Psalm might be called "The Song of the Sojourner." A question is asked, "Lord, who shall sojourn in Thy tent? Who shall dwell in the hill of Thy holiness?" In the answer given we have the characteristics mentioned which must belong to the spiritual pilgrim, who would abide in the fellowship of God (Rev. 7. 14, 15). He must be—

I. Upright in his Walk. "He that walketh uprightly." "He that saith he abideth in Him ought himself also so to walk, even as He walked" (1 John 2. 6). They must walk by faith who would walk uprightly in the midst of a wicked and perverse generation. God can have no fellowship with unrighteousness.

II. Truthful in his Heart. "Speaketh the truth in his heart" (v. 2). Their hearts must be clean who would abide in the tabernacle of Him who "looketh upon the heart." "The pure in heart shall see God." When the truth is not in the heart, the lips are prone to be deceitful.

III. Charitable to his Neighbour. "He backbiteth not with his tongue...nor taketh up a reproach against his neighbour" (v. 3). A truth-loving heart never uses a backbiting tongue. He cannot help *hearing* reproaches against his neighbour, but he does refrain from "taking

them up. " If evil reproaches were but let alone by God's
people they would soon rot.

IV. **Careful of his Company.** "In his eyes a vile
person is contemned, but he honoureth them that fear the
Lord" (v. 4). Like Mordecai, he can offer no respect to the
vile and haughty Haman. He is a companion of all them
that fear the Lord. He who walks with God, as Noah and
Enoch did, will be separate from sinners.

V. **Faithful to his Promise.** If he swears or gives his
solemn promise to do a thing, he will do it, even to his own
hurt, and change not (Judges 11. 35). This faithfulness
is but a faint imitation of the faithfulness of Him, "who,
for the joy that was set before Him, *endured the Cross*"
(Heb. 12. 2). "Having loved His own, He loved them unto
the end. "

VI. **Merciful in his Dealings.** "He taketh no reward
against the innocent" (v. 5). He will not seek to take
advantage of the ignorant or the poor; he will not be
guilty, as some lawyers are, of taking a reward against the
innocent. To him bribery is robbery. He will not wear
Christ's livery and deny Him honest service (Num. 22. 18).

VII. **Stablished in his Character.** "He that doeth
these things shall never be moved. " The storms and floods
of earth cannot move him out of his place, because his life
is rooted in the will of God. He is like a tree planted by
rivers of water; ye shall not know when drought cometh.
This is the man who abides in the tabernacle of God's
service, and who dwells in the holy hill of His presence.

A GOODLY HERITAGE.
PSALM 16. 5-11.

"THE Lord is the portion of mine inheritance, and of my
cup...yea, I have a goodly heritage. "

I. **The Nature of It.** It is—

1. LARGE. "The Lord is the portion of mine inheritance." The infinite wealth of the character of God Himself is the portion of the believer's cup. No wonder that he has to say, "My cup runneth over." "The Lord is my portion, saith my soul" (Lam. 3. 24); "I know *whom* I have believed," saith the apostle (2 Tim. 1. 12).

2. PLEASANT. "The lines are fallen unto me in pleasant places" (v. 6). Experiences that would otherwise have been desert wastes, have, by the presence and goodness of God become "pleasant places." In this portion we are made partakers of the inheritance of the saints in light. These are the ways of pleasantness and the paths of peace.

3. ETERNAL. "The LORD is the portion of my cup" (v. 5). It will take all eternity to dip up this river of pleasure with the little cup of our life. The portion is divinely suited to the needs of the eternal spirit of man. God's gift of eternal life is the gift of Himself.

II. **The Effect of It.** The conscious possession of such a goodly heritage must powerfully influence the life. There will be—

1. PRAISE. "I will bless the Lord who hath given me counsel" (v. 7). All who have been counselled by His Holy Spirit, and constrained to believe in, and yield themselves to God, have very much to bless Him for. "Ye have not chosen Me, but I have chosen you" (John 15. 16).

2. FELLOWSHIP. "I have set the Lord always before me …He is at my right hand." "Always before me." What an inspiration and comfort in the midst of all the trials and turmoils of life! What a source of restfulness of spirit, with regard to all that was before him! If the miser, or prosperous man of the world, loves to set his possessions before him, so does the man of God; but how different their nature and results.

3. **Stability.** "Because He is at my right hand, I shall

not be moved. " The man who always sets the Lord before him is little likely to be moved away from the hope of the Gospel. All the popular winds of adverse doctrine cannot move him. His heart is fixed, trusting in the Lord.

4. Gladness. "Therefore my heart is glad, and my glory rejoiceth" (v. 9). His *heart* is glad, because it is healed and satisfied. This is not an attempt at rejoicing, like many of the world's "get-ups"; it is the natural or inevitable consequence of a certain condition or attitude of soul. "We joy in God through our Lord Jesus Christ" (Rom. 5. 11).

5. GUIDANCE. "Thou wilt shew me the path of life" (v. 11). Though this holy path of life may be narrow, the trusting soul is confident that He will reveal it moment by moment, and step by step. The path of the high Christian life is the path of continual faith and continual obedience. Day by day we need to be shown the path He would have us follow

6. HOPE. "In Thy presence is fullness of joy; in Thy right hand are pleasures for evermore" (R. V.). Although now the sons of God, "it doth not yet appear what we shall be, but we know that when He shall appear, we shall be *like Him.* " Although His presence is *with us* now, we have not yet passed into the fullness of the blessing of His presence in the glory-land. He holds in His right hand, reserved for us, "pleasures for evermore. " "Blessed Hope!" (Titus 2. 13).

PRAYER AND TESTIMONY.
PSALM 17. 1-8, 15.

THERE must always be a vital relationship between prayer and testimony. Those who are most powerful in prayer are most likely to give the most powerful testimony. The songs of David are just about equalled with his prayers,

Influence for God springs out of influence with God. Observe here—

I. **The Things Asked from God.** David prays for—

1. DIVINE ATTENTION. "Hear the right, O Lord, attend unto my cry" (v. 1). It is for the glory of His Name that He attends to the *righteous* cry of His children. God has a quick ear to "hear the right." No mother or physician can give such close attention to our need as our heavenly Father.

2. DIVINE UPHOLDING. "Hold up my goings in Thy paths" (v. 5). He knows that it is not in man to direct his steps (Jer. 10. 23). By the help of His gracious hand we are kept from stumbling. Our footsteps will slip when we cease to lean upon His strength. He is able to keep the feet of His holy ones (1 Sam. 2. 9, R.V.).

3. DIVINE MANIFESTATION. "Shew Thy marvellous lovingkindness" (v. 7). He pleads for a further revelation of God's character in His kindness, lovingkindness, marvellous lovingkindness. It is so excellent that it constrains men to put their trust under the shadow of His wings (Psa. 36. 7). This marvellous lovingkindness finds its perfect manifestation in and through Jesus Christ.

4. DIVINE PROTECTION. "Keep me as the apple of the eye; hide me under the shadow of Thy wings" (v. 8). They will surely be securely kept who are hidden beneath His wings, and guarded as the apple of the eye. His pinions are long and powerful, and one is more jealous of the eye than any other part of the body. The *strength* and the *carefulness* of God are more than enough to save from our "deadly enemies!"

II. **The Testimony Given for God.** We are assured by the Psalmist that God had—

1. PROVED HIM. "Thou has proved mine heart" (v. 3).

The *heart*, that is so prone to be deceitful, must first be dealt with. The good seed is only fruitful in a "good and *honest* heart" (Luke 8. 15).

2. VISITED HIM. "Thou hast visited me in the night" (v. 3). The heart is proven that it might be visited in mercy and grace. He visits in the night of quiet restfulness, in the night of darkness and sorrow. He knows when to visit, and what to bring. "Behold, I stand at the door" (Rev. 3. 20).

3. TRIED HIM. "Thou hast tried me, and findeth no evil purpose in me" (R.V., *margin*). The trial of your faith is precious; when perfectly sincere, it will be to His praise and glory (1 Peter 1. 7). When our hearts or secret purposes condemn us not, then have we confidence towards God.

4. SUSTAINED HIM. "By the word of Thy lips, I have kept me from the ways of the violent" (v. 4, R.V.). By taking heed to His Word, any young man may cleanse his way (Psa. 119. 9). We are kept by the power of God through *faith*—faith in His word. Man shall not live by bread alone, but by every word of God. The prayer of our Great High Priest was, "Sanctify them through Thy truth: Thy word is truth" (John 17. 17).

5. ANSWERED HIM. "I have called upon Thee, for Thou wilt answer me, O God" (v. 6, R.V.). He testifies that the reason why he prays is because God answers Him. "Let your requests be made known unto Him" (Phil. 4. 6).

6. SATISFIED HIM. "I will behold Thy face...I shall be satisfied when I awake with Thy likeness" (v. 15). Such a glorious prospect is enough to make the heart sing for joy, even now, when we but see through a glass darkly. God's *likeness* is His best and greatest gift. The more like Him we become now, the deeper will our soul satisfaction be.

THE GOD OF SALVATION.

PSALM 18. 1-3.

FROM the heading of this Psalm we learn that it was written as a song of DELIVERANCE. The first three verses contain a manifold revelation and a manifold obligation.

I. **The Revelation.** This is a revelation of the character of Jehovah as a Saviour. In verse 2 eight terms are used that are suggestive of so many aspects of His saving grace—

1. For REFUGE, He is *My Rock.* The unchangeable Rock of Ages.

2. For PROTECTION, He is *My Fortress.* "His Name is a strong tower; the righteous runneth into it and is safe." "The Lord encampeth *round about* them that fear Him" (Psa. 24. 7).

3. For OPPRESSION, He is *My Deliverer.* "Deliver us from evil, for Thine is the Kingdom, and the power" (Matt. 6. 13).

4. For WORSHIP, He is *My God.* It is written, "Him only shalt thou worship."

5. For WEAKNESS, He is *My Strength.* They that wait upon the Lord shall exchange strength. "My strength is made perfect in weakness."

6. For DEFENCE, He is *My Buckler.* Put on the whole armour of God, and over all the buckler, or shield of faith.

7. For POWER, He is *My Horn.* "All power is given unto Me; go ye therefore." Who shall resist Him?

8. For PROSPECT, He is *My High Tower.* Those seated in heavenly places have got a delightful view. From their high tower they can see the land that is "fairer than day."

II. **The Obligations.** Such marvellous privileges of grace have also gracious responsibilities. What are they? To—

1. LOVE HIM. "I will love Thee, O Lord" (v. 1). The

first and great commandment was: "Thou shalt love the
Lord thy God." Surely such manifestation of His love
should constrain us. Let it be also a thing of the *will*
(1 Cor. 13. 13).

2. TRUST HIM. "In Him I will trust" (v. 2). God
has done everything for us, and is willing to be everything
to us, but when there is no heart trust, the door of the soul
is barred against Him.

3. PRAISE HIM. "Who is worthy to be praised" (v. 3).
Those who "call upon the Lord" are most likely to praise
Him. He is worthy. Think of all He hath done, and of
His long-suffering mercy. "Worthy is the Lamb, to
receive glory and honour."

THE GREAT DELIVERANCE.

PSALM 18. 4-20.

THIS most majestic Psalm was sung by David, not as a
king, but as "the *servant* of the Lord." The key-note is
struck loudly at the beginning. "I will love the Lord...I
will trust the Lord...I will call upon the Lord...so shall
I be saved." Love, trust, prayer, assurance. If there are
great heights here, there are also terrible depths. To lift
from the deepest depth, up to the highest height, is the
glory of the grace of this Deliverer. While this Psalm
records the experiences of a soul passing from death unto
life, it is also prophetic of the sufferings, the death, and
resurrection of the Lord Jesus Christ.

I. **The Need.** His need was great for He was compassed about with the—

1. "SORROWS OF DEATH" (v. 4). To a soul without hope
these sorrows are most pungent. It is the sorrow of losing
every earthly blessing, of entering into the darkness of
despair. The Philippian jailer felt the pangs of them.
(Acts 16. 30).

2. SORROWS OF MEN.   "Floods of ungodly men made me afraid." In times of soul conviction, the enemy is sure to come in like a flood. The world's mind and ways are against the purpose of his heart.

3. "SORROWS OF HELL" (v. 5).   "The cords of Sheol were round about me" (R.V.). Fearful cords that would drag the soul down to eternal death. The joys of Heaven are best known by those who have felt the "sorrows of Hell."

II. **The Confession.**   "In my distress I called upon the Lord, and cried unto my God" (v. 6).   He was in real distress, and so his prayer was unfeigned, and his confession wholehearted.   When a man's distress is as keenly felt as this, he has no hope of saving himself by any work he can do, or by anything he can give.   The sorrows of Hell make sin-convicted souls feel that only the power and grace of almighty God can meet their need.

III. **The Deliverance.**   In answer to this cry of distress he says that—

1. "HE CAME DOWN" (v. 9).   To do this, He had to bow the Heavens.   The language here is prophetic of the coming and sufferings of Christ.   There are always signs and wonders wrought when He comes down in answer to the agonising cry of human need (vv. 7, 8).

2. "HE TOOK ME, He drew me out of many waters" (v. 16).   If we are to be *drawn out* of the many waters of our sins and sorrows, He must take hold of us, and we must be perfectly submissive to His drawing power.   Resist not the grace of God.   When He does take hold, it is unto a perfect salvation.

3. "HE DELIVERED ME from my strong enemy" (v. 17).   Your adversary, the Devil, is a strong enemy, but a stronger than he has come to seek and to save (Heb. 2. 14, 15).

4. "HE BROUGHT ME forth also into a large place" (v. 19). Whom the Lord sets free are free indeed. Out from the power of Satan, into the *Kingdom* of our Lord Jesus Christ. This is indeed "a large place," for it stretches into the ages of eternity. It takes a large place to meet all the aspirations of an immortal spirit. Resurrection ground.

5. "HE DELIGHTED IN ME" (v. 19). He delivers because He delights in saving the objects of His love. "He loved me and gave Himself for me." His is no mechanical, or perfunctory salvation. He *"delighteth* in mercy." Our trust in Him delights His soul.

6. "HE REWARDED ME" (v. 20). "He is a Rewarder of them that diligently seek Him." He never said to any, "Seek My face in vain." A clean heart, and clean hands, the Lord will recompense (v. 24). "O taste and see that the Lord is good" (Psa. 34. 8).

THE GOD OF DELIVERANCES.

PSALM 18. 25-39.

I. His Manner of Working. He reveals His—

1. MERCIFULNESS TO THE MERCIFUL (v. 25). "With the merciful Thou wilt shew Thyself merciful." The mercifulness of men can never rise to the mercifulness of God. Human mercy is to be measured by the Divine.

2. PERFECTION TO THE PERFECT. "With the perfect *man,* Thou wilt shew *Thyself* perfect" (R.V.). The perfection of men is to be seen in the light of the perfection of God. The man with the "upright heart" desires this, "Shew me Thy glory."

3. PURITY TO THE PURE. "With the pure Thou wilt shew Thyself pure" (v. 26). The pure in heart shall see a God that is infinitely purer. The desire after holiness is thus encouraged by this promise.

4. FROWARDNESS to the FROWARD. "With the froward

Thou wilt shew Thyself froward. " The *frowardness* (lit.) of man, turning away from God, will be met with the frowardness of God. If man chooses to be perverse toward God, then they have the perversity of God to deal with.

5. PURPOSE IN SO DEALING WITH MEN. "For Thou wilt save the afflicted, but the haughty Thou wilt bring down" (v. 27, R.V.). If there is in us a mercifulness, a perfection, or a purity that is unreal, then the manifestation of His character is to rebuke pride and lead to repentance. His purpose is to save honest seekers, and to bring down the proud boasters.

II. **His Manifold Mercies.** All God's gifts are deliverances.

1. He gives LIGHT. "Thou wilt light my lamp...My God will lighten my darkness" (v. 28). In Him was life, and the life was the light of men.

2. He gives COURAGE. "By Thee I have ran through a troop; and by my God have I leaped over a wall" (v. 29). Troops of troubles and walls of difficulties need not hinder the man of faith.

3. He gives STRENGTH. "It is God that girdeth me with strength" (v. 32). Loins girded with the Word of God will be strong to do exploits.

4. He gives STABILITY. "He maketh my feet like hinds' feet" (v. 33). The hind is sure-footed, and can walk and leap with safety in slippery places.

5. He gives WISDOM. "He teacheth my hands to war" (v. 34). We war not with flesh and blood, but with principalities...and wicked spirits. For this battle Divine wisdom is needed.

6. He gives PROTECTION. "Thou hast given me the *shield* of Thy salvation" (v. 35). The salvation of God is a shield as long as our life, and as broad as our need.

7. He gives HONOUR.   "Thy gentleness has made me great. "   The gentleness of almighty grace brings wonderful promotion to the whole nature of the spiritual man.

8. He gives VICTORY.   "Thou hast girded me with strength; Thou hast subdued under me those that rose up against me" (v. 39).   "Thanks be unto God who giveth us the victory, through our Lord Jesus Christ. "   "Great deliverance giveth He" (v. 50).

THE WORD OF GOD.
PSALM 19.

WHILE the Heavens declare the glory of God, the Bible declares His will.   The speech of the Heavens is silent, "their voice is not heard" (R.V.).   But even His eternal power and Godhead can be understood by the things that are made (Rom. 1. 19, 20).   We have to come to the written and Incarnate Word for the *doctrine* of God.   In verses 7-9 six different terms are used to express the fullness and preciousness of *His word*.

I. **It Converts the Soul**, because it is *perfect* (v. 7).   It takes a perfect instrument to accomplish such delicate and powerful work as this.   The soul needs conversion: the sword of the Spirit can do it (James 1. 18).

II. **It Makes Wise the Simple**, because it is *sure* (v. 7).   It is sure because it is given by inspiration of God (2 Tim. 3. 15).   It makes wise unto salvation all who are simple enough to believe it.

III. **It Rejoiceth the Heart**, because it is *right* (v. 8).   It is the right thing for all the needs of the heart, so the heart rejoices in the receiving of it.   The poor, hungry soul that finds great spoil (Psa. 119. 16).   "Thy Word was the joy of my heart" (Jer. 15. 16).

IV. **It Enlightens the Eyes**, because it is *pure* (v. 8).

As the weary Jonathan had his eyes enlightened by partaking of the honey, so doth new light and vigour possess us when we taste the pure honey of His Word. The eyes are opened to see wondrous things. "Every word of God is pure." "Thy Word is a lamp" (Psa. 119. 105).

V. **It Endureth for Ever**, because it is *clean* (v. 9). It is the very thing a young man needs to cleanse his way (Psa. 119. 9). It is uncorruptible, and so endureth for ever. It does, and can, offer everlasting life, because the word itself is everlasting.

VI. **It is Altogether Righteous**, because it is *truth* (v. 9, *margin*). It is altogether right—right in its every warning and demand, counsel and promise. It is not only true, it is the TRUTH, and, therefore, cannot possibly be wrong on any point.

VII. **It is Most Desirable**, because it is better than *gold*, and sweeter than *honey* (v. 10). It is better than the best, and sweeter than the sweetest of all earthly things.

VIII. **It is Most Needful**, because it both *warns* and *rewards* (v. 11). It warns both servants and sinners of the danger and doom of unbelief. It assures the obedient of a glorious reward. It is both a law and a Gospel, a hammer and a fire, a beacon light, and bread from Heaven.

INTERCESSION AND CONFIDENCE.
PSALM 20.

WHILE it is good to pray for ourselves, it is gracious to pray for others. A powerful incentive to intercessory prayer is a satisfied and thankful heart.

I. **An Example of Intercession**. Here are seven requests that the Psalmist would put into prayerful lips. A sevenfold blessing which God is able to bestow.

1. "The Lord HEAR thee" (v. 1). It is a wonderful

privilege to have the God of Heaven bending His ear like a fond mother to the confidential whisperings of a child.

2. The Lord DEFEND thee (v. 1). To be defended by "the NAME of the God of Jacob," is to have power with God, and to prevail (Gen. 32. 28).

3. The Lord HELP thee. "Send thee help from the sanctuary" (v. 2). Help from the place of His holiness is sanctifying help. Provision was made for this (1 Kings 8. 44, 45).

4. The Lord STRENGTHEN thee. "Strengthen thee out of Zion," by the supplications of the people of God. Perhaps the *oneness* of the body of Christ may be suggested here.

5. The Lord REMEMBER thee (v. 3). "Remember all thy offerings," all thy gifts, and sacrifice for Him. May He have thee in everlasting remembrance. "I know thy works and labour of love."

6. The Lord SUPPLY thee. "Grant thee thy heart's desire" (v. 4, R.V.). To obtain this, there must be a delighting in the Lord (Psa. 37. 4). "The desire of the righteous is only good" (Prov. 11. 23).

7. The Lord FILL thee (v. 5). They are truly filled who have all their petitions fulfilled. "He filleth the hungry with good."

II. **An Example of Confidence.** A confidence—

1. In the SALVATION of God. "We will rejoice in Thy salvation" (v. 5). It is a salvation worth rejoicing in, because of its greatness, its costliness, and its fullness.

2. In the CAUSE of God. "In the Name of our God we will set up our banners." The banner of truth (Psa. 60. 4), of victory, of progress. His Kingdom cannot be moved.

3. In the FAITHFULNESS of God. "Now know I that the Lord saveth His anointed" (v. 6). Blessed are they that

know this joyful sound. This is experimental knowledge of Divine faithfulness.

4. In the NAME of God. "Some trust in chariots, but we will remember the Name of the Lord" (v. 7). To remember His Name is to remember His revealed character, and this is all sufficient to faith (2 Chron. 32. 8).

5. In the POWER of God. "They are brought down... but we are risen" (v. 8). He casteth down the proud, but the lowly in heart He lifteth up. Hold fast the confidence which you had at the beginning. Pray and trust.

THE JOY OF SALVATION.

PSALM 21

THE prayers in the preceding Psalm seem to find their fulfilment in the first nine verses of this Psalm. The one appears to be the perfect complement of the other, when compared verse by verse. "In Thy salvation," he says, "how greatly shall he rejoice" (v. 1). Note then—

I. **The Joys of the Saved.** In this state of blessedness there is the joy of—

1. HEART SATISFACTION. "Thou hast given him his *heart's* desire" (v. 2). God's great salvation is for the heart. He only knows to the full its nature and its need.

2. ANSWERED PRAYER. "Thou hast not withholden the request of his lips." What a privilege to ask and receive of Him who is the Creator of the universe, and the Father of our spirits.

3. PROVIDENTIAL GOODNESS. "Thou preventest (goeth before) him with the blessings of goodness" (v. 3). The God of goodness goeth before him with his blessing, and goodness, and mercy followeth after him (Psa. 23).

4. CROWNED WITH HONOUR. "Thou settest a crown of pure gold upon his head." All the glory of this world

cannot be compared with the pure gold of Divine favour (Matt. 4. 8).

5. ETERNAL LIFE. "He asked life of Thee; Thou gavest him length of days for ever and ever" (v. 4). "The *gift* of God is eternal life." His gift, like Himself, belongs to the eternal ages.

6. DIVINE FELLOWSHIP. "Thou hast made him exceeding glad with Thy countenance" (v. 6). This is the presence that brings fullness of joy (Psa. 16. 11). The reconciled countenance of God is the most soul-gladdening vision that man can ever have. Our fellowship is with the Father, etc.

7. PERFECT ASSURANCE. "Through the mercy of the Most High, he shall not be moved" (v. 7). He knows in whom he has believed, and is persuaded that He will keep.

8. SONGS OF PRAISES. "So will we sing and praise Thy power" (v. 13). His saving and satisfying power is worthy of our loudest song, for it will be our longest, for as the God of salvation we shall praise Him for ever.

II. How this Salvation is Received.

1. BY ASKING. "He asked life of Thee, and Thou gavest it" (v. 4). "If thou knewest the gift of God, ye would ask of Him" (John 4. 10). "Ask and ye shall receive."

2. BY TRUSTING. "The king trusted in the Lord" (v. 7). Without *faith* it is impossible to please Him (John 3. 36).

III. The Miseries of the Unsaved. They shall be—

1. FOUND OUT. "Thine hand shall find out all Thine enemies" (v. 8). Those who reject His *Word* of mercy will be apprehended by the *hand* of justice.

2. SORELY TROUBLED. "Thou shalt make them as a fiery oven in the time of Thine anger" (v. 9). Despised

and rejected love must be met with fury and indignation. The "wrath of the Lamb" awaits those who tread under foot the "blood of the Lamb."

3. MISERABLY DISAPPOINTED. "They intended evil... they imagined...which they are not able to perform" (v. 11). In different ways, men still command that the sepulchre of Christ be made sure, but all such devices result in wretched failure. No matter how often men, by their wicked works and ways, crucify and bury Christ God will raise Him from the dead. No wisdom or counsel can stand that is against the Lord (Prov. 21. 30). "The wages of sin is death" (Rom. 6. 23).

HIS SUFFERINGS AND GLORY.
PSALM 22.

THIS is a prophetic declaration of "The sufferings of Christ and the glory that should follow." It is not only "The Psalm of the Cross," but also of the Crown and the Kingdom. These sufferings cannot be David's. Who "pierced his hands and feet?" Who "parted His garments, and cast lots upon His vesture?" (v. 18). These words are the tender breathings of the Holy Spirit, through this holy man of old. Here the Spirit testifies beforehand the sufferings of Christ.

I. **The Nature of His Sufferings.** He was—

1. DESERTED. "My God, My God, WHY hast Thou forsaken Me?" (vv. 1, 2). This is a mysterious and awful *why*. The question of sin and judgment is in it. He was forsaken of God because "He was made a *curse* for us."

2. REPROACHED. "A reproach of men, and despised of the people" (v. 6). Although God hid His face from Him, there was no reproach on His part. The reproach and the scorn came from wicked men, for whom He suffered.

3. Derided. "Commit thyself unto the Lord...let Him deliver Him, seeing He delighteth in Him" (v. 8, R. V.). They mocked at His faith in God as a vain thing. They laughed at His weakness, as an evidence of failure and presumption.

4. Emptied. "I am poured out like water" (v. 14) He emptied Himself and became of no reputation. He poured out His soul unto death. He gave all that He had.

5. Humbled. "Thou hast brought Me into the dust of death" (v. 15). He was brought to the dust, through His own voluntary humility. "He humbled Himself, and became *obedient* unto death."

6. Pierced. "They pierced My hands and My feet" (v. 16). They nailed Him to a Cross. They crucified the Lord of Glory.

7. Shamed. "I may tell all my bones...They part My garments among them." The death of the Cross was the most painful and shameful of all deaths (John 19. 23, 24). They put Him to an open shame. "He suffered for us, the Just for the unjust, that He might bring us to God" (1 Peter 3. 18).

II. The Glory that was to Follow.

1. The Declaration of His Name. "I will declare Thy Name" (v. 22; see Heb. 2. 12). "Wherefore," because of His sufferings and death, "God hath highly exalted Him, and given Him a Name that is above every other name." The preaching of His *Name* is the preaching of His holy and wondrous saving characters.

2. The Assurance of His Grace. "He hath not despised nor abhorred the affliction of the afflicted" (v. 24). "The meek shall eat and be satisfied" (v. 26). Grace and truth came by Jesus Christ. "My grace is sufficient for thee." "Hearken diligently unto me, and eat ye that which is good, and let your soul delight in fatness" (Isa. 55. 1, 2).

3. THE TRIUMPH OF HIS CAUSE. "All the ends of the world shall remember and turn to the Lord...for the Kingdom is the Lord's, and He is the Ruler over the nations" (vv. 27, 28, R.V.). The rejected King shall yet rule over the earth (Zech. 14. 9). "The kingdoms of this world shall become the Kingdom of our Lord and of His Christ" (Rev. 11. 15). He died for us, that He might be Lord both of the living and the dead. "Thine is the Kingdom, and the power, and the glory, for ever" (Matt. 6. 13).

THE ALMIGHTY SHEPHERD.
PSALM 23.

AMONG all the Psalms, the twenty-third is the "pet lamb" of the flock to many. Beecher called it the "Nightingale Psalm, small, and of a homely feather, singing shyly out of obscurity; but, oh! it has filled the air of the whole world with melodious joy." After the Psalm of the Cross comes the Psalm of Life, and *fullness of blessing*. The path of this pilgrim is like the shining light that shineth more and more till the day of perfection. Let us follow him step by step. There was—

I. Decision. "The Lord is my Shepherd." His personal choice was made as to whom he would follow. He would not follow his own heart nor the blind reasonings of men; he would claim Jehovah as his Saviour and Guide and not be ashamed to say so.

II. Assurance. "I shall not want." The godless, although strong as young lions, do lack and suffer hunger, but they that seek the Lord shall not want any good. "My God shall supply all your need." He has his Shepherd's promise, and he believes it.

III. Rest. "He maketh me to lie down in green pastures, and beside the waters of rest" (*margin*). The rest of faith in the Lord is a rest that is calm and refreshing. He does not say "rest," without leading into the best place where it can be found—in His love—green pastures.

IV. **Restoration**. "He restoreth my soul." If through self-confidence, or discontent, we should stray from His paths of greenness, He is gracious enough to forgive and restore. He, only, can restore the backsliding soul (1 John 1. 1).

V. **Guidance**. "He leadeth me in the paths of righteousness." The paths that are *right* may not always be the paths that seem easiest. Bunyan's pilgrims found it "easy going" over the stile which led to the castle of Giant Despair. His leading is for His own *Name's sake*.

VI. **Courage**. "Though I walk through the valley of the shadow of death, I will fear no evil." The shadow of death is a dreadful thing to the man whose portion is in this life. But there is no evil to fear when the Shepherd is near (Isa. 43. 2).

VII. **Fellowship**. "Thou art with me." The heavenly pilgrim is always in good company. The Lord stands by when all men forsakes (2 Tim. 4. 16, 17). His presence is always sufficient at all times.

VIII. **Comfort**. "Thy rod and Thy staff they comfort me." The club and the crook of the shepherd were the instruments of defence and deliverance. What they were to the sheep, the Word of the Lord is to us. It is a club to beat off our enemies, and a crook to guide or lift those who have fallen into a pit or ditch. The sword of the Spirit doth comfort me.

IX. **Provision**. "Thou preparest a table before me in the presence of mine enemies." He knows when and how to feed His flock. We have a meat to eat that they know not of.

X. **Enduement**. "Thou anointest my head." This

anointing, or unction from the Holy One, is significant of authority and power. Kings and priests were anointed. Ye are a kingdom of priests unto God (Acts 1. 8).

XI. **Satisfaction.** "My cup runneth over." The God of grace gives good measure, pressed down, shaken together, heaped up, running over. The holy anointing must go before the overflowing (see John 7. 37, 38).

XII. **Prospect.** "Surely goodness and mercy shall follow me...and I will dwell in the house of the Lord for ever." Goodness to supply, and mercy to forgive, all the days of this life; and a mansion is prepared beyond this life, where we shall be for ever with the Lord (John 14. 1-3).

Psalm 23 (again).

1. **Beneath me**, "green pastures." 2, **Beside me**, "still waters." 3, **With me**, "my Shepherd." 4, **Before** me, "a table." 5, **Around me**, "mine enemies." 6, **Upon me**, "anointing." 7, **After me**, "goodness and mercy." 8, **Beyond me**, "The house of the Lord."— *Selected.*

———

THE ASCENT OF MAN.
Psalm 24. 3-6.

In the twenty-second Psalm we have the Lord's sorrowful descent to man. Here is the way of man's ascent to the Lord.

I. **The Goal.** "The hill of the Lord...His holy place." The hill of the Lord is the holy place of His presence. Mount Zion stands for the tabernacle or habitation of God (Psa. 55. 1). The highest ambition of the soul should be the fellowship of God—the fellowship of Him to whom the earth belongs, and the fullness thereof (v. 1).

II. **The Way.** "Who shall *ascend*?" The way of sin and impurity is downward, but the way of holiness is ever *upward.* The ascent of this mount is the ascent of every faculty in man. No one can climb this hill without having their own moral, spiritual, and intellectual being invigorated.

III. **The Pilgrim.** The characteristic features of this hill-climber are given:—

1. His HANDS must be *clean.* "He that hath clean hands." Not hands washed in water, like Pilate's, but washed in innocency, like David's (Psa. 26. 6). We cannot ascend to Him with the lie of a deceitful motive in our right hand. Let the wicked forsake his ways, and let him return to the Lord. The laver stood outside the door of the tabernacle, at which the approaching priest must wash his hands.

2. His HEART must be *pure* (v. 4). Holiness is something that has to do with the heart, and without holiness no man shall see the Lord. "The pure in heart shall see God." It is with the heart that man believeth *unto righteousness.* It is when the seed of the Kingdom falls into an "honest heart" that it brings forth fruit.

3. His SOUL must be *humble.* "Who hath not lifted up his soul unto *vanity.*" When vanity, or spiritual pride, gets into the soul, then there is an end to growth in grace. If we would ascend into the holy hill of the Divine likeness, there must be no vain lifting up of ourselves.

IV. **The Attainment.** "He shall receive the blessing from the Lord, and righteousness from the God of his salvation." The blessing of perfect rightness with God is a crown of life within the reach of every spiritual pilgrim. *The blessing* of the Lord embodies every needful and desirable thing.

V. **The Application.** "This is the generation of them that seek Him" (v.6). This is the character and attitude

of the true seed of Abraham—the father of the faithful.
This is the generation that belongs to the *re*-generation.
These are the marks of the children of God, who climb
the hill of holiness into the Father's house.

_____

ELEMENTS OF SUCCESSFUL PRAYER.
PSALM 25. 1-11.

THE Psalms have been called by Dr. A. Murray "The
prayer book of God's saints." In this book, the spirit of
prayer, and the spirit of praise are twin spirits; they are
indivisible. This psalm would teach us how to pray.

I. Elements of Prayer.

1. WHOLEHEARTEDNESS. "Unto Thee, O Lord, do I
lift up my soul" (v. 1). What is the use of lifting up our
voice, or our eyes, unto God, if the *soul* is not in them.
God's ear is not to be charmed by such soulless music.
We find Him when we seek Him with the whole heart.

2. FAITH. "O my God, I trust in Thee." We cannot
taste the goodness of the Lord by mere talk; the tongue of
the soul must touch Him. Faith is the hand that lays
hold of His promise.

3. DESIRE FOR HIS WAYS. "Shew me Thy ways, O
Lord; teach me Thy paths" (v. 4). This implies a
forsaking of our own ways (Isa. 58. 6), and a readiness to
follow His footsteps. "Yield yourselves unto God."

4. DESIRE FOR HIS TRUTH. "Lead me in Thy truth,
and teach me" (v. 5). This must be the longing of that
heart in which the Holy Ghost is, for "when He, the Spirit
of truth, is come, He will guide into all truth" (John 16. 13).
A craving after the mind and will of God, is a powerful
factor in prevailing prayer.

5. DESIRE FOR HIS HONOUR. "For Thy goodness'
sake, O Lord" (v. 7). "For Thy Name's sake, O Lord"
(v. 11). To plead His Name is to plead His nature. His

goodness stands for His character (see Exod. **33**. 18, 19;
34. 5, 6). When He "sanctifies His great Name among the
heathen" (Ezek. **36**. 23), He makes *Himself* known as
the Lord God, merciful and gracious. "If ye ask anything
in My Name I will give it. "

6. PATIENCE. "On Thee do I wait all the day" (v. 5).
Let your requests be made known unto God, but let patience
also have her perfect work. There is no virtue in waiting,
unless we are waiting *on* HIM. "They that wait upon the
Lord shall renew strength. "

7. CONFESSION. "Remember not the sins of my youth,
nor my transgressions" (v. 7). There must be no hiding of
sin; no glossing over the trangressions of earlier days.
Those who would deal with a holy and righteous God must
be perfectly honest in the purposes of their heart. "God is
not mocked. "

II. **Encouragements to Prayer.** "Let your requests
be made known unto God. "

1. Because He is GOOD AND UPRIGHT (v. 8). God is
love, and God is light. The goodness of a Father is here
associated with the uprightness of a righteous sovereign.

2. Because He TEACHES SINNERS (v. 8). What condescension: the Almighty God willing to become the sinner's
teacher. His desire is to lead us in His way. He teacheth
savingly and to eternal profit.

3. Because He GUIDES THE MEEK (v. 9). He does not
guide a man because he is rich, or learned, for all cannot
attain to these, but any man may be *meek*, and learn
heavenly wisdom.

4. Because "ALL THE PATHS OF THE LORD ARE MERCY
AND TRUTH unto such as keep His Word" (v. 10). Mercy
and truth, constitute the daily need of the heavenly
pilgrim. Mercy, to forgive, and to cleanse; truth, to
guide, to strengthen, and to satisfy. To get out of the
Lord's paths, is to get out of the channel of supply.

FEATURES OF A WHOLE-HEARTED CHRISTIAN
PSALM 26.

I. **He Desires to be Tested by God.** "Judge me, O Lord...Examine me, O Lord" (vv. 1, 2). It is a small matter to him, to be judged of men, who seeks the judgment of God. He who can pray, "Search me, O God, and know my heart; try me, and know my thoughts," lives above the fear of man (Acts 23. 1).

II. **He has Faith in God.** "I have trusted also in the Lord, therefore I shall not slide" (v. 1). God has become the greatest reality in the world to his soul, and in Him he hath put his trust. His heart condemns him not, because he has confidence toward God (1 John 3. 21).

III. **He Adheres to the Word of God.** "I have walked in Thy truth" (v. 3). To walk in His truth is to walk in His way, and so walk in the light. He chooses the will of God as revealed in His Word, rather than the imaginations of his own heart.

IV. **He Separates Himself from the Enemies of God.** "I have not sat with vain persons, neither will I go in with dissemblers" (v. 4). The evil communications of the worldling corrupt the good manners of the child of God. "Wherefore come out from among them and be ye separate."

V. **He Offers Sacrifices unto God.** "I will wash mine hands in innocency: so will I compass Thine altar, O Lord" (v. 6). The sons of Aaron washed their hands at the laver ere they compassed the altar of incense (Exod. 30). The man that had to leave his gift at the altar and be reconciled to his brother was taught to first wash his hands (Matt. 5. 23). "The sacrifices of God are a broken spirit."

VI. **He Testifies for God.** "That I may publish with the voice of thanksgiving, and *tell* of all Thy wondrous works" (v. 7). He is most thankful and willing to tell of

that most wonderful work of God in his own heart and
experience. "Great and marvellous are Thy works, O
Lord;" Thy works of mercy and grace in the sinful souls
of men; Thy work of redemption by the Cross of Thy
beloved Son.

VII. **He Loves the House of God.** "I have loved the
habitation of Thy house, and the place where Thy glory
dwelleth" (v. 8, R.V.). He loved the house because of
Him who dwelt therein. When his soul thirsts for the
"courts of the Lord" it is because he was thirsting for the
"living God" (Psa. 84. 1, 2). They are idolaters who love
the *habitation* of God rather than God HIMSELF.

VIII. **He Praises God.** "In the congregation will I
bless the Lord" (v. 12). He is not ashamed to praise the
Lord with his *whole heart* (Psa. 3. 1). He has often asked
the Lord to bless him, but he does not forget to "bless the
Lord." "Whoso offereth praise glorifieth Me" (Psa.
50. 23).

THREEFOLD CORDS.
PSALM 27

THE thoughts in this most precious Psalm seem to run in
triplets.

I. **A Threefold Need** (v. 1).

1. LIGHT. "The Lord is my light." The world needs
light. Christ is the light of the world. Satan hath
blinded the minds of men.

2. SALVATION. "The Lord is...my salvation." He
took me from a fearful pit.

3. STRENGTH. "The Lord is the strength of my life."
He established my goings. This threefold need is met only
in the Lord (Phil. 4. 19).

II. **A Threefold Desire** (v. 4).

1. To "DWELL in the house of the Lord." To dwell in

His house is to "Abide in Him." It is an expression of holy affection for the Lord Himself.

2. To "BEHOLD the beauty of the Lord." This was the good part that Mary chose, when she sat at the feet of Jesus. To learn of Him is to behold His glory.

3. To "INQUIRE in His temple." If any man lack wisdom, let him ask of God. The temple door of the Holy Scriptures is always open to inquirers. Counsel not with the ungodly (Psa. 1. 1)

III. A Threefold Privilege (v. 5).

1. HIDDEN IN HIS PAVILION. In the time of trouble, sheltered in the great pavilion of His special providence (Rom. 8. 28).

2. SECRETED IN HIS TABERNACLE. In the secret of His *presence*, as well as His power, doth He hide from the pride of man. The life that is hid in God can never be found out by His enemies.

3. SET UPON A ROCK. His feet, or ways, are established on a sure foundation. His life is not built up on the shifting sands of human theories.

IV. A Threefold Assurance (vv. 8-10).

1. OF HIS FACE. "When Thou saidst, Seek ye My face; my *heart* said unto Thee, Thy face, Lord, will I seek." The pure in heart shall see the face of God in His Son, in His Word, and in His Providence.

2. OF HIS FELLOWSHIP. "Thou hast been my help; leave me not." He hath said, "I will never leave thee," so that we may boldly say, "The Lord is my Helper" (Heb. 13. 5, 6).

3. OF HIS FAVOUR. "When my father and mother forsake me, then the Lord will take me up." The Good Shepherd carries the weary, or forsaken lambs in His arms. Those who forsake their father, the Devil, will find favour with the Lord (Hos. 14. 3).

V. A Threefold Prayer (vv. 11, 12).

1. FOR TEACHING. "Teach me Thy ways." His ways are ways of pleasantness. He teacheth *savingly.*

2. FOR GUIDANCE. "Lead me in a plain path, because of mine enemies." We are best able to use "plainness of speech" when our feet are walking in a plain path. We walk by faith, and not by sight.

3. FOR DELIVERANCE. From "The will of mine enemies." As David has his Doig, and Christ His Judas, and Paul his Coppersmith, so every true servant of God may have those from whom he needs deliverance.

VI. A Threefold Encouragement (vv. 13, 14).

1. To BELIEVE. "I had fainted unless I had believed." Troubled on every side, yet not distressed (2 Cor. 4. 8-10), because our faith is in God. Peter fainted while on the water because he doubted.

2. To WAIT. "Wait on the Lord." Wait on Him because the expectation of faith is from Him (Psa. 62. 1-5). All who truly wait on Him will yet be able to say, "Lo, this is our God" (Isa. 25. 9).

3. To WORK. "He shall strengthen thine heart, be of good courage." "Whatsoever thy hand findeth to do, do it" (Eccles. 9. 10), for His strength is made perfect in weakness. _____

A STRIKING CONTRAST.
PSALM 28.

THIS Psalm opens with a strange request, "Be not silent to me: *lest*" (vv. 1, 2). It is not every one who dreads the miseries of a *silent* God. They must have had deep experiences of God who get so alarmed at His silence. Alas, for those who interpret His silence as meaning peace. Note the contrast here—

I. The Character of the Wicked. They are—

1. MISCHIEVOUS IN THEIR NATURE. "They speak peace

to their neighbours, but mischief is in their hearts"
(v. 3). They may have fair lips, but the poison of asps
is under their tongues. Their hearts are deceitful. "Full
of wounds...and putrifying sores."

2. FOOLISH IN THEIR ACTIONS. "They regard not the
works of the Lord, nor the operation of His hands" (v. 5).
They are indifferent to their highest and best interests.
They heed not the voice of God in creation and in grace.
The operation of His hand in providence, and in their
own individual lives is systematically disregarded. "A
brutish man knoweth not" (Psa. 92. 5, 6).

II. **The Character of the Godly.** They are—

1. PRAYERFUL. "He hath heard the voice of my
supplications" (v. 6). God is not silent for ever to the cry
of His people. Although at times He may answer "never
a word," yet the pleading saint knows that He hears every
word. "Pray without ceasing."

2. BOASTFUL. "The Lord *is* my strength and my shield...
and I *am* helped" (v. 7). He is full of boasting, but not
in himself, his boast is in God. He will glory in the
Lord, because He hath done great things for him.

3. TRUSTFUL. "My heart trusted in Him." The heart
of man finds its true refuge and source of supply in the heart
of God. It is the sum of all blessedness when our hearts
answer to the heart of our Heavenly Father. With the
heart man believeth unto righteousness.

4. JOYFUL. "My heart greatly rejoiceth." The
trusting heart is sure to be a joyful heart. Faith in God
produces joy in God. A happy heart is a continual feast.

5. PRAISEFUL. "With my song will I praise Him."
The Christian's hero is Christ. His song shall be
of Jesus. This is the "new song" put into the heart and
lips of those redeemed by grace.

6. HUMBLE. "He is the saving strength of His anointed"

(v. 8). HE is. What have we that we have not received?
It is because of what *He is*, not because of what *we are*,
that we glory in the Lord. All is yours, for ye are Christ's
and Christ is God's.

7. HOPEFUL. "Save Thy people, and bless Thine
inheritance, feed them, and lift them up" (v. 9). They
confidently expect that all God's people will be saved,
blessed, fed, and lifted. What an encouragement this is
for others to trust in Him. There will be a great lifting up
when the Redeemer and Bridegroom appears (1 Thess.
4. 17).

THE POWERFUL VOICE.
PSALM 29.

In the preceding Psalm David speaks of the "operation of
His *hands*;" here, amidst the terrors of a thunderstorm, he
sings of the *voice* of the Lord. The Psalmist does not confound nature with the personality of God. He "gives unto
the Lord the glory due unto His Name" (v. 2). The voice
of the Lord is not a mere noise, it is a message. This voice
we hear in all the riches of its majesty and glory in the
person of His Son. "God hath in these last days spoken
unto us by His Son." This voice of the Lord, in its
"breaking," "making," "dividing," "shaking," and
"discovering" power may prefigure the influence and
effects of the voice or Word of Jesus Christ. It is a—

I. **Universal Power.** "The voice of the Lord is upon
the waters" (v. 3). Metaphorically, these waters may
represent the nations of the earth. The voice of God's
word is for every people, tribe, and tongue. "Go ye into
all the world and preach the Gospel to every creature."

II. **Majestic Power.** "The voice of the Lord is full of
majesty" (v. 4). There is a God-like dignity about the Bible
which belongs to no other book, it is full of majesty. The
Gospel of Christ is the *power of God* to every one that

believeth. The word of God asserts its own majestic character by being "quick and powerful." It has all the nobility of "Spirit and life."

III. **Breaking Power.** "The voice of the Lord breaketh the cedars" (v. 5). The strongest of *nature's* growths are bowed and broken by its pressure. "Is not My Word a hammer?" Saul in Jerusalem, was like a cedar in Lebanon, but on the way to Damascus he was broken down.

IV. **Separating Power.** "He maketh them (cedar branches) to skip like a calf" (v. 6, R.V.). His Word can not only break down, but can also break into pieces; separating branch from branch, tearing them away from their roots. A storm of Divine truth makes havoc with old associations and conservative habits and manners.

V. **Dividing Power.** "The voice of the Lord divideth the flames of fire" (v. 7). Every word of God is a flame of fire, and He can divide them as the lightning flashes are divided. He can make His tongue of flame to rest upon every holy head (Acts 2. 3). God's Word makes great distinctions. It is a divider of soul and spirit, of sinners and saints. The voice of the Lord is a terror to some, it is heavenly music to others.

VI. **Shaking Power.** "The voice of the Lord shaketh the wilderness" (v. 8). Yes, the *wilderness*, in all its desolation, barrenness and hopelessness; whether that wilderness is your heart, your home, or your city, the power of the Word of God can shake it, and make it to tremble into a transformation (Isa. 35. 1-7).

VII. **A Life-giving Power.** "The voice of the Lord maketh the hinds to calve" (v. 9). Because of the awfulness of God's thunderings, the hinds, through terror, were made to calve. It is when God's Word thunders and lightens most, that Zion's travail for the birth of souls becomes greatest. It is by His mighty Word of truth that souls are still being "born again."

VIII. **Stripping Power**. "The voice of the Lord... strippeth the forest bare" (v. 9, R.V.). The hidden depths of the heart of the forest are laid bare by His discovering voice. The Word of God is a *discerner* of the thoughts and intents of the heart. The fig-leaves of man's covering cannot stand this storm.

IX. **God-glorifying Power**. "In His temple everything saith glory" (v. 9, R.V.). Every iota in the great temple of nature saith "glory." So doth every thing in the temple of His revealed Word—Jesus Christ. So ought every thing in the temple of these bodies, which are His. "The Word was made flesh, and dwelt among us, and we beheld His glory." Not one thing of all that He hath spoken shall fail, everything shall say "glory."

A SONG OF SALVATION.
Psalm 30.

"Thou hast lifted me up" (v. 1). This may be regarded as the key note of this Psalm, sung at the dedication of the house of David. The salvation of God is fitly expressed by a lifting up? He was lifted up—

I. **From the Power of his Enemies**. "Thou hast raised me up, and hast not made my foes to rejoice over me" (v. 1, R.V.). The grace of God that bringeth salvation to all men, lifts up the believing soul out of the kingdom of darkness and tyranny, into the Kingdom of light and liberty. More than conquerors, over self and sin through Him who loved us.

II. **From all his Diseases**. "Thou hast healed me" (v. 2). Only He who forgiveth all our iniquities, can heal our diseases (Psa. 103. 3). A nature that is morally unsound can only be cured by moral and regenerative influences. "The Blood of Christ cleanseth from all sin."

III. **From the Place of Death.** "Thou hast brought my soul from the grave" (v. 3). Sheol was the abode of the dead. Speaking figuratively, he had by the grace of God been delivered from a state of spiritual death. There are many souls that are as dead to the things of God as if they were in their graves. It is the Spirit that quickeneth.

IV. **From Going Down to the Pit.** "Thou hast kept me alive, that I should not go down to the pit" (v. 3). Or, "Thou hast separated me from among them that go down to the pit" (see R.V., *margin*). He was saved from the company and influence of them that were perishing in their sins. Deliver from going down to the pit, for I have found the ransom.

V. **From Weakness and Failure.** "Lord, by Thy favour Thou hast made my mountain to stand strong" (v. 7). By God's *grace* the mountain of his faith had been made to stand strong. His strength had been made perfect in weakness. Unbelief says, "I shall die in my nest" (Job. 29. 18), but faith says, "My mountain is strong."

VI. **From Sorrow and Sadness.** "Thou hast turned my mourning into dancing. Thou hast loosed my sack-cloth, and girded me with gladness" (v. 11, R.V.). Our God transforms the inner life of Zion's mourners, by giving them beauty for ashes, the oil of joy for mourning, and the garment of praise for the spirit of heaviness (Isa. 63. 1).

VII. **From Praiseless Silence.** "To the end that my glory may sing praise to Thee, and not be silent" (v. 12). There are those who profess to know God, but they glorify Him not as God, neither are they thankful (Rom. 1. 21). He hath saved us with a great salvation that our praises may abound unto Him, and not be silent (Eph. 5. 19, 20).

THE BLESSED LIFE.

PSALM 31.

THERE are bright rays of light, and dark gloomy shadows here. But the blessed life can be lived in the midst of "nets," "lying vanities," and "lying lips." It is in circumstances like these that we can best prove the saving grace of God. Let us try and catch some of the features of the life of faith as revealed in this song. There was—

I. **Confidence.** "In Thee, O Lord, do I put my trust" (v. 1). The blessed life must have its source in God, who is blessed for evermore. We do not begin to live till we trust in Him (John 3. 36). To receive by faith the life-giving One is to receive the right of Sonship (John 1. 12).

II. **Committal.** "Into Thine hand I commit my spirit. Thou hast redeemed me, O Lord God of truth" (v. 5). The *redeemed* spirit must be entirely committed to the Redeemer. "Ye are not your own, for ye are bought with a price." The life of faith is a life of continual and unreserved surrender to the will of God. Self-sacrifice in the will of God is a very different thing from self-sacrifice outside that will.

III. **Confession.** "Have mercy upon me, O Lord, for I am in trouble,...my strength faileth...I am forgotten as a dead man, I am like a broken vessel" (vv. 9-12). It is no new thing for a man to feel nothing but weakness, and worthlessness, after he has solemnly and heartily given himself to God. It may be very painful to discover that, instead of strength and fullness, there has come the consciousness that we are but as *dead* men, and *broken* vessels! But these are the first evidences that the consecration has been real and effectual. Crucified with Christ, having the broken and contrite heart.

IV. Petition. "My times are in Thy hands, deliver me ...make Thy face shine upon Thy servant" (vv. 15, 16). Having committed his spirit and his "times" into the hand of God, he now pleads for the shining of His face. God requires perfect honesty of heart, in confession and in prayer. The shining of HIS FACE is the perfect remedy for those who are "forgotten as a dead man." The longing of every holy heart is for the "light of His countenance" (Psa. 4. 6).

V. Adoration. "Oh, how great is Thy goodness" (v. 19). Those who are wholly yielded to God will find their soul's satisfaction in the goodness of God. The ripest fruit of faith is adoration. The goodness of God in His Son Jesus Christ is so great that we must admire and adore.

VI. Praise. "Blessed be the Lord: for He hath shewed me His marvellous kindness" (v. 21). Although the tongue can never express the overwhelming sense of God's goodness, that at times fill the soul, yet it cannot remain silent. Bless the Lord, O my soul, Praise Him, praise Him for His marvellous works of love and mercy. Join now in the new and everlasting song, "Worthy is the Lamb that was slain."

VII. Exhortation. "O love the Lord, all ye His saints. ...Be of good courage" (vv. 23, 24). The heart that is full of the goodness of God will eagerly long for others to *love* Him, *trust* Him, *serve* Him, and to *hope* in Him. O ye separated ones, love the Lord, and let love lead to courage in His service, and He shall strengthen your heart. The blessed life is a life of faith in God for ourselves, and of faith in His Gospel for others.

SAVED AND KEPT.

PSALM 32.

THIS well-known Psalm might be studied in the light of the ninth chapter of the Acts. It describes the experiences of a soul passing from the sorrows of conviction into the joys of salvation. There is—

I. The Need of Salvation.

1. SIN IMPLIED. "Transgression...sin...iniquity" (vv. 1, 2). Three words that describe three different phases of guilt. Those who would reckon with God must face the question of *sin*. All have sinned. All have gone astray (Isa. 53. 6).

2. SIN DISCOVERED. "Day and night Thy hand was heavy upon me; my moisture was changed as with the drought of summer" (v. 4, R.V.). He tried to keep silence, but the heavy hand of God made him "roar all the day long." It is hard to kick against the pricks of God's goading truth. The moisture of the natural man quickly dries up when the convicting breath of God's Spirit comes.

3. SIN CONFESSED. "I acknowledged my sin unto Thee" (v. 5). As long as the prodigal son tried to cover his sin, he did not prosper, but when he cried, "Father, I have sinned," he found mercy. "If we confess our sins, He is faithful and just to forgive us" (1 John 1. 9).

4. SIN FORGIVEN. "Thou forgavest the iniquity of my sin" (v. 5). Now he has entered into the "blessedness of the man whose transgression is forgiven, whose sin is *covered*." God's forgiving grace goes deep down, taking all guile out of the spirit (v. 2). Not only forgiven, but *renewed* in the inner man.

II. The Blessedness of the Saved. They are—

1. HIDDEN. "Thou art my hiding place" (v 7). **God** Himself becomes their refuge and hiding place. Hidden from the strife of the foolish and poisonous tongues of men, and from the day of His wrath, against all ungodliness, your life is hid with Christ in God.

2. TAUGHT. "I will instruct thee and teach thee in the way which thou shalt go" (v. 8). The forgiven ones are to be all taught of God, who teacheth *saving*, from the ways of error, and to *profit*, both for this life, and that which is to come. Ye have the anointing of the Holy One, and need not that any man teach you (1 John 2. 27).

3. GUIDED. "I will guide thee with Mine eye." Sweet promise, as it implies that His eye is to be always upon us for good, so that we may see His face and enjoy His fellowship. We are not to be guided like the ignorant horse, or stubborn mule, with bit and bridle, but like obedient children, who can read the *mind* of God, in the eye of His Word.

4. GUARDED. "He that trusteth in the Lord, mercy shall *compass* him about" (v. 10). "Thou shalt *compass* me about with songs of deliverance" (v. 7). Compassed about with *mercy* and *songs* of deliverance; what a blessed environment. The heart garrisoned with forgiving mercy and songs of triumph. What a contrast to the "tribulation and anguish" that surrounds the soul of the evil doer (Rom. 2. 9).

5. GLADDENED. "Be glad in the Lord, and rejoice... and shout for joy" (v. 11). Not unto us, but unto THY Name, be all the glory. He begins by taking us up out of the fearful pit of sin, then puts the new song in our mouth. Praise to our God! "Rejoice in the Lord alway, for He changeth not."

REJOICE IN THE LORD.

PSALM 33. 1-12.

THERE are abundant reasons here why God's people should
"Shout for joy in the Lord" (Newberry). It is a blessed
choice to leave the doubters and join such shouters. The
source of the believer's joy is not in the world, nor in
themselves, but in the Lord. They sing unto Him a "new
song" (v. 3), because they have been made new creatures,
who enjoy new delights. They rejoice in the Lord because
of—

I. **His Word**. "The Word of the Lord is right" (v. 4).
It is the right thing for the souls and lives of men, because
of its converting and enlightening power (Psa. 19. 7, 8).
The Word of God is powerful, for by it the Heavens were
made (v. 6). It is the incorruptible *seed* that endureth
for ever.

II. **His Works**. "All His works are done in truth"
(v. 4). Every stone built by Him is perfectly plumb.
All His works are perfect. All His works in grace, as well
as in creation, are done in truth. He is a *just* God, and a
Saviour. If Christ is the way and the life, He is also the
truth. To be saved by grace is not to be saved at the
expense of truth, for "grace *and* truth came by Jesus
Christ" (John 1).

III. **His Lovingkindness**. "The earth is full of the
lovingkindness of the Lord" (v. 5, R.V.). Everywhere, to
those who have eyes to see, the tokens of His goodness may
be seen. But it is in Christ Jesus that His marvellous
lovingkindness finds its fullest manifestation. Yet in the
earth, the outer court of His temple, "He maketh the sun
to rise on the evil and on the good, and sendeth rain on the
just and on the unjust" (Matt. 5. 45). "God loved the
world" (John 3. 16).

IV. **His Power.** "Let all the earth fear the Lord...for He spake, and it was done, He commanded and it stood fast" (vv. 8, 9). Man may make void God's word, but He never speaks in vain. What He hath promised, He is able also to perform. Power belongeth unto God, and He giveth power to the faint, therefore, rejoice in the Lord.

V. **His Knowledge.** "The Lord bringeth the counsel of the nations to naught. He maketh the thoughts of the people to be of none effect" (v. 10, R.V.). It is a joy of God's children, that He knows all about the secret desires of the ungodly, and that He taketh the wise in their own craftiness (1 Cor. 3. 19). "Ye thought evil against me, but God meant it for good" (Gen. 50. 20). He can sanctify adverse things to the furtherance of the Gospel (Phil. 1. 12, 13).

VI. **His Faithfulness.** "The counsel of the Lord standeth for ever, the thoughts of His heart to all genera- tions" (v. 11). The *thoughts of His heart*, revealed in His Word, shall stand for ever. Man is famous for his "vain thoughts," but precious are Thy thoughts, O Lord, because they are infinitely great, and good, and true, and faithful.

VII. **His Grace.** "Blessed is...the people whom *He hath chosen* for His own inheritance" (v. 12). Grace is not an after-thought with God, it belongs to His eternal character, it is an essential attribute of His nature, for we are chosen in Him, before the foundation of the world, and now blessed with all spiritual blessing in Christ (Eph. 1. 3, 4). The grace that hath chosen us is to be made sufficient for us, therefore rejoice in the Lord, and again I say, rejoice.

JUBILIATION.

Psalm 34. 1-10.

In the original, the verses of this Psalm begin with the letters of the Hebrew alphabet, indicating, perhaps, that special care has been bestowed on its composition. The occasion of it—when David played the fool before Abimelech—was anything but creditable to the king. Nevertheless he would joyfully praise the Lord for His great deliverance. These words seem to be the expression of a soul in an ecstasy of delight. The more keenly we feel our own foolishness and guilt, the more loudly shall we praise the God of our salvation. About this exuberant joy, note—

I. **The Nature of It**. It is—

1. SPIRITUAL. "I will bless the Lord" (v. 1). God is a spirit, and the spirit that finds its highest and deepest delight in "blessing the Lord," has something infinitely better than natural riches.

2. CONTINUAL. "I will bless the Lord *at all times*, His praise shall *continually* be in my mouth." At all times and in all circumstances He is ever the same, so that our praises should never cease. Even the *earth* yields its increase to a praising people (Psa. 67. 5-7).

3. UNSELFISH. "O magnify the Lord *with me*, and let us exalt His Name *together*" (v. 3). The praiseful heart longs for others to join in, and share the happy service.

II. **The Causes of It**. He had experienced Divine—

1. INTERPOSITION. "I sought the Lord and He heard me" (v. 4). Another testimony to the power of prayer. The God of law is also the God of grace.

2. SALVATION. "Delivered me from all my fears... saved out of all his troubles" (vv. 4-6). We must needs be saved from all our sins to be saved from all our fears.

The salvation of God goes down to the "uttermost" of human need, and lifts to the "uttermost" of Divine grace.

3. PROTECTION. "The angel of the Lord encampeth round about them that fear Him" (v. 7). As the mountain was full of horses and chariots to the opened eyes of Elisha, so doth the power of God encompass His people as with a tabernacle (Psa. 27. 5).

III. **The Influence of It.** This holy joy constrains—

1. To INVITE. "O taste and see that the Lord is good" (v. 8). The sweetness of the Gospel of God, like the sweetness of honey, is best explained by tasting it. Those who have proved its preciousness, long for others to share its blessedness.

2. To AFFIRM. "Blessed is the man that trusteth in Him …They that seek the Lord shall not want any good thing" (vv. 8-10). They confidently testify to the goodness and faithfulness of God, because of their own experience.

3. To EXHORT. "O fear the Lord, ye His saints… Come ye children hearken unto Me" (vv. 9-11). The note of warning must be sounded, as well as the notes of invitation and personal testimony. It is as needful for *saints* to fear the Lord as for *children* to hearken to the voice of those who know Him and can teach the way of life (v. 12).

AN EXPERIENCED TEACHER.
PSALM 34. 11-22.

"COME, ye children, hearken unto Me; *I will teach you* the fear of the Lord" (v. 11). To teach the fear of the Lord is to teach how to know the Lord, and live in the enjoyment of His favour and presence. As *children* then, let us sit down at the feet of this great teacher and learn what he has to say about the way of life and blessedness.

As a man of experience, he sets forth the truth in order. He speaks—

I. **About Desire**. "What man is he that *desireth* LIFE" (v. 12). The anxiety of the soul must be after the right and proper object to begin with. The heart that longs to "see good" has come to the gate of the narrow way.

II. **About Evil**. "Keep thy tongue from evil...depart from evil" (vv. 13, 14). Those who would seek life must be ready to be separated from all their sins. To run this race every weight and sin must be laid aside (Heb. 12. 1). Let the wicked forsake his way, etc.

III. **About Peace**. "Seek peace" (v. 14). He does not teach us that we should *make* peace, but *seek* it. Christ hath made peace by the Blood of His Cross. Seek the peace of God, and follow peace with all men (Heb. 12. 14).

IV. **About Prayer**. "The eyes of the Lord are upon the righteous, and His ears are open to their cry,...the righteous cry and the Lord heareth" (vv. 15-17). Apart from the Lord Jesus Christ no man is better able to instruct in the art of prayer than David. God and prayers were tremendous realities to him. "Ask and ye shall receive."

V. **About Nearness**. "The Lord is nigh unto them that are of a broken heart" (v. 18). Let us give special heed to this teaching. Broken-heartedness is a condition of true fellowship with God. He knoweth the proud afar off. "The sacrifices of God are a broken spirit" (Psa. 51. 17). The Holy One that inhabiteth eternity dwells with him that is of a contrite and humble spirit (Isa. 57. 15).

VI. **About Affliction**. "Many are the afflictions of the righteous; but the Lord delivereth him out of them all" (v. 19). The Lord's people are not saved from afflictions, but saved in them, as Daniel was in the den of lions, and the Hebrews in the furnace of fire. "In the world ye shall have tribulation, but be of good cheer, I have overcome the world." Troubled on every side, but not distressed (2 Cor. 4. 8).

VII. **About Perseverance.** "None of them that trust in Him shall be condemned" (v. 22, R.V.). None shall pluck them out of My hand, He is able to keep from stumbling all those that trust in Him. By faith we are saved from guilt and sin, by faith are we kept day by day from the condemning influences that are ever about us and within us. "I am the Way, the Truth, and the Life" (John 14. 6).

_____

FALSE WITNESSES.
PSALM 35.

IF any man would live godly, he must suffer persecution.

I. **His Cowardly Enemies.** "False witnesses did rise up; they laid to my charge that I knew not; they rewarded me evil for good (vv. 11, 12). In mine adversity they rejoiced" (v. 15). In this he became a partaker of the sufferings of his Lord (Matt. 26. 59-61). Even because of *love*, some will become our adversaries (Psa. 109. 4). Those who are out of sympathy with Jesus Christ will be out of sympathy with His faithful followers.

II. **His Attitude Towards Them.** "But as for me, when *they were sick*, my clothing was sackcloth...and my prayer returned into mine own bosom" (v. 13). All those, so called, imprecations in this Psalm should be read in the light of this statement. He who fasted and prayed for his enemies, when they were in trouble, was not likely to pronounce curses upon them. As Newberry points out, these "texts" should be read in the future tense. "They shall." Well David knew what the future would be of those who raised false charges against God's people, and who rejoiced at their halting (v. 15, R.V.). Our Lord's command is, "Love your enemies, bless them that curse you,...and pray for them that despitefully use you," even although your prayer should "return into your own bosom," as it sometimes does.

III. **His Petitions to God.** "Strive Thou, O Lord, with them that strive with me...and stand up for mine help" (vv. 1, 2, R.V.). He pleads for—

1. DIVINE ADVOCACY. "Strive *thou* with them." The servant of Christ must not strive, seeing that he has an advocate with the Father who is Jesus Christ the *Righteous*. Vengeance belongeth unto the Lord; commit thy ways unto Him. GOD is our refuge.

2. DIVINE DELIVERANCE. "Lord, how long...rescue my soul from their destructions" (v. 17). He who is our Redeemer and Lord will not fail to rescue the souls of His trusting ones from all the destructive plans and purposes of His and our enemies. His Name was called Jesus because He shall save.

3. DIVINE JUSTICE. "Judge me, O Lord my God, according to Thy righteousness" (v. 24). Those who have found refuge in His mercy will find strength in His righteousness. "It *is* a righteous thing with God to recompense tribulation to them that trouble you" (2 Thess. 1. 6).

IV. **His Joyful Resolution.** "My soul shall be joyful in the Lord...All my bones shall say, Lord, who is like unto Thee" (vv. 9, 10). "My tongue shall speak of Thy righteousness, and of Thy praise all the day long" (v. 28). When we make our appeal to God, we must in confidence leave the matter in His hands, *rejoicing* that He is able, and *praising* because He will. Those who are joyful in the Lord are best able to speak of His righteousness.

UNDER HIS WINGS.

PSALM 36. 5-9.

THE Psalmist begins here by laying bare the secret thoughts and intents of the wicked man's heart. "There is no fear of God before his eyes; he flattereth himself in his own eyes" (vv. 1, 2). Does the denial of *God* not always spring from the desire for *self*-flattery? How different it is with those who are joyfully resting beneath the shadow of His wings. Note the—

I. Attitude Mentioned. "Under the shadow of Thy wings" (v. 7). They are there because they have "put their trust" in the Lord their God. There is no other way of getting under the saving, protecting power of God but by faith. It was because Ruth *believed* that she found refuge under the wings of the Lord God of Israel (Ruth 2. 12). The feathers of God's wings are the words of His Gospel. "His truth shall be thy shield" (Psa. 91. 4; Matt. 23. 37).

II. Reasons Given. "Therefore" (v. 7). This word suggests the wherefore—

1. "Thy MERCY is in the Heavens" (v. 5). Being in the Heavens, it is high enough to overtop all the altitudes of human guilt. "As far as the Heavens is high above the earth, so great is His mercy toward them that fear Him" (Psa. 103. 11).

2. "Thy FAITHFULNESS reacheth unto the skies" (v. 5, R.V.). The clouds may come and go, but the sky, in all its purity, remains eternally the same, so with the faithfulness of God. He is faithful that hath promised, and that faithfulness will not fail till the objects of it reacheth the skies (1 Cor. 1. 9).

3. "Thy RIGHTEOUSNESS is like the mountains of God" (v. 6, R.V.). The righteousness of God! Who

can rise up to it? It is like the great mountain top
that pierces the clouds, where no human foot has ever
trod. Who can by searching find out God? But He
hath made Christ to be unto us Righteousness, even
the righteousness of God, which is unto all and upon
all them that believe.

4. "Thy JUDGMENTS are a great deep" (v. 6). If His
righteousness is as high as Heaven, His judgments are as
deep as Hell. "O the *depth* of the riches both of the
wisdom and knowledge of God!" There is no escape from
His justice but under the wings of His mercy.

5. "Thy LOVINGKINDNESS is precious" (v. 7, R.V.).
Precious indeed is the lovingkindness of God, who in the
Person of His Son hath spread the wings of His proffered
grace over a perishing world. "Herein is love."

III. **Blessings Enjoyed.** All those who are under
His wings are in the place of—

1. ABUNDANT SATISFACTION. "They shall be abundantly satisfied" (v. 8). The Hebrew word is "watered"
(R.V., *margin*). The provision of His grace will be found
amply sufficient for those who hide in Him. He shall make
them to drink of the *river* of His own pleasure (v. 8, l.c.).
"At His right hand there are pleasures for evermore."
Jesus cried, "If any man thirst let him come unto Me and
drink." To come to Him is to come to the "*fountain* of
life" (v. 9; John 4. 14).

2. CLEARNESS OF VISION. "In Thy light shall we see
light" (v. 9). In the light of His presence we see clearly
the light of His truth. To trust in Him is to pass out of
darkness into His marvellous light. In His marvellous
light, we see light, on sin, on self, on death, on
immortality, and eternal life (John 8. 12).

COUNSELS FOR CHRISTIANS.

PSALM 37. 1-9.

IN Newberry's "Englishman's Bible" there are seven words in these verses printed in heavy letters, indicating that they are emphasised in the Hebrew. Those words stand out as stepping stones into the blessed life of faith and fullness. Here they are—

I. **Fret Not.** "Fret not thyself because of evil-doers" (v. 1). Be not envious at the foolish, when you see the prosperity of the wicked (Psa. 73. 3). Be content with such things as ye have. Knowing that "all things work together for good to them that love God." All things are yours, for ye are Christ's.

II. **Trust.** "Trust in the Lord, and do good" (v. 3). To be content, without trusting in the Lord, is no virtue, it is imbecility or madness. God's *amen* is given to our faith, "*Verily* thou shalt be fed." Faith is an active grace, therefore be not slothful, but followers of them who through faith and patience inherit the promises (Heb. 6. 12).

III. **Delight.** "Delight thyself also in the Lord: and He shall give thee the desires of thine heart" (v. 4). We may well question our *trust*, if it does not lead to "*delight* in the Lord.*" We cannot delight in Him, unless we believe that He is the chief and perfect good of the soul.

IV. **Commit.** "Commit thy way unto the Lord...and He shall bring it to pass" (v. 5). Where there is perfect trust and delight in the Lord, there will surely be a perfect committal of ourselves, and all our ways and purposes unto Him. The life that is wholly committed will be free of all anxious thoughts (Matt. 6. 25). We are encouraged to cast *all* our care upon Him, for He careth for us (1 Peter 5. 8).

V. Rest. "Rest in the Lord" (v. 7). This rest is the result of a whole-hearted committal. In this quietness and confidence ye shall find your strength (Isa. 13. 15). Rest in the Lord, for the battle is not your's, but His.

VI. Cease. "Cease from anger and forsake wrath" (v. 8). If your trust is in the Lord, cease from self and from man. Wrath and strife are the works of the flesh (Gal. 3. 19, 20). "He that hath no rule over his own spirit is like a city that is broken down, and without walls" (Prov. 25. 28).

VII. Wait. "Wait upon the Lord" (v. 9). "Wait patiently for Him" (v. 7).. This word is most needful. After having committed all to Him, and ceased from our will and way, there is a danger of growing weary in well-doing. Wait, "Ye have need of patience, that *after* ye have done the will of God, ye might receive the promise" (Heb. 10. 36). They that wait upon the Lord shall have such manifestations of Himself as shall renew their strength.

––––––––

SEVEN CHARACTERS, AND THEIR PORTION.
PSALM 37. 10-37.

IT is what men *are*, not so much what they think, say, or do that determines their character, relationship, and portion in the sight of God.

I. The Evildoer: he shall be cut off (v. 9). "Bloody and deceitful men shall not live out half their days" (Psa. 55. 23). Like chaff, the wind shall drive them away.

II. The Meek: he shall inherit the earth; and delight himself in the abundance of peace (v. 11). The meekest Man the world ever saw "had not where to lay His head," but He and His followers shall yet judge the world.

III. The Lawless: the Lord shall laugh at him (vv. 12, 13). Those who refuse to obey the call of God's grace, and cast away the cords of His commandments from them, shall be rewarded with the laugh of His derision (Psa. 2).

IV. The Righteous: the Lord shall uphold him (v. 17). Those who bear the image of the Heavenly Father shall be upheld with His everlasting arms.

V. The Good: the Lord shall order his steps, and delight in his way (v. 23). The walk that is ordered by the Lord will be a delight to His heart. The "good man" seeks to get the highest good, and to do the greatest good.

VI. The Saint: he shall not be forsaken; he shall be preserved for ever (v. 28). God can never forsake His holy ones, since the Holiest One of all was forsaken on their behalf. They shall be preserved for ever, for they are the heirs of eternal life (1 Peter 1. 5).

VII. The Perfect: his end is peace (v. 37). His end shall be perfect peace, because the peace of God already rules in his heart. The peace of God which passeth all understanding can never pass away. In these leading words we may easily trace a gradation of experience in the Godly life. The *meekness* of contrition, the *righteousness* of faith, the *goodness* of grace, the *saintship* of holiness, and the *perfection* of glory.

———

THE RIGHTEOUS MAN.
Psalm 37. 10-34.

As compared with the "righteousness of God," by nature "there is none righteous." The truly righteous man is the man whose *iniquities* are forgiven, whose moral nature has been "made straight" and who now lives the *upright* life. The blessedness of such a man is here beautifully portrayed.

I. His Little is Blessed. "A little that a righteous man hath is better than the riches of many wicked" (v. 16). Although there is but little meal in his barrel, it never

goes done. With his little, he has always the blessing
of the Lord which maketh rich, and addeth no sorrow
(Prov. 10. 22).

II. He is Upheld by the Lord. "The Lord upholdeth
the righteous" (v. 17). His strength is not in himself, but
in the faithful and strong hand of his God (Isa. 41. 10).
He is upheld upon the sinking billows, like Peter, where no
faithless feet can ever go. "I have prayed for thee that
thy faith fail not" (Luke 22. 32). He maketh my feet like
hinds' feet, to stand in slippery places.

III. His Inheritance is Everlasting. "The Lord
knoweth...the upright; and their inheritance shall be for
ever" (v. 18). If he has *little* on the earth, he has "an
inheritance incorruptible, and undefiled, and that fadeth
not away, reserved in Heaven" (1 Peter 1. 4). Being an
heir of God, he is an heir of the eternal joys and glories that
belong to Him; pleasures that are at God's right hand for
evermore.

IV. He is Merciful and Gracious. "The righteous
sheweth mercy, and giveth" (v. 21). He has learned by
the example and Spirit of his Lord, that "it is more blessed
to give than to receive." He has had mercy and grace
shewed him, and as he has *freely* received, he freely gives.

V. He is Never Forsaken. "I am old, yet have I not
seen the righteous forsaken, nor his seed begging bread"
(v. 25). This *old* man's testimony is most precious and
encouraging; he had never seen the righteous forsaken nor
his seed in destitution. "Believe on the Lord Jesus Christ
and *thou* shalt be saved *and thy house*" (Acts 16. 31).

VI. He is Endowed with Heavenly Wisdom. "The
mouth of the righteous speaketh wisdom...the law of his
God is in his heart" (vv. 30-32). When the *Word of God*
is hid in the heart, then out of the *good treasure* of the heart

he can bring forth good things (Matt. 12. 35). "It is not ye
that speak, but the Spirit of your Father which is in you."

VII. **The End is Peace.** "Behold the upright, for the
end of that man is peace" (v. 37). He does not need to
pray, like Balaam, "Let me die the death of the righteous,"
for he has already peace—the peace of God—and the
blessedness of the peacemaker is now his; he is a child of
God (Matt. 5. 9). "My peace I give unto you" (John
14. 27).

VIII. **His Salvation is All of God.** "The salvation of
the righteous is of the Lord...because he trusts in Him"
(vv. 39, 40). He is saved by grace, through faith. There
is nothing in himself to boast of; his life-long salvation is
the result of his life-long trust in the mercy and power of
his God and Saviour. As Daniel was "taken out of the
den, with no manner of hurt found upon him, *because he
believed in his God*" (Dan. 6. 23) so will He save us from
this present evil world, because we trust in Him.

SIN'S MISERIES, AND THE WAY OF ESCAPE.
PSALM 38.

THIS Psalm of "Remembrance" which reminds us of a
boiling pot, in which there are many unsavoury ingredients,
is in marked contrast to the preceding Psalm. We may
partly misunderstand David, if we forget that he acted not
only as king of Israel, but also as Israel's national poet.
This is the language of one who remembers the horrors of
the pit out of which he has been dug. It fitly describes—

I. **The Miseries of Sin.** Sin, when it is finished
bringeth forth death. See here how it operates in the
awakened sinner. There is—

1. CONVICTION. "Thine arrows stick fast in me" (v. 2).
It is not at the sinner God shoots at so much as at his sins

His arrows are sharp and pierce to the core of the evil. The Word of God is a discerner of the heart.

2. DISORDER. "There is no soundness in my flesh" (v. 3). His whole moral nature was discovered to be diseased, and out of order. This is a most humbling revelation. The heart has been found out as a deceitful traitor, and all its actions discovered to be polluting and disorderly.

3. UNREST. "Neither is there any rest in my bones because of my sin" (v. 3). The strongest features in his character were shaken and troubled at the thought of *sin*. The whole fabric of his moral nature was disturbed. Real conviction of sin is as an earthquake in the soul—universal disturbance.

4. OPPRESSION. "Mine iniquities are...as an heavy burden they are too heavy for me" (v. 4). Too heavy for *me*? yes, but not too heavy for Him, who bore our sins on His own body to the tree. What can a man do with a burden that is too heavy for him, and who cannot cast it off? O wretched man! who shall deliver?

5. CORRUPTION. "My wounds stink and corrupt because of my foolishness" (v. 5). This is no exaggerated figure of speech; it is the sober statement of one who has seen and felt sin in its true character and effects. There is no balm in Gilead, no physician on earth that can heal those deep-seated festering wounds.

6. HELPLESS. "I am feeble and sore broken" (v. 8). His whole nature was completely *benumbed*, and powerless to throw off the foul malady. "Without strength" is the condition of all under the torpid blight of sin.

7. DARKNESS. "As for the light of mine eyes, it has gone from me" (v. 10). All the light of hope he had before has died out. Darkness covers the face of his deep.

II. **The Way of Escape**.

1. CONFESSION. "I will declare my iniquity" (v. 18).
A full declaration is needed. He that covereth his sin
shall not prosper, but "if we confess our sins, He is faithful
and just to forgive."

2. CONTRITION. "I will be sorry for my sin" (v. 18).
This is the godly sorrow that worketh repentance to
salvation. The confession that does not spring from
contrition of heart is mockery. It is he that confesseth
and *forsaketh* his sin that finds mercy.

3. FAITH. "In Thee O Lord do I hope: Thou wilt hear,
O Lord my God" (v. 15). "Believe on the Lord Jesus
Christ and thou shalt be saved" (Rom. 10. 9, 10).

TAKE HEED.
PSALM 39.

THIS resolution of the psalmist to "take heed to his ways"
is a note of reminder to us. Let him that thinketh he
standeth take heed lest he fall. Mark those things which,
like David, we should give special attention to. I will take
heed to—

I. **My Ways** (v. 1). I will scrutinise my motives, my
habits and manners. I will not think them right because
they are *my* ways. I will search out whether they are in
harmony with God's word and ways.

II. **My Mouth**. "I will keep my mouth with a bridle
(muzzle) while the wicked is before me" (v. 1). God
is often judged by the ways and mouths of His people,
therefore there is need at times for the muzzle. The man
that offends not in word is a perfect man (James 3. 2).
Walk in wisdom toward them that are without (Psa.
141. 3).

III. **My Heart**. "My heart was hot within me" (v. 3).

Blessed are the hot in heart where the holy fire burns while
they muse on the things of God, for their tongues shall
speak of His praise. Take heed lest there be in any of you
an evil heart of unbelief, or a lukewarm heart of indifference.

IV. My End. "Lord make me to know mine end"
(v. 4). What shall my end be? is a most important
inquiry. Balaam desired that his last end may be like the
righteous, but he did not take heed to his end, so he fell
numbered with the enemies of God.

V. My Days. "Behold Thou hast made my days
(lifetime) as hand-breadths" (v. 5, R.V.). As our lifetime
is made up of a few hand-breadths, we have need to take
heed to each one of them; to "number them that we may
apply our hearts unto wisdom" (Psa. 90. 12).

VI. My Hope. "My hope is in Thee" (v. 7). Take
heed that your hope is in the Lord, and not in yourself or
your circumstances. We are saved by hope, but hope that
is seen is not hope (Rome. 8. 24). Those whose hope is
in God will be filled with all joy and peace in believing, for
He is the God of hope (Rom. 15. 13).

VII. My Transgressions. "Deliver me from all my
transgressions" (v. 8). To transgress is to backslide; to
fail to *take heed* to it is to fall from grace, and allow sin to
have dominion over us (Rom. 6. 14). Although we may
fall, we may rise again for the Lord is the Deliverer of His
people.

VIII. My Prayer. "Hear my prayer, O Lord, and give
ear to my cry; hold not Thy peace at my tears" (v. 12).
Take heed to your prayers, see that they are the *sincere*
expression of your inmost heart, and that they are offered
in no cold and formal manner. They are all the better of
being soaked with tears.

SAVED AND SATISFIED.

PSALM 40. 1-5.

THE first few verses of this favourite Psalm give us the experiences of a soul passing from darkness into light—from the miseries of a lost condition into the joys of a full salvation.   He was—

I. **Distressed.**   In "an horrible pit" and "miry clay" (v. 2).   Our sins are the cords by which we are let down into the dismal darkness to sink in the mire.   It is an horrible awakening when one makes the discovery that this is their condition.   The pains of Hell get hold of such.

II. **Heard.**   "He inclined unto me, and heard my cry" (v. 1).   What a mercy that this pit is not bottomless, and that the gracious ear of God is still within reach. Jonah cried out of the belly of Hell and was heard.

III. **Saved.**   "He brought me up" (v. 2).   His arm is not shortened that it cannot save, it is long enough and strong enough to lift the penitent sinner, "up out of" the pit of horrors and the treacherous mire.   Others may divert and amuse the imprisoned soul, God only can bring him *out*.

IV. **Established.**   "He set my feet upon a rock, and established my goings" (v. 2).   It is a mighty deliverance, from the sinking miry clay of our own thoughts to the rock of God's eternal truth, and to have our ways so established that we are *kept* from falling back into our former condition.   The Lord thy keeper.

V. **Gladdened.**   "He put a new song in my mouth, even praise unto our God" (v. 3).   This new song belongs to the new life of faith.   It is a song of praise unto the Lamb who is worthy, for He was slain and has *redeemed* us to God by His blood (Rev. 5. 9).   He puts this song only into the mouths of those whose feet *He* has set upon the rock.

VI. Used. "Many shall see it, and fear, and shall trust in the Lord" (v. 3). The change is so great that many can't help *seeing* it; it is so manifestly of God, that they will be led to *fear* and to *trust* in the Lord. The testimony of a sound, happy, consistent life, must be fruitful.

VII. Satisfied. "Blessed is the man that trusteth in the Lord...Thy wonderful works...Thy thoughts to usward... if I would declare and speak of them, they are more than can be numbered" (vv. 4, 5). He is satisfied that the man who trusts in the Lord has entered into the *blessed* life. He finds that the works, and thoughts of God, on his behalf, are so wonderful and numerous, that they are unspeakable. When the eyes of our understanding have been enlightened, then we may know what is the hope of His calling, and the exceeding greatness of His power to usward who believe (Eph. 1. 18-20).

MESSIANIC FEATURES.
PSALM 40. 6-10.

THERE is much in this Psalm that might have been fitly spoken by the Lord Jesus Christ. Some of these statements can hardly be applied to David (vv. 6-8). Surely the Holy Spirit, the Revealer of Christ, rested upon the Psalmist when he uttered these prophetic words. There are here some—

I. Features of His Character. In him there was the—

1. OPENED EAR. "Mine ears hast Thou opened" (v. 6). When the slave had his ear bored it was a token of entire *submission* to his master's will (Exod. 21. 6). The Lord God bored the ear of His Son, and He was not rebellious, neither turned He back (Isa. 50. 4, 5). This figure is used to denote the entire devotion of the Son to the Father's will.

2. SURRENDERED LIFE. "Burnt offering and sin offering hast Thou not required; then said I, Lo, I come" (vv. 6, 7). When there were no more sacrifices required at the hands of the Jewish priesthood, then Christ came. He came, not to offer sacrifices for sin, but to *give Himself*, an offering unto God. His life was yielded to God for the purpose of redemption. He is "the end of the law for righteousness" (Rom. 10. 4).

3. FULFILLED WORD. "In the volume of *the book* it is written of me" (v. 7). All that was written in the law of Moses, and in the Prophets and in the Psalms concerning the Messiah, found their perfect fulfilment in Him (Luke 24. 44). So ought His Word to be fulfilled in us.

4. EMBODIED LAW. "Thy law is within my heart" (v. 8). He not only obeyed the law, but the law of His God was so deeply engraven in his heart as to constitute His very nature. His meat was to do the will of Him that sent Him (John 4. 34). This is what the Holy Ghost seeks to do in us, by making us partakers of the Divine nature.

5. JOYFUL SERVANT. "I delight to do Thy will, O my God" (v. 8). It is a delight to do His will, when His Word is hid in the surrendered heart (Rom. 7. 22). This is the secret and character of the "holy life," when the self-will is lost in the delightsomeness of the will of God.

6. FAITHFUL PREACHER. "I have preached righteousness: I have not refrained: I have not hid: I have declared: I have not concealed" (vv. 9, 10). As a faithful witness, He kept back nothing that was profitable. Having the Spirit of the Lord upon Him, He preached the Gospel to the poor (Luke 4. 18, 19). He was manifestly declared to be an epistle of God.

II. Aspects of His Ministry. Christ's life and teaching was a revelation of the—

1. Righteousness of God.   "I have published righteousness" (v. 9, R.V.).   The law and the prophets *witnessed* to the righteousness of God, but Jesus Christ alone can *impart* it to all them that believe (Rom. 3, 21, 22).

2. Faithfulness of God.   "I have declared Thy faithfulness" (v. 10).   Every miracle that Christ performed, every prayer that He uttered, was a declaration of the faithfulness of His Father to His Son, and to His Word. He walked by faith, and received from God all that He needed, thereby proving His faithfulness.

3. Salvation of God.   "I have declared...Thy salvation" (v. 10).   Salvation through the grace of God was the *central* theme of our Lord's ministry.   This salvation which *began* to be spoken by the Lord: how shall we escape if we neglect it? (Heb. 2. 3).

4. Lovingkindness of God.   "I have not concealed Thy lovingkindness" (v. 10).   God is love, and His love and kindness had a new *unveiling* in the gift of His Son. Jesus Christ never concealed the fact that *Himself* was the expression of the lovingkindness of the Father to a perishing world.   "Last of all He sent His Son."   Herein is love.

5. Truth of God.   "I have not concealed...Thy truth" (v. 10).   The truth as it is in the character of the Father has been manifested to us in the character of the Son.   No essential feature belonging to the nature of God was concealed by Him.   He is *the Truth*; neither more nor less can be said of Him than what is said of God: "I and My Father are one."   Let us thank God that He who is the *Truth*, is also the *Way* and the *Life*.

THE BLESSEDNESS OF CONSIDERING THE POOR.

PSALM 41. 1-3 (*see next Psalm*).

THE word "blessed" here is in the plural, "Oh, the blessednesses" of such.

I. He will be **Delivered** in time of trouble (v. 1).

II. He will be **Preserved** and *kept* in life (v. 2).

III. He will be **Blessed** upon the earth (v. 2).

IV. He will be **Saved** from his enemies (v. 2).

V. He will be **Strengthened** in time of weariness (v. 3).

VI. He will be **Comforted** in time of sickness (v. 3).

THE SUFFERINGS AND CONSOLATIONS OF THE SAINT.

PSALM 41. 4-13.

According to the Hebrew divisions, this Psalm ends the first Book.

I. His Sufferings. He suffers from—

1. EVIL SPEAKING. "Mine enemies speak evil of me" (v. 5).

2. EVIL THINKING. "When shall he perish?"

3. EVIL WHISPERING. "They whisper together against me" (v. 7).

4. EVIL PLOTTING. "They devised my hurt."

5. EVIL WORKING. "Lifted up his heel against me" (v. 9).

II. His Consolations. He is comforted with the—

1. KNOWLEDGE OF GOD. "But Thou, O Lord" (v. 10).

2. FAVOUR OF GOD. "I know that Thou favourest me" (v. 11).

3. FAITHFULNESS OF GOD. "Mine enemy doth not triumph over me."

4. POWER OF GOD. "Thou upholdest me" (v. 12).

5. PRESENCE OF GOD. "Thou settest me before Thy face" (v. 12).

SIN.

THE juice of the manchineel tree is said to be so poisonous that when it touches the blood it works death with awful rapidity. Yet its appearance and fruit look most beautiful. Outwardly, it is very attractive; inwardly, it is a deadly poison. How like sin this is! Its very attractiveness is its greatest danger. It beguiles by promising much; it ends in destruction. "Sin, when it is finished, bringeth forth death."

FALSE AND REAL.

PROFESSOR Robinson once found a plant growing most luxuriantly in a coal-mine. Its form and qualities being quite new to him, he had it removed to his garden and carefully attended. But the plant soon languished and died, but from its roots there sprang up a new, fresh form of life, which he easily distinguished as the common tansy. The pit-life of the tansy was unreal and deceptive, as the lives of all are who are living in the pit of spiritual darkness. Not until we get transplanted into the light of the Kingdom of God do we become really true to the deeper instincts of our nature. "*He* took me from the fearful pit."

EXPOSITORY OUTLINES.

New Testament.

THE SHEPHERD.

JOHN 10. 1-10.

"Now, the training strange and lowly,
Unexplained and tedious now:
Afterward—the service holy
And the Master's "Enter thou."
—F. R. HAVERGAL.

THESE "Verily, verily's" of our Lord, which might be
rendered, "In most solemn truth," never seem to be used at
the beginning of a discourse, but always to illustrate, or
emphasise some preceding statement; so that the last part
of chapter 9 is closely connected with the opening verses
of chapter 10. Those hirelings, who cast the man out
because he said that Christ opened his eyes, are here
contrasted with the true shepherd, who cares for the sheep.
The allegory of this chapter, like the parable in the
fifteenth of Luke, is given to us in three different sections.
We have (1) the sheepfold and the (under) shepherd (vv.
1-10); (2) the Good Shepherd giving His life for the sheep
(vv. 11-18); (3) the safety of the sheep (vv. 25-30).

I. **The Sheepfold.** This was an enclosure, into which
the sheep were put for safety during the night (v. 1).
This may have reference to the old theocracy, that position
of privilege, which belonged to the Jews as God's chosen
and protected people, and into which no man could
honourably enter, but by the door of birth—the seed of
Abraham; or it may represent that new provision of security
which Christ Himself was about to establish for His sheep,

through the giving of His life for them. It is a *sheep*fold, there is no mention of goats here.

II. The Entrance. There is an entrance, but only *one*. "I am the Door of the sheep" (v. 7). It is through Him who died for them that they enter into the safety and quiet of this spiritual and heavenly fold. "He that entereth in by the door is a shepherd of the sheep." The sheep and the true shepherds all enter in by the same door. There is none other Name whereby we can be saved (Acts 4. 12). He is no shepherd of the sheep who has not, first of all, appropriated Christ for himself, as the Way, the Truth, and the Life. If he enters not by this door into the sheep-fold ministry, "the same is a thief and a robber," and those sheep which have entered by the door will not follow him. Christ is the only open door into the salvation of God, and, praise Him, it is open for all "I am the Door: by Me if *any man* enter in, he shall be saved" (v. 9).

III. The Porter. "He that entereth by the door... to him the porter openeth" (v. 3). It is a marvel to us how commentators should ignore or belittle the porter, lest they should press the allegory too far. In point of fact, the porter is second in importance to Him who is the Door, and undoubtedly represents the ministry of the Holy Spirit. Who abode with the sheep, and was their only comforter during the weary hours of night? The porter. Who could take the Door (Christ) and open it and close it at His will? The porter. Who alone had the power to admit a shepherd into the fold? The porter (Acts 13. 2). All who would enter in by the door shall have the porter's help and encouragement. It is the Spirit who takes the things of Christ and shows them to the seeking soul.

IV. The Shepherd. "He that entereth in by the door is a shepherd of the sheep" (v. 2, R.V., *margin*). The reference here is to the under shepherd, who has the liberty of the porter (Spirit) to go in and out, and to lead, and feed the sheep. The hirelings in chapter 9. 34, cast out the true sheep of Christ's flock. They know not the voice of strangers. It is important to note the nature of the shepherd's work and influence as stated here. It is—

1. PERSONAL. "He calleth his own sheep *by name.*" There is no mistaking the purpose of a true shepherd when he comes into the sheepfold. He has not thought of thrashing or amusing the sheep, his chief object is to call them out into a larger place of blessing. To this end he deals with them definitely and personally. All the faithful under-shepherds of Christ's flock rightly divide the Word: they call the sheep by their proper names, and seek their individual good.

2. PROGRESSIVE. "He leadeth them out." It is not enough that the sheep are safe and at rest in the fold, they have to be lead out into fresh healthy pastures. The fields at the disposal of the shepherds are as broad, far reaching, and as rich as the whole Revelation of God. But those who have not examined those rich pasture lands will not be likely to lead the sheep into them.

3. EXEMPLARY. "He goeth before them." The true shepherd *leads* by example, as well as by precept. He does not say, "Go," but "*Come.*" He goeth before them in doctrine and in practice (Titus 2. 7). Not as lords over God's heritage, but as examples of the flock (1 Peter 5. 3). Paul wrote to Timothy: "Be thou an example of the believers in *Word,* in *conversation,* in *charity,* in *spirit,* in *faith,* in *purity.*" To the Corinthians he said: "Be ye followers of me, even as I also am of Christ." The *shepherd* leads into green pastures, and by the still waters, not into the howling wilderness of that "higher criticism," which offers only doubt and perplexity to a hungry soul.

3. PROTECTIVE. "A stranger will they not follow...for

they know not the voice of strangers" (v. 5). The true
sheep know the voice of a true shepherd, and will not be
led away by the call of a stranger, who has climbed up by
some other way. Some religious teachers have the form of
godliness, but deny the *power* thereof (Holy Spirit); from
such turn away. The sheep that have a faithful shepherd
are too well taught to become the followers of any hireling,
or thief, who may don the shepherd's attire.

V. **The Intruders.** "He that entereth not by the
door, but *climbeth up some other way*, the same is a thief and
a robber." It does not matter much what that "other
way" is, so long as it is *another way*, it is an ignoring and a
denial of Him who is the Door—and of Him who is the
Porter—a denial of Christ, and of the Holy Spirit. Those
who will not enter by the door of grace into this Kingdom
will have some *climbing* to do, and in the end rewarded
only as thieves and robbers. The "other way" that some
prefer is the way of legalism, or learning, human *works*, or
human *wisdom*. They will climb away for years to get into
the fold, rather than submit to enter by the door. But all
such climbers are, in their hearts, at enmity with the
Shepherd and the sheep, and seek only their own base and
selfish ends. "The same is a thief." There is no other
way for a sheep, or a shepherd, for salvation or service, but
by the Lord Jesus Christ, who is the Door. "I am the Door:
by Me if any man enter in, he shall be saved."

THE GOOD SHEPHERD.
JOHN 10. 11-18.

THE Lord Jesus Christ is the good or perfect Shepherd.
All that ever came before Him—*in His stead*—or that shall
yet so come, are thieves and robbers. There is only one
Good Shepherd who can lay down His life for the sheep
and take it again (v. 18). There is perhaps no image of

Christ that has so powerfully appealed to the imaginations of men in all ages as the "Good Shepherd." Let not the familiarity of the term rob us of the great sweetness and depth of precious teaching that it reveals.

I. "He Giveth His Life for the Sheep" (v. 11). This is the outstanding characteristic of the Good Shepherd. He is not only ready to sacrifice His life in defence of the sheep, but has a *command* from the Father to *lay down* His life for the sheep (v. 18), that the sheep might have life through Him in abundance (v. 10). The scope of the teaching cannot be limited to the mere metaphor. The metaphor is used to help us to grasp the fullness of the truth. That Christ taught redemption here is surely beyond doubt, when He said, "Therefore doth My Father love Me, because I lay down My life that I might take it again" (v. 17; Heb. 13. 20). The Father loved the Son because He willingly obeyed this command to lay down His life for the salvation of all who would enter in at this door into the sheepfold (1 Peter 2. 25).

II. His Sheep Hear His Voice. "They shall hear My voice" (v. 16). Every soul who would follow Christ must individually hear His voice. That voice may be heard through the written Word, or in the preaching of the Gospel, but it will be recognised as His voice and His call to a new and separate life. Christ's first message was to the Jewish flock, but He had other sheep—multitudes of them—which were not of that flock, but which belonged to every kindred and tongue, and people, and nation, "them also," He said, "*I must bring*," for the death that He was about to die was to be "the propitiation, not only for our sins (Jews), but also for the whole world" (1 John 2. 2). This present dispensation is the time of the bringing in of the "other sheep" which He has, as the gift of the Father, and they are hearing His voice, through the preaching of

the Word, and following Him.   To Him is the gathering of
the people to be.

III. He Knows His Sheep.   "I know My sheep"
(v. 14).   As to the extent or limit of this knowledge,
it is impossible, except by sheer presumption, to define.
He knows their name, their nature, and their need.   The
Lord does not judge as man judgeth, by outward appearance; He judgeth the heart.   He discerns the hidden
spirits of men, whether they are merely carnal or Christ-
like.   All His sheep have a love for, and a disposition like
the Shepherd Himself.   "If any man love God, the same is
known of Him" (1 Cor. 8. 3).   The Good Shepherd does not
judge His sheep by their *cry*, for many will say on that day,
"Lord, Lord," to whom He will say, "I never knew you."

IV. His Sheep Know Him.   "And am known of
Mine" (v. 14).   This knowledge is akin to that which exists
between the Father and the Son (v. 15).   This affinity
is the deepest and most sacred of all relationships.   We may
know Him as we know the sun that shines in the Heavens,
and yet know but little of Him.   The sheep know the
Shepherd because He has manifested Himself to them, so
we "know that the Son of God is come, and hath given us
an understanding that we may know Him that is true"
(1 John 5. 20).   "I know whom I have believed" (2 Tim.
1. 12).   This is eternal life, to know Him and Jesus Christ
whom He hath sent.

V. His Sheep are Owned by Him.   "He who is an
hireling, *whose own* the sheep are not" (v. 12), is here
contrasted with Him who laid down His life for the sheep,
as an evidence that they are *His own*.   The flock of God
hath been purchased by His own blood (Acts 20. 28).
Jesus was speaking as the Good Shepherd when He said to
Peter, "Feed *My* lambs...Feed *My* sheep" (John 21).
"Ye are not your own; ye are bought with a price."

VI. He Cares for His Sheep. "The hireling fleeth because he careth not for the sheep," but the true Shepherd is very careful over *His* sheep (v. 13). The wolf-like Satan finds his greatest enemy in the Shepherd of our souls. It is the privilege of the sheep to be without carefulness, for "He careth for you," therefore cast all your care upon Him (1 Peter 1. 7). The Shepherd is most careful about the *safety* and *supply* of the sheep—about their defence and their food. His wisdom and His power are being continually exercised on their behalf. "Lo, I am with you alway, even unto the close of the age."

VII. His Sheep shall all be Gathered into one Flock. "There shall be one flock and one Shepherd" (v. 16). Meanwhile, His sheep are in every clime and country, speaking almost every language under Heaven, and divided by many sectarian folds, but all have heard His voice, and know Him, and are known by Him, having by one Spirit been baptised into one body. But when the Chief Shepherd shall appear, those who are still living on the earth shall be caught up with those who have gone to sleep, and so shall we ever be with the Lord. Wherefore, comfort one another with these words (1 Thess. 4. 16-18). In the ever-green pastures of the Heavenly Kingdom He shall lead *His flock*, and they shall follow the Lamb whithersoever He goeth. "The Lord is my Shepherd...and I shall dwell in the house of the Lord for ever" (Psa. 23. 1 and 6).

THE SAFETY OF THE SHEEP.
John 10. 22-30.

It was winter, and Jesus was walking in the porch of the temple called "Solomon's," when the Jews, who were bewildered about the character and doings of Jesus, came about Him, saying, "How long do you mean to keep us in suspense? If Thou be the Christ tell us plainly" (v. 24).

He had been telling them all along by His *words* and *works*, but they believed not (v. 25). Never man spoke more plain than He, but to those who are wilfully or judicially blind, such evidence is of little value. "Ye believe not," said Jesus, "because ye are not of *My sheep*" (v. 26). By their persistent unbelief they proved themselves unfit to enter the sheepfold of His chosen ones. "They could not enter in because of their unbelief" (Heb. 3. 19). This question of the Jews gives Him an opportunity of explaining more fully the relationship and privilege of His sheep.

I. **Their Relationship.** They are His by—

1. SOVEREIGN GRACE. "My sheep hear My voice, and I know them" (v. 27). "All we like sheep have gone astray; we have turned every one to his own way." The Lord might have passed us by in our waywardness and misery, but in love and in mercy He spoke. If *He* did not speak, the sheep would never hear His voice, and never follow Him. "My voice!" There is no other voice like His. To *hear it* is to turn and live, or die in sin. "By grace are ye saved through faith."

2. DELIBERATE CHOICE. "They follow Me." They hear Him, believe Him, and follow Him. They choose to obey His voice, rather than the voices of the world, or the whisperings of their own heart. To follow Christ is to renounce self and forsake all that would hinder the soul from abiding in His presence and obeying His Word.

II. **Their Security.** They are perfectly safe, because—

1. THEY HAVE ETERNAL LIFE. "I give unto them eternal life" (v. 28). The verb is in the present, and might be read, "I am giving them the life of the ages." This life is the *gift* of Him who laid down His life for the sheep—a gift that is continuous, running on into the endless ages of futurity. Who but the Eternal One could make such a

promise and bestow such a blessing? "The gift of GOD is eternal life" (Rom. 6. 23).

2. THEY ARE THE GIFT OF THE FATHER. "My Father... gave them Me" (v. 29). The sheep of Christ are the "elect according to the foreknowledge of God the Father" (1 Peter 1. 2). "All that the Father hath given Me shall come to Me" (John 6. 37). They are secure because they are possessed with a life suited for the ages of eternity, and because they are the chosen ones of the Father "before the foundation of the world, that they should be holy and without blame before Him in love...to the praise of the glory of His grace" (Eph. 1. 3-6). It was for such Christ prayed when He said, "Holy Father, keep through *Thine own* Name those whom *Thou hast given Me.*"

3. THEY ARE IN CHRIST'S HAND. "Neither shall any pluck them out of My hand." Of them which Thou hast given Me have I lost none (John 18. 9). His *hand* stands here for the almightiness of His power—a power as gentle as a mother's touch, as strong as the eternal God. No foe is able to wrest us from His hand. The sheep are saved by the gift of Divine life, and by the grip of Divine power. They are made partakers of a new nature and the subject of a new environment. They are in His heart of grace and in His hand of safety.

4. THEY ARE IN THE FATHER'S HAND. "None is able to pluck them out of My Father's hand" (v. 29). "My Father is greater than all...I and My Father are one." The sheep are in the all-embracing power of the Son, as the Son is in the all-embracing power of the Father. "The glory which Thou gavest Me I have given them, that they may be one, even as We are" (John 17. 22). The security of the Son is virtually the security of the sheep. As He is in the hand of the Father, so are we in the hand of the Son.

Accepted and kept in the Beloved, the *oneness* of the Son
with the Father is a powerful guarantee (v. 30).

5. THEY HAVE HIS PROMISE. "They shall never perish."
The negative here is doubly strong, and might be rendered,
"They shall *never*, NEVER perish" (v. 28). The infallible
Word of the eternal Son stands like an adamantine wall
between the helpless sheep of His fold and perdition. The
breaking of that Word would be the breaking down of His
own character. One "jot or tittle" of His Word cannot
possibly fail. Thus we have strong consolations who have
fled to Him as the Refuge and Shepherd of our souls.

LAZARUS.
JOHN 11.

THE Hebrew form of the name Lazarus is Eliezer—God my
Helper. Surely a fitting name for one who was so mightily
helped by God. The history of Lazarus is, in a spiritual
sense, the history of all who have passed from death unto
life. Note the various stages in his remarkable experience.
There was—

I. **Sickness**. "A certain man was sick" (v. 1). "He
whom Thou lovest is sick" (v. 3). Loved by the Lord,
yet smitten with sickness. Through some cause or other,
soul-sickness is almost invariably the prelude to enlarged
and deeper spiritual blessing. When Jesus heard of it, He
said, "This sickness...is for the glory of God" (v. 4).
Yes, blessed be His Name, for that sickness which brings us
down to the place of death, that the Son of Man might be
glorified in doing a marvellous work in us and for us. The
Holy Spirit must convince of sin before He quickens into
newness of life.

II. **Death**. "Jesus said unto them plainly, Lazarus is
dead" (v. 14). This sickness was not unto eternal death,

but unto that death which in a very singular way made
Lazarus a fit subject for the *resurrecting* power of the
Son of God. Real sin-sickness is only unto the death of
self-love and self-will, that the power of Christ might be
manifested. Sin, when it is finished, bringeth forth death.
When the Spirit convinces of sin, of righteousness and of
judgment, it is the passing of the sentence of death upon
the sinner. All hope of salvation from any other source
had to be abandoned. "Sin revived, and I died" (Rom.
7. 9).

III. **Life.** "He that was dead came forth" (v. 44).
The *life-giving* power of Jesus Christ could only be manifested in the case of a *dead* man. If Lazarus had only been
in a swoon, or in a sleep, there would have been no glory to
God in his awakening. Christ Jesus came into this world
to save sinners. It would bring no glory to Him to give
life or salvation to those who did not need it. Before the
Apostle Paul could say, "Now I live," he had to say, "I am
crucified." Resurrection life can only come where there
has been death. We must die to self if we would live unto
God. To share with Christ His resurrection power, we
must needs go to the Cross and the grave with Him. If
we refuse to die, we refuse to enter into the new and
fruitful life. "Except a corn of wheat die, it abideth
alone" (John 12. 24).

IV. **Liberty.** "Jesus said, Loose him and let him go"
(v. 44). It ill becomes one who has been raised from the
dead by the power of God, to be in bondage to any man,
or the customs and habits of men, especially those manners
and customs that belong to the dead. As in nature, so in
grace, where there is a fullness of life there will be the
bursting open and a breaking forth from the old dead forms
and habits. All that we can do for our dead is to bind
them and bury them, but how different when, with a loud

voice, the Son of God speaks to them. The man that has been liberated from death and the grave, must not be hindered by any fashion of grave clothes. Whom the Son of God makes free are free indeed. The relatives of those saved by Christ may do much to bind or loose their lives for His service. The Lord's command to the friends of Lazarus was, "Loose him and let him go" (John 11. 44). What a crime in His sight if they had refused to obey. See that ye refuse not.

V. Communion. "Lazarus was one of them that sat at the table with Him" (chap. 12. 2) What a blessed privilege to company with Him who has given us to know in our own experience that He is the "Resurrection and the Life." To those who have passed from death unto life there is no fellowship to be compared with His. As like draws to like, so must the resurrected spirit draw to Him who is the Resurrection. Every time we sit down prayerfully to study His Word, we are sitting at the table *with Him*, listening to His voice, and receiving food for our souls. Are you one of those who *sit* at this table with Him?

VI. Testimony. "By reason of him, many of the Jews went away and believed on Jesus" (chap. 12. 11) The power of his testimony lay, not so much in what he was able to say, as in what he was. The fact that he had been raised from death and corruption by the word of Jesus Christ, was in itself a most convincing witness to His Divinity and Messiahship. The greater the work of grace wrought in us by God's mighty power, the greater will be the force of our testimony for Him. The influence of Christ's risen life in us should be the leading of others to "believe on Jesus."

VII. Suffering. Because of the converting power of this new life in Lazarus "the chief priests consulted that they might put him to death" (chap. 12. 10). His old life brought no persecution, but now he has the happiness of those who are reproached for the Name of Christ (1 Peter 4. 14). It is beyond the power of the enemy to kill or destroy the resurrection life. Your life is hid with Christ in God. "If any man suffer as a Christian, let him not be ashamed, but let him glorify God on *this behalf*" (1 Peter 4. 16).

————

JESUS.
John 11.

The Gospel of John is like the rending of the veil, it opens up the way for us into the Holiest of all. Much of the personal glory of the Son of God will be unseen by us, if we fail to discern what His sayings and doings reveal concerning *Himself*. In this chapter we have several bright glimpses of this inner glory, glimpses such as we have everywhere throughout the Gospels.

I. His Divinity. When Jesus heard of the sickness of Lazarus, He said, "This sickness is not unto death, but for the glory of God, that the Son of God might be glorified thereby" (v. 4). This prophetic language is full of meaningless mystery if Jesus Christ was nothing more than the "best of men." Although He *emptied* Himself as the Divine One, that He might live and die for us, He was still *Himself*, the eternal Son, in the bosom of the Father. He knew that this sickness had come that He, as the Son of God, might be glorified thereby.

II. His Love. "Now Jesus loved Martha, and her sister, and Lazarus" (v. 5). While Jesus Christ was Divine, He was also perfectly and purely human. He loved all with that love of God which is the love of pity and compassion, for even those who are His bitterest enemies, but the Marthas, the Marys, and the Lazaruses are the special objects of His affection and delight. He can only delight with His whole heart in those whose hearts are opened with delight toward Him. It is not possible for such love as His to rejoice in iniquity.

III. **His Faith.** "Are there not twelve hours in the day?" etc. (vv. 7-9). These very suggestive words were spoken to His disciples, in answer to their alarm at His proposal to cross over from Peræa, where the Jews of late had sought to stone Him. There were to be twelve hours in His working day, and but eleven had passed. He must work the works of Him that sent Him while it is day (John 9. 4). He did believe that His life was "immortal till His work was done," and so He would walk *in the day* that He might stumble not. Faith in God never leads to laziness or fatalism. He that believeth shall not make the haste of flurried excitement, but they shall make steady progress, despite all the oppositions of the forces of Hell. "Are there not twelve hours in the day?"

IV. **His Joy.** "I am glad" (v. 15). The conjunction here is most remarkable. "Lazarus is dead, and I am glad; glad for *your sakes* to the intent that ye might believe." He was glad that He was not there to save Lazarus from dying, that He might have the opportunity of raising him from the dead, that they might see His glory and believe in Him. Mark the secret of Christ's gladness—glad to have the chance of manifesting His power that others may *believe in Him*, so that they might be blessed by Him. This was the joy that was set before Him when He endured the Cross. The nature of Christ's gladness is totally different from that which is sought for by the sinful sons of men.

V. **His Indignation.** "When Jesus saw her wailing, and the Jews also wailing, He was moved with indignation in the Spirit" (v. 33, R.V., *margin*). Why all this wailing *now* that HE had said, "Thy brother shall rise again," and that "I am the Resurrection and the Life?" In the face of His words and in His presence, this wailing was surely to Him the wailing of unbelief. He groaned in Spirit with a holy anger because of their slowness of heart to believe all that He had said unto them.

VI. **His Compassion.** "Jesus wept" (v. 35). Those tears were as "drops of grief" from the loving heart of our Great High Priest, who is touched with the feeling of our infirmities (Heb. 4. 15). What a contrast between the hypocritical tears of those would-be mourners and the tears of the pure-hearted Son of God. The voice of these tears seems to have spoken louder than His words, for, "*Then* said the Jews, Behold how He loved Him." If these teardrops were pearls of love, what shall we say of those blooddrops wept in the Garden of Gethsemane? "Greater love hath no man than this." There is a way through Christ's tears, as well as through His words, to the heart of God the Father.

VII. **His Power.** "He cried with a loud voice, Lazarus come forth, and he that was dead came forth" (vv. 43, 44). This was the cry of Him who is "the Resurrection and the Life." "Resurrection," one has said, "is not an impersonal fate, but a personal effect." It is not the natural result of any known law, but the supernatural outcome of a Divine personal act. In Christ was life, and the life was the light of men. He speaks and it is done. As when Christ, who was the Life, appeared at the grave of Lazarus, Lazarus also appeared with Him, through the power of His Word; so "when Christ, who is our Life, shall appear, then shall we also appear with Him in glory" (Col. 3. 4). While on earth our Lord had to do with death in three different stages: the child on the death-bed, the young man on the bier, and the man in the grave. It was only in this last stage that He spoke with a *loud voice*. The raising of Lazarus was a

manifestation of that power that shall one day with the
voice of a trumpet awaken the dead, and as the vile body
of Lazarus was changed (v. 30), so shall it be in the
resurrection (Phil. 3. 20, 21). This corruptible must put
on incorruption. He that heareth His Word now, and
believeth on Him.. is passed from death unto life (John
5. 24).

___

A SUPPER SCENE.
JOHN 12. 1-8.

ACCORDING to Matthew and Mark, this supper which
"they" made for Jesus, was in the house of Simon, who had
been a leper, and may have been a united effort, with the two
families, to do honour to Jesus and His disciples because
of the raising of Lazarus from the dead, and, perhaps, the
healing of Simon. It took place six days before the passover, which meant six days before His death and burial.
It must have been a hallowed time. Let us think of—

I. Mary, the Sacrificer. While others rejoice to sit
at the table with Jesus, and learn of Him, Mary, who had
before sat at His feet, feels impelled by the love of her
heart to embrace this opportunity of proving her faith and
affection by personal sacrifice. To her, at that time, it was
more blessed to give than to receive. There surely must
be seasons in our lives when we shall find it more blessed
to sacrifice than to seek, to give than to take, to praise
than to pray. See the *nature* of it. "Mary took a pound
of ointment of spikenard, *very costly*." Judas reckoned its
value at "three hundred pence"—more correctly, *shillings*
As money goes now, it would mean probably about £60.
The costlier the better for Mary's deep purpose of love.
Hypocritical worshippers are content to give the Lord the
lame and the blind, the odd coppers and the spare moments.
They never cross the threshold of the sanctuary of self-
sacrificing service.

See the *manner* in which it was given. She "anointed the feet of Jesus, and wiped His feet with her hair." It is possible to give even a costly gift in such a way as to sting the soul of the receiver. The Lord loveth a cheerful giver. Mary not only offered Him her precious treasure, but her personal glory was also laid at His feet and surrendered to His service. The ointment was all the more precious to the Saviour because the soul of the offerer was in it. See the *influence* of it. "The house was filled with the odour of the ointment." Such a self-sacrificing act could not pass without being *felt* by all who saw it. Such costly offerings, made for such a sacred purpose, are sure to betray themselves (Prov. 27. 16). A consecrated life has always a sweet odour to Christ and His faithful disciples.

II. Judas, the Criticiser. The only one who did not appreciate the holy deed of Mary was Judas. The "odour of the ointment" poured upon the Son of God had no sweet savour to him, "because he was a thief," and would rather have had the "three hundred shillings" in his bag for his own advantage. His hypocritical plea was, that it might have been sold and the money given to the poor. "Not that he cared for the poor." Surely the Saviour of sinners was more interested in the poor than he was. He who was rich, for our sakes became poor. "To what purpose is this waste?" (Matt. 26. 8). Judas, the son of perdition, could not see that the breaking of this alabaster box, and the pouring out of the fragrant treasure upon the Person of Christ was the consecrating of both to the greatest possible service. It is noteworthy that the word "waste" used by Judas is literally the same word used by our Lord in referring to him as the "son of *perdition*." Where the spirit of self-seeking is there is blindness to the honour and glory of the Lord Jesus Christ. Mary's vision of Jesus was such that it constrained her to surrender all. **Judas**

could not see beyond the black shadow of his own sinful self-interest.

III. **Jesus, the Justifier.** "Then Jesus said, Let her alone; against the day of My burying hath she kept this." He understood the full significance of this singularly solemn service, and always puts the highest value upon such gifts. The costly offering was in no sense wasted on Him. To His soul, in view of His death and burial, it had a sweet savour. "Let her alone." The Son of God who sacrificed Himself for sinners will never put any hindrance in the way of a believing, grateful heart showing its devotion to Him to the fullest extent. He knows that such love and sacrifice will have its corresponding reward (Mark 14. 9). "Let *her* alone." Well He knew that there are so few who care to go this length in honouring Him. She broke through all the forms of etiquette, and gave to Christ exceeding abundantly above all that *they* would have asked or thought of. Such a spontaneous outburst of self-sacrificing affection was to Jesus the principal part of the feast. Love feasts on love. Here He had a meat to eat that others knew not of. "The poor," he said, "always ye have with you, but Me ye have not always." But those who reckon it waste to pour out wealth for the cause of Jesus Christ will not be likely to break *their* treasure boxes in behalf of the poor. The best friends of the poor have always been those who are the most devoted friends of Jesus Christ. The love of Christ constraineth us.

DEATH, LIFE, AND SERVICE.
JOHN 12. 20-26.

PROBABLY these Greeks who desired to see Jesus came from the same city as Philip and Andrew, and may have been personally known to them. Philip and Andrew did what they could to bring about an interview, but seemingly failed. The closing words in verse 36 are very significant in this connection. "These things spake Jesus, and departed, and did *hide Himself from them.*" But while He hid Himself from them, the things which He spake were in themselves a new and fuller revelation of the Christ which He wished them to see. He who would "see Jesus" as God desires Him to be seen, must see Him as "a corn of wheat falling into the ground and dying, and bringing forth much fruit."

I. Death. "Except a corn of wheat fall into the ground and die, it abideth alone." A corn of wheat *in the process* of dying is here alluded to. As applied to His own preparation for the Cross, the reference is full of solemn suggestion. As a corn of wheat must *fall into the ground* before it will die, so He had to condescend to come into the place of death before He could reap the fruits of resurrection life. When Christ came into this world He came into the place of death. His coming was the falling of the corn of wheat into the ground, but *except it die,* it abideth alone. A seed that had lain in the hand of a mummy for 3000 years, remained alone, but when, by another hand, it fell into the ground and did die, then it brought forth fruit. The process of dying is the process of yielding up everything to those forces that are opposed to stationary barrenness. Just as the buried seed slowly surrenders its all, so is its new capacity created for fruitfulness. The life of Jesus Christ, which ended in the shameful death of the Cross, was like the life of the corn-seed in the ground— there was no reserve, no keeping back, the treasures of His marvellous nature were wholly surrendered. "He came not to be ministered unto, but to minister, and to give His life." He died for us   What was true of the Christ as "a corn of wheat" is also true of the Christian, except he die—to the old self-life—he abideth alone. It is by being "alway delivered unto death for Jesus' sake, that the life also of Jesus is made manifest in our mortal flesh" (2 Cor. 4. 11).

II. **Life.** "But if it die, it bringeth forth much fruit." The life that is yielded up by the dying seed conditions and prepares the way for another and more fruitful life. Christ died, and therefore did not abide alone. The life that He yielded up has been abundantly fruitful in an ever-increasing harvest of resurrected souls. The possibilities of Jesus Christ as seed-corn dropped, as it were, from the hand of the Heavenly Father into the soil of humanity, are the possibilities of GOD. He shall see His seed, because His soul was made an offering for sin. Christ died, but like a corn of wheat, He was born anew—begotten again in resurrection fruitfulness. In this new life, in Him and in us who have died unto sin, there is the abiding power of eternity. Herein is My Father glorified, that ye bear much fruit, but "that which thou sowest is *not quickened except it die*" (1 Cor. 15. 36). If the seed refuses to die, the quickening power refuses to act. The Holy Spirit, the *Quickener*, can only work this *newness of life* where there is death. This new Divine life, begotten out of the death of the self-life, is the life that glorifies God in bearing much fruit. He that soweth to the flesh shall out of the flesh, as out of poisoned soil, reap corruption.

III. **Service.** "If any man serve Me, let Him follow Me." To *follow Him* is the highest and holiest of all service. To follow Him is to go on continually denying self. We cannot be following Him in His life of perpetual self-denial unless we are prepared daily to lose our own life. He that loveth his (own) life shall lose it, and he that maketh his own life of no account shall keep it unto life eternal (v. 25). Christ loved not His own life, but yielded it, day by day, unto the will of the Father, and so served Him by following Him. Our service must be of the same

nature, as we have, through grace, been brought into the
same privilege. Now are we the sons of God. In essence,
then, this service is *self-denial* for the sake of Jesus Christ.
But think of the blessedness of it. "If any man serve Me,
him will My Father honour." The Father honoured the
Son for such a service; He will also honour all who so follow
His footsteps. They will be honoured with His presence,
His peace, and His power, and "where I am, there shall
also My servant be." "If any man will come after ME, let
him deny *himself*" (Matt. 16. 24). To go after a self-
denying Christ is impossible without the denial of self.
We must deny our own thoughts, will, power, interests—
everything that would hinder His will, power, and interests
from being accomplished in us and by us.

THE LIGHT OF THE WORLD.
JOHN 12. 44-50.

OUR Lord's ministry on earth was first prophetic, then
priestly. John's reference to the lament of the prophet
Isaiah, in verses 38-41, may be regarded as the close of
Christ's work as a Prophet, and here the beginning of His
work as a Priest.

I. **His Relationship to the World.** "I am come a *Light*
into the world." In Him was no darkness at all. The
purity and power of ineffable light was in Him, to meet
the needs and solve the problems of a guilty and benighted
world. "*I* am come." There is no other light powerful
enough to scatter the darkness of a world. He comes, not
as a citizen to share our sorrows, or as a patron to protect
our rights, but as a Light to *reveal*. This was the world's
first great need.

II. **The Nature of this Light.** It was the light of the
great Heavenly Father's will revealed in the Son. "I have
not spoken of Myself," He says, "but the Father which

sent Me, He gave Me a command what to say, and in what words to speak" (v. 49). The body of Jesus Christ was as a lantern, the light that was in Him was the Light of God, the manifestation was through His words and works. These words and works reveal infinite love and mercy, hand in hand with infinite power and holiness. The shining was perfect, for He could say, "He that seeth Me, seeth Him that sent Me" (v. 45).

III. **The Purpose of the Light.** "I am come not to judge the world, but *to save the world*" (v. 47). The purpose of every lighthouse is salvation. Light is a great saviour from death and destruction. There were those who were opposed to gas light, when first introduced in 1807, but it was declared that the new light had done more for the reduction of crime than all the laws of Parliament since the days of Alfred. The light of Christ is sin's greatest enemy. To see a Father's love in the life and death of His beloved Son is to see our own need and God's only remedy. He has not come as a light to shine out judgment, and condemnation, but that the world *through Him* might be SAVED (John 3. 17).

IV. **How this Light is Received.** "Whosoever believeth in Me shall not abide in darkness" (v. 46). This heavenly and saving Light shines into the hearts of those who with the heart believe in Him. This faith cometh by hearing. "If any man hear My words," etc. Hear His words, believe them, yield to them, and the light of life will possess the soul. While ye have this light, believe in it, obey it, follow it, trust it. It is as real and as free as the light of the sun. Having believed in Him as the Light of your life, *confess* Him, and be not hindered by the fear of man, or the desire for their praise (see vv. 42, 43; Heb. 11. 27). To believe in Christ is to believe also in Him who sent Him (v. 44). We honour the Father when by faith we receive the salvation, which is Christ Jesus (John 6. 40).

V. **The Consequences of Rejecting the Light.** If those who believe in Him "shall not *abide* in darkness," then those who believe not are *abiding in darkness.* Light has come into the world, yet men love darkness rather than the light, because their deeds are evil. To abide in darkness is to abide in death. To reject this light is rebellion against the will of God. They shall lie down in sorrow who prefer the sparks of their own kindling to the light of eternal truth. But although men reject those illuminating *words,* or message of God in Christ, and cling to the delusions of darkness, they are not done with this light, they must face it again in its more fierce and withering form, for He says, "The word (message) that I have spoken, the same shall judge him in the last day" (v. 48). The light that has been rejected, lest it should consume their sin, will become a consuming fire for sinners. As every flower reflects the colour that it rejects, so every Christ-rejecter will be manifested in that day (John 3. 19-21).

CHRIST'S LAST TOKEN OF LOVE.
JOHN 13. 1-17.

THE passover and the supper, linked together here, is most significant. The passover commemorated deliverance from Egyptian darkness and bondage; the supper supplied the emblems of redemption from the darkness and dominion of sin. What Pharaoh was to the Israelites, Judas was to Jesus Christ, and the consequences were much alike. the sudden destruction of the enemy, and the triumph of the Lord and His people. It was here, at the supper, that Christ gave to His disciples the farewell token of His self-humiliating love to them. Let us try and think afresh of—

I. **What He Did.** "He rose from the supper, and laid

aside His garments, and took a towel, and girded Himself
...and began to wash His disciples' feet and to wipe
them." To wash the feet of guests, at a feast, was the work
of a *slave*. "He made Himself of no reputation, and took
upon Him the form of a servant" (Phil. 2. 7). This was the
attitude of the Lord Jesus from the beginning. "He came
not to be ministered unto, but to minister (serve) and to
give His life" (Matt. 20. 28). The Lord would have our
feet (walk), as well as our hearts, clean.

II. When He Did It. "When He knew that His
hour was come that He should depart...unto the Father
(v. 1)...that the Father had given all things into His
hands, and that He was come from God, and was going
to God" (v. 3). This lowly act of personal humiliation
and service was performed, as it were, in view of the awful
death of the Cross and the glory that was to follow. The
near prospect of the agony of Gethsemane, the desertion of
His washed disciples, and the eternal glory of the Father,
did not prevent Him from humbling Himself to attend to
their present need. How easy it is for us to get so taken
up with our own sufferings or successes as to become self-
centred and proud, or unsympathetic. He pleased not
Himself, but lived and died for us.

III. How He Did It. He did it *lovingly*. "Having
loved His own...He loved them unto the end" (v. 1).
Love beamed in His eyes, love throbbed in His words,
love dropped at His fingers. His touch was as gentle as
a mother's. He did it *voluntarily*. Neither law nor
custom required that HE should wash their feet. He did
it of His own free will and choice. It was an expression
of the reality and depth of His inventive grace and love.
He did it *perfectly*. We may be well assured that when He
washed their feet they would be well washed. All His

words are perfect. "The blood of Christ cleanseth us from *all* sin" (1 John 1. 7).

IV. Why He Did It. "I have given you an example, that ye should do as I have done to you" (v. 15). Let this mind be in you which was also in Christ Jesus (Phil. 2. 3-5). Feet-washing is a very delicate business, and must be done in the Spirit of Jesus, for it is not pleasant to flesh and blood to have our faults pointed out. There is a way of doing it that may be more offensive than profitable. To rebuke a brother or sister in an unkind manner is like washing their feet in frozen water, and let us also take heed that the water is not boiling hot with temper. Let us not forget that it is more difficult for some Christians to keep their feet (walk) clean, as in their daily calling they have more dirty paths to tread, because they are more frequently in contact with the soiling influences of the world. Humbling and painful as the work may be, Christ's example teaches us that the work at times has to be done. There will always be those who, like Peter, are ready to say, "Thou shalt never wash my feet," but a little kindly explanation may turn it into a gladsome experience. But woe unto those who refuse to accept the blessing offered through Christ's humiliation. They have no part with Him (v. 8; John 3. 5).

SELF-EXCOMMUNICATED.
JOHN 13. 21-30.

OUR Lord had just been washing the feet of His disciples; giving them a final example of His humiliation and self-forgetting service. After this, John tells us that "He was troubled in spirit."

I. The Cause of Christ's Trouble. "One of you shall betray Me" (v. 21). The cause of His perturbed spirit was not the fact that within a few hours He would be

crucified, but that *"one of you,"* His chosen companions
and friends, would *betray* Him.   Well He knew that they
were "not all clean" (v. 11).   His tender compassionate
heart was troubled, not on account of Himself, but because
of the fearful ingratitude and guilt of that "one" who had
already "lifted up his heel against Him" (v. 18).   Think
of all that Judas had seen and heard of Jesus, and of the
place he occupied, and the confidence that was reposed in
him (allowing him to carry the bag), and think also of
falling from such an height of privilege into a hopeless
perdition.   He hath no pleasure in the death of the wicked.
"He was troubled in spirit."

II. **The Token of Christ's Love.**   "When He had
dipped the sop, He gave it to Judas" (v. 26).   In giving
the morsel first to Judas, Christ was not only showing to
John who should betray Him, but He was also proving to
the traitor that although He knew all that was in his evil
heart to do, He loved him to the end.   Had He not also
washed his feet? washed off the very dust contracted by
that secret visit to those murderous priests.   If Judas, or
any others, will sin their soul to doom, they will never find
any occasion in Him, whose love is stronger than death.
Did the Lord Jesus hope that this humiliating act of
washing the feet of Judas would soften his hard and deceitful heart?   If so, how terribly suggestive are the words
which follow: "And after the sop, Satan entered into
him."   The tokens of a Saviour's love had no effect in
closing the door of his heart against the entrance of the
Devil.   Satan is always ready to take full advantage of
every opportunity.   Those who reject the grace of God, in
Christ Jesus, become the willing dupes of the Devil.

III. **The Departure from Christ's Presence.**   "He
then having received the sop, went immediately out,
and it was night" (v. 30).   He *went* out.   Christ did not

cast him out. He preferred to go out into the night, rather than abide in the light. He loved the darkness rather than the light, because his deeds were evil. He went out; his choice was finally made. Think of what he went out from, and what he went out to.

1. He went out from THE BEST COMPANY ON EARTH, into the company of God-hating, Christ-rejecting murderers.

2. He went out from THE RULE AND SERVICE OF THE SON OF GOD, into the rule and slavery of Satan.

3. He went out from THE PLACE OF LIGHT AND HOPE, into the night of darkness and despair.

4. He went out FROM THE OFFER OF ETERNAL BLESSED-NESS, into the place of eternal doom.

He apparently did not go out as one in a rage; he went out quite orderly, as one who had something of more importance to *do*; something of more importance to *get*. But in turning away from the love of Christ, at this particular moment, he was rejecting his last chance of salvation. Having refused Christ's place, there is nothing for him now but "his own place" (Acts 1. 25)—perdition. Judas may have imagined that his betrayal of the Master, for thirty pieces of silver, would not seriously affect Him, as He was well able to save Himself from the hands of His enemies; but every betrayer is guilty of the body and blood of the Lord. The blood of every Christ-rejecter will be on his own head. "Ye *will not* come to Me that ye might have life" (John 5. 40).

AN INFALLIBLE CURE FOR HEART TROUBLE.
JOHN 14. 1-4.

THERE were several reasons why the hearts of His disciples became troubled or affrighted at this time. Judas had left the company; the Lord had been speaking of going away, and had just been warning Peter that before the cock would crow he would deny Him thrice. Our hearts also may often get troubled when we look at the signs of the times, or when we look within at our own sins and failures. *Heart* trouble is a common malady, but the word and work of Jesus Christ is a perfect remedy. He came to bind up the broken heart. When Jesus said, "Let not your heart be affrighted," He at the same time poured the oil of comfort upon the troubled waters. In this prescription for a troubled heart, given by the Great Physician, there are seven comforting elements.

I. The Power of Christ. "Ye believe in God, believe also in Me." GOD, ME. To "believe in Me" is to believe in God. "I and My Father are One." What a comfort to a sinful, sorrowful soul to know that He who suffered and died for sinners has all the authority and power of Almighty God. "All power," He says, "is given unto Me in Heaven and in earth" (Matt. 28. 18). Trembling soul, affrighted at your own guilt and at coming death and judgment, let not your heart be troubled, believe in Him.

II. The Many Mansions. "In My Father's house are many mansions" (v. 2). The "many mansions" is another way of saying there is plenty of room. The reception room of the Father's house is large enough for all, and there are multitudes of private apartments for the individual comfort of the redeemed. You may be in straights here and now; there may be no room for *you* in the world's inns; although, like the Master Himself, you may not have where to lay your head—let not your heart be troubled, in our Father's house are many mansions.

III. The Prepared Place. "I go to prepare a place for you." He went to the Cross and the grave to prepare salvation for us. He went out of the grave, rising from the dead that He might prepare eternal life for us. He ascended into Heaven that He might prepare a home for

us. The *prepared* place will correspond with the preparedness of the soul here, by the work of the Holy Spirit. The
measure of our enjoyment of the Kingdom of Heaven will be
according to the measure of our spiritual capacity. Hence
the importance of growing in grace now, and in the
knowledge of God. The place prepared for the Apostle Paul
would not be quite the same as that prepared for the penitent
thief. Let not your heart be troubled, the place prepared
for *you* will be in every way exactly suitable to you.

IV. **The Coming Again.** "I will come again." When
He says, "*I* will come again," He surely does not mean
death. He who is the *Life* can never be compared to *death*.
Neither did He mean the Holy Spirit. The Holy Spirit
had not yet been given. He did not die "for our sins."
He meant what He said, for "the Lord *Himself* shall
descend from Heaven with a shout," therefore comfort
one another with these words (1 Thess. 4. 16-18). Let not
your heart be troubled about the loved ones who have
fallen asleep in Jesus, for in that day "them will He bring
with Him," and we shall be "caught up *together*" (1 Thess.
4. 17). Neither let your heart be affrighted at the things
that are coming to pass on the earth, for "He shall reign
till He hath put all enemies under His feet" (1 Cor. 15. 25).

V. **The Great Reception.** "I will come again and
receive you unto Myself; that where I am there ye may be
also." To be received by Him is to have the honour of the
Father and of the Kingdom conferred upon us. His prayer
on our behalf will then have its perfect fulfilment, "Father,
I will that they also, whom Thou hast given Me, be *with
Me where I am*: that they may behold My glory" (John
17. 24). "If any man serve Me...where I am, there shall
also My servant be." Let not your heart be troubled
although the world despise and reject you, there is a
glorious reception awaiting you at the Coming of the Lord.

VI. The Eternal Home. "Where I am, there ye may be also." Meanwhile the mists of earth partly blinds our eyes to the glories of that place where He is. God hath exalted Him far above all principalities and powers, and given Him a Name that is above every name. He is seated at the right hand of God, crowned with glory and honour; and where He is, there His beloved bride shall be, to behold His glory, and to glory in beholding it. The place of honour purchased by the Lord Jesus Christ, as the Redeemer, is to be shared by the redeemed. Let not your heart be troubled although your circumstances here may be mingled plentifully with trials and sorrows, all tears will be wiped away when at home with Him where He is.

VII. The Blessed Assurance. "Whither I go ye know, and the way ye know" (v. 4). Blessed be His Name, we know *where* He is gone, and also *the way* into His presence. He is gone to prepare a place for us, and He Himself is the Way (v. 6). The way to where He is is the way of faith in Him. Faith *in* Him always leads *to* Him. "The way *ye* know." There is a way that seemeth right unto men, but the end is death, instead of life and glory. Let not your heart be troubled, the way may at times be rough and thorny, and narrow, and may seem long, but five minutes at home with Jesus will abundantly compensate for all the inconveniences of our pilgrim life. The way ye know, and it should be enough for us that it is the way.

_____

CHRIST AND THE FATHER.
John 14. 6-21.

When Philip said to Jesus, "Lord, shew us the Father, and it sufficeth us," he was giving expression to the deepest, the most secret, and mysterious longing of the human soul. The curious, critical eye can never look upon

the face of God; it is the pure in heart that see Him.
Philip, like multitudes in every age, was perfectly sincere
in his desire, but slow to believe that Jesus Himself was
the visible expression of the invisible God. "He that
hath seen Me hath seen the Father" (v. 9). In this chapter
our Lord dwells much upon this fact, perhaps in answer
to Philip's request. Christ's relationship to the Father
can only be understood, in any measure, by thinking
deeply into Christ's own statements concerning it. The
hypothesis of the Rationalist is of no value in the face of
His own plain declarations. From His teaching we learn
that—

I. He Dwelt in the Father. "Believest thou not
that I am in the Father" (v.10). The home of His soul
was the bosom of God. As a Son He abode in the love
of His Father, delighting in His will. He dwelt in the
Father that He might be ever with Him for the glory of
His Name among men (See 1 John 4. 12-16).

II. His Father Dwelt in Him. "Believe Me that I
am in the Father and the Father in Me" (**v. 11**). The
Father, in all the riches of His glorious character, abode
in the Son for the edification and salvation of man. He
pleased not Himself; yea, more, He *emptied* Himself,
that the Father might be gloried in Him. Being in the
Father, He dwelt in eternal love; the Father being in
Him, the love of God was thus manifested.

III. He is the Revelation of the Father. He said to
Philip, "If ye had known Me ye should have known My
Father also; from henceforth ye know Him and *have seen
Him*. He that hath seen Me hath seen the Father" (vv. 7-9).
He is the image of the invisible God (Col. 1. 15). This
is the cause of that halo of glory that surrounds the char-
acter of Jesus Christ, making it unapproachably unique

among the sons of men. The revelation of Jesus Christ
on earth was the apocalypse (unveiling) of the Father.
To know Christ in His true inward character. is to *know*
the Father.

IV. **His Words were the Words of the Father.** "The
word which ye hear is not Mine but the Father's which
sent Me" (v. 24). This doctrine, in one form or another,
is emphatically declared about ten times in this Gospel.
It is that deep far-reaching truth, which the critics of
Christ and His teaching so often forget or deliberately
ignore. "My doctrine" He says "is not Mine, but His
that sent Me" (chap. 7. 16). "I speak to the world
those things which I have heard of Him" (chap. 8.
26-28). To reject His words is to reject the message
of the Eternal God and Father to men, and to perish in
sin and ignorance.

V. **His Works were the Works of the Father.**
"That the world may know...as the Father gave Me
commandment, even so I do" (v. 31). The Father's
commandments were the secret motives of His life. Just
when He was about to finish His career of obedience unto
death, He said: "I have kept My Father's commandments" (John 15. 10). He had power to lay down His
life and to take it again, because He had received "this
commandment of His Father." His wonderful works,
as well as His wonderful words, were manifestations
of the Father's grace and power in operation through
the Son. "Believe Me that I am in the Father, and
the Father in Me; or else believe Me for the very *work's
sake*" (v. 11).

VI. **His Desire was that the Father should be
Glorified in Him.** "Whatsoever ye ask in My Name,
that will I do, that the Father may be glorified in the Son"

(v. 13). That the Father may be glorified He pleased not Himself, but spoke the words and did the works of His Father; and now promises to answer prayer in His Name, that the Father, who is represented by the Son, might be glorified *in* the Son. It is surely this Divine fact that explains the value and power of His Name in prayer (John 16. 24).

VII. **He is the Way to the Father.** "I am the Way... no man cometh unto the Father but by Me" (v. 6). To miss Christ as the Way, the Truth and the Life, is to miss the Father, for the Father is in Him and He is in the Father. "This is the true God and eternal life." He is the *Way* to the Father, because He is the *Truth* about the Father, and the very *Life* of the Father. Christ as *The Way*, must be received by *faith*, as well as Christ the Truth and the Life. To come to Him as the Way, is to forsake our own way and to trust in Him as the Truth and the Life and so come into fellowship with the Father in Him and through Him (Eph. 2. 18).

VII. **To Love Him is to be Loved of the Father.** "He that loveth Me shall be loved of My Father, and I will love him and will manifest Myself to him" (v. 21). To love the Lord Jesus Christ is to love the Father and to be loved in a very special manner by Him. The effect of this mutual love is a further and fuller manifestation of Christ Himself as the image of the Father to the heart of the loving one. What a comfort to know that because we love the Son of God we are being loved by God, and that that great love of His can find no higher reward to give His lovers than a fuller, deeper experience of His Son, Jesus Christ. Oh, the depths of the riches that are in Him. How keenly the apostle must have felt this truth when he said: "If any man love not the Lord Jesus Christ, let him be accursed at His coming" (1 Cor. 16. 22).

LOVE'S REWARD.

JOHN 14. 21-24.

THE words of the Lord Jesus Christ are as fathomless as
His unsearchable nature. "God is Love," Christ is the
perfect manifestation of that love. "He that loveth Me,"
He says, "shall be loved of My Father, and I will love him
and will manifest Myself to him." In these words we have
the promise and condition of the greatest spiritual
inheritance that God in Christ can bestow upon a human
soul.

I. **The Promise.** "I will manifest *Myself* to him."
The revelation of *Himself* is the redeemed soul's greatest
solace. The purpose of the Hóly Spirit in us is to take the
things of Christ and show them to us. The quickened
spirit of man must seek and yearn for God. "My soul
thirsteth for God," said the Psalmist. What Christ has
done meets all the needs of a sinner; what Christ *is* meets
all the needs of a servant. Philip may have been ignorant,
but he was surely honest when he said: "Shew us the
Father and it sufficeth us" (v. 8). Let me see and know
the true God and then I shall be satisfied. He had not
yet understood that to see Jesus Christ was to see the
Father (v. 9). This is the true God and eternal life.
To meet this deep spiritual need in Philip, Christ manifested *Himself* to him. What a revelation this must have
been to Philip. See how our Lord answered the somewhat
similar question of Judas (not Iscariot): "How wilt Thou
manifest Thyself unto us and not unto the world?" (v. 22).
The Lord's answer to this most important question is
pregnant with vital teaching. He will manifest Himself
in the Spirit of the Father to the man that loves Him by
"coming unto him and making His—or Their—*abode with
him*" (v. 23). This manifestation is not outward, or
external; it is the coming of the Divine life and character

in fresh and fuller power into the inner man. The *indwelling* presence of God is the most central, the most solemn and influential reality with which the Christian has to do. The craving of a pure heart is to see God. In times of sorrow, loneliness, weariness, fruitlessness, and failure, our real need is expressed in one word: "Himself." We cannot possibly make too much of this fact and privilege of grace, that Christ eagerly desires to *manifest* HIMSELF as the Healer of all diseases, the Source of all fruitfulness, and the Victor in every fight. Whenever and wherever He manifests Himself, results worthy of Himself will be accomplished. When He showed Himself after His passion it was "by many infallible proofs." Although the two men on the way to Emmaus knew Him not when He appeared, yet did He make their *"hearts burn* within them while He talked to them." When He manifested Himself to Mary, there followed confession and *commission* (John 20. 16, 17). When He manifested Himself to His unbelieving disciples, He first *rebuked* them (Mark 16. 14), then when He had showed them His hands and His feet they were *glad*, and He breathed on them, saying, *"Receive ye the Holy Ghost"* (John 20. 20-22). The result of His appearing to doubting Thomas was confession and *worship* (John 20. 26-28). His appearing to the disciples by the sea shore turned their failure into great *success* (John 21). Three times did the Lord manifest Himself to the Apostle Paul for the purpose of *encouraging* him in His service (Acts 23. 11; 18. 9, 10; 27. 23, 24). To the suffering and dying Stephen He revealed Himself as the glorified One (Acts 7. 55). In the light of all this let us seek to grasp the significance and preciousness of this promise: "He that loveth Me...I will *love him*, and *will manifest Myself to him.*" The manifestation of Himself to us is His infinitely gracious way of meeting and satisfying our every need. But how will He manifest Himself unto us and not unto the world? This brings us to the second point, namely—

II. The Condition. *"He that loveth Me."* This promise of Christ is for ever true, and this simple condition is for ever availing. Christ *will* manifest Himself to those who *love Him.* It is possible to be wise and scholarly, faithful and enthusiastic, and yet destitute of that deep joy and satisfaction which comes through the manifestation of Himself to the *loving* heart. Thank God, this greatest of all blessings is not promised to the learned, or the laborious, but to the loving. "Lovest thou Me?" was our Lord's pressing question after manifesting Himself to His disciples by the sea of Galilee. The heart must become very sensitive that would receive and retain the image of the Son of God as revealed by the Holy Spirit. It is love, not knowledge, that creates capacity for Christ. Intense loving is more pleasing to Him than deep thinking. He who loves the Lord with all his heart will live in the continual vision of His comforting presence and matchless glory. The condition is love; but the proof of love is the "keeping of His words"—or teaching. "He that hath My words and keepeth them, he it is that loveth Me...If a man love Me, he will keep My words...He that loveth Me not keepeth not My words" (vv. 23, 24). John, in his first epistle, restates this truth very plainly: "Whoso keepeth His word (teaching), in him surely is the love of God perfected" (2. 5). The soul in which that love is perfected will be honoured with the apocalypse (unveiling) of Jesus Christ. It was to John, the most loving of His disciples, that the book of "The Revelation of Jesus Christ" was given (Rev. 1. 1). The love of God can only be perfected in that heart where love answers to love. It is impossible to keep His words and to grow under His teaching, as He desires we should, unless there is in us a

growing love and devotion to Christ's person and work.
In these days of intellectual and moral activity, let us
be diligent to keep our hearts right with God, otherwise
there will be no manifestation of HIMSELF as the sum of all
power, and blessing, and success.

OBEDIENCE.

JOHN 14. 23, 24.

"IF a man love Me, he will keep My words: and My
Father will love him, and We will come unto him, and make
our abode with him. He that loveth Me not keepeth not
My sayings: and the Word which ye hear is not Mine, but
the Father's which sent Me."

Obedience is the necessary consequence of love.

FRUIT-BEARING.

JOHN 15. 1-8.

ISRAEL, as a vine, was brought out of Egypt and planted
in Canaan, after the heathen had been cast out like weeds
(Psa. 80. 8). This vine, though noble, and of a right seed,
soon degenerated into a strange plant to God (Jer. 2. 21).
But Jesus Christ is the TRUE Vine, brought down from
Heaven and planted in the earth. He was the faithful and
true witness. There was nothing in Him to create a feeling
of "strangeness" or disappointment in the heart of God.
He was true to God, true to His own nature, true to His
environment, and to the sons of men. But the principle
thought here is that, as a Vine, He is true to those who are
associated with Him as branches, so that they might bring
forth fruit. Note the—

I. **Source of Fruit**. "The vine." The branch cannot
bear fruit of itself (v. 4). "Apart from Me, ye can do
nothing" (v. 5, R.V.). Impoverished branches in this vine

is no evidence of an impoverished vine, for God giveth not the Spirit with limitations to Him (John 3. 34). All the treasures of wisdom and knowledge, of grace and power, are in Him, even the "fullness of the Godhead." "From Me is thy fruit found" (Hosea 14. 8).

II. **Removal of the Fruitless.** "Every branch in Me that beareth not fruit He taketh away" (v. 2). "If any man abide not in Me, he is cast forth as a branch and is withered" (v. 6). This may refer to those who are in Him *religiously*, but not *spiritually*: those who have been from their birth brought up in the form of godliness, but who have never known the power and sweetness of His fellowship. There is an outward resemblance to the vine branch, but no production of the vine fruit, so the husband-man deals with it as having no connection with the vine. Such a branch "cast forth" can do nothing else but *wither*. Apart from Christ, there is no saving or preserving power in man. It is only those whose roots are in the river of God whose leaves shall not wither (Psa. 1. 3). These withered branches are gathered, not by the angel reapers, but by *men*, who cast them into the fire of testing, and they are burned. A religious, Christless life will never be of much use to men, far less to God. Like savourless salt, they are good for nothing.

III. **Pruning of the Fruitful.** "Every branch that beareth fruit, He cleanseth it, that it may bear more fruit" (vv. 2, 3). There are growths about the Christian life, as there are about the vine, which do not tend to fruitful-ness, shoots that show signs of a vigour which is only fit for the pruning knife. The riches of the grace of God is seen here in seeking to make the fruitful more fruitful. Those fit for His service He desires to make more fit. The process may be painful, to have *our* new-born desires and fresh efforts nipped off and thrown away as hindrances;

but His will be done. The heart life is to be kept pure by *faith* (Acts 15. 9). The pruning knife is the Word of God which is sharp and powerful...discerning the thoughts and intents of the heart. "Now are ye clean through the Word."

IV. **Nature of the Fruit.** "Bear much fruit, *so* shall ye be My disciples" (v. 8). That branch is a true disciple of the vine that bears much of the fruit of the vine. We are the true disciples of Christ when His character manifests itself in our lives. What the sap of the vine is to the branch, the Spirit of Christ is to the Christian. The fruit of the Spirit is love, joy, peace, etc., because the Spirit Himself is all this, and when He has free access into our hearts, and full control of them, His own personal characteristics will appear as fruit in our lives.

V. **Condition of Fruitfulness.** "He that abideth in Me and I in him, the same bringeth forth much fruit" (v. 5). The human side is, "He in me;" the Divine, "I in Him." "The branch cannot bear fruit of itself... no more can ye except ye *abide* in Me" (v. 4). "In *me*," that is, in my flesh dwelleth no good thing, but in HIM all fullness dwells. His grace will be perfected in us, as we by faith abide in Him. Constant contact with Him implies the attitude of continual receptiveness, "I in Him." To abide in Him is to abide in His Word, His will, and His work, then God works in us both to will and to do of His good pleasure.

VI. **Results of Fruitfulness.** "Herein is My Father glorified, that ye bear much fruit; so shall ye be My disciples" (v. 8). The results are twofold: the Father is glorified, and our true discipleship is proven. It is to the honour of the husbandman that the tree brings forth fruit abundantly. It is also to the credit of the tree that it so proves its good character by its works. Where there

is wholehearted discipleship there will be fruitfulness **and**
a life glorifying to the Father. Fruit is the natural
outcome of a faithful following of Christ, as well as an
evidence of it. The life lived in Christ, and for Him, is
the only God-glorifying life. "Much fruit" means much
love, much joy, much peace, etc.

BRANCHES, DISCIPLES, FRIENDS.

JOHN 15.

THESE are not empty titles, the Lord Himself is the Author
of each of them, but they are each conditioned with something else. The first with abiding, the second with
fruitbearing, the third with obedience. These three names
are suggestive of three different experiences.

I. As Branches, we Receive. "I am the Vine, ye are
the branches" (v. 5). This process and privilege of
receiving of the fullness that is in Christ cannot begin until
we as branches have been broken off the old fruitless Adam-
stock, and grafted into Him who is the second Adam, the
True Vine. The precious sap of this Vine (Spirit) will
never minister to the pride of the old selfish sinful life.
But having been planted into Christ, we now live by faith
that is in Him. The branch cannot live apart from the
vine, no more can ye. To live apart from Christ is to be
dead while we live. "Because I live ye shall live also"
(John 14. 19), if ye abide in Me. The life of the branch,
then, is a life of *continual appropriation*. The call of the
vine to the branch is to take, take, take. "Let him that is
athirst, take." "If any man thirst, let him come unto
Me and drink." This receiving of the sap by the branch
was to manifest itself in fruitfulness To be filled with the
Spirit is to be filled with the fruit of the Spirit, as it is
possible to grow apples of different quality on the same
stock, so, by the same Spirit there may be different

manifestation, according to the character of the branch. While our union with Christ is the death of our sinful life, it is not the death of our individuality. In every Christian life the whole fruit of the Spirit should be found (Gal. 5. 22, 23), but, as a rule, in the lives of Christians, some one or two aspects of this fruit are often found prominent, this may be partly due to the nature of the recipient. Still, "the wind bloweth where it listeth."

II. **As Disciples, we Follow.** "So shall ye be My disciples" (v. 8). In continuing the metaphor of the vine and branches here, the idea is, that the branch truly follows the vine, when it abides in it, and when by the power imparted to it, it faithfully carries out the purpose for which the vine had been given. So, by an adherence to the mind and will of our Lord, and by the bringing forth of much of the fruit of the Spirit, we are declaring ourselves to be walking in His footsteps. "If ye continue in My Word, then are you My disciples indeed" (John 8. 31). This discipleship implies a readiness to sit at His feet, like Mary, and to learn of Him who is the Great Teacher come from God. It implies also a willingness to believe every word He says. How can His words *abide in us* if they are not received by faith (v. 7). How can we follow His example if we do not live and walk by faith in the Word of God as He did. Another mark of discipleship is love one to another (John 13. 35).

III. **As Friends, we Commune.** "Ye are My friends... I have called you friends (not patients), for all things that I have heard of My Father I have made known unto you" (vv. 14, 15). A friend comes closer to the heart than a servant, "A servant knoweth not what his Lord doeth." It is a very sacred and humbling privilege to walk among men as the friends of Jesus Christ. As His friends, living in communion with Him, we become—

1. Sharers of His SECRETS. "The secret of the Lord is with them that fear Him" (Psa. 25. 14). It was of him who was "the friend of God" that God said, "Shall I hide from Abraham that thing which I do?" The deep heart purposes of the Son of God are revealed to those who live in fellowship with Him. In the light of His presence they see light clearly. They walk among the gloomy shadows of a sinful world, with the secrets of life, peace, and eternal glory in their souls.

2. Sharers of His SYMPATHIES. As a devoted wife becomes a partaker of her husband's likes and dislikes, so does the friend of Jesus, through close contact with Him, becomes imbued with His thoughts and feelings. They love all that He loves and hate all that He hates. They are in real heart sympathy with Him in His desire to honour the Father, and at the same time to love, and seek to save, the sinful sons of men.

3. Sharers of His SUFFERINGS. "The world hated Me... because ye are not of the world...therefore the world hateth you" (vv. 18, 19). Christ suffered because of His unlikeness to the world. His true friends will fare little better. Christ suffered in His daily life because of His sympathy with God His Father, and His separation from the sins and false conception of His age. The more we become like Him the more shall we feel the power of those forces in the world which were opposed to Him.

4. Sharers of His CONSOLATIONS. "For as the sufferings of Christ abound in us, so our consolation also aboundeth by Christ" (2 Cor. 1. 5). To be made a partaker of His sufferings, is to become an heir of His consolations. Such consolations are neither few not small, good measure, pressed down and running over. What the Father was to the Son, the Holy Spirit, the Comforter is to us an ever present, all sufficient compensation for all the sorrows and sufferings incurred through our sympathy with Christ, and service for Him. If we suffer, we shall also *reign* with Him, that is consolation indeed.

———

"I AND YOU."

John 15. 12-26.

In this chapter alone Christ uses the first personal pronoun with *studied emphasis* eleven times. In each case the chief importance of the words spoken lie in the character of Him who speaks. In these impressive I's of His there is the thought of—

I. Grace. "I have loved *you*" (v. 12). *You* who sometime were afar off, but are now made nigh: you who were once in ignorance of Me, and walked according to the course of this world. I *have loved* you with a love that can only be compared with that love wherewith the Father hath loved Me (v. 9). "Ye know the grace of our Lord Jesus Christ, that though He was rich, yet for your sakes He became poor, that ye through His poverty might be rich."

II. Separation. "I chose you out of the world" (v. 19, r.v.). "The whole world lieth in wickedness" (John 5. 19). To be chosen of Christ is to be called out of the world into His fellowship and Kingdom. In this fellowship ye shall be partakers of His sufferings, for the world that hated Him will hate you. The Cain-spirit that seeks to slay those more righteous than themselves is ever with us (1 John 3. 12). We are chosen out of the world like Noah, that we might be saved from it, and become witnesses against it. By faith, like Abraham, we must go out.

III. Friendship. "I have called you friends" (v. 15). To be called friends by Him who is God's best Friend is an honour indeed. It was a blessed day for Mordecai when he was declared the friend of the king (Esther 6. 11). *Servants* have kitchen privileges, but *friends* have parlour opportunities. Anywhere in the Lord's house is an honour and a blessing, but covet earnestly the best gifts. He will call *you* friend if ye abide in Him.

IV. Teaching. "All things...I have made known unto you" (v. 15). He is the great Teacher come from God. As He sought to instil into the minds of His disciples the things that He heard of His Father, so by the Holy Spirit does He still make known the will of the Father, for all things are now delivered unto Him, and the Spirit takes the things which are His and shows them unto us.

V. Responsibility. "I have chosen you...that ye should bring forth fruit" (v. 16). Having called His disciples friends, and having instructed them in the things concerning Himself, He expects them to be something else than mere *patients* in a doctor's hands. The love that has grown into friendship must go on ripening into fruitful service. A fruitless branch never serves the purpose of the vine. A barren Christian profession is a misrepresentation of Christ. *"Chosen* and *ordained* to bring forth fruit" (v. 16). If the fruit of the Spirit is not manifest in our lives, we are falsifying both our calling and our ordination.

VI. Brotherly Love. "I command you that ye love one another" (v. 17). Love is the bond that is to hold His people one to another amidst the hatred and opposition of this world. It is His *command*, His *new* commandment which is the sum of the whole law. Have this salt of love in *yourselves*, and there shall be peace one with another (Mark 9. 50). Not to love one another is an act of rebellion against the rule of Christ.

VII. Promise. "I will send you...the Spirit of truth" (v. 26). The word Comforter in this verse may be translated "Helper." This promised "Helper" is the "Spirit of truth." This "Spirit of truth the devil-deluded world cannot receive, because it seeth Him not, but He shall be *in you*" (John 14. 17). In promising the Spirit, Christ promised every needful thing for life and service. He is the Spirit of truth, of grace, of burning, and of power. What a Helper He is! How fruitless our testimony without Him! "I will send Him unto *you*." "Receive ye the Holy Ghost."

THE GREAT HELPER.
JOHN 16. 7-15.

THE Lord Jesus Christ is mighty to *save* a sinner; the Holy Spirit is mighty to *help* a saint. The word "Comforter" has been variously translated. The terms "Advocate," "Paraclete," "Helper," have been used. In Romans 8. 26, we read that "The Spirit *helpeth* our infirmities"— literally *taketh hold with me*. The same word is used in Luke 10. 40, but nowhere else in the New Testament. "Bid her therefore that she *help me.*" The Holy Spirit has come, as one who is willing and mighty to "take hold with me," that I might be helped in doing the will and work of God.

I. **The Condition of His Coming.** "If I go not away, the Helper will not come unto you, but if I go, I will send *Him* (not it) *unto you*" (v. 7). Christ had to go, taking humanity into the character and presence of God, before the Spirit could come, bringing divinity into the character and presence of man (Acts 2. 33). The bodily absence of the Redeemer was to ensure the spiritual presence of the Helper. The Spirit could not be given till Jesus was glorified (John 7. 39). The coming of the Helper was the proof that Christ's atoning work was perfected, and that the Father, Son, and Spirit, were all most desirous that men should be *helped* into possession of the present and eternal fruits of the saving work of Jesus Christ.

II. **His Mission in the World.** "I will send Him unto *you*; and He, when He is come, He will convict the world in respect of sin, and of righteousness, and of judgment" (v. 8, R.V.). While the Spirit's attitude to the Church is that of an Helper, His attitude to the world is that of a Convicter. There are three things the world needs to be convicted of: Sin, righteousness, and judgment.

1. "Of SIN, because they believe not on Me" (v. 9). The great sin of the world, in the eyes of the Holy Spirit, is unbelief—believing not the Son of God. His mission is to glorify Christ (v. 14), and the first thing He does is to convict of the sin of rejecting His Word and sacrifice.

2. "Of RIGHTEOUSNESS, because I go to My Father." Christ could not go to His Father until He had gone to the Cross and the grave as an atonement for sin. To go to His Father, He must rise again from the dead. His resurrection and ascension secures for us that righteousness which His death for our sins had prepared. He died for our offences, He rose again for our *justification* (Rom. 4. 25). On the Cross He was made sin for us; now at the Father's right hand He is made of God unto us righteousness (1 Cor. 1. 30). This is the righteousness that the world needs, and that the Holy Spirit seeks to convict it of. Our own righteousnesses are as filthy rags in His sight.

3. "Of JUDGMENT, because the prince of this world hath been judged" (v. 11, R.V.). As surely as the prince of this world (Devil) has already been judged, and brought under condemnation by Christ's death and resurrection, so has every unbeliever. "He that believeth not hath been

judged already" (John 3. 18, R.V.). This is the judgment, that the light is come into the world, and men love the darkness rather than the light. The Spirit has come to convict concerning judgment. All down through these ages the Holy Spirit has been, as it were, prosecuting the world, bringing it to judgment, because of its criminal attitude toward the Son of God. How is this work done? Does the Spirit use any medium, through which He convicts the men of the world? The last clause of verse 7 should surely not be separated in thought from verse 8. "If I depart, I will send Him *unto you*, and when He is come—unto you—He will convict the world." It was when the Spirit had come with power unto Peter, that the three thousand were "*pricked* in their heart," on the day of Pentecost. A powerless Christian, or a powerless Church will never be successful in convicting the world of sin, of righteousness, and of judgment. This needed work cannot be done in any other way, but by the Holy Ghost, the Almighty Helper.

III. His Mission to the Church.

To the redeemed of God the Holy Spirit has come—

1. As a GUIDE INTO ALL TRUTH. "Howbeit when He, the Spirit of truth, is come, He will guide *you* into all the truth" (v. 13, R.V.). He is the Spirit of truth, because He has come out from Him who is "The Truth," in His person and doctrine. He guides into the truth, because the Spirit searcheth into the deep *things of God* (2 Cor. 2. 10). O soul, thirsting for the truth as it is in Jesus, receive the guidance of this heavenly Helper; ask Him, and depend upon Him to do it. This holy anointing teacheth you all things and is truth (1 John 2. 27).

2. As a REVEALER OF THE THINGS OF CHRIST. "He shall glorify Me; for He shall take of Mine, and shall declare it unto you" (vv. 14, 15). He helps us all He can,

by taking the things that *are Christ's*—by right of His
sufferings and death —things purchased for His people by
His own blood; and to declare them, or make them known
unto us, that He might glorify the Son, by filling up
and making fruitful the lives of His redeemed ones (John
15. 8).   Blessed Helper, help me to enter into this most
precious inheritance.   "All things are yours, for ye are
Christ's."

3. As an Example of Self-abandoned Service.   "He
shall *not speak from Himself*; but whatsoever things He
shall hear, these shall He speak; and He shall declare
unto you the things that are to come" (v. 13, R.V.).   His
ministry was one of entire self-abnegation.   As Christ
sought, through self-emptying, to glorify the Father, so
the Holy Spirit likewise sought to glorify the Son: we
also, through self-renunciation, must honour the Holy
Spirit.   The Son of God spake not from Himself (John
14. 10, R.V.).   Neither did the Holy Spirit, neither
should we.   Self-will, and self-wisdom, and every other
form of self-assertiveness, is a usurping of the Holy Spirit.
If we would have the help of the Spirit in our ministry for
Christ, we shall not speak from our own authority, but
whatsoever things we shall hear—from Him—these shall
we speak, and shall declare the *things that are to come.*

A LITTLE WHILE.

John 16. 16-23.

In these verses, the words, "A little while," are repeated
seven times over, as if they were of special significance.
From the fact that our Lord, in explaining the meaning of
them, used the parabolic form, we may infer that different
applications may be made of them (v. 25).   "A little
while, and ye shall not see Me...and ye shall be sorrowful...

but I shall see you again, and your heart shall rejoice...
and in that day ye shall ask Me no question." These
precious words may easily have a threefold meaning.
As the

I. Historical. "A little while, and ye shall *not* see
Me." It was but "a little while"—a few hours—and
Christ was buried out of their sight, though in a *borrowed*
grave, yet *sealed* with the royal signet. The interval
between His death and resurrection was, indeed, to them
a time of "sorrow" and "lamenting," but to the world a
time of rejoicing (Luke 24. 17). The world's feasts go on
more merrily in the absence of the Saviour from sin, but
the Christian can find a feast nowhere where He is not.
"A little while, and I shall see you again, and your heart
shall rejoice." Their hearts did rejoice when, after three
days, they saw Him again in resurrection power and glory.
"*Then* were the disciples glad when they saw the Lord"
(John 20. 20). "They worshipped Him, and *returned* to
Jerusalem with great joy." "In that day" they did ask
Him no question. The fact of His appearing to them as
the Risen One was itself the answer to all their doubts and
questionings. He who had power to rise from the dead,
had power to perform His every promise. In a dark and
cloudy day, the relative value of other lights may be dis-
puted, but when the sun breaks out in all his glorious
majesty, there is no questioning his all-sufficiency to meet
the need.

II. Personal. "A little while...ye shall be sorrowful
...but I will see you again, and your heart shall rejoice...
in that day ye shall ask no question." The sorrowful
"little while" of His called-out ones is *now*, while their
Lord is absent, and the world is rejoicing. "In the world
ye shall have tribulation" (v. 33), but His "I will see you
again" is the hope of his suffering saints. Through the

gathering gloom we look for the breaking of the day, when we shall see Him face to face. Just now we may see as but through a glass darkly; there are many things that we cannot possibly understand, mysterious movements of the providence of God, and of the Holy Spirit, that at times sorely perplex our eager spirits, many things we should like explained. Yes, but *"in that day* ye shall ask Me no question."　One look into the glorified face of our redeeming Lord will hush at once every restless feeling and every anxious thought. So satisfied shall we be when we see HIM, that we shall not be able to ask Him any question. So perfect will be our acquiescence to *His will* in everything.

> "Not a surge of worry, not a shade of care,
> Not a blast of hurry moves the spirit there."

III. Dispensational. These words of our Lord may also be prophetic of that time when He will come again, taking to Himself *His right* to rule and reign over this world for which He died. The Church of God is now passing through its "little while" of sorrow, this is its time to "weep and lament, but the world shall rejoice." In the latter days perilous times will come. But the Church's hope lies in His promise, "I will see you again, and your heart shall rejoice, and your joy no man taketh from you." She, like a woman in travail, hath sorrow now, but when THE MAN is born *into the world*, she shall remember no more her anguish for joy (v. 21). God's people just now are sadly divided and full of questionings, but on that day when HE *shall appear* in the glory of His power, as King of kings and Lord of lords, "ye shall ask no questions." All human questionings are for ever set at rest in the presence of the glorified Son of God. Angels ask Him no questions, but it is our great privilege *now* to "Ask that we may receive" (v. 23).

CHRIST'S GIFTS TO HIS OWN.
JOHN 17.

IN approaching this chapter we feel as if we were passing
through the veil into the holiest of all. This prayer of our
Great High Priest, just before He offered Himself upon the
altar of the Cross as the sacrifice for the sin of the world,
is in itself a great unveiling of holy things. Here every
petition is a revelation, every declaration a discovery.
From these—Christ's own words—we shall note first of all
some of the blessings He has conferred upon His own.
Observe the—

I. **Life of God.** "Thou hast given Him authority
over all flesh, that...to them He should give eternal
life" (v. 2, R.V.). This eternal life consists in knowing
God and Jesus Christ whom He hath sent (v. 3). To
know Him is to be made a partaker of His nature, to be
adopted into His family as "sons and daughters of the
Lord God Almighty." When Christ condescended to take
upon Him the likeness of sinful flesh, God gave Him
authority over *all flesh*, that He might give this life to all
who believe.

II. **Name of God.** "I have manifested Thy Name
unto the men whom Thou gavest Me out of the world"
(v. 6). The life and work of Jesus Christ was "the Lord
proclaiming the Name of the LORD, the Lord God, merciful
and gracious, longsuffering, and abundant in goodness
and truth." In manifesting the *Name* of God, He was
manifesting His nature. He could truly say, "He that
hath seen Me hath seen the Father." But only those given
Him "out of the world" could receive this gracious
revelation. "The world by wisdom knew not God."

III. **Words of God.** "I have given them the words
which Thou gavest Me" (v. 8). This thought is frequently
expressed in this Gospel (chaps. 12. 49; 14. 10). Those

who have been made alive unto God must feed upon
the words of the Living God. "Man shall not live by
bread alone, but by *every word* that proceedeth out of the
mouth of God." Christ Himself is the truth, because the
words He spake were the very words and doctrines taught
Him by the Eternal Father. "I and My Father are One."
One in nature and in purpose, One in will, in deed, and in
truth. "The words that I speak unto you are spirit and
life." As He lived by faith in those words given Him, so
shall we. "Believe, and thou shalt see."

IV. **Service of God.** "I am glorified in them" (v. 10).
As the Father was glorified in the Son (v. 4), so the Son
is to be glorified in His own. The words of God have been
given us as they were given to Jesus Christ His Son, for a
very definite and gracious purpose, that God might be
glorified in faithful and successful service (v. 4). The
privilege of working for Him is a precious gift. Alas, that
so many should neglect to stir up this gift. How is Christ
to be glorified in us unless there is whole-hearted surrender
to His will and work, as He was to the will and work which
the Father gave Him to do? Was not this what the
apostle meant when he said, "Christ shall be magnified in
my body, whether it be by life or by death?" (Phil. 1. 20).

V. **Glory of God.** "And the glory which Thou hast
given Me I have given unto them" (v. 22, R.V.). What
glory was this that Christ received from God the Father,
and passed on to His disciples? Did not this glory consist
in God's nature and Name, His words and work, which
were given to the Son, and which in grace He has imparted
to His followers? As He is, so are we. There is, besides,
the glory that is yet to be revealed when we shall be with
Him where He is (v. 24). As God gave Him the glory
of Sonship and heirship, so hath He given this glory to us
who believe (John 1. 12). The purpose of this manifold

gift is, "that *they* all may be one," even as Christ and the
Father are One (v. 22). What would be the results if this
glory was really witnessed by the world?

VI. Love of God. "I made known unto them Thy
Name, *and will make it known* that the *love* wherewith Thou
lovedst Me *may be in them*" (v. 26). Christ hath made
known, and will go on making known the Name (character)
of God, that His nature which is love may be continually
nurtured in us. This He does by the gift of the Holy
Ghost, who sheds this love abroad in our hearts (Rom.
5. 5). It is surely a heart-searching thought that our Lord
should close His great unveiling priestly prayer with this
testimony, that the purpose for which He had faithfully
declared the Name of God was that the *love* which God had
for His Son might be *in us*. Has this grace of the Lord
Jesus Christ been in vain to us? Are we rejoicing in the
depth, the fullness, and the eternity of this love? Is this
love being revealed to others through us, as it has been
revealed through Christ to us?

———

CHRIST'S PETITIONS FOR HIS OWN.
JOHN 17.

THIS is one of the chapters of which Baxter in his "Saint's
Rest" says, "It is of more value than all the other books
in the world." But the veil that is over the heart needs to
be taken away, before the hidden glory can be seen. This
is not a prayer for the world. "I pray not for the world."
His cry for the perishing world came out of His agonised
heart while hanging on the Cross (Luke 23. 34). Here
He pleads for those that had been given Him out of the
world. He prayed that they might be—

I. Kept by the Father. "Holy Father, keep them in
Thine own Name which Thou hast given Me" (v. 11). To be
kept *in His own Name* is to be kept in His own character

and likeness; is to be continually acknowledged and
claimed as His own sons and daughters. They are to be
kept in that *Name* which Christ had manifested to them
(v. 6). "The Name of the Lord is a strong tower, the
righteous runneth into it and are safe" (Prov. 18. 10).

II. **Happy in Themselves.** "Now I come to Thee...
that they may have My joy fulfilled in themselves"
(v. 13). He who was the "Man of Sorrows and acquainted
with grief," was no stranger to that joy which is in the
Holy Ghost (Rom. 14. 17). If His joy had been in Himself
alone, how could He impart it to others? But being in
the Holy Spirit, this He could and did give. The Lord's
people are not asked to put on a smiling face without
possessing a smiling heart. This holy personal joy is the
joy of true *fellowship* with the Father, and with His
Son Jesus Christ, in the *communion* of the Holy Ghost
(1 John 1. 3, 4).

III. **Protected from the Devil.** "I pray...that Thou
shouldest keep them from the evil one" (v. 15, R.V.).
Christ knew, from personal experience, the subtle dangers
that lay in being tempted of the Devil, so He prays here
that we might be kept from yielding to his illuding devices.
"When ye pray, say, Lead us not into temptation, but
deliver us from the evil one" (Matt. 6. 13, R.V.). "He
that is begotten of God keepeth *Him*, and the evil one
toucheth him not" (1 John 5. 18, R.V.). While we by
faith keep hold of *Him* who has destroyed the works of
the Devil, God will keep us by His mighty power from
the evil one.

IV. **Holy unto God.** "Sanctify them in Thy truth...
for their sakes I sanctify Myself, that they also might be
truly sanctified" (vv. 17, 19, *margin*). As He consecrated,
or set Himself apart *for us*, He prays that we may be
consecrated (set apart) *for Him*. He says, "As the Father

sent Me into the world, even so have I sent them into the world" (v. 18). He delivered the same message to His disciples after His resurrection (John 20. 21). Ye are not your own, ye are, in the purpose of His grace, separated unto Himself, "therefore glorify God in your body and your spirit, which are His."

V. Useful unto Others. "Neither pray I for these alone, but for them also which shall believe in Me through their word" (v. 20). Then Christ expected that others would believe on His Name *through* them; that the "other sheep" which were not of this little fold, were to hear *His voice* "through *their word*," and be brought into the one flock under the one Shepherd (John 10. 16). Let your light so shine—that light which He hath shined into your hearts—that others, seeing the good works of God in you, may glorify your Father which is in Heaven. He hath blessed us, that we might be made a blessing. Let us see that the Holy One is not limited in His saving grace by our unbelief (Psa. 78. 41).

VI. United One to Another. He prayed also, "That they all may be one" (v. 21). There is here a double union. His request to the Father is that as *brethren*, they might be one in themselves, and as *sons*, they might be "one *in us*...as Thou Father art in Me, and I in Thee." How blessed Christian fellowship would be, if it resembled the fellowship that exists between the Father and the Son. That *they* may be one as *we* are, is the longing of Christ's heart (Gal. 3. 28). The anticipated outcome of this is, "That the world may believe that *Thou hast sent Me*." The world still needs to know that *love* of God which sent His Son to save it (John 3. 16).

VII. Glorified with Christ. "Father, I will that they also, whom Thou hast given Me, be with Me where I am, that they may behold My glory" (v. 24). When *He*

shall appear, we shall be like Him. Here we are more
familiar with the sufferings of Christ than with the glory
which is now His with the Father; but our afflictions,
which are light compared with His, are working out for us
as His afflictions wrought out for Him, "an exceeding and
eternal weight of glory" (2 Cor. 4. 17). If we suffer with
Him, we shall also be glorified together with Him. Our
eyes have often been dimmed with tears while beholding
His sufferings, but all tears shall be wiped away and every
heart questioning hushed when we behold His glory. We
cannot say of the prayers of Christ, as with the prayers of
David, that "they are ended," for they are still being
fulfilled. May we, through our sanctified lives, help to
give Him these desires of His heart.

THE CHRISTIAN'S RELATIONSHIP TO
THE WORLD.
JOHN 17.

I. They are Taken Out of the World. "The men
which Thou gavest Me out of the world" (v. 6). The *world*,
as such, is a ruined mass, lying in the lap of the evil one;
being coddled by the illusions and guided by the false
principles of the god of this world; but the followers of
Jesus Christ have in spirit been lifted up out of the whole
thing, as out of an horrible pit and miry clay, and have
been established in the Kingdom of our God, and of His
Christ, which is righteousness, and peace, and joy in the
Holy Ghost. "Ye are not of the world, even as I am not
of the world."

II. They are Distinguished from the World. "I
pray for them: I pray not for the world" (v. 9). As soon
as we become separated in spirit from the world, we come
under a new set of laws in the Kingdom of grace. We are
dealt with as *children* of God, not as the mere offspring of
His creative power. Christ loves His own with a love

which is peculiar to His own. While He has the love of pity for the world, He has the love of pleasure for His own. Because they are in heart for Him, He in heart and power is for them; so all things work together for good to them that love Him.

III. **They are In the World.** "But these are in the world" (v. 11). As to their spirit and purpose, they are out of the world, but as to their bodily presence and influence, they are still in the world. In the world, but not of it, even as Christ was (v. 16). In the world, not as a branch in the vine, but as a light in the darkness; not as a member in the body, but as a physician in the hospital. In the world, not as a "man of the world," but as a "man of God"; not as its slave, but as its victor.

IV. **They are Hated by the World.** "The world hath hated them, because they are not of the world, even as I am not of the world" (v. 14). There was no hatred until He had given them the Word of God. "I have given them Thy Word, and the world hath hated them." This God-given *Word*, when received, so revolutionised their minds and hearts that the world did not know them, and so contrary did they become to the world's ways and maxims that they hated them. The worldly wise and the worldly prudent cannot receive those precious things which God is prepared to reveal unto babes (Matt. 11. 25). The *hatred* of the world is a trifling matter to those whose hearts are filled with the *love* of God.

V. **They are Kept from the god of this World.** "I pray...that Thou shouldest keep them from the evil one" (v. 15, R.V.). He does not pray that we should be taken out of this world, but kept from the evil one who rules in it. We need not weary to get out of this world so long as we can be made a perpetual miracle and monument of His keeping power in it. We are surely at perfect liberty to claim, for the honour of Christ's own Name, the daily fulfilment of this prayer in our own lives. Our beloved gourds may wither, but His promise cannot.

VI. They are Sent into the World. "As Thou hast sent Me into the world, even so have I also sent them into the world" (v. 18). Every Spirit-anointed one is sent to preach good tidings (Luke 4. 18). As Christ was sent into the world to seek and save that which was lost, so also are we. As He was an ambassador for God, so also are we for Jesus Christ (2 Cor. 5. 20). As He was not sent on His own charges, so neither are we. As He was in the world, not on His own account but as a *Sent One*, so are we. Those sent by Him will be equipped by Him for the work, as He was equipped by the Father which sent Him. "As My Father hath sent Me, even so send I you" (John 20. 21).

VII. They are Indwelt for the Salvation of the World. "I in them, and Thou in Me...that the world may know" (v. 23). As the Father was in the Son, so the Son desires to be in us, that the world may know the love of God. Christ fulfilled, in a perfect manner, all required of Him, but what miserable counterfeits many of us are. The Son has given Himself as freely to us as the Father gave Himself to the Son, that His great love might triumph in us and through us. As God so loved the world that He gave His Son, so doth the Son so love the world that He gives His Spirit-filled followers, and for the self-same purpose. "Christ liveth in me," says Paul (Gal. 2. 20), and all the world knows to what a God-honouring result. The one thing needful that this world needs to know is THE LOVE OF GOD; not only God's love to the *world*, but His love to *His Son*, and to them that love Him. "That Thou hast loved them as Thou hast loved Me." May this love be shed abroad in our hearts, and out through our hearts into this cold Christ-neglecting world around us.

REVELATIONS IN THE GARDEN.

JOHN 18. 1-11.

EVERY circumstance in which Jesus Christ was placed, somehow or other, became the occasion of a further revelation of His wondrous character. Wherever He was, He, in His unique Personality, could not be hid. In these few verses we see some rays of His heavenly glory breaking through the dark cloud of His earthly weakness. Here is a revelation of—

I. **His Habit of Prayer.** "Judas...knew the place; for Jesus oft-times resorted thither with His disciples" (v. 2). Although Christ possessed the *spirit* of prayer, He believed also in the *place* of prayer. When one gets familiar with their surroundings, the mind is more free for intercourse with the unseen and eternal. In the matter of frequent praying, as well as in suffering, the sinless Son of God has left us an example.

II. **His Knowledge of the Future.** "Jesus therefore, knowing all the things that were coming upon Him, went forth" (v. 4, R.V.). He knew that "all things that are written by the prophets concerning the Son of Man shall be accomplished," for the Scriptures must be fulfilled (Luke 18. 31). Our knowledge of the future must be derived from the same source. If we had the faith that Jesus Christ had in those words uttered by men full of the Holy Ghost, then would we be among those wise men which discern the signs of the times.

III. **His Confession Concerning Himself.** "I am He" (v. 5). They declared that they were seeking Jesus of Nazareth. He confessed that He was that Nazarene. *Reproach* had been associated with that Name, and He willingly accepts it and bears it. It was as if they said, "Where is that despised and rejected One?" He answered,

"I am He." This solemn "I AM HE" of the Son of God may be looked upon as His answer to all who seek Him, whether through love and mercy, or hate and derision. It is with *Him* all have to do.

IV. **His Power Over His Enemies.** "As soon as He had said unto them, I am He, they went backward, and fell to the ground" (v. 6). It was good for them that they had the ground to fall on. The same power that drove them back might have as easily driven them into Hell. This manifestation of His power was His last convincing proof that, apart from His own will, they had no power at all against Him. "No man taketh it from Me, but I lay it down of Myself" (John 10. 18).

V. **His Love for His Own.** "If, therefore, ye seek Me, let these go their way" (v. 8). These words are full of solemn significance, as they reveal Christ's attitude toward the powers of darkness and the sheep of His pasture. He was no hireling to flee when the wolf cometh. What He here said to His enemies He could say with a deeper meaning to that "death and the curse" which was coming upon Him. "If, therefore, ye seek *Me*, let these go their way." As our Substitute and Surety, His chief desire was the salvation of His people. Christ is the end of the law for righteousness to every one that believeth.

VI. **His Submission to His Father's Will.** "The cup which My Father hath given Me, shall I not drink it?" (v. 11). He knew the Father's love too well to refuse even that awful cup of suffering that was just now being put into His hands. He was so perfectly at one with the Father's purposes that His meat was to do His will and to finish His work. As the weapons of His warfare were not carnal, neither are ours, yet they are mighty, through obedience to God, to the pulling down of strongholds. By

His surrender and obedience unto death, He triumphed in resurrection power. He hath left us an example that we should follow His steps.

———

CHRIST'S SUFFERINGS AT THE HANDS OF MEN.

JOHN 18.

HE suffered by being—

I. **Betrayed by the Hypocritical.** "Judas also, which betrayed Him, stood with them" (v. 5). He who companied with Christ, and shared the fellowship of His disciples, now takes his stand among the enemies of his Lord, and lends his influence towards His downfall. "Woe unto you hypocrites."

II. **Defended by the Passionate.** "Simon Peter having a sword, drew it and smote the high priest's servant, and cut off his right ear" (v. 10). The Lord had as little need for Peter's passion as for his sword. The wrath of man works not for the praise of God. There is a zeal for Christ and His cause that must be more painful than pleasing unto Him.

III. **Smitten by the Unreasonable.** "Jesus answered, If I have spoken evil, bear witness of the evil; but if well, why smitest thou Me?" (v. 23). It is easier for pride and prejudice to sneer and to smite than to face the truth. Self-seeking men are ever ready to justify themselves if it should be at the cost of smiting the character of the Saviour. But the clouds that would hide the face of the sun cannot hinder its progress.

IV. **Denied by the Cowardly.** When Simon Peter was charged with being "One of His disciples, he denied it, and said, I am not" (v. 25). The Lord and His cause still suffers much through the cowardliness of His professed

followers. There are other ways than Peter's in denying
Christ. He did it with his tongue; we may do it with
our feet, or by our general conduct. When the act or
behaviour is more in keeping with the enemies of Christ
than with His Word and teaching it is practically a denial
of Him.

V. Shunned by the Self-righteous. "Then led they
Jesus...unto the hall of judgment...and they themselves
went not into the judgment hall, lest they should be defiled,
but that they might eat the passover" (v. 28). Any thing
or place was clean enough for Jesus, but *they* must preserve
their (supposed) ceremonial holiness. "They strain at a
gnat, and swallow a camel." This is what one has called
"putid hypocrisy." These, like all other self-righteous
bigots, would seek the blessing without the Blesser; they
would have the passover without Him who is the Passover
(1 Cor. 5. 7). They are like men crying for light and
closing their eyes to the sun.

VI. Questioned by the Ambitious. Pilate asked three
questions of Jesus, and profited nothing by them: (1) "Art
Thou the King of the Jews?" (v. 33); (2) "What is
truth?" (v. 38); (3) "Whence art Thou?" (chap. 19. 9).
By such questions the Christ was "oppressed and afflicted,"
so He "opened not His mouth." Men animated by selfish
and impure motives still oppress Him, whose Divinity is
clear as the sun, by their questionings regarding His
character and teaching. He that *doeth* His will shall know
of the teaching whether it be of God (John 7. 17).

VII. Mocked by the Frivilous. "The soldiers platted
a crown of thorns, and put it on His head...and said, Hail,
King of the Jews" (chap. 19. 2). These men of war set
Him who is the Prince of Peace at *naught* (Luke 23. 11).
To them the kingdom of Caesar is everything, the Kingdom
of God nothing, material things important, but spiritual

things ridiculed and laughed at. Truly they know not what they do, who trifle with the Person of the Lord Jesus Christ (Rev 1. 17, 18).

> "I have seen the face of Jesus,
>   Tell me not of aught beside;
> I have heard the voice of Jesus,
>   All my soul is satisfied."

MARY MAGDALENE.

JOHN 20. 1-18.

JOHN was that disciple whom Jesus loved, but Mary Magdalene was surely that disciple who pre-eminently loved Jesus. She loved much because she had been forgiven much (Luke 8. 2). Behold her—

I. **Anxiety.** She came "early, when it was yet dark, unto the sepulchre" (v. 1). The darkness without was nothing to her who had had the lamp of heavenly love burning in her heart. Was it *only* to see the sepulchre she came? Was there not a tremulous restlessness about her feelings that some unusual thing was about to happen?

II. **Disappointment.** "They have taken away the Lord out of the sepulchre, and we know not where they have laid Him" (v. 2). It never was more blessedly true than in this case, that our disappointment is God's appointment. In search for a dead Lord, she finds but an empty grave. He is "away" not that she might lose Him but that she might—to her heart's satisfaction—find Him.

III. **Sorrow.** "Mary stood at the sepulchre weeping" (vv. 11-13). Peter and John, at her report, ran together to the sepulchre and looked in and returned again to their own home, but Mary stood, as one bound to that tomb by the cords of faith and love. So intense were her desires, and so blinded were her eyes by sorrow, that "the angels in white sitting, the one at the head, and the other at the feet, where the body of Jesus had lain," never seemed to awaken a suspicion in her mind that the Lord was *risen.* Yes, it is possible to be so overwhelmed with our imaginary loss that we fail to grasp God's greatest blessing.

IV. **Mistake.** "She supposing Him to be the gardener," etc. (v. 15). Even in resurrection power our Lord had still the *likeness* of sinful flesh. Why did she not know Him? The likelihood is that she was so perfectly absorbed in thought that she was blind to all outward objects— "Swallowed up with overmuch grief." The love of her heart was all right, but the theory of her head was all wrong. It will save us much sorrow and disappointment to have a correct creed as well as a devoted life. He was risen, *as He said*, but they believed Him not.

V. **Discovery**. "Jesus saith unto her, Mary. She *turned herself* and saith unto Him, Rabboni" (Master) (v. 16). She needed to have her eyes *turned* away from herself and from the grave, to see Him who is the Resurrection and the Life. The word of Jesus caught her ear and sunk into her heart. He called her by her name and claimed her as His own (Isa. 43. 1). His sheep hear His voice. No one who ever seeks the Lord Jesus Christ ever finds a dead or powerless Saviour. The deepest cry of a living soul is for a living God (Psa. 42. 2).

VI. **Boldness.** "Touch Me not" (v. 17). She evidently fell down and was about to embrace His feet, when Jesus stood back saying, "Touch Me not, for I am not yet ascended to My Father." Another little disappointment to her ardent heart and another lesson to her that she must learn to walk by faith and not by sight. No mortal hand was allowed to *touch Him*, who died as the sinner's Substitute, until He had presented Himself to His Father for acceptance as our Redeemer and High Priest. Afterwards every doubting Thomas was invited to thrust his hand into His side that he might feel the mark left by the spear wound.

VII. **Obedience.** "Jesus said unto her, Go to My brethren and say unto them...Mary came and told the disciples" (vv. 17, 18). She tarried in the garden until she was endued with the power of a great commission. What a message was Mary's, the Gospel of *Sonship*; "*My* Father, and *your* Father," in the power of the Resurrection. Her love is rewarded by being made the first herald of His resurrection power. "He that loveth Me...I will *manifest Myself* unto him." The vision of the glorified Christ makes a willing servant (Acts 9. 6).

DOUBTING THOMAS.

JOHN 20. 24-29.

THAT evening of the first day of the first resurrection week was an ever memorable one. The hearts of the disciples were full of fear and wonder at the things which had happened (v. 18). They had met with closed and bolted doors, for fear of their enemies, to reconsider the whole situation. But He who died to save them set all their doubtings and their fears at rest, by suddenly appearing among them, speaking peace and breathing into them a foretaste of Pentecostal power and blessing. All Christ's acts here are full of significance. (1) He spoke the word of "*Peace*" to them; (2) He revealed *Himself* as the Crucified One (v. 20); (3) He *Commissioned* them (v. 21) ; (4) He *Endued* them (v. 22); (5) He promised them success in His business (v. 23). Now what about Thomas? If Peter was rash with his tongue, Thomas was slow in his mind (chap. 14. 5). Observe his—

I. **Lost Opportunity.** "But Thomas...was not with

them when Jesus came" (v. 24). Why he was absent
is not stated, but it is at least suggestive that *he* was
absent. He must have known of the meeting, but being
incredulous regarding the resurrection of Christ, he
probably had given up all hope, feeling utterly perplexed
and ashamed. In refusing to assemble with His brethren
he only strengthened his unbelief and lost the faith-
confirming fellowship of the Lord. Those out of fellowship
with the body of believers need not expect to enjoy the
fellowship of Christ.

II. **Emphatic Denial.** When the disciples said unto
him, "We have seen the Lord," he said, "Except I see...
I will not believe" (v. 25). He was faithless (v. 27).
His heart was hardened against the truth of "the resurrection." His "*I will not*" reveals the desperate
antagonism that was in his nature. He would walk by
sight, not by *faith*. It is little short of madness to set one's
self against the united testimony of the disciples of Jesus
Christ. The imperious "I will not believe" of the haughty
and prejudiced mind can never make the faith of God of
none effect. "Believe, and thou shalt see."

III. **Humbling Rebuke.** Thomas gained nothing but
sadness and separation from his independent attitude. He
did not, however, miss the next meeting of the disciples,
"after eight days," for "Thomas was with them." Again
Jesus appeared and saith to Thomas, "Reach hither thy
finger...and be not faithless, but believing" (v. 27).
He had now, according to the grace of the Lord Jesus
Christ, an opportunity of "handling the Word of Life,"
but as soon as HE comes within touch, the hand of unbelief
is paralysed. What the disciples could not do in a week's
reasoning, Jesus Christ did in a moment by His Word.
Unbelief is the most shameful of all things when Christ
Himself is seen. How Thomas must afterward have

repented over his treatment of the testimony of his believing friends. Are *we* not losing much blessing just now for the same reason, refusing to believe those who have experienced a fullness of blessing to which we, in our unbelief, are utter strangers? May He so reveal Himself to us that every doubt will be ashamed before Him.

IV. **Confession of Faith.** "Thomas answered and said unto Him, My Lord and my God." He hath seen, and he hath believed, but the blessedness of the man who hath not seen and yet hath believed could never be his (v. 29). However, he hath believed, and that with all his heart. His words were few, but profound, and came from the uttermost depths of His soul. There was in them a confession—

1. Of His DEITY. "My *God.*"
2. Of His AUTHORITY over him. "My *Lord.*"
3. Of his PERSONAL SURRENDER to Him. "*My* Lord and *My* God."

————

HOW JESUS SHOWED HIMSELF.
JOHN 21. 1-14.

AFTER His resurrection no one could see Jesus through mere curiosity or by accident. Neither Mary nor the two men who walked with Him on the way to Emmaus knew Him till He *revealed Himself* to them. None but disciples ever saw Him in His resurrection body. The vision now is a spiritual one; only those who *believe* shall *see* the glory of God in the Person of the risen Christ. "On this wise shewed He Himself" on that memorable morning.

I. **The Time.** It was—

1. AFTER A NIGHT OF FAILURE. "That night they caught nothing" (v. 3). In those days of quiet testing Peter got somewhat restless and said, "I go a-fishing. They

say unto him, We also go with thee." They followed
Peter, and they caught nothing. Disappointment and
defeat may prepare us for a new manifestation of the grace
and power of Jesus Christ To labour without His presence
and blessing is like putting our treasure in a bag with holes.
Failure in business may be a good preparation for spiritual
success.

2. AT THE BREAKING OF THE DAY. "When the day was
now breaking, Jesus stood on the shore" (v. 4, R.V.).
Sorrow may endure for the night, but joy cometh in the
morning when He appears He was there, but they knew
Him not There is always the breaking of a new day when
Christ shows Himself afresh to the weary soul. Every
vision of Him is a new and fuller dawning of the heavenly
day.

II. **The Manner.** Our Lord followed the example
of no man. He had His own unique way of showing
both Himself and His doctrine. He began to reveal
Himself by—

1. LEADING THEM TO CONFESSION. "Children, have ye
aught to eat? They answered Him, No!" (v. 5, R.V.).
This was an honest confession of failure. They had taken
nothing, so they made no attempt to make it look like
something. They had nothing, neither for themselves nor
for others, and they said so; and by so doing put themselves in a position to be blessed by the Lord. Beware
of misrepresentation and exaggeration. Christ is interested
in our reports.

2. TESTING THEIR FAITH. "Cast the net on the right
side of the ship, and ye shall find" (v. 6). They had toiled
all night to no purpose, and now that the day was breaking
they had given up all hope. But the authoritative voice of
that stranger on the shore, so full of promise, was heard,
and immediately obeyed. There is always a ring of

certainty about the Word of the Lord Jesus. To *hear* it is to have our hearts tested by it.

3. Turning Failure into Success. "They cast therefore, and now they were not able to draw it for the multitude of fishes" (v. 6). They obeyed, and their faith was abundantly rewarded. By this sign which followed, John was constrained to say, "It is the Lord." This is the *Lord's* doing; John feels that it is so like Him. Yes, it is just Christlike to turn our total defeat into unprecedented success, through the giving of His Word and the believing of it. It is in "this wise" that sinners are converted, and fruitless Christians made wise to win souls.

4. Providing for their Wants. "As soon as they came to land they saw a fire of coals, a fish, and a loaf" (v. 9, R.V., *margin*). Even in His resurrection body the Lord was not unmindful of the bodies of His cold and hungry disciples. This is another *revelation* of His love and care for His own. It was not, perhaps, a sumptuous feast, but it was according to His manner as the Shepherd of His flock. "The Lord is My Shepherd, I shall not *want*." "My God shall supply all your *need*" (Phil. 4. 19). The Son of God is always before us in His providential arrangements.

5. Having Fellowship with Them. "Jesus said unto them, Come and break your fast...Jesus then cometh and taketh bread, and giveth them, and fish likewise" (v. 12, 13). Now, "none of the disciples durst ask Him, Who art Thou?" None but the Lord Himself could act in this manner, showing such grace and power. Christ has a way of *giving*, whereby He Himself is made known (Luke 24. 30, 31). He gave Himself for us. The *law* demands, but the *grace* of God that has come to us in Christ Jesus delights to give. It is an ever memorable experience to have our long spiritual fast broken by the

blessings provided for us, and offered to us by Him who
died for us and rose again. Eat, O friends! Come and
dine. "Behold, all things are now ready" (Matt. 22. 4).

———

"IF I WILL."

JOHN 21. 15-22.

AFTER they had dined, the Lord showed Himself in another
way to Peter, when He searched the secrets of his heart
with that threefold question, "Lovest thou Me?" This
was Peter's final examination for the Gospel ministry. It
had to do with the *heart* more than the head. It was a
test of *love*. There can be no truly educated ministry
without a whole-hearted devotion to the Person of Jesus
Christ. It was because of Peter's confession of *love* he
received his commission to serve, "Feed My lambs." After
the Lord had signified to Peter by what painful death he
should glorify God, Peter made no protest, accepting it at
once as the good will of God, but he became anxious to
know how John was to end his earthly journey, "What
shall this man do?" Jesus said, "If I will that he tarry
till I come, what is that to thee? Follow *thou* ME." This
reply of Christ to Peter's question of curiosity is a further
revelation of His unique methods and matchless character.
"If *I* will." This is an *I* that stretches from the deepest
depths to the highest heights; its arms reach out to all
time past and to the eternity to come. These words of
Christ are a revelation to us of His—

I. **Views of Life.** His eye was always on the great
essentials of true existence. He allowed no place for mere
personal curiosity. "What is that to thee? Follow thou
ME." Here is the true centre around which our lives
should move, and from which they must receive their
guiding and inspiring principles. We must be more
anxious to follow Christ than to contrast our experience

with the experience of others, either in their life or in their death.

II. Methods of Working. "If I will that HE tarry... what is that to thee?" His dealings with His disciples is not in any stiff mechanical fashion, not after the rigid law f uniformity. The wealth of Christ's wisdom and power cannot permit of this. Each individual disciple will have His special consideration and providence. He calleth His own sheep by *name*, which means *nature*, and will deal with them for their highest good and His highest glory.

III. Divine Power. "If I will." What a WILL this is! What a refuge for the weary trembling soul! His will is not a burden for us to carry, but a pillow on which to rest. Think of the dignity, authority, almightiness, that lie in these words, like strength in a giant's limb. He has but to *will* and it shall be done, for His will is done in Heaven and among the inhabitants of the earth. If He wills to bless thee and keep thee, then thou shall be blessed and kept. How safe and right our life is when yielded to His will!

IV. Abiding Presence. "Follow thou Me." By His Word and Spirit, lo, He is with us alway, even to the end of the age. He has left us an example that we should follow His steps. "Follow thou Me." Is this possible now that He is risen in newness of life, and seated in heavenly glory? Yes. It is *His will*. Whatever is His will for us is possible to us. Think of the *privilege* of following Him whom angels delight to honour, and of the tremendous *possibilities* associated with such a life.

V. Second Advent. "Till I come" (v. 22). This is at least the third time in this Gospel that our Lord definitely refers to His coming again (chaps. 14. 3; 16. 22). Throughout the New Testament there are something like 603 references to this subject. He has come as a suffering

Saviour. He shall come as a glorious King. The hope of the Church is the *Cross* of Christ, the hope of the world lies in the *throne* of Christ When He comes again it will not be in grace, but to assert His *right* and reign. "Then the kingdoms of this world shall become the Kingdom of our God and of His Christ." Blessed hope! This heavy-laden world, staggering on through the ages with its ever-gathering burden of sin and woe into ever-deepening darkness, shall, at the coming of the Lord Jesus Christ, be saved and filled with His glory (Heb. 10. 37).

"HE HELPED ME."
PSALM 116. 3-9.

A PERSONAL TESTIMONY.

1. His CONDITION,   "The sorrows of death...the pains of Hell...I found trouble" (v. 3).
2. His CONFESSION.   "I was brought low" (v. 6).
3. His PETITION. "I called upon the Name of the Lord" (v. 4).
4. His SALVATION. "He helped me...He delivered my soul...mine eyes...and my feet" (vv. 6-8).
5. His RESOLUTION.   "I will walk before the Lord" (v. 9).
6. His CONSOLATION.   "Rest, O my soul, for the Lord hath dealt bountifully with thee" (v 7).

TRANSFORMING GRACE.
1 CORINTHIANS 15. 9, 10.

1. His Past: "I persecuted the Church of God."
2. His Present: "An Apostle."
3. How this great change was wrought: "By the grace of God."

BIBLE READINGS.

THE CHURCH, WHICH IS HIS BODY.

EPHESIANS 1. 22-23.

THIS is a simple statement, but it reveals a wondrous mystery. The Church is the body of Christ. How precious and beautiful is the thought that every believer—every truly converted soul—is a living member of the living mystical Body of Christ, and precious to Him as the apple of His eye. Being baptised or planted into Christ, we are made partakers of His Divine nature, and so become heirs of that eternal life. As members of His body we are part of Himself. This metaphor is very suggestive.

I. **The Church, as His Body, is the Visible Proof of His Presence.** I cannot see your spirit; you cannot see mine; but our bodies are alike visible. The presence of a *living* body is the evidence of the presence of a living invisible *spirit*. The world cannot see the invisible Christ who dwells in His Body the Church, but it can see the body. It can see you and me. Does Christ so live in us that our lives evidence the presence and power of an unseen Saviour? Every Jew is a proof that Abraham lived. Every Christian is a witness to the *living* Christ, as surely as a living hand proves a living head (Eph. 5. 23-30).

II. **As His Body, the Church is Animated by a Divine Spirit.** "You hath He quickened." The life is God-given. It is His own life. Because "I live ye shall live also." It is God who dwelleth in you. In every living human body there is a human spirit. The Church of Christ is a Divine body and is indwelt by a Divine spirit. Every branch in the vine must be possessed by the life-sap of the vine. Do we realise that as members of His body the source and power of our life is in Him alone? Just as the hand is dependent on the head, and waits the energising of the will, so our spirits depend on Christ, our Head, and are animated by His Spirit (1 Cor. 6. 17; Eph. 4. 4).

III. As His Body, its Members are all One. The head controls every member of the body, and each member is connected with each other because of its connection with the head. As members of Christ, we are members one of another, and should have the same care one for another (1 Cor. 12. 25). There are different functions for the members, but there are in the sight of Christ, the Head, no divisions—"all one in Christ." Oh, that, as individual members, we may live and work under the power of this soul-raising truth—in honour preferring one another (Rom. 12. 5; Col. 1. 18).

IV. As His Body, each Member is Dependent upon the Head. Without the head the body would be nothing but a corrupt lifeless corpse. The body exists for the head and not the head for the body. From the head each member receives its authority. Child of God, remember this. If the hand is enabled to perform any cunning workmanship it is because the wisdom of the head has been imparted. He is made of God unto us wisdom (Rom. 14. 7, 8; Eph. 2. 21, 22).

V. As His Body, it is Subject to Suffering. Christ as "the Head once wounded" is now beyond the reach of the smiter; but His body, the Church, is still exposed to scorn and persecution. How sweet to know that the Head is in deepest, closest sympathy with *each* suffering member. "Inasmuch as ye did it unto these, you did it unto Me." When Saul was persecuting the members of His body, Jesus said to him, "Why persecutest thou *Me*?" O Christian, bear patiently. If the head, who feels the pang more keenly than the member, complains not, why should the member? These things may be permitted for edification. "Tribulation worketh patience" (2 Tim. 3. 10-12; Matt. 19. 29; Phil. 3. 8).

VI. **As His Body, its Members are His Instruments of Service.** The body is the servant of the head; the Church is the servant of Christ. The head has no way of working out its purposes but through the body. So Christ, as the living, thinking Head of His Body, the Church, is pleased to accomplish His will, and work out His gracious purposes through the members of His body. What a privilege! "Workers with Him." "Weapons of righteousness unto God" (Rom. 6. 13, *margin*). "Ye are not your own." No; ye are the hands and feet, the eyes and tongue of Christ. It is God who worketh in you, both to *will* and to *do*. If every member of His body were fully yielded to His will, what mighty things would be accomplished. Who could withstand *Him*? (1 Cor. 6. 15-20; Rom. 12. 1).

VII. **As His Body, it is Amply Provided for.** Bodies are often ruined through thoughtless heads, and sometimes great heads are hindered because of weak and deformed bodies. It is the work of the head to lay up in store for the body. What stores of grace and truth, what powers of sufficiency dwell in Christ for us, as members of His Body. A *withered* branch is no honour to the vine. A powerless, half-starved Christian is a discredit to Christ. "My God shall supply all your need according to His riches in glory *by* Christ Jesus." If ye, being evil, know how to feed, protect, and clothe your own bodies, will Jesus Christ your Lord not much more care for His? "O ye of little faith" (Matt. 6. 32; Phil. 4. 6; Psa. 34. 9-10).

VIII. **As His Body, the Church cannot see Corruption.** The Body of Jesus, which was a type of His Church, was abused, bruised, and broken, but it did not

see corruption. The Church as His body may be marred
and outwardly weak, but is indwelt by the Spirit of God.
Just as surely as the *Body* of Jesus was glorified on the
mount of transfiguration, so surely shall His body, the
Church, be transformed with resurrection beauty and
filled with the glory of God. He, as the Head of the Body,
has already ascended. The body, which is still on earth,
will likewise one day be "caught up." "We shall not all
sleep (die), but we must all be changed. It doth not *yet*
appear what we shall be, but we know that when He shall
appear we shall be like Him, for we shall see Him as He
is" (Col. 1. 21, 22; Eph. 5. 27, Cant. 4. 7; Jude 24, 25).

WALK WORTHY OF THE LORD.

"TEACH me, O Lord, the way of Thy statutes, and I shall
keep it unto the end. Give me understanding, and I shall
keep Thy law; yea, I shall observe it with my whole heart.
Make me to go in the path of Thy commandments; for
therein do I delight. Turn mine eyes from beholding
vanity; and quicken Thou me in Thy way" (Psa. 119.
33-37). "It is God who worketh in you both to *will* and to
do" (Phil. 2. 13).

I. **The Christian Life as a Walk.** It implies—

1. PILGRIMAGE. Here we have no continuing city; we
are pilgrims and strangers on the earth: sojourners with
the Lord (Lev. 25. 23). Our citizenship is in Heaven.

2. SELF-DENIAL. "If any will come after Me," said
Jesus, "let him deny himself" (Matt. 16. 24). Must
be prepared to give up the riches, pleasures, and honours
of the world, to find our all in Himself.

3. SEPARATION (Col. 3. 1, 2). If *we* be risen with
Christ our affections are risen out of the world with Him.

Outside the camp; not of the world. "Transformed by the renewing of your mind" (Rom. 12. 2).

4. SUFFERING (1 Peter 2. 20, 21). If any man will live godly he must suffer. The world which hated Christ will not love His friends (John 15. 15-19). *Here* we have fellowship with His suffering; by and by with His glory.

5. PROGRESS. We cannot be standing still while we are walking. "The path of the just is as the shining light, shining *more and more* unto the perfect day." The sphere of this walk is in the heavenlies. We *mount up* as on eagle wings; *then*, when we are up, we run and are not weary, walk and are not faint. Don't believe in the coming-down theory.

II. The Christian's Companion in the Walk.

It has been said, "A crowd is not company: one good companion makes good company." We have—

1. A DIVINE COMPANION (2 Cor. 6. 16). While sceptics are crying out, "Where is God?" the Christian is walking with Him day by day.

2. AN ALMIGHTY COMPANION (Gen. 17. 1). Surely these words should hush every doubt, silence every complaint, and calm every fear.

3. A PLEASANT COMPANION (Amos 3. 3). The pleasures of companionship depend largely upon our *oneness* of purpose and feeling. What a blessing to be agreed with God—one in heart and purpose.

4. AN EVER-PRESENT COMPANION (Psa. 116. 9). "Lo, I am with you always." "I will never leave thee, nor forsake thee." He is "a *present* help in the time of need" (Psa. 46. 1).

5. A CLOSE COMPANION (2 Cor. 6. 16). No earthly friend can be so near as He. Not only does He walk with us, but He dwells *in us*.

6. A FAITHFUL COMPANION (Heb. 11. 5). He takes His companions with Him. "Where I am, there shall My servants be." He is a Friend that loveth at all times.

7. A COMFORTING COMPANION (Psa. 23. 4). He knows how to speak a word to him that is weary. His rod and staff—strange comforters in the eyes of the world—comfort us.

8. AN EXEMPLARY COMPANION (1 John 2. 6). We are to walk as He walked. How did He walk? He walked by faith, and always did those things which pleased the Father.

III.. The Manner of the Christian's Walk.

1. IT SHOULD BE BY FAITH (2 Cor. 5. 7). We received Christ Jesus by faith, and we are to walk in Him as we received Him. It is neither by sight nor feeling, but by faith, as He walked.

2. IN NEWNESS OF LIFE (Rom. 6. 4). As risen with Christ, we are to show forth this newness of life by seeking those things which are above, and turning not back to the sins of the old life (2 Peter 1. 9).

3. WITH HUMILITY (Micah 6. 8). If we continually realise with whom we walk, it will surely constrain us to "walk in the fear of the Lord."

4. IN THE SPIRIT (Gal. 5. 16). The best way to keep tares out of the bushel is to fill it with wheat. Abide by the law of the Spirit and you will not fulfil the lusts of the flesh.

5. IN HIS TRUTH (Psa. 86. 11). According to the truth of God. Jesus Christ Himself is the Truth; let His Word dwell in you richly.

6. IN LOVE (Eph. 5. 2). If we walk with Him who loved us and gave Himself for us, it much becomes us to walk in love.

7. IN WISDOM (Col. 4. 5). This is needed, when we remember those who are without, and how they watch our steps and read the book of our lives.

8. WORTHY OF GOD (1 Thess. 2. 12). That is, worthy of God who is calling you and walking with you. One false step might bring His Holy Name into dishonour. "Hold Thou up my goings" (Psa. 17. 5)

IV. The Privileges of the Christian Walker. He is—

1. RECONCILED (Amos 3. 3). There can be no fellowship without agreement. Justified, and at peace with God. Old things have passed away.

2. CLEANSED (Isa. 35. 8, 9). Only the clean can walk the way of holiness. The path of the redeemed is the path of righteousness. Abiding with Him, His blood keeps cleansing (1 John 1. 9).

3. INDWELT (2 Cor. 6. 16). Possessed by Him with whom we walk. Blessed mystery; a secret the unrenewed cannot know.

4. ILLUMINED (Psa. 84. 11). Not only walking in the light of His favour, but having the light of the knowledge of God shining in the heart. Children of the light.

5. DELIVERED from fears, from iniquity (Psa. 119. 3-45). In His good company we are saved from much bad company.

6. COMFORTED (Acts 9. 31). The comforting Spirit walks with those who walk with God, taking the things of Christ and showing them to them.

7. HAPPY (Psa. 128. 1). Happy is every one who walketh in His ways. His ways are ways of pleasantness. Miserable, says the wicked spirit. Happy, says the Holy Spirit.

8. HONOURED (Rev. 3. 4). They that walk in the light shall walk in white. They journey to a land where there is no night. Shall they weep again? No, never; but shall reign with Him for ever (Rev. 20. 5).

FOR CHRIST'S SAKE.

OUR prayers usually end with these words, "For Christ's sake." We desire that God should look upon the face of His Beloved Son, and deal with us according to the merit of our Suffering Substitute. But this is only one side of this great truth   God also desires *us* to look upon the face of His Son, and for Christ's sake, suffer, serve, and glorify the Father. This is the true motive for Christian life and work. How much will a mother suffer for her child's sake? For Jonathan's sake, David was willing to bless the house of Saul. For Christ's sake we are to—

I **Forgive**   "Forgiving one another, even as God for *Christ's sake* hath forgiven you" (Eph. 4. 32). God for Christ's sake hath forgiven us, so we for Christ's sake are to forgive others, even until seventy times seven (Matt. 18. 21, 22). It is so *Christlike* to have compassion and pity, and a heart ready to bless and forgive (see Col. 3. 12, 13). For His sake we are to—

II. **Serve One Another.**   "Ourselves your servants *for Jesus' sake*" (2 Cor. 4. 5). The Son of Man came not to be served, but to serve, and to give His life; so he that will be chief among the followers of Christ will be the *servant* of all Paul gloried in this, that he "made himself servant unto all, that he might gain the more" (1 Cor. 9. 19). The service of each member, when done for "Christ's sake," is done for the good of the whole body, not otherwise. Menpleasers add nothing to the perfecting of the Body of Christ. For His sake we are to be—

III. **Always Delivered unto Death.**   "We which live are always delivered unto death *for Jesus' sake*, that the life also of Jesus might be manifested in our mortal flesh" (2 Cor 4. 11). For His sake self is to be continually surrendered unto death, "Killed all the day long," that the life of the now glorified Jesus might be manifested in us. Only those save their lives who lose them for His sake (Matt. 10. 39). The seemingly painful and death-like gloom of such an experience may cause some to fear this entire abandonment of self unto death; but dying for *His sake* is the way into the liberty and power of His risen *life*. For Christ's sake the martyrs faced the sword, the flaming fagots, and the floods, and entered into rest. If we suffer for Him, we shall also reign with Him. The muffled cry of the Christ-despising is still, "Save thyself and come down from the Cross." Let our answer be, "I am crucified with Christ, nevertheless I live, yet not I, but Christ." For Christ's sake we should—

IV. **Take Pleasure in Afflictions.** "I take pleasure in infirmities, in reproaches, in necessities, in persecutions, in distresses *for Christ's sake*; for when I am weak, then am I strong" (2 Cor. 12. 10). Wherever Christ is, there is salvation and the restfulness of Heaven; therefore bring Him into all your "infirmities," "reproaches," "necessities," "persecutions," and "distresses." This is part of our inheritance in Christ, for "it is *given* unto us, not only to believe, but also to suffer for His sake" (Phil. 1. 29) For His sake we are to—

V. **Strive Together in Prayer.** "I beseech you brethren *for the Lord Jesus Christ's sake*...that ye strive together with me in your prayers to God for me" (Rom. 15. 30). As Christians we may differ in many things, but surely we may all agree in this, that for the Lord Jesus Christ's sake we will pray for one another. Yes, there are sharp and ugly crooks in some disciples' characters, but for *His sake* we ought to strive together in prayer. The full depth of the possibilities of prayer has never yet been fathomed. For His sake we must also—

VI. **Labour Patiently.** "I know...thou hast borne, and hast patience, and *for My Name's sake* hast laboured,

and hast not fainted" (Rev. 2. 3). A fitful worker is as
untrustworthy as a fitful lover. It is easy to lose patience,
and to faint when the labour is not directly "for His
Name's sake." The secret of perseverance and victory lies
in doing all as unto Him. The work given us to do is HIS
work, and must be done in His Name, and for His sake.
Therefore, for His sake labour patiently for the salvation
of the lost, and the sanctification of the saved. "Consider
Him...lest ye be wearied and faint in your minds."

> "I will not work my soul to save;
>   That my Lord hath done,
> But I will work like any slave
>   For the sake of God's dear Son."

Moreover, we must be willing for His sake to be—

VII. **Counted Fools.** "We are fools *for Christ's sake*"
(1 Cor. 4. 10). In the eyes of the world a fool is one who,
perhaps through mental weakness, is incapable of entering
into the business and pleasures that engross the multitude,
and whose mind is occupied, perchance, with some trivial,
worthless thing; or he is a man with a strong self-will that
is constantly leading him into difficulties and disappoint-
ments. Those who are fools for Christ have a business, and
pleasures, and prospects, that Christless eyes have never
seen. Fools, because they hold lightly the material, and
grasp with firm hand the eternal. The things of the
Spirit of God are foolishness to the natural man (1 Cor.
2. 14). To die to live, is wiser than to die to be lost.

YOUR MASTER.
"ONE IS YOUR MASTER, CHRIST" (Matt. 23. 8).

"WHAT kind of a master have you?" asked an Irish tramp
of a farm servant, who was busy in the field. "He is a
good master when you give him all his own way." "Och,
sure, so is the Devil," was his comment. But although

you do give the Devil all his own way he never can be a *good* master; but give the Lord Jesus Christ His own way, and you will find Him the Good Master, and His service the best and sweetest of all. His will is the only true and lasting good; to be in it is to be in the best of all environments, and the surest and safest way to abiding peace and eternal success. "Good is the will of the Lord." "Ye call Me Master...and so I am." What about the servants?

I. The Servant's Relationship. "You are not your own, for you have been redeemed at infinite cost" (1 Cor. 6. 20, Weymouth). His servants have been bought with a price, the value of which is for ever beyond the grasp of man's finite mind. It does not become those bought with *His blood* to be servants of men (1 Cor. 7. 23). Redeemed by Him, and for Him, "therefore glorify God in your body and in your spirit, which are God's."

II. The Servant's Motive. "I love my master...I will not go free" (Exod. 21. 5). The experience of this Hebrew is that of all those who have yielded themselves heartily to the service of Jesus Christ, they fall in love with their Master, and count His service the greatest liberty and sweetest delight. The love of Christ constraineth us. We love Him because He first loved us. *Love* is the fulfilling of the law, not duty.

III. The Servant's Work. "The Son of Man...gave... to every man his work" (Mark 13. 34). "To each one his special duty" (Weymouth). The Son of Man does not lay upon every servant the same task; the gift of work is according to the character of the vessel, or the ability of the worker. A vessel made meet for the Master's use will be put by Him to the highest possible use. Let us not say "What can I do?" but "What wilt *Thou* have me to do?" "Christ is over His own house; whose house are we?"

(Heb. 3. 6). Therefore the ordering of the vessels and the service is in His hands. "What is that in thine hand?"

IV. **The Servant's Supply.** "He called his ten servants, and delivered them ten pounds, and said unto them, Occupy till I come" (Luke 19. 13). When He gives the work, He gives the power to carry it out. Each servant received his pound, and each pound meant a Pentecost; it was an enduement with power, to occupy his place till he should come again. "The manifestation of the Spirit is given to every man to profit withal." Let us take heed that we are trading (serving) with His gift (Holy Spirit) and not depending on our own acquirements, to the neglect of His pound and the ruin of our own testimony.

V. **The Servant's Encouragement.** "Lo, I am with you alway, even unto the end of the age" (Matt. 28. 20). This is not only the promise of His presence, it is the assurance of His co-operation. "The Lord is with thee... go in this thy might" (Judges 6. 12-14). As servants, we are His property, to do His work, using His means and enjoying His presence and help. In this holy service we have nothing that we have not received, but in this lies the secret of our confidence. We take His yoke upon us, and so learn of Him who walks in the yoke with us (Phil. 4. 13).

VI. **The Servant's Reward.** "Well done, good and faithful servant...enter thou into the joy of *thy* Lord" (Matt. 25. 21). As ye have shared your Master's service and sufferings, ye shall also be sharers of His joy. In His right hand there are pleasures for evermore (Psa. 16. 11, R.V.). None shall pluck us out of this hand. But the servant of Jesus Christ has a mighty reward *now* as well as awaiting him, for the Spirit of God is in him, and the honour of the Father upon him, as well as the joy of the Lord before him. Eternal life is a gift, but it is the overcomers who sit with Him on His throne (Rev. 3. 21). This

reward is not for being saved, but for being faithful
servants and sufferers for His sake. "If we suffer we shall
also reign with Him."

————

HINDRANCES TO PRAYER.
"That your prayers be not hindered" (1 Peter 3. 7).
There is surely something wrong when we sow much in
prayer and bring in little reward. That your prayers be
not hindered, see that ye—

I. **Love the Lord**. "Delight thyself also in the Lord,
and He shall give thee the desires of thine heart" (Psa.
37. 4). Is thy *heart* right with God? It is the nature of
love to seek *Himself*, and to those who love Him hath He
promised to manifest Himself. Delight also in His *Word*
if your petitions are to be unfettered in their approach
(John 15. 7).

II. **Confess Sin**. "If I regard iniquity in my heart, the
Lord will not hear me" (Psa. 66. 18). Sin discovered in
the heart, and unconfessed before God, remains a barrier to
prayer. Such sins hide His face from you that He will not
hear (Isa. 59. 1, 2). The Lord looketh upon the heart,
there must be no secret controversy there with Him—no
traitor in the camp. It is not a question as to what others
may think of me. If I regard iniquity there, then I must
deal with it if I would prevail with God.

III. **Put away Idols**. "These men have set up their
idols in their heart...should I be inquired of at all by
them" (Ezek. 14. 3). An idol is anything that is set up in
the forefront of our affections, taking the place of God.
Seen or unseen by men, it is erected before His face. It
may take the form of Pleasure, Fashion, Friends, Business,
Sin, or Self. There is no room *in the heart* for an idol and
the Holy Spirit. The heart must be cleansed if the spirit
of prayer is to prevail.

IV. **Deny Self.** "Ye ask, and receive not, because ye ask amiss, that ye may consume it upon your pleasures" (Jas. 4. 3, R.V.). The desire after our own personal pleasure strangles multitudes of prayers. The petitions are right in themselves when we plead for wisdom, power, grace, or the salvation of our friends; but if our motive is *our own pleasure,* we ask amiss. Has not our Lord said, "If any man would come after Me (in prayer), let him deny himself?" God still hides many things from such "wise and prudent" self-seekers.

V. **Be Steadfast.** "But let him ask in faith, nothing wavering; for he that wavereth...let not that man think that he shall receive anything of the Lord" (Jas. 1. 6, 7). There is no stability about a wave; it is utterly purposeless, being driven about with the wind, a creature of mere circumstances. The prayer of persevering faith storms the fort of blessing. A prayer may be like a wave tossed up against the throne of God, through the force of some tempestuous trial, but this is not a wavering prayer. "All things, whatsoever ye ask in prayer, believing, ye shall receive."

VI. **Consider One Another.** "Likewise, ye husbands ...giving honour unto the wife as unto the weaker vessel, and as being heirs together of the grace of life; that your prayers be not hindered" (1 Peter 3. 7). What is true of husbands is true also of wives, and, in a great measure, of sons and daughters, brothers and sisters, and of the whole *household of faith.* They are *"heirs together* of the grace of life"* (1 Peter 3. 7). All one in Christ Jesus, and the lack of giving honour one to another, especially the weaker vessels, acts as an hindrance to prayer, because it is a grieving of the Holy Spirit, and a dishonouring of the Father's love and the Saviour's redeeming grace. *Agreement* with one another is a powerful condition of prevailing prayer, so much so that, "If *two* of you shall agree on earth as touching anything that they shall ask, it shall be done for them of My Father which is in Heaven" (Matt. 18. 19).

LIFTED.

"WHEN THEY CAST THEE DOWN, THEN THOU SHALT SAY, THERE IS LIFTING UP" (Job 22. 29).

YES, thank God, although we may at times be cast down, and our characters almost dismantled by merciless hands, we can still hope in God, for His hand is not shortened that it cannot save, we can confidently say, "There is lifting up."

I. **The Need.** In Luke 13. 11 we read of a poor woman who had a spirit of infirmity eighteen years, and was bowed together, and could in *no wise lift up herself*. Such were some of us, "bowed together" by the love of the world that we could in no wise lift ourselves above it, and, like the publican, we could not lift up so much as our eyes unto Heaven. At that time without strength.

II. **The Lifter.** "But Thou, O Lord, art...the Lifter up of my head" (Psa. 3. 3). When the head is lifted above the whelming flood, the life is saved. Man in his helplessness and guilt needs such a lift that only God in His infinite mercy and power can give. Christ is not only the Breaker up of the sin-closed way, but the Lifter of the sin-bound head (Psa. 27. 6).

III. **The Provision.** "I, if I be lifted up from the earth will draw all men unto Me" (John 12. 32). Our Almighty Lifter had Himself to be lifted on the Cross, lifted from the grave, and lifted to that throne that is "high and lifted up," that He might be the Lifter up of His people. His love is an uplifting power: "Thou hast loved my soul out of the pit of corruption."

IV. **The Condition**. Those whom He lifts up are described as being *needy*. "He raiseth the poor out of the dust, and lifteth the needy out of the dunghill" (Psa. 113. 7). It belongs to the character of God to choose the weak things, and to exalt the lowly. His mercy seeks the guilty, His power the weak, His wisdom the ignorant, and His love the lost. Again, He lifts up the *humble*. "Humble yourselves in the sight of God, and He shall lift you up" (James 4. 10). He that exalteth *himself* shall be abased, but he that humbleth himself shall be exalted. Wherever there is true humbling of ourselves before God, His mighty uplifting hand will be manifested in due time (1 Peter 5. 6).

V. **The Manner**. The Lord took Peter's wife's mother "by the hand and lifted her up" (Mark 1. 31). Ezekiel the prophet says, "So the Spirit lifted me up and took me away" (chap. 3. 14). There is still lifting up by the hand of faith and by the Spirit of power. It is the Spirit that quickeneth the whole man, lifting the entire character into the upper regions of faith, where as on eagles' wings we can run and walk without growing weary or faint.

VI. **The Results**. There is—

1. The uplifted FACE of reconciliation. "Then thou shalt have thy delight in the Almighty, and shall lift up thy face unto God" (Job 22. 26). Once afar off, with face earthward and Hellward, but now Godward.

2. The uplifted HEAD of confidence. "Lift up your heads, for your redemption draweth nigh" (Luke 21. 28). Saved from all fear amidst the perilous times of the later days, when men's hearts are failing them for fear when the powers of Heaven are being shaken.

3. The uplifted HANDS of supplication and consecration. "I will lift up my hands in Thy Name" (Psa. 63. 4). Hands that used to hang down in feebleness and idleness

now lifted up in holy intercession for others, and offered as empty hands to God to be filled for His service and glory.

4. The uplifted VOICE of praise and testimony. "They shall lift their voice, they shall sing...they shall cry aloud" (Isa. 24. 14). The ransomed of the Lord shall return, and come to Zion with songs and everlasting joy upon their heads. Cry aloud, and shout, *thou* inhabitant of Zion, for the Lord hath done great things for thee. Say to those who are cast down, or who are wallowing hopelessly in the sinking mire of sin: "THERE IS LIFTING UP."

THE TABERNACLE OF GOD.

EXODUS 40. 17-35.

LET us think of—

I. **The Meaning of It**. Everything here is typical of things spiritual. Paul, in his epistle to the Hebrews, speaks of them as "The shadow of heavenly things," "The patterns of things in the heavens," "The figures of the true" Those blind to spiritual things can see neither beauty nor meaning in this wonderful arrangement. It was God's own picture to His people of "good things to come." Open Thou mine eyes to behold wonderful things here in Thy Tabernacle.

II. **The Purpose of It**. It was to be a sanctuary for God, that He might dwell among them (Exod. 25. 8). God so loved His people, whom He had redeemed, and delivered from the bondage of Egypt, that He desired a place for Himself, that His presence might abide with them. Does He not still desire to abide in every soul whom He hath saved by His grace? Then let us make Him a sanctuary in our own hearts, that He may dwell with us. "Ye are the temple of God."

III. **The Time of its Setting Up**. "In the first month,

on the first day of the month, the tabernacle was reared
up" (v. 17). Is it not significant that this House of God
was to be set up on "New Year's day?" Does not this
indicate that it was to be a *new beginning* for them? They
were to begin the year with God in their midst—as a
Pilgrim with them. The only *new start* worth making is to
begin with God. If He is with us, then certainly prosperity
in the highest sense will follow.

IV. **The Structure of It.** The manner of its get-up was
simple, yet everything had to be made and set in order
according to the pattern shown to Moses on the mount.
The sockets, which formed the *foundation* (v. 18), were of
solid silver, made from "atonement money" (Exod 38),
so that these golden boards actually stood upon that which
represented "Redemption"—the price of souls. Like this
Tabernacle in the wilderness, the "Church of God" has no
other standing than on that which has been paid (the blood
of Christ) as a ransom for the soul. These boards, built
upon the sockets of "Ransom," and "fitly knit together,"
and strengthened by the "bars thereof"—as encircling
arms of power—represent our standing in Christ, and our
union one with another within the everlasting arms of
Divine strength and faithfulness.

V. **The Contents of It.** The Tabernacle was divided
into three parts: "The Holiest of all," "The Holy Place,"
and the "Court." In the "Holiest" was put the Ark which
contained the law, the lid of which formed the *"Mercy-
seat,"* where God promised to meet with them (vv. 20, 21).
Christ has *covered* the broken law, and formed a mercy-seat
for us. Then, in the "Holy Place" there was the *Table*
with its bread, meaning *fellowship* with God in Christ. The
Candlestick, with its branches (v. 24), which speaks of
testimony in the power of Christ. The *Golden Altar*
(vv. 26, 27), with its sweet incense, speaking of acceptable

prayer in the Name of Christ. Then outside the door of the Holy Place stood the "*Altar* of burnt-offering"—the place of sacrifice, indicating that the *first need* of the people in their approach to God was *Atonement* (v. 29). The altar points to the Cross of Christ. Between the Altar of Sacrifice and the door of Communion, they set the *Laver* (v. 30), with its water for cleansing, teaching the need of the Holy Spirit's cleansing by the Word of Christ. There must be Substitution before true fellowship with God.

VI. The Glory of It. "The glory of the Lord filled the Tabernacle" (v. 34). The glory of it was the *manifest* presence of God. As it was with the Tabernacle, so was it with the life and work of the Lord Jesus Christ. It was crowned with a supernatural manifestation. He showed Himself alive by many infallible proofs (Acts 1. 3). When the glory of His Holy Presence is seen, then men feel like Moses, "Not able to enter in" without atoning blood.

———

BACKSLIDING.

HEBREWS 3. 12.

I. The Subjects. "Take heed, *brethren!*" Only those who have been made nigh unto God can backslide from Him.

II. The Cause. "An evil heart of unbelief." Unbelief is in itself the fruit of an evil heart.

III. The Manner. "Departing from the living God." The trust of the heart turning away from God to something else.

IV. The Preventative. "Take heed!" Examine yourselves.

GOSPEL OUTLINES.

THE GREAT SALVATION.

"How shall we escape if we neglect so great salvation?"
(Heb. 2. 3).

I. **This Salvation is Great**. Great, when you think of
the greatness of Him who saves. He is the Heir of all
things, the Maker of the worlds, the brightness of the
Father's glory, the express image of His Person, who
upholdeth all things by the word of His power, and is
much better than the angels (Heb. 1. 2-4). Great, when
you think of the awful condition from which He saves,
from the guilt and dominion of sin, and delivers from that
death which is the wages of sin, and from the wrath of
God which must for ever rest upon sin and sinners. Great,
when you think of the happy position into which He
saves—brought into the family of God, justified from all
things, made sons and daughters and heirs of eternal life,
having the promise for the life that now is, as well as the
life which is to come. Great, when you think of the
unspeakable price He paid for our salvation. Not corruptible things, as silver and gold, but His own precious
blood. It took the *sacrifice* of Himself to purge our sins
and He willingly, lovingly, gave His all.

II. **This Salvation may be Neglected**. It is neglected
every time the opportunity of being saved is let slip. We
ought to give the more earnest heed to the things which we
have heard, lest at *any time* we should let them slip.
Because to let the chance slip *any one* time may be letting
it slip for the *last* time. Many neglect salvation by
neglecting the Lord's day. To neglect the Word of God,

the Gospel of God, the strivings of the Spirit of God, and the Providence of God, is to neglect salvation. The process of neglecting, like the process of drifting, may be painless and unconscious, but it is the more dangerous on that account. You may neglect it without hating it or denying it. The Osbtinates, who refuse to go forward, and the Pliables who turn back, equally neglect salvation.

III. **This Salvation, if Neglected, Leaves no Escape.** This question, "How shall we escape if we neglect?" is one which the wisdom of God cannot answer, although some men in the pride of their own hearts have attempted it. How shall the merchant escape ruin if he neglects his business? How shall we escape hunger if we neglect food? How shall we escape darkness if we neglect the light? How shall we escape the wages of sin if we neglect the Atonement for sin? How shall we escape the wrath of God if we neglect the Gift of God? How shall we escape the doom of the lost if we neglect the Saviour of the lost? How shall we escape the condemnation of Hell if we neglect the salvation of Heaven? "Behold, now is the accepted time." One of the most melancholy sights of earth is a Christless old age.

DECISION.

"How long halt ye between two opinions? If the Lord be God, follow Him; but if Baal, then follow him" (1 Kings 18. 21).

It is sometimes needful to "halt between two opinions," if the proper course of action is not quite clear, but when the right and the wrong stands out in naked reality indecision becomes sin. It is with spiritual things, as with the temporal, the wavering and the lukewarm cannot succeed. The young man who cannot make up his mind as to what business he should follow is in danger of being ruined. In religion, as in politics, no progress can be made, no definite testimony can be given, so long as the mind is not clear, and the will emphatic. In these, and other matters, a halting man is a useless man, worse than useless, for he is a stumbling-block to others. The scene on Mount Carmel is an object lesson on the need of instant decision for God. Elijah's call is needed now as much as then.

I. **Where the People Halted.** "Between *two* opinions." To them this simply meant—

1. BETWEEN TWO RELIGIONS. There were only two. The religion of Baal and that of Jehovah. The one was the product of man's darkened imagination, the other was a revelation from Heaven. The heart of man and the heart of God are the only two possible sources of religious thought. Here is the halting ground of multitudes— between the thoughts of men and the thoughts of God. To halt here is to halt—

2. BETWEEN TWO MASTERS. Between Baal and Jehovah, between the false and the real, between super-stition and revelation, between the tyranny of ignorance and fear, and the freedom of light and truth. The one represents the prince of darkness, the other the Prince of Peace. The design of the one is to destroy, the purpose of the other is to save. His servants ye are to whom ye yield yourselves. Let not sin have dominion over you. There is no communion between these two masters: no fellowship between light and darkness, between Christ and Belial. There is no agreement between the temple of God and the house of idols. Ye cannot serve these two masters; your choice lies between them.

II. **Why the People Halted.** Some thing, or things, must surely have been hindering them from confessing the

Lord as their God.   They may have been deterred as many
in our day are—

1. BECAUSE OF THEIR NUMBER.   Their name was legion
who had entered the broad road of God-rejection.   It is
comparatively easy to go right, or wrong, while going with
the multitude, but a man is his own miserable comforter
when he tries to console himself by saying, "If I am not
right there are a great many like me."   Though hand join
in hand, the wicked shall not go unpunished.   "Broad is
the way that leadeth to destruction, and many there be
which go in thereat."   It is poor comfort, when on a
sinking ship, to know that *many* are perishing with you.
To remain undecided for Christ because many are doing it
is a sad betrayal of moral weakness.   Although Baal and
the groves had 850 prophets, and Jehovah only one, yet to
be with Him was to be in the majority and on the side of
victory and blessing.

2. BECAUSE OF THEIR FEAR OF MAN.   Some halted,
doubtless because they feared the wrath of the king.   It
was very different with the parents of Moses (Heb. 11. 23).
Ahab was the enemy of God, and the troubler of Israel.
He sought to banish the worship of Jehovah out of the land,
and because of him many were afraid to acknowledge the
Lord.   They *halted*, perhaps because they were convinced
that the policy of Ahab and Jezebel was base and
revolutionary, but they had no courage to take their stand
for Jehovah.   The fear of man bringeth a snare.   When
Luther was told that all the world was against him, he
said, "Well, I am against the whole world."   "Why halt ye?
If the Lord be God, follow Him."   Better is it to grieve and
forsake the enemies of God than remain an enemy to God.

III. **The Unsatisfactory Nature of such a Position.**
"*How long* halt ye?"   Every moment one halts between
holiness and sin, between Christ and the world, is likely to

weaken the will power and reduce the life to a waste heap
for God and a coming eternity.   To remain undecided for
God and righteousness to say the least—

1. It is Foolish.   It is like the donkey in the fable,
which died of starvation because it could not decide which
of the two bundles of hay to eat first.   Moses was wise when
ᴀe "chose rather to suffer affliction with the people of God,
than to enjoy the pleasures of sin for a season."   Rebekah
was wise when she said, "I will go."   The poor Indian
woman knew in whom she had believed when, after having
been robbed of all her goods, she said, "I would rather die
a poor Christian than a rich heathen."

2. It is Dangerous.   Indecision has been the ruin of
many.   Remember Lot's wife.   To *decide* means literally
"to cut off" that which is unnecessary.   Then "cut off"
from that state of sin and doubt, and, like Mary, choose
the better part.   The undecided are always easily overcome.   When Charles I., after having been defeated at the
Battle of Naseby, was about to make another charge upon
the troops of Cromwell, one of his courtiers caught the
bridle of his horse and turned him aside from the path of
honour.   Charles had not the courage to rebuke him.   Who
would have dared to have done this with Cromwell?

CONVERSION.

"Verily, I say unto you, except ye turn and become as little
children, ye shall in no wise enter into the Kingdom
of Heaven" (Matt. 18. 3, r.v.).

This was Christ's answer to some of His own *disciples*, who
had been asking that somewhat half-curious, self-confident
question, "Who is the greatest in the Kingdom of Heaven?"
They are not all properly converted who are the professed
followers of Jesus Christ.   Three things here should be
noted—

I. The Need of Conversion. "Except ye turn and become as little children, *ye shall in no wise enter the Kingdom of Heaven.*" We may be disciples, in a sense, and yet be unfit for the Kingdom of God. Those who don't need to be converted are those who, at some time or other, have been converted, for "All we like sheep have gone astray." There may be an outward conformity where there is an inward deformity. The tree needs to be made good before the fruit can be good; the fountain of the heart must be cleansed if the streams of thought and feeling are to be pure. The Kingdom of Heaven cannot be entered by those who selfishly seek their own good, and not the glory of God. Not to submit to the will and purpose of God is to rebel against this Kingdom, which is the "rule of the Heavens."

II. The Nature of Conversion. "Except ye *turn.*" It is a turning about—a turning from self-confidence and self-rule unto the rule of God. Saul was thoroughly converted when he said, "Lord, what wilt Thou have me to do?" He had turned from His own self-made plans and purposes to the will of his Lord and Saviour. In one sense we need to be converted very often, for every time we turn aside, like Bunyan's pilgrims, into any By-Path Meadow that leads us out of fellowship with the Lord, we need another conversion, another *turning back*, if we would enter again into the peaceful Kingdom of Heaven. Christ "suffered for us, the Just for the unjust, that He might bring us to God." If we have not been *turned unto God* we are yet unconverted; and if we have been thus converted, and are not now walking in the light and joy of His presence, it is quite clear that we need another turning about. "Turn ye, turn ye, why will ye die?"

III. The Evidence of Conversion. "Become as little children." The little child which "Jesus set in the midst of them," was for them an object lesson of self-abasement and trustfulness. Those who are wholly turned to God are as open minded and submissive as little children. They are very conscious of their own weakness, and free from all unholy ambition and secret intrigue. They are harmless, affectionate, and sincere, without duplicity and hypocrisy. To become as a *little child* is to have the past blotted out and forgiven, and to begin life anew after another and more heavenly fashion. It is only when a man gets converted, and becomes again a little child, that he can have all the prospects and opportunities of a lifetime before him. He has not yet begun to live in a real, true sense, if he has not been *turned to God*. "God is angry with the wicked every day; if he turn not, He will whet His sword" (Psa. 7. 11, 12).

ASSURANCE.

"THESE THINGS HAVE I WRITTEN UNTO YOU THAT BELIEVE ON THE NAME OF THE SON OF GOD, THAT YE MAY KNOW THAT YE HAVE ETERNAL LIFE" (1 John 5. 13).

I. **The Persons to be Assured.** "You that believe." To believe on the Name of the Son of God in John's day was to take up the ignominy of the Cross. The object of faith is not Christianity as a system, or the Bible as a book, but the Son of God as a living, abiding Personality. It is not written, "*Believe* and be saved," but "Believe *on the Lord Jesus Christ* and thou shalt be saved" (Acts 16. 31). The faith that does not take hold of Christ is a dead faith. To be assured of salvation we need more than faith in things, we need faith in HIM.

II. **The Blessing to be Assured Of.** "Eternal life." This is something different from, and something better than, mere eternal existence. Devils know about eternal existence, but they know nothing experimentally of eternal

life. This life stands for the sum of all good, here and hereafter. As the acorn seed contains within itself, potentially, all the power and majesty of the oak, so does this life, begotten in us by the Holy Spirit, contain the fullness of joy and glory that is yet to be revealed.

III. **The Blessedness of Being Assured.** "Ye may know." This word "know" is a favourite one with John. In these few verses (13 to 20) he makes use of it seven times. If you are a believer in Jesus Christ and don't know that you have eternal life, "ye may know." It is not only a possibility, but it is your privilege to know. This assurance is needful for the comfort and joy of salvation. How can we thank God for the gift of eternal life, if we are not sure that we have it?

IV. **The Ground of this Assurance.** "These things have I *written* unto you...that ye may know." Assurance does not come through any special revelation from Heaven, apart from the *written Word*. "He that hath the Son hath life" (v. 12). These words, inspired by the Holy Spirit, and penned by the apostle, are for you who believe, that ye may know that ye have eternal life. Not to receive this testimony is to make God a liar, and rob your soul of this blessed confidence. A little orphan girl, happy in the knowledge of Christ as her Saviour, was asked how she knew that she was saved, said, "He says it, and that's enough for me." Is it not enough for you?

THE NEW CREATION.

"IF ANY MAN IS IN CHRIST, HE IS A NEW CREATION; THE OLD THINGS ARE PASSED AWAY: BEHOLD, THEY ARE BECOME NEW" (2 Cor. 5. 17, R.V., *margin*).

I. **The Condition of It.** "In Christ." "If any man is in Christ he is a new creation." This implies that we have fled to Him for shelter and salvation—as the man-slayer

fled to the City of Refuge—taking refuge in His atoning
work. In Christ, as the branch is in the vine, for strength
and supply; in Christ, as the member is in the body, for
sympathy and service.

II. **The Nature of It.** "A new creation." It is a
reformation in a very radical sense. "We are *His workmanship*, created in Christ Jesus" (Eph. 2. 10). There is a *new
life*. Born, not of blood, nor of the will of the flesh, nor of
the will of man, but of God. There is a *new mind*.
"Renewed in the spirit of the mind" (Eph. 4. 23), and able
now to comprehend something of the character and power
of God in Christ Jesus. There is a *new heart*. The
affections that were alienated from God are now centred in
Him. There is a *new spirit*. The Spirit of God now bears
witness with our spirits, implying oneness of purpose in
service and testimony. There is a *new song*, because there
has been a new revelation of Divine mercy and grace
(Psa. 40. 1-3).

III. **The Results of It.** "The old things are passed
away; behold they are become new." With the new
creation then comes new views of *sin*. Sin is now seen to
be a crime and a curse, and the old view of it being a debt,
or a misfortune, passes away. There comes also new
views of *self*. Self is now seen to be a worthless, unclean
thing, and it too becomes an "old thing" only fit to pass
away. The old unscriptural views of *Christ* pass away, and
new Spirit-inspired views take their place. Jesus Christ
is no longer a Saviour waiting for us at a death-bed, but a
present, living reality in the daily life. The old things
which used to interest us in the *world* are passed away, and
behold, new interests have been awakened. In the old life
the pleasures and profits of the world were the objects of
our desires, but now the desire is for the salvation of the

world. It used to be the place of amusement for self, but now it is a workshop for Christ.

IV. The Privilege of It. "If any man." The door into this new and better life stands open for all. "Any man," no matter how weak and helpless, no matter how sad and sinful, "any man," no matter how old and forgetful if he steps out of sin-ruined self into Christ, will instantly become a new creation. For, in Christ, God is reconciling the world unto Himself.

GRIEVE NOT THE HOLY SPIRIT.
EPHESIANS 4. 30.

IT is solemnly possible to grieve the Holy Spirit, because He is a gracious, loving, tender *Personality*. It is not possible to grieve or vex a mere influence. The *wind* bloweth where it listeth, you cannot grieve the wind; but the breath of the Holy Spirit is the breathings of the very heart of God. All the attributes of God are attributed to the Holy Spirit. He is the Spirit of truth, of wisdom, of life, and of power. To grieve Him is to hinder His loving and merciful operations in the heart, and thereby impoverish our lives, and stultify our most earnest efforts in the service of Christ.

I. By Unholy and Profitless Talk (see vv. 29 and 31). Communications that are not "to the use of edifying," but which have a *corrupting* influence must be a grief to Him who is "Holy," and who has come to take the things which belong to the incorruptible Christ and show them to us. The Spirit of Truth can have no fellowship with frivolous talk and evil speaking.

II. By Ignoring His Presence. If our earthly friends dealt with us as we often deal with the Holy Spirit, we would be sorely offended. To live in the same house with

one and be seldom recognised must be a great hardship.
Mutual recognition is absolutely essential to the main-
tenance of real friendship.   Don't grieve Him by the
coldness of forgetfulness.

III. **By Rejecting His Teaching**. It was by rebelling
against His leading that Israel "vexed His Holy Spirit"
(Isa. 63. 10). The Spirit is ever seeking to lead us into the
truth as it is in Jesus, that we might be sanctified and made
meet for His use. We grieve the Spirit, when through
prejudice or unbelief, we refuse to accept His teaching,
or to obey His leading. If we are not *growing* in
grace, and in the knowledge of God, we may well
suspect ourselves of disobedience to the Lord the Spirit.
It must be a great grief to Him that His gracious work
should in any way be hindered in us or through us, as
Christ is dishonoured thereby, and His chief purpose is
to glorify Him.

IV. **By Conniving at Things which He Hates**. The
Holy Spirit is opposed to sin in every form. All worldliness and self-seeking are antagonistic to His nature and
mission. If we found any of our personal friends winking
secretly at things which they knew our souls abhorred,
how deeply we would be grieved at such a discovery. Are
we more sensitive than the Holy Spirit is? If we are
ashamed to rebuke what He rebukes, and to exalt what He
exalts, then we are not in the fellowship of the Spirit.
Grieve not the Spirit by encouraging the ungodly in their
sin. Remember Samson.

V. **By Grieving the Children of God**. Uncharitable
thinking which leads to uncharitable *speaking*, must grieve
Him who is the Spirit of *love* and of *unity*. Whatever tends
to alienate the affections of God's people, one from another,
is a striving against the workings of the Holy Ghost.
"That they all may be one," was the prayer of Christ.

"That they all may be one," is the purpose of the Spirit. To hinder this *oneness* is to grieve the Spirit by marring the unity of the Body, which He is so eager to maintain.

VI. By Serving the Lord in Our Own Strength. The Holy Spirit has come that we might have power to witness for Christ; to speak and labour in *our own* strength is a denial of His mission, and must be a great grief to His heart. How very sad it must be to the mighty Holy Spirit to see the servants of Christ, whom He has come to empower, substituting fleshly energy and worldly policy for His subduing, quickening presence. When the Spirit is grieved by such self-assertiveness, the evidence of it is apparent in a formal, fruitless life. A grieved Spirit not only means a powerless testimony, but also a lack of the enjoyment of the love of God in the heart. If this love is to be shed abroad in our hearts, we need the *communion* of the Holy Spirit; this we cannot have if our manner of life and service is opposed to His mind and will. We may have our lamps, and we may have a measure of light, like the foolish virgins, but if we have not that reserve of oil which is to be found in the presence of an ungrieved Spirit, we will be ashamed before Him at His coming.

"I OBTAINED MERCY."
1 TIMOTHY 1. 16.

I. He needed **mercy**. According to his own confession, he was the "chief of sinners" (v. 15). He was a ringleader among the enemies of Christ. Nothing but *mercy* could meet his need. He did not need more worldly wisdom or a better man-pleasing life; he needed the mercy of God to forgive his sin and save his soul from death. Divine mercy covered all his deep, dire need.

II. He **obtained** mercy. He did not obtain it by any

work or merit of his own. *He* obtained it just because God in His infinite grace *gave* it to him. He obtained it because he readily *accepted* the gift when offered to him. There is no other way for us to obtain mercy than by receiving it.

III. He obtained mercy **through Christ Jesus** (v. 15). There is none other name under Heaven, none other channel between Heaven and earth, through which the stream of God's forgiving and saving mercy can flow. The only price by which we can obtain the mercy of God is the precious Blood of Christ. When the Lord said to Saul, "It is hard for thee to kick against the pricks," it was His merciful call to surrender. The mercy and the victory came when Saul answered, "Lord, what wilt thou have me to do?" God is rich in mercy through Jesus Christ His Son.

IV. He obtained mercy **that Jesus Christ might shew forth all longsuffering in him.** Not only that he might be saved from a life of rebellion and coming wrath, but that he may become a lantern through which the long-suffering goodness and patience of Christ might shine forth. The longsuffering Christ was revealed to him and in him, that He might be revealed through him. The obtaining of mercy has to do with the honour and glory of God, as well as with our own salvation.

V. He obtained mercy, **that he might be a pattern to them which should hereafter believe on him.** In obtaining mercy, he not only became an exhibition of the grace of God, but an example to encourage all those who desired to trust Jesus Christ, with the view of obtaining that mercy which means "life everlasting." Seeing, then, that the conversion of Saul is to be taken as a *sample* of the saving mercy of God, what great encouragement there is for sinners of every age to believe on the Lord Jesus Christ. It is said that Abraham Lincoln gave orders to his doorkeepers never to turn away anyone petitioning for life. All the doorkeepers of the House of God have the same instructions. If you are seeking life, eternal life, here is mercy for you. Have you obtained it?

DARKNESS AND DAWN.

"THE PEOPLE WHICH SAT IN DARKNESS SAW GREAT LIGHT; AND TO THEM WHICH SAT IN THE REGION AND SHADOW OF DEATH, LIGHT IS SPRUNG UP" (Matt. 4. 16).

"DARKNESS" as emblematic of an unsaved state, is very frequently referred to in the unerring Word of God. Salvation is represented as a being "called *out of* darkness *into* His marvellous light." Those who have experienced this change, cannot but be perfectly conscious of it. In this verse there is a description of—

I. **Man's Condition without Christ.** "The people which sit in darkness."

1. Darkness implies a state of IGNORANCE. Christ is the Light of the World; to be ignorant of Christ is to be in darkness about the Father, for "no man knoweth the Father but the Son, and he to whom the Son will reveal Him."

2. Darkness implies SUPERSTITION. Where there is no light there is sure to be false and exaggerated views of things. The light of God's truth always reveals the foolishness of man's wisdom. His darkened mind cannot think the thoughts of God, and so he builds castles which have no foundation but in the air of his own fancy.

3. Darkness implies DANGER. The position is described in the text as being "*in* the region and shadow of death." To be in the malarial region of unforgiven sin, is to be in the shadow of the second death. Those who are in darkness cannot see the shadow; this makes their condition all the more perilous. To be in ignorance of Christ the

Saviour is to be already in the region of death, having no fitness for the regions beyond, of eternal life and glory.

4. Darkness implies a condition of HELPLESSNESS. "They *sat* in darkness." When the light dawned upon them they were *sitting* in darkness, as if they did not know where to go or what to do. This is the attitude of those who have, through failure and disappointment, come to an utter end of themselves. All the sparks of their own kindling only made the darkness the more dense. It was when they discovered their own helplessness and hopelessness, that the "great light sprung up" (Matt. 4. 16). The darkest hour is the hour before day-break.

II. **God's Effectual Remedy.** "The people which sat in darkness saw *great light*." The light that has come through the appearing of Jesus Christ is indeed a "great light." Those who are not satisfied with sunlight will never be satisfied with any light, for there is no greater than this. Those who do not find the light of Christ sufficient for the darkness of their hearts and lives, will for ever remain in darkness, for there is no greater light than this. There is nothing like light for overcoming darkness. Christ is that light, and this true light now shineth.

As darkness is emblematic of ignorance, superstition, danger and helplessness, so light is emblematic of knowledge, truth, safety and power. This light has come as God's message of hope "To them which sit in the region and shadow of death" (Matt. 4. 16). Alas, that so many should condemn themselves, by preferring the darkness to the light, because they love the deeds that are evil (John 3. 19). There be many who have *seen* this "great light," but there are few who follow it. While ye have the light, believe in it, and ye shall not walk in darkness, but shall have the light of life.

RESCUE WORK BY ANGELS.

GENESIS 19. 1.

"THERE came two angels to Sodom." *Angels* in *Sodom*! What a contrast. The brightest and holiest of servants in the darkest and wickedest cities. Even slumwork may become angelic. These messengers of mercy and of judgment are examples to all who desire to rescue the perishing. Notice—

I. **Where they Went.** They went to "Sodom" (v. 1). A city reeking with iniquity, and they went conscious that their eyes and ears must see and hear things that would pierce their souls with an agony of pain and distress, but they were prepared to suffer, they were willing even to "abide in the street all night" (v. 2). Those who would seek the salvation of others must be ready to sacrifice their own comfort and ease.

II. **Why they Went.** They went because the Lord sent them (v. 13). They did not go because they felt that the wickedness of the city demanded that *something* should be done, or because they had nothing else more urgent to do. No. They went with a definite commission at the bidding of the Lord. They realised that the work was not theirs, but God's. They had come in His Name, and in His strength, to do His will among them, and it would be done. The servants of Christ will soon grow weary in well-doing if they have not this perfect assurance, that they are in the very place and doing the very work He has sent them to do.

III. **What they Went to Do.** They went to preach instant salvation and coming judgment. "Up, get you out of this place, for the Lord will destroy this city" (v. 14). They had no scheme of social reform to propose. Those Sodomites were condemned already. There was no alternative left them but to escape or perish. The eyes of these Heaven-sent messengers were wide awake to the real facts of the case, so that they could do nothing else but press home their one message of warning and hope. They spoke and acted as those who believed in the "wrath to come," and who saw the peril of those who were disposed to "linger" through indecision (v. 16). There was no time like "*now*" to them: "Behold, now is the day of salvation." So urgent were these evangelists that they literally laid hold of Lot, his wife, and his two daughters (v. 16). *Personal* dealing they felt was a pressing necessity if souls were to be rescued from the approaching doom. Why should preachers of the Gospel not be as earnest and as urgent as these two heralds were? Have they not as definite a message to deliver? Is there not the same danger of destruction awaiting those who believe not, nor obey the Gospel? (1 Thess. 5. 3). "This one thing I do" which characterised these "sent ones" is a special feature in all those who have been called of God and sent. He maketh His ministers a *flame* of fire.

THE TRUE AND THE FALSE REFUGE.

"A MAN SHALL BE AN HIDING PLACE" (Isa. 32. 2).
"THE REFUGE OF LIES" (Isa. 28. 17).

Two hiding places are brought before us here. The one is the refuge of truth, the other is a refuge of lies. The one is a *Man*, the other is an imagination. The first is a revelation from God, the second is an invention of man. All men feel their need of a refuge of some kind or other, but all men are not equally safe in their place of refuge. It is of vital importance that we should know now the true from the false. It will be too late for the self-deceived to find out this distinction when their "refuge of lies" is being swept away. Here then are some of the features of the true, God-appointed refuge. The true refuge is the place of—

I. Conscious Safety. "A man shall be an hiding place *from the wind*, and a *covert from the tempest.*" Those who have fled to the Man Christ Jesus, as a refuge for the soul, are now being sheltered from the wind and tempest of sin and judgment The wind round about them may be as bitter and terrible as ever, but they *are being saved* from its power, and they know it. Their refuge saves them. Is your refuge saving you from being turned aside by the sudden blasts of sin and the pressing storms of iniquity. If your hiding place—that in which you trust—is not sheltering you day by day, then your refuge is a refuge of lies.

II. Friendship and Communion. "A *man* shall be an hiding place." This is the man who is God's fellow (Zech. 13. 7). All those who have fled for refuge to the true hiding-place are in the fellowship and friendship of the Lord Jesus Christ. They are reconciled to God, and rejoicing in Him. They know assuredly that *God* is their refuge and strength. Does your hiding-place bring you into contact and communion with God? Does that in which you trust for salvation make Christ unspeakably precious to your soul? If your refuge is not *in Him*, it is a refuge of lies that the judgment of hail shall sweep away, and the waters of desolation overflow. God's only refuge for the sin-smitten souls of men is the MAN who was smitten for sin. "Other refuge have I none." "I flee to *Thee* to hide me" (Psa. 143. 9).

III. Rest and Refreshing. "A man shall be...as rivers of water in a dry place." Those who have found the true refuge of the soul know of it and enjoy it, for they now drink the living waters of satisfaction. In their place of hiding they find the source of abiding blessing. Their Rock of refuge has become a fountain of delight. Here everlasting springs abide, and never-withering flowers. They heard the Divine call, "If any man thirst, let him come unto *Me* and drink;" they obeyed, and found in Him salvation from the wind and the tempest of sin and wrath, and waters of cleansing and refreshing. Does your hiding place bring cleansing for your soul, and yield refreshing streams for your thirsty heart. If you are not happier and holier through that in which you trust for salvation, your hiding place is, in the sight of God, only a "refuge of lies." If that so-called *faith* of yours is not saving you from your sins, and bringing refreshing and gladness into your life, then it is a delusion; it is not faith in Jesus Christ, for all that believe in Him are justified from all things. A dying infidel was exhorted by his companion to "Hold on." "I am quite willing to hold on," said the dying man, "if I knew what to hold on by." He had no Christ, and so had no hope, for all refuges of lies will be swept away.

> "Jesus, Lover of my soul,
> I will to Thy bosom fly "

GOD-SHINE.

"GOD HATH SHINED IN OUR HEARTS" (2 Cor. 4. 6).

WHEN the blessed sunshine breaks out from behind the thick clouds of darkness, there is no mistaking the fact that a great change has taken place. This is just such a change as takes place in the benighted soul of man when the *light* of the knowledge of God breaks through the darkness.

I. **The Source of this Shining.** "GOD hath shined." This light is not of man's kindling. Out of the darkness within no such light could ever be produced. Only He who could "command the light to shine out of darkness" could cause such a light to shine in the sin-darkened hearts of men. The light of the knowledge of God is the light of God Himself. It is a definite and direct act of the infinite mercy and goodness of God upon the individual soul. "God hath shined." God, who is Light, and in whom is no darkness at all, is still shining through His Son Jesus Christ, by His Word.

II. **The Place of this Shining.** "God hath shined *in our hearts.*" The brightest thing in Heaven is the darkest place on earth. This God-shine in the heart brings with it a double revelation. It shows by way of contrast how dark the heart by nature was, and how hopeless it was for it in itself to create such a soul-satisfying light. It is also a revelation of the character and presence of God in the heart. This is not so much a light created by God, as it is the light of the *presence* of God in the heart. Into every dark crevice of the soul this shining has come. It is the nature of light to cast its influence over everything that is anywhere within its reach. In shining into the *heart* this light enters into every act and deed of the life, into every thought and feeling and motive of the soul's activities. *God* hath shined His light, and wisdom has come to take the place of our darkness and ignorance. The god of this world had *blinded* the mind, but the God of Heaven hath shined in our hearts to give the light of the knowledge of God (v. 4).

III. **The Purpose of this Shining.** "To give the light of *the knowledge of the glory of God, in the face of Jesus Christ.*" This shining of God, in His glorious grace, upon and in the heart, gives us to know something of that glory that has come to God in and through His Son Jesus Christ. God hath shined in our hearts in answer to the atoning death of His Son, by which His Holy Name has been glorified. This shining assures us of much more than the *existence* of God, it is the manifestation of His glory—the glory of His *saving* grace—in the face or character of Jesus Christ. As all the colours of nature are in one single ray

of pure white light, so all the attributes of God are perfectly harmonised and embodied in this revelation of
Himself. *Knowledge* is light, but the knowledge of the
glory of God which is radiant on the face of Jesus Christ,
is the brightest and most effectual light that ever pierced
the darkness of a human heart. It is a light that transforms the whole inner man, and that adorns with the
beauty of the Lord; it is the dawning of that great eternal
day upon the soul, which will never be followed by the
darkness of night but which will brighten as the hours and
years go by, until the *perfect* day of perfect likeness, face
to face. God hath shined. Walk in the light and ye shall
not stumble.

A DREADED BLESSING.

"FOR THE MORNING IS TO ALL OF THEM AS THE SHADOW OF DEATH"
(Job 24. 17, R.V.).

THE moral nature of any man must be sadly perverted,
when the bright rays of the morning dawn are to him as
the shadows of death. All rebels against the light are
lovers of iniquity (v. 13). "Men love darkness rather
than the light, *because* their deeds are evil."

I. **The Contrast.** "The morning...the shadows of
death." The difference is that of day and night, life and
death, good and evil.

1. The "morning" is suggestive of PLEASURE. "Light is
sweet, and it is a pleasant thing for the eye to behold the
sunshine." How beautiful and fresh is the morning dawn,
with all its new revelations and silent benedictions. What
a lovely emblem of the dawn of spiritual life in the soul.

2. The "morning" is suggestive of PRIVILEGE. With the
morning light comes all the opportunities and possibilities
of a new day. The darkness as a difficulty in the way of
general labour is removed and the generous sunshine pours

its cheering beams into every needy corner where its
progress is not obstructed The voice of the morning is,
"Awake, awake, put on strength." Behold now is the
day of salvation. "The night cometh when no man can
work."

3. The "shadow of death" is suggestive of GATHERING
DARKNESS. The bright, hopeful light has died away, and
the thick gloomy clouds of darkness are spreading quickly
over the sky. Those who have been thankfully using the
daylight have entered into rest, while those who have been
idling away their time have lost their opportunity.
Spiritually, this is a very melancholy condition to be in.

4. The "shadow of death" is suggestive of FUTURE
HOPELESSNESS. It is that awful shadow which is the certain
forerunner of eternal separation. *Death* is not far away
when its shadow has come. What prospect can a man
have of re-establishing his lost character when the shadow
of death is already upon him? While death does not end
all, it is the end of all opportunity, as far as this life is
concerned.

II. **The Anomaly.** "The morning is to them *as* the
shadow of death." This is a most unnatural and wretched
state to be in. It betrays a condition of perfect moral
disorder; an inherent unfitness for the enjoyment of God's
order of things. Why should God's brightest gifts be to
them as the darkness of doom? Why should the light of
the Gospel be to some as the shadow of death, instead of the
morning dawn of the light of life? The more brightly this
light of truth shines, the more dark does the sky of their
self-created hopes become; so, to them the "morning" of
God's light of salvation is as the shadow of death—

1. Because it awakens the FEAR OF DISCOVERY. Like
the thief, the murderer, and the adulterer, they love the
darkness better than the light, because it is better suited

for their vile purposes. The morning light is as it were the death blow to their ungodly prospects. That which is good very good, is to them bad, because it exposes and condemns their own badness. Those who wrap themselves up in the garment of self-righteousness cannot bear the glare of God's unsullied truth, because it reveals their boasted righteousness to be nothing but filthy rags. They would rather have the pleasures of darkness, the delusive joys of sin, to the pure delights of holiness that comes to us through the shining of His Word. The man who is afraid of Heaven's light is an enemy to God at heart. He that loves the light comes into the light that his life and character might be tested and purified. To them who love not the Lord Jesus Christ, His coming again, as the Bright and Morning Star, will be to them indeed as the shadow of death, for they will be consumed by the brightness of His coming.

A DIVINE COMPLAINT.

"My people doth not consider" (Isa. 1. 3).

THOUGHTFULNESS about the things of the world, and thoughtlessness about the things of eternity, is a very common sin among the people of God. Superficial thinking leads to superficial living. The ox knoweth his owner, and the ass his master's crib, but how often the Lord's people fail to recognise their Owner, or the blessings He provides for them. Inconsiderateness is a great hindrance to the growth of spiritual life and to usefulness because it is dishonouring to God. Mere talk and mechanical action will never be a substitute for solemn heart reflection. If we would take time to meditate until the fire burns, our testimony would not be so powerless and fruitless. "My people doth not consider." This is the language of wounded love. Think on some of those things which *we* fail to consider as we ought, and of which God might justly complain. "My people doth not consider"—

I. The Pit out of which they have been Digged, or they would be more Humble. How ready we are, like Israel, to forget our bondage in Egypt, and as we look upon other worldly, sin-sodden lives, fail to remember that such were some of us.

II. The Cost at which they have been Redeemed, or they would be more Thankful. Not with silver and gold, but with that blood which speaks of the sacrifice of Divine love and of life. Have I considered it sufficiently that the peace which I now enjoy was purchased by the blood of Christ's Cross, and that it is mine, not for any good in me, but because of His infinite mercy and grace?

III. Their Relationship to Him who Saves, or they would be more Restful. "Ye are not your own." Ye belong to Christ. Have we thought deep enough into this blessed truth? As members of His body, will He not be very careful over us? Why take anxious thought about your physical life; does not your Father know that you have need of these things? "Let not your heart be troubled, ye believe in God, believe also in *Me*."

IV. Their Privileges as Sons, or they would be more Joyful. Because ye are sons, God hath sent forth His Spirit into your hearts, that ye might cry "Abba— My Father," and that He might in answer to that cry "supply all your need."

V. Their Responsibility as Servants, or they would be more Watchful. *Now* is the acceptable time for self-sacrificing service, as well as the day of salvation. To-day if ye will hear His voice, harden not your hearts. All who have received the Gospel become custodians of it, and are responsible to the Master for it. Watch ye, therefore.

VI. **The Gift of the Holy Spirit, or they would be more Fruitful.** "Know ye not that your body is the temple of the Holy Ghost in you, which ye have of God." Do you reckon on Him as a Teacher and Comforter, and as the Endurer of power? Do you consider Him all-sufficient for you in the work of God?

VII. **The Glory that is Coming, or they would be more Praiseful.** The glory that is yet to be revealed in and through the redeemed of God, is the glory that belongs to the eternal Son of God. They shall *see* His face, they shall be *like* Him, and shall be *with* Him where He is. Consider your ways, and consider Him, for a book of remembrance is written before Him for them that *thought upon* His Name.

―――

"SPRING UP, O WELL!"

NUMBERS 21. 17.

At the beginning of the journeyings of the children of Israel, Moses was commanded to *smite* the rock in Horeb that water may flow forth for the thirsty people. Now, nearly forty years after, he is told to *speak* to the rock, but in anger he smote it twice, for which disobedience he was prevented from entering the promised land (20. 10-12). That Rock was Christ, says the Apostle (1 Cor. 10. 4), and as such it was not the purpose of God that it should be smitten *twice*. He suffered *once* in the end of the age to put away sin. Now we have but to *speak* to the Rock that the refreshing stream may spring up. This sweet little word—"Spring up, O well"—contains—

I. **A Suggestive Metaphor.** "A *well*." A well within a rock. This rock is Christ, the Fountain of living water. Like Jacob's well, it is *deep*, deep as the fathomless fullness of God. The waters in this well represent the

unsearchable riches of Christ—that which is abundantly
able to satisfy all the needs of a human soul.

II. **A Felt Need.** "*Spring up*, O well." Spring thou
up in my thirsty soul, for I have been to the broken cisterns
of earth, and am disappointed, and perishing of thirst.
Spring up, O well, in this desert life of mine, that has
hitherto brought forth no fruit unto God. My heart
thirsteth for God, yea the living God.

III. **A Great Encouragement.** This well can "spring
up," so that its life-giving stream may be within the reach
of every needy one. There is a tremendous pressure in
this spring. It is the pressure of infinite love, a force
that can send its influence into the deepest depths of need,
and up to the highest heights of satisfaction and spiritual
attainment.

IV. **A Simple Means.** "Spring up." *Speak* ye to the
rock. This rock is waiting to yield its treasures to those
who ask. *Speak*, you don't need to shout Your speech
need not be eloquent. Prayer is a very simple thing when
it is real. The remedy for soul-thirst is to speak to the
rock. *Speak* to it when your heart is smitten with barrenness and death. *Speak* to it when burdened with the dying
need of others. Speak to it believingly, and the waters
will gush out, then ye shall be able to "*Sing* unto it."

THE DIVINE VISITOR

"Behold I stand at the door and knock" (Rev 3. 20).

Christ *knocking* at the door is a proof that He has come
very *near*, and that to bless us. It also implies His
willingness to come in, and the heart's reluctance to let
Him in. Man's nature is like a house with many rooms.
The Lord knocks at the door of each apartment that He
might have access to the whole house of Mansoul.

I. He Knocks as a Redeemer *that He might save.*
Save the sleeping conscience from sleeping the sleep of
death.   As the One who paid the ransom for the soul, He
knocks that He might get into possession of His blood-
bought property, that it might be saved from the
destructive hands of the enemy.   "If any sinful man opens
the door I will come in to Him" (Rev. 3. 20).

II. He Knocks as a Physician *that He might heal.*
He knows that all the inmates of this house of Mansoul are
sick and in need of His healing touch.   The whole head is
sick, the heart faint, and the hands and the knees are feeble.
There is, in fact, "no soundness," the whole inner life
has been polluted with the poison of sin.   Behold, thy
Healer is at the door.   "If any sin-sick man opens the
door I will come in to him" (Rev. 3. 20).

III. He Knocks as a Teacher *that He might instruct.*
He is the great Teacher come from God who can anoint the
eyes of His pupils with the heavenly eye-salve, that they
may see and understand heavenly things.   The minds,
blinded by Satan, can be beautifully illumined by Him
who is the Wisdom of God.   "If any unlearned man opens
the door I will come in to Him" (Rev. 3. 20).

IV. He Knocks as a King *that He might rule.*   A life
that is self-centred is a ruined one.   As Lord He knocks
that He might so get into that life which He hath redeemed
by His life as to govern and control it for its own good and
His glory.   Until the King is enthroned within, the soul is
under the bondage and tyranny of foolish and presumptuous
self.   He wishes the government of your life to be upon
His shoulders, that there might be no mismanagement in
the affairs of the soul.   Although He is "King of our
lives," He does not compel, He knocks.   "If any man
opens the door I will come in to him" (Rev. 3. 20).

V. He Knocks as a Merchantman *that He might enrich*. He knows the poverty of those who say that they are rich and have need of nothing. Unsearchable riches are in *Himself*, and infinite mercy and love has brought Him to the very door of your impoverished life that you might be filled out of His fullness. "I counsel you to buy of ME gold refined in the fire, that you may become rich" (Rev. 3. 18). You buy without money when you let the Merchant in. "If any poor man opens the door I will come in to him" (Rev 3. 20).

VI. He Knocks as a Bridegroom *that He might woo*. His desire is not only to save, heal, teach, rule, and enrich, but to have the *fellowship* of those whom He hath blessed. He knocks at the door of the heart because He seeks admission into the affections. Three times Peter heard this knock, "Lovest thou Me" (John 21. 15). Because He loves us so much, He is very jealous of our affections. If you have admitted Him as Saviour and King, surely you will give Him with your allegiance the love of your heart and the fellowship of your life. His love constrains Him to knock that our love might constrain us to open, so that every barrier between the soul and Christ may be removed, and unbroken communion enjoyed. "If anyone listens to My voice and opens the door I will come in" (Rev. 3. 20).

CHRIST THE END OF THE LAW.

"FOR CHRIST IS THE END OF THE LAW FOR RIGHTEOUSNESS TO EVERY ONE THAT BELIEVETH" (Rom 10. 4)

I. What is the Law? As God's revealed standard it is "holy, just, and good," therefore a revelation of His holiness, justice, and goodness. The source of the law is holy, the character of it is just, the purpose of it is good.

II. What is the End of the Law? "Christ is the end of the law." This blessed fact may be interpreted in different ways. The end of the law, for a thief, is the prison; for a murderer, it is the rope. The end of the law for all sinners, is condemnation or Christ. The end of a book is to instruct; of a watch, to keep time; or a lamp, to give light; the end of the law is to bring us to Christ. It came as a tutor (slave) for this very purpose (Gal. 3. 24). The end of the avenger of blood is to kill, and in seeking to do so he often chased the manslayer into the city of refuge.

III. Why did Christ become the End of the Law? It was "for righteousness." He did not come to act in defiance of the law, but to fulfil it. He was made under the law, that its holy and just claims might be perfectly satisfied in Him. He became obedient unto death, and so brought to an end the righteous demands of the law against all those who are in Him. He is now made of God unto us *"righteousness"* (1 Cor. 1. 30).

IV. To Whom is Christ the End of the Law? "To every one that believeth." "By Him all that believe are justified from all things" (Acts 13. 39). The end of an unalterable law to Daniel, in the eyes of his enemies, was the *lions' den*, but to him *God* was the end of that law for deliverance. To those who are out of Christ, there is no end to the demands and threatenings of that offended and insulted law. Only those who are ignorant of the righteousness of God would ever go about seeking to establish their own. To submit to the *righteousness* of God is the only wise thing to do, and you do this when you cease from your own works and believe on the Lord Jesus Christ, who made an end of the law, and brought in for you everlasting righteousness.

PULLED OUT OF THE FIRE.

JUDE 23

WHAT is more alarming than an outbreak of fire? What excitement! What consternation! What strenuous, self-sacrificing efforts to save the perishing inmates from the blazing tenement. The fire of sin broke out in Eden, and has spread over the whole world. The only way of escape is by that ladder which Jacob saw, which reaches from earth to Heaven (John 14 6) Think of the—

I. **Nature of Sin** It is compared here to "fire." Fire is an element that can neither be weighed nor measured. Who can set a boundary to the workings of sin, or reckon up its capabilities and effects? The nature of sin, like fire, is to mar or destroy all that comes within its grasp that is not able to resist its mighty influence. Sin is an unquenchable fire, as far as the wisdom and power of man is concerned.

II. **Danger of the Sinner.** As he needs to be "pulled out" of the fire, it is clear that he must be *in the fire*. He is living under the power and dominion of sin, therefore, *in* sin. He may be utterly unconscious of his awful position, but the end is destruction all the same. To be in a state of sin is to be in a state of condemnation. Sin, like fire, when it is finished, bringeth forth death.

III. **Work of Rescue.** "Pulling them out of the fire." There are only two ways whereby a brand can be saved from the burning: either put out the fire, or pull out the brand. Men cannot put out the fire of sin, so sinners must be pulled out of the fire. In this world of sin the Church is God's fire brigade—a rescue party sent to pull men out of the fire. There is no escape from sin's destructive power but by being *separated* from it. The love of Christ is the constraining motive.

FIRE IN AN ASYLUM.

On the 27th January, 1903, fire broke out in a London lunatic asylum. Of the 300 inmates, 50 perished and 250 had to be literally *pulled out of the fire.* While the work of rescue was going on, these poor insane creatures behaved in such a way as to remind us very forcibly of how insane sinners behave when their salvation is earnestly sought after by others. It was reported that—

"Some laughed at the mention of fire." Only fools could laugh at a calamity like this. Fools make a mock at sin. Only those who are morally insane would dare to trifle with the fire of sin.

"Some said they would not leave their bed in the night and go out." They would not consent to leave their present enjoyment, even to save their lives. There are many like this, who prefer the pleasures of a condemned state to the joys of salvation. Their madness is self-evident by the choice they make.

"Some were found hiding under the bed from the fire." In their refuge of lies, they said, "Peace, peace, when there was no peace." No one but a fool can suppose that a bed of ease or of indifference is any protection against a consuming fire. Be sure your sin, like a fire, will find you out.

"Some seemed to fancy that the rescuers had made the fire." They were blamed for trying to "burn them up." You would think, to hear some people speak, that preachers were the makers of Hell, and the disturbers of the peace, by seeking to convince men of sin and to pull them out of their perishing condition. Of course in making a charge like this they only prove that they are beside themselves.

"Many of them fought against their rescuers, biting and tearing their hair out." What a melancholy picture; what a sad proof of insanity—warring against those who were

sacrificing themselves for their deliverance. It is no uncommon experience for those who seek to pull men out of the fire of sin to have their Christ-like efforts gnashed upon with their teeth, and to have their merciful motives torn to pieces. Only spiritual lunatics could behave in this fashion.

"*Some were heard knocking at a closed door to get out, when it was too late.*" It must have been a terrible awakening to come to their senses and find themselves imprisoned in a devouring fire. Those who refuse to be pulled out of the fire of sin will perish in it. "How shall ye escape, if ye neglect so great salvation?"

"*Every sane man and woman went to the rescue.*" The time was short; the doom of the unsaved was certain; the work was great and urgent; every other interest was set aside; the one thing needful was the salvation of souls. All sane Christians make it their chief business to get souls pulled out of the fire of sin. Are you out or in?

"ASK FOR THE OLD PATHS."
Jeremiah 6. 16.

In these days the spiritual pilgrim comes to many a cross road, so that there is need for *standing* and *asking* for the old paths if there is any doubt in the mind as to their real whereabouts.

I. **Why ask for the Old Paths?** Because the *new* ones are delusive and destructive. The new paths are men's miserable substitutes for the grand old "highway" of God, which only beguile the unwary into Doubting Castle, the habitation of Giant Despair. Even though an angel from Heaven should preach a new Gospel, let him be accursed. Ask for the old paths, and be steadfast therein.

II. **What are the Old Paths?** The old paths are the

paths that were trodden by Abel, Abraham, Moses, David, Elijah, and all the prophets and apostles, who believed God and accepted His Word as a lamp to their feet, and the testimony of His Son as the sure foundation of their hope. The *revealed will* of God is the old unerring path that leads to peace and paradise. This is the old light that is as trustworthy as the sun; the new lights are mere "will-o'-the-wisps" dancing about the bogs. The old paths are sprinkled with the blood of atonement; the new with the rose-water of men-pleasing.

III. **Why we should Walk in the Old Paths.** Because there we find—

1. THE BLOOD OF CHRIST TO JUSTIFY. All pilgrims in the "old paths" are forgiven, and justified through the blood of His Cross; the new path wanderers know nothing of this.

2. THE WORD OF GOD TO SATISFY. They have not followed cunningly-devised fables, but the true light that shineth in this dark place. The testimony of Jesus is the spirit of prophecy. The plausible theories and philosophies of men may beguile for a time, but they cannot bring abiding satisfaction to the heart and conscience.

3. THE POWER OF THE SPIRIT TO SANCTIFY. The makers of the new paths have no place for the quickening, sanctifying, enduing power of the Holy Ghost. Along their new and tardy way there is no missionary enthusiasm, no felt need of being filled with the Spirit, no joy in the Holy Ghost, no glorying in the Cross of Christ, no conversions from sin and self to God. The old paths are the paths of peace, pleasure, and power, because they are the paths in which the Son of God still walks in company with His followers. "Ask for the old paths, where is the good way, and walk therein, and ye shall find rest for your souls."

AN OPEN DOOR FOR YOU.

"Behold, I have set before thee an open door" (Rev. 3. 8).

When out of work, honest tradesmen have often to say, with heavy heart and weary feet, "I can't get an opening." How sad a world it would be if there was no opening for weary, sin-burdened souls in the love of God, or the grace of Jesus Christ. The work of Christ was the work of an Opener. Sin had closed the door into every spiritual privilege, but He who has now the keys of death and of hades hath set before us—

I. **The Open Door of Salvation.** "I am the Door, by Me, if any man enter in, he shall be saved." This is a door of escape from the wrath of God, from the guilt and pollution of sin, from the fear of man, and the tyranny of self. It is for you, therefore you may have boldness to enter in by the blood of Jesus. Come now.

II. **The Open Door of Instruction.** The privilege of being "taught of God" is open for all. If any man lack wisdom, let him ask; the door into the Divine audience chamber is now open through the Name of Jesus. He can not only "open to you the Scriptures," but also anoint your eyes with such an eye-salve as shall make you see wonderful things in His Holy Word. He can also make you of quick understanding, wise in Christ.

III. **The Open Door of Prayer.** Others have won great victories by prayer. The same door by which they entered into fullness of blessing and triumph is open for you. "If ye ask anything in My Name." Moses, Elijah, David, Daniel, Paul, Luther, Knox, Muller, Quarrier, and hosts of other mighty ones, owed almost everything to this open door. Who can tell all the profit you shall have if you pray unto Him? (Job. 21. 15). Enter now.

IV. **The Open Door of Fellowship.** This is another

glorious privilege that is open to all saints. "If ye draw nigh unto Me, I will draw nigh unto you" (James 4. 8). The Lord needs no very urgent constraint to come and abide with us. The deepest yearning of His loving heart is that we should "abide" in Him. His difficulty with us is our closed door against Him. "Behold, I stand at the door and knock."

V. **The Open Door of Power.** Undoubtedly some have more spiritual power than others. How? Have they got into special favour with God through some hidden private door? Hath He not declared that "All power is given unto *Me*, go ye therefore" (Matt. 28. 18, 19). Go ye therefore to Him and for Him. "He giveth power to the faint, and to them that have *no might* He increaseth strength" (Isa. 40. 29). He hath set this open door before you. Wait upon Him, and ye shall change strength.

VI. **The Open Door of Service.** If you are a son, go work to-day in His vineyard; the door is open for you, and your work is waiting on you. What can I do? Do what you are told, "Go, and work." Christ does not compel us to serve or follow Him, but He commands and invites. Who then is willing to consecrate his service to the Lord, service of heart and voice, of mind and means? In every foreign mission field, wide doors, and effectual, are set open before us.

VII. **The Open Door of Heaven.** "I go to prepare a place for you." Those who are Christ's have no fear of ever getting this door closed against them. He has opened it, and no man shutteth. Let us be faithful now, taking full advantage of the privileges offered us, that so an abundant entrance shall be ministered unto us on that day, when we come to enter through this gate into the city. Beware of acting the part of the foolish virgins who were outside when "the door was shut."

THE DEATH OF CHRIST.

Isaiah 53. 10, 11.

WHAT the sun is to the Heavens and the earth, the death of Christ is to the Bible and to Christianity. Look at—

I. **The Nature of It.** "It pleased the Lord to bruise Him, He hath put Him to grief." The Rationalist can only see in Christ's death a martyr to Jewish malice and Roman contempt; but it pleased Jehovah to bruise Him. "He spared not His own Son, but delivered Him up for us all." He was bruised between the upper and nether millstones of God's justice and man's guilt. He could say, "No man taketh My life from Me, I lay it down of Myself." His was a voluntary, God-ordained sacrifice.

II. **The Purpose of It.** "To make His soul an offering for sin." What an infinite depth of difference there was between *"His soul"* and *"sin."* Only God can fully judge the value of the one and the demerit of the other. The greatness of the price reveals the awfulness of the condition. He poured out the treasures of His soul, that the sin of my soul might be taken away. The price was all-sufficient in the sight of God, and so the redemption is eternal.

III. **The Result of It.** "He shall be satisfied." A woman forgetteth her travail, for joy that a man is born into the world. He shall see of the travail of His soul, but shall He ever forget it? He shall rejoice that a bride has been born into the world, and shall be satisfied when she is safely brought home to the marriage festival and to His eternal glory. We also shall be satisfied when we awake in His likeness. Meanwhile, by life and lip we are to show forth the saving, sanctifying, satisfying power of His death till He come.

THREE ASPECTS OF SALVATION.
LUKE 15.

IN this chapter we have three parables, representing three conditions of the lost, and showing three persons seeking the lost. These parables were spoken to the Pharisees and Scribes, who murmured, saying, "This man *receiveth* sinners." They show the kind of sinners He does receive, and how He does receive them. We observe—

I. A Threefold Aspect of the Lost. The—

1. LOST SHEEP—representing those who are lost to *safety*. Outside the fold means outside the count. There were ninety and nine—the lost one was not counted. The lost sheep was in danger, exposed and helpless, typical of those who are *thoughtlessly* lost, unconscious of their condition.

2. LOST MONEY—representing those lost to *usefulness*. As long as this piece of silver was lost, it was unfit to be used—good for nothing. It was not lost out in the desert, but in the house. It is possible to be in the house of God and yet lost to usefulness, like the Scribes and Pharisees, to whom these words were spoken. It is possible to have a saved soul and yet have a lost life. To be out of the hand of Him to whom we belong as redeemed ones, is to be in a condition of uselessness. When a piece of money is lost it is not only the base metal that's lost, but all the good that money might do.

3. LOST SON—representing lost *fellowship*. Out of communion with the Father: a condition of degradation and dishonour brought about by a deliberate choice and wilful separation from His presence. Thus is the backslider lost to fellowship with God through his love of the world.

II. A Threefold Salvation. In these three parables we may see the desires and longings of the Father, Son, and Holy Spirit toward the lost ones.

1. THE SHEPHERD SEEKS THE LOST SHEEP TO SAVE IT. Here we have the work of the Son revealed. He goes *after* the lost, leaving His all behind, in order that He might find it. At great *sacrifice* He seeks to save.

2. THE WOMAN SEEKS THE LOST SILVER TO USE IT. This suggests the mission of the Holy Spirit. The money is lost in the house. She lights a candle and sweeps the house. Dust and darkness usually are the causes why the Holy Ghost cannot get hold of our lives to use them. The light of the truth has to be brought from without, and the dust of inward corruption stirred up within, that confession and surrender may be made. The unsaved one has just to be outside the fold to be a lost soul; the saved one has just to be outside the control and touch of the Holy Spirit to be a lost life. He, like this woman, seeks to save those lost to a life of service for God.

3. THE FATHER SEEKS HIS LOST SON TO HAVE FELLOWSHIP WITH HIM. The Father does not go forth to seek; He *waits* and longs for the coming prodigal. The loss of love is a great loss. He calls on the backsliding ones *to return*, and promises healing to such. It is sad to find Christians in this terrible plight—out of fellowship with God. For such two things are needed: (1) To come to themselves. (2) To come back to their Father.

III. **A Threefold Rejoicing.** There is joy in Heaven over the salvation of—

1. A LOST SOUL. The value is unspeakable, the joy is never-ending.

2. A LOST SERVANT. Grieve not the Holy Spirit. Yield yourselves unto God. Ye are bought with a price.

3. A LOST SON. Love restored, and the peace and fellowship enjoyed. In this threefold salvation—the heart of God the Father, God the Son, and God the Holy Ghost—one heart, is made glad.

SEED THOUGHTS.

METAPHORS OF BELIEVERS
In 2 Corinthians.

Epistles, chap. 3. 3; Ministers, chap. 3. 6; Vessels, chap. 4. 7; Workers, chap. 6. 1; Temples, chap. 6. 16; Sons and Daughters, chap. 6. 18.

FELLOWSHIP WITH ONE ANOTHER.
1 John 1. 7.

Here are several powerful reasons why believers ought to keep in fellowship with one another:—

1. All are born of the same Father (John 1. 13).
2. All are bought with the same Price (1 Cor. 6. 20).
3. All are members of the same Body (Col. 1. 18).
4. All are taught by the same Spirit (John 16. 13).
5. All are walking in the same Path (2 Cor. 5. 7).
6. All are serving the same Master (Matt. 23. 8).
7. All are heirs of the same Inheritance (Rom. 8. 17).

SEVEN GREAT FACTS IN JOHN 3.

1. The gift of God (16), ... *Love.*
2. The mission of Christ (17), ... *Salvation.*
3. The work of the Spirit (8), ... *Quickening.*
4. The need of man (3), ... *New Life.*
5. The way of life (14, 15), ... *Believing.*
6. The consequence of unbelief (18, 19), *Condemnation.*
7. The evidence of faith (21),   .. *Works.*

CHRIST'S SEVENFOLD PRAYER FOR HIS PEOPLE IN JOHN 17.

1. That they might be *kept through His Name* (11).
2. That they might have *His joy in themselves* (13).
3. That they might be *sanctified* (17-19).
4. That they might *all be one* (21, 22).
5. That they might be a *blessing to others* (20).
6. That they might *possess the Father's love* (26).
7. That they might *behold His glory* (24).

DIVINE THOUGHTFULNESS.

"THINK UPON ME, MY GOD, FOR GOOD" (Neh. 5. 19).

I. GOD DOES THINK UPON US.

    1. He thinks upon our *Past,*   ..   Jer. 2. 2.
    2. He thinks upon our *Present,*   ..   Ezek. 16. 60.
    3. He thinks upon our *Future,*   ..   Ezek. 16. 62.

II. GOD DOES THINK UPON US FOR GOOD. It is good for us that:

    1. His thoughts are *Great,*   ..   Isa. 55. 9.
    2. His thoughts are *Many,*   ..   Psa. 40. 5.
    3. His thoughts are *Peaceful,*   ..   Jer. 29. 11.
    4. His thoughts are *Comforting,*   Hosea 2. 14.

COURAGE.

HAVE the courage—

    1. To *Obey* like Abraham,   Gen. 12. 4; Heb. 11. 8.
    2. To *Suffer* like Moses, ... Heb. 11. 25.
    3. To *Flee* like Joseph, ... Gen. 39. 12.
    4. To *Stand* like Elijah, ... 1 Kings 17. 1.
    5. To *Persevere* like Daniel, ... Dan. 6. 10.
    6. To *Venture* like Peter, ... Matt. 14. 28, 29.
    7. To *Testify* like Paul, ... Acts 26. 22, 23

THE CHRISTIAN'S ENVIRONMENTS.

THEY are seen—

1. Among Lions, ... Psa. 57. 4.
2. Among Thorns, ... S. of S. 2. 2.
3. Among Scorpions, ... Ezek. 2. 6.
4. Among Wolves, ... Luke 10. 3.
5. Among Tares as Wheat, ... Matt. 13. 30.
6. Among the Heavenly Host,   .. 2 Kings 6. 17.
7. Surrounded by the Lord Himself,   Psa. 125. 2.

THE WAY TO GOD.

1. A Needed Way, ... Psa. 63. 1.
2. A New Way, ... Heb. 10. 19, 20
3. A Finished Way, ... 1 Peter 3. 18.
4. A Personal Way, ... John 14. 6.
5. A Safe Way, ... Heb. 7. 25.
6. A Free Way, ... Heb. 10. 20-22.
7. A Blessed Way, into all needed help, Heb. 4. 14-16.
8. An Unfailing Way, ... James 4. 8.

THE SAVING CALL.
LUKE 19. 5.

THE Call of Jesus Christ is—

1. A *Gracious* Call,   ..   He might have passed by.
2. A *Personal* Call,   ..   "Zaccheus."
3. An *Urgent* Call,   ..   "Make haste."
4. A *Humbling* Call,   ..   "Come down."
5. An *Affectionate* Call,   "Abide at thy house."
6. An *Assuring* Call,   ..   "I must."
7. An *Effectual* Call,   ..   "He made haste."

FAITH.

1. The Ear of Faith, ... 1 Kings 18. 41.
2. The Eye of Faith, ... 2 Kings 6. 17.
3. The Feet of Faith, ... Genesis 5. 24.
4. The Hand of Faith, ... Acts 3. 7.
5. The Heart of Faith, ... Rom. 10. 10.

CONDITIONS OF FELLOWSHIP.

LUKE 24. 29.

1. Consideration, "The day is far spent."
2. Invitation, .. "Abide with us."
3. Importunity, "They Constrained Him."
4. Result, .. "He went in to tarry with them."

A GREAT OPPORTUNITY.

ISAIAH 53. 6.

1. Whom? "Seek ye the Lord." 2. Why? "Because He is near." 3. When? "While He may be found." 4. How? "Seek...call." Who? "Ye."

FAITH AND SIGHT.

"HE who pinneth faith to bodily sight, to the earthly and visible, doth himself expose it to change, since all things visible are temporal, and only the invisible is eternal" (2 Cor. 4. 18).—*Gerlach.*

ORIGINAL ILLUSTRATIONS.

DISAPPOINTED WORKERS.

It has been proved that when a bird's nest has been robbed several times she builds her last nest in a more slovenly fashion. So much is she influenced by disappointment, and such results are very natural to all who are depending upon their *own works*. However things may turn out, the Christian worker must never become slovenly in his or her service for Christ. Do the last as carefully as the first, and the least as heartily as the greatest. "Whatsoever thy hand findeth to do, do it with all thy might," for ye serve the Lord Christ. Angels are never disappointed, neither are they at any time slovenly in their work. They obey and worship. "Go thou and do likewise."

SELF-APPROBATION.

The peculiar, self-conceited manners of the turkey cock are very generally known. It is so cowardly that it will fly from the most insignificant animal that dares to face it boldly; but if it can only succeed in frightening a child or a little pet dog, it will strut about the yard displaying its plumage with as much pride as if it had conquered a bull. Did you ever see what might be vulgarly called a turkey cock Christian worker? He is one who will do nothing for the Lord that implies self-sacrifice, or is likely to damage the plumage of *his own* good name in the eyes of worldly men, but who, when he does accomplish anything with seeming success, makes such an ado about it that everybody within a mile must know of it. They think others should praise them, while they are glorying in their own self-conceit.

CRABBED.

A CRABBED person is one who is usually tormented or avoided—one who is supposed to be crab-like. Yet who has not at times been ensnared in the toils of this crab? It appears that hermit-crabs are extremely *crabbed*. They will fight almost to the death with each other over a few empty shells, not a whit more suitable for them than the one they already possess. Self-seeking and covetousness always lead to crabbedness. Put off the old man with his deeds, and put on the new, and be content with such things as ye have.

THE ENCHANTMENT OF NEARNESS.

DISTANCE does not always "lend enchantment to the view." Wordsworth said, on looking at a cataract two miles off, that it was "frozen by distance." The matchless love of God, the joys of salvation, and the service of Christ are to a great many "frozen by distance." In the spiritual Kingdom nearness always lends enchantment to the view. The altogether loveliness of Christ grows increasingly as we grow in nearness to Him. It is those who are *afar off* that see no beauty in Him, and who are not enchanted by Him. "Let us draw near."

PERFECT SOUNDNESS.

IN an American locomotive shed there is an instrument something like a piano, for testing engines. The sound of each part of the engine, when in a perfect state, is in unison with the corresponding note in the testing machine. The slightest flaw in any of the parts will cause a discord, and so reveal its weakness. The Word of God is a perfect testing instrument for man's character and life. If our thoughts and acts are not in harmony with it, it is because there is some defect in us somewhere. The character that is perfectly sound will be in perfect accord with this Divine instrument.

CONVERSION.

THE emigrant sailing-ship, in passing from Europe to Australia has to go through a region called by seafaring people the "Equatorial Doldrums." This region is noted for rains and clouds, perplexing calms, and baffling winds; but the sunny land lies beyond. The emigrant soul, in passing from death to life, must go through the equatorial doldrums of conversion. The experiences here are not always the same. To some it may be a distressing calm— the painful stillness of unanswered prayer. To others it may be a region of tempest and fearful agitation. Some go quickly through, while others lie helpless for weeks and months. Anyway, don't be content to abide there. Press on to the sunny land of assured salvation (Rom. 7. 24, 25).

LOST OPPORTUNITY.

IT is said of Sir I. Newton that once having dismounted from his horse to lead him up a hill, the horse slipped his head out of the bridle, but Newton, oblivious to what had happened, went on holding the bridle till he reached the hill top, and turned to remount. While he, in his mind, was busy here and there, the horse was gone. Let us take heed, lest—while we are engrossed with other things—the opportunity of salvation does not slip away from us for ever.

THE NEW LIFE.

IT is a singular characteristic of the cuckoo that it never lays its eggs in its own nest. It deposits them in the nests of other smaller birds, where they are hatched. When the young cuckoo is strong enough it hoists the other occupants of the nest outside, and takes entire possession. This conduct seems very selfish and ungrateful, but it illustrates the process of the new life in the soul. "The expulsive power of a new affection," as Dr. Chalmers termed it. The new life, like the young cuckoo, has come from a different source—born from above. It is expected to take entire control of the whole being, and is to become a herald of the spring-time of salvation, bringing gladness and hope to others.

POWER OF CIRCUMSTANCES.

A MAN went down from Jerusalem to Jericho and fell among thieves. If you or I had gone down that way at that time we would likely have met with the same fate. We have not fallen among thieves, just because we have not been brought up among them. "In a vacuum," says Ganot, "liquids fall like solids, without separation of their molecules." Where there is no resistance, every material thing falls with the same rapidity—a feather as quick as a stone. Who can tell how much we owe to the restraining circumstances into which we have been born. Might not many of those thieves and drunkards have been as moral and religious as we are if they had got the same chance? Let this awaken thankfulness and sympathy.

REGENERATION.

IT is a well-known fact, although it is an ever-increasing wonder, that a caterpillar changes into a butterfly. There is certainly very little resemblance between the two, yet every butterfly has been a caterpillar. The butterflies can truthfully say, as they look at the poor caterpillars, "Such were some of us, but we are changed." So every saint has been a sinner, but a wonderful work has been wrought in them. The caterpillar sinner knows nothing of the delights of the butterfly saint. The only way a caterpillar can enter into the joys of the butterfly life is by being made a "new creature"—by being, in a sense, "born again." The cabbage-loving caterpillar has no capacity for the new-born movements and delights of the butterfly. No more can the carnal nature of man enter into the enjoyment of the things of God without being born again.

SHAM PROFESSORS.

THE fox is said to be the prince of all schemers. When it sees that escape is impossible it will sometimes feign death, and allow itself to be kicked and carried by the tail over one's shoulder without showing any signs of life; but as soon as opportunity offers itself it will scamper with all haste back to its old quarters. Foxy professors are not uncommon. They mingle with God's people, sing and talk as they do. You imagine them all right, but as soon as an opportunity comes in the form of some worldly amusement they decamp. It is not altogether impossible for even a Christian to feign himself dead to the world, and sin, while attending a holiness convention, and then, after these holy restraints are withdrawn, to play the fox and scamper back to the old life of selfishness.

A WARNING TO IDLERS.

TAKE heed, lest there be in any of you an evil heart of *laziness*! When bees have finished the business of swarming, and the workers have discovered that there are no lack of queens, then they with one accord fall on the drones, who are massacred without mercy. Thus Nature, in these busy bees, passes the sentence of death upon the useless idler. This is also a law in the spiritual world. Those Christians who will not work for the good of Christ's cause among men will be visited with the blight of death upon their spirits. No idler in the vineyard can possibly live in health and prosperity of soul. "Son! go work to-day!" He that will not do the work of God should not eat the food of God.

IMAGINARY GREATNESS.

FROUDE tells us that "Pompey was a weak man, ignorant of himself; and unwilling to part with his imaginary greatness, he was flung down by the cruel forces of the world." The forces of this present evil world are always too mighty for those clothed in the armour of "imaginary greatness." Only in the "armour of God" can we *stand*.

HANDFULS ON PURPOSE

SERIES VIII

PREFACE

WITH the *eighth* volume I feel constrained to offer my sincerest thanks to all who have so heartily assisted is making these books known to those who have been longing for such help as they afford, and who have been in turn truly thankful to God for them. Testimonies as to their usefulness have been innumerable.

One of the best proofs of their suitability to meet a felt need is the ever increasing demand for them by those who are busy in the thick of the fight. The assurance that many Christian workers have found them strengthening, and refreshing to their own souls, has brought much refreshing to the heart of the author. It was with this object in view that they were first offered for publication. It is but a small and ordinary matter to present thoughts to the mind, but it is, in our way of thinking, a very great matter to be able in any measure to put some freshness and inspiration into a weary, languid heart. The Word of God, as revealed in the "Scriptures of Truth," is the infallible weapon of the Holy Spirit. Our strength and our victory lie in getting into the citadel of God's mind, and in allowing and reckoning on the current of His will flowing through us, and so accomplishing His own merciful and gracious purposes with us. In His will, in His work, and in His way there is no failure and no defeat.

Brethren, be strong in the Lord, and in the power of His all-conquering might. Take that sword, the Word of God, which is the only sword the Holy Spirit believes in and uses, "Praying always with all prayer in the Spirit, and supplication for all saints, and for me."

Yours sincerely in His service,

JAMES SMITH

GENERAL INDEX OF SUBJECTS

OLD TESTAMENT STUDIES

NEW TESTAMENT STUDIES

BIBLE READINGS

Handfuls on Purpose

Old Testament Studies

DEEP CALLETH UNTO DEEP.

PSALM 42, 1-7.

THE key words to this pathetic Psalm are, " My Soul " and " My God." These are two great deeps, and the one calleth unto the other. The natural phenomenon referred to in v. 7, " Deep calleth unto deep at the noise of Thy waterspouts," may have awakened this line of thought and expression. The deep, dark cloud, calling unto the deep sea, by the voice of a whirlwind, creating a waterspout, that may have burst in the hills, flooding the river, and again making for the deep of the sea. Two deeps ; one above, and one beneath ; the God of heaven, and the soul of man. " As the hart panteth after the waterbrooks, so panteth my soul after Thee, O God." Deep calleth unto deep.

I.—MAN'S SOUL IS A GREAT DEEP. As a spiritual and immortal being, there is in him almost fathomless depths.

1. There is a great deep of NEED, "My soul thirsteth." This deep saith, satisfaction is not in me. No. Apart from God "darkness is upon the face of the deep." The Godless soul of man is but a yawning

gulf of emptiness and thirst.   This well is deeper than
Jacob's.

2. There is a great deep of POSSIBILITY.   In another place the Psalmist says," The heart is deep "
(Ps. 64, 4).   There is a great depth of capacity in it for
pain or pleasure, weal or woe.   The depth of its
capacity is the depth of its possibility.   Who can
reckon up the full capabilities of a human soul ?

3. Man's soul is also a great deep of RESPONSIBILITY.
Being an immortal spirit, eternal consequences are
involved in its thoughts and actions.

II.—GOD IS A GREAT DEEP.   The Living,
Almighty, Self-existent and Eternal God.   Who can by
searching find out the limits of the Almighty ?

1. HIS THOUGHTS are deep (Ps. 92, 4).   His thoughts
are perfectly consistent with His character.   They come
out of the great depths of His Infinite mind.

2. HIS WISDOM and KNOWLEDGE are deep.   " O
the depth of the riches both of the wisdom and knowledge of God, how unsearchable." (Rom. 11, 33-34).
God is *the* " deep thinker," and in the great depth of His
wisdom and knowledge there is for us an unsearchable
depth of *riches*.

3. HIS LOVE is deep (Eph. 3, 18-19).   We need to
be rooted and grounded in it, to be able to comprehend,
with all saints, what is its breadth, and length, and
depth, and height.   His love is as deep as His fathomless
heart.   The love that gave Jesus to die.

4. His RESOURCES are deep.   He clave the rock
and gave them water to drink out of the great depths
(Ps. 78, 8-15).   In Christ, our Spiritual Rock, there

dwelleth all the fulness of God. He is able to do exceeding abundantly.

III.—THE ONE DEEP CALLETH UNTO THE OTHER. The deep of man's need calleth unto the deep of God's fulness ; and the deep of God's fulness calleth unto the deep of man's need. Between our emptiness and His all-sufficiency there is a great gulf, but, thank God, it is not yet fixed. Deep calleth unto deep. The deep mercy of God needs our emptiness, into which it might pour itself. Man needs God, God needs man. Nothing can fully meet the depth of our need but the depth of His Almighty fulness. Out of His depths hath He cried unto me : Out of my depths have I cried unto Him (Ps. 130, 1). This is the mind and work of the Spirit, for the Spirit searcheth the deep things of God. Then, my soul, ' Launch out into the deep," and " dwell deep."

THINGS TOUCHING THE KING.
PSALM 45.

The King referred to here, who is called " God," and whose throne is " for ever and ever," can be none other than the Messiah. The heart of the writer is so filled with the riches of such a soul-warming vision that it *overflows* like a boiling pot (v. 1, R.V.). A full heart makes a ready or eloquent tongue. A clear soul-ravishing sight of the glories of Christ, and His Bride, the Church, is the best preparation for a powerful testimony (Acts 4, 20). Note what these " things " are.

I.—HIS BEAUTY. " Thou art fairer than the children of men ; grace is poured into Thy lips " (v. 2).

He is the chiefest among the thousands, in earth or in heaven. His mouth is most sweet, because of the grace that has been poured into His lips. No man ever spake like this Man. He is fairer than the children of men, because He is the express and unsullied image of the heavenly Father, full of grace and truth.

II.—HIS SWORD. "Gird Thy sword upon Thy thigh, O most mighty" (v. 3). Beauty and might are gracefully wedded in the Person of Christ. On his lips, grace ; on His thigh, a sword. The Word of God is either grace that saves, or a sword that severs. This sword is two-edged . . . . dividing . . . . and discerning (Heb. 4, 12). During these days of grace and salvation, the sword is upon the *thigh* of Him who is most mighty, but the time shall come when it shall be in His *hand* (2 Thess. 1, 8-9).

III.—HIS CAUSE. "Because of truth and meekness and righteousness" (v. 4), Christ, in vindicating truth, meekness, and righteousness, is vindicating His own character and our need. He is the Truth. He is meek and lowly in heart. He is the Lord our righteousness. The untruthful (not true to God, and men), the proud, and the self-righteous, are opposed to the cause of the Lord Jesus Christ. To love the truth, to possess a meek spirit, and to act righteously is to be in harmony with His will, in line with His purpose, and in the likeness of His character.

IV.—HIS ARROWS. "Thine arrows are sharp in the heart of the King's enemies" (v. 5). The King knoweth His enemies. His arrows are sharp, and they go straight to the *heart*, where the enmity and deceit lurks. They cut so deep that no earthly remedy can heal the wound (Acts 2, 37). These arrows are as swift as light, as straight as truth, and as unerring as the wisdom of God. Sooner or later they shall reach every heart at enmity with the King.

V.—HIS THRONE AND SCEPTRE. " Thy throne, O God, is for ever and ever ; a sceptre of equity is the sceptre of Thy kingdom " (v. 6, R.V.). The seat and method of His government are eternally the same. His throne is the symbol of eternal dignity, and His sceptre of everlasting righteousness. Every attribute of His kingly character is in favour of righteousness, and opposed to wickedness (v. 7). This is He who was made *sin* for us, that we might be made the *righteousness of God* in Him. Therefore God hath anointed Him with the oil of gladness above His fellows. He shall see of the travail of His soul, and shall be satisfied. His Divinity is undeniable.

VI.—HIS GARMENTS. " All Thy garments smell of myrrh, and aloes, and cassia, out of the ivory palaces " (v. 8). All His vestments have an unmistakable heavenly fragrance about them, because they are HIS. He is *in* them. His presence gives a new perfume to every environment. All the doctrines of His Word are as His sweet-smelling garments, that speak of the fulness and freeness of the riches of His grace. Although our eyes see Him not, yet are we conscious of the nearness of His presence by the fragrance of His garments.

VII.—HIS QUEEN. " At Thy right hand doth

stand the queen in gold of Ophir " (v. 9, R.V.). The queen of the Kingly Son of God is the Church, which is the Bride of the Lamb ; her destined place is at His " right hand," and her adorning is with the purest golden glory. Through His grace He will present it to Himself a glorious Church, not having spot or wrinkle or any such thing. Seeing that the marriage of the Lamb is coming, it becometh the Bride to make herself ready (Rev. 19, 7-8).

VIII.—HIS DAUGHTER. " The King's daughter in the inner part of the palace is all glorious " (v. 13, R.V., marg.). This Bride occupies the unique relationship of being both queen and daughter. He calls her " My sister, My spouse." She is a daughter because *born* of God ; she is a queen, because, with Him (Christ) she is seated in heavenly places, crowned with honour and glory. In the inner palace of the King she is now *all* glorious, who once like Him, and for Him, was despised and rejected of men (Isa. 61, 10). She can now truly say, " The King hath brought me into His chambers ; we will be glad and rejoice in Thee " (Ca. 1, 4). Have you accepted His loving invitation, and put on His proffered wedding garment ? (Matt. 22, 11).

PRICELESS POSSESSIONS.
PSALM 46.

This is the song of the Christian warrior. All who have put on the whole armour of God, to resist the principalities and powers of evil, will, like Luther, sing it often. Each note of this Psalm is an inspiration There are in it—

I.—AN INFALLIBLE REFUGE. " God is our Refuge and Strength." The life that is " hid in God " is surely as safe as God can make it. The eternal spirit of man needs the " Eternal God as a Refuge " (Deut. 33, 27). To hide in God, is to hide in His Love, and in His Mercy, and in His Power. This means not only perfect safety, but also perfect self-abandonment to God, to His will and work.

II.—AN IMMOVABLE CONFIDENCE. " Therefore will not we fear, though the earth be removed," etc. (vv. 3-4). What has the removing of the *earth* to do with a soul that is dwelling in GOD ? His house is built on the eternal Rock, therefore the rain, floods, or winds cannot shake it (Matt. 7, 25). The Lord, in whom we trust, is " Mightier than the noise of many waters." Let not the din of the world's tumult drown this sweet note of restfulness.

III.—AN INFINITE SUPPLY. " There is a river, the streams whereof make glad the city of God " (v. 4). New rivers of delight flow out for the soul that has found its refuge in God ; they drink now of " the river of *Thy pleasures* " (Ps. 36, 8). They are led by the still waters of God's great thoughts, and refreshed and strengthened by the living streams of eternal truth. The supplies for the new man are found in his new hiding place (Isa. 32, 2).

IV.—AN UNFAILING COMFORT. " God is in the midst . . . . God shall help . . . He uttered His voice . . . The Lord of Hosts is with us " (vv. 5-7). His abiding presence is our continual protection, and the guarantee of rest in service (Ex. 33, 14-15). When God, by His Spirit, is in the midst of thee, and when He uttereth His voice, then the earth, and the things of the earth melt.

V.—AN ASSURING PROSPECT. " Come, behold . . . what desolation He hath made . . . He maketh wars to cease," etc. (vv. 8-9). There is here a backward look and a forward look. He hath made desolations of men's works and ways in the past, and He will yet break, and cut to pieces, the instruments of destruction, and make wars to cease, unto the end of the earth (Isa. 2, 4). The angelic song at the Nativity, " Peace on earth and goodwill among men," will yet be perfectly fulfilled at the coming of the King.

VI.—A PEACEFUL ATTITUDE. " Be still, and know that I am God." Only those who have faith in God can possibly be still, when circumstances are apparently adverse. But it is in this stillness of soul that we learn to know God. " In quietness and in confidence shall be your strength " (Isa. 30, 7-15). Stand still and see the salvation of God. Hush, and let God utter His voice.

VII.—A TRIUMPHANT RESULT. " I will be exalted . . . I will " (v. 10). The Lord above shall be exalted in that day, when He becomes the Refuge and Strength of His people. It is so now, in our individual experience ; it will be so then, in His coming kingdom, when He shall be all and in all to His own.

THE GREAT CHANGE.
PSALM 51.

David had grievously sinned, and Nathan, at the command of God, had done for him what the Holy Spirit does for us. " Convinces of sin." The penitential language of this Psalm is always appropriate on the lips of a soul passing out of the agonies of conscious guilt, into the joys of forgiving grace.

I.—CONFESSIONS. Here it was deep and real " I *acknowledge* my transgressions." There was no further attempt to cover it up. " Against Thee, Thee only, have I sinned." He is conscious that his secret sin was an open insult to the name and character of God, as every sin is. " Thou desirest truth in the *inward* parts " (v. 6). He feels now more keenly than ever that God looketh on the heart. Hypocrisy, like faith and truthfulness, is a thing of the heart (Luke 11, 39). It is to such confessors that the Faithful and Just One gives forgiveness and cleansing (1 John 1, 9).

II.—PETITIONS. Where there are such confessions there will also be petitions. The vessel of the heart needs not only to be emptied of the evil, but filled with the good. His first petition is for the—

1. MERCY OF GOD. " Have mercy upon me, O God " (v. 1). Nothing but *mercy* can meet his case, and that mercy must be the mercy of God. No convicted sinner would dare to ask for justice or righteousness, only the self-righteous are presumptuous enough to think of this. Then he pleads for—

2. CLEANSING FROM SIN. "Wash me *thoroughly*
. . . and cleanse me from my sin" (v. 2). The remedy
must be as thorough as the disease. Where sin abounded,
grace did much more abound. God's infallible cure for
the guilt and pollution of sin is "The blood of Jesus
Christ, His Son." (1 John 1, 7).

3. EXPIATION FROM GUILT. "Purge me with
hyssop, and I shall be clean" (v. 7). "Expiate me by
a sin offering" is another rendering. The hyssop had
to do with the blood of the lamb (Ex. 12, 22). God's
forgiveness is always on the ground of expiation. If
the conscience is to be purged from dead and sinful
works, it must be by "the blood of Christ, who through
the eternal Spirit, offered Himself without spot to God."
(Heb. 4, 19).

4. REGENERATION OF HEART. "Create in me a
clean heart, O God" (v. 10). The remedy would not
be perfect that only dealt with past sins and present
guilt ; the *heart* which is "deceitful and wicked" must
be changed. The clean heart is a new creation. It is
a heart destitute of the love of sin, and filled with the
love of God. It is a condition described in the New
Testament as being "born again" (John 3, 3).

5. RENEWAL OF SPIRIT. "Renew a right spirit
within me." With the new heart comes the new spirit
within us, and upon us (Ezek. 36, 25-27). There cannot
be the right spirit where there is not the clean heart.
The hearts that were purified by faith were filled with
the Holy Ghost (Acts 15, 8-9). The absence of the
right spirit is the evidence of indwelling sin.

6. RESTORATION OF JOY. " Restore unto me the joy of Thy salvation " (v. 12). As a backslider, this joy had faded out of his life, but with the new heart and right spirit it was sure to return. At least, the way was open now for the return of this bright bird of Paradise into his life. Sorrow may endure for the night of confession, but joy cometh in the morning of forgiveness and renewal. There is a joy in His salvation, a joy that should never be lost.

7. PRESERVATION BY HIS POWER. " Uphold me with Thy free Spirit" (v. 12). Now that he has been set free from the law of sin and death, he longs to be *kept* in this condition of spiritual freedom. " Hold Thou me up." As one who had been burned with the fire of sin, he now dreads it. Although we have had the cleansing power of His blood, we still need the upholding power of His Spirit. He is able to keep us from falling.

III.—RESULTS. Where there has been a decided work of grace, signs will follow. He had—

1. A DESIRE TO WIN SOULS. " Then will I teach transgressors Thy ways ; and sinners shall be converted (turned) unto Thee " (v. 13). When, by experience, we have learned " Thy ways," we have something worth teaching ; something that transgressors need to know. It is a great work to convert a sinner (Jas. 5, 19-20). If God hath blessed us, it is that we might be made a blessing. He that winneth souls is wise.

2. A DESIRE TO PRAISE GOD. " O God of my salvation ; my tongue shall sing *aloud* of Thy righteous-

ness ; " and again, " O Lord, open Thou my lips, and
my mouth shall shew forth Thy praise " (v. 15).   Those
saved by the Lord have a double debt to pay.   They
are debtors to the unsaved—to teach them *His* way—
they are debtors to God, to praise Him.   " Whoso
offereth praise glorifieth Me " (Ps. 50, 23).

A BLESSED EXPERIENCE.
PSALM 57, 1-2.

In these two verses the way of salvation is set
before us in a very expressive manner.   Observe there
is—

I.—DANGER.   " Until these calamities be over-
past."   Saul was threatening the life of David, but his
danger was nothing compared to the danger of those
who are under the threatening judgments of God.
His wrath against sin is a terrible calamity for the
sinner (John 3, 36).

II.—PRAYER.   " Be merciful unto me, O God,
be merciful unto me."   This is the language of one
who is very sensible of his danger and need.   *Mercy* is
the crying need of those who have been awakened
to a sense of their real condition.   " God be merciful
unto me, the sinner."

III.—PROVISION.   " The shadow of Thy wings."
How gracious is our God, that He should stand, as
with outstretched wings, waiting and willing to receive
and shelter all who take refuge beneath them.   " O
Jerusalem . . . how often would I have gathered . . .
as a hen gathereth her chickens under her wings "

(Matt. 23, 37). The shadow of His wings means the shadow of God.

IV.—FAITH. "My soul trusteth in Thee ; yea, in the shadow of Thy wings will I make my refuge." The outspread wings of divine grace can only save those who trust and accept. "Ye would not" was the only hindrance in the way of Jerusalem sinners being saved. If the Israelites could not enter into the joy of the Promised Land, it was "because of unbelief" (Heb. 3, 19).

V.—DELIVERANCE. "I cried unto God . . . that performeth all things for me." God's salvation is perfect. *He* performeth every needed thing. It is His way, that when He begins a good work in you, to per·form it until the day of Jesus Christ (Phil. 1, 6). Salvation is of the Lord.

WAITING UPON GOD.
PSALM 62, 1-8.

Twice in this Psalm does David speak of his soul "waiting" or being "*silent* unto God" (R.V., marg.). This silence is profoundly significant. It is about as ominous in us as when it was in heaven for the "space of half an hour." It is so difficult for us, at times, to be perfectly still before God, as an instrument whose silent cords wait the divine touch. Let us think of—

I.—HIM, ON WHOM WE SHOULD WAIT. "My soul waiteth upon God." My soul, pause and think of Him at whose door thou dost wait. He that cometh to God, must believe that He is, and that HE

is the rewarder of them that diligently seek HIM. Wait
on Him as the Israelites waited on the moving of the
Pillar of Cloud. To move without Him is to move
without the promise and the presence. To wait God's
guidance and *incoming* for power and progress, is as
the seaman, waiting on the rising of the tide, and the
deepening of the river channel, that he may go forth
in safety with his precious cargo.

II.—WHY WE SHOULD WAIT ON GOD.
Because of what He is. "He only is my Rock, my Salvation, my Defence" (v. 2). It may seem an awkward
figure of speech to be waiting on a "Rock," but the
sense is of tremendous importance. It is to wait on
the coming of irresistible strength and stability. He
alone is to be our Strength, our Saviour, and Defender.
I need Him as "my Rock" (Strength), to stand in the
midst of all the evil forces of the *world*. I need Him as
"my Salvation," to deliver me from the subtle temptations and lusts of the *flesh*. I need Him as "my
Defence," to save me from the wiles and fiery darts of
the *devil*. "My soul wait thou *only* upon God" (v. 5).

III.—HOW WE SHOULD WAIT. We should
wait as those who expect the fulfilment of His Word,
and the manifestation of His character. "My expectation is from Him . . . I shall not be moved." (vv. 5-6).
It is the believing and expectant heart that looks for
the opened windows of heaven, and the poured-out
blessing (Mal. 3, 10). "Open thy mouth *wide*, and I
will fill it" (Ps. 81, 10). It is only when every other
door is closed, and every vain desire of self silenced,

that we are in a position to prove Him, and to say truly, " My expectation is from Him." When we are thus shut up to faith in Him, we may also say, " I shall not be moved." They that wait upon the Lord shall renew their strength.

IV.—THE RESULT OF WAITING UPON GOD. There will be a clear and encouraging *testimony* to His faithfulness. " Trust ye in Him at all times, pour out your heart before Him ; God *is* a refuge for us " (v. 8). From experience he can say to the people : At all times, trust Him, for all things *pour out* your heart to Him ; for He is a refuge, and a present help to those who wait upon Him. They that wait upon Him are blessed, and made a blessing to others.

THIRSTING FOR GOD.
Psalm 63, 1-8.

This is the language of the Psalmist while wandering in the wilderness of Judah. It is an experience which is typical of those who have discovered their real need in the wilderness of this world's unsatisfactory pleasures and profits.

I.—THE NATURE OF THIS THIRST. " My *soul* thirsteth for Thee, my *flesh* longeth for Thee " (v. 1). It is the thirst of an aching *spirit*, and an impoverished *life*. Man is a soul ; he is a spirit. There is a yawning gulf within his being, that all the material blessing of the world cannot fill. This *soul* thirst is an internal evidence of its kinship with God.

II.—THE OBJECT OF IT.   " My soul thirsteth
for Thee . . . longeth for *Thee.*"   Only those who know
God will thirst after Him.   The hart panteth after the
waterbrook, because it knoweth the refreshing efficacy
of the flowing stream.   There are souls that are smitten
with intense thirst, but they know not what they really
need, so they rush to the broken cisterns, that can hold
no water.   They will not acknowledge that it is God they
need.   O living, restless soul, it is the living, restful God
you need (Ps. 42, 2).

III.—THE CAUSE OF IT.   " In a dry and thirsty
land, where no water is."   The land in which we dwell
is in itself a dry, thirsty place—there is no water in it ;
absolutely nothing belonging to it that can meet this
deep soul-need of man.   Our best environments, apart
from the enjoyment of the presence of God, is but a
howling wilderness to the awakened.   A clamouring
emptiness, that only mocks the true hunger of the soul.
This world offers the thirsty one everything but the one
thing needful.

IV.—THE MOTIVE OF IT.   " To see Thy power
and Thy glory " (v. 2).   This is a bold and large demand.
What a satisfactory vision ; to see the power and glory
of God ; to see the power of His saving grace and the
glory of His matchless character.   In the sanctuary of
His Holy Word, this refreshing revelation is made.   In
the Person of His Son, His power and glory can be seen.
If any man thirst, let him come unto Me and drink
(John 7, 37).

V —THE CONFIDENCE OF IT.   " My soul shall

be satisfied as with marrow and fatness " (v. 5).   Where
this thirst has been created, it is the forerunner of rich
and lasting blessing.   God Himself becomes the portion
of whosoever so seeks Him.   He makes them to drink
of the river of His pleasures (Ps. 36, 8).   The soul is
not to be satisfied with theological bones, but with
marrow, and fatness ; the " *finest* of the wheat."

VI.—THE GUIDANCE OF IT. " My soul fol-
loweth hard after Thee " (v. 8).   When once the thirsty
roots of a tree find the river, they follow after it.   Those
who have found soul-satisfaction in God will abide by
the " Fountain of living waters."   If we have found in
Him full salvation, let us follow hard after Him in consecrated service.   Blessed are they that hunger and
thirst after righteousness, for they shall be filled.

JOYFUL IN GOD.
PSALM 66.

The soul that has thirsted *for* God, and found satisfaction *in* Him, will surely make a joyful noise *to* Him.
We may shew forth our joyfulness in God—

I.—BY PRAISING HIS NAME.   " Sing forth the
honour of His name " (v. 2).   His *name* is all that He
Himself is (Isa. 9, 6).   Sing out His glorious grace ;
His everlasting love and Almighty power.   It will take
all eternity to shew forth all the honours of that wonderful name.

II.—BY GLORYING IN HIS WORKS.   " Come
and see the works of God " (v. 5).   The Lord hath done
great things for His people Israel (vv. 6-7).   Has he not

C VIII

done great things for us ?　His work of salvation is both
" honourable and glorious " (Ps. 111, 3). Think of the
pit out of which ye have been digged, and let your
joy in God abound.

III.—BY CONFESSING HIS FAITHFULNESS.
" O bless our God . . . which holdeth our life, and
suffereth not our feet to be moved.　Thou hast tried
us . . . Thou broughtest us out into a wealthy place "
(vv. 8-12).　There have been temptations ; there has
been the furnace of trial, that has tested us as silver.
There have been the " net," the " fire and water," but,
praise His name, the end has been " a *wealthy* place."
He is faithful who hath promised.

IV.—BY YIELDING TO HIS CLAIMS.　" I will
go . . . I will pay . . . I will offer " (vv. 13-15).
" Go " into His House of *worship* ; " pay " the vows of
consecration ; " offer " the sacrifice of *service.* The joy
of worship ought to be accompanied with the joy of
sacrifice and service.　Arise, and go up to Bethel, the
place of vision and consecration.

V.—BY PERSONAL TESTIMONY.　" Come and
hear . . . and I will declare what He hath done for
my soul " (v. 16).　Those who have no testimony for
God, know nothing of the joy of God.　It is those who
have " *received* the Atonement," that joy in God, through
the Lord Jesus Christ (Rom. 5, 11).　The Psalmist's
testimony is three-fold.　First.—To the fact of his own
joyfulness.　" He was extolled with my tongue " (v. 17).
Second.—To the fact that God does answer prayer,
" God hath attended to the voice of my prayers " (v. 19).

Third.—To the fact that an unclean heart hinders prayer. " If I regard iniquity in my heart, the Lord will not hear me " (v. 18). " Make a joyful noise unto God."

A CRY OF DISTRESS.
PSALM 69, 1-5.

This Psalm ought to be read, on our knees, as coming from the lips of the suffering Son of God. In the opening verses we may hear the cry of a soul in utter desperation for the salvation of God. The reasons for it are very apparent. There was a sense of—

I.—DANGER. " Save me, O God ; for the waters are come in unto my soul " (v. 1). His soul is like a vessel in a stormy sea that had sprung a leak. The waters of sorrow and fear have come in upon him. He had been struggling hard to keep them out, but has failed. The waters have prevailed, and the danger is great. A ship in the sea is natural, but the sea in a ship is dreadful.

II.—HELPLESSNESS. " I sink in deep mire, where there is no standing " (v. 2). In the deep miry sea of sin a man can do nothing else but *sink*, for there is absolutely " no standing " there. A man must get out of this horrible pit before his feet can stand on the rock. The law of sin and death, like the law of gravitation, can do nothing for us while in the miry deep. " There is no standing."

III.—HOPELESSNESS. " I am come into deep waters, where *the floods overflow me* " (v. 2). The waters came into his soul, now he is come " into deep waters."

And, like one sinking within the tide mark, the billows begin to dash over him.   The figure used here is most expressive to describe the sinner's inability to deliver himself from the guilt of his own sin.   He might as well attempt to turn the tide as the wrath of God against sin.

IV.—WEARINESS.   " I am weary of my crying." He speaks now as a child that has grown utterly tired and exhausted by its own efforts.   We are not heard merely because of our much crying.   We have to get to an end of our praying self, as well as our working self.

V.—THIRSTINESS.   " My throat is dried."   This figure is that of a man ready to perish in a burning, sandy desert.   His crying has brought only a deeper sense of need.   Floods overflowing him, yet dying of thirst.   These are the agonies of a soul struggling for deliverance from worldliness and sin (Isa. 55, 1-2).

VI.—BLINDNESS.   " Mine eyes fail while I wait for my God."   He is now like one on a watch-tower, whose eyes are weary and dim through eagerly straining after something that he has failed to see.   No hopeful discovery can he make.   In me, that is, in my flesh, dwelleth no good thing.

VII.—ENEMIES.   " Mine enemies . . . are mighty " (v. 4).   They are also numerous as " the hairs of mine head."   The enemies of the human soul, in its quest after God and salvation, as mighty as " Principalities, Powers, and Wicked Spirits."   And more in number than the hairs of the head.   It is a great escape from the kingdom of darkness to the kingdom of God. The whole condition, then, is one of intense impotency and hopelessness, apart from the grace and power of God.

VIII.—CONFESSION. " O God, Thou knowest my foolishness, and my sins " (v. 5). Confession is needed. Our *sins* are there, there in our own hearts, like drowning waters ; there around us like the deep mire. Our *foolishness* must also be confessed ; in getting into the mire and hoping to save ourselves by an agonising effort. God *knows* it, therefore hide it not. Make full and frank acknowledgment to Him.

IX.—PETITION. " Save me, O God " (v. 1). " My prayer is unto Thee, O Lord, in an acceptable time (v. 13) . . . Deliver me out of the mire . . . and out of the deep waters (v. 14) . . . Draw nigh unto my soul and redeem it " (v. 18).

1. It was offered to the right One. " Unto Thee, O Lord."

2. It was for the right purpose. " Salvation and deliverance out of the mire."

3. It was in the right season. " An acceptable time " (2 Cor. 6, 2).

A JOYFUL TESTIMONY.

Psalm 71, 15-24.

There is in it—

I.—SALVATION. " My mouth shall shew forth Thy righteousness and Thy salvation " (v. 15). How could he shew forth His salvation if he had not experienced it ?

II.—RESOLUTION. "I will go . . . and I will make mention" (v. 16). The saved ought to *go*, and go in "His strength," making mention of His character (Rom. 1, 16).

III.—CONFESSION. "O God, Thou hast taught me" (v. 17). This is a thankful acknowledgment of His grace and wisdom. It is the privilege of the saved to be "taught of God" (John, 14, 26).

IV.—PETITION. "Now also when I am old . . . forsake me not; until I have shewed Thy strength and Thy power" (v. 18). This is a grand "Old Age Pension," to be able, when "grey-headed," to shew forth the strength and power of God. Why should the aged lose their spiritual freshness? The Vine is still the same, if the branch abides it will be fruitful.

V.—ADORATION. "O God, who is like unto Thee?" (v. 19). Those who have witnessed, and experienced, the great things of God, cannot but be filled with adoring gratitude.

VI.—EXPECTATION. "Thou . . . shalt quicken me again . . . Thou shalt increase my greatness, and comfort me on every side" (vv. 20-12). He had seen "great and sore troubles," so he expects to receive great and precious blessings. This is the language of one who knows by experience God's searching, gracious methods with His own.

VII.—EXULTATION. "I will praise Thee . . . will sing with the harp . . . My lips shall greatly rejoice when I sing unto Thee . . . My tongue shall also talk of Thy righteousness all the day long " (vv. 22-24). Oh, how great, how satisfying, is the goodness of our God. Taste and see. He is the Fountain of Life. Bless the Lord, O my soul (Ps. 103, 2-4).

THE MILLENNIAL REIGN.
PSALM 72.

This wonderful Psalm is called " A Psalm of Solomon," but a greater than Solomon is here. The reign of Solomon, the king's son, was doubtless one of comparative peace and righteousness, but " All kings did not fall down before him," nor did " *All* nations serve him," nor shall " the whole earth be filled with his glory." But all will be literally fulfilled when the Son of God appears in power and great glory. What are the characteristics of this blessed age, as revealed in this Psalm ? There will be—

I.—UNIVERSAL RIGHTEOUSNESS. " He shall judge Thy people with righteousness " (v. 2). This righteousness is the righteousness of God (v. 1). The righteousness of men is as filthy rags compared with this. " Behold a king shall reign in righteousness " (Isa. 32, 1). The law shall come from His lips, and shall never be thwarted by the selfish cross-purposes of man. " He shall break in pieces the oppressor " (v. 4). The greed of the miser and the haughty pride of the tyrant shall be crushed by the power of His judgment. The poor in spirit shall be the blessed ones in His kingdom (Matt. 5, 3). All presumptuous rule and authority shall be put down when he reigns.

II.—UNIVERSAL REVIVAL. " He shall come down like rain upon the mown grass ; as showers that water the earth " (v. 6). *He*, like the rain, shall *come down* from heaven. He shall come down in a time of great need *upon the mown grass*. Grass that has been mown is in great danger of being burned up at the roots. He shall come as *showers* that water the earth. Showers indicate distinct seasons of definite blessing. The effect of long-delayed rain is the renewal of the whole face of Nature ; the result of His coming upon a mown humanity will be a mighty reviving and refreshing from the presence of the Lord. Everything shall live whither this river cometh (Ezek. 47, 9).

III.—UNIVERSAL PROSPERITY. " In His days shall the righteous flourish ; and abundance of peace " (v. 7). The burden of national armament will, then, be rolled away (Isa. 2, 4). Righteousness, not force, will be the popular governing principle in " His days." Wickedness, and deceit, in every form, like unclean bats, will not be able to shew face in the bright day of His glory. Thy kingdom come, Thy will be done on earth, as it is in heaven.

IV.—UNIVERSAL DOMINION. " He shall have dominion from sea to sea, and . . . unto the ends of the earth " (v. 8). Every other kingdom shall be broken in pieces (Dan. 2, 24). Then shall the heathen be given Him for His inheritance, and the uttermost parts of the earth for His possession (Ps. 2, 8). He came that " the *world*, through Him, might be saved " (John 3,

17). Every knee shall yet bow to Him, and every tongue confess Him as Lord.

V.—UNIVERSAL SUBJECTION. " The kings . . . shall bring presents . . . and other gifts. Yea, all kings shall *fall down* before Him ; all nations shall *serve* Him. His enemies shall lick the dust " (vv. 9-11). The tongues of many scoffers are eloquent now, but they shall lick the dust when He cometh (Micah. 7, 17). The world needs a Ruler. As the queen of Sheba, hearing of the fame of Solomon, came to prove him, so shall the kings of the earth be constrained to come to Him who is the King of kings, and Lord of lords. The kingdoms of this world shall become the kingdom of *our* Lord, and of *His* Christ (Rev. 11, 15). He shall reign for ever and ever.

VI.—UNIVERSAL BLESSING. " There shall be an handful of corn . . . the fruit shall shake like Lebanon . . . the *city* shall flourish like *grass* of the earth. His name shall endure for ever . . . and men shall be *blessed in Him*. All nations shall call Him blessed " (vv. 16-17). When the city flourishes like the grass, there will be no place found for the slum. Men are blessed *in Him* now by faith, men shall be blessed in Him *then* by sight ; and so blessed that all nations shall call Him blessed, because He is the universal Blesser (Eph. 1, 3). Then will be fulfilled the angelic saying in Luke 2, 14.

VII.—UNIVERSAL GLORY. " Blessed be His glorious name for ever ; and let the whole earth be

filled with His glory " (v. 19). The glory of this name
which now transfigures the soul, will then transfigure
the world. For the earth shall be filled with the knowledge of the glory of the Lord, as the waters cover the
sea (Hab. 2, 14). This is the work of Him who is
" glorious in holiness, fearful in praises, doing wonders."

A GREAT PROBLEM SOLVED.
Psalm 73.

In judging things by their outward appearances,
the Psalmist says, " My feet were almost gone ; my
steps had well-nigh slipped " (v. 2). These are " perilous times " for the trusting soul, when the Providence
of God seems to contradict the Word of God. As in the
vision of Ezekiel, so in God's dealing with men, there are
" wheels within wheels."

I.—THE PROBLEM. It was great and complex.
Here are some of the things that staggered his senses.

1. He saw the prosperity of the wicked (v. 3).

2. He saw that they had " no bands (pangs) in
their death " (v. 24).

3. He saw that they are not " troubled . . . and
plagued like other men " (v. 5).

4. He saw that " pride was to them as a chain
ornament about their neck " (v. 6, R.V.)

5. He saw that " they have more than heart could
wish " (v. 7).

6. He saw that they " speak loftily and set their
mouth against the heavens " (vv. 8-9).

7. He saw that they were wilfully ignorant of God, saying, " How doth God know ? " (v. 11).

Then he adds, with something like irony in his tone, " Behold, these are the ungodly, who prosper in the world " (v. 12). Is it in vain, he asks, that I have "Cleansed my heart and *washed my hands in innocency* ?" (v. 13). Does it matter nothing what a man *is* ? Is there no principle of righteousness over-ruling the affairs of men ? Does it pay best to be wicked and God-defiant ? " For all day long have I been plagued " (v. 14). The problem of the sufferings of the righteous, and the prosperity of the wicked, is ever before us. Judged from a merely mundane standpoint, the mystery is insoluble. The man of the world, whose eyes stand out with fatness, can say, sneeringly, " How doth God know ? "

II.—THE SOLUTION. " When I thought how I might know this, it was too painful for me ; *until* I went into the *sanctuary of God*, and *considered* their *latter* end " (vv. 16-17, R.V.). The whole situation is, indeed, " painful," apart from the revelation of " the sanctuary of God." But when considered in the light of that revelation from God, which bears directly upon " this *latter* end," things are seen in their true perspective. In His light we see light clearly. Things take on a new and different character when seen in the light of Eternity. Temporal prosperity may only be the primary and deceptive symptoms of a fatal disease. In this holy and enlarged vision He saw—

1. That they were " set in slippery places " (v. 18).

2. That they would be "cast down into destruction."

3. That they would "become a desolation in a moment" (v. 19, R.V.).

4. That they would be "utterly consumed with terrors."

5. That God would "despise their image" (v. 20). This new view withers up the roots of envy. Who would covet the position of a man who was to be famous for an hour, and a fool for a year? The wicked have their portion in this life, but are miserable bankrupts in the end (Luke 16, 25).

III.—THE SOUL RESTED. Having now seen the puzzling problems, as it were, with new eyes, he makes full confession of his "foolishness" and "ignorance," and declares himself as a *beast* before God. Beastly eyes can only see the earthly and the outward (v. 22). The ungodly live but the life of the "brutish man" (Ps. 92, 6) ; but why should the godly judge such things, from a *brutish* man's standpoint? Having discovered his mistake, and acknowledged his foolishness, he proceeds to reckon up the blessings which belong to him as a man of God, in contrast to the portion of the man of the world. What are they?

1. He has the companionship of God. "Nevertheless, I am continually *with Thee*, Thou hast holden me by my right hand" (v. 23).

2. He says, "Thou shalt *guide me* with Thy counsel" (v. 24).

3. He is sure that God will "Afterwards receive

Him to glory." This is a very different *afterward* than that referred to in verse 18.

4. He feels that there is "None upon the *earth* that he desires beside Thee " (v. 25). The brutish man knows nothing of this *earthly* blessing.

5. He is confident that although his "flesh and heart faileth, God is the strength of his heart and his *portion for ever* " (v. 26).

6. He knows by experience that it is "*good for him* to draw near to God " (v. 28). It is good for us that we *can* draw near to *Him*.

7. He testifies "I have put my trust in the Lord God, that I may declare all Thy works " (v. 28). Social problems seen in the light of God's sanctuary must lead to a fresh and fuller declaration of the mighty *works* of God.

CONDITIONS OF BLESSING AND FAILURE.
PSALM 81, 8-16.

These words in this part of the Psalm are of tremendous significance, as they contain God's own testimony unto His people as to what He expected from them ; as to what they should have expected from Him ; and as to why they failed to receive His choicest blessings.

I.—A MERCIFUL ENTREATY. He pleads with them (1) to "*Hearken* unto Me " (v. 8). He must have the attentive ear, if divine wisdom and power are to be. imparted. (2), "There shall *no strange god* be in thee." He entreats that nothing should be allowed to take His place in the heart's affection, or as an object of confidence. It is surely easy to yield all for Him, when He offers to be all to us. (3), To " *Open thy mouth wide* and I will fill it " (v. 10). A " wide mouth " means large expectations. The proof that He is able, and willing, to meet the largest demand that our faith can make, is in this : " I am the Lord thy God, which brought thee out of the land of Egypt." He who can save to the uttermost, can satisfy to the deepest. Hearken, Believe, Expect.

II.—A GRACIOUS PURPOSE. The love that delivered our souls from the pit of sin longs to enrich us with the gifts of His grace. He says, " Oh that my people had hearkened unto Me, and walked in My ways " (v. 13), then He would have done three things for them. 1. He would have *subdued their enemies* (v. 14). Victory would have been theirs if they had followed Him. It is dishonouring to Him that His people should be in bondage to the powers of darkness. 2. He would have made the *haters of the Lord submit unto Him.* (v. 15). They would have been used in bringing their souls to God. His people's unbelief hindered Him from subduing and conquering His enemies. A solemn lesson for us. 3. He should have *fed them* also with the *finest* of the wheat, and satisfied them with honey out of the rock (v. 16). His purpose is to subdue enemies, save sinners, satisfy saints.

III.—A SORROWFUL COMPLAINT. "But My people would not hearken to My voice ; and Israel would none of Me " (v. 11). They rejected His *word* by not hearkening to His *voice*, and in rejecting His word they rejected *Himself*, " would none of Me." How gracious is our God, that He laments the lack of opportunity to bless His people. His word and Himself are so vitally connected, that to refuse the one is to reject the other.

IV.—A MISERABLE CONDITION. " So I gave them up into *their own* hearts' lusts ; and they walked in *their own* counsels " (v. 12). To be " given up " by Him, because of stubbornness and unbelief, means utter defeat in the presence of the foe ; the enemies are *not* subdued. Sinners are not converted unto God, and there is no feeding on the " finest of the wheat " no glad satisfaction, with " honey from the rock." A powerless, and a fruitless Church, is the painful evidence that God's voice is being unheard and unheeded, and that we are " walking in *our own* counsels," guided by the wisdom of men, to the neglect of the wisdom of God. Those who are more anxious for the words of men than the Word of God, are preferring chaff to the wheat. Men fed on chaff make poor soldiers. God's desire is to make His people " more than conquerors." " Hearken diligently unto Me, and eat ye that which is good."

THE REASON WHY.
Psalm 86, 1-7.

Here are seven reasons urged by this petitioner why God should answer him. There are many objective reasons arising from God's own character and promises, but those here are all subjective. There is—

I.—MY NEED.   " O Lord, hear me ; for I am poor and needy."   Our poverty and helplessness is a powerful plea at the door of infinite mercy and grace.

II.—MY GODLINESS.   " Preserve my soul, for I am godly " (v. 2).   This is no empty boast ; **to be** godly is to seek the glory of God.   This godliness is profitable as an agreement in prayer.   Many ask amiss for lack of it.

III.—MY FAITH.   Save Thy servant that *trusteth* in Thee.   Faith can honestly make an appeal to the faithfulness of God.   His trusting *servant* shall doubtless triumph in His saving power (Isa. 26, 3).

IV.—MY IMPORTUNITY.   " For unto Thee do I cry all the day long " (v. 3, R.V.).   This is another powerful element in prayer.   Has not our Lord declared that " because of his importunity he shall give him as many as he needeth."

V.—MY WHOLEHEARTEDNESS.   " Rejoice the soul of Thy servant ; *for* unto Thee, O Lord, do I lift up *my soul* " (v. 4).   The soul of true prayer is the lifting up of the soul (1 Sam. 1, 15).   An undivided heart is a conquering heart.

VI.—MY EXPERIENCE.   " For Thou, Lord, art . . . plenteous in mercy unto all them that call upon Thee " (v. 5)   His past experience and knowledge of the character of God is another reason for expecting present help.

VII.—MY ASSURANCE.   " I will call upon Thee ; *for Thou wilt* answer me " (v. 7).   " I will, for Thou wilt." This is the confidence that is never put to shame. Believe, and thou shalt see.

A WORKER'S PRAYER.
PSALM 90, 12-17.

This Psalm, which begins the fourth section of this book, is entitled "A Prayer of Moses, the man of God." The petitions offered in these closing verses are suggestive of the Christian worker's needs. He prays for—

I.—INSTRUCTION. "Teach us to number our days, that we may get us an heart of wisdom" (v. 12, R.V.). *Wisdom* is the principal thing (Prov. 4, 7); those who are taught to number their days of service on earth will seek it, and they that are wise redeem the time. We need divine teaching on this point to save us from folly and frivolity.

II.—RESTORATION. "Return, O Lord, how long?" Fellowship with Him has been lost, and the loss is keenly felt, which is a hopeful sign. The Lord is ready to return to the help of His servants "when He seeth that their power is gone," and there is none to help (Dan. 32, 36). The restoration of His presence is the restoration of the soul.

III.—SATISFACTION. "O satisfy us early with Thy mercy." His *mercy* can satisfy, and it will come early when there is true repentance toward God. His compassions fail not. His purpose is to satisfy (Ps. 36, 7-8).

IV.—COMPENSATION. "Make us glad according to the days wherein Thou hast afflicted us." This

D VIII

is a bold request. But the height of our joy will be according to the depth of our mourning (Ps. 126, 5-6). The depth of the valley is measured by the altitude of the hills. The arm that is strong to smite is equally strong to save. The long night of trial will surely have a long day of triumph.

V.—MANIFESTATION. "Let Thy work appear . . . . and Thy glory" (v. 16). He is but a poor servant of God who does not intensely long for the unmistakable *appearance* of His work and glory. This is the clamant need of the Church in these back-sliding days. His servants ought to see **His** working, and **to** have His glory *upon* them (R.V.).

VI.—SANCTIFICATION. "Let the beauty of the Lord our God be upon us" (v. 17). Thy people shall be willing in the day of Thy power, *in the beauties of holiness* (Ps. 110, 3). The sum of God's character is "Holiness." The Holy One of Israel. As the flower is beautified by the sun, so must all be adorned with the glory of His presence. This is the will of God, your sanctification.

VII.—CONFIRMATION. "Establish Thou the work of our hands upon us." Our *work* needs to be established by God, as well as our *feet* (Ps. 40, 2). What is the value of our work, if the Lord is not working with us, and *confirming* the work? (Mark 16, 20). "My speech and my preaching," says the Apostle, "was not with enticing words of man's wisdom, but *in demonstration of the Spirit* and of power." This was the divine confirmation that "their faith should not stand in the wisdom of men, but in the power of God." How are we to know that our work is of God, if *He does not bear witness*, as of old, both with signs and wonders, and divers miracles, and gifts of the Holy Ghost, according to His will ? (Heb. 2, 3-4).

THE FRUITS OF LOVE.
PSALM 91, 14-16.

" Because he hath set his love upon Me, therefore "

I.—I WILL DELIVER HIM. The first fruit of a surrendered heart is salvation. Freedom from the guilt and power of sin. The law is fulfilled in one word, " Thou shalt *love*." David set his heart on God ; see how God delivered him ! (1 Sam. 17, 50). So with Joseph, Daniel, and Paul.

II.—I WILL EXALT HIM. "Set him on high " (v. 14). After salvation comes exaltation ; or rather, to be saved is to be exalted : taken out of the fearful pit. If we have been crucified with Christ we have also been raised together with Him.

III.—I WILL ANSWER HIM (v. 15). What an inspiring promise this is ! Let your requests be made known unto God. Here is His own assurance that if you have set your love upon Him, He will answer you. If love to Him is our motive, then we shall not ask amiss (Jas. 4, 3).

IV.—I WILL BE WITH HIM. This is the promise of His fellowship in the day of our trouble. If He is with us then we can fear no evil (Ps. 23). God knows that His abiding presence is a continual necessity for guidance, strength, and victory.

V.—I WILL HONOUR HIM. We honour Him by setting our love upon Him. So " Them that know Me I will honour " (1 Sam. 2, 30). Seek the honour that comes from God *only ;* and His special favour will be manifested in your life (John 12, 26)

VI.—I WILL SATISFY HIM. He shall be satisfied with " length of days " (marg.), which, to us, implies the privilege of everlasting joy and service. Our days upon the earth, if lived in His love, will be as long as are needful for the honour of His name. He gives to His own eternal life, and they shall be satisfied when they awake in His likeness.

SING UNTO THE LORD.
PSALM 95, 1-8.

There are many groans in the Psalm, but there are also those spontaneous outbursts of wholehearted praise to God, that could only come from souls full to overflowing with love and thankfulness. " O come, let us sing unto the Lord "—

I.—HOW SHALL WE SING UNTO THE LORD ?

1. JOYFULLY. "Make a joyful noise to the Rock of our salvation " (v. 1). That Rock was Christ (1 Cor. 10, 4). He is worthy to be praised. Be joyful, not doleful, in the Lord.

2. THANKFULLY. " Let us come . . . with thankfulness " (v. 2). Have you not very much to be thankful for ? Think of what He has done *for* you, *in* you,

with you, and promised *to* you. Thanks be unto God for His unspeakable gift.

II.—WHY SHOULD WE SING UNTO THE LORD ? Because—

1. He is OUR SALVATION (v. 1). He Himself is our salvation, and this salvation is firm as a " Rock," He is *ours* because we have trusted Him, and are safe.

2. He is GREAT. " The Lord is a great God, and a great King " (v. 3). He is our loving God, and ever-lasting King (Jer. 10, 10) ; the God of our salvation, and the King of our redeemed lives. " One is your Master, even Christ."

3. He is STRONG. " In His hand, deep places ; the strength of the hills is His " (vv. 4-5). The strength of the hills is His, and He is yours, in whose hand the deep places are. All power is given unto Me. " Go ye therefore " (Matt. 28, 18-19).

4. He is HOLY. " O come, let us worship . . . let us kneel before the Lord our Master " (v. 6). Ours is a holy privilege to kneel before HIM, and worship. We are not only workers, but worshippers. The spirit of humble adoration is our best fitness for service. It is on bowed knees that the victory is gained (Ezra 9, 5 ; Dan. 6, 10 ; Eph. 3, 14).

5. He is GRACIOUS. " We are the people of *His* pasture, and the sheep of *His* hand " (v. 7). How gracious is our God to call *us* the people of *His* pasture, and the sheep of *His* hand. How green and refreshing His pastures are ; how safe and happy are the sheep that's guided, fed and protected by His hand. See

how **God** pastured His people even in " the wilderness," and led them into the green fields of Canaan " I am the Good Shepherd, and know My sheep, and *am known of mine.*"

NOTES IN THE NEW SONG.
PSALM 98.

In the last verse of Psalm 96 we read · " He cometh, for He cometh to judge the earth." In the first verse of Psalm 97 : " The Lord reigneth, let the earth rejoice." Now this Psalm begins with " O sing unto the Lord a new song . . . for His holy arm hath gotten Him the victory." (1), The COMING ; (2), The REIGNING ; (3), The REJOICING. In this new song there is the—

I.—Note of WONDER. " He hath done marvellous things " (v. 1). " Who is like unto Thee, O Lord, glorious in holiness, fearful in praises, doing wonders " (Ex. 15, 11 ; Rev. 15, 3). The Incarnation, the Crucifixion, and the Resurrection are wonders of the highest order. Wonders of grace.

II.—Note of VICTORY. " His right hand, and His holy arm hath gotten Him the victory." His holy *arm* may represent His Son (Isa. 53, 1). His right *hand—* the Holy Spirit. By His arm and hand is *salvation* accomplished (R.V.). It is Christ that redeemeth ; it is the Spirit that quickeneth.

III.—Note of MERCY. " The Lord hath made known His salvation " (v. 2). He has not only provided salvation by grace, but has also published it abroad in mercy. Every invitation of His Gospel, every copy

of the Bible, every Spirit-inspired messenger, is a proof
of God's desire that men should know the joyful sound
of His salvation (Isa. 45, 21-22 ; Mark 16, 15).

IV.—Note of FAITHFULNESS. " He hath remembered His mercy and His faithfulness " (v. 3, R.V.).
He who was faithful to the Israel of God, will be faithful
to the Church of God. Faithful is He that *called* you.
What His mercy hath promised, His faithfulness will
perform. Believe ye that I am able to do this ?

V.—Note of GRACE. " All the ends of the earth
have seen the salvation of our God " (v. 3). This, of
course, is prophetic, and will be actualised when " The
Lord reigneth." See the abounding grace of our God
in seeking the salvation of " all the ends of the earth."
All flesh shall see the salvation of God (Luke 3, 6).
Meanwhile, whosoever calleth upon the name of the
Lord shall be saved.

VI.—Note of PRAISE. " Make a joyful noise
unto the Lord . . . rejoice and sing praise " (v. 4).
This note of adoration is the keynote of the " New
Song," (Rev. v. 9-12). Because the Salvation of God
has been great and marvellous, let the praise be loud
and long.

VII.—Note of HOPE. " For He cometh to judge
the earth : with righteousness . . . and the people
with equity " (v. 9). We, according to His promise,
look for new heavens, and a new earth, wherein dwelleth
righteousness (2. Pet. 3, 13-14). The whole creation
shall be delivered from the bondage of corruption, when

the children of God enter into their glorious liberty
(Rom. 8, 21). This is the self-purifying hope (1 John
3, 3). O sing unto the Lord this new song.

THE "I AM'S" IN PSALM 119.

It has been said that this Psalm "Contains the
anatomy of experimental religion, the interior lineaments
of the family of God." Its twenty-two sections, are
so many strings of pearls, linked together by the letters
of the Hebrew Alphabet, and representing every phase
of Christian experience. It is a song of joy and rejoicing in the *Word of God*, which is referred to under
ten different names. Luther set a high value on this
Psalm, declaring that he "would not take the whole
world in exchange for a leaf of it." Note some of
the "I AM's."

I.—"I AM A STRANGER IN THE EARTH"
(v. 19). There is nothing in all the earth that can fully
meet the needs of a "Man of God." He has not where
to lay his *heart*, as Christ had not where to lay His head.
Holy men of old "All died in faith declaring plainly
that they *seek* a country" (Heb. 11, 13-14). The man
of the world is no stranger in the earth, it is his home ;
but the Christian's citizenship is in heaven.

II.—"I AM A COMPANION OF THEM THAT
FEAR THEE" (v. 63). Strangers in a foreign land,
who have come from the same country, naturally draw
one to another (Mal. 3, 16). These, in fellowship with
God, should be found in fellowship with one another.
Surely those who are to be our companions in eternity

should be our choice companions now. Such a testimony is greatly needed.

III.—" I AM BECOME LIKE A BOTTLE IN THE SMOKE " (v. 83). Through adverse circumstances I am like a shrivelled " Wine-skin " (Josh. 9, 4). A bottle *in the smoke* is in the place of trial and testing ; while in this evil world, the Christian must come into contact with its smoky influence, and must patiently endure as seeing Him who is invisible like the Hebrews in the fiery furnace : and like Job.

IV.—" I AM THINE, SAVE ME " (v. 94). Though in the smoke of perplexity and helplessness, it is comforting to be able to say " I am Thine." Thy property, (Acts 20, 28), Thy workmanship (Eph. 2, 10), He can as easily save us *in* the smoke, as the youths in the furnace of fire, and also *from* it, without the smell of it on the garments.

V.—" I AM AFFLICTED ; QUICKEN ME " (v. 107). " He suffered . . . that He might succour them that are tempted " (Heb. 2, 18). Divine *quickening* is the remedy for a sorrowing, sinking soul. The affliction may be heavy, but with His " abundant life " there will be an easy victory. He quickens the languid heart by His word of promise and spirit of power.

VI.—" I AM AFRAID OF THY JUDGMENTS " (words) (v. 120). Every truly quickened soul will tremble at His Word, and into such, He will look, (Isa. 66, 5). It is a characteristic of the tender obedient child. All heaven must be astonished at those who do not fear the Lord (Rev. 15, 4). This is not the fear that hath torment.

VII.—" I AM THY SERVANT " (v. 125). Thy willing slave, since Thou hast ransomed me from the slavery of sin (Rom. 6, 16-20), as Thy servant, "give me understanding," teach me what Thou wilt have me to do—not my will, but Thine be done.

VIII.—" I AM SMALL AND DESPISED" (v. 141). This is his own, and the world's estimation of the servant of God. Small, compared with the full stature of Jesus Christ, and despised as He was ; but fear not thou *worm* Jacob ; I WILL HELP thee saith the Lord. He can use small things.

THE "I WILL'S" IN PSALM 119.

I.—" I WILL PRAISE THEE " (v. 7) ; ("Give thanks unto Thee " R.V.). To this great end are the people of God formed (Isa. 43, 21). The qualification for it is " Uprightness of heart." The means to this end is the saving grace of God.

II.—" I WILL OBSERVE THY STATUTES," (v. 8, R.V.). An heart that is right with God, will be attentive to His words. The observer of the times must be an observer of His truth—to be wise.

III.—" I WILL MEDITATE IN THY PRE-CEPTS " (v. 15). The ungodly are not so ; they would cast these cords from them, but His Words are deep, and sweet to the obedient heart. " Thy words were found and I did eat them." The result was joy and rejoicing (Jer. 15, 16), see John 1, 14

IV.—" I WILL DELIGHT MYSELF IN THY STATUTES " (v. 16).　The meditating heart will soon be a delighted one.　Ainsworth reads it " I will solace and recreate myself."　His words both comfort and renew, in midst of life's worries and sorrows.

V.—" I WILL RUN THE WAY OF THY COMMANDMENTS " (v. 32).　Those who " observe, meditate and delight " in His Word, will soon be found running in the way, with an heart greatly enlarged. " Following afar off," or " Faint yet pursuing," is the condition of many.　They who *run* this race keep looking unto Jesus, who is the Way, the Truth and the Life (Ezra 7, 9).

VI.—" I WILL WALK AT LIBERTY " (v. 45). Augustine said " I gave my will to mine enemy, and he made a chain, and bound me with it."　Those who give their will to Christ are free indeed (John 8, 31). Sin is slavery ; Obedience to His Word is Liberty (John 8, 34).

VII.—" I WILL SPEAK OF THY TESTIMONIES . . . AND NOT BE ASHAMED " (v. 46).　Those who walk at liberty through Him, will surely speak freely for Him (Dan. 3, 16-81.)　It was so with Paul (Rom. 1, 16).　Preach the word, and be not ashamed, remember (Mark 8, 38 ; Rev. 21, 8).

VIII.—" I WILL GIVE THANKS AT MIDNIGHT " (v. 62).　Blessed are all they who can rise up in the midnight of their sorrow and gloom, and give

thanks unto the Lord. See Acts 16, **24, 25** ; the darkness and the light are alike to Him.

IX.—" I WILL NEVER FORGET THY PRE-
CEPTS " (v. 93). No, never ! for Thy words have
brought light, and life, and sustenance to my soul.
They shall guide me into eternity and abide with me
there. " They are spirit, and they are life " (John 6, 63).
I shall never forget *them*, because I shall never forget
THEE.

SOME " I HAVE'S " IN PSALM 119.

I.—" I HAVE GONE ASTRAY LIKE A LOST
SHEEP " (v. 176). A lost sheep can do nothing else
but go astray (Isa. 53, 6). Think of what we wander
from, in going astray—from God and His Word : think
of where we wander to. The Shepherd's purpose is
to seek and save the lost.

II.—" I HAVE SOUGHT THEE WITH MY
WHOLE HEART " (v. 10). This is the right object,
sought in a right manner (Ps. 27, 4). For the sheep
astray, there is only the " wormwood and the gall "
(Sam. 3, 19) of weariness, danger, and disappointment.
In Him is life. Seek the Lord.

III.—" I HAVE REJOICED IN THE WAY "
(v. 14). In the way of His testimonies there is joyful
deliverance, His ways are ways of righteousness. Faith
leads into the promised land of the " unsearchable
riches of Christ." Stand, and ask for the old paths,
where is the good way (Jer. 6, 16).

IV.—" I HAVE DECLARED MY WAYS " (v. 26). " My ways," no matter how crooked, foolish and fruitless they have been, it is good to declare them all in His ear. We must declare *His* ways to others, but our own wayward ways to Him.

V.—" I HAVE CHOSEN THE WAY OF FAITH-FULNESS " (v. 30, R.V.). This is a courageous and needful choice. He hath chosen to be faithful to us ; why should we not *choose* to be faithful to Him ? The choice is to be made, between faith, and faithlessness ; between Barabbas and Christ. He stuck to His choice (v. 31).

VI.—" I HAVE REMEMBERED THY NAME " (v. 55). The Name of the Lord is a wonderful solace " in the night of trouble and perplexity ; " for what God is, that is His name (Ex. 34, 5-7). As ointment it has been poured forth in the person and work of His Son.

VII.—" I HAVE BELIEVED THY COMMAND-MENTS " (v. 66). This is a noble confession. What mischief and failure are constantly being produced in Christian living for lack of faith in the Words of God. The Lord hath promised, and " I have believed." Can we so say ?

VIII.—" I HAVE REFRAINED MY FEET FROM EVERY EVIL WAY " (v. 101). There are many evil ways that may look pleasant and profitable, but are not in keeping with His Word. We walk by faith, not by sight. The *easy* way may be an evil way, like Bunyan's pilgrims in By-path meadow. It was

" easy going," but it led to Doubting Castle.　To " keep
His Word," we must refrain our thoughts and actions
from the ways of the ungodly.

IX.—" I HAVE LONGED FOR THY SALVA-
TION " (v. 174).　The daily Salvation of the Lord is an
experience much to be longed for.　We should long for
it in all its fulness.　Those who hunger and thirst after
such righteousness, shall be filled.　We also long for the
salvation of the Lord, when we long for the salvation
of the sinner.　Surely the saved will long for this.
Those who long for His coming again long for His final
salvation.

MY SOUL, A WEANED CHILD.
PSALM 131, 2.

1.　My Soul is as a *Child*—helpless.　But confident
in a Mother's love, having had experiences of her special
care.

2.　My Soul is as a *weaned child*—Suffering.　The
mystery of an unexpected refusal ;　a new method of
treatment.

3.　My Soul is *as* a weaned child—submissive.
The gift denied, but the Mother embraced.　**The** rest
of faith and love.

REASONS FOR PRAISE.
PSALM 138.

" I will praise Thee with my whole heart " (v. **1**).

1.　Because Thou *Answeredst* me (v. 3).

2.　Because Thou didst *Encourage* me (R.V.),

3. Because Thou wilt *Revive* me (v. 7).
4. Because Thou shalt *Protect* me (v. 7).
5. Because Thou wilt *Perfect* that which concerneth me . . . (v. 8).

SELF-EXPOSURE TO GOD.
PSALM 139, 23-24.

1. *Search me*, for I seek Thy Salvation.
2. *Know me*, for I seek Thy Fellowship.
3. *Try me*, for I seek Thy Service.
4. *See me*, for I seek Thy Comfort (R.V. marg.).
5. *Lead me*, for I seek Thy Guidance.

PRAYER AND ARGUMENT.
PSALM 143, 8-11.

1. Cause me to *Hear* : for in Thee do I trust (v. 8).
2. Cause me to *Know :* for I lift up my Soul unto Thee.
3. *Deliver* me (for) I flee unto Thee to hide me (v. 9).
4. *Teach* me : for Thou art my God . . . (v. 10).
5. *Quicken* me : for Thy Name's Sake . . . (v. 11).

A TESTIMONY.
PSALM 144, 1-2.

Blessed be the Lord, for He is—
1. My Strength in my helplessness.
2. My Kind One (marg.) in my destitution.
3. My Fortress : my refuge of Safety.
4. My High Tower in my days of darkness
5. My Deliverer, when my enemy oppose.

6. My Shield : when fiery darts are about.

7. My Confidence : " In Whom I trust."

PRAISE THE LORD.
PSALM 146, 8-10.

Here are seven reasons why He should be praised :

1. *He looseth the Prisoners.* The prison speaks of guilt and bondage. Christ came to preach deliverance to the Captives (Luke 4, 18). Whom the Son makes free are free indeed. See Acts 12, 7.

2. *He openeth the Eyes of the Blind.* This implies moral and spiritual *darkness.* The " recovering of sight to the blind," was another feature of Christ's mission (Luke 4, 18). Believe and thou shalt *see.*

3. *He raiseth the Bowed-down.* Those like the woman in the Gospel who " could in no wise lift up herself " (Luke 13, 11), bowed with the burden of grief or guilt, the deformity of sin, He raiseth up—by His Word of cheer and Arm of Power (2 Cor. 7, 6).

4. *He Loveth the Righteous.* Those who are *right* with Himself, and for Himself, will be loved by Him (John 14, 23). He draws nigh to those that draw nigh to Him.

5. *He Preserveth the Stranger.* He deals with the stranger, as with the fatherless and the widow (Deut. 27, 19 ; Jer. 7, 6-7). Alike, helpless and destitute, " Ye are no more strangers " (Eph. 2, 19).

6. *He Upholdeth the Fatherless and Widow* (R.V.) His loving heart beams through His merciful eyes. Our helplessness is no hindrance to His power.

7. *He turneth the Way of the Wicked upside down.*
He disapproveth the devices of the *crafty* (Job 5, 12).
The *way* of the ungodly, with all its pleasures and
expectations shall perish (Ps. 1, 6). Upside down is
a very positive and complete change.

WISDOM'S CALL.
PROV. 1, 20-29.

The book of Proverbs is said to " Represent the
very science of practical philosophy." It is divided
into two sections ; Chapters I.—IX., WISDOM'S WAYS,
and chapters X.—XXXI., WISDOM'S WORDS. These
words " The fear of the Lord, which is the beginning
of knowledge " (v. 7) may be taken as the keynote of
the book. They occur thirteen times. These Proverbs
are literally " Comparisons " in practical " parables."
The WISDOM personified here (8, 12) stands for the
highest intellectual sagacity, and the purest moral
character, and finds its perfect fulfilment in the Person
and Character of the Lord Jesus Christ, who is " The
Wisdom of God," and who is " made of God unto us,
Wisdom, Righteousness, Sanctification and Redemption." In this cry of Wisdom, let us hear the cry of
Christ. We can hear in it the voice of—

I.—COMPASSION. " Wisdom crieth without . .
in the streets, in the openings of the gates " (v. 20).
The message is for the " man in the street," as well as
the ruler at the gates. It is the compassionate cry of
infinite mercy and fulness (John 7, 37). This voice
seeks to ring in every street, city, and county. It is the

E VIII

cry of God's Evangel to a perishing world. Three
classes are addressed—the " Simple," the " Scorner,"
and the " Fool."   The weak, the wayward, and the
worthless : He came, not to call the righteous, but
sinners.

II.—REPROOF.   " He crieth . . . how long, ye
simple ones . . . Turn you at my reproof " (vv. 22-23).
These three classes are typical. (1). The SIMPLE are
rebuked for being easily led ; yielding themselves
thoughtlessly to the influence of others, and not taking
time to " Stand still, and ask for the good old paths."
They are the willing dupes, in mind and heart, to
unprincipled or ungodly men. (2). The SCORNER is
reproved for his delight in scorning ! Taking pleasure
in ungodliness is about the climax of human guilt. Such
glory in their shame, for the sake of a fetid applause,
they receive from a corrupt humanity. (3). The
FOOL is charged with " hating knowledge ! " At
enmity with Wisdom.   He *loves* the darkness rather than
the light, which is abundant proof of his madness.
He hates Wisdom, because it is opposed to his supreme
folly.   Such are the attitudes of many toward Christ.

III.—ENTREATY. " Turn ye at my reproof "
(v. 23). Wisdom, like Christ, calls, and entreats, but
will not compel. " Turn *ye*." The responsibility is
with the hearer. He appeals to the will : to the reason.
" Come now, and let us reason together saith the Lord."
Regeneration is the work of the Spirit, but *conversion*—
turning about—is the work of man.   " Repent, and be
converted," is His command.   " Turn ye ! turn ye, for

Why *will* ye die ? " Ye will not come to Me that ye might have life. Your face is away from Him who is the Way, the Truth, and the Life ; turn you at My reproof.

IV.—PROMISE. " Behold, I will pour out my Spirit unto you, and I will make known my words unto you " (v. 23). He will meet the real need of the Simple, the Scorner, and the Fool, by imparting to them His own regenerating Spirit, and making them to receive and understand His precious, soul-satisfying words. He promises, not to change their circumstances, but to transform their character. God's law is perfect, and so is His remedy for the silly, sneering, sinful souls of men. Salvation is of the Lord.

V.—LAMENTATION. " I have called, and ye refused . . . and would none of my reproof " (vv. 24-25). This is the language of wounded love, like that in Matt. 23, 37. His " call " was refused, His " stretched out hand " was disregarded, His " counsel " was set at naught. His " reproof " they would have none of. His " Call," His " Counsel," His " Entreaty," and His " Reproof " had been alike fruitless, because of the stupidity and hardness of their heart. He willeth not the death of any, but how sad that many should prefer death to life.

VI.—JUDGMENT. " Because . . . ye refused . . . I also will laugh at your calamity." " I will mock when your fear cometh," etc. (vv. 26-29). There is nothing more certain than this, that *fear cometh* upon all the ungodly sooner or later. Those who have wilfully rejected His call of Mercy, will find their Call of Fear rejected. Christ had His Calamity on the Cross, the Christ-despiser will have his when He sees Him on His Throne. The depths of the horrors of perdition may partly explain the depths of the horrors of the Crucifixion. Here deep calleth unto deep. Man's crowning crime is : that he hates the knowledge of God, and chooses not His fear (v. 29). Behold now is the day of Salvation ; now is the seed-time of eternal life. In vain shall we call upon Him in the winter of Judgment, if we neglect the summer of His Grace and Mercy.

WISDOM'S PRECIOUSNESS.
Prov. 3. 13–20.

Christ is the Wisdom of God, and to them that believe He is precious. Those who have put on Christ have such an adorning that all the material glories of earth are not to be compared with it. "She is more precious than rubies." From these verses we may learn something of her, or His—

I.—GREATNESS. The Lord *by wisdom* hath founded the earth " (v. 19). " In the beginning was the Word, and the Word was with God, . . . All things were made by Him, and without Him was not anything made that was made " (John 1, 1-4). " O Lord, how manifold are Thy works, in wisdom hast Thou made them all." God, by Jesus Christ, created (Eph. 3, 9). God, by Jesus Christ, Redeemed.

II.—RICHES. " Length of days is in her right hand, and in her left riches and honour " (v. 16). The treasures of true Wisdom are the treasures which belong to Jesus Christ. "Length of days," "Riches," "Honour." Everlasting life, unsearchable riches, and the Right Hand of God. In Him is Life, and the treasures of Wisdom and knowledge, and all the fulness of God ; He is *crowned* with glory and honour. With long life doth He satisfy those to whom He hath shown His Salvation (Ps. 91-16).

III.—INFLUENCE. Wisdom has a mighty influence.

1. On the HEART. "Happy is the man that findeth Wisdom" (v. 13). The yoke of Wisdom is easy, her burden is light. To find the Wisdom of God is to find rest to the soul, light to the eyes, and joy to the heart. To find Wisdom (Christ) is to find the holy, blissful, all-conquering will, and mercy of God. A man cannot make such a find without being renewed in the whole inner man.

2. On the LIFE. "The merchandise of it is better than the merchandise of silver" (v. 14). Those who find Wisdom, find a new object in life, and a new sphere of action. To trade with Christ, and work for Him, is more profitable than the best investment on earth. "The gain thereof is better than fine gold."

III.—DESIRABILITY. "All the things thou canst desire are not to be compared unto her" (v. 15). It is not possible for you to desire anything better than this. Paul knew this when he said : "What things were gain to me, those I counted loss for Christ." You may desire great and many things, but the affections of the heart can never be set on a more worthy and needful object than the Wisdom of God, as revealed in His Well-beloved Son. Wisdom's ways " are ways of pleasantness, and all her paths are peace " (v. 17). By faith Moses desired the better part, when he esteemed the reproach of Christ greater riches than the treasures in Egypt. Christ is the gift of God, covet earnestly this best gift. Those who have Him, though poor, yet can make many rich, as having nothing, yet possessing all things " Wisdom is the principal thing, therefore get Wisdom. Exalt her, and she shall promote thee " (4, 7-8)

IV.—ACCESSIBILITY.   " She is a tree of life to them that *lay hold* upon her " (v. 18). . How can I, so weak and foolish, get possession of this Wisdom ? It is not for scholars, but for sinners.   *Lay hold* on eternal life.   She is not only life to those who lay hold upon her, but " a *tree* of life," a *well* of water springing up ; not only a stream of blessing, but a *fountain* within ; Accessible !   Yes.   Whosoever will may come.   Him that cometh unto Me I will in no wise cast out.   Incline thine *ear* unto Wisdom, and *apply thine heart ;* for with the heart man believeth unto righteousness (see chap. 2, 1-6).   Now then, " take fast hold of Wisdom, let her not go ; keep her, for she is thy life " (4, 13).   " Unto you, O men, I call ; and my voice is to the sons of men " (8, 4).

WISDOM'S CHARACTER.
PROV. 8, 12-36.

Here again, as in chapter 2, 20-23, we have in the opening verses of this chapter a revelation of Wisdom's

agonizing attitude towards men. The voice of Wisdom,
like the light of the sun, is unto all men. This voice,
like the voice of the sun, may be silent, but it is withal
the Voice of God, because it is the voice of Character.
The world may close its ears to the cry of the Christ,
but it cannot stifle that pleading voice. " Unto you
O men, I call ; and my voice is to the sons of men."
How Christ-like are the characteristics of Wisdom.
Observe—

1. *Wisdom's Personality.* " I wisdom dwell with
prudence" (v. 12). Here the Personality is divine ;
qualities are claimed which belong properly to the Eternal
Son. God is Love, God is Light, and God is Wisdom.

2. *Wisdom's Powers.* " I have strength. By
me kings reign, and princes decree judgment " (vv.
14-16). His name shall be called Wonderful, the
Mighty God. The Everlasting God, the Creator of
the ends of earth, never is weary ; and He giveth
power to the faint, and increaseth the strength of the
helpless (Isa. 40, 28-29). There is no power but of
God. All power is given unto Me.

3. *Wisdom's Offer.* " Those that seek me diligently shall find me " (v. 17, R.V.) If any man love
Me, he shall be loved of My Father, and I will love him
and will manifest Myself unto him. Heavenly Wisdom
is imparted to the open, diligent heart. Christ reveals
Himself as a reward to the diligent seeker. Ye shall
find Him when ye shall search *for* HIM with all your
heart (Jer. 29, 13). Seek ye *first* the Kingdom of God.
Behold, now is the accepted time.

4. *Wisdom's Wealth.* "Riches and honour are *with me ;* yea, durable riches and righteousness. My fruit is better than gold" (vv. 18-19). Her *riches* can only be given with *honour ;* her durable riches with righteousness. Christ's unsearchable and eternal riches are connected with His holy and eternal righteousness. To be eternally rich we must be eternally right. In Him all fulness dwells. "Wherefore do ye spend money (wealth) for that which is not bread ? and labour for that which *satisfyeth not.* Hearken diligently unto Me," etc. "I counsel thee to buy of Me, gold tried in the fire, that thou mayest be rich" (Rev. 3, 18).

5. *Wisdom's Grace.* "I lead in the way of righteousness . . . That I *may cause* those that love me *to inherit substance.* And I will fill their treasures" (vv. 20-21). Not only are her hands full of riches, but her heart is full of love and mercy, seeking to lead others into the joyful possessions of her treasures. It is not difficult for the anointed eye to see Jesus here. He leads into Righteousness, that He might lead into an incorruptible inheritance. Oh ! the riches of that Grace which " causes us to love Him " that we might be made partakers of His infinite riches, and so have the treasury of the heart filled out of His fulness (Rom. 5, 17).

6. *Wisdom's Testimony.* The wonderful language used in this passage (vv. 22–31) could only come *truthfully* from the lips of one who was, and is, co-equal with God.

He was *possessed* by Jehovah in *the beginning* (v. 22).

He was *exalted from everlasting*, or ever the earth was (v. 23).

He was brought forth, *before* the fountains, the mountains, or the hills (vv. 24-25).

He was present when God *prepared* the heavens, etc. (vv. 26-29).

He was *with* God as a *Master Workman*, and was daily His delight, rejoicing always before Him (v. 30, R.V.).

His delight was with the *Sons of Men* (v. 31).

This was the Word that was made flesh, and dwelt among us. This is the One, who being in the form of God, took upon Him the form of a servant, and became obedient unto death, even the death of the Cross.

7. *Wisdom's Counsel.* " Now, therefore, my sons, hearken unto me ; for blessed are they that keep my ways " (v. 32, R.V.) "This is My Beloved Son, Hear ye Him." What a privilege to hear His words, and to receive His invitation. Oh, the madness of turning a deaf ear to Him. The blessing that maketh rich is to be found in Him, His ways are ways of pleasantness, as well as safety.

8. *Wisdom's Promise.* " For whoso findeth me findeth life, and shall obtain favour of the Lord " (v. 35). *Life* and divine *favour* are alone to be found in Him who is the Wisdom of God, and the Power of God. " I am the Way, the Truth, and the Life, no man cometh unto the Father but by Me." I am come that ye might have life. He that hath the Son hath life."

9. *Wisdom's Warning.* " He that sinneth against me wrongeth his own soul. All they that hate me love death " (v. 36). To sin against God is to make for

self-destruction. To kick against His goadings is to
wound our own feet and prefer death to life. We sin
against Him when we refuse to believe His Word and
submit ourselves to Him. In so sinning against Him,
against His love and merciful pleadings, we wrong our
own soul by compelling it to abide in a condition of
spiritual darkness, guilt, and condemnation. Your sin
of unbelief and rebellion may not wrong God, but is a
terrible wrong to your *own soul.*

WISDOM'S PROVISION AND INVITATION.
PROV. 9, 1-6.

In this chapter we have not only the pressing call
of Wisdom, but also the clamorous invitation of Folly
(v. 13). The foolish woman seeks to *imitate* her who is
the expression of the Wisdom of God. The wonder-
workings of God will always have their counterfeits
in the workings of the devil. The one leads to the
heights of heaven, the other to the " depths of hell "
(v. 18).

WISDOM'S PROVISION. The provision indicated
here is sevenfold. There is—

1. *The House.* " Wisdom hath builded her house "
(v. 1). It is a house of Refuge, and a place of holy and
heavenly fellowship. It is large, and in every way
fitted for its great purpose, and perfectly becoming the
character of the builder. See Eph. 2, 20-22 ; 1 Pet.
2, 5.

2. *The Pillars.* " Wisdom hath hewn out her
seven pillars." The pillars indicate strength and sta-

bility. *Seven* is the perfect number. This building is supported by that which is perfect in character. Here are seven pillars which belong to this spiritual Temple, The Lord God: (1), "Merciful"; (2), "Gracious"; (3), "Long-suffering"; (4), "Abundant in goodness and truth"; (5), "Keeping mercy for thousands"; (6), "Forgiving iniquity, transgression, and sin"; and (7), "Will by no means clear the guilty" (Justice). Ex. 34, 6. The doctrines of Jesus Christ are pillars of truth, and are as stable as the attributes of God.

3. *The Sacrifices.* "Wisdom hath killed her beasts." Wisdom hath made her sacrifices. Ample provision could only be made through the shedding of blood, the forfeiture of innocent life. God so loved the world that He gave His Son. It pleased the Lord to bruise Him. He hath put Him to grief. In this sacrifice there was the pouring-out of divine love, and life. WISDOM hath done it, although man in his ignorance and pride of intellect would protest against it.

4. *The Wine.* "Wisdom hath mingled *her* wine." The wine mixed by the wisdom of the world can only bring "woe, sorrow, contention, babbling, wounds, and redness of eye" (23-30). This is neither worldly wine, nor a worldly mixture. It is Wisdom's own wine, and Wisdom's own mixture. The wine is pure, and the spices are pure, the blend is the richest that thirsty, languid souls can ever drink. Christ's wine of joy is mingled to suit each individual case. It is always a wholesome mixture. The Lord hath another mixture for a different class of people (Ps. 75, 8).

5 *The Table.* "Wisdom hath furnished her table" (v. 2). The wisdom of God hath put upon the table of His grace every needful blessing. His table is well furnished. My God shall supply all your need. Many don't realise their manifold need, and so cannot appreciate the value of Wisdom's provision.

6. *The Servants.* "Wisdom hath sent forth her maidens" (v. 3). The feast being ready the heralds of His grace are sent forth with free invitations. Wisdom hath *her own* servants, as well as her own house, and a table. Salvation is of the Lord.

7. *The Call.* "Wisdom crieth upon the highest places of the city." It may be the servant's voice, but the call is that of "Wisdom." We are ambassadors for Christ. It is God that beseeches by us (2 Cor. 5, 20). The call is urgent, it is from the *highest places* of the city that all may hear. It is a Call. 1, To *Turn.* "Turn in hither." It implies conversion from the broken cisterns of the world to the well-furnished table of the Lord. 2, To *Come.* "Come, eat of My bread, and drink of the wine which I have mingled" (v. 5). Come and eat of that which the Wisdom of God has so abundantly provided, the bread of strength, and the wine of gladness and inspiration. 3, To *Forsake.* "Forsake the foolish and live" (v. 6). Folly saith : "Stolen waters are sweet" (v. 17). The wisdom of this world is foolishness with God. Come out from among them, and be ye separate, saith the Lord. 4, *To go.* "Go in the way of understanding" (v. 6). Having turned to the Lord and received of His gifts, we now go in His way, learning

of Him. He shall guide you with all truth when you follow Him, leaning not on your own understanding (3, 4-7). Come and take, then go and work.

ETERNITY IN THE HEART: A KEY TO ECCLESIASTES.

CHAPTER 3, II.

Newberry's rendering of this text enables us to see the meaning of this book in a clearer light. "He hath set *eternity* in their heart, *without which* no man can find out the work that God maketh from the beginning to the end." The word translated "world" here only occurs in one other place, where the meaning is ages, or eternity. This book deals with "things under the sun" : the mundane things of earth, seen in the light of Nature's revealer. The "Preacher" begins with "Vanity of Vanities," then proceeds to demonstrate the truthfulness of his convictions. He gave "his heart to *search out*," and to "*see* all the works that are done under the sun," and to "*prove*" his *heart* with every earthly good. He made "great works," and "withheld not his *heart* from any joy." Yet he pronounced it "all vanity and vexation of spirit." So deeply did he drink of all the waters of the world's pleasures that he said : "What can the man do that cometh after the king?" (2, 12). What man can have any chance of satisfying his heart with the material things of earth, when *he*, the richest and wisest man on earth, failed ? Why did he fail so miserably after such an earnest, favourable and exhaustive experiment ? Here is the answer : "God hath set *eternity* in the heart." That which belongs to eternity cannot find its counterpart in those things which are only temporal. Although there is " a *time* " to every purpose *under* the heavens, there is nothing circumscribed by time that is not " vanity and vexation of spirit " to that which is eternal. As God hath set eternity in the heart, He means to set eternal things there. Observe—

I.—THE FACT OF IT. "Eternity is in the heart." In its very constitution, as the workmanship of God. The heart, here, may stand for man's essential character, as distinct from the lower animal creation. When Duncan Matheson prayed, "Lord stamp eternity upon my eyeballs," he was uttering words which revealed the most profound characteristic of the human soul. God hath set eternity in the heart by setting there the *thought* of it, the *desire* after it, *kinship* to it, and *capacity* for it.

II.—THE EVIDENCE OF IT. The evidence of this truth is apparent in the universal belief in immortality found among the early Egyptians. Babylonians, Persians, Hebrews, Hindus, Chinese, South Sea Islanders, Druids and Celts. But perhaps one of the most convincing proofs of it may be seen in the universal *restlessness of the human heart.* Towards the things of this world, like the sea, it is ever crying : " Give, Give," and never fully satisfied therewith. One of the wealthiest men in modern times declared to a friend " I am not to be envied ; How can my wealth help me ? I would give you my millions if you could give me your youth and health." Youth and health in themselves could only enable him to repeat his own and Solomon's abortive experiment. "Man's life consisteth not in the abundance of things which *he possesseth*," but in the things which God possesseth. Surely the *capacity* of the human heart for the love and fellowship of the eternal God is an argument of no mean force. The heart's desire, in its truest and best moments, is for the " things which are eternal." Even pagan philosophers have acknowledged this. " The presage of a future life," says Cicero, "is most discoverable in the greatest and most exalted souls." When the glamour of sunny circumstances vanishes in some calamity or domestic affliction, then the deeper and more enduring instincts of the soul assert themselves.

III.—THE PURPOSE OF IT. " Without which no man can find out the work that God maketh." It takes the attribute of eternity in the heart to contemplate the character of God and His work Eternity in the heart is—

1. A *Witness* to the Eternity of God. It has been set there as a testimony to the fact of His eternal Personality, and man's kinship to Him.

2. A *Protest* against Worldly-mindedness. Just as a man can profit nothing by gaining the world, and losing his life, so the eternity in the heart can only be deceived by loving and resting on the things of time— he layeth up treasure for himself and is not rich toward God (Luke 12, 19-21). Those who "*mind*" earthly things " are enemies of that Cross which stands for heavenly and eternal things.

3. An *Incentive* to seek eternal things. The fact that God hath set eternity in the heart, is surely meant to be a powerful incentive to seek those things which are above. " Like draws to like."

4. An *Evidence* of God's love. Let the deep in the heart call unto the deep that is in God. God hath set that deep there that He might fill it out of the deep of His own infinite fulness.

5. A *Warning* against the neglect of Salvation. To neglect eternal salvation is to choose eternal death. Eternity is in your heart whether it is found or lost. " Son, daughter, give Me thine heart." He who hath set eternity in it is best able to meet and satisfy its every need.

THE SONG OF SONGS.

CHRIST'S DESIRABLENESS.

CHAPTER 1, 4.

This " Song of Songs which is Solomon's " is seldom sung by self-seeking souls. To many carnal Christians it is either too mystical or spiritual to be of any practical interest. It is a Song parable of Love, or spiritual friendship, and must be interpreted as such. The language is uniformly metaphorical, perhaps, that it might be easily and growingly applicable to spiritual relationships. The two leading personalities assume the character of Bridegroom and Bride, suggestive at once of Christ and the Church. This is confirmed by the *intenseness* of the language used throughout by both parties, revealing deep and tender feelings. The first to speak is the Bride. This sudden outburst of burning desire reveals—

I.—HER ESTIMATION OF HIS CHARACTER.
She declares that—

1. His *love* is better than wine. She knew this because she had had some experience of it. Wine here stands for the exhilarating and luxurious pleasures of the world. But His love is more effectual, coming from a better source, and producing better and more lasting results. Wine is man-made, love is of God (Rom. 8, 38-39).

2. His *Name* is an ointment poured forth. His name is His character, a precious ointment, that contains all the ingredients needed to heal the wounds of humanity (Acts 3, 16). This ointment hath been *poured forth* in Word, and in blood, that its efficacy may be tested and enjoyed (2 Cor. 8, 9). This pouring forth of saving virtue implies God's generosity and man's opportunity and responsibility. "Therefore do the virgins (pure hearts) love Him," while the harlots pass Him by. It is to the glory of Christ that He is loved by the purest of minds. The savour of His name is eternally satisfying (Acts 4, 12). "Unto you which believe He is precious."

II.—HER DESIRE FOR HIS APPROVAL.
She longs for—

1. His *Personal favour.* "Let Him kiss me," etc. Him . . . me. Her aching heart, empty and lonely, yearns for a token of *His love.* Nothing else can satisfy. It is not enough to hear of His love, or see others re-

F VIII

joicing in it, " Let *Him* kiss *me*." Personal contact needed. His kiss is a token of affection, favour, and friendship. This grace can only come from Him. God breathed into Adam—kissed him—and he became a living soul. Matt. 4, 4.

2. *His Personal Influence.* " Draw me, we will run after Thee " (v. 4). Having been reconciled, she longs to follow. Christ is God's magnet to draw souls to Himself (John 6, 44). His influence over the life should be an unceasing *draw*. He draws by His Word and His Cross, wherever He is " lifted up." This prayer of the Bride is a proof of her love for Him, and devotion to Him. Her self-denial will affect others, " *we* will run." The more powerfully our lives are influenced by Christ the more swiftly shall we run after Him, and the more likely are we to move others. It is better to draw than to drive. If His influence does not draw us after Him, there are other influences that will certainly draw us from Him. He will have a willing people in the day of His power.

III.—HER EXPERIENCE OF HIS FELLOW-SHIP. Her prayer has been answered. He has drawn and she did run, and the results have been abundantly satisfying. We now find her—

1. *Companying with Him.* " The King hath brought me into His chambers " (v. 4). These chambers represent His own personal possessions. All His unsearchable riches are at her disposal. His peace, His rest, His joy, His wealth, what a portion ? These present possessions represent the full Salvation Christ

desires to give those who lovingly follow Him. *He* brought her in, she never could have entered His chambers without His liberty and guidance. The way into the Holy of Holies is now open to every blood-washed Spirit-led soul (Phil. 3, 12-14).

2. *Rejoicing in Him.* " We will be glad and rejoice in Thee." With loving kindness has she been drawn, and with infinite plenty hath she been satisfied. The Bridegroom did it all for her, so she will rejoice in Him. It is always with gladness and rejoicing that anyone is brought into this King's palace (Ps. 45, 15). There is no night there ; it is a banqueting-house, with a canopy of love. All my springs, both the upper and nether—for soul and body—are in Thee.

3. *Testifying of Him.* " We will make mention of Thy love " (v. 4, R.V.). His love, like Himself, cannot be hid. His love, like Jonathan, constrained Him to strip Himself for our adorning (2 Cor. 8, 9). Shall it not also constrain us to speak forth its praise ? At this world's " Babel Streams " the heavenly minstrel can only sit and weep if he has no other fountain opened. Make mention of His love, for it is better than the world's wine. It is not a plant that grows among the weeds of Nature's garden, it is an exotic from above (Rom. 5, 5). The " *upright* " love Him, although the learned and the fashionable may reject Him (1 Cor. 6, 29).

> " O cold ungrateful heart, that can from Jesus turn,
>
> When living fires of love within His heart doth burn."

HER CONFESSION AND APPEAL.
CHAPTER I, 5-7.

I.—HER CONFESSION. " I am black, but comely." To many this is a seeming contradiction, if not a perfect absurdity, but it is a very fit expression of the two-fold nature of the Bride's character, even although she has been brought into His chambers of wealth and beauty. She describes herself as—

1. " *Black* as the tents of Kedar." These tents of Kedar, or of the Bedouin, who led a nomadic life in Arabia, were blackened by the sun, and uncomely. Like our own carnal mind it is black, and can be nothing else.

2. " *Comely* as the curtains of Solomon." The graceful and costly curtains of Solomon could only be seen from within. The king's daughter is all glorious within, if the outward appearance should look black in the eyes of others. In the flesh life there is no good thing, but in the Spirit life there is the beauty of the Lord. While in our sins, we, like the Ethiopian in his native land, were unconscious of our blackness. But wondrous grace, her blackness did not disqualify her for receiving His Comeliness. See Ezek. 16, 14 for the secret of perfect beauty.

II.—HER EXPLANATION. She suffered from different causes. " I am black," she says, because—

1. " The *sun* hath scorched me " (v. 6, R.V.). Look not with disdain upon me. I am black because I have been long and severely *exposed*. If we had been

born and brought up in Africa the sun would have blackened us too.   How many are born into conditions where they are morally blackened ere they know what it means.   Christ does not despise us although the complexion of our character may have been changed by exposure and sin.

2.   " My *Mother's sons* were incensed against me " (R.V.).   Her " Mother's sons " may represent those unspiritual church members, which are her professed brothers and sisters.   They don't like her dusky appearance ;   they are grieved and angry that *she* should have such favour shewn her by the King.   The proud and the jealous have no appreciation of the *grace* of the Lord Jesus Christ.   Persecuted by your own household.

III.—HER OCCUPATION.   " They made me the keeper of the vineyards."   This looked like a very lowly task for the bride of a king.   She offered no objections ;   she willingly gives herself to the service of the thankless for His sake.   Although the task was common and arduous she humbly accepts the situation.   Those who love the Lord and are beloved by Him will have their pride and patience tried in their service for Him.   " Mine own vineyard," she says, " have I not kept."   Was she to blame for this ?   We think not. The word " But " supplied here, which is not in the Hebrew, has had much to do with the misunderstanding of the statement.   A free rendering might be " They made me guardian of that which belonged to others, and so devoted was I to their interests that I sacrificed my own.   She made herself of no reputation, denying

herself for the good of others. This is the true attitude
and business of the Church. In this Christ Himself has
set us an example. "He saved others, Himself He
could not save." Self-forgetting love is the chief mark
of the Bride of Christ and the real motive to all missionary enterprise. There are, of course, those who are so
engrossed about the vineyard of the body that they
neglect the vineyard of the soul.

IV—.HER APPEAL. "Tell me, O Thou whom
my soul loveth " (v. 7). It was first " Kiss me," then
" Draw me," now it is " Tell me." This indicates progressive experience. The appeal is to Him who is the
object of her soul's love. There is " none other name "
to her. Those who love the Lord must love Him with
the *whole* heart. She makes three requests—

1. **Tell** me where Thou *feedest* Thy flock. This
implies that He has a flock, and that He feeds them.
His flock was given Him by the Father, redeemed by His
blood, and fed by His Word. He feeds them among the
green pastures of His revealed truth. He feeds His
flock where He Himself is, as the Bread of Life (John
14, 21).

2. **Tell** me where Thou *resteth* Thy flock at noon.
His people need rest as well as food. She feels her need
of both, and seeks after them. Rest at *noon* from the
burdensome heat of wearisome toil and oppressive circumstances. Where does He rest them ? Under the
shadow of His love and faithfulness.

3. **Tell** me . . . Why should I be as *one that is
vailed*, beside the flock of Thy companions? (R.V.). To be

a vailed one is to be one unknown to others. The Lord has many companions—*Sunday* companions—to whom this devoted Bride is unknown. She asks, "Why should I be as one unknown to them, who company with Thee?" Her heart yearns for fellowship with all who profess to love her Beloved. But alas, the true Bride of Christ is still as a vailed one to those who have only the form of godliness denying the power. Why it should be so is often a wonder to the sincere follower of Christ.

HIS ANSWER AND ENCOURAGEMENT.
CHAPTER I, 8-11.

In verse 8, the Bridegroom gives His gracious answer to the Bride's urgent request, "Tell me."

I.—HIS WORDS OF APPRECIATION. "O thou fairest among women." He knows how to speak a word in season to the weary. What constitutes beauty in His sight may be unattractive to the purblind multitude. To her *He* is the "Chiefest; to Him *she* is the "fairest." The deciding factor is love and personal devotedness. So is it with Christ and His Church.

II.—HIS WORDS OF COUNSEL. In answer to her question He now tells her—

1. *Where she is to go.* "Go thy way forth by the footsteps of the flock." The *footsteps* of His flock in every age have been the footsteps of *faith* as taught in the eleventh chapter of Hebrews. To "go forth" in this direction implies a definite act of the will, and a readiness to be separated from all that would hinder

It is along this path that He feedeth His flock. " Seek
the old paths, where is the good way," and beware of
the " New " (John 14, 6). New revelations, and New
theologies that are not in accordance with the " footsteps of the flock " are to be rejected and avoided.

2. *What she is to do.* " Feed thy kids beside the
shepherd's tents." The kids are the young of the flock
in which she has become specially interested. Personal
devotion to Christ leads to an earnest desire after the
good of others. Our Lord's " Lovest thou Me " was
accompanied with " Feed My lambs," and always is.
The kids were to be associated with the flock, and so are
to be fed " beside the shepherd's tent. ' Their tents
were pitched for the convenience of the flock. The place
where the shepherd feeds his sheep is the place where
to feed the lambs, and what is " green pastures " to
the one will be " green pastures " to the other. There
is but one Lord, one faith.

III.—HIS WORDS OF COMPARISON. " I have
compared thee . . . to a steed in Pharaoh's chariot "
(v. 9, R.V.). This is His comparison, and must be full of
significance. It suggests—

1. *Soundness.* The King would have no blem-
ished steed in His chariot. The blind and the lame had
no place there. In God's service, moral, spiritual, and
intellectual soundness is required. Salvation from the
deformity of sin needed—

2. *Dignity.* The royal steed must be dignified in
its every action. A slovenly, cumbrous gait does not
become such. The servant of Jesus Christ must walk

worthy of the Lord. " Lift up your heads." Your citizenship is in heaven.

3. *Strength*. Pharaoh's chariot steed is no weakling ; it is clothed with power, and can smell the battle afar off (Job 39, 25). Paul's soul was prancing like a steed when he said, " I can do all things through Christ which strengthened me."

4. *Activity*. Always ready for action is another characteristic of the full bred, highly-developed steed. Liveliness of disposition belongs to the perfect man in Christ Jesus. " Ready to every good work " (Titus 3, 1). Always abounding in the work of the Lord.

5. *Submissiveness*. The steed in the kingly chariot, with all its pomp and power, is very sensitive and obedient to the guiding hand. So is the Bride under the constraining love of Christ and His Holy Spirit. Willing and Obedient.

6. *Honours*. The steed of Pharaoh's chariot was called to Royal service. It was associated with the king for his work and pleasure. Bearing him whither he would. We are also co-workers together with Him, who is King of Kings. Called to bear His name among the heathen (Acts 9, 15). Take My yoke upon you.

THE BLESSED FELLOWSHIP.
CHAPTER I, 12-17.

After the Bride's request and the Bridegroom's answer and encouragement, comes a season of refreshing communion.

I.—WHERE? "At the King's table" (v. 12). The King has a table—that which displays His marvellous provisions—the Word. The King "*sits*" at His Table" (R.V.) ready to welcome each invited guest. It would be an unsatisfying table if the King Himself were not there. Such is the "Lord's Table" (Luke 12, 37). The Scriptures, as the table of the King, testify of Him. Great God, what a spread.

II.—HER EXPERIENCES. She declares, *while* the King sat at His table—

1. That *His spikenard* sent forth its fragrance (v. 12, R.V.). As this sweet-smelling shrub, in a congenial atmosphere poured forth its fragrance, so in the warmth of His presence, her afflictions flowed out copiously. When His Spirit is received in fulness, then the love of God, and love to God, will be shed abroad in our hearts.

2. That *her Beloved* was to her as a bundle of myrrh. The more love we have for Christ, the more fragrant and precious will He become to us. Not only myrrh, but as a *bundle* of it. We are told that Eastern ladies carried myrrh in their bosoms to impart fragrance to the person. Christ in the heart, makes a fragrant life. To some He is but a "root out of a dry ground." To them that believe, He is precious.

3. That His position was *on her heart*. "A bundle of myrrh . . . that lieth betwixt my breasts" (13, R.V.). Betwixt the breasts is the seat of the heart— the place where Christ delights to rest. He dwells in the heart by faith (Eph. 3, 17).

III.—HIS WORDS OF COMFORT TO HER. Now the Bridegroom responds to the glowing testimony of the Bride. She has honoured Him ; He honours her. He says—

1. " Thou art fair " (v. 15). She has become very pleasant in His eyes. Those to whom Christ is precious, are precious to Christ. The more beauty we can see in Jesus, the more of His beauty will be seen in us. To be fair in His sight is better than being fashionable with the world.

2. " Thine eyes are as doves " (R.V.). The eyes are expressive of character. In those eyes He sees simplicity and purity. The dove nature is seen in the dove's eyes. How different are the eyes of the hawk and the fox : the eyes of the unclean and the deceitful. Her whole nature had been subdued into the purest and tenderest devotion. This is the beauty which the King so greatly desires (Ps. 45, 11).

IV.—HER WORDS OF RESPONSE TO HIM. She says—

1. " Thou art fair, my Beloved, yea pleasant " (v. 16). Fair and pleasant characterises the Bridegroom. Beautiful to the eye, and pleasant to the heart. He satisfies the vision and meets all the needs of the soul.

2. "Our couch is green " (R.V.). The resting place of these mutual beloveds is as pleasant and refreshing as the Love of God. They rest in His Love. They have both been made to lie down in green pastures.

3. " Our House has beams of cedars " (R.V.). The house of the Church, in which both Bride and Bride-

groom delight, being built on a Rock ; its beams are strong and enduring. Cedar wood is the most durable of timbers—sometimes called shittim wood. The superstructure is built to *Stand*.

4. "Our Galleries are firs" (R.V., Marg.). The galleries may refer to steps of ascent, or to a series of balconies for outward prospect. The fragrant firs and the enchanting outlook, that widens the horizon, as they arise, platform above platform. Such is the progressive experience, and growing delight of those who abide in fellowship with Him. Three times over, she uses the word "Our" not "My." What have we, that we have not received from Him, and what is Ours, is also His. It is mutual enjoyment.

TIMES OF REFRESHING.
CHAPTER 2, 1-7.

In His Chambers, and in His Presence, she is in the enjoyment of rich refreshing. "In Thy Presence is fulness of joy." The conversation is the sweetest and most endearing. Notice—

I.—HER CONFESSION. "I am a Rose of Sharon, a Lily of the Valley" (R.V.). These words are often quoted as spoken by the Bridegroom, but they are the words of the Bride, and express her lowly opinion of herself. The Rose of the plain and the Lily of the valley were only common, modest flowers. She feels that in herself, she is no better than others. But God hath chosen the poor of this world rich in faith and heirs of the kingdom (Jas. 5, 2 ; 2 Cor. 8, 9).

II.—HIS APPRECIATION. " As a Lily *among thorns*, so is My love among the daughters." A lily is the symbol of beauty, of purity, and of humility. To Him, she is a lily arrayed in a beauty more glorious than that of Solomon's, but her position on earth is as one " among thorns." Thorns represent the uncharitable, uncomely, unprofitable, and hurtful. Their tendency is to choke the Word of life—their end is to be burned. The lily is *among* the thorns, not of them, as the wheat grows among the tares. There were saints in Cesar's household. Their position is one of suffering and testimony.

III.—HER BLISSFUL TESTIMONY. Observe that it is all of Him. She refers to—

1. *His Character.* " As the tree (citron or orange) among the trees . . . so is my Beloved among the sons " (v. 3). She is a lily among thorns, He is an orange tree among the fruitless trees of the wood : the sons of men. He is "the Tree of Life." None ever found " nothing but leaves " here. This tree with its thick deep green foliage, and ever ripe and luscious fruit is the coveted place of shelter and refreshing to the weary-burdened, thirsty pilgrim (Isa. 32, 2). This unique tree yields its fruit every month. Let him that is athirst, come.

2. *His Shadow.* " I sat under His shadow with great delight." There are other shadows, like Jonah's gourd, under which we may sit with fear. Only under *His* shadow can we sit with " great delight." Here only is security, love, power, and satisfaction. The fruit of His labour and suffering is sweet ; Pardon, peace, and hope. It is sweet to the taste of a weary, hungry,

thankful heart. Many have their taste so depraved by eating the deceptive apples of Sodom, that they desire not the fruit of the Tree of Life.

3. *His Banqueting House.* This is suggestive of joyful company, and abundant provision. The House of Prayer is a banqueting house, where the soul is refreshed and strengthened with His grace and truth, being filled with the Spirit. " He brought me ! none else could. He leads me into the place of fulness of blessing."

4. *His Banner.* " His banner over me was love." This banner is the symbol of His conquering love ; under it she has a triumphant entrance. Our liberty of access comes through His prevailing love. " He loved me, and gave Himself for me." This King sets His banner over all His possessions. It is the banner of love, because all the forces of love in His Kingdom are represented by it.

5. *His Hands.* " His left hand under my head, and His right hand doth embrace me." She who has such a warm place in the heart of His love, will not fail to have a secure place in the hands of His power. His left hand for support, and His right hand for protection. " Underneath are the *everlasting arms.*" He fainteth not. The beloved of the Lord shall dwell is safety by Him (Deut. 33, 12). None is able to pluck His loved ones out of His hand (John 10, 28-30).

PROOFS OF HIS LOVE.
CHAPTER 2, 8-13.

" The voice of my Beloved " (v. 8). She hears His voice , it is the voice of love, a love that delights to manifest itself in unmistakable words and actions.

1. He *Comes*. "Behold, He cometh." The great distance which separated Him and her, could only be bridged by Him, through infinite love. He comes *powerfully*, "leaping upon the mountains." He comes *joyfully*, "skipping upon the hills." He comes to seek and to save.

2. He *Stands*. "He standeth behind our wall." There is no wall that can keep Him out, but "*our* wall." The wall of indifference and unbelief. Yet He condescends to stand behind it. Break down this wall, and you will see the King.

3. He *Looks*. "He looketh in at the windows" (v. 9, R.V.). He takes advantage of every opening to get into touch with our needy souls. No lover can be more interested in his sweetheart than He is about His own. Every desire after Him is a window through which He can look into the soul.

4. He *Reveals*. "He sheweth Himself through the lattice" (R.V.). It is the fondest longing of His gracious heart to shew Himself, in all the wealth of His character, to the lonely loving heart. "He that loveth me . . . I will manifest Myself to him" (John 14, 21).

5. He *Speaks*. "My Beloved spake" (v. 10) She has no doubt at all that it is *His* voice she hears. What other voice could be so sweet, so surpassingly charming ? There is no mistaking it.

6. He *Invites*. "Rise up, my love, my fair one, and come away." He has come that He might take her to Himself, and into the fair summer land of His Grace.

" Come away," away from all that harms or hinders, into
His ways and works, where there is peace and power.
As sinners we go *to* Him, as disciples we go *after* Him, as
friends we go *with* Him.

7.   He *Encourages.*   The characteristics of spring
mentioned here (vv. 11-13) are metaphorical of the *new*
life.   It is spring-time in the soul, when the Sun of
Righteousness casts His warm reviving beams upon it.
All the blessings of this new life have their source in Him.
In these words of cheer, spoken to the Bride by the
Bridegroom, we have " The Gospel of Christ," which
assures us that—

(1).   " The winter (of Death) is past " (v. 11).
You hath He quickened who were dead.   All in Christ
are a new creation . . . All things are become new
(2 Cor. 5. 17).   Passed from death into life, from winter
into summer.

(2).   " The rain (of Judgment) is over and gone."
As Noah, after the flood, stepped out into a new world,
so Christ, by His death on the Cross, brings us out of
condemnation into the glorious liberty of " newness of
life " (Rom. 8, 1).

(3).   " The flowers (of promise) appear on the
earth."   After the death and resurrection of Christ,
the promises of God, spring up in fresh beauty and power,
as plentiful as the flowers of the field.   " The promise is
unto you," pluck these precious gifts, and make your
life beautiful and fragrant.

(4).   " The time of Singing (Praise) is come."   It
well becometh the mornings of spring to be vocal with

song. The dawn of the new morning of spiritual life
is a time when every bird within the cage of our being is
set a singing. " Praise ye the Lord," sing and make
melody in your heart, for the Lord hath done great things
for you.

(5). " The voice of the turtle (Holy Spirit) is
heard in our land." While the flowers of promise appear
in the earth—offered to all, the assuring voice of the
Spirit only is heard in our land. To receive the promised
Spirit, as the Comforter and Guide, we must know the
Power of His Cross, (Gal. 3, 13-14).

(6). The season of Fruitfulness is at hand. " The
fig tree ripeneth her green figs, and the vines are in
blossom " (v. 13). There is now the prospect of a
priceless ingathering. This is the stage referred to in
John 15, 16. Blessing for others must be one of the
results of our Union with Him (Hosea 14, 8).

(7). The Call is repeated. " Arise, my love, my
fair one, and come away." Arise, don't keep sitting in
the place of darkness and doubt. Thou art " my love,
the joy of my heart," come away into the full enjoyment
of all this Heaven-sent Spring brings within your reach.
In His Presence is fulness of joy. Wilt thou go with this
Man ?

MUTUAL DELIGHT.
CHAPTER 2, 14-17.

To her, He is the " chiefest among the thousands,"
to Him, she is the " fairest among women." The
fellowship of such must be sweet. Observe here—

G VIII

I.—HER SECURITY. As His own *dove*—the emblem of purity and affection—she is—

1. " In the *clefts* of the Rock," for *safety* (v. 14). She dwells on high (Isa. 33, 16), far above the reach of the cruel fowler, in the cleft of the Rock of Ages, kept by the power of God. The strength of Hills, which is His, is also hers.

2. " In the *secret places* of the ascent " (Newberry), for *progress*. Her position is one of safety, her privilege is one of advancement. The Rock of defence is frequently associated with the secret place of privilege (Ps. 27, 15 ; Isa. 33, 16). The power of the Spirit is associated with the blood of the Cross. As sons, we are in the cleft of the rock, as servants, we are " in the secret places of the stairs."

II.—HIS LONGING FOR COMMUNION. He desires of her two things, He says—

1. " Let Me see *thy countenance* . . . for it is *comely*." Comely with the beauty that He has put upon it, by satisfying her heart with His love and goodness. Lift up thy face unto God—His heart yearns to see His own light in your eyes, and to have fellowship with thee. Then—

2. " Let Me hear *thy voice*, for it is *sweet*." It is sweet to Him to hear *thy* voice in prayer to Him, in praise of Him, and in testimony for Him. The voice may be weak and trembling, but to Him it is sweet. Let Him hear it often, for there are so many other voices that must be harsh and painful to His gracious ear.

III.—HIS CAREFULNESS OVER THEIR POS-
SESSIONS. " Take *us* the foxes, the little foxes, that
spoil the vineyards, for *our* vineyards are in blossom "
(v. 15, R.V.). The vineyards may represent spheres
of service. Into the sacred enclosure foxes, or false
teachers, have come (Ezek. 13, 4). There are also " little
foxes," playful, innocent things in a way, but they
spoil the vines. The Bride and Bridegroom are co-
partners in this business ; what touches the vineyard,
affects them both. If we are vitally united to Christ,
we shall be vitally interested in His cause. What is to
be done with the foxes ? " Take them." Deal with
them as foxes.

IV.—HER JOYFUL CONFESSION. " My Beloved is mine, and I am His " (v. 16).

1. *His, by Grace and Choice.* His, because He
hath set His love upon me, and hath chosen me as His
own. He loved me, and gave Himself for me.

2. *His, by Faith and Self-surrender.* " I am His ! "
He gave Himself for me, and I have given myself for
Him. Ye are not your own, ye are bought with a price.
This is a union that is indissoluble in death or eternity.

3. *His, until the Day break.* Just now, her sphere
of action, in fellowship with Him, is among the shadows :
but when that great " day " dawns, these shall " flee
away." She is His, as really in the place of suffering, as
in the day of glory. Yea, though I walk through the
valley of the shadows . . . I will fear no evil, for
Thou art with me (Ps. 23, 4).

4. *His, until He comes again.* " Turn, my Beloved, and be Thou like a young hart upon the mountains of division " (R.V., Marg.). The young hart can speedily overcome the hills and valleys, which separate. When Christ comes again, He will come " quickly" the mountains that presently hide His visible presence, and *divide* His waiting people, will flow down at His Appearing. The cry of the Bride is, " Come, Lord Jesus, come quickly."

A SORROWFUL NIGHT.
CHAPTER 3, 1-4.

These verses tell us of a lost fellowship, and a midnight search.

1. *The Search.* " I sought Him." Why ? What had happened ? Something had separated these lovers. When the Holy Spirit is grieved, fellowship with the Lord is broken. She sought Him because she was deeply sensible of her loss. The more precious the Lord is to us, the more sorrowfully shall we miss His presence.

2. *The Time.* " By night." It is always night to the loving heart when He is not there. Distance from Christ implies darkness ; for He is the Light of Life.

3. *The Manner.* (1), She sought Him on His *bed*. The bed is a place of ease and inactivity. But He is not found here ; for the search is still in a slothful fashion. (2), She sought Him in the *Street*, she is out of her bed now, and into Society. But even in the city, she is seeking for the living among the dead. Lost fellowship

with Christ is not restored in this manner. (3), She sought Him among the *Watchmen* (v. 3). "Saw ye Him?" Alas, even the Watchmen of Zion are not always in personal touch with Him. She has also to pass them by.

4. *The Discovery.* "I found Him whom my soul loveth" (v. 4). When her own plans and methods and efforts had been exhausted, He revealed Himself unto her. She made this joyful discovery when *alone*. Mary made a like discovery after a somewhat similar search (John 20, 11-16), "I found *Him*." There was no possibility of her mistaking another for Him. He only could satisfy her loving, trusting heart.

5. *The Result.* Having found Him, she says— (1), "I held Him." She held Him fast, with the heart grip of faith, like one clinging for very life. She held Him, conscious of her own need, and of His inexpressible preciousness. (2), "I brought Him into my mother's house." If He had been earlier brought into her mother's house, she might have saved herself this time of weary searching. Fellowship with Jesus Christ is sweet, but it is all the sweeter when He is brought into the home circle. If you cannot bring your mother and your brethren to Jesus, bring Jesus to them.

HIS BED, HIS CHARIOT, AND HIS CROWN.
CHAPTER 3, 7-11.

These words, "Bed, Chariot, Crown," are all emphasised in the Hebrew.

I.—HIS BED. " Behold, His bed." His bed represents the place of divine rest.

1. *It was well defended.* " Threescore valiant men are about it." The place of His rest is strongly protected. " He shall not fail, nor be discouraged." Neither the power, the number, nor the devices of the enemy can disturb the rest of the Lord. To enter into His rest is to be saved indeed. " Come unto Me, and I will give you rest." His defenders are all " expert in war " (v. 8).

2. *The reason why.* " Because of fear in the night." We wrestle not against flesh and blood . . . but against the rulers of the *darkness* of this world (Eph. 6, 12). The foes that seek to disturb His rest, and ours, are mighty, but they that are for us are greater. The weapons of our warfare are not carnal.

II.—HIS CHARIOT. This is His " Car of State" (R.V., Marg.). Like the Salvation of the Lord—

1. *It was devised by the King.* " King Solomon made himself a chariot " (v. 9). The plan, the purpose, and the material were all his own devising. So was it with the Chariot of the Gospel. The whole scheme of Redemption is according to the choice and mind of God. Man's thoughts have no place here.

2. *It was costly.* " He made the pillars thereof of silver, the bottom of gold." Solomon was not only the wisest, but the richest man of the age, he only could provide the materials for such a costly Car of State. Silver and gold stands here for preciousness and perfection. The means of our Salvation was indeed a

costly provision. Not silver and gold, but the precious blood of Christ.

3. *It was comfortable.* It was " inlaid with love " (R.V., Marg.). The covering was the purple of royalty, but the lining was that of *love*. This phrase in itself is ample warrant for seeking spiritual significance in this Song. In this wonderful chariot there is Love all around. What a blessed experience. You have to get inside to know what is the length, the breadth, the depth, and the height of this love, which passeth knowledge.

4. *It was for others.* " For the daughters of Jerusalem " (v. 10). O ! ye daughters of Zion, this is the royal provision for you to take you to the King's palace. Written all round the Chariot of our Salvation, are these words, " Whosoever will, may come." If any man enter in he shall be saved and satisfied.

III.—HIS CROWN. "Go forth . . . and behold King Solomon with the crown " (v. 11). Yes ! the chariot paved with love leads to the vision of the crowned King.

1. *When did He receive it ?* It was " in the day of his espousals, and in the day of the gladness of his heart." When Christ was resurrected and enthroned, it was the day of His betrothal to His redeemed Bride, and a day of great gladness to His heart.

2. *Who gave Him the Crown ?* " The crown wherewith His Mother crowned Him." The *Mother* is the embodiment of Love and grace. God is Love. Love sent Jesus Christ, the Son, and love crowned Him.

" On His head are many crowns." Behold your Bridegroom cometh, crowned with glory and honour. Go
forth to meet Him, and to be for ever with Him

HER PERSONAL BEAUTY.
CHAPTER 4, 1-6.

" Behold, thou art fair, my Love : behold, thou
art fair." This is not the Bride's own estimate of herself, but His. The features of the physical body are
here used as a similitude of the Church's moral beauty.
The outward appearance is taken as an analogy of the
inward character.

1. Her *Eyes* are like dove's. Meek and affectionate. The love of her heart beams out in her eyes.
" The light of the body is the eye." Like Him, she is
meek and lowly in heart.

2. Her *Hair* is like a flock of goats. Her hair as
a vail of covering gracefully hides her person, as a
flock of goats on Mount Gilead. The Bride is modest,
not self-assertive, and even her modesty is majestic
as the stately march of a flock of goats.

3. Her *Teeth* are like a flock of ewes that are newly
shorn (v. 2, R.V.). Numerous as a flock, and *clean* as a
newly-shorn lamb. The teeth of the Bride are not set
on edge, after the sour grapes of the world. They are
not spoiled by eating that which is not good (Isa. 55, 2).
They are not like lion's, for devouring one another.

4. Her *Lips* are like a thread of scarlet. They
have a healthy colour, and are well defined, because they
speak the language of the Crucified One. The lips of

those who preach the " blood of His Cross " must become like a thread of scarlet.

5. Her *Speech* is comely. Because it is seasoned with the salt of His Spirit, and because it is the language of a faithful loving heart. The speech of those who speak of Him, who is altogether lovely, must be comely. No corrupt communication can proceed out of her mouth.

6. Her *Temples* are like a piece of pomegranate. They are well developed, and indicate the highest wisdom. Her Bridegroom is made unto her wisdom and righteousness. Those that are Christ's are wise in Him.

7. Her *Neck* is like the tower of David (v. 4). Strong, straight, and dignified. She is not stiff-necked. The carriage or bearing of the Church of Christ ought to be in keeping with her glorious destiny as the Lamb's wife. Why should the saint walk with his head bowed to the earth, as if he were the conquered foe of the world ?

8. Her *Breasts* are like young roes which feed among the lilies (v. 5). The breast is the symbol of *Affection*. They are like " *young* roes," because they possess all the vigour of youth, and all the warmth of a first-love. These affectionate desires have pleasant pastures : they " feed among the lilies." He satisfieth the longing soul with good.

9. Her *Purpose*. " I will get me to the mountain of myrrh . . . until the day break and the shadows flee away " (v. 6). The " mountain of myrrh," and " hill of frankincense " fitly represent " heavenly

places in Christ Jesus." This is the abiding place of
His people now, until the day of His Appearing break,
and the shadows of this earthly life of sorrow and suffering flee away before the glory of His Presence.

HER CHARACTER AND INFLUENCE.
CHAPTER 4, 7-15.

The many titles given here by the Bridegroom, to
the Bride, are a revelation of His high appreciation of
her character and preciousness to Him. His invitation
is most expressive, " Come with Me " (v. 8). His heart
longs for unbroken communion.

1. Come and *Walk* with Me (Col. 1, 10).   Agreement.

2. Come and *Talk* with Me (Luke 24, 17).   Prayer.

3. Come and *Work* with Me (1 Cor. 3, 9).   Service.

4. Come and *Suffer* with Me (Luke 14, 26-29).
Fellowship.

5. Come and *Rejoice* with Me (Matt. 25, 21).
Reward.

6. Come and *Dwell* with Me (John 14, 2-3). Glory.

Now observe the various titles used as indicating
her character in His sight.

I.—HER CHARACTER. He speaks of her—

1. As a *Friend* without spot. " Thou art all
fair, my friend : there is no spot in thee " (v. 7, Newberry). The Church is Christ's friend in this present
evil age, and should be holy and without blemish before
Him in love (Eph. 5, 27).

2. As the *Companion* of His Choice. "Come with Me . . . from the lion's dens ; from the mountains of leopards " (v. 8). Christ has not only chosen us, but by following Him, we are delivered from the power of those spiritual lions and leopards whose dens are still in high places (Eph. 6, 12).

3. As a *Sister* and *Bride*. He calls her "My Sister, my Bride (v. 9). "Spouse" should always be read "Bride" (R.V.). This double relationship comes by *birth* and *betrothal*. Like Eve, the Church is "bone of His bones and flesh of His flesh"—Sister—and also God's gift to Him as an helpmeet—Bride. His Incarnation and Resurrection explain these two facts.

4. As a *Garden* enclosed (v. 12). A garden enclosed is a place of private pleasure and profit. The Church is Christ's own private and delightsome property It is well enclosed, protected by the walls of His almighty power and everlasting love. Separated unto Him.

5. As a *Fountain* sealed. There are treasures and possibilities connected with the Church that have not been revealed. Our life is hid with Christ in God. " When He shall appear then shall we also be manifested with Him.

6. As a *Well* opened. "A well of living waters and *streams* from Lebanon " (v. 15). While about her there is much that is as yet sealed, or hidden from the eyes of others, there is also much that cannot be hid. The Church of God is a channel through which flows streams of living waters. In each redeemed and satis-

fied soul there is a well of water springing up into everlasting life (John 4, 14).

II.—HER INFLUENCE WITH HIM. What a
confession the Bridegroom makes when He says to her :
" Thou hast *ravished* My heart " (v. 9). This is the
only place where this word is used in the Bible. He had
yielded His whole heart to her and she had *taken it
away* (R.V., Marg.). How had she succeeded in so
captivating and keeping His heart ?

1. With her *Looks*. " Thou hast ravished My heart
with one of thine eyes." Being single-eyed, her whole
body was full of heavenly light. Looking unto Jesus with
the clear confident eye of faith is delightsome to Him.

2. With her *Love*. " How fair is thy love . . .
better is thy love than wine " (v. 10). Our eye will
never ravish His heart, unless He sees our heart in it.
Be not deceived, He is not mocked. He who loved the
Church, and gave Himself for it, desires to see of the
travail of His soul, and to be satisfied in it.

3. With her *Lips*. "Thy lips, O My Bride, drop as the
honeycomb" (v. 11, R.V.). The words of her testimony
are sweet to Him. The Bridegroom was sanctified in
her heart, so she was ready always to give a reason of
the hope that was in her (1 Pet. 3, 15). Let the redeemed
of the Lord *say* so, for no other lips have such a sweet
story to tell as they. Honour the Lord with thy lips.

HER PRAYER AND HIS ANSWER.
Chapters 4, 16 ; 5, 1.

1. THE PRAYER. The Bridegroom has just been
comparing her to " A garden enclosed . . . with

plants . . . and pleasant fruits . . with trees of frankincense . . . and chief spices " (4, 12-15). Now her intense desire is that she, as a garden, might be worthy of Him ; and abundantly pleasing to Him, so she prays—

1. For the Coming of the Wind. " Awake, O north wind, and come thou south " (4, 16). The *Awakening* and the *ripening* influence of the Holy Spirit are urgently needed if our lives are to be fruitful unto God. As the " North wind," He convicts ; as the " South," he comforts and guides into all truth, that we may grow in grace and knowledge.

2. For the Outflowing of the Spices. " That the spices thereof may flow out." The spices—or new graces of the character—would not flow out if they were not there. It takes the wind, or breath of the Spirit, to make them flow out right over the walls, in *testimony* to the riches of His grace (Zec. 4, 6).

3. For the Satisfaction of her Beloved. " Let my Beloved come into His garden and eat His precious fruits " (R.V.). She acknowledges that as a garden she is His ; and that all she has, and is, are for Him. What have we that we have not received ? It is His desire and should be our delight that He should come into our lives and make personal use of all the products of the Holy Spirit in us. Ye are not your own. The fruits of the unrenewed life are but sour grapes to Him.

II.—THE ANSWER. To her anxious request He gives a speedy reply—

1. He comes. " I am come into My garden " (v
1). He comes *into* His garden : into the sacred enclosure of the heart, and there manifests Himself,
claiming it as His own. " *My* garden." When we
yield ourselves unto God, our members will become
weapons of righteousness for Him.

2. He accepts. " I have gathered My myrrh,
I have eaten My honeycomb, I have drunk My wine,"
etc. He has willingly and joyfully accepted for His
own use, all that had been so freely offered Him. What
is consecrated to Him will surely be accepted by Him,
and used for the honour and glory of His name.

3. He invites. " Eat, O friends : drink, yea,
drink abundantly, O beloved." See now His eager
desire that others should share His precious provision.
Let all who are *friendly* to Christ, shew their friendliness
by accepting of His proffered blessings. Eat. Christ's
gifts cannot be received too freely, there is no danger
of excess here. " Drink abundantly " (Rev. 22, 17).

HER SLOTHFULNESS AND ITS SORROWFUL RESULTS.
CHAPTER 5, 2-8.

After a season of " abundant " feasting and fellowship, there is the danger of yielding to selfish ease (v. 1).
Let not His abounding grace lead to self-confidence and
apathy. The experience here is that of a backslider.
Why should backsliding follow times of refreshing ?

1. *Her Sleep.* " I sleep, but my heart waketh."
This describes a condition of spiritual inactivity while

the *conscience* is still awake. This is not the sleep of death (Eph. 2, 1), but of indifference and neglect. Beware of sinning wilfully after that ye have believed.

2. *Her Awakening.* The voice of my Beloved knocketh, saying, " Open to Me." She knows that it is His voice that knocketh, but she only hears it in a dreamy fashion. How tender is His call. " Open to Me, My sister, my love, My dove." The door of self-sufficiency now stands between her and Him. See Rev. 3, 17-20.

3. *Her Excuse.* " I have put off my coat, how shall I put it on?" etc. (v. 3). A very little thing is an excuse for a backslider. She had put off her coat, and washed her feet, with the intent of self-indulgence. How should she be disturbed, and *her* purposes thwarted? She has fallen from her first love.

4. *Her Repentance.* " I rose to open to my Beloved " v. 5). Her *heart moved* when she saw His hand put in by the hole of the door (v. 4, R.V.). When her heart moved she moved. Backsliding always begins with the heart. If there is even a hole in the door, His merciful hand will find it out, and seek a wider opening.

5. *Her Discovery.* " I opened to my Beloved, but my Beloved . . . was gone " (v. 6). While she opened the door her hands and fingers " dropped with myrrh " (v. 5). His gracious act in putting His hand on the lock made it very pleasant for her to open to Him, but when His fellowship is lightly esteemed it will be with-

drawn. Be not deceived, God is not mocked (Heb 12, 17).

6. *Her Self-reproach.* "My soul failed when He spake" (v. 6). He had spoken to her (v. 2), but instead of instant obedience, she began to make excuse (v. 3) Now, like Peter, she mournfully remembers her guilt and failure. She knows exactly where the sin lay. She had preferred selfish ease to obeying Him.

7. *Her Miserable Condition.*—

(1). Fellowship broken. "I sought Him but could not find Him." Sin leads to separation. We may not be conscious of it at the time, but when the Spirit is grieved our communion with Christ is interrupted.

(2). Prayer unanswered. "I called Him, but He gave me no answer." If we would ask and receive, we must *abide* in Him (John 15, 7). She has ceased to be right with Him, so her prayers do not avail (Jas. 5, 16).

(3). Testimony lost. "The watchmen found me . . . . smote me . . . wounded me . . . took away my vail from me" (v. 7). So changed was she that the city watchman did not know her. Stripped of her vail, she was brought to both sorrow and shame. Backsliders will always suffer in a measure from faithful watchmen, they must be reproved and rebuked, and made ashamed of themselves that they might more keenly feel their guiltiness in disobeying their Lord and Redeemer.

8. *Her Appeal.* "I charge you . . . that ye tell Him that I am sick of love" (v. 8). She was cast

down, but not destroyed. She pleads with those who are in touch with Him to speak to Him on her behalf— to pray for her. The Lord turned the captivity of Job when he prayed for his friends. It is a Christ-like ministry to make intercession for transgressors. It is wise to seek the help of others, that we might be lifted into a higher, Christian experience. " Brethren, pray for us." But one must needs be " sick of love " to make such a request as this.

HER DESCRIPTION OF HIS PERSON.
CHAPTER 5, 9-16.

These " daughters of Jerusalem," as nominal professors, do not help the Bride in her search for her Beloved ₍v. 8). They acknowledge her character as the " fairest among women," but to them her Beloved is no more than any other beloved. It is only a matter of personal choice and devotion. But their question, " What is thy Beloved ?" etc., stirred up her deeper emotions to give this full and glowing testimony to His matchless beauty, and incomparable character. She *knows* Him, whom she has believed.

1. *He is white and ruddy* (v. 10). As a Nazarite He was " whiter than milk, and more ruddy than rubies" (Lam. 4, 7). White and pure as the Son of God, ruddy and healthy as the Son of Man. Divinely pure and beautifully human.

2. *He is the Chiefest among thousands.* In the building He is the chief Corner-Stone. Among the brethren He is the First-born. Among the resurrected

H VIII

He is the First-begotten. He is the Alpha and Omega
The First-born of every creature.

3. *His head is as the most fine gold.* Here is perfect purity of thought and the perfection of wisdom.
His thoughts are not only pure, but very precious.

4. *His locks are bushy and black.* His is the beauty
of divine youthfulness and strength. The same yesterday, to-day, and for ever.

5. *His Eyes are as doves'* (v. 12). They are full of
tenderness and compassion. They are also " fitly set."
They see things in their true light (2 Chron. 16, 9).

6. *His Cheeks are as a bed of spices* (v. 13). Lovely,
fragrant, *attractive.* There was that about our Lord
that drew and fascinated. Even the children were
influenced by it. He is fairer than the children of men.

7. *His Lips are like lilies.* They are pure and full
of grace ; for grace hath been poured into them (Ps.
45, 2). They drop sweetness.

8. *His Hands are as rings of gold.* (v. 14, R.V.).
Precious and endless in their working. How manifold
are Thy works (Ps. 104, 24). I have graven thee upon
the palm of My hand (Isa. 49, 16). Into Thine hand I
commit my spirit (Ps. 31, 5. 2 Tim. 1, 12).

9. *His Body is as bright ivory* (R.V.). Ivory,
" overlaid with sapphires," is surely symbolic of purity
and incorruptibility. God would not suffer His Holy
One to see corruption. On the mount of transfiguration it was seen to be overlaid with sapphires shining
like the sun

10. *His Legs are as pillars of marble* (v. 15)
They are strong and unfailing. He is the Rock, His
work and ways are perfect (Deut. 32, 4). He fainteth
not.

11. *His Aspect is like Lebanon* (v.r.). There is a
unique dignity about His general appearance that
makes Him pre-eminent among the sons of men, as
Lebanon among the hills.

12. *His Mouth is most sweet* (v. 16). Never man
spake like this Man (John 7, 46). Never man had such
a message as this Man. His mouth is most sweet, for
in Him dwelleth all the fulness of the Godhead ; full
of grace and truth.

13. *He is altogether lovely.* All the *loveliness* of
God is revealed in Him. What is more lovely than
love. God is Love. He that dwelleth in love dwelleth
in God.

Now, says the Bride, " *This* is my Beloved, and
this is my Friend." Who would not covet such a
relationship ?

THE ANXIOUS INQUIRERS.
CHAPTER 6, 1-3.

It is not to be wondered at that after the Bride's
magnificent testimony to His " altogether lovely "
character (vv. 10-16) we should immediately meet with
seeking souls. If Christ, in all His glorious fulness,
was more frequently preached, there would be no dearth
of results.

1.—THE INQUIRERS. These are the daughters or virgins of Jerusalem. They are nominal professors, members of the visible Church, who are as yet strangers to Jesus Christ. Their lives are morally clean, but they have no personal experience of His power and fellowship.

1. Whom they seek. They seek *her Beloved.* " Whither is thy Beloved turned aside ? that we may seek *Him* with thee." They seek Him of whom they have just heard. Him who is so full of grace and truth, the Mighty to save, and to satisfy. Hearing should lead to seeking. Whom seekest thou ?   (John 20, 15).

2. Where they seek. " Whither is thy Beloved gone. O thou fairest among women." They seek Him through her, who has been made fair through His comeliness put upon her. Her *fairness* was her likeness to Him, which made her testimony all the more effective. Those whose character has not been beautified by the grace of Christ will not be privileged to *win* souls.

II.—THE DIRECTIONS GIVEN. She is able to tell them where He can be found. He is—

1. In His garden. " My Beloved is gone down into His garden " (v. 2). He delights to wander in the garden of His Word, the " Scripture of Truth." There ye shall meet with Him. Every book of the Bible is a " bed of spices."

2. Feeding His flock. " My Beloved is gone down . . . to feed (His flock) in the gardens." Here He refreshes and strengthens His people, who, like Him, take delight in this garden. " Thy Word was found, and

I did eat it." Man shall not live by bread alone, but by *every word* that proceedeth out of the mouth of God. Faith cometh by hearing, and hearing by the Word of God.

3. Gathering lilies. " Gone down into His garden . . . to gather lilies." His loved ones are like lilies (2, 2), here He gathers them, receiving them to Himself, and making them a delight to His soul. He who gathers the lambs in His arms says, " Him that cometh unto Me I will in no wise cast out."

III.—HER PERSONAL TESTIMONY. " I am my Beloved's, and my Beloved is mine " (v. 3). I am His, because I have given myself to Him. He is mine because He has given Himself for me. He is mine, because I have accepted Him ; I am His because He has accepted me. We should be able and ready to give a reason for the hope that is in us to all those that ask. Such personal testimony is always encouraging to anxious inquiries.

SYMBOLS OF HER UNIQUE CHARACTER.
CHAPTER 6, 4-10.

It would seem that each time she extols His virtues, speaking of the goodness and loveliness of His character (vv. 2-3), He in turn extols the virtues of the Bride. They who honour the Lord shall be honoured by Him. To her, " He is altogether lovely " (v. 16). To Him, she is " the choice one " (v. 9).

1. *Beautiful as Tirzah* (v. 4). Tirzah was a royal residence, a place renowned for its *beauty* (1 Kings

14, 19). The Church, true and clean, is a beautiful and delightful residence of her Lord. " I in you." The beauty of the Lord our God upon us.

2. *Comely as Jerusalem.* " Zion," like the Church, is " the perfection of beauty " (Ps. 50, 2). Beautiful for *situation,* none so favoured and honoured as she. Like Jerusalem, she is well protected, the mountains of God are round about her. The comeliness of her God is upon her (Ezek. 16, 14).

3. *Hopeful as the Morning.* " She looketh forth as the morning " (v. 10). Her prospects are bright Her cause is as the shining light (of the morning) that shineth more and more, until the perfect day dawns. She has a blessed hope (Matt. 13, 43).

4. *Fair as the Moon.* The moon is the chief light of the world in the absence of the sun. Ye are the light of the world. " Occupy till I come." The moon's fairness is but the reflection of the unseen sun. So the Church.

5. *Clear as the Sun.* While the moon is not so brilliant as the sun, it is equally faithful in fulfilling its appointed mission. The Church ought to be as clear as the Christ in its doctrine, motives, and life. This one thing I do.

6. *Terrible as an Army* (v. 10). This word " terrible " here and in v. 4 only occurs once elsewhere in the Bible (Hab. 1, 7). It means *Awe-inspiring* as bannered hosts. There are tremendous possibilities in " bannered hosts." Banners here are the symbols of unity, conviction, courage, and confidence. The Church

in its goings forth on its divinely-inspired mission, with its unfailing resources, its God-given armour and un-conquered Leader, should be an awe-inspiring sight. Is this what the Church is to-day?

THE BRIDEGROOM'S VISIT.
CHAPTER 6, 11-13.

1. *The Place.* "I went down into the garden of nuts." The Church, as a whole, is compared to a garden, and His people to nuts, whose lives are sweet to Him, and well protected. Our life is hid with Christ in God. He "went down." All His dealings with us implies a going down on His part. He humbled Himself.

2. *The Purpose.* "To see the fruits" (v. 11). And whither the vine flourished, and the pomegranates budded. He came seeking fruit, and to see how His green plants prospered. The tree that is planted by the rivers of water should bring forth fruit in its season (Ps. 1, 3). Every tree planted by our Lord has *river* privileges, and is therefore without excuse. In Me is thy fruit found. See John 15, 1-5.

3. *The Effect.* "Or ever I was aware, My soul (desire) set Me among the chariots of My princely people" (v. 12, R.V.). Suddenly, His chief desire was to identify Himself with the martial movements of His beloved and princely people. Those who would bring forth fruit unto Him, by their life and testimony, shall have the joy-inspiring presence of their Lord and Saviour. "Lo, I am with you." Pentecost is the expres-

sion of His sudden desire to go forth with His princely people in their service for Him.

4. *The Call.* " Return, return, O Shulamite ; return, return, that we may look upon thee " (v. 13). "Shulamite " is the feminine for Solomon, and might be rendered, Return, O Solomonite. She is called by the King's own name, as the disciples of Jesus Christ was called " Christians " first at Antioch. Perhaps this call is in response to her anxious inquiry in chapter 5, 8. If His soul is to abide with His princely people, they must with their whole soul return to Him. Fruitfulness is con- ditioned by His abiding in us, and we in Him."

5. *The Question.* She now ventures to ask : " Why will ye look upon the Shulamite ? " (v. 13). What will ye see in her ? She has nothing that she has not received worth looking at. It is all by the grace of God that we are what we are. Although " in me, that is, in my flesh, dwelleth no good thing." Yet He desires to see His own comeliness and workmanship in us.

6. *The Answer.* His reply is wonderful. He sees, as it were, " The advance of two companies " (R.V., Marg.). There are before His eyes two great and happy companies, constituting the whole redeemed family of God. A joyful company in heaven, and a joyful company on earth, both singing the song of the conquering blood of the Lamb. Rejoice in the Lord.

WORKERS TOGETHER.
Chapter 7, 10-13.

In the first part of this chapter He gives another description of the personal virtues of His Bride. He begins with referring to her "beautiful feet," and ends with comparing her mouth to wine that causeth "the lips of those that are asleep to speak" (v. 9). The testimony of the Church ought to lead to the awakening of those that are asleep to speak forth the praise of His glorious Name. There is here—

1. *Confession.* "I am my Beloved's," and His desire is toward me" (v. 10). Joyful and fruitful service is impossible until our own personal relationship with Christ is properly adjusted. If His desires are to be toward me, and His love fill My heart, He must be the beloved of my soul. I must be wholly His.

2. *Consecration.* "Come, my Beloved, let us go forth into the field," etc. (v. 11). Her heart is now enlarged, so she longs to go forth into the field of missionary service. She knows that without Him she can do nothing. She says, "let *us* go. The "fields," the "villages," and the "vineyards," may represent three aspects of service. The evangelist, the pastor, and the teacher. Whether our work is in the open field, gathering the villagers, or ministering to the vineyards, we equally need the presence and power of our loving Lord with us.

3. *Resolution.* "*There* will I give Thee my love" (v. 12, R.V.). If we do not give Him our love, *then*, in the place of service, with all its trials and difficulties, we are giving him nothing. The love of Christ must constrain us. Are there not those who are more ready to give Him their labour than their love. Here in this

world of sin and sorrow, He gave us His love, here, amidst the toil and strife, give Him thy love.

4. *Satisfaction.* " At our doors are all manner of precious fruits, new and old, which I have laid up for Thee, O my Beloved " (v. 13, R.V.). In union with Him, the fruits will be precious and plentiful. The workers' souls will be abundantly refreshed, and fruits will be " laid up " for their Lord and Master, that He may see of the travail of His soul, and be satisfied. Just now, we are workers *together* with Him !

LOVE'S LONGING.
CHAPTER 8, 1-5.

Wherever there is intense love, there will be un. mistakable proof of it.

I.—HER PASSIONATE DESIRE is seen in her longing.

1. To have the liberty of a *Sister.* " O, that Thou wert as my brother, I would kiss Thee, yea, and none would despise me " (v. 1, R.V.). She is eager to make a public profession of her love and devotion to Him. It is so becoming to shew love for a brother, without provoking the sneer, or suspicion of others. Why should the public expressions of our love to Christ lead to ridicule, any more than to a brother or a sister ? The world understands natural, but not spiritual relationships.

2. To bring Him into her *Mother's house.*

The " Mother's house," or household, may repre-sent the Assembly of His people. The Church at

Laodicea had great need of one such to bring the rejected Christ inside. The household of faith should profit by the special individual experience of each.

3. To *cause Him to drink* of spiced wine. There is a burning desire to refresh and cheer His soul with the best. What shall I render unto the Lord for all His benefits ? The wine of our natural love, spiced with the divine love shed abroad in our hearts, is ever pleasing unto Him.

4. To have her whole person *supported and protected by His power.* " His left hand under my head, His right hand should embrace me " (v. 3). The more we know of the love of Christ, the more shall we seek to trust Him. Those who have taken refuge in the Eternal God shall have underneath them the everlasting arms (Deut. 33, 27). The *head* that is resting on His hand shall be without anxious thoughts (Matt. 6, 25).

II.—HER NOTE OF WARNING. " I charge you . . . that ye stir not up my Love until He please " (v. 4). She warns the daughters of Jerusalem against saying or doing anything that would tend to produce disturbing influences. True love to Christ is jealous for His Will and Work. We must learn to wait on Him, " until He please."

III.—HER MANNER OF WALK. " Who is this that cometh up from the wilderness leaning upon her Beloved ? " (v. 5). The virgin daughters ask this question, one of another, as they look at the walk of the Bride with the Bridegroom. Observe—

1. Where she is ; " In the wilderness." It is a picture of " the Church in the wilderness " (Acts 7, 38). In the world, but not of it. Pilgrims and strangers on the earth.

2. Where she was going ; " Up from the wilderness." This is not our rest ; we look for a city, whose builder and maker is God. Up from the sphere of service and suffering to the place of rest and reward.

3. How she went ; " Leaning upon her Beloved." Walking with Him, and resting on Him, is the Christian pilgrim's joy and privilege.

THE BRIDEGROOM'S WORDS OF COMFORT.
Chapter 8, 5-7.

This is one of the most impressive passages in the whole Book. It contains His definition of His own love. He declares—

I.—WHAT HE HAD DONE FOR HER. " I awakened thee" (v. 5, R.V.). The first impulse of the new life came from Him. " He first loved us." He found us asleep, and insensible to His nearness, His grace, and His goodness. You hath He quickened who were dead.

II.—WHAT HE DESIRES TO BE TO HER. He pleads with her to set Him—

1. " As a Seal upon her heart." When Christ Himself is fixed on the heart, then the actions of the life become as His signet, revealing the impress of His character (Hag. 2, 23). When this seal is on the heart.

then every thought and feeling is stamped with His image.

2. "As a Seal upon her arm." When the arm is made bare for service, the Seal of His authority and power should be visible. The Seal of Christ and of His Holy Spirit must first be in the heart for life and love before it can be on the arm for power and service.

III.—WHAT HE HAS FOR HER. Infinite love.

1. A love that cannot die. "It is as strong as death." Death is strong, but it is not stronger than His love. The strength of this love is the strength of the lover.

2. A love that cannot be quenched (v. 7). Although the enemy comes in like a flood, it cannot quench this love, which is indeed "A very flame of the Lord" (v. 6, R.V.). A fire that shall never go out. "I have loved Thee with an everlasting love." The many waters of sorrow and suffering cannot quench it. Herein is love (1 John 4, 9-10).

3. A love that cannot be drowned. "Neither can the floods drown it." It cannot be extinguished, neither can it be overwhelmed or buried in the depths. It will succeed in manifesting itself.

4. A love that cannot be bought. "If a man would give all the substance of his house for it, he would utterly be contemned." (v. 7). A man can no more purchase the love of God, than he could purchase the Son of God. All the *substance* of man, moral or material, is utterly worthless as a price for His love. God doth not sell

His love, He commendeth it toward us, while we are
yet sinners (Rom. 5, 7-8).

A PLEA FOR OTHERS.
Chapter 8, 8-10.

She has just had another and a fuller revelation of
His unquenchable love, and the result of it is : anxiety
for others.   When the love of God is shed abroad in our
hearts, we will fall in love with the loveless.

I.—THE BRIDE'S INQUIRY.   It was regarding
" a little Sister " (v. 8).   Although the unconverted are
lower in standing than the children of God, there is still
kinship between them—Sisters.

1.   The Sister's defect.   " She hath no breasts."
The breast is emblematic of *Affection*.   She hath no love
in her heart.   This is a most lamentable condition to be
in, but it is exactly the state of every unrenewed soul.
No love for Jesus Christ.

2.   The difficulty.   " What shall we do for our
Sister in the day when she shall be spoken for ? "   Yea,
even she will be spoken for by Him whose name is Love,
and who died for us even while we were yet sinners.
What shall we do for her, who is so loved by Thee, and
who has no love in response to Thee ?   This is a problem
that is still with us.   He loves the loveless, " I called
. . . ye refused."

II.—THE BRIDEGROOM'S REPLY.   There are
two possible results.

1.   She may be built up.   " If she be a *wall*, we
will build upon her a palace of silver " (v. 9).   If there

is any *stability* in her, and if she is willing to receive all
that we can give her, then the breasts of her affection
will be lifted up like a "turret of silver" (R.V.).
Love begets love, we love Him because He first loved us.

2. She may be nailed up. "If she be a *door*, we
will enclose (fix) her with boards of cedar." If she prove
as unstable, and as easily moved about with every
wind, as an unfixed door, through which all or anything
may go, then we will nail her up, and make her to feel
her bondage and helplessness. If souls are not won by
love, then they will be condemned by the law. The
Bride and Bridegroom co-operate in the work of
winning souls.

III.—HER PERSONAL TESTIMONY. She now
gives a little bit of her own experience—

1. "I am a wall" (v. 10, R.V.). I am steadfast
and trustful. I will not be moved. I know whom I
have believed. This is not vain boasting.

2. "My breasts are like towers." My affections,
she says, rise up unto Him like towers in the skies.
She loves Him with all her heart.

3. "I, in His eyes . . . found peace" (R.V.).
Where there is stability of purpose and a heart of
love, there will be the enjoyment of His favour and
peace (Col. 2, 7). By the grace of God, I am what I am.

CLOSING WORDS.
CHAPTER 8, 11-14.

In the closing words of this matchless Song we have
reference made to—

I.—THE KING'S POSSESSION. "Solomon had a vineyard at Baal-hamon," which means "the place of a multitude" (v. 11). The Church, or vineyard of the Lord, is in the place where the multitude is, because it is intended to be a blessing to the multitude.

1. What He did with it. "He let out the vineyard to keepers." This vineyard needs to be kept, and all called of God and empowered with the Holy Spirit, are put in trust with the affairs of their Lord and King. They occupy for Him.

2. Why he let it out. "For the fruit thereof." The purchase of this vineyard cost Him much (Acts 20, 28). Those who reap the advantage of it, are responsible to the King. Mark 13, 34.

II.—THE BRIDE'S RESOLUTION. "My vineyard, which is mine (myself) is before me ; Thou . . . must have a thousand"—the full amount. Each worker in the vineyard will have reward—two hundred, but *Thou* must have a thousand. Honour must be given to whom honour is due ; but the Lord must be exalted far above all.

III.—THE BRIDEGROOM'S INJUNCTION.

1. To whom spoken ? To her "that dwelleth in the gardens" (v. 13). She who dwelt in the clefts of the rock" (2, 14) now dwells in the gardens of separation and delight. The rock for safety, the vineyard for work, the garden for pleasure.

2. To what purpose? He says to her, "The companions hearken to thy voice : cause *Me* to hear it." It is good that others should hear our voice in testi-

mony, but it is better that He should hear it in praise and prayer. Thy Redeemer loves to hear thy voice. Cause Him to hear it often.

IV.—THE FINAL INVITATION. This book of "Unvailings," like the book of "Revelation," closes with an earnest cry for the coming of the Bridegroom in His power and glory. "Make haste, my Beloved" (v. 14). Come quickly, "like a roe or a young hart upon the mountains." This is the attitude of a faithful loving, longing Bride. This is our hope. "For our citizenship is in heaven, from whence also we wait for a Saviour, the Lord Jesus Christ, who shall fashion anew the body of our humiliation, that it may be conformed to the body of His glory, according to the working whereby He is able even to subject all things unto Himself." (Phil. 3, 20-21, R.V.). Even so, come, Lord Jesus.

———————

New Testament Studies.

THE INFANT CHURCH.

Acts 1.

The infant Church was mighty in its infancy. The present-day snare of *precedency* was unknown in those early days of simple, child-like trust, when everything seemed to be sprinkled with a dewy resurrection freshness. May this newness of life be ours. To this end let us look at some of those features which characterised the members of the infant Church, and let us ask ourselves whether we as His sheep have the same marks upon us?

1. *They were in fellowship with their Risen Lord.* "To whom He *showed Himself* . . . and assembled together with them" (verses 3 and 4). The resurrection of Christ was an unquestionable fact to them. He had now become their very life. "Christ our life." They had each personally experienced the power of His presence—a presence which not one of the unbelieving ever knew. Do we know what that means?

2. *They received the promise of the Holy Ghost.* "Ye shall be baptised with the Holy Ghost not many days hence" (verse 5). This great "promise of the Father" (verse 4) is made to every heaven-born child of God, and should be as definitely accepted as the promise of eternal life. This promise was not given that they might be more fully justified before God, but that

God might be more fully justified in them before the world (Ezek. 38, 16). See Acts 19, 2.

3. *They were obedient to His Word.* " Then returned they unto Jerusalem, . . . and went up into an upper room " (vv. 12-13). The Lord had told them to wait for the fulfilment of the promise, so they had come to *wait.* They did not gather together to discuss the manner, the time, or extent of the promised outpouring, but to WAIT. They had made up their minds simply to do their Master's bidding, and leave the rest with Him. " Go thou and do likewise."

4. *They were united in Spirit.* " These all continued with one accord in prayer and supplication " (verse 14). Why should they pray when they had His sure word of promise ? Was not the very certainty of the promise a powerful incentive to wait and to pray ? A Pentecostal day will come at any time when there is the same unity of spirit and persistent, believing prayer (Matt. 18, 19-20).

5. *They honoured the Scriptures.* " Peter stood up and said, Men and brethren, this scripture must needs be fulfilled," etc. (vv. 15-20). Peter and the one hundred and nineteen that were with him had no difficulty at all as to David being the author of Psalm 69, and that he spoke prophetically under the guidance of the Holy Ghost (2 Tim. 3, 16). He who handles the Word of God so as to foster discredit has grieved the Holy Spirit, and done the work of the devil.

6. *They brought their difficulties to the Lord in prayer.* " Thou, Lord, knowest the hearts of all :

show whether of these two Thou hast chosen " (21-24). Two had been named to fill the one office. They were quite willing to sink their own individual preferences, and accept him whom the Lord should commend. As it was then, so is it now. Only the called of God will succeed. If any man lack wisdom let him ask of God. The *infant* Church was mightier than the *aged* Church of the present day. Why? Well, Why? The clamant need of the church is :—

1. A new revelation of the Risen Christ.
2. A fuller experience of the power of His Resurrection.
3. An unwavering faith in His Word.
4. A fresh baptism of the Holy Ghost.
5. The spirit of unity amongst believers.
6. Believing prayer.

THE EMPOWERED CHURCH.

Acts 2, 1-13.

A praying Church will always be a powerful Church. The true and real influence of a Church does not consist in the number or social position of its members, not in the stateliness of the building, nor in the largeness of its contributions, but in the presence and *power of the Holy Ghost*. Where the ministry of the Spirit is absent, the Church is but a breathless body. " It is the Spirit that quickeneth." Observe—

1. *Where they were.* " They were all with one accord in one place " (v. 1). They were in " one place " just because they were all of " one accord." This is a condition of heart that is absolutely necessary to the

receiving of the power of the Holy Spirit. To be filled
with the Spirit we must be emptied of all self-seeking
and uncharitableness. When brethren dwell together
in unity, then the Lord will command His blessing.

2. *When the Blessing came.* "When the day of
Pentecost was fully come." According to the type,
that was fifty days after (Christ as) the sheaf of first-
fruits was presented as a wave offering (Lev. 23,
15-16). God's workings are always in harmony with
the "fulness of time" (Gal. 4, 4). He does nothing
prematurely ; there is an eternal fitness in the divine
seasons. There is an *earthly* as well as a heavenly
counterpart in all the arrangements of Him whose work
is perfect. The Holy Ghost is still ready to come upon
all those who are *ready* to receive Him. They that wait
upon the Lord shall exchange strength.

3. *How the Blessing came.* "Suddenly, as a
mighty, rushing wind, and as cloven tongues of fire"
(vv. 2-3). It did not come through a process of growth
or development ; it was not evolved out of their own
inner consciousness ; it was the direct gift of the Father
in answer to their believing prayer, and in fulfilment of
His own gracious promise. It came as "mighty wind"
and as "tongues of fire," symbolic of a personality that
cannot be limited or controlled by the mere will of man
(John 3, 8).

4. *To whom the Blessing came.* "It sat upon *each*
of them, and they were *all* filled with the Holy Ghost"
(vv. 3-4). God is no respecter of persons ; every
waiting, believing heart was filled with the Spirit.

They each received the like gift, although the *manifestation* of the power in their individual lives was different ; yet it was the same Spirit. The lesson undoubtedly for us is that every believing disciple of Christ may and should be " filled with the Holy Ghost." More than that, each one in that upper room baptised of the Holy Spirit was perfectly conscious of the fact. In this respect between the first century and the twentieth there is no difference (Luke 11, 13). The same God is rich unto all that call upon Him.

5. *The Effects Produced.* These were twofold : (1) Upon themselves. " They were *filled*, and spake with *other tongues*, as the Spirit gave them utterance." They were possessed and controlled by the mighty power of God. As earthen vessels they were charged with heavenly treasure a precious gift that is for ever hidden from the worldly-wise and revealed only unto babes (Matt. 11, 25). (2) Upon others. " Many were amazed and marvelled ; . . . others mocked " (vv. 7-13). The coming of the Holy Spirit is always certain to be a telling innovation. There is no hiding of His power. It is such an unearthly movement that ungodly philosophers are all amazed and in doubt, saying one to another, What meaneth this ? (2 Cor. 10, 4). This was in truth a " wealthy " church, it was rich in spiritual power and fruitfulness.

THE WITNESSING CHURCH.
ACTS 2, 14-36.
" This Jesus hath God raised up, whereof *we all are witnesses* " (v. 32).

A quickened Church, or a quickened soul, will be certain to give Jesus the pre-eminence. Had not Christ said that " When He, the Spirit of Truth, is come, He shall glorify Me ? " (John 16, 13-14). The Church or the individual that is not glorifying Jesus Christ as the crucified and risen Son of God cannot be filled with the Spirit. We are assured of this, that the Holy Ghost will not give His glory to another than Jesus Christ, in whose name He has come, and whose work He seeks to continue on earth. So when " Peter, filled with the Spirit, stood up with the eleven and lifted up his voice " it was to preach " Jesus and the Resurrection." Spirit-filled men have no other theme. We shall note, briefly, the outstanding features of Peter's Pentecostal testimony, and here he speaks as the mouthpiece of the whole Church. He testified—

1. *To the Transformation of his Brethren.* " These men are not drunken, as ye suppose " (v. 15). There was undoubtedly a very marked change in their behaviour. They were intoxicated sure enough, but not with the world's wine, as they supposed, for they were filled with the new wine of the Kingdom of God. But the *natural man* cannot understand the things of the Spirit of God, for they are foolishness unto him (1 Cor. 2, 14).

2. *To the Fulfilment of Prophecy* (vv. 16-21). At the marriage at Cana, the best wine—the gift of Christ—was kept to the *last.* So in " these last days " the best wine has been given in the coming of the Holy Ghost. Between this promise made to Joel and the

fulfilment there lay twenty-four generations ; but His faithfulness faileth not.   The Spirit has been given, but " *all flesh* " have not yet been touched with the flame of this life-quickening fire.   But surely this also will come to pass.   Let us join the Lord's remembrancers, and pray for it.   The testimony of a living Church must be to God's faithfulness to His Word.

3.   *To the Divine Approval of Jesus of Nazareth.—* " A man approved of God " (v. 22).   The works that Jesus did were the works that no other man could do (John 15, 24).   His " miracles, wonders, and signs " were incontestable evidence of His holiness and super-human power, of His actual oneness with the invisible and almighty Father (John 14, 10-11).   This Man approved of God still waits His approval of men.

4.   *To the Guilt of Rejecting Christ.*   " HIM . . . *ye have taken,* and by wicked (lawless) hands have crucified and slain " (v. 23).   Peter, filled with the Holy Ghost, knows no fear, and sees no contradiction between " the determinate counsel of God " and the terrible law-lessness of those who crucified His Son (Luke 22, 22). After Pentecost, the first act of the Holy Spirit upon the ungodly was to convince of murder.   What is sin ? Sin is lawlessness, rebellion, usurpation.

5.   *To the Power of His Resurrection.*   " It was *not possible* that HE should be holden of death " (v. 24). He who claimed to be " the Resurrection and the Life " proved His claim by rising from the dead (John 10, 17). As it was not possible for the powers of death and hell to hold Him, neither is it possible for them to hold those

who by faith are in Him (John 5, 24-25 ; 2 Cor. 4, 14).
A witness to the power of His resurrection must have a
resurrection experience (1 Peter 1, 3).

6. *To the Inspiration of David.*   David spoke concerning Christ, for he " *foresaw* the Lord *always* before
his face " (v. 25, and Ps. 16, 8.)   As the One who, according to the promise of God, " He would raise up to
sit on His throne " (v. 30).   To deny the prophetic
character of the *Psalms of David* is to reject the testimony of the Holy Ghost by whom Peter now was speaking (Luke 24, 44).   Those moved by the Holy Ghost
are " holy men " and are never moved to declare things
which are inconsistent.

7. *To the Certainty of Christ's Exaltation.*   The
coming of the Holy Spirit was not only the fulfilment of
a promise, but also the guarantee that He who had been
crucified was now " by the right hand of God exalted "
(vv. 33-36), and made " both *Lord* and Christ."   Although all authority has been given Him, He still waits
with outstretched arms to give " gifts unto men "
(John 1, 12).   When Christ's death, resurrection, and
exaltation are firmly believed and emphatically preached
signs and wonders will be done in His name.

THE POWER OF THE GOSPEL.
Acts 2, 37-47.

Peter's sermon was in the power of the Holy Ghost,
so there were " signs following."   There was—

1. *Deep Conviction.*   " When they heard they
were pricked in their heart " (verse 37).   " They felt

the nails wherewith they had crucified Christ sticking
fast in their own hearts as so many sharp daggers."
When the Spirit of Grace is poured out, sinners are sure
to see Him whom *they have pierced* (Zech. 12, 10).
He came to convince of sin (John 16, 8). How shall
they hear without a preacher, and how shall they preach
with convicting power unless they are sent ?

2. *Open Confession.* " Men and brethren, what
shall we do ? " This burning question (Acts 9, 6 ; 16,
30), wrung from Spirit-pierced hearts, declares this fact,
that salvation must come from God. "What shall I do?"
A convicted sinner never knows of himself what to do.
It is not in man. But when frank and full confession is
made the guiding light will speedily dawn (1 John 1, 9).

3. *Plain Directions.* " Repent and be baptised
every one of you, . . . and ye shall receive the gift of
the Holy Ghost, for the promise is unto you " (vv. 38-40).
Peter's word was not, " Reform, and be more civilised,"
but " Repent, and be baptised." To *repent* was to
change their minds completely regarding Jesus Christ,
whom they rejected ; and to be *baptised* implied the
renouncing of the old life, and an open confession of
Christ as their Lord. In doing this they would receive
the gift of the Holy Ghost, that they might be endued
with power to overcome the world and be witnesses unto
Him who died and rose again. Have you received the
Holy Ghost since you believed, " for the promise is
unto *you* ? " (v. 39).

4. *Joyful Reception.* " **They** gladly received His
Word " (v. 41). The offer of " the remission of sins "

through repentance was like cold water to a thirsty soul ; they gladly received it. No condemned criminal ever received a free pardon more willingly than they accepted the offer of mercy. This is the Gospel that God is commanding all men everywhere to repent and believe. Three thousand brought in, " but yet there is room."

5. *Steady Progression.* " They continued steadfastly in doctrine, fellowship, breaking of bread, and in prayers " (v. 42). They were God-made converts, and so the true signs of an inward transformation are clearly evident. These were—love for the *Word*, love for *one another*, love for their *absent Lord*, and love for private and public *prayer*. Being grafted into the living Christ, they became possessed with His Spirit, and grew in grace and in the knowledge of their Lord and Saviour.

6. *Hearty Co-operation.* " They were together and had all things common " (vv. 44-45). This, perhaps, not of necessity, but because of their warm affection for one another, and practical mutual interest. This spirit is very beautiful, and reveals the wonderful influence the love of God has when shed *abroad* in our hearts. Jesus Christ had given His all for them ; now they were prepared to give their all for Him and for one another (Eph. 5, 2). What hinders the continuance of this spirit of brotherhood ? Lack of faith in God, worldliness, and selfishness.

7. *Great Jubilation.* " Gladness of heart ; praising God " (vv. 46-47). Repentance is the narrow gate that leads into the happy home of a heavenly Father's heart. The hearts that were pierced with conviction

now praise God for salvation.　Weeping may endure for a night, but joy cometh in the morning (Acts 10, 43).

This Gospel in the power of the Spirit is still the power of God—

To pierce with conviction the heart of sin.

To compel men to confess their need.

To bring the joy of forgiveness to a believing heart.

To keep in fellowship those who obey.

To turn self-denial into a great delight.

To fill the heart with praise to God.

To make the life a testimony for God.

A WORK OF POWER,
Acts 3, 1-26.

"**Is** Christianity a failure ? "　We might as well ask is the sunshine a failure ?　The Christianised paganism that is being substituted for Pentecostal life and power is a failure because it offers hungry souls stones for bread—it never touches the unutterable need of the human heart.　It was very different with Peter and John, filled, as they were, with the Spirit of prayer and of power.　In this chapter we have :—

I. *A Picture of Need.* "A certain man lame . . . laid daily at the gate " (vv. 2-3).　He was both *poor* and *helpless*.　But he was willing to be laid *in the way* of getting help—"at the gate called Beautiful."　He was not too proud to beg or to lay his deformity in the path of prayer.　If he had been ashamed to confess his need he probably never would have experienced the healing power of the name of Jesus.

2. *A Work of Faith* (vv. 4-6). Peter and John said, " Look on us ! " and the lame man, having such a door of hope opened, gave heed unto them "expecting something." Men filled with the Holy Spirit are sure to awaken expectancy in the minds of others. They had neither "silver nor gold," but they had something infinitely better ; they had faith in the saving name of the risen Christ. Calvary and Pentecost are God's remedy for lame and helpless humanity.

3. *A Miracle of Grace.* " Immediately his feet and ankle bones received strength " (vv. 7-9). Having been healed through the power of the name of Jesus (v. 16). He gives an unmistakable testimony to it by "*leaping, walking,* and *praising* God." Then *did* the lame man leap as a hart (Isa. 35, 6). When a poor, lame, hopeless soul comes into contact with Him who is the Resurrection and the Life, there will be a joyful transformation ; the *place* of the beggar is forsaken for the place of the worshipper (v. 8).

4. *An Awakening of Wonder.* " All the people ran, . . . greatly wondering." Peter said, " Why look ye so earnestly on us ? " (vv. 11-12). The amazed and bewildered people could only see the *instruments* that were in the hands of the invisible wonder-working Saviour. Peter and John were the channels of a " power and holiness " not their own, but Christ's. All power is given unto Him, and Pentecost means the imparting of that power to His disciples, for the glory of His name.

5. *A Charge of Guilt* (vv. 13-16). Peter, quick to take advantage of this sudden awakening of interest, charged them with the " denial of the Holy One," and " killing the Prince of Life," then declared that " faith in the name of Him whom they had killed had made " this man strong." Thereby proving that God had raised Him from the dead. Every redeemed and healed soul is a witness to the fact of Christ's resurrection (2. Tim. 1, 10).

6. *An Offer of Mercy* (vv. 17-21). We think we see the tear in Peter's eye when he said : " Now, brethren, I wot that through ignorance ye did it . . . Repent and be converted, that your sins may be blotted out." Their sins were very great, but the *blood* of Jesus Christ, whom they had crucified, was able to cleanse them all away. By thus repenting the times of refreshing from His presence would come unto them.

7. *A Word of Warning.* " Every soul that shall not hear that prophet shall be destroyed " (vv. 22-23). To despise the messenger of the Lord is to despise Him that sent Him (Luke 10, 16). He that heareth these sayings of Mine and doeth them shall be likened to a wise man. Hear, and your soul shall live.

THE CHALLENGE AND THE DEFENCE

Acts 4, 5-23.

In preaching " Jesus and the Resurrection," Peter and John were thrusting the sword of truth right into the hearts of the king's enemies. If Jesus who was crucified has risen again then they are the vilest sinners on the face of the earth, for by consent they had killed the Holy Son of God. If Christ is not risen, then all preaching and faith are alike vain (1 Cor. 15, 14).

1. *The Challenge.* " By what power, or in what name, have ye done this ? " (vv. 5-7, R.V.). The *power* was self-evident in the healed man ; the *name* was a mystery. Was it Satanic or Divine ? The challengers were numerous and influential. " Rulers, elders, scribes, the high priest, and as many as were of his kindred." How could they rejoice in the healing of this lame-born beggar, when their own personal dignity was in danger of being lowered in the eyes of the people ?

2. *The Defence.* Peter being " filled with the Holy Ghost " was ready to give a faithful and courageous reply (vv. 8-12). His searching words were to ring out to " all the people of Israel " that it was through the power of " the name of Jesus of Nazareth, whom they had crucified," that this man was made whole, and that he was a standing witness to the resurrection of Jesus, and to their own guilt. The stone which they had cast aside as unfit for use had been lifted up by God and made both the *foundation* and the *chief corner* of a new and better structure. On this foundation only spiritual living stones could be built, and by this " Head of the *corner* " both Jews and Gentiles were to be made one. " All one in Christ Jesus." Other foundation

can *no man* lay ; " for there is *none other name* under heaven given among men whereby we must be saved."

3. *The Results.* (*a*) They marvelled at the boldness of Peter and John (v. 13). But they had to confess that, although they were " unlearned and ignorant men," they had stamped on their characters the features of Jesus. God had chosen the foolish things to confound the wise (1 Cor. 1, 27). The treasures of God's grace are still hid from the wise and prudent, and revealed to humble, trustful babes (Matt. 11, 25). (*b*) They were silenced when they beheld the man that was healed standing with them (v. 14). Transformed lives by the power of the Risen Christ are the best apologetics for Christianity. In the cause of Jesus Christ, *words* are mere empty prattle, without the power of the Holy Ghost (1 Cor. 4, 19). (*c*) They were moved by a guilty fear (vv. 15-18). They could not deny that " a notable miracle had been done," but they were anxious that it should " spread no further ! " What amazing perversity ! By their speaking *in the name of Jesus* great good had been done, but they would " command them not to speak any more in the name of Jesus." They could speak as long as they liked in their own name—as long as no souls were saved —but they were not to preach Christ and Him crucified in the power of the Spirit, for that would work such revolutions as would upset their peaceful theories, and spoil the regular quiet and decorum of their manner of worship. The descendants of these unbelieving formalists are still among us ; who would rather have the

order and quiet of a graveyard that the stir of a revival by the Spirit of God.   (*d*) They let them go (vv. 19-23). Peter and John would not lower the banner one single inch, for they " could not but speak the things which they had seen and heard."   Being " let go " they found their own company—those who were possessed by the same Spirit—members of the same heavenly family. To which company do you belong ?

THE APPEAL TO GOD.

ACTS 4, 23-31.

" Being let go they went to their own company." It is an old saying that " fowl of like feather flock together."   Just as when the needle is set free from every hindrance, it will gravitate to the pole, so those hearts kindled with the same spiritual flame will be powerfully attracted one to another.   This love for those who love the Lord is an evidence of heavenly kinship, and a mark of our separation from the world. As soon as Peter and John had " reported," they all fled together in prayer to their city of Refuge, which was the God of their Risen Lord.   Prayer is the secret of all strength and consolation, while as servants we suffer for His name.   Let us notice some things about this appeal :—

1. *It was Believing.*   " Lord, THOU art God." They did not pray into unresponsive space, they talked into the very ear of God.   " He that cometh to God must believe that *He is.*"   Their God was the God

K VIII

" which *made* heaven, earth, sea, and *all that in them is.*"
The God of creation, not of evolution.

2. *It was United.* " They lifted up their voice
to God with *one accord* " (v. 24). They had already
proved the value of united prayer. They would
trust to see the power of it again. They seemed never
to forget the words of their now Glorified Master. " If
two of you shall agree," etc. (Matt. 18, 19). United
believing prayer is one of the mightiest weapons God
has put within the reach of His people. Every Church,
no matter how small, has this sword of overcoming
power hanging at its girdle. O that it were unsheathed.
Alas, that it hath slept so long in the scabbard of unbelief.

3. *It was Scriptural* (vv. 25-28). These holy men
of God, possessed by the same Spirit which taught the
prophets of old, are neither afraid nor ashamed to make
mention of David as the author of Psalm 2, and to
interpret his words as the infallible testimony of the
Holy Ghost. It will give power to our petitions if
the Word of God dwells in us richly. The Polychrome
Bible is the gallows on which Higher Criticism will yet
be hanged.

4. *It was Definite.* " *Now*, Lord grant that with
all boldness they may speak Thy Word" (v. 29). How
could they speak the *Word of God* with boldness, if they
did not know assuredly what was the Word of God ?
They prayed for, and expected, an immediate answer.
" *Now*," they spread out their needs as Hezekiah did
the letter, and with the same sudden, overwhelming
manifestations (Acts 14, 3). There is a great difference

between *saying* prayers and making a direct personal appeal to God for a present declaration of His saving power.

5. *It was Christ-Honouring.* "That signs and wonders may be done by the name of Thy Holy Child Jesus" (v. 30). They were far more concerned about the honour of Christ than the honour of the Church. This is always characteristic of Spirit-filled lives. If the NAME of Jesus does not get the prominence, signs and wonders will not be done by the "stretching forth of His hand." Our self-sufficiency will always paralyse the wonder-working hand of the Holy Spirit.

6. *It was Answered.* "And when they prayed the place was shaken ; they were all filled with the Holy Ghost, and spake the Word of God with boldness" (v. 31). To be *filled* with the Spirit is God's answer to all our needs as His servants and witnesses. There is a great difference between speaking the *Word of God* and giving the *opinions* of men about it. The one is the wheat, the other is the chaff (Jer. 23, 28). The order here is Suggestions, Praying, Shaking, Filling, Testifying.

TESTING TIMES.
ACTS 4, 32-37 ; 5, 1-16.

The power of a Church will be according to the measure by which that Church is filled with the Holy Ghost. When a Church is of "one heart and of one soul," it is an evidence that there is no controversy among them ; then they look every man "not on his own things" (4, 32-37). The proof that we love God is that we "love our brother also." The story of Ananias and Sapphira is an unquenchable beacon of warning to all who would live godly ; it is like some terrible hand with five dreadful fingers. Here they are—

1. *Human Deceitfulness.* Ananias and Sapphira had beautiful names, but they had crooked and deformed natures. Like the other disciples, they sold their possession, but, unlike the others, they "kept back part of the price." They put on the sheep's skin, but they were still goats at the heart. They went a *long way* in the Christian life in laying a part at the apostles' feet, but they went the *wrong way* in pretending that they were giving *all*. Like Achan, they hoped to enrich themselves by deceiving the Lord. The heart must be "deceitful above all things," for it would deceive the very God of Heaven.

2. *Satanic Influence.* "Why hath Satan filled thine heart to lie against the Holy Ghost ?" (v. 23). This "Liar from the beginning" still seeks to deceive by *filling the heart* with thoughts that are opposed to the Spirit of God. Beware of his "fiery darts"—those burning desires to honour self more than God. With regard to the service of Christ, *first* thoughts are usually best. Their first thought was to give all, their second was to *keep back part* of the price. Whatever would *hinder* us from seeking *first* the Kingdom of God and His righteousness is of the world, the flesh, or the devil.

3. *Unexpected Detection.* It must have been an awful awakening to Ananias when he had laid the money at the apostles' feet, expecting their benediction,

to hear instead those soul-piercing words, " Ananias,
why hath Satan filled thine heart to lie against the Holy
Ghost ? " The sins of the *heart* cannot be hidden from
God any more than the blood of a murdered Abel. Men
filled with the Holy Ghost, like Peter, are quick to detect
the lying spirit of the devil in a false professor. Try the
spirits, whether they are of God (1 John 4, 1). Remember Lot's wife, and also the man without the
wedding garment (Matt. 22, 12).

4. *Divine Judgment.* " Ananias, hearing these
words, fell down, and gave up the ghost " (v. 25). There
was but little time, between the flash of conviction and
the stroke of vengeance. He may not even had time
to say, " God be merciful to me, a sinner." He that
hardeneth his neck shall suddenly be cut off. He that
covereth his sin shall not prosper. He may go a long
way round about, but some time, and that suddenly, the
great searchlight from the Throne of God will break
in upon him, bringing irretrievable self-condemnation
and death. Let false professors beware, for no human
disguise will ever hide a heart-lie from Him who is the
Truth.

5. *Fatal Disappointment.* It is extremely sorrowful to think of his wife coming in about " three hours
after, not knowing what was done," expecting, perhaps,
to find her husband exalted to a place of honour, and
with the same lie on her lips and in her heart, to be met
with the same sudden and overwhelming retribution.
God is no respecter of persons ; the same sin meets with
the same condemnation. Sapphira may have been a

beautiful woman, as her name indicates, but outward
comeliness is no shelter for inward deceit. This startling vindication of the holiness of God had a very
salutary effect in putting a wholesome fear into the hearts
of many (v. 13), and magnifying the power of God
in the life and testimony of the apostles (John 14, 12).

APOSTOLIC BOLDNESS.
ACTS 5, 17-42.

One of the most pronounced effects of Pentecost was
the bringing of the disciples into a closer and more vital
relationship with Jesus as their risen Lord. By this
fiery baptism were they all made " one body," and,
planted together in the likeness of His death, were also
made in the likeness of His resurrection (Rom. 6, 5-6).
So that they now knew Him in the power of His resurrection and the fellowship of His sufferings. No one can
enter into the heaven-born *fellowship* of *His* sufferings
who has not entered into the soul-sanctifying power of
Pentecost. The disciples were not able, nor were they
asked, to take their God-given stand for Him, who was the
Truth and the Crucified, until they were all filled with the
Holy Ghost. Neither can we without the same equipment.

1. *They suffered for Him.* They were put " in
the common prison " (v. 18). They well knew that it
was their love and their likeness to Jesus Christ that
brought this persecution upon them ; it was " for His
name." If any man would live godly he must suffer.
The words of their Master were now being fulfilled in
them (Luke 21, 12). The rulers were filled with in-

dignation and fear for the doctrine of the apostles had filled Jerusalem, and, if true, it proved them to be the murderers of the Son of God (v. 28). Those who preach a doctrine like this, that drives guilt and condemnation home to the hearts of self-righteous men, will also know what it is to suffer.

2. *They were encouraged by Him.* " The angel of the Lord brought them forth and said, " Go, stand and speak all the words of this life " (vv. 19-20). Those who are faithful to God, their Saviour, have miracles of mercy wrought for them that others can never understand. This new deliverance and fresh commission must have been a mighty buttress to their faith. They were to go and speak to the people all the words of THIS LIFE. This life, which was divine and eternal, and was offered to all who repent of sins and believe in the Lord Jesus Christ (1 John 5, 11). Those who would speak *all* the words of " this life " will always have plenty to speak about, and these are *the words* that *the people* need.

3. *They were devoted to Him.* " Behold the men whom ye put in prison are standing in the temple and teaching the people " (vv. 21-25). They were not disobedient to the heavenly vision. These Spirit-taught men knew nothing worth living for apart from doing the will of God. The desire to please Jesus Christ was the overmastering passion of their souls. One is your Master, even Christ, and if we are true to Him, we shall speak out, and live out, all His revealed will. To substitute our own thoughts for the " Words of this Life " is to deny the Lord, and to become false witnesses.

4. *They were fearless for Him.* " We ought to obey God rather than man," etc. (vv. 29-32). Although they had just escaped from prison they were not afraid to look the enemies of Christ in the face and say, " God hath raised up Jesus, whom *ye* slew and hanged on a tree. The Spirit of God had come to " convince the world of sin " through the lips and lives of those in whose heart He dwells. The sin-convicting power of the Holy Ghost is hindered and thwarted by the downright poltroonery of many of Christ's ambassadors. The fear of man bringeth a snare, not only to the soul of the preacher, but also to the Gospel which he preaches.

5. *They were joyful in Him.* " They rejoiced that they were counted worthy to suffer shame for His name " (vv. 41-42). They did not lift up their hands in pious horror at the thought of doing anything to bring *shame* upon their own name if Jesus was to be honoured thereby. Only those filled with the Spirit can take pleasure in reproaches for Christ's sake (2 Cor. 12, 10). We are not ashamed of our Scottish martyrs who suffered as Christians, but we may well be ashamed of those who are ashamed to suffer for His name's sake (1 Peter 4, 13-16).

SERVING AND SHINING.

Acts 6, 1-15.

The portion before us here may be divided into two sections :—

I. A NEW TRIAL. The number of the saved had grown rapidly, and so the work of administering

help to the needy ones was becoming increasingly
difficult.

1. *The Complaint* (v. 1). The Greek-speaking
Jews " murmured because *their* widows were neglected."
This neglect could not be wilful. It is pleasing to note
how careful these early brethren were about the interests
of their sorrowing, suffering sisters.

2. *The Remedy*. " Look ye out men full of the
Holy Ghost," etc. (vv. 2-4). There are two important
lessons for us here, the first is, that to minister "the Word
of God " is a more urgent business than doling charities
to the poor ; and the second, that even for the simple
work of distributing gifts among the needy the filling of
the Holy Spirit was needed. The Lord would not have
the poor of His people relieved *in the manner* in which a
man may relieve the hunger of his dog ; but in the
tenderness and compassion of the Spirit of Grace, that
the receiver may be doubly blessed thereby. It is not
of God that the poor among His flock should be constantly reminded of their pauperism. All those who
have seen that God-inspired work among the orphans at
Bridge-of-Weir must feel thankful to God for the absence of the very smell of the " charity-workhouse "
system.

3. *The Results*. " They chose Stephen, a man full
of the Holy Ghost . . . and the Word of God increased "
(vv. 5-7). These seven men, whom they had " looked
out," were not chosen because of their social position or
scholarship, but because they were " filled with the
Spirit ; " this is the indispensable equipment for accept-

able service in the eyes of the glorified Christ.   The
Word of God is sure to increase in power and fruitfulness through the ministry of such men.   If the " Word
of God " is not *increasing* in its hold upon the hearts and
lives of its hearers it is because it is preached in the
spirit of doubt and fear, instead of in the power of the
Holy Ghost.

II.   A NEW TESTIMONY.—Stephen's *face* became a witness to Stephen's *faith.*

1. *See Him Serving.*   Being "full of faith and
power, he did great wonders " (v. 8).   The secret of
Stephen's wonder-working influence is an open one, and
within the reach of every servant of Christ.   He had
two mighty hands—" faith and power "—and with these
it became easy for him to do great things.   This strength
is not something we may put off or on, like a garment, it
belongs to the *constitution* of our spiritual manhood
(Acts 1, 8).

2. *See Him Suffering.*   Stephen was never more
like his Master than when they sought false witness
against him (Matt. 26, 59).   Truly they hated him
without a cause.   In this fiery trial he was filled with a
wisdom and spirit that " they were not able to resist,"
thus experiencing the fulfilment of the Lord's promise
(Luke 21, 15).   Men filled with the Holy Spirit are sure
to stir up the enmity of the carnal mind.   But greater is
He that is in you, than he that is in the world (1 John 4).

3. *See Him Shining.*   All those who sat in judgment on him " looking steadfastly, saw his face as it had

been the face of an angel." The glory of his transfigured soul—by the indwelling Spirit of God—shone
through his eyes as the windows of that body of his
which was the temple of the Holy Ghost. This was a
new witness to the sanhedrim, of the resurrection and
glorification of Jesus of Nazareth, whom they crucified,
and in whom Stephen trusted. It is the Spiritual *Life*
within us that is the *light* that shines through us. " The
life is the light of men." Let your light so shine.
But our light will be darkness, unless, like Stephen,
we are filled with the Spirit of Life (2 Cor. 3, 18). Covet
earnestly the best gift.

APOSTOLIC CHARACTER.

Acts 7, 51-60.

Stephen's defence is a masterpiece of spiritual
policy and power. He did not begin his address by
saying, " Ye stiffnecked and uncircumcised in heart."
No ; but with these very courteous words—" Men,
brethren, and fathers, hearken." He that winneth
souls is wise. We might observe here :—

1. *His Knowledge of Scripture.*—This Spirit-filled
man had a clear and comprehensive grasp of the doing
and purposes of God in Old Testament history. The
knowledge of the will of God will always be a mighty
weapon in the hand of anyone full of the Holy Ghost.
The Spirit of God will have but little to work on, unless
our hearts are filled with the words of God. This is the
secret of successful prayer (John 15, 7). It is the

honest heart which hears the Word and keeps it, that brings forth fruit (Luke 8, 15).

2. *His Faithfulness.* " Ye stiffnecked . . . ye do always resist the Holy Ghost " (vv. 51-53). A man filled with the Spirit cannot but be courageous, for the Kingdom of God ; the truth burns like a fire in his bones, while sin, and the things of eternity, stand out before his anointed eyes in the clear light of Him who sits at the right hand of the Father in heaven. They are in an awful condition who *resist* the Holy Ghost by the stiffness of their wills and the hardness of their hearts. They may be " cut *to* the heart " (v. 54) by a faithful testimony, but unless they are " pricked *in* the heart " (vv. 11-37) they will " gnash with their teeth," and die in their sins.

3. *His Vision.* While " they gnashed on him with their teeth," he saw the " glory of God." Our heavenly Father has always rich compensation for His suffering children. Seeing " Jesus standing on the right hand of God " is a wonderful balm for the wounds made by the teeth of the enemy. This revelation to Stephen is the vision that is ever before the mind of those who, like him, are enabled by the power of the Holy Ghost, through faith, to look up " steadfastly into heaven." It is the work of the Spirit to reveal the things of Christ to the believing heart (John 16, 14). To have the vision of the soul filled with the glory of the exalted Redeemer is to have the life consciously " hid with Christ in God."

4. *His Martyrdom* " They stoned Stephen, call-

ing upon God and saying . . . Lord, lay not this sin to their charge " (vv. 57-60). This first martyr for Christ was a witness to that overcoming grace of God in the heart which constrains to pray for them " which despitefully use you." If the death of Stephen was but the means in the hand of God of sending the goads of conviction into the soul of that " young man whose name was Saul " (9, 5), then it was a death that has helped to open up a channel of life and blessing to the world. The Kingdom of Jesus Christ never suffers defeat through the killing of His followers. The blood-stained prayers of those saints who suffer martyrdom for His name's sake, God in grace will mightily avenge, " The blood of the martyr is the seed of the Church."

5. *His Mercifulness.* " He kneeled down and cried, Lord lay not this sin to their charge." The love of a merely natural heart never constrained any one so earnestly to seek the highest good of those who were committing the greatest personal wrong. This last cry of the dying martyr is a convincing proof of the transforming power of the love of Christ in the heart. This merciful spirit manifested in Stephen's last breath toward those sin-blinded murders is the spirit Jesus Christ has sent into the world to seek and save it. " This sin " which they were committing was an awful one. They were destroying the temple of the Holy Ghost. If Stephen had not been filled with the Holy Ghost he would not have been stoned. " Inasmuch as ye have done it unto one of the least of these, ye have done it unto Me."

THE CITY'S AND THE CHURCH'S NEED.

Acts 8, 1-25.

We may learn from this portion :—

1. *That Persecution is not an Unmixed Evil* (vv. 1-5). If the Church at Jerusalem had been allowed to remain in the very comfortable position into which they had settled down (chap. 4, 32) it would have been a long time before " the regions beyond " would have had the Gospel of Christ preached unto them. The wind of persecution " scattered abroad " the good seed of the Kingdom, which sprang up into fresh harvests of souls for the glory of God. What is true in the history of the Church is true also in the individual experience, so that we may glory in tribulations (Rom. 5, 3 ; Matt. 5, 11-12).

2. *That the Great Need of a City is Christ.* " Philip went down to the city of Samaria and preached Christ unto them . . . . and there was great joy in that city " (vv. 5-11). No field of labour could possibly look more unpromising than Samaria did at that moment. Simon the sorcerer, an agent of the devil, had got the people by the ears, for " they all gave heed unto him, from the least unto the greatest," and were completely bewitched by him. They were so carried away with " lying wonders " that they had *no wits* left for sober judgment. What better are the multitudes in our cities and towns to-day, who are bewitched by the deceitfulness of riches, the excitement of gambling, the love of pleasure, the allurements of Satan, and the deceitfulness of a heart at enmity with God. Slum souls, grovelling in the mire

of iniquity, loving the darkness rather than the light.
Philip, being full of the Holy Ghost, preached Christ unto
them.   Holy Ghost men have no other remedy but God's
to offer sin-blinded souls being driven into perdition.   He
did not preach science and philosophy, history, morality,
or the "learned results of criticism." He preached
CHRIST, as the sin-bearing Redeemer, and *unclean*
spirits were cast out and useless, crippled lives were
healed and restored, "and there was great joy in the
city." The joy of souls emancipated from the deluding
powers of darkness.

3.   *That all Believers Should Receive the Gift of the
Holy Ghost* (vv. 14-17).   Samaria had "received the
Word of God"—the message of life declared to them by
Philip, through Christ—but as yet the Holy Ghost
"had fallen upon none of them." They had been converted, but they had not yet been anointed.   To Peter
and John the *receiving* of the Holy Ghost was as definite
a blessing as the receiving of the forgiveness of sins.
In apostolic days the gift of the Holy Ghost accompanied the remission of sins.   Paul's first question to the Ephesian converts was, "Have ye received
the Holy Ghost since ye believed?" (Acts 19, 1).   He
was anxious that they not only should be disciples, but
that they should be powerful witnesses for Christ.   The
receiving of the Holy Ghost is as absolutely necessary for
service as the receiving of Christ is for salvation.

4.   *That the Power of God cannot be Purchased with
Gifts*.   Simon said, "Give me this power," and offered
to purchase the gift of God with money (vv. 18-25).   The

power of the Holy Ghost cannot be given as a *reward* for anything that man can do or give ; it is the " Gift of God." Is it not possible for us to be offering this prayer of Simon's in another form ? We would not, perhaps, say, " Give me this power," for I am rich, but in our hearts we may have been saying, " Give me this power," for I am clever, or for I am earnest. God does not barter with man about the Holy Spirit. Let your prayer be, " Give me this power," for I am *weak ;* and believe that ye receive, and ye shall have (Isa. 40, 29-31 ; Luke 11, 13).

SOUL-WINNING.
Acts 8, 26-40.

There are several examples set before us here, to which we shall do well to take heed. There is an example of—

1. *Anxiety of Soul* (vv. 27-28). It was no trifling curiosity that brought this Ethiopian nobleman, this chancellor of the exchequer, up to Jerusalem to worship. He was, doubtless, an earnest seeker after the soul-satisfying truth of God, and as an honest, anxious inquirer, he had, meanwhile, laid everything else aside that he might seek this one thing needful. He came to Jerusalem that he might *hear ;* he searched the Scriptures that he might *see.* Those who seek with all their heart will speedily find (Jer. 29, 13).

2. *Obedience to God.* When Philip received the call to " Arise and go . . . . he arose and went " (vv. 26-27). His desire was to do the will of God, whether

that was in the quiet of " the desert," or in the excitement of a mighty spiritual revival. He went out, like Abraham, by faith, not knowing whither he went. This was God's way of meeting those Spirit-begotten longings that were in the heart of that anxious Ethiopian pilgrim. In some way or other the earnest prayers of the needy will be answered, while they use the means within their reach. God could have blessed the eunuch without Philip's aid, but it hath pleased the Lord to make those who are filled with the Spirit *co-workers* together with Him.

3. *Enthusiasm for Souls.* At the bidding of the Spirit " Philip *ran* thither to him " (v. 29-30). Only those whose hearts have been enlarged by the Spirit of God will run in the way of His commandments. Men filled with the Holy Ghost will always be at home in dealing with an anxious soul. Real enthusiasm in the work of God is a rare accomplishment in these cold, intellectual, critical days. Those who would be wise to win souls must be willing to " run and *join themselves* to their chariots ; " to get alongside of them, not as unfallen angels, but as fellow-pilgrims to eternity, seeking, by the help of the Holy Spirit, to lead them to a saving knowledge of Jesus Christ.

4. *Faithfulness to the Bible.* The anxious Ethiopian was reading the prophet Isaiah at chapter fifty-three ; Philip, filled and guided by the Holy Ghost, began at the *same scripture*, and preached unto him Jesus " (vv. 32-35). We have teachers among us now who are evidently filled and guided by another spirit, for they would gravely rebuke the modern Philips for such

L VIII

a *misuse* of the Bible. But "*All* Scripture is given by inspiration of God, and is profitable for *doctrine*." And "they are they which testify of Me," said the Son of God. Philip preached unto him *Jesus*. *Who* else can meet the need of a sin-smitten soul? What other *preaching* could be of any avail?

5. *Readiness to Confess.* "Faith cometh by hearing." The eunuch heard the Gospel from the lips of Philip, and believed and was saved. Now, he was ready and willing to be cut off from his own religious beliefs and habits, and to confess Christ in baptism. To him it was an outward sign of his inward fitness to join the family of the redeemed in the House of God on earth, and be numbered with the joint-heirs of Christ. Faith should always be accompanied with confession (Rom. 10, 9-10).

6. *Happiness in Christ.* "He went on his way rejoicing" (v. 39). Being justified by faith, he had peace with God, now he goes on his way rejoicing in hope (Rom. 5, 1-2). The darkness is passed, the true light now shines in his heart. What a change Jesus brings into the life when He is received and trusted. The great majority of business men go on their way plotting and scheming, instead of *rejoicing*, because they are strangers to the blessedness of the man whose sins are forgiven (Ps. 32, 1-11).

SAUL'S CONVERSION.
ACTS 9, 1-19.

The claims of all other religions can be met by mere outward conformity, but Christianity demands the regeneration of the inner man. Even unconverted men like Saul, as touching the law, may live blameless lives in the sight of men, but the *converted* man is one whose whole heart has been *turned* to God. The process is here exemplified in the experience of Saul. We see him—

1. *As a Rebel.* "Saul *yet* breathing out threatenings," etc. (v. 1). *Yet*, after all the evidences he had had of the resurrection of Jesus Christ in the life and testimony of Stephen, witnessing the triumphant death of a Christian is seldom enough to slay the enmity of the human heart against the revealed will of God.

2. *As a Prisoner* (vv. 2-4). He was apprehended by a "light from heaven." The search-light of God was turned upon this religious burglar on the way to Damascus to rob the Church of its living treasure. There is nothing the evil-worker dreads more than the *light* (John 3, 20). From this moment Saul could speak of himself as the "prisoner of Jesus Christ" (Phil. 1). Like many another sinner, he was apprehended "suddenly." The light of truth flashed into the heart by the power of the Holy Spirit is still God's way of subduing rebels to Himself. The pressure of the light was so overwhelming that he fell to the earth. This light, like the Word of God, was quick and powerful, sharper than any two-edged sword (Heb. 4, 12). The weapons of our warfare are not carnal.

3. *As an Inquirer.* "Who art Thou, Lord?" Along with the arresting LIGHT there came a "*voice*, saying, Why persecutest thou Me." When the *truth* comes in the power of the Holy Ghost there is always a

voice with it, making the sinner feel that it is with HIM, not *it*, that he has to do. This question reveals the terrible blindness of Saul's heart and mind—he knew Him not. How could he possibly *know* Him and live at enmity with Him. It was very different with Stephen (vv. 6-55). But light from the Lord is sure to lead to an honest inquiry after Him.

4. *As a Convert.* " Lord, what wilt Thou have me to do ? " (v. 6). " Trembling " at the discovery of his past sin and guilt, " and astonished " at the greatness of the Lord's mercy and grace, he asks this question, as a true penitent, ready and willing to yield himself to do His will. This is conversion. Not the talking about religious duty, but the entire surrender of the whole being to the person and service of the Lord Jesus Christ. Saul repented at once, as soon as he discovered the error of his ways (Matt. 18, 3). As a disciple he was easily *led* (v. 8).

5. *As a Worshipper.* " Behold he prayeth " (v. 11). Saul had frequently said his prayers, but now he prayed. Now his renewed heart yearned for fellowship with the risen Lord, who had revealed Himself to him. A young convert once said—" Before I was converted I prayed to myself, but now I pray to God." Those who don't know Jesus Christ as their own personal Saviour can only draw nigh unto Him with the lips ; they worship they know not what.

6. *As a Witness* (vv. 15-19). Before this he was a vessel fitted for destruction, but now " he is a chosen vessel "—having been cleansed and transformed by the

grace of God—" to bear My Name," as precious treasure " before the Gentiles." As a vessel, he was made strong, for he was to " suffer great things " for His Name's sake. He was often cast down, but not destroyed. As a vessel, he was made meet for the Master's use, being " filled with the Holy Ghost " (v. 17). We have this treasure in earthen vessels, that the excellency of the power may be of God and not of us. Saul's conversion and equipment for Christ's service has been given for a *pattern* to them which should *hereafter* believe on the Lord Jesus Christ (1 Tim. 1, 16). Be ye filled with the Spirit.

SAUL'S TESTIMONY.
Acts 9, 20-31.

Paul, in writing to the Galatians, refers to his conversion in very striking language. He says—" It *pleased* God, who called me by *His grace*, to *reveal* His Son *in me*, that I might *preach Him*." The words here put in *italics* give us the whole Gospel in brief. Saul was not disobedient to the heavenly vision.

1. *A Courageous Stand.* "Straightway he preached Christ as the Son of God " (v. 20). It was impossible for Saul to be a Unitarian, or for any one who, like him, has been transformed in heart by the power of the resurrected Christ. He who was an enemy to Jesus, now becomes one of His most successful recruiting sergeants. He was not ashamed of the Gospel of Christ (Rom. 1, 16).

2. *A Suggestive Question.* " Is not this he that destroyed them ?" etc. (vv. 21-22). Yes ; this is he, yet

it is not he, for Saul the persecutor has died, and Saul the preacher has been quickened from the dead. The lion has been converted into a lamb, and a religious icicle has suddenly become a flame of holy fire. Henry Martyn said—" If I could see a Hindoo convert, I would see the dead raised." Who can explain the process of resurrection ? So is every one that is *born* of the Spirit (John 3, 8).

3. *A Vigilant Enemy.* " They watched the gates day and night to kill him " (vv. 23-25). The more "Saul increased in *strength* " the more bitter did the enemies of Christ become. All those who would grow in grace may be prepared for a growing opposition in some quarters. The subjects of the " Kingdom of God " will surely be despised by the subjects of the " Kingdom of Satan." But the servant of Christ need fear no evil, there will always be a " basket " or a hole in the wall for them in time of need. It is said that " man is immortal till his work is done."

4. *A Confession of Discipleship.* " He assayed to join himself to the disciples " (v. 26). When Saul offered himself as a member to that Church of Jerusalem which he had so lately persecuted, " they were afraid of him "—perhaps thinking this was another of his dodges to catch them—" and believed not that he was a disciple." But as he had been brought into the fellowship of Jesus Christ, he longed for the fellowship of the saints. It is a certain sign of discipleship when we love the people of God, and seek the company of the redeemed.

5. *A Brotherly Act.* " Barnabas took him and de-

clared unto them how he had seen the Lord " (vv. 27-28).
This " son of consolation " did a most gracious work in
smoothing the way for this new convert.   There are disciples still who seem slow to believe the testimony of
those who have been *suddenly* transformed by the grace
of God.   It will ever be a blessed and Christ-like ministry to help those who are misunderstood.

6.   *A Confirming Testimony*.   " He spake boldly in
the name of the Lord Jesus " (v. 29-30).   The fact of Saul
being changed was very soon apparent.   He was now doing
the same work for which Stephen was stoned, and in the
same fearless and powerful manner, because he was animated by the same heaven-born motives. (Gal. 1, 15-16).

7.   *A Grand Result*.   This result was five-fold.
(a) They had *peace* (v. 31, R.V.).   How sweet this calm
was after the fiery tempest of persecution.   How sweet
peace is after the inward battle of sin and unbelief.
(b)   They were *edified*.   Built up in the holy faith,
strengthened by the study of the Scriptures.   (c)   They
walked in the fear of the Lord.   Their daily life was lived
in the presence of Him who said—" Lo, I am with you
alway."   (d) They had the *comfort of the Holy Ghost*.   The
promised Comforter had come (John 14, 16), they had
received Him, and were now experiencing the blessedness of His indwelling.   (e) They were *multiplied*.
Success is absolutely certain to any Church bearing these
characteristics.   Peace, wisdom, comfort are still being
eagerly sought after by the restless " men of the world."
O, that they could see these blood-bought gifts exhibited
in the lives of Church members to-day.

THE VICTORY OF FAITH.

Acts 9, 32-43.

For a time the name of Saul drops out of the record, and the halo of divine glory is seen on Peter. To him was given the keys of the kingdom, and he used them well in opening doors for others. He came down to see the saints. "How sweet to mingle with such kindred spirits here"—and the poor paralysed Æneas was able to bless God for his visit. "He had kept his bed for eight years" (v. 33). Like a man sick and paralysed by sin, he was utterly helpless and hopeless, apart from the saving power of God. "Peter said unto him, Jesus Christ maketh thee whole." This bold declaration recalls Peter's unstaggering faith in his risen Lord, and, according to his faith, so was it done unto him. Peter knew that it was glorifying to the name of Jesus that he should venture much in Him.

HIS VICTORY AT JOPPA.—

1. *Why he Went.* The disciples sent unto him two men desiring that "he would not delay but come" (vv. 36-38). They had been suddenly plunged into sorrow through the death of their beloved Dorcas What a mercy that Peter, the man of Pentecost, was only a few miles off. The more we are filled with the Holy Spirit, the more shall we be able to minister the consolation of Christ to the needy.

2. *What he Saw.* With tearful eyes the widows showed him "the coats and garments which Dorcas made." While the great battles of Roman Emperors

have been forgotten, the gracious deeds of Dorcas are being held in everlasting remembrance. Every " Dorcas Society " is a monument to her immortal memory. Whatsoever we do *for the glory of God* shall be as gold and silver and precious stones ; all the testing fires of time and coming judgment shall never be able to efface their beauty, or dim the memory of them in the mind of God (1 Cor. 3, 11-14).

3. *What he Did*. The several acts of Peter here in raising Dorcas from the dead may be suggestive to us as to how we may be successful in *restoring* souls to the new life which is in Christ. (*a*) " He put them all forth " (v. 40). This was a work that God *only* could do, so he gets alone with God. Everything that would in any way distract our faith in Him must be put out. (*b*) " He kneeled down and prayed." Special definite prayer is needed. Peter's whole soul was centred on this one thing. When Elijah prayed for rain we may be sure that at that time he prayed for nothing else. When a beggar cries for everything he usually gets nothing. (*c*) He called on her by name. " Tabitha, arise ! " It is not enough that we speak to God, we must speak to the people, and speak to them *personally*, and as if we expected them to hear and believe at once. Peter did not say, " Tabitha, I hope you may see your way to get up soon," but, " ARISE ! " In the name of the Risen Christ, arise from the dead. (*d*) He gave her his hand and lifted her up. This is a beautiful touch of real *sympathy* and tenderness. If we would *lift up* new-born souls, we must not only speak the

truth, but speak it in *love*. As soon as she "saw Peter," she felt the uplifting power of his compassionate hand. (*e*) "He called the saints and presented her alive." He would have them all rejoice in this victory through the grace of God. The result was that "many believed in the Lord." Such results are sure to follow where there is definite, prayerful dealing with God for the deliverance of souls from the power of death.

DIVINE PREPARATION.

Acts 10, 1-23.

Cæsarea was the headquarters of the Roman Governor. Cornelius was captain of the one hundred Italians who formed the bodyguard. The Jewish and the Gentile streams meet and mingle in Peter and Cornelius. The time had come for the overflowing of the river of grace that had so long been limited to the narrow channel of Israel. "It was the bursting of the chrysalis, in which the life has been preserved indeed, but confined." Let us look at—

I. CORNELIUS THE PETITIONER.—

1. *His Character.* "Devout, feared God, gave alms, and *prayed alway*" (v. 2). This is a very brief biography of a great man, who dared to be holy in the most unlikely circumstances. Do we wonder that his influence was such that *all his house* feared God? A man may be a brave soldier, and yet be a religious coward.

2. *His Vision* (vv. 3-6). He who prays much will see much. God is ever ready to unlock the treasures

of His grace to the humble seeking heart. The vision came about the ninth hour—the hour of prayer (chapter 3, 1). It brought him a message of personal assurance (v. 4), and also a plain word of direction (v. 5). When God answers our prayers there is no doubt about it, everything is so perfectly clear and God-like.

3. *His Obedience.* As soon as the heavenly messenger was departed, he sent to Joppa, about thirty miles off, for Peter (vv. 7-8). The willing and trustful heart will never seek a more convenient season than *now*. It is such joy to the man of prayer to *know* the will of God that it becomes his delight to do it.

II. PETER THE PREACHER.—

1. *His Call to Cæsarea.* " Send to Joppa and call for Peter " (v. 5). God could easily have made the angel His messenger to bring to Cornelius all the light and comfort he needed, but He chooses *redeemed* ones to be co-workers together with Him in the preaching of the Gospel.

2. *His Love of Prayer* (vv. 9-10). Time never hangs heavily upon those who delight in secret fellowship with the Lord. While the dinner was being cooked, Peter was pleading, perhaps, that his way might be made plain as to where he should next go to preach Christ.

3. *His Strange Preparation* (vv. 11-23). The vision of the " great sheet " or " vessel " let down from heaven was certainly intended as a revelation to Peter of the gracious purpose of God to gather all sorts into

His kingdom, through faith in Christ Jesus. When
the hungry apostle saw this strange lot, and was asked
to receive them, he refused to have anything to do with
them. He would have no fellowship with the " common
and unclean." But these, " all manner of four-footed
beasts, wild beasts, creeping things, and fowls of the
air," represented all manner of sinners, wild sinners,
creeping, grovelling, earth-worm sinners, and intellectual, high-flying sinners, but no longer " common or
unclean," for God hath cleansed them by the blood of
Christ, through faith in His name. They were all
one *in* the " vessel," even as we are " all one in Christ
Jesus," both Jew and Gentile. The little " creeping
thing " was equally safe with the strong beast or the
fowl of the air, all tied up together in the bundle of
life. They were taken from the earth, but their abode
was in the heavenlies ; they were sent back to the earth
as a testimony to the cleansing power of God. Wild
beasts and creeping things, such were some of you, but
ye are washed.

The effect of this vision on Peter was that he was
now ready and willing to preach the Gospel to *every*
creature (vv. 42-43).

THE APOSTOLIC GOSPEL.
Acts 10, 38-44.

It was a very warm reception Peter got from
Cornelius. No medical professor ever had a more
hearty welcome from any pain-stricken patient. He
received him as one shut up in a besieged city would

receive the General of the relief force. Blessed are the feet of them that bring good tidings. " He fell down at his feet " (vv. 23-26). Then Peter went in and " talked with him." As they each rehearsed their individual experience, it became abundantly clear to both that God had been guiding them, and that they were both brought together to witness a very definite manifestation of His grace and power (vv. 27-33). Peter's vision prepared him to go wherever God should send him. The vision of Cornelius prepared him to receive all that God should give him (v. 33). In this we have a very decided example of how God may prepare a people and a preacher when times of reviving are about to come from His presence. The spring of blessing began on both sides in *secret* prayer, where every heaven-born revival has its human origin. Peter never preached to a more interested audience than this, and although the meeting was small, the results were mighty and far-reaching, because he preached unto them, JESUS.

1. *Jesus, the Anointed One.* " God anointed Jesus of Nazareth with the Holy Ghost " (v. 38). This anointing took place at Jordan when the Spirit of God, like a dove, lighted on Him (Matt. 3, 16). " Him hath God the Father sealed," who was His eternal Son, and into whose hands the salvation of sinners and the glory of the Father have been committed.

2. *Jesus, the Compassionate One.* " Who went about doing good." Having been " anointed to preach the Gospel to the poor " (Luke 4, 18), His pitiful eyes

were ever on the look-out for humble, needy souls,
that He might bless them with His good. O, the depth
of that GOOD that was in Him.

3. *Jesus, the Mighty One.* " Healing all that were
oppressed of the devil." He preached deliverance to
the captives, for He had come that He might destroy
the works of the devil (1 John, 3, 8). The devil op-
presses with the burden of darkness, of doubts, and of
hopeless despair, affecting the mind, the heart, and
future prospects. He not only *delivers* from the thraldom of the devil, but *heals* the wounds sin and Satan
had made. He was mighty, for the Almighty One was
with Him (v. 38 ; John 14, 10).

4. *Jesus, the Suffering One.* "Whom they *slew*
and *hanged* on a tree " (v. 39). What condescension and
gracious self-emptying is this ? He who delivered
others from the oppressive death-grip of the devil
submits to be oppressed to death at the hands of men.
They *slew* that loving, tender heart of His with their pride
and unbelief before they *hanged* that weak, exhausted
body on the tree. He suffered for us, the Just for the
unjust.

5. *Jesus, the Risen One.* "Him God raised up
the third day." "God loosed Him from the pangs of
death, because it was NOT POSSIBLE that He should be
holden of it " (Acts 2, 24). The love of God for His Son
and for those for whom He died, made it *impossible* that
death should keep Him. Being raised from the dead,
He is " *declared* to be the Son of God *with power* "—with
power to save and keep all who believe on His name.

6. *Jesus, the Exalted One.* " Ordained of God to be the Judge of *quick* and *dead* " (v. 42). All judgment hath been committed unto the Son, because He is the Son of *Man* (John 5, 22-27). In 2 Cor. 5, 10 we have the judgment of the quick—those *alive* unto God. In Rev. 20, 11-15 we see Him judging the dead—those who have died in their sins.

7. *Jesus, the Universal Saving One.* " Whosoever believeth in Him shall receive remission of sins " (v. 43). " Through His name " the door of Mercy and Access has been thrown wide open, and through this open door the voice of divine entreaty is now being heard in the Gospel. When this door is shut no man will be able to enter in (Luke 13, 24-25).

The effects of Peter's sermon were most manifest. He preached Jesus, and " signs and wonders " followed (vv. 44-48).

PETER'S TESTIMONY.
Acts 11, 1-18.

Every new move of the Spirit of God is likely to stir up doubtful questionings in the hearts of some conservative Christians. The Church has not yet learned to hail with joy *any* Spirit-directed innovation that brings glory to God in the salvation of sinners. They contended with Peter for having fellowship with Gentiles, although they knew that they had " received the Word of God " (vv. 1-3). We ought always to be liberal-minded as the Holy Ghost is, otherwise we are narrow-minded. Where did we learn that the Gospel

was only to be preached on a certain day in the week in
a stated place at a fixed hour ? Is not the Church of
God an army on a campaign against the enemies of
Christ and of righteousness ? Would any nation permit
its army to fight only one day in the week, and allow
its foes to do their deadly soul-destroying work all the
other six days ? Peter had carried the holy war into
the enemies' country, and had gained a glorious victory,
but was now gravely charged with imprudence by those
who had preferred to stay at home. Peter's defence
is beautiful for its humility and simplicity. If it was
analysed we might find in it—

1. *A Spirit of Prayer.* " I was in the city of
Joppa praying " (v. 5). Those who are possessed by
the spirit of prayer will always find a time and place for
the purpose of prayer Yes, " in the city," as well as
out of it. If the fire of divine love has been kindled in
the heart, flaming tongues of holy desires will leap
God-ward.

2. *A Heavenly Vision.* This " vessel, let down
from heaven by four corners " (v. 5), was to Peter, as
we have seen, a revelation of the purposes of God in
relation to the Gentiles. The secrets of heaven are still
revealed to those who wait upon God in secret prayer.
Such exchange their own weakness for the uplifting
strength of His manifested will (Isa. 40, 31).

3. *A Definite Commission.* " The Spirit bade me
go." Men of faith and prayer hear voices and see
visions that other mortals are quite incapable of understanding (2 Cor. 12, 4). Under the guiding Spirit of

God things will also be done that will look foolish and absurd in the eyes of the worldly wise. We cannot be filled with the Spirit to excess.

4. *A Special Preparation.* " He showed us how he had seen an angel in his house " (vv. 13-14). Cornelius was also prepared like Peter for fuller blessings through prayer. The soil of the centurion's heart was made ready for the seed of the Word. " He shall tell thee *words*, wonder-working words, words whereby ye shall be saved." Words, in the power of the Holy Ghost, are spirit and life.

5. *A Divine Manifestation.* " As I began to speak, the Holy Ghost fell on them " (vv. 15-16). The Spirit who bade him go sealed Peter's testimony for Jesus by His coming down in mighty power upon the hearers, baptising them into the mystical body of Christ, and so making of twain, one new man.

6. *A Silencing Question.* " What was I, that I could *withstand God ?* " (vv. 17-18). Well done, Peter ! That was a dexterous stroke with the sword of defence. What could he do, being caught in the rush of that heavenly wind that " bloweth where it listeth." He could no more withstand the pressure of the Spirit of God than Saul of Tarsus could withstand the " light from heaven." " When they heard these things they held their peace and glorified God." They saw the hand of God in it, and they had grace enough to praise Him for it, although they themselves had no hand in it. Is this the grace wherein we stand ?

M VIII

THE REVIVAL IN ANTIOCH.

ACTS 11, 19-26.

Antioch was the eastern capital of the empire. There was a great exhibition on in this metropolis, not of human art and industry, but of the mighty saving grace of God. Such an unprecedented show, that it was well worth the while of Barnabas going all the way from Jerusalem to see it. Those who would travel back in the line of history to the purity and power of primitive Christianity must take care that they don't lose their way in that " valley of the shadow of death," called " The Dark Ages." The pure light of the Gospel shines most brightly at the dawning of this new day :—

I. THE REVIVAL AT ANTIOCH.—

1. *The Origin of it.* " The persecution that arose about Stephen " drove those nameless disciples " as far as Antioch." In this case the wrath of man was made to praise the Lord (Ps. 76, 10). They thought evil against the Church, but the Lord meant it for good (Gen. 1, 20). The things which happened unto them fell out rather unto the furtherance of the Gospel (Phil. 1, 12).

2. *The Means of it.* There was first the " preaching of the Word " (v. 19), " preaching the Lord Jesus " (v. 20). There was, second, " the *hand* of the Lord with them." The Word of the Gospel of Christ is the weapon in the hand of the Holy Spirit (1 Thess. 1, 5). We preach Jesus, and the hand of the Lord

works wonders. Thus we are labourers with God (1 Cor. 3, 9).

3. *The Results of it.* " A great number *believed* and *turned* unto the Lord." The turning of the heart to the Lord is the evidence of having believed. The great end of all preaching should be to turn men unto the Lord. John Owen said, long ago, that " Ministers are seldom honoured with success unless they are *continually aiming at the conversion of sinners.*" This is a true witness.

II. THE VISIT OF BARNABAS.—Observe—

1. *What He Was.* " He was a good man, full of the Holy Ghost and of faith " (v. 24).   He was an all-round *good man* (Acts 9, 27), baptised with the Holy Ghost and full of faith in the Gospel, which he preached, expecting direct results. These are the elements which constitute the *gift* of the evangelist.

2. *What He Saw.* " He saw the *Grace of God* " (v. 23).   A Roman philosopher could only see in this movement " a vile superstition," where the Spirit-anointed eyes of Barnabas saw " the grace of God." A man's inward character determines what he shall see. The Athenians saw, with great pride, their many gods ; but Paul saw " the city wholly given to idolatry."   There are things which can only be " spiritually discerned," and the " Grace of God " is one of them.   When *you* go into a city, what seest thou ?

3. *What he Felt.* " He was glad."   His heart was filled with joy at seeing the work of God prosper,

although he had no hand in it. A man's *character* is
unmistakably revealed by what saddens or gladdens
him. As a man thinketh in his heart, so is he.

4. *What he Did.* " He exhorted them all . . . to
cleave unto the Lord." To cleave unto Him as the
branch does to the vine (John 15, 4). As a helpless
child would do to its mother ; and as a *faithful* follower
and friend, " with full purpose of heart." Be ye
steadfast and unmovable (1 Cor. 15, 58). He also
sought for Saul to help him in the work (vv. 25-26).
It is a great matter to be able to set others to work for
God. It was here and at this time, that disciples were
first called Christians. What a sweet, suggestive title.
They were called after the name of Christ because they
had *believed* on Him, and *turned* to Him, and were now,
with full purpose of heart, *living* for Him. Would that
all who are called Christians in our days had these
marks of the sheep of Christ. How sad to have a name
to live, and yet be dead.

PERSECUTION AND DELIVERANCE.

ACTS 12, 1-17.

The infant Church was not rocked in the cradle
of ease, or nursed in the lap of luxury. It had early to
face the fiery baptism of persecution. Herod thought
that he had done a fine stroke of business when he discovered that the killing of James with the sword had
" pleased the Jews " as well as himself. So he proceeded
to gain further honour by apprehending Peter also. But

He that ruleth in the heavens said, " So far, but no farther." Herod had already got to the end of his tether. Look at Peter—

1. *His Perilous Condition.* Peter was kept in prison, guarded by sixteen soldiers (vv. 4-5). The sentence of death seemed hanging over him ; in *himself* he was utterly helpless and hopeless. Such is the condition of all those who are under the power of the god of this world (John 3, 18).

2. *His Faithful Remembrancers.* " Prayer was made without ceasing unto God for him " (v. 5). Thank God, all the forces of earth and hell cannot close the door of prayer—this highway to heaven—this secret blood-stained path into the very audience chamber of the King of kings. We may not be able to speak to our friends personally, who are suffering affliction for the cause of Christ, or who may be led captive by the devil at his will, but we can speak to God on their behalf. The prayer of faith will *save*. Many have been pulled out of the fires of sin, as Peter was pulled out of prison, by " effectual, fervent prayer."

3. *His Peaceful Submission.* " That same night Peter was sleeping between two soldiers " (v. 6). That *same night* that Herod was to bring him forth to condemnation and death Peter's mind was so calmly resting in the good will of God, that he went to sleep as sweetly as a babe in its crib, rocked by a loving mother's hand. It is well known that Argyle, the martyr, had to be awakened out of his sleep that morn-

ing he was executed. *Easy* lies the head that wears a crown of holy innocency. Even on the cold, damp pavement of a dungeon the Grace of God can make us to lie down as in green pastures.

4. *His Supernatural Deliverance.* " The angel of the Lord came," etc. (v. 7). Soldiers are poor clumsy things in the presence of an angel, yet not more clumsy than the ways of men are, compared with the ways of God. His salvation is perfect. There was the *Divine Presence.* " The angel of the Lord " in personal touch with the needy one. There was the *Light shining in the prison.* Into the place of darkness the light of heaven came (2 Cor. 4, 6). There was the *smiting* of the prisoner, the awakening touch of the Messenger of God. " When He, the Spirit of Truth, is come, He will convince." There was the *call,* " Arise up quickly ! " God hath commanded all men everywhere to repent, and believe the Gospel. There was the *offer of liberty.* " His chains fell from his hands." The Gospel of Christ offers liberty to the captives " (Luke 4, 18).

5. *His Instant Obedience.* " And so he did." Peter was wise enough neither to argue nor object. He was profoundly conscious that " Salvation is of the Lord, and that his privilege was to trust and obey. Salvation had come to his prison-house ; he gladly accepted it as God's message to his soul. Be ye not disobedient to the heavenly vision.

6. *His Perfect Assurance.* " Now I know of a surety that the Lord hath delivered me " (vv. 10-11). No conqueror ever had a more triumphant march than

Peter had from the State prison to the street. Those soldiers in charge of his life remained blind and dumb as he passed them by, and the ponderous gate swung open at his approach. How could he be anything else than SURE that he was saved, after such an experience of the mighty power of God (Dan. 6, 22). Do you know of a surety that the Lord hath delivered you ?

7. *His Joyful Testimony.* " He *declared* unto them how the Lord had brought him out of the prison " (vv. 12-17). It was a wonderful story that Peter had to tell ; the story of God's salvation is always so. While Peter continued knocking at their door, it was God's answer to their prayers seeking admission, but they would hardly believe it. Those who have been delivered by the Lord should not be ashamed to confess Him by telling how great things He hath done for their souls.

THE CALL OF BARNABAS AND SAUL.

ACTS 13, 1-12.

After a missionary in China had been showing them the folly of idols, and had preached Jesus to them, one old man said—" Stop and tell us, for we *cannot find the door.*" How sad to think of the multitudes who are groping in the dark for the door of eternal life and cannot find it. How shall they hear without a preacher, and how shall they preach except they be *sent*. The Holy Ghost is very desirous to thrust out labourers ; pray ye Him. The young Church at Antioch had grown in number and power. Among the notable converts was

Manaen, who had been a companion of that Herod who ordered the death of John the Baptist, and who mocked the Lord Jesus Christ, " setting Him at naught." But by the grace of God he was plucked as a brand out of the fire. As the members of this Church " served and fasted," the Holy Spirit met their real need by pressing home to their hearts this message of definite direction, " Separate Me Barnabas and Saul." Perhaps they had been waiting on the Lord for special guidance, as to how they might further the cause of Christ when this unmistakable call came—

1. *It was a Divine Call.* " The Holy Ghost said," etc. (v. 2). They were as surely " called of God " as was Aaron. As all *fitness* for this service must come from Him, so also must the *call*. The Holy Ghost will never choose a man possessed by the spirit of the world as an ambassador of the Kingdom of Christ.

2. *It was a Personal Call.* " Barnabas and Saul." There was no room for questioning as to whom the Lord meant, neither was there any occasion for envy or jealousy. The Holy Spirit divideth to every man severally as He will (1 Cor. 12, 11). Not everyone that saith Lord, Lord, is fit for the service of God. " No man taketh this honour unto Himself but he that is called of God " (Heb. 5. 4).

3. *It was a Call to Separation.* " Separate Me," etc. Barnabas and Saul were to be separated unto the Holy Ghost, that He might breathe the will of God through them, as He had done with the *holy men* of God in old time (2 Peter 1, 21). To be used of the Holy

Spirit we must be separated from the world, and entirely yielded unto HIM, as vessels meet for His use. But we are not to suppose that those who *remained* in Antioch were not separated unto God. We can live the separated life anywhere by living for His glory.

4. *It was a Call to Work.* " For the work whereunto I have called them." Only those who are *new* creatures in Christ Jesus can have a hand in the work of this " new creation." We are not called to ease and idleness, but to be " workers together with Him," who hath called us into this holy calling. Have we entered into this work whereunto God, the Spirit, hath called us ? Or are we *idlers* in His vineyard ?

5. *It was a Call which met the Approval of the Brethren.* " They sent them away " (v. 3), but not without " fasting and prayer." It would be a great blessing to the Church and the world to-day if the Church was anything like so willing to recognise, and send forth, those who have been called of the Holy Ghost to do the work of an evangelist. By their fruit ye shall know them. These holy men were " solemnly ordained," not with dinners and toasts ! but with " fastings and prayer." There were no " hip, hip, hurrahs ! " but there was a solemn doing of the will of God. Many modern ordinations are a scandal to the cause of Jesus Christ.

6. *It was a Call, Followed by Mighty Deeds.* How can we believe that we are called and empowered by God if " signs and wonders " worthy of God are not being done through us in His name ? (vv. 5-12). Two

wonders were wrought here by Barnabas and Saul
(*a*) The overcoming of the sorcerer. This "child of
the devil" and "enemy of all righteousness" was
smitten with temporary blindness. The *works* of the
devil were destroyed. (*b*) The conversion of the deputy
(v. 12). The salvation of the governor of the island,
and the silencing of Elymas, the enemy of God, were
surely works worthy of the Holy Ghost, unto whom
Barnabas and Saul had been separated.

THE GOODNESS OF GOD.

ACTS 13, 13-43.

Paul and Barnabas had penetrated to the far away
Antioch in Pisidia, and on the Sabbath day they quietly
took a seat among the worshippers in the synagogue.
Being asked, as strangers, if they had a word for the
people, " Paul stood up " and delivered such a " word "
as they had never heard before. This first recorded
address of the great Apostle to the Gentiles may be entitled, " The Goodness of God." Paul may have taken
the pattern of it from that great address of Stephen's,
which must have been to him most memorable. He
deals with—

I. THE GOODNESS OF GOD REVEALED IN
HIS DEALINGS WITH ISRAEL.—(1) *They were
Chosen* (v. 17). God had been pleased, through grace,
to make them His people, chosen, not for good in
them, but as the monuments of His mercy (Deut. 7,
6). (2) *They were Delivered* (v. 17). When they were

strangers in the land of Egypt, " with an high arm He
brought them out." He saved them from the house of
bondage. (3) *They were Preserved* (v. 18). For forty
years His long-suffering patience bore with their mur-
murings and unbelief. Yet, as a people, they were
kept from perishing (Ps. 95, 9-10 ; 2 Peter 3, 9). (4)
They had a place Prepared for Them (v. 19). Seven
sinful Canaanitish nations were cast down and destroyed, that they might have a possession. The forces
of iniquity have all to be overcome ere the children of
God can enter into their inheritance. (5) *He Supplied
Their Need.* He gave them judges, a prophet, and a
King. Then He *raised up* David, a man after His own
heart (vv. 20-22). David was a type of Jesus Christ,
as a man *raised up* by God, to do His will among the
people. Paul, true to his mission, at once links on the
Christ to the seed of David, and shows next—

II. THE GOODNESS OF GOD REVEALED
IN HIS SON JESUS CHRIST.—(1) *He was Given
According to Promise* (v. 23). He was the rod out of
the stem of Jesse, and the branch out of his roots (Isa.
11, 1). Prepared in eternity, and raised up in the fulness
of time as a Saviour. (2) *He was Heralded by John* (vv.
24-25) as the Baptiser with the Holy Ghost and fire,
whose shoes he was not worthy to loose. (3) *He was
Condemned by the Rulers* (vv. 26-29). Paul makes it
clear that Christ was *slain* by those who found " no
cause of death in Him," thus bringing out the awful
enmity of the natural heart against the Holiness of God.
(4) *He was raised from the Dead* (v. 30). This was a

startling dogma for the apostle's hearers. **Dogmatic**
was he ? Yes ; as dogmatic as the Son of God. He
spake as one having authority (1 John 1, 1). If a man
cannot speak dogmatically on these great verities of
the Gospel, then let him hold his peace, for he has no
message from God to the people ; and there is plenty
of sickly namby-pambyism in the world already. (5)
He was Preached by Eye-witnesses of His Resurrection
(vv. 31-37). We have not followed cunningly-devised
fables. The resurrection of Christ is quite in harmony
with His unique life and testimony. Christ's death and
resurrection are the two pillars of the bridge of GRACE.
(6) *He is now able to Save all who Believe* (vv. 38-39).
" All that believe *are* justified. This is another blessed
dogma (Rom. 3, 28). No. The law of Moses could
never do this. It is through His blood the forgiveness
of sins come (Eph. 1, 7).

III. THE WARNING AGAINST DESPISING
THIS GOODNESS.—" Beware, therefore," etc. (vv. 40-
41.) Despisers are sure to perish. God is still working
this work of salvation in our days, in the hearts and lives
of all who believe. Yet there are many who still " despise, and wonder, and perish " in their unbelief, although
a man—saved and transformed by the power of this
Gospel—declare it unto them. Behold, therefore, the
" goodness of God " as exhibited in the life, death, and
resurrection of Jesus Christ as the Saviour of Men, and
let thy heart be bowed and broken by repentance.
These words of Paul were to many as good news from a
far country, so they wanted to hear them again the

next Sabbath. No other story can bear to be repeated so often as this.

RESULTS OF PAUL'S PREACHING.

ACTS 13, 42-52.

Somehow or other, wherever these first preachers of the Gospel went, they succeeded in creating a stir. If they " turned the world upside down " it was because the world was wrong side up. Men who have been made, as it were, into new bottles, and filled with the new wine of the kingdom of God—the Holy Spirit— cannot possibly act as ordinary mundane mortals. They are intoxicated by a new possession that excites to a holy enthusiasm for the eternal honour of the Lord Jesus Christ. It is impossible for a man full of the Holy Ghost to be cold and formal ; the Word of God burns in his bones as an unquenchable fire ; he cannot but speak the things which he has *seen* and *heard*. The effects of Peter's sermon were emphatic and varied—

1. *There was a Desire to Hear.* " The Gentiles besought that these words might be preached to them the next Sabbath " (v. 42). The Gospel had been so preached that morning that a real thirst had been created in the hearts of many to hear it again. There were many anxious inquiries at the close of Peter's address (v. 43). " After meetings " are no new thing.

2. *There was a general Awakening.* " The next Sabbath day there came almost the whole city together to hear the Word of God " (v. 44). It must have been

an intensely interested audience that Paul and Barnabas
addressed that day. We should see the multitudes
oftener crowding together " to hear the Word of God "
if they were sure that the Word of God was going to
be preached. Much of the present-day preaching does
not seem to stir up any interest whatever in the Word
of God. Multitudes of sermon hearers are in total darkness as to what the Bible teaches.

3. *There was Bitter Opposition.* " The Jews were
filled with envy, and spoke against Paul," etc. (v. 45).
There was no fear of Paul ever bringing himself under
that woe that comes upon those of whom " all men
speak well of." The proud, envious Jews, like the
Prodigal's " elder brother," could not rejoice in that
Grace of God which saves *sinners* and transforms them
into sons. Those who would preach " the Word of God "
must be prepared for the " contradiction and blasphemy"
of self-righteous, religious sinners, who are entirely out
of sympathy with God in the salvation of the lost. But
their opposition only stirred up the apostles to greater
boldness, and to bring a more direct charge against
them (v. 46). How sad to think of those who, in the
pride of their heart, judge themselves unfit to receive
everlasting life as the *gift* of God's grace through Jesus
Christ, His Son.

4. *There was Joy among the Gentiles.* " They were
glad and glorified the Word of the Lord " (v. 48).
See Rom. 15, 9-12. These " other sheep " which were
not of this Jewish fold were heartily glad to get into those
life-giving pastures of His Word. The hungry Gentiles

are fed, while the self-satisfied Jews are sent empty away.   To the *poor* the Gospel is preached with God-honouring results.   " Ye will not come to Me that ye might have life."

5. *There was Apparent Defeat.*   " They expelled them out of their coasts " (v. 50).   It is melancholy to think of " devout and honourable women " lending their influence to such an unholy and dishonourable cause.   They may cast out the servants of God, but they cannot cast out the seed of the Word that has been sown in the hearts of the people.   No ; the purpose of God in the lives of His chosen and consecrated servants can never suffer defeat.   All things work together for good to them that love God (Rom. 8, 28).

6. *There was Grace Triumphant.*   " The disciples were filled with joy and with the Holy Ghost " (v. 52). When the preachers were expelled from them God gave them a greater blessing in filling them with the Holy Ghost, and so sealed them unto the day of the final redemption (Eph. 1, 13).   These young disciples were rejoicing over a new found treasure, which they knew would enrich them during all the ages that were yet to come, while these persecutors had yet to reckon with that dust which the apostles shook off their feet against them.

MISSIONARY EXPERIENCE.

Acts 14, 1-20.

In Iconium, Paul and Barnabus " *so spake* that a great multitude believed . . . boldly in the Lord," so

that He " granted signs and wonders to be done by their
hands " (vv. 1-3). Signs and wonders are not likely
to be *granted* where the Word of God is so preached that
a great multitude are sent to sleep. Preaching " boldly
in the Lord "—not in the strength of our carnal wisdom
and fleshly energy—will certainly be accompanied with
the witness-bearing power of the wonder-working presence of God (Heb. 2, 4 ; Mark 16, 20). Wherever God
grants signs and wonders to be done, you may look for
persecutions (vv. 4-6). The rulers of darkness will
always oppose a violent disturbance of their kingdom.

I. AN EXAMPLE OF FAITH.—This man, who
had been " a cripple from his mother's womb," was a
picture of *helplessness* (vv. 8-9). He had never walked,
and in all likelihood never hoped to walk. Such liberty
and joy were not seemingly for him. Have we ever
thanked God for the use of our feet. But this same man
" heard Paul speak," and that faith which " cometh by
hearing" sprung up as a new-born faculty in the sorrowful soul of the cripple. He hears, and he believes, that
the Risen Saviour is able to heal him. See, there is a
new light in his eye, it is the light of that new hope that
is born of the Spirit of God, through the preached Word.
He has " faith to be healed," and the Spirit-taught
apostle is quick to perceive it, and calls him to " Stand
upright on thy feet ! " (v. 10). And he "leaped and
walked." He *leaped* before he walked, not only for joy,
but perhaps also because he had never yet learned to
walk. This great change was none the less real because
it came *suddenly*.

II. AN EXAMPLE OF FOLLY.—When these idolatrous Lycaonians saw the well-known cripple leaping and walking, they foolishly supposed that *their* gods had come down in the likeness of Paul and Barnabas The gods of idolaters are deaf and dumb and dead. How could they heal a poor cripple, and where could they "come down" from ? (vv. 11-13). But from their blind enthusiasm, let us solemnly learn how possible it is for us to be very earnest over religious notions that are only imaginary and delusive. How thankful we should be for the written Word of God, which is as a light shining in darkness, whereunto we do well to take heed. Any amount of " oxen and garlands " will never make a wrong thing right. They called Barnabas, Jupiter ; and Paul, Mercurius ; but these heathen Galatians are ·not the last of those who have attempted to adapt the things of God to their own idolatrous practices (Jude 4).

III. AN EXAMPLE OF FAITHFULNESS.—It is possible that Paul and Barnabas may not have understood the people when they spake " in the speech of Lycaonia," but as soon as their purpose of sacrifice was known they were quick to make a vehement protest against all forms of man-worship. They " rent their clothes " as an outward sign of inward horror—of hearts rent with agony at the thought. So jealous were they of the honour of God, that nothing pained them so deeply as that they, as the servants of Christ, should have the place in their thoughts and minds that their Lord and Master alone should have. The longing of their hearts and the object of their lives was to " turn them from

these vanities unto the Living God" (vv. 14-18). They
were " men of *like passions* with themselves," but what
a difference the grace of God had made. Elijah was a
man of like passions as we are, but how few of us can
pray as he did (James 5, 17). How differently Herod
acted when the people worshipped him. " He gave not
God the glory," and immediately the angel of the Lord
smote him (Acts 12, 22-23). Seek the honour that comes
from God only (Dan. 4, 37).

IV. AN EXAMPLE OF FICKLENESS.—In a
few days after they " stoned Paul, drew him out of the
city, supposing he had been dead" (v. 19). There is not
much between the world's honours and its frowns, between its " garlands" and its stones. To-day they cry,
" Hosanna ! " to-morrow, " Crucify ! " What a Friend
we have in JESUS, the same yesterday, to-day, and for
ever.

HELPING THE SAINTS.
ACTS 14, 19-28.

" Once was I stoned " is the name of one of the
medals Paul received for his faithfulness to Jesus
Christ (2 Cor. 11, 25). There is not much between the
praises and the anathemas of an ungodly crowd (vv.
18-19). Woe be to them who seek their happiness in the
favour of men, instead of the favour of God. It was
perhaps while Paul lay outside the city of Lystra, as one
dead, that he had that " unspeakable " experience of
being " *caught up* into paradise," so that whether " in
the body or out of the body he could not tell " (2 Cor.
12, 3-4). If so, see how the Lord can compensate His

suffering servants that they might be able to " glory in tribulations also." After preaching the Gospel in Derbe and making many disciples (v. 21, R.V.), they began their great return journey, which was crowded with holy deeds and crowned with abundant results.

1. *They Confirmed the Souls of the Disciples* (v. 22). This is a very needful work, if young believers are to be saved from backsliding. To confirm a soul in the faith is to strengthen that soul against the temptation and assaults of the world, the flesh, and the devil. Deal tenderly with young converts, show them the whole armour of God, and tell them how to put it on. Give them line upon line, and perhaps a little of your own experience, if you have any.

2. *They Exhorted to Continue in the Faith.* The Christian fight is a fight of *faith.* FAITH, fighting against feelings, failings, and appearances. As ye have therefore *received* the Lord Jesus—by faith—so walk ye in Him. Continue trusting in the promise of God against everything that seems opposed, and so make God true, if it should make every man a liar. This is the victory that overcomes the world, even our faith. There is a great need for *faith,* for it is " through much tribulation that we enter into the kingdom of God " (v. 22). In the world ye shall have tribulation, but faith clings to Him who hath said, " Be of good cheer ; I have overcome the world."

3. *They Ordained Elders in every Church* (v. 23). It was needful, in the absence of the apostles, that suitable and trustworthy men should be elected as rulers

and teachers. They would likely be appointed by the
vote of the people. All men are not fit to *rule* and to
" labour in word and doctrine." Since the beginning
there have been those who, through divine grace, and
a more entire consecration of themselves to God, have
become better qualified for spiritual service than others.
Covet earnestly the best gifts.

4. *They Commended them to the Lord.* After being
called they were handed over to the Lord as His own
private property that He might use them as it may
seem good in His sight. Do you think this would be a
hardship ? It is glorious liberty. Ye are not your own,
for ye are bought with a price.

5. *They Preached the Word* (v. 25). Oh, what a
Word was this that filled and fired their souls with an
unquenchable desire to labour and suffer for the salvation of men and the glory of the name of Jesus Christ.
From the day of Paul's conversion to the day of his
translation you never find him " off duty." He was
as much a witness for Jesus out of the pulpit as in it.
" To me to *live* is Christ."

6. *They Rehearsed all that God had done* WITH
THEM (v. 27). It was a wonderful story of grace they
had to tell. The Lord had done not only great things
for them, but great things *with* them. There be many
who are ever ready to tell us what God has done *for*
them, but we long most of all to hear what God has been
able to do *with* them. If you are saved, God hath
wrought a great work for you. If you are consecrated,
God will do a great work with you.

THE DISPUTE ABOUT WORKS.

ACTS 15, 1-35.

I. THE CAUSE OF THE DISPUTE (vv. 1-2).—
It arose about as to whether the Gentile converts should
be circumcised " after the manner of Moses " or not.
Those brethren that came down from Jerusalem were
so strong in their arguments for it as to make it " necessary to salvation." These nameless men, which disturbed the peace of the Church with this controversy,
are the forerunners of a class still extant, who are not
famous for spirituality of mind or success in the Lord's
work, but who are for ever ready to put those right who
are being greatly owned and blessed of God. The most
unspiritual are usually the greatest sticklers about
forms. Paul and Barnabas, who had seen so much of
the *grace of God*, hotly opposed this attempt to bring
them back into bondage. So keenly did Paul feel it that
in writing to the Galatians shortly after, he says : "If ye
be circumcised, Christ shall profit you nothing " (v. 2).

II. THE CONFERENCE AT JERUSALEM.—It
was agreed to submit the case to the General Assembly
at Jerusalem (vv. 2-21). So the evangelists hastened
thither. After they had given their report, " declaring
all things that God had done with them," the burning
question was at once introduced by certain converted
Pharisees, who had enough of their old nature still in
them as to make it hard for them to believe that
Gentiles could be saved " without the works of the law."
After " much disputing," Peter rose up and addressed

the Assembly as one clothed in the authority of God. He spoke of what his eyes had seen of the power of the Gospel among the Gentiles, how God had " given them the Holy Ghost, even as He did unto us," putting no difference between them, " *purifying their hearts by faith.*" There was great stillness in the court when Barnabas and Paul again addressed the audience (v. 12) on the special subject before them, taking care to show that the wonderful works wrought among the Gentiles were the works of God. The river of His grace is always too broad for the narrow channel of man's pride or prejudice. The next to speak is James—a man deeply taught in the Scriptures. He shows from the Word that it was the purpose of God to take out of the Gentiles " a people for His name," and takes the further liberty of submitting to the Church the divine programme of the present dispensation. A people " for His name " are *now* being taken out, through the preaching of the Gospel of Christ. This is James's *first* point. The *second* is the return of the Lord : " After this I will return." *Third*, the restoration of Israel : " Build the tabernacle of David." *Fourth*, the Millennium : " That the residue of men might seek after the Lord " (vv. 14-17). In closing his magnificent address, he makes this wise proposal : That the Gentile converts should not be troubled about forms that were not vital to their life and usefulness, but that they should be asked to abstain from those heathenish practices that were so common around them (v. 20)

III. THE RESULTS.—James's motion was carried unanimously. Letters of congratulation and sympathy were sent by special messengers to all those affected by this controversy. It was a cause of great joy to them when they heard that " it seemed good to the Holy Ghost to lay no unnecessary burden upon them " (v. 28). The goodness of the Holy Ghost in this respect is not always acknowledged by those who rule in some ecclesiastical courts. The true object of Church government is not to advocate or elaborate men's opinions, but to find out the mind of the Holy Spirit of God, and to do it. Where the Spirit of the Lord is, there is *liberty*.

THE CRY OF THE HELPLESS.
ACTS 16, 9-15.

Paul and Silas had been " *forbidden of the Holy Ghost* to preach the Word in Asia," and when they assayed to go into Bithynia, the " *Spirit suffered them not.*" These are facts full of deep significance to every servant of the Lord Jesus Christ. They reveal how completely the Holy Spirit has control over their lives. It is the mission of this Great Teacher come from God to guide us into all truth, and to carry on the work of God through the lives of those who are wholly yielded up to Him. Our subject may be divided into three parts—

1. *The New Call.* " Come over into Macedonia, and help us " (v. 9). It now became plain to Paul why the Holy Spirit had been closing other doors in his face. Macedonia needed the *help* that Paul and Silas, apostles of the Cross of Christ, were able to give.

What *help* could *they* have given if they had not been possessors of the grace of God and the knowledge of His saving power, through the death and resurrection of His beloved Son.   The best help anyone can get is to be lifted out of a life of sin and hopelessness into a life of holiness and victory.   How the vision came to Paul we need not stop to inquire, it was simply the Lord's way of revealing His will to His servant (Rom. 10, 14-15). May we not hear this cry for help, in a muffled fashion, rising in one form or another from every grade of social life to-day ?

2.   *The Immediate Response.*   They at once obeyed, " assuredly gathering that the Lord had called them to preach the Gospel unto them " (v. 10).   Paul and the Gospel were so vitally joined together that an open door to him meant an open door for the Gospel of Christ. When Paul said, " To me to live is Christ," he was stating not an article in his creed, but the all-absorbing principle of his heaven-born existence.   Let us beware of being disobedient to any heavenly vision that may be beckoning us into new spheres of service, or into higher and fuller experiences of the deep things of the Spirit of God.   It is only those who, like Paul and Silas, have had their lives enriched with the grace and power of Jesus Christ that can render the *help* that is needed to those who sit in darkness and the shadow of death and despair.

3.   *The Blessed Results* (v. 13-15).   They were not long in finding out the place of prayer.   It may have been a spot by the river-side, set apart as a public

oratory, because of its natural adaptations. In this roofless " house of prayer " Paul and Silas sat and spake the wonderful words of life to the women which resorted thither. The interest centres in a " certain woman named Lydia, *whose heart the Lord opened.*" She had been a worshipper of God, but now the door of her heart was opened to receive the message of the Gospel, sent to her by the Lord, through His servants. Take note that the " Word of Salvation " sent from God to man is not so much for the head as for the *heart*. With the heart man believeth unto righteousness. The *open* heart will always be " attentive unto the things " spoken by the servant of God, and God is sure to open hearts for the reception of the message that *He hath sent.* Another evidence of the open heart is a willingness to confess Christ and a love for the fellow-ship of the people of God (v. 15). We can never work out our own salvation until God hath worked it in us. Some hearts are opened as with the gentle kiss of light (2 Cor. 4, 6), others have been broken open as with a rod of iron. To open the heart to the Lord is to give Him the control of all the springs of the life. Son, give Me thine heart.

THE JAILOR'S CONVERSION.
ACTS 16, 16-40.

These incidents remind us of a picture gallery, where you have different scenes grouped together, and that, perhaps, strike you most by way of contrast. Shall we look at each separately ?

1. *A Picture of Demoniac Possession.* " A damsel possessed with a spirit of divination " (v. 16). How sad to think of this nice-looking young woman, wholly given over to the control of a deceitful, wicked spirit. She was the property of several sin-hardened wretches, who probably sold her half-mad ravings as the oracles of God. What she cried after the apostles on their way to the prayer meeting was quite true (v. 17), but then the words had such a hollow, fiendish ring about them that " grieved " Paul ; so, by faith in the name of Jesus Christ, he " commanded the evil spirit to come out of her."

2. *A Picture of Selfishness and Cruelty* (v. 19-24). " When her masters saw that the hope of their gains was gone," because the poor girl was now delivered from the soul-maddening power of the devil, instead of being thankful to God for such an emancipation, and because her salvation touched their pockets, they sought the ruin of the servants of God. " The *love* of money is the root of all evil." The spirit that possessed her masters was no better than the spirit which possessed the deluded damsel ; for greed of gain they would traffic in the *souls* of their fellow-creatures.

3. *A Picture of Heaven-Born Happiness.* " Paul and Silas prayed and sang praises unto God " (v. 24). Although lying in the deepest, darkest hole of that miserable prison, with bleeding backs and aching limbs, the joy of the Lord so filled their hearts that they were able also to " glory in tribulation." What but the grace of God could make anyone sing in such circumstances.

" The prisoners heard them." Might not this have been one of the reasons why God permitted His servants to be cast into prison. These fellow-prisoners also share in the victory which God wrought, for " everyone's bonds were loosed."

4. *A Picture of Divine Intervention.* " Suddenly there was a great earthquake," etc. Paul and Silas *resisted* the devil in the damsel, but no doubt they *prayed* for those who had despitefully used them and persecuted them (Matt. v. 44). Having calmly and joyfully trusted in God, the mighty, wonder-working hand of God is now stretched out for their deliverance. Truly, when they prayed " the place was shaken." This was a fulfilment of Psalm 10, 15.

5. *A Picture of Sudden Conversion* (vv. 27-31). It was a very dark moment in the experience of the jailor when he drew out his sword intending to commit suicide ; but it was immediately followed by the brightest experience he ever had. " He called for a light " that might guide his feet into the inner prison of the suffering saints, but when he cried, " Sirs, what must I do to be saved ? " he was calling for another light that might guide his feet into the paths of righteousness and peace and joy in the Holy Ghost. Then they told him words whereby he and *all his house* should be saved (v. 31). Just as he had been saved from self-destruction through the word of the apostle— " Do thyself no harm, for we are all here "—so can he be saved from the power of sin and the wrath of God by " believing on the Lord Jesus Christ " (John 3, 16).

6. *A Picture of Joyful Fellowship* (vv. 32-34).
What a change. A few hours before this the jailor
was fastening their feet in the terrible stocks. Now he
is bathing their wounds, taking them into his house,
and spreading the best he has before them, eating with
them, " and rejoicing, believing in God with all his
house." He had been suddenly awakened out of his
sleep, but now he was at one with the servants of God,
and with them enjoying an early hallelujah breakfast—
such a scene as would do credit to a modern Salvation
Army " glory feast."

SPECIAL MISSIONS.

ACTS 17, 1-14.

It was a long journey from Philippi to Thessalonica (about 100 miles) for two men who had just
lately been beaten with " many stripes." But as the
sufferings of Christ abounded in them, so also did the
consolation of Christ (2 Cor. 1, 3-6). About one year
after this Paul reminds the Thessalonians that their
entrance unto them was after they " had suffered and
were shamefully entreated at Philippi " (1 Thess. 2).
It was often at great personal sacrifice that these early
apostles preached the Word.

I. EXPERIENCES AT THESSALONICA.—

1. *Where they went.* There was a synagogue of
the Jews there, " and Paul, as his manner was, went in."
There seems to have been no synagogue at Philippi, the
only recognised place of worship being the place by

" a river side, where prayer was wont to be made "
(chap.16, 13). The manner of this evangelist, wherever he
went, was to seek out the " house of prayer," because
there was there liberty given for prayer and exhortation.

2. *What they did.* " Paul reasoned with them out
of the Scriptures." He proved to them, from Moses,
the Prophets, and the Psalms that Messiah must suffer
death and be raised again from the dead, and that Jesus
of Nazareth, whom he preached, was that same Anointed
One. " This Jesus whom I preach." This preacher
was never ill off for a text. He was so in love with
Jesus, as his Redeemer and Lord, that he could glory in
no one else. No one can preach the Gospel of Christ
as it ought to be preached, unless it is the all-absorbing
passion of their soul.

3. *How they succeeded.* " Some believed, and
some were moved with envy " (vv. 5-9). The Gospel,
in the power of the Holy Ghost, is either a savour of
life or death, of justification or condemnation, according
as it is received or rejected. In either case a change of
attitude toward God will take place. If the enmity is
not slain thereby, it is likely to be embittered. "The baser
sort " are always ready to oppose the Kingship of Jesus.

II. THEIR EXPERIENCES AT BEREA.—In
obedience to the Word of their Lord, " If they persecute you in one city, flee to another," they set off by
night for Berea, a distance of sixty miles. They found
the people here—

1. *Open-hearted.* " They received the Word with
all readiness of mind " (v. 11). Their minds were not

sealed with prejudice ; they were quite prepared to give this new doctrine a careful and favourable consideration. The minds of many Gospel hearers are like a well-trodden footpath in a field ; the seed may. fall *on* it, but it never gets a chance of entering *into* it. There is no readiness to receive the Word.

2. *Noble-hearted.* " They searched the Scriptures daily whether these things were so." A willingness to bring all teaching to the test of the " Scriptures of truth " is an evidence of nobility of mind (v. 11). What could be more noble than a soul eager to know and obey the mind of God ? There is something fatally wrong with our thoughts and opinions if they cannot stand the test of God's revealed will as found in His Word. If we are building on a sandy foundation, surely the sooner we find out our folly and danger the better.

3. *Honest-hearted.* " Therefore many of them believed" (v. 12). Having been convinced of the truth of Paul's teaching, after searching the Word for themselves, they were honest enough to believe it. When a good and honest heart hears the Word, it keeps it and brings forth fruit with patience (Luke 8, 15). Be honest with God. If any man will do His will, he shall know whether the teaching is of God (John 7, 17).

PAUL AT ATHENS.
ACTS 17, 15-34.

The reason why Paul came to Athens is stated in the previous verses. It may simplify the lessons here just to put them in this modern form—

1. *The Preacher.* Paul. A man learned in all the wisdom of the philosophers. A man who had been soundly converted by God to a special revelation of Jesus Christ. A man with a definite commission from the Risen One. A man who had already suffered much in the service of Christ. A man with a soul ablaze with love for his fellow-men, who knows no fear, and who is prepared to face all the wisdom of the Greeks, in the name of his Lord and Master. A preacher who has always a message, and who is never ashamed to tell it out.

2. *The Preparation.* "While he waited, his *spirit was stirred* in him" (v. 16). The city was stocked with thirty thousand gods, many of them magnificent works of art. But Paul was no mere sight-seer. He looked upon things in the light of the revelation of God in Christ and of eternity. While others could only see Grecian handiwork in Athenian "devotions," this man of God saw "the city wholly given to idolatry." The man whose eyes God hath opened will look upon "the things which are unseen." In many of our towns or cities there are signs of "religious devotions" that are not of God enough to stir the spirit of any preacher who has the heaven-lit eyes of the apostle.

3. *The Pulpit.* "Then Paul stood in the midst of Mars' Hill" (v. 22). That was after he had been in the synagogue and the market place preaching unto them "Jesus and the Resurrection." As the lonely evangelist stood in the midst of that open-air court, while the Athenian dignitaries rested on these rock-

hewn seats, he was occupying the leading pulpit of the city. It was a bold stand that he took, but he believed that the Lord who stood by him, was worthy of the highest place in this philosophical centre. Paul counted this a great privilege for his Master's sake.

4. *The Audience.* " Ye men of Athens " (v. 22). No preacher ever addressed a more critical congregation ; they made it their life's business to inquire into every new thing (v. 21). In the Epicureans, he had a company of high-minded Rationalists, whose god was their belly ; the Stoics extolled virtue, but denied human responsibility and future judgment. In them Paul was face to face with the wisdom of Socrates and Plato, but in him they were face to face with the " wisdom of God." The world by wisdom knows not God.

5. *The Sermon.* It was not read, it was poured out of a burning heart. The *subject* was " HIM." Whom therefore ye ignorantly worship, *Him* declare I unto you. This preacher always found a short cut to Christ because he gloried in Him (Gal. 6, 14). The *Heads* of this wonderful sermon are very clear. He preached (*a*) The Existence and Creative Power of God. " God that *made* the world," etc. This was a blow at the Epicurean theory of evolution or " chance." (*b*) The Spiritual Character of God (v. 25). He is not worshipped " with men's hands." Out of the *heart* are the issues of life. (*c*) The Universal Brotherhood of Man. " Made of *one blood* all nations." (*d*) The overruling Providence of God. He hath determined the times before appointed (v. 26). (*e*) Man's Need of God, " They should

seek the Lord." (*f*) The Universality of the presence of God. "He be not far from every one of us" (v. 27 ; Isa. 55, 6). (*g*) That God Himself is the source of all Life. "In Him we live, and move, and have our being" (v. 28). How much more fully is this truth realised by those whose "life is hid *with Christ* in God ?" Then came the *Application*—(*a*) Something we ought *not to do*. "We ought not to think that the Godhead is like unto gold," &c. (*b*) Something we ought *to do*. We should *repent*, for "God hath commanded all men everywhere to repent" (v. 30) ; and "because He hath appointed a day in which He will judge the world by Jesus Christ" (v. 31 ; Rom. 2, 16).

6. *The Results.* (*a*) Some mocked (v. 32). The doctrine of the resurrection and final judgment cut at the roots of their selfish lives and false philosophy. What made Felix tremble, made them *mock*. Any fool can do that. (*b*) Some hesitated. "We will hear thee again," they said. They wavered, and lost their opportunity, for they never heard him again (v. 33). (*c*) Some believed. The Gospel is the power of God unto salvation to everyone that believeth.

PAUL AT CORINTH.
Acts 18, 1-17.

Athens was perhaps the hardest field in which the apostle had ever attempted to sow the good seed of the kingdom. The wisdom of this world is one of the strongest forts of the kingdom of Satan. Paul writes no epistle to the Athenians. When he visited Corinth, the

O VIII

capital of Achaia, he must have found it a busy and populous centre of commerce. Let us look at him here—

I. AS A TENTMAKER.—" Because he was of the same craft he abode with them and *wrought*" (v. 3). It was a principle with Paul that if any man "*would not* work, neither should he eat." Rather than burden anyone with the responsibility of his board and lodgings, he would labour night and day (2 Thess. 3, 8). Paul was *courageous* enough to preach the Gospel to the Athenian professors at the Mars' Hill University ; he was also *humble* enough to act as a journeyman tentmaker in the workshop of Aquila. *Whatsoever* ye do, do it heartily as unto the Lord.

II. AS A REASONER.—" He reasoned in the synagogue every Sabbath " (v. 4). Paul did not reason with them merely to bring them over to his way of thinking, or to prove his own superior scholarship ; he reasoned with them "*out of the Scriptures*" (chap. 17, 2), that he might bring them over to the mind of God concerning His Son Jesus Christ. If the *will of God*, as revealed in the Scriptures of truth, has not become the governing and impelling factor in our lives, then is our preaching vain, and men will remain in their sins. Many preachers nowadays, instead of reasoning *out of the Scriptures*, go out of the Scriptures to *reason*. Instead of giving the people bread, they offer them luminous dust.

III. AS A WITNESS.—" He testified to the Jews that Jesus was the Christ." He not only could reason with them over an open Bible, but he could also give his own *personal* testimony to the Messiahship and saving power of Jesus, who was called Christ. Had he not seen Him, and heard Him, and been transformed by His wondrous grace ? (Acts 9). Mere finger-post preachers may be *correct*, but they are always cold, and stiff, and lifeless. God never sent anyone to preach Christ who had not first Christ revealed in them (Gal. 1, 16). " We speak that we do not know."

IV. AS A PROTESTANT.—" When they opposed . . . he said, Your blood be upon your own heads ; I am clean " (v. 6). He protested against the unreasonable opposition and wilful blindness of these Jews by turning his ministry specially to the Gentiles. That very dust that he shook off his raiment will remain as a witness against them. It is a very solemn thing to grieve the Spirit of God, so that the message of the Gospel, which is the message of Life, is turned into a sentence of death (Ezek. 3, 18-19).

V. AS A SOUL-WINNER.—" Many of the Corinthians hearing, believed " (vv. 7-8). His turning away from the Jews was the salvation of these Gentiles. If *you* don't come into the marriage feast of the Gospel, another will, for every seat will be occupied when the King comes. But the apostle's testimony among the opposing Jews was not in vain ; it never was. Among the converts he had " Crispus, the *chief ruler* of the synagogue." My Word shall not return void.

VI. AS ONE BELOVED BY GOD.—" Then spake the Lord to Paul," etc. (vv. 9-10). If there was

any lingering doubt or fear in Paul's mind as to the wisdom of turning away with the Gospel from his own kins-
men, this message from the Lord would give him perfect
rest.   There was in it (1) a word of *cheer*, "Be not
afraid ; " (2) a word of *counsel*, "Speak and hold not thy
peace ; " (3) a word of *assurance*, "I am with thee ; " (4)
a word of *promise*, "No man shall hurt thee ; " (5) a word
of *hope*, "I have much people in this city." They are
always blessed who are heaven's favourites.

VII.   AS ONE DESPISED BY MEN.—"The Jews
made insurrection with one accord against Paul" (vv.
12-17).   Woe unto you when *all* men speak well of you.
The more intently anyone seeks the glory of God in the
salvation of souls, the more bitter will those self-righteous
religious formalists become.   They beat Sosthenes in
the presence of a *careless* governor (Gallio), but as to
Paul, it happened unto him just as the Lord had said.
"No man shall set on thee to hurt thee." Be thou
faithful.

PAUL AT EPHESUS.
ACTS 19, 1-20.

Paul did a great service in bringing Priscilla and
Aquila to Ephesus.   Next to winning souls, there is no
greater work than putting others in the way of doing
better service for God.   Jealousy is a cruel monster that
would hinder us from rejoicing in the success of others.
It was surely the guiding hand of God that brought
Apollos into contact with these two deeply taught
disciples (chap. 18, 26).   If they were not eloquent themselves, they were able, by the grace of God, to sharpen

the sword of the mighty Apollos. He knew only John's baptism, and evidently was a stranger to the mighty baptism of the Holy Spirit. He was a fervent, eloquent, diligent believer in the Lord, but he lacked what many preachers still lack, a definite baptism of the Holy Ghost. Apollos was not too proud to sit at the feet and learn of those who were less scholarly, but more deeply spiritual, than himself. Humility is a characteristic of all who are prepared to be used in the work of God.

Paul, having again visited Jerusalem, returned to Ephesus. His heart must have been cheered in finding there " certain disciples " (v. 1). His first question was a searching one—" Have ye received the Holy Ghost since ye believed ? " He did not wish these young believers to be, like Apollos, strangers to this gift of the Ascended Christ. The apostle knew that without this they were in great danger of backsliding, or of living fruitless and powerless lives. It was well that he did, for they had not even heard of the Spirit of Pentecost, having only known the " baptism of John." But as soon as they heard of this *second blessing* they at once yielded themselves, that they might receive it. " Then the Holy Ghost came on them, and they spake with tongues." No one ever yet received the baptism of the Holy Spirit without *signs* following. It is impossible for anyone to be filled with the Spirit and yet no supernatural works following. How will ever the world be convinced that God is in us if no God-like wonders are being wrought ?

The Church of God will never be anything else, in the eyes of an ungodly world, but an impotent thing, beating the thin air until experimentally this great truth is grasped. God will not give His glory to another on earth save the Holy Spirit. This is a question of urgent and tremendous importance for every believer in Jesus Christ. " Have ye received the Holy Ghost *since* ye believed ? " Pentecost must follow Calvary in the experience of every one that would honour God by a life of service. And we say it in all tenderness, the will of God is not being done in the lives of those who are not filled with the Spirit.

For two years Paul spake of the " things concerning the kingdom of God " (v. 10). Some believed not, but all that dwelt in Asia *heard* the Word of the Lord Jesus. Whether men received the message of God or not, Paul sounded out the " Word of Life." He did not seem to trouble himself much about *results*. He knew the Word would not return void to Him who sent it. His great business as a preacher was to make men *hear*.

The miracle of the " handkerchief " seemed to excite the jealousy and emulation of the vagabond Jews ; they, too, would work miracles for their own glory in the name of " Jesus, whom Paul preached " (v. 13), but the demon-possessed " overcame them and prevailed against them." The victory of the man with the evil spirit over those would-be exorcists was proof enough that they were not sent by God, and that they were not possessed by the Holy Ghost. No one can be a match for the devil in his own strength. The powers of darkness will always prevail against those who are not in themselves right with God. " Jesus I know, and Paul I know, but who are ye ? " said the demon. It is a startling fact that devils know no enemies but those filled with the Spirit and in living touch with God. It is by " He that is in you," who is " greater than he that is in the world," that we overcome the world, the flesh, and the devil.

WORLDLY WISDOM.
ACTS 19, 21-41.

" No small stir " was created in Ephesus through the faithful testimony of Paul. When the Word of God is preached in the power of the Holy Ghost sent down from heaven, it is as a two-edged sword piercing and dividing asunder the things that affect both soul and spirit. It is the flash-light of the Eternal Throne of God cast upon the iniquitous thoughts and acts of men, and is always sure to produce a consternation when it suddenly falls upon those who love the darkness rather than the light.

Demetrius became almost demented when he saw that his idolatrous " craft was in danger." It mattered nothing to him how many souls were being blessed of God, in being redeemed out of heathen darkness, so long as his purse was not affected. This silversmith, like many others, could be very religious so long as it brought him a good income. He showed real " worldly wisdom " in gathering together " the workmen of like occupation " to protest against the teaching of Paul. It would be good for us if we were half so earnest in contending for the truth as those men were for their heathenish superstitions.

In connecting " this our *craft*" with the " great goddess Diana," Demetrius did a magnificent stroke of business. His craft and his god were to stand or fall together. Is there not a more urgent lesson here for every Christian worker ? Is our work for Christ so vitally connected with Him that His honour waxes or wanes according as we succeed or fail in His service ? As through the work of Demetrius and his associates' *images* of their god were made and circulated among the people for the glory of Diana, so, through the work of Paul and his companions in labour, *images* of his God were being created and circulated for His glory and honour in those souls that had been transformed by the Holy Spirit. Here the powers of the kingdom of Satan and the forces of the kingdom of Christ meet in terrible conflict. Do we wonder that " the whole city was filled with *confusion* ? " These enemies of God were blinded by the smoke of their own guns. In their desperation they caught two of Paul's companions and made a rush for the public oratory (theatre), that their triumph might be all the more conspicuous. Paul, the fearless, would at once have faced those lions in their own den, but his trustworthy friends advised him not to " adventure himself" (v. 31). The scene in the theatre was like the troubled sea casting up mire and dirt. " Some cried one thing, and some another." Confusion reigned ; for the greater part of the mob knew not for what reason they had come together. But like all other narrow-minded, sin-blinded bigots, they could say *one* thing, and for the space of two hours they kept saying it: " Great is Diana of the Ephesians ! " What is the use of us crying up the greatness of our God if we ourselves act like a lot of silly imbeciles. It is easy to preach on the *faithfulness* of God while we show by our acts that we are living in unbelief. The town clerk seemed to be a man worthy of his honourable position ; faithful, clear-headed, and reasonable. He knows how to manage the tumultous crowd by first speaking a word of praise for the world-renowned city and its goddess (v. 35). Then, in substance, he declares, seeing that the God which ye worship is the greatest that ever came from heaven, and that the things which ye believe are infallible, and "cannot be spoken against," ye ought to show the reality of your faith by being calm, and not doing anything rashly. How very applicable all this is to those who believe in the Lord Jesus Christ. Is He not great ? Did He not come down from heaven ? Has He not spoken things which cannot be overthrown ? Ought we not then to be "quiet, and do nothing rashly ?" He that believeth shall not make haste. When we know that greater is He that is for us than all that can be against us, surely we can well afford to be quiet and do nothing rashly. They that wait on the Lord shall renew their strength.

A MIDNIGHT MEETING.

ACTS 20, 2-12.

One prominent characteristic of the great apostle of the Gentiles was his intense carefulness over young believers, that they might be established in the faith (v. 2). He counted no personal sacrifice too great so that they might be made strong in the Lord, to live and witness for Him. It is not enough that we are saved :

we are saved to *serve*. We fail in our ministry if we
do not lead young converts into the secret joy and
power of His service. It is a great matter to lead a soul
into the saving knowledge of Christ, but it is an equally
important matter to lead a soul into active work for
God. A soul yielded to Christ is a soul saved, but a *life*
given to Him is a life saved. We are not rewarded at
last for being saved, but for works done in His name
and for His glory. It might help us to grasp the teaching of this portion more easily if we look at—

1. *The Speaker*. "Paul preached unto them,
ready to depart on the morrow" (v. 7). His stay at
Troas was short, only "seven days," but it was a memorable time. Who could ever forget a sermon by Paul ?
When the soul of a preacher is aflame with heaven-born
fire, the bread of life is sure to be served in season. It
is possible even to preach the truth in such a way as to
sicken even a hungry soul. The Gospel of the Love of
God must be served hot if men are to receive it gladly.
We feel perfectly sure that Paul would give no countenance to read sermons.

2. *The Time*. "The first day of the week, when
the disciples came together to break bread." The "first
day of the week," which is our Sabbath, is a day for
which we should continually thank God. It is the
memorial of Christ's resurrection, and the "breaking of
bread" was the memorial of His death. Paul seems to
have waited the whole week to get this opportunity of
ministering the Word to them. Were there no Sabbaths,
how few, even in our own Christian country, would ever

think of going to hear the Word of God. Let us pray
that the sanctity of it may be long preserved.

3. *The Place.* " The upper chamber, where there
were many lights " (v. 8). Ever since Pentecost, the
disciples seem to have a special liking for the " *upper*
room"(chap. 1, 13). Being an all-night meeting, they had
need of lights, but perhaps the *"many* lights" suggests
the willingness of all the disciples to provide abundance
for the occasion. The natural consequence would be
the heating of the atmosphere to an excessive degree,
which may partly account for the window being open,
and the sleepy young man falling over.

4. *The Speech.* " Paul continued his speech
until midnight " (v. 7), and after taking some refresh-
ment, he " talked a long while, even till break of day "
(v. 11). The people who clamour for short sermons
are not likely to be found at a midnight meeting.
From the attitude of some modern church-goers, you
would think that they look upon listening to the preaching of the Word of God as a kind of penance that should
be made as short as possible. They are perfectly satisfied with the smallest crumb of the heavenly bread for
their souls, then they go home and have a dinner with
five courses. It is quite true that there are some sermons long at five minutes, while others are short at
fifty. Everything depends on the man and the message

5. *The Interruption.* " Eutychus sunk down with
sleep and fell from the third loft " (v. 9). This young
man suffered severely for his " first sleep in the kirk ; "
he nearly lost his life. Are there not multitudes in our

own days who are running the risk of losing their souls through the same drowsy habit, and with only about the tenth part of the provocation that befel Eutychus ? Immediately Paul ran to the help of the unfortunate man, and by " embracing him " restored him again to consciousness, to the great comfort of the disciples. Are there not—in another sense—many *fallen* ones lying within our reach who might be *restored* to a new and better life if only they were *embraced* by the arms of Christian love and faith ?   We shall never be successful in " lifting the fallen " unless we can take them into the affections of our hearts.

A PERSONAL TESTIMONY.

Acts 20, 13-27.

Paul's company sailed into Assos, he arranged to meet them there, preferring himself to walk the distance, which was only a few miles ; perhaps that he might have a quiet time of meditation by the way, or that he might have some further opportunity of preaching the Gospel. A true Christian can enjoy the presence of God in the highway, just as much as anywhere else.   It is said of a certain man of God that he used to walk along the road with his hat off, so conscious was he of the nearness of the presence of the Lord.   Paul faithfully kept his appointment, as every honourable man should, (v. 14). There are some who always study to be late.   If they cannot be notable in one way they will in another.   It is he that is faithful in the least that will be honoured in the much.

To save time they passed by Ephesus and halted at Miletus, from whence Paul sent for the Ephesian elders, that he might leave with them his last parting message. His words to them were in the form of a personal testimony. It was no egotism that moved the apostle to give them this perfect photograph of his own spiritual character as a servant of Christ. We feel profoundly thankful to him for it, as it gives us a true picture of what every servant of the Lord Jesus Christ should be. Let us carefully look at it.

1. *He was Humble.* " Serving the Lord with all humility " (v. 19). There is no room for pride, or selfish boasting where the Spirit of the " meek and lowly in heart " rules. The Lord can never be *served* in any other way but in " all humility of mind." Brokenness of spirit is an essential condition even of *fellowship* with Him, and there can be no real service for Him out of the communion of the Holy Ghost. His humility is further seen in his working with his hands for the support of himself and those who were with him (v. 34). He was not ashamed to call himself " the least of the apostles " and to declare that it was " by the *grace of God* I am what I am."

2. *He was Compassionate.* He served the Lord " with *many tears* and temptations " (v. 19. " He ceased not to warn every one night and day *with tears* " (v. 31). Paul's ministry was not a cold, formal, glass-eyed business. His words were moist with the heart-dew of divine love and tenderness. Many preachers use the words " I tell you," but how few can add, " even

weeping." (Phil. 3-18). We might as well throw stones
at the people, as *heartless* words of wisdom. The truth
must be spoken in love. The man who cannot weep
over the enemies of the Cross of Christ fails to make
full proof of his ministry. We can weep over our own
sorrows and losses, and if the interests of Jesus Christ
were as real to us we would also weep over His. Servant of God, is your *heart* right ?

3. *He was Faithful.* " I kept back nothing that
was profitable," etc (vv. 20-21). He taught from house
to house, both Jews and Greeks, preaching *repentance*
towards God, and *faith* towards our Lord Jesus Christ,
and shunned not to declare the *whole counsel* of God
(v. 27). Paul had no theories of man to defend, he had
a revelation of God to declare. It is a most lamentable
fact that one of the most prominent doctrines of this
great apostle—repentance toward God—has almost
died out of the modern sermon. To seek popularity,
and the praise of men, instead of to declare the whole
counsel of God, is to become a traitor to Christ, and a
stumbling-block to the souls of men. Only the *faithful* shall be rewarded (Luke 19, 17).

4. *He was Submissive.* " I go bound in spirit
unto Jerusalem . . . but none of these things move
me " (vv. 22-24). Although Paul had the witness of the
Holy Ghost that " in every city bonds and afflictions
waited for him," there was no offence in his heart at
this painful providence. In nothing that the finger of
God touched was he offended. He believed that *all
things* work together for good to them that love God

(Rom. 8, 28) " Bonds and afflictions " are not in themselves evidences that we have erred, and so need them as *chastisements ;* they are often conditions necessary to the discipline of the soul, for further and deeper experience of the things of God. Our Lord's sufferings were in no sense corrective, but served, in one way, as a background for the manifestation of His glorious character.

5. *He was Devoted.* " Neither count I my life dear unto myself, that I might finish the ministry . . . of the Gospel of the grace of God " (v. 24). To publish the Gospel of the grace of God was a thing more dear to Paul than his own life. It was his meat and drink to do the will of his Redeemer and Lord. He could say, " To me to live is Christ." The Gospel is never preached as it ought to be, unless by those who are more desirous to glorify God than themselves. He who seeketh " great things for himself " is morally unfit for the service of Christ. If any man would come after ME, let him *deny himself.*

6. *He was Courageous.* " I have not shunned to declare unto you the whole counsel of God " (v. 27). No " fear of Man " could fetter the tongue of this faithful witness. A full-orbed Gospel had been revealed to him, and at any personal cost he was determined that not one ray of it should be hindered from shining through him. The perfect *love* with which the heart of Paul was filled cast out all *fear.* He loved the Lord Jesus Christ and the souls of men too intensely to keep back anything that was profitable (v. 20). It is a base and false charity that shuns to declare the whole counsel of God.

FAITH AND FAILURE.

ACTS 21, 1-36.

"St. Paul was a great trader of Christ both by land and sea." So said John Trapp, and it is a most suggestive saying. No merchant could more urgently push his wares than Paul pushed the things of the Kingdom of God. Wherever he went, whatever he did, it was always as an ambassador for Christ. To him religion was no cloak, to be thrown off or on as occasion demanded. It was the bone and sinew and vital breath of his being. As Saul, he was crucified with Christ ; as Paul, he had no existence but in Him and for Him. "To me to live is Christ." Note here some further things about him—

1. *His Sorrowful Prospect.* While on his way to Jerusalem, he was warned at least twice of dangers, and of certain imprisonment, if he should go there at that time (vv. 4-11). He knew before this—by the Holy Ghost—that bonds and afflictions awaited him in every city (vv. 20-23). In his unconverted days, he "profited much in the Jew's religion" (Gal. 1, 14) in that he was honoured and praised of men ; but all was sacrificed for Him, who had called him by His grace, and who had promised to show him what great things he must suffer for His sake. He was called into the fellowship of Christ's sufferings.

2. *His Fearless Faith.* Paul's reply to their united entreaty was short and decisive. "I am ready" (v. 13). Ready, not only to be bound, but to die for

the name of the Lord Jesus. The secret of peace and
victory in the face of all trial and persecution is to
connect the NAME of the Lord Jesus with it. He who
can say confidently, " Who shall separate me from the
love of Christ ?" will also be able to add " We are more
than conquerors through Him." " I am ready." What
a ring of unstaggering confidence there is in this. How
much has been lost politically, commercially, morally,
and spiritually for the want of being *ready* when the
crisis came. It was " they that were *ready* " who went
in when the Bridegroom came ; they who were *getting
ready* were shut out.

3. *His Powerful Testimony.* " He declared what
things God had wrought among the Gentiles" (vv. 17-20).
Having arrived at Jerusalem, and having been warmly
welcomed by the brethren, Paul gave them another
chapter out of his life's book, thrilling with the wonders
of the grace of God. Those who by faith attempt
much for God, will have experiences that will glorify
God (v. 20). If we would see the wonder-working
power of God, we must needs " launch out into the
deep "—into the deep of God's fathomless grace, and the
unsearchable riches of His Son. Believe and thou shalt see.

4. *His Compromising Meekness* (vv. 21-26). Seeing that there were so many in Jerusalem who believed
that Paul's teaching led the converts to " forsake
Moses," the elders persuaded him to show his devotion
to the law of Moses by shaving his head, and joining
himself with those four men who were about to present
themselves as observers of the law of the Nazarite

P VIII

(Num. 6, 13-18). This was intended to shut the mouths of those who madly cavilled against the apostle's preaching, and showed the great humility of Paul, when he submitted to it for their sakes. He was willing to be made all things . . . that he might save some.

5. *His Conspicuous Failure* (vv. 27-31). The very means he used to disarm the enemy became the cause of offence. He had shaved his head through the fear of man ; now he is caught in the snare. We cannot but think that, in his willingness to please the brethren, and perhaps to justify himself in the eyes of men, he for the time being failed to " stand fast in the liberty wherewith Christ had made him free." But in any case trouble was sure to come upon him in Jerusalem, for the Holy Ghost had already witnessed to this, and the beloved Paul seemed in no way disappointed with the terrible consequences.

6. *His Rescue by the Soldiers* (vv. 32-36). This was a sad scene. The worshippers of the temple of God going about to kill him, whose body was the temple of the Holy Ghost. Religious *formalists* are always at war with the Spirit of God, for where the Spirit is there is liberty. The chains of the Roman soldiers were more merciful than the tongues of these hypocrites. But a man of God is immortal till his work is done.

PAUL'S DEFENCE, A GOSPEL.
ACTS 22, 1-21.

Paul's life is an exhibition of what the grace of God can do. Even in the most trying and unexpected circumstances, he could possess his soul in patience. See his beautiful courtesy, "*May* I speak unto thee?" (vv. 21-37) and note his wonderful wisdom and courage when he asked, as a "Jew of Tarsus and a *citizen* of no mean city," he might be allowed to speak to the people What a blending of giant strength with child-like simplicity. Having received permission to speak from the stairs of the castle, he addresses the religious rabble, not as blood-thirsty enemies, but as "Men, brethren, and fathers." His defence takes the form of a personal testimony. He is not so anxious to justify himself before the people as to show them what great things God had done for him. He refers to himself here—

1. *As a Learned Jew* (v. 3). He was no ignorant bigot, no prejudiced Gentile, but a Jew born in the famous *free* city of Tarsus, and educated at the feet of the great Gamaliel: a Hebrew of the Hebrews. Paul's natural gifts and high-class training made him one of those men that were not to be easily deceived.

2. *As a Zealous Persecutor.* "I persecuted *this way* unto the death" (v. 4). *This way* refers to the way of Christians, the way he now walked. In carrying out the unenlightened conviction of his heart, he thought he *ought* to oppose the things connected with the name of Jesus (Acts 8, 3). The "I thought" of the unregenerate man is always contrary to the mind of God. There is a religious enthusiasm that has not been kindled by the holy fire from heaven, but by the fire of hell.

3. *As a Conquered Foe.* "I fell unto the ground" (vv. 6-7). A sudden burst of soul-convicting light from

the presence of the glorified Saviour, overwhelmed the haughty Saul ; smiting him to the earth. What other power could have arrested such a sinner and subdued such a determinate will ? When God speaks it is with convincing power. What can speak more effectively than *light ?* By the light of His Word He still brings rebel souls to the dust. Is not My Word a hammer and a fire, saith the Lord. With this hammer God, the Spirit, can break the rocky heart to pieces.

4. *As a Humble Inquirer.* " And I answered, Who art Thou, Lord ? . . . What shall I do, Lord ? " (v. 8-10). Those questions reveal a radical change in the mind and heart of Saul, but between the first and the second there comes the *revelation of Jesus* Himself to his soul. When anyone is *ready* to obey the light and the voice of God's Word they will not be left long in ignorance of the saving power of Jesus. But, Who art Thou ? should be followed with, What shall I do ? for we are saved to serve (Luke 1, 74).

5. *As a Comforted Believer.* " Brother Saul, receive thy sight " (vv. 11-13). At first he " could not see, for the glory of that light " had blinded his eyes to every earthly object. The light of the glory of God is always an eye-blinding light to the glory of this world. " *Brother Saul.*" How soothing this salutation would be, coming from the lips of the saintly Ananias ; and as an evidence that the Lord, whom he had met, desired to bless him, he received his sight, a new sight for the new world into which he had now entered. With him old things had passed away, and all things had now become new.

6. *As an Instructed Disciple.* " God hath chosen thee, that thou shouldst know His will . . . and be His witness unto all men " (vv. 14-16)   He was called to be a witness to the resurrection of Christ, as one born out of due season.   The Gospel which he preached was not received of man, but by the *revelation* of Jesus Christ (Gal. 1, 12).   Through Ananias he learned more fully the purpose of God in calling him.   Have we learned all that God, by His grace, means us to be and to do ?

7. *As a Divinely Commissioned Apostle* (vv. 17-21) It was while *praying* in the temple that the vision of God came, saying, " Make haste   . out of Jerusalem.   . . Depart, for I will send thee far hence unto the Gentiles."   Is it not usually while *praying* that the vision of God's will is made known ? (Acts 9, 11 ; 30) Ask and ye shall receive.   As a " chosen vessel," Paul was not sent on his own charges, but was filled with the wealth and power of the name of Jesus (Acts 9, 15). He was divinely called, divinely commissioned, and divinely equipped.   So is it with all the true servants of the Lord Jesus Christ.

A DAY OF TRIAL AND A NIGHT OF CHEER.

ACTS 23, 1-24.

After spending a night in the rocky fortress of Antonia, Paul was brought down to answer for himself before the chief priests and all their council.   The leading points in this portion will perhaps be more easily grasped if we put them thus—

1. *An Honest Confession.* " I have lived in all good conscience before God until this day " (v. 1). To have a conscience " void of offence toward God " was the constant ambition of the apostle (chap. 24, 16). There are some whose consciences are seared as with a red-hot iron, through their many refusals to obey the Word and will of God. A good " conscience " is one in perfect harmony with the mind of God, and is the guarantee of a blissful life.

2. *A Holy Indignation* " God shall smite thee, thou whited wall," etc. (vv. 2-4). This may seem harsh, but the pure righteous soul of the prisoner was so grieved that the man exalted to administer *justice* should, through *personal* hate, order him to be smitten " contrary to the law." The high priest's business was to condemn the wicked, and not to smite the righteous (Deut. 21, 5). We are told that in the beginning of the Jewish wars this same priest was actually smitten to death by a captain of the Jews.

3. *A Skilful Attitude.* " But when Paul perceived," etc. (v. 6). Paul was a man whose *eyes* the Lord had opened, and so was quick to take in a situation. He was wise as a serpent, but not so poisonous, because he had also the harmlessness of the dove. In declaring himself a Pharisee, and a believer in the resurrection, he was stating that which was absolutely true, for none could be more jealous for the truth of God that he.

4. *A Divided Jury.* " There arose a dissension between the Pharisees and the Sadducees " (vv. 7-10)

Before this they both cried, "Away with this fellow from the earth," but now the Pharisees attempt to justify Paul by saying, "Perhaps an angel hath revealed it to him." This was also a side-thrust at the Sadducees, who denied the existence of angels and spirits. We have here an old exhibition of a modern sin, that of putting partyism, personal passions, and interests before the truth of God and the general cause of righteousness.

5. *A Divine Encouragement.* "The night following the Lord stood by him and said, Be of good cheer, Paul" (v. 11). It was a blessed night, luminous with the glory of His presence, and his soul comforted with His word of promise. How easy it is for the faithful Saviour to meet the need of His suffering saint. He can speedily turn our prison house into a "palace beautiful." While Madame Guyon was lying in a French prison, she said "the very stones of her prison shone like rubies in her eyes." He knows how and when to speak a word to the weary.

6. *A Dastardly Plot* (vv. 12-15). These forty fanatics, who bound themselves neither to eat nor drink until they had killed Paul, doubtless thought that they were doing God's service, but such take good care never to consult God about it. There is no night black enough to hide such murderous plans from the eye of the Lord. The counsel of the wicked shall come to naught, their words shall not stand (Isa. 8, 10).

7. *An Unexpected Discovery* (vv. 16-24). This son of Paul's sister was a brave young lad. He evidently

had overheard the plot, perhaps those cruel men were so intent on their fiendish purpose that they paid no heed to the boy near by. The boy *heard*, *believed*, and *acted* at once. To go up to the castle on a prisoner's behalf was a bold venture, but *love* constrained him. His timely effort was crowned with success. He was the means of saving the life of his beloved uncle. *Procrastination* is not only the " thief of time," but it is also the thief of souls and of heaven. What thou doest, do quickly.

PAUL BEFORE FELIX.
ACTS 24, 1-27.

The journey from Jerusalem to Cæsarea was over sixty miles. To Paul it was a triumphal march out of the clutches of his would-be murderers. The Lord knows how to deliver the godly. Five days later the high priest with the elders, and the orator, Tertullus, arrived as the accusers of the prisoner. The priest and the elders had made the bullets, and hired this eloquent orator to fire them ; but he missed the mark, for Felix had knowledge of " that way." Look at—

I. THE ACCUSATION.—After Tertullus had spoken some flattering words to the voluptuous Felix, he launched four terrible charges against the holy apostle. (1) *A Pestilent Fellow*. A man whose character is thoroughly diseased, and a danger to the morals of the people. (2) *A Mover of Sedition*. A disturber of the national peace, and an enemy to the Roman Government. (3) *A Ringleader of the Nazarenes*. A religious fanatic.

A man who has gone crazy over the supposed resurrection of Jesus who was crucified. (4) *A Profaner of the Temple.* A rank heretic. A man who has no regard for the true worship of God. The charge was as foul as the prince of darkness could make it. The image of the " father of lies " was stamped upon it.

II. THE DEFENCE.—Paul makes no attempt to flatter the governor, but is glad to mention the fact that Felix had been for " many years a judge of the nation," and was well able to understand the nature of the case (vv. 10-11). (1) *He Denies the Charge* (vv 12-13). What else could he do but hurl their hate-kindled darts back to their own bosoms with the challenge that they " cannot prove the things whereof they accuse me." (2) *He makes a confession* of his *faith* in the Word of God (v. 14). Of his *hope* toward God, and the resurrection (v. 15). Of the *purity* of his *aim* in seeking " always to have a conscience void of offence " (v. 14). Because of the true, child-like simplicity of his character, Paul could not but speak out the deep and tender feelings of his soul. These things formed the very tissue of his spiritual life. (3) *He gives an Explanation* (vv 17-21). He tells, in simple, truthful language, what in reality did happen. The *truth* always suits best, and the honest and the upright love it.

III. THE DEFERMENT.—When Felix heard these things he made up his mind to do nothing till Lysias, the chief captain of the Roman band at Jerusalem, should come and explain matters more fully to him (vv. 22-23) Meanwhile Paul was to have liberty and

the privilege of seeing the friends who may call on him.
The honest man has scored a victory.

IV. THE PRIVATE HEARING.—Felix, willing to
entertain his wife, who was a Jewess, and also evidently
believing that Paul's name was one to conjure with,
sent for him, and had a private interview, which reveals : (1) *A Courageous Prisoner.* Called to explain
to them the cause of his " faith in Christ," he did not
fail to *reason* with them of " righteousness, temperance,
and judgment to come." He took this quiet opportunity to rebuke the noble sinners personally. Truly,
he sought not great things for himself. (2) *A Cowardly
Judge.* Although he trembled at the truthful words of
his blameless prisoner, yet he "sent for him" and " bound
him," just as he thought it might bring gain or honour
to himself (vv. 26-27). But Paul lived before another
Judge, whose mercy and grace had never failed him
(Acts 23, 1). Those who dare for Jesus Christ, can
dare to stand alone. Felix was convicted—he trembled—but he was not converted. His conscience condemned him, but his stubborn will, through fear of
man, or of woman, refused to yield. He proposed
to consider this matter when he had a more convenient
season. How readily we are to forget that there are
two sides to a " convenient season." We cannot make
a spring season at will. A farmer may have more
time to sow his seed in the winter, but what would
it profit him ?

The most convenient of all seasons for getting
right with God, is when His Word is pricking us to

the heart, and when we are trembling under the power of it.

PAUL'S APPEAL UNTO CÆSAR.

Acts 25, 1-12.

Paul had now been two years in prison. A new governor had just arrived (Festus) to take the place of Felix This was a new opportunity for those " Chief of the Jews " whose hearts were still full of murderous hate at the apostle, and they were quick to take advantage of it—

1. *A Cunning Plot.* They sought the favour of Festus that they might persuade him to send for Paul to Jerusalem, so that they might have a chance of killing him by the way (vv. 2-3). They were not privileged to kill Paul, but they were surely guilty of murder in the sight of God. " He that *hateth* his brother is a murderer." The Lord looketh upon the heart.

2. *A Reasonable Proposal.* It must have been very disappointing to these enemies of the apostle when Festus refused to yield to their sinister request (vv. 4-5). Cæsarea, being the Roman headquarters, was the proper place for trial. As many of them as were *able*—having sufficient time and means—and we may add, sufficiently hardened in heart, could go with him and " accuse this man." But it was not *justice* these Jewish rulers wanted, it was the *death* of him who preached " Jesus and the Resurrection."

3. *A Renewed Charge.* The next day, after Festus arrived, Paul was brought out for the third time to be

examined. The complaints of the Jews were many and grievous. They were as numerous and as black as so many lying tongues could make them, but not one of them could they prove. It has been said that "truth seldom goes without a scratched face." He who Him-self was the TRUTH had a face more marred than any man's. Those who live at enmity with God will always love the darkness rather than the light. Christ said they hated Me *without a cause*, and they will also hate you.

4. *A Renewed Denial.* All the vile charges they brought against Paul could not bring the faintest tre-mor to his heart, or blush of shame to his cheek ; he had not " offended in anything at all." Those who live before God with a good conscience need fear no evil (chap. 23, 1), for greater is He that is *in them* than he that is in the world. It is the Spirit of God in the believer that wars against the wicked spirit that works in the children of disobedience (Eph. 2, 2).

5. *A Strange Request.* Festus said to Paul, " Wilt thou go up to Jerusalem to be judged ? " Why does the judge ask the prisoner as to where he might be judged ? He is now wavering, and, being desirous to favour the Jews, he becomes " double-minded and un-stable in his ways " (Isa. 1, 6-8). Those who would have the light of truthfulness to shine in their lives must, in heart, walk in the light.

6. *A New Weapon.* When the wide-awake apostle saw that his judge was likely to be bribed over to the side of his bloodthirsty enemies, he unsheathed an un-expected, but mighty, weapon of defence. " I appeal

unto Cæsar." As a Roman citizen, not proved to be a criminal, he had this right. When Festus answered, " Unto Cæsar shalt thou go," it was another victory for the man of God. The finger of God is clearly seen in this. Had not the Lord told him just a little while ago that he must witness of Him at Rome (chap. 23, 11). Now he has the promise of being taken there free of all charge, to preach the Gospel in Rome also. Truly, God moves in a mysterious way, making all things work together for good to them that love Him.

PAUL AS A WITNESS FOR GOD.

ACTS 26, 1-32.

When King Agrippa came to Cæsarea to salute Festus, the new governor, he was told the story of Paul, the prisoner ; how the charges brought against him had not been proven, and how he had " appealed to Cæsar." Festus was quite pleased that Agrippa should hear him on the morrow, in the hope that this might help him out of the " unreasonableness " of sending a prisoner to Augustus without being able to " signify the crimes laid against him." So Paul is brought out once more and permitted to speak for himself. The apostle's defence was the story of his *conversion*—this was always his apologetic for Christianity. Like the sword of Goliath, " there is none like it." It so affected Festus that he thought Paul had gone mad through " much learning ; " it so touched the conscience of Agrippa that he said, " Almost thou persuadest me to be a Christian." Look at Paul's defence, then, as revealing the characteristics of a true Christian—

I. HE IS A CHANGED MAN (vv. 9-15).—Once he did many things contrary to the name of Jesus. Now he was His bond-slave. The change was radical and complete, wrought not by the will of the flesh, nor the will of man, but of God. He was born from above. No one can be a Christian without being " born again." A new *nature* is needed before we can *see* the things of the kingdom of God, or enjoy the fellowship of Christ, the only begotten of the Father.

II. HE IS AN EMPOWERED MAN.—Empowered by the Lord Jesus Christ to be a witness unto Him by opening the eyes of sin-blinded men, and turning them from the power of Satan unto God (vv. 16-18). God does not send us a warfare on our own charges (Acts 1, 8). The evidence that a man is sent by God is that he does the work that none others can do by their own strength and wisdom. *Signs* must follow those who *believe.*

III. HE IS AN OBEDIENT MAN.—"I was not disobedient unto the heavenly vision " (v. 19). To be disobedient to the heavenly call is to seal our own spiritual doom. Neither did he dishonour Him who had called him by *immediately* conferring with flesh and blood (Gal. 1, 15-16). He settled the matter right off with the Lord Himself as to what he would do.

IV. HE IS A DIVINELY HELPED MAN.— " Having therefore obtained help of God, I continue

unto this day" (vv 21-22).   He had been often persecuted, but never forsaken; cast down, but not destroyed
He had experienced the promise of his Lord—" I will
never leave thee "   Every *faithful* servant of Christ will
be able, at the close of life, to raise an Ebenezer to the
honour of His name.   Hitherto hath the Lord helped us.

V.   HE IS A DEVOTED MAN.—" Saying none
other things than those . . . that Christ should suffer "
(v. 23).   Paul was wholly yielded up to the interests of
Christ and His cross.   He meant it when he said, " To
me to live is Christ.   I am determined to know *nothing*
among men save Jesus Christ and Him crucified."
Unless our lives are entirely yielded up to Him our
testimony for Him will be powerless and fruitless.

VI.   HE IS A MISUNDERSTOOD MAN.—Fes-
tus said, " Paul, thou art beside thyself ;   much learning
doth make thee mad " (v. 24).   The *natural* man receiveth not the things of the Spirit of God, they are
foolishness unto him.   To those who are in a perishing
condition " the preaching of the cross is foolishness "
(1 Cor. 1, 18).   The disciple is not greater than his Lord
Did they not say of Christ, He hath a devil and is
mad ? (John 10, 20).

VII   HE IS A COURTEOUS MAN.—" I am not
mad, *most noble* Festus."   Honour to whom honour is
due.   The grace of God will always teach a man to be
civil   There is no man on earth who can better afford
to honour the nobility than the Christian, for he himself has been exalted into the ranks of the blood-royal
of heaven.   Children of God.

VIII. HE IS A FAITHFUL MAN.—" King Agrippa, believest *thou* the prophets ? " This personal appeal to the king must surely have come to him with startling suddenness, while it reveals the simple, fearless courage of the man whose heart God had transformed, and perhaps a real longing for the spiritual and eternal well-being of Agrippa. Paul had always an eye on his Master's business ; pulling men out of the fire of sin.

IX. HE IS A SATISFIED MAN.—When Agrippa confessed that he was " Almost persuaded to be a Christian," see how quickly Paul shows him that it is the better part. " I would to God that thou and all . . . were altogether *such as I am*, except these bonds " (v. 29). There was not a richer or happier man in Cæsarea than Paul. The peace of God was in his heart, and the unsearchable riches of Christ were his.

PAUL'S SHIPWRECK, OR THE POWER OF FAITH.
ACTS 27, 1-44.

The taking of Paul the apostle to Italy was one of the most important and far-reaching undertakings ever attempted by the powerful Government of Rome. The coming of that lonely prisoner was the coming of the Ambassador of Heaven to establish a new and everlasting kingdom among the Gentile nations of the earth. It was the planting of that new tree, the leaves of whicl. will ultimately heal the nations. Behold how great a matter a little fire kindleth. We cannot go into detail here, but will seek some spiritual lessons from the outstanding features. We note—

I. A PERILOUS POSITION.—" Exceedingly tossed with tempest . . . neither sun nor stars . . . and all hope taken away " (vv. 17-20). We can scarcely imagine a more agonising predicament. Such is a true picture of those who have been awakened by the Holy Spirit to a real sense of their guilt and danger as sinners in the sight of God. Tossed with fear and alarm, without seeing any guiding light, and all hope of salvation taken away. At that time ye were without Christ, having no hope (Eph. 2, 12).

II. A MERCIFUL REVELATION.—" The angel of God stood by me, saying, Fear not, Paul . . God hath given thee all them that sail with thee " (vv. 23-24) The effectual, fervent prayer of this righteous man hath availed much (James 5, 16). It was doubtless in answer to Paul's earnest pleadings that this answer was given.. What a victory of faith it was. Are we not reminded here of God's answer to the cry of Christ's heart, " I will give Thee the heathen for Thine inheritance ? " All who sail in the same boat with Jesus Christ will be eternally given to Him.

III. A FAITHFUL PROCLAMATION.—" Wherefore, sirs, be of good cheer, for I believe God " (vv. 22-25). It was a " glad and glorious Gospel " that Paul had to preach to those whose souls were sinking in despair It was, indeed, the *Gospel of Salvation.* " There shall be no loss of any man's life." It was a Gospel of *cer-*

Q VIII

tainty to Paul, for he adds, " I believe God that *it shall be*, even as it was told me." Such is the Gospel of Christ to all who, like Paul, have received it as a revelation from God. Only those who *believe* the Word of God have any Gospel of *certain salvation* to preach.

IV. A NECESSARY CONDITION.—" Except these abide in the ship, ye cannot be saved " (v. 31). Paul warns the soldiers that if the *sailors* are allowed to desert the ship, they could not be saved (v. 30). There is no inconsistency between the sovereign grace of God and the responsibility of man in the use of prescribed means. The promise was that " all would be saved;" the condition was, " *abiding* " in the ship. The Gospel of Christ offers salvation to all, but the condition is, believe in Him and abide in Him.

V. A COMPASSIONATE EXHORTATION.— " Wherefore, I pray you to take some meat, for this is for your *health* " (v. 34). No shepherd could be more careful over his flock than Paul is over those 276 fellow-passengers. He seeks not only their salvation, but their *health* and comfort. But God's order is *salvation* FIRST, then health, and better houses if you will. The Holy Ghost is the agent in every God-sent revival, and He *never* begins with the *social* conditions of men, always with their sinful, sorrowful spirits. But here note that *eating*, as well as *abiding*, is a condition of full salvation. " Thy *Word* was found, and I did eat it."

VI. A WONDERFUL TRANSFORMATION.— " Then were they all of good cheer " (v. 36). What a contrast between the experiences mentioned in verse

29, "all hope taken away," and verse 36, "good cheer."
What has made the difference? The *promise* of salvation. After they had got the assurance that none of
them would perish, they were able to eat with gladness
of heart. It is so with all those who, by faith, receive
the promise of God in Christ Jesus (Acts 16, 31). Those
who have had their feet taken out of the fearful pit of
despair and planted upon the rock of God's Word will
have the " good cheer " song put in their mouth (Psalm
40, 2-3).

VII. A PERFECTED SALVATION.—" And so
it came to pass that they escaped all safe to land " (v.
44). Not all in the same way ; not all at the same time ;
but all enjoyed the fulfilment of the same promise of deliverance. If they had not been obedient and abode in
the ship, they would not have got the " boards " and
" broken pieces " to float them ashore. It is always
safe to trust God and obey His will. " *None* perish that
Him trust." Christ shall lose none of those whom the
Father hath given Him (John 6, 39) ; in some way or
other all shall come safely to the heavenly land. But
how shall we escape if we *neglect* so great salvation.
From Paul's action at this crisis we may learn the value
and power of individual faith in God.

PAUL AMONG THE BARBARIANS.
ACTS 28, 1-10.

" They all escaped to land." This seems to have
been the third time that Paul had " suffered shipwreck "

(2 Cor 11, 25). There are few who have ever had such vivid glimpses of heavenly things as Paul, and few who have ever had to *suffer* so much for the cause of Christ. It would appear that every new spiritual experience needs its counterbalance of suffering. We observe here—

I UNEXPECTED KINDNESS.—" The barbarous people showed us no little kindness " (v. 2). Although the inhabitants of this island were not *Romans*, they were not savages. They had the " milk of human kindness " in their hearts. The fire was a welcome sight to those who had just come out of the sea into the drenching rain and biting cold. The Lord has many a way of scattering crumbs of comfort to those who fear His name (John 21, 9). Doubtless Paul looked upon this fire as if it had been kindled by the hand of Jesus Christ.

II. HUMBLE SERVICE.—" Paul gathered a bundle of sticks." The great apostle of the Gentiles did not think it beneath him to go a-searching for fuel to help to dry the clothes of those soldiers and sailors who were his companions in tribulation. He had learned from his Master that the way to be greatest of all is to be the servant of all. The deeper our experience is of the greatness of God's grace the more generous and attentive shall we be to those *little* things that minister to the good of others. Paul did not need to be told to "*mend the fire*" before he did it. " Consider one another to provoke unto love and good works."

III. ANOTHER TRIAL.—" There came a viper out of the heat, and fastened on his hand, and he shook off the beast into the fire." Why should the self-humbling effort of the apostle to comfort others be rewarded with the sudden grip of a poisonous viper ? Why ? Paul does not know, but he believes that " all things work together for good to them that love God." Those who would sacrifice themselves for the warming up of their shivering fellow-creatures need not be surprised although the *heat* should bring to life some torpid snake that will seek to fasten itself to that hand of mercy. Is it a temptation to sin, either in thought or act, shake the slimy thing off into the fire from whence it came, and possess your soul in patience.

IV. FALSE JUDGMENT.—These islanders, judging by appearance, thought first that Paul must be a murderer, then they believed him to be a god (vv. 4-6). When the viper succeeded in catching him, they condemned him, but when he conquered the viper they adored him. There is not much between the frown and the favour of those who know not the truth as it is in Christ Jesus. The world is always ready to applaud those who succeed, and is quick to believe in the worthlessness of the man who happens to become the prey of that venomous snake called calumny. It was such a viper that came out of the heat and fastened on Joseph while in Potiphar's house, but he shook it off, and felt no harm (Gen. 39, 13-14). The devil often spoils his pictures by using a brush that is too big.

V. GENEROSITY REWARDED.—Publius was entertaining an angel unawares when he received Paul and lodged him and others for three days (v. 7). He was amply recompensed for his kindness in the healing of his father by this mysterious prisoner. In some way or other God will compensate those who give even a cup of cold water to His disciple. Paul the prisoner was still Paul the apostle. No circumstance in which he was placed could ever mar his authority or stain the purity of his apostolic mantle.

VI. NEEDS SUPPLIED.—" They honoured us, and laded us with such things as were necessary " (v. 10). They had lost their all by the shipwreck, but now, because of the merciful wonder-working power of Paul, all their needs for the journey to Rome were supplied. Truly the presence of this man of God among them was the salt that saved them from the corruption of death. The ungodly do not know how much they owe to the presence of those who believe in God. Judgment could not fall upon Sodom until Lot was taken out (Gen. 19, 22). When the " preacher of righteousness " was shut up in the ark then the flood came.

PAUL'S MINISTRY IN ROME.
ACTS 28, 11-31.

The entrance of Paul into Rome, although unknown and unheeded by the multitude, was a greater event than the coming of an army of soldiers or the arrival of a fleet of battleships. He was as a corn of wheat cast into the ground to die, but destined to bring forth such fruit as would be a blessing to the nations of the earth. The possibilities of one single life, wholly yielded to God, and possessed by His Holy Spirit, are, for us, incalculable.

Paul's life and testimony have been given as an *example* to them who should hereafter believe (Phil. 3. 17).

I. THE CHEERING SALUTATION.—When Paul saw the brethren who had come to meet him, " he thanked God, and took courage " (v. 15). Appii Forum is about twenty-seven miles from Rome, but some of the weaker brethren could only go the length of " the Three Taverns," a distance of seventeen miles. The angel-like ministry of encouraging the hearts of God's tried and suffering servants is quite within the reach of all the brethren who care to make a little self-sacrifice for their sakes. Don't wait till they come to you for sympathy, go and meet them. There are wonderful comfort and consolation in *mutual* faith and love (Rom. 1, 12).

II. THE PRELIMINARY CONFERENCE.— After three days Paul, who was " suffered to dwell by himself, called the chief of the Jews together," etc. (vv. 16-22). Although he had suffered so much at the hands of his Jewish brethren, yet his heart's desire and prayer to God for Israel was that they might be saved (Rom. 10, 1). He tells them of his sufferings in Jerusalem, and the reason why he was " bound with this chain." They had heard about this sect that was " everywhere spoken against," and were desirous of hearing from his own lips what he had to say about it. No man on earth could better tell them the story of the Gospel of Salvation.

III. THE STORY TOLD.—On the day appointed for this special purpose " there came many to him into his lodging," etc. (v. 23). Has there ever been any-

where such a " lodging-house " gathering as this ?
A prison turned into a church, the prisoner the preacher;
the subjects were " The Kingdom of God and the Things
Concerning Jesus." The arguments are drawn from
Moses and the prophets, and the sermon lasted " from
morning till evening." Once more, note that Paul, ever
since his conversion, knew *nothing among men* save
Christ and Him crucified. Why should it be otherwise
with preachers now ?

IV. THE DIFFERENT RESULTS.—" Some be-
lieved, and some believed not " (v. 24). Yes, thank God,
" *some* believed." Wherever Christ is faithfully preached
some will believe and be saved, while others will prefer,
through unbelief, to remain vessels of wrath, instead of
being changed into vessels of mercy. The preaching of
the cross is to them that perish foolishness. No matter
how clearly the word of salvation is preached, it will not
profit unless the *hearing* of it is mixed with *faith* (Heb.
4, 2). By grace are ye saved through faith.

V. THE FINAL MESSAGE.—These are solemn
and decisive words recorded in verses 25-29. They contain Paul's last words of warning and rebuke to his impenitent brethren according to the flesh. They had
eyes and ears, but they failed to use them in a proper
manner, because their *heart* had become gross and
sensual through pride and self-righteousness (v. 27).
There are none so blind as those who don't want to see.
Those who have " pleasure in unrighteousness " will
not believe the truth, but will readily believe a lie unto
their own condemnation (2 Thess. 2, 11-12).

VI. THE TWO YEARS' MINISTRY.—For two whole years in his own hired house, and with a soldier to guard him, Paul kept an open door for inquirers after the "things concerning the Lord Jesus Christ." With all confidence he preached, "no man forbidding him." Here several of Paul's richest epistles were written. How much the Church of God owes to Paul's imprisonment eternity alone can reveal. It was out of Bedford jail that Bunyan's "Pilgrim's Progress" came. It is often out of the depths of our deepest trials that our richest fruits are found.

THE BLISSFUL LIFE.

PSALM 100.

The metrical version of this psalm has been recognised almost by universal consent as the churches' National Anthem. It is a psalm of blissful experiences. There is—

I. A BLISSFUL KNOWLEDGE.—"Know ye that the Lord He is God." It is a great thing to *know* assuredly that the Jehovah of the Bible, in whom we trust, is the God of the whole earth, and of the whole universe.

II. A BLISSFUL RELATIONSHIP.—"It is He that hath made us, and we are His." "We are His people, and the sheep of His pasture" (R.V.). With regard to our character, we are His workmanship, created in Christ Jesus (Eph. 2, 10). With regard to our safety and provision, we are the *sheep of His pasture* (John 10, 27-28).

III.   A BLISSFUL SERVICE.—" Serve the Lord with gladness, come before Him with singing " (v. 2). You would almost think from the appearance and tone of some religious meetings that we should serve the Lord with sadness, and come before Him with whining.   His service is joyful when His servants are holy and hopeful.

IV.   A BLISSFUL FELLOWSHIP.—" Enter into His gates with thanksgiving, and into His courts with praise " (v. 4).   To enter within His gates and courts was to come into the place of personal communion. Since our Great High Priest went into the holiest, through the *rent vail*, this privilege of fellowship is now ours continually.

V.   A BLISSFUL OBJECT.—" His Name " (v 4).   As there are fathomless depths of riches in Nature, so are there boundless depths of spiritual wealth in *His Name*.   His Name is Wonderful.   His Name is a Strong Tower.   To know His Name is to trust in Him.

VI.   A BLISSFUL TESTIMONY.—" The Lord is good ; His mercy is everlasting.   His truth endureth " (v. 5).   The Lord is good—He is *Love*.   Can anything be more desirable ?   His mercy lasts ; it is neither fickle nor uncertain.   His truth stands unchanged and unchangeable.   He is the Way, the Truth, and the Life.   " Let the redeemed of the Lord say so."

REASONS FOR BLESSING THE LORD.
PSALM 103, 1-5.

Call upon thy soul to bless the Lord, to bless His holy Name, because--

I. HE PROVIDETH ALL HIS BENEFITS.—
" All His benefits ! " What does this all mean ?
Nothing that would benefit man hath He kept back.
In the gift of His Son He hath pledged Himself to
supply all our need (1 Tim. 6, 17).

II. HE FORGIVETH ALL INIQUITIES.—Because of His infinite compassion, He keeps mercy for
thousands, forgiving iniquity. He must either punish
iniquity or forgive it, He cannot change its character.
Light can have no fellowship with darkness.

III. HE HEALETH ALL DISEASES.—*Ini-
quities* refer to acts, but the *disease* to the polluted
spring from whence the acts came. Every part of
man's moral nature is diseased. " In me, that is, in
my flesh, dwelleth no good thing." But His healing
power, the blood of Christ, cleanseth from all sin.
See Ps. 107, 17-22.

IV. HE REDEEMETH FROM DESTRUCTION
(From *the pit*, R.V., Marg.). He not only forgives and
heals, but delivers from the sphere of darkness and
disease ; brought into a purer atmosphere, into the
Kingdom of His own dear Son, and so saved from unclean and destructive influences.

**V. HE CROWNETH WITH LOVING KIND-
NESS.—**The loving kindness of God makes a very
beautiful and comfortable crown for the head. Those
who have been *healed* of all their diseases will be crowned
with honour in their life and testimony (Ps. 5, 12).

VI. HE SATISFIETH WITH GOOD.—" All His benefits " are spread out for the blood-washed soul. They shall be " made to drink of the river of *His plea-sures* " (Ps. 36, 8). The pure in heart shall see God. God only can satisfy with good, and only those saved and healed by the Lord can be satisfied with that which is pure and good. The carnal mind cannot love the things of God. Redemption implies capacity for good.

VII. HE RENEWETH LIKE THE EAGLE.— The eagle renews its youth by an outward regeneration. The soul that has been saved and satisfied is regenerated both within and without. Those born from above have youth renewed, because they are a new creation in Christ Jesus.

BELIEVERS' PRIVILEGES.
PSALM 105, 1-4.

In these few verses there is a seven-fold privilege indicated.

I. GIVING THANKS TO HIM.—" O give thanks unto the Lord." The giving of thanks implies the consciousness of great favour bestowed. " Thanks be unto God for His unspeakable gift."

II. CALLING UPON HIM.—" Call upon His Name." Liberty of access to *Him*, and to plead His own Name, is a greater privilege than we have ever yet realised. John 14, 14.

III. WORKING FOR HIM.—" Make known His deeds among the people." His mighty acts of grace, in Christ Jesus, are well worthy of being made known. The people are perishing for lack of such knowledge. Preach the Word.

IV. SINGING TO HIM.—" Sing unto Him, sing psalms unto Him." Yes, make a joyful noise unto the Lord, who hath done such great things for us. In heaven, with thundering voice, the harpers harp with their harps (Rev. 14, 21). Worthy is the Lamb now to receive the praises of our hearts and lips.

V. MEDITATING ON HIM.—" Meditate ye on all His wondrous works" (R.V., Marg.). There is a time to speak, and a time to sing, but there must also be a time to *think*. " Think on these things." One of our Lord's last words to His disciples was : " Remember Me." See Malachi 3, 16.

VI. GLORYING IN HIM.—" Glory ye in His Holy Name." To glory in His Name is to glory in Himself. We may well glory in Him, who is all glorious in Himself, and whose love and grace have been poured into our desolate lives, that we might be saved and satisfied.

VII. TESTIFYING FOR HIM.—" Seek the Lord, and His strength. Seek His face evermore." Those who have seen His blessed face, in Jesus Christ, cannot but counsel others to seek it. His face is His favour, it is worth seeking for, it is for " evermore." The Lord and His saving strength is the clamant need of the human soul. " Seek the Lord while He may be found."

THE GOD OF DELIVERANCES.

PSALM 107.

In this psalm we have a four-fold picture of " the redeemed of the Lord " (v. 2).

I. FROM WEARINESS TO REST (vv. 4-8).— Here are three words which fitly express the substance of each section—Destitution, Petition, Salvation ; or, Need, Prayer, and Deliverance.

1. THEIR DESTITUTION. They were " wanderers in the wilderness," as those who had lost their way, in " solitary ways," bye-paths, perplexed and wearied. They were " hungry and thirsty," their souls clamouring for what they could not get. " Their soul fainted in them," sank down in despair. Utter failure of works.

2. THEIR PETITION. " Then they cried unto the Lord " as a last resort. Shut up to faith. Heaven's ear, like heaven's door, is always open to the cry of need.

3. THEIR SALVATION. " He delivered them." He only could. How ? By leading them forth by " *the right way*." Led into truth, out of error and deception, that they " *might go* to a city of habitation," to a place of fellowship and plenty. Oh, praise Him for His goodness.

II. FROM DARKNESS INTO LIGHT (vv 10–15)—

1. THEIR CONDITION. They were sitting " in darkness," they knew not where they were. They

were " in the shadow of death "—a place of imminent danger. " In affliction and iron "—a condition of painful bondage. And this because they " *rebelled* against the words of God " they were defeated; " heart *brought down* with labour." They were helpless. " None to help."

2. THEIR PETITION. " Then they cried unto the Lord." It was high time. What a mercy that they had some one to cry to who is mighty to save.

3. THEIR SALVATION. " He saved them . . . brought them out of darkness . . . and broke their bonds asunder." In His deliverance there is light and freedom. Eph. 5, 8 ; Luke 4, 18. Oh, praise the Lord for His goodness.

III. FROM SICKNESS TO HEALTH (vv. 18-21).—

1. THEIR CONDITION. " Their soul abhorreth all manner of meat." They were so sick of their old life and its pleasures that nothing belonging to it was enjoyed. " They drew near unto the gates of death." Dying of starvation. Results of deep conviction.

2. THEIR PETITION. " Then they cry unto the Lord." This is the cure for those that are sick of the world and its mocking pleasures. Isa. 55, 2.

3. THEIR SALVATION. " He saved them." He despised not any. How this was done. " He sent His Word, and healed them." His Word *believed* is always efficacious in the soul (Matt. 8, 8). He " delivered them from their destructions." His *healing* powers rescue the life from death and destruction.

IV. FROM DANGER TO SAFETY (vv. 23-31).--

1. THEIR DANGER. " They stagger like a drunken man." Driven to and fro, tossed with tempest. Mental bewilderment. They are " at their wits' end." At the point of utter despair. Undone. " Their soul is melted." All courage and hope gone. Woe is me. Who shall deliver me ?

2. THEIR CRY. " Then they cried unto the Lord." It takes a lot to make some men stagger God-ward.

3. THEIR DELIVERANCE. " He bringeth them out," as He brought Israel out of Egypt when at their " wits' end." " He maketh the storm a calm " when He comes aboard the troubled soul (Matt. 8, 26) " He bringeth them into their desired haven." Whom He bringeth out, He desires to bring in. Out of the Kingdom of Satan into the Kingdom of His dear Son. Oh, that men would praise the Lord for His goodness and wonderful works.

THE WORKS OF THE LORD.
PSALM III.

As is the workman, so is the work. The works of the Lord are—

I. GREAT (v. 2).—They are as unsearchable as Himself. All His works praise Him, because they are a credit to the Worker. This is evident in His work of Creation, Redemption, and Providence (Ps. 104, 24). His work is great in every sense as to quality, variety, utility, and Eternity.

II. DESIRABLE. "Sought out of all them that have pleasure therein" (v. 2). His *works* are expressions of His *thoughts*, and such thoughts are very deep and precious (Ps. 92, 5). What depth of thought there is in the Redemption by Jesus Christ. How earnestly this work is sought out by all them that have pleasure therein. It is a profitable search.

III. HONOURABLE.—"His work is honour and majesty" (v. 3, R.V.). There is a becoming dignity about the work of Creation and Redemption that reflects great honour on the Worker. The salvation of Jesus Christ by the Cross brings eternal glory to His Name. "The Lord is holy in all His works," and notably in the work of the Cross.

IV. MEMORABLE.—"He hath made His wonderful works to be remembered" (v. 4). His works of grace and mercy in behalf of His people are to be held in everlasting remembrance. Who can forget the day of their conversion to God, the day of deliverance from guilt and sin, and the dawn of His light and peace in the soul?

V. POWERFUL. "He shewed His people the power of His works" (v. 6). Israel saw the mighty power of His working in their salvation from Egypt, in their passing through the Red Sea, and across the opened Jordan, and in the downfall of the walls of Jericho. But what hath God wrought *for us*, and *in us*? Hath He not shewed us the power of His work by the Cross for us, and by the Holy Spirit in us?

R VIII

VI. TRUTHFUL. "The works of His hands are truth and judgment" (v. 7, R.V.). They are in perfect truthfulness to the needs of the case. His work of grace and of salvation is exactly what we need, and all we need. Just and true are the ways of the King of saints (Rev. 15, 3). He is the Way, the Truth, and the Life.

VII. ETERNAL. "They stand fast for ever and ever" (v. 8). Man's works, like himself, will wither like the grass, but the Word and work of the Lord shall stand for ever. Our righteousnesses rot like filthy rags, but the work of His regenerating Spirit, the renewing of the Holy Ghost, stands fast for ever. I give to My sheep eternal life, and they shall never perish. It is God who worketh in you both to will and to do of His good pleasure. "His work is perfect."

WHAT SHALL I RENDER?
Psalm 116.

"What shall I render unto the Lord for all His benefits toward me?" (v. 12). This is a deeply *personal* and sensible consideration.

I. WHAT ARE HIS BENEFITS TOWARD ME? There is—

1. AN INCLINED EAR. "He hath inclined His ear unto me" (v. 2). He hath not turned His ear away from me, but, like an anxious father, He hath bent His head to listen to the cry of His child. What a

precious privilege to have the listening, sympathetic ear of God.

2. DELIVERANCE FROM DEATH (v. 3). " Thou hast delivered my soul from death, mine eyes from tears, and my feet from falling " (v. 8). We have this victory through our Lord Jesus Christ (1 Cor. 15, 55-57; Rom. 6, 23).

3. BOUNTIFUL TREATMENT. " The Lord hath dealt bountifully with thee " (v. 7). Out of His own fulness and in infinite grace hath He supplied all your need. Luke 15, 22-23.

4. FREEDOM FROM BONDAGE. " Thou hast loosed my bonds " (v. 16). The bonds of sin, doubt, and fear have been snapped. Liberty to serve with gladness the Great Deliverer.

II.   WHAT SHALL I RENDER UNTO HIM ?

1. I WILL LOVE HIM (v. 1). " We love Him because He first loved us." I will yield Him the affection of my heart because He hath loved my soul out of the pit of corruption.

2. I WILL CALL UPON HIM. Yes. " As long as I live " (v. 2). This is a very expressive way of shewing our gratitude to GOD. This method would not serve with man.

3. I WILL REST IN HIM. " Return unto thy rest, O my soul " (v. 7). I will shew my confidence by resting my soul entirely in Him. This He desires. Matt. 11, 28-29.

4   I WILL WALK WITH HIM (v. 9). I will order

my daily life in all its details as before His eyes. To this life was Abraham called (Gen. 17, 1). I will choose Him as my constant companion (2 Cor. 5, 7).

5. I WILL SPEAK FOR HIM (v. 10, R.V.). I will testify to what He hath done for my soul. My lips shall speak His praise, and my tongue shall not be silent.

6. I WILL TAKE FROM HIM (v. 13). We render honour to Him by taking more from Him. This is not after the manner of men. I will shew Him how much I appreciate His grace by drinking more deeply of the "Cup of Salvation."

7. I WILL OFFER TO HIM. "I will offer to Thee the sacrifice of thanksgiving . . . I will pay my vows unto the Lord." (vv. 17-18). The sacrifice of thanksgiving may not seem a very costly gift, but it is well pleasing unto God (Heb. 13, 15-16). Render to Him the calves of your *lips* (Hosea 14, 2). And let the vows of devotion and service made to Him be duly paid *in the presence of His people*.

Bible Readings.

FAITH.

MARK 11, 22.

Consecration to God and faith in God ought to characterise every servant of God. And who can tell the limits of the possibilities of such ? There are many believers in Jesus, but few consecrated to Him. Fewer still who actually prove His faithfulness in fulfilling all His promises.

I. THE NATURE OF FAITH.—Faith is the substance of things hoped for, etc. (Heb. 11, 1). Faith acknowledges the things unseen, and acts as if they were visible. So Noah built the ark (v. 7). So Moses forsook Egypt (v. 27). "Seeing Him who is invisible." "Blessed is he who hath not seen and yet hath believed" (Isa. 20, 29). Through faith Jacob coveted the birthright (Gen. 25, 31). And because Esau could not *see* its value he dispised it and sold it. "Oh, I *see* it" is not equivalent to "Oh, I *believe* it." For with the *heart* man believeth (Rom. 10, 10). God judgeth the heart. A clear head is no evidence of a believing heart.

II. THE OBJECT OF FAITH.—" Have faith in GOD " (Mark 11, 22). Means must be used, but means must not be the object of trust. They are but the ditches we dig. God must fill them (2 Kings 3, 16). God can be trusted to fulfil every promise He hath made, for "God is faithful" (1 Cor. 10, 13). He says, "I *will not* suffer My faithfulness to fail" (Ps 89, 33). And again, "My covenant I will not break. Nor alter the thing that is gone out of My lips" (Ps. 89, 34). How, then, can His *power* be doubted. *Nothing* shall be *impossible* with God. "Is anything too hard for Me?" (Jer. 32, 27). The object of our faith is "One who cannot lie," One who cannot change, One who cannot fail.

III. THE GROUND OF FAITH.—The WORD OF GOD which liveth and abideth for ever (1 Peter 1, 23). "He that believeth as the *Scriptures hath said*" (Isa. 7, 38). Every word of God *is purified* (Prov. 30, 5). There is no dross, nothing to be put away. To be received just as it is given. We are to desire the *sincere* milk of the Word. Many seek to boil it down before receiving it. They attempt to refine what God has already purified. The Word is not only pure, but "sure." "Sure Word of prophecy." The Word of the Lord shall stand for ever (Isa. 40, 8). Because it is already "*settled in heaven*" (Ps. 119, 89). Then the ground of our faith is as faithful and true as the Object of it.

IV. THE EXERCISE OF FAITH.—Abraham believed God (Rom. 4, 5), and went out, not knowing whither he went (Heb. 11, 8). He had but "His Word," as we have. Caleb believed God when he said "Let us go up at once and possess it" (Num. 13, 30). God had promised to give them the land, and he believed. although the difficulties were great and numberless

Peter believed when he said, "Nevertheless (although there seemed nothing but failure), at *Thy word* I will let down the net" (Luke 5, 5). His *word* was all he had, but it was enough. And he even ventured to walk on the sea with a " Come " from Jesus. Paul exercised faith when he said, " I believe God, that it shall be *even* as it was *told me*" (Acts 27, 25). Do you ?

V. THE ENCOURAGEMENT OF FAITH.—Believe and thou shalt see (John 11, 40). Did Abraham not believe and see when made rich ? And Caleb ? Peter believed and saw a great draught. What was Joshua's testimony ? " There failed not aught which the Lord had spoken. All came to pass " (Josh. 21, 45). What was Solomon's testimony 400 years after ? " Blessed be the Lord, there hath not failed *one word* of all which He promised" (1 Kings 8, 56). Again, in Mark 14, 16, we read, the disciples *went forth* and found, as He *had said* unto them. If they had not gone forth they could not have proved the truthfulness of His word. Is there a single case where faith has been disappointed in all the Revelation of God ? And if not, will there ever be one ?

VI. THE NEED OF FAITH.—*Have faith* in God. He cannot do many mighty works through us, because of our unbelief. " If ye have faith as a grain of mustard seed *nothing* shall be impossible unto you " (Matt. 17, 20). *All things whatsoever* ye ask, believing, ye *shall* receive (Matt. 21, 22). " *All things* are yours, for ye are Christ's." This is either true or it is not true. If it is not true, we can have no confidence in God

If it is true, then why is it not our experience ? Might Jesus not say to us : "O fools and slow of heart to believe *all* that I have spoken. Let the question be faced. " Believe ye that I am able to do this ? " (Matt. 9, 28). If He can say to you, "Great is *thy* faith," you may also expect that it shall be unto you, " even as thou *wilt.*"(Matt. 15, 28).

VII. THE RESULT OF FAITH.—Many wonderful results are recorded in Heb. 11. It would be impossible to mention all the possibilities of faith, since it is written, "according to *your* faith it shall be done unto you." There is no limit given. We are straightened in ourselves. " If thou canst believe, all things are possible to him that believeth " (Mark 9, 23). Elias prayed, and it rained not by the space of three years and a half. He prayed again, and the heaven gave rain (James 5, 17-18). Hezekiah trusted in the Lord God, and there was none like him (2 Kings 18, 5). There are none to-day like those who trust God.

A CONSECRATED LIFE.

1 Samuel 3.

In looking over the facts recorded regarding the early years of Samuel's life, they seem suggestive of the experiences of a soul that has been born of God, and wholly devoted to Him. We see him—

I. ASKED OF THE LORD (chap. 1, 20).--Hannah looked upon Samuel as one given from God in answer to many tears and much bitterness of soul (v. 10),

A Consecrated Life. 257

after being mocked and misunderstood by him who should have sympathised and helped (v. 14). How much do we owe to Christ, to His tears and prayers, and bitterness of soul, for our life from above. How little we think of our being given to Christ by the Father in answer to His prayers. " Born from above " is true of every child of God. We must believe that we are the " given " of God. One of the " All that the Father hath given Me." Our *citizenship* made sure.

II. CONSECRATED TO THE LORD (chap. 1, 28).—He is now given back to the Lord, to belong to Him, " as long as he liveth." That which is truly God's ought not to be withheld from Him. " I live, yet not I, but Christ in Me." This life, then, should be given back to God " as long as he liveth." " Ye are not your own." Keep not back part of the price. Hannah's conduct with her first and much loved child might seem hard to the carnally minded, but she could say, " My heart rejoiceth " (chap. 2, 1). Those who surrender all to God can always rejoice. Every child of God ought to be wholly God's. If we are the gifts of the Father to His Son Jesus Christ, for what purpose is it ?

III. MINISTERING BEFORE THE LORD (chap. 2, 18).—He was but a young minister (being a child). It was but little he could do. It was but little he knew, for the Lord had not yet revealed *Himself* to him (chap. 3, 7). But although he was both weak and ignorant, that did not hinder him from doing what he could. He believed although he understood little. Jeremiah said, " Ah, Lord God. I cannot speak, for I am a child "

(Jer. 1, 6). God wants us to be children first, before
we are men in service (child-like spirit). But the
willing child will become the wise man. It is in our
weakness we must come. He gives power to the weak.

IV. WAITING ON THE LORD (chap. 3, 10).—
The Lord had spoken twice to Samuel, and he ran to
Eli. He is not the only one who has run to man at the
voice of the Lord. Paul says, " Immediately I conferred not with flesh and blood." To know His will,
we must *wait* on Him with open ears. Speak, Lord,
for Thy servant heareth. It is a good point gained
when we are willing to know what the will of the Lord
is, but *waiting* is willingness in practice. How natural
for us to run out and in and serve man, but how different
to be silent before the Lord.

V. TAUGHT BY THE LORD (chap. 3, 11-14).—
While waiting Samuel learned what the will of the Lord
was. Those who are taught in the deep things of God
are those who wait much on God. To be unwilling to
wait is to be unwilling to be taught, and just to do our
own will. When God teacheth, the ear shall tingle that
hears the tidings. The *word of the Lord* will not be in vain.
Paul's preaching was "in demonstration of the Spirit, and
of power." The divinely commissioned will be divinely
taught, the Bible is a dry book to those who wait not

VI. WITNESSING FOR THE LORD (chap.
3, 18).—Though he at first feared (v. 15) to shew the
truth to Eli, yet afterwards he told him *every whit*, and
hid nothing. Could he be a faithful servant and keep back

part of the truth ? Many Gospel hearers might justly complain that the half has not been told them. The preachers either have no vision (v. 15) or else they fear to shew it. How can a man be a witness if he has had no vision. He is like a servant out of work ; he may busy himself here and there, but he has no reward from his labour. The faithful will know God's counsel, and will declare it all (Acts 4, 20).

VII. WALKING WITH THE LORD (chap. 3, 19).— " The Lord was with him, and did let none of His words fall to the ground." If we are faithful to God He will prove Himself faithful to us. " He *dwells with the humble* and the contrite " (Isa. 57, 15). We cannot *climb* to abiding fellowship with God. It is not the result of our efforts, but the flowing forth of great grace into the depths of the broken spirit. As the waters abide in the deep so will God dwell with the humble.

VIII. ACKNOWLEDGED AS OF THE LORD (chap. 3, 20).—" And all Israel knew that Samuel was a prophet of the Lord." How did they know ? Just because he declared the truth of God. And God was with him. The one that lives in the presence of God will be acknowledged as belonging to God. " They took knowledge of them that they had been with Jesus " (Acts 4, 13), when they saw their *power* and *boldness* (see margin, v. 20). Faithfulness to God is what all expect from a servant of God. If the world sees not this, the conclusion must be either we are hypocrites, or else there is no God.

IX. PRIVILEGED BY THE WORD OF THE

LORD (chap. 3, 21).—" The Lord *revealed Himself* to Samuel by the *Word of the Lord*. The Word is the instrument through which we must know Him. It is the Christian's telephone, and our ear must be attentive to His Word if we would know His mind and will. We cannot know Himself apart from this. In shutting out His Word we shut the appointed means of communication between our souls and God. " They have rejected the Word of the Lord, and what wisdom is in them ? " (Jer. 8, 8-9).

DIVINE ENCOURAGEMENT.

The Lord Jesus Christ never sends anyone a warfare on their own charges. He takes the responsibility of supplying all the need of those who go forth at His bidding to do His will (Phil. 4, 19). No man ever attempted to run a greater business than the apostle of the Gentiles, because no man was ever more deeply convinced of the wealth and wisdom of his PARTNER in the business. Lo, I am with you. In the following texts we have a six-fold revelation of how Paul was encouraged by his Lord and Master in his great missionary labours.

I. BY A SPECIAL CALL TO SERVICE (Acts 22, 18-21).—It was *while praying* in the temple at Jerusalem—shortly after his conversion—that he heard this definite call from God—" Depart, for I will send thee far hence unto the Gentiles." No one has ever accomplished any great work for Christ who has not been conscious of a distinct call from Him to do that work. The service of God, like any other *Governmental* service, implies a definite engagement, and a mutual understanding as to terms. The Holy Ghost, as God's representative on earth, is the only agent authorised by Him to hire labourers for His vineyard (Acts 13, 2 ; Heb. 5, 4). He was encouraged

II. BY A SPECIAL WORD OF PROMISE.— " Be not afraid . . . for I am with you " (Acts 18, 9-10). Faith in the promise of His presence is the secret of courage and boldness in the service of the Lord. He does not say that no man shall *oppose* thee, but " No man shall *hurt* thee "—as a witness for Him. This promise was fulfilled to the letter. He was often thrashed and imprisoned and maligned, but as a *witness* for Christ no man or devil was able to hurt him. He finished his course with joy, because he fought the good fight in faith. Hiding in God, no weapon that is formed against us can prosper. This is the heritage of the servants of the Lord (Isa. 54, 17).

III. BY A SPECIAL MESSAGE OF CHEER.— " Be of good cheer, Paul, for thou must bear witness also at Rome " (Acts 23, 11). The news that a fortune had been left him would not have been half so cheering to the heart of Paul at any time as that he was going to be permitted to preach the Gospel of Christ in Rome also. How very considerate our Lord is. He is always ready in one way or other to drop into the troubled hearts of His servants some word that brings consolation and comfort. He knows how to speak a word to the weary. This Good Shepherd is specially careful

over those sheep whose lives are endangered through
following Him.. The Christian life should be one of
" good cheer," because every good thing is ours in
Christ Jesus (Rom. 8, 28).

IV. BY A SPECIAL ASSURANCE OF SALVA-
TION.—" Fear not, Paul. God hath *given* thee all
them that sail with thee " (Acts 27, 23-24). What
a gift this was ! What a triumph of faith and prayer !
What an encouragement this would be to him, in his
future ministry, to expect great things from God, and
to look for many souls for his hire. Blessed is he that
believeth, for there shall be a performance of those
things which were told him from the Lord (Luke 1, 45).
They that are wise win souls.

V. BY A SPECIAL IMPARTATION OF
POWER.—" The Lord stood with me and strengthened
me" (2 Tim. 5, 17). *Five* times he did receive forty stripes,
save one, and *six* times did the Lord manifest Himself
to him in times of need. When all men forsook him
(v. 16), and were ashamed of him and his testimony,
his faithful and glorified Master stood by him, as one despised and rejected with him, but mighty to save and to
help. Many a foreign missionary knows what this
means when they have been left to stand alone for the
cause of Christ.

VI. BY A SPECIAL SUPPLY OF GRACE.—
" He said unto me, My grace is sufficient for thee " (2
(Cor 12, 9). The Lord was not pleased to remove the
thorn, which was to Paul as a " messenger of Satan,"
but He was greatly pleased to give him as much of His

grace as would enable him to triumph gloriously over the affliction. The servants of Christ must not expect the source of every difficulty and sorrow to be removed ; but they must expect "grace sufficient," like the incoming tide, to lift their souls like a ship above the threatening rocks. Who would not glory in their infirmities to be a partaker of the power of Christ ?

ETERNAL LIFE.

"He lives who lives to God alone,
And all are dead beside ;
For other source than God is none,
Whence life can be supplied."

I. THE SOURCE OF THIS LIFE.—

1. IT COMES FROM THE ETERNAL FATHER (Jer. 10, 10, marg.). He who inhabiteth eternity is the Fountain of this living water. The living God, and King of eternity. Born of God.

2. IT IS OFFERED THROUGH THE ETERNAL SON (Rom. 6, 23). "The same was in the beginning with God" (John 1, 2). "The Word was made flesh and dwelt amongst us." This is that eternal life : the Good Shepherd who gave His life for the sheep.

3. IT IS BEGOTTEN BY THE ETERNAL SPIRIT (Heb. 9. 14). "You hath He quickened who were dead," It is the Spirit that quickeneth. Salvation is of the Lord.

4. IT IS ORDERED BY AN ETERNAL PURPOSE. Chosen in Him before the foundation of the world

(Eph. 1, 4). Promised before the world began. A
precious truth demanding simple faith (Heb. 11, 3).

5. It is Sustained by Eternal Things (2 Cor.
4, 18). The things of this world cannot satisfy the
desires and affections of this eternal and God-given life
(Col. 2, 1-3).

6. It is Destined for Eternal Glory (1 Peter
5, 10). It has come from God, and is going to God.

II. THE POSSESSION OF THIS LIFE.—

1. It is not Inherited by Works (Matt. 19, 16).
By the deeds of the law shall no flesh be justified in
His sight (Rom. 3, 20). To offer works as a price is to
make God a debtor (Rom. 4, 4).

2 It is the Promise of God. (1 John 2, 25).
The promise of the true God that inhabiteth eternity.
This promise is the word of life. He speaks and it is
done.

3. It is a Gift (Rom. 6, 23). Divine life can
alone come from God. It must be given for it cannot
be bought. What was lost through sin can only be
attained through grace.

4. It is in Christ (1 John 5, 11). It hath pleased
God that this fulness should dwell in Him ; in Him
who is alive for evermore. He that hath the Son hath
life.

5. It is received by Faith (John 3, 15). Not of
works, lest any man should boast. This is the work
of God that ye *believe*. Grace shuts up to faith.

6. IT CONSISTS OF KNOWING GOD (John 17, 3). The *living* they praise Thee. I know whom I have believed. I know My sheep and am known of Mine Whom sayest thou that I am ?

7. IT CONSISTS OF HAVING GOD (John 6, 54). " As many as received Him," etc. (John 1, 12). Knowing and having the Eternal One is being in possession of eternal life. It is not having hope, but having the Christ who is our hope.

III. THE FULNESS OF THIS LIFE.—This fulness is seen—

1. IN THE SOURCE FROM WHENCE IT COMES (Isa. 57, 15). The unchanging and Almighty One. This blessing comes from " the high and lofty One " like the cool, refreshing stream which flows from the high and lofty hills, crowned with eternal snow.

2. IN THE PURPOSE OF THE GIFT. God so loved the world that He gave His Son (John 3, 16). He knew all that the world needed, and He knew that in giving His Son, He was giving the world everything it needed.

3. IN THE LIFE OF CHRIST (1 John 1, 1-2). What love and wisdom, grace and power, were manifested in the life of Jesus ! All fulness dwells in Him who is the image of the invisible God.

4. IN THE PROMISES OF GOD (John 10, 28). What promises are ours in Christ ! Having given us His Son, how will He not with Him also freely give us all things ?

5. IN THE LIVES OF GOD'S PEOPLE. Those who
S VIII

have subdued kingdoms, wrought righteousness, obtained promises, out of weakness were made strong
waxed valiant in fight, and turned to flight the armies
of the aliens (Heb. 11, 33-34). His riches are seen in
His kindness towards us (Eph. 2, 7).

IV. THE POWER OF THIS LIFE.—It is eternal,
and so possesses all " the power of an endless life "
(Heb. 7, 16). This life has in it—

1. A SIN-HATING POWER (John 12, 25). It being
a holy life—divine nature—it instinctively abhors
that which is un-Christ-like.

2. A WORLD-DESPISING POWER (1 John 2, 15).
This eternal life, born and nourished by things unseen,
cannot love this present evil world.

3. A SELF-FORGETTING POWER (Mark 10, 30). A
life that finds its highest good in being good and doing
good. The life of Jesus manifested in our mortal flesh
(2 Cor. 4, 11).

4. A SINNER-LOVING POWER. Although sin is
hated, the sinner is loved for Jesus' sake. " Love your
enemies, pray for them that persecute you."

5. A HOPE-INSPIRING POWER (Titus 1, 2). Each
individual believer, standing before God, resting in His
will, is a confirmed and joyful optimist.

6. A DEVIL-CONQUERING POWER. In this eternal
life there is such a power of *resistance* when exercised
by faith that the devil must flee from you (James 4, 7).

7. A GOD-GLORIFYING POWER. Having been
made *alive* unto God, we must glorify Him in our bodies

and spirits, which are His, and look for the time when He shall be glorified in His saints, and admired in all them that believe (2 Thess. 1, 10).

THE SAYINGS OF JESUS: A REVELATION OF HIMSELF.

Each saying of Jesus is a ray of divine light. The sun can only be seen by the light which itself emits. So Jesus, the Light of the World, can only be understood by " the sayings concerning Himself."

I. THE SAYINGS OF JESUS REVEAL THE DIVINITY OF HIS OWN CHARACTER.—He manifests Himself—

1. AS THE FIRST AND THE LAST (Rev. 1, 8). A striking declaration of the eternity of His Being.

2. AS HAVING POWER OVER DEATH AND HELL (Rev. 1, 18). The keys are the emblems of authority. He carries them, because through dying He has purchased the right.

3. AS THE FULFILLING OF PROPHECY (Rev. 22, 16) As David's Lord, He is the Root ; as David's Son, He is the Offspring ; as the predicted Messiah, He is the Bright and Morning Star.

4. AS THE SACRIFICE OF SIN (John 12, 32). The lifting up of the brazen serpent was typical of the lifting up of the bruised Son that *wounded* ones may be healed.

5. AS THE LIGHT OF THE WORLD (John 8, 12).—He will be better understood as our Light, when we have received Him as our Life.

6. As the Way, and the Truth, and the Life (John 14, 6). He is the Life to save, the Truth to satisfy, and the Way to walk.

7. As the Bread of Life. He is the Bread of God (John 6, 33), satisfying all the claims of God. He is the Bread of Life, to satisfy all the wants of man. Also, angels' food.

8. As the Source of Fruitfulness (John 15). Everything the branch needs may be found in the Vine— Abide.

9. As the Source of Power (Matt. 28, 18). The power is in Himself ; abiding in Him we abide in power.

10. As the Resurrection and the Life (John 11, 25). He alone can resurrect dead souls into life. He will resurrect the bodies of His saints into the glorious image of His own eternal life.

II. REVEAL HIS OWN RELATIONSHIP TO THE FATHER.—

1. He was Sent by the Father (John 8, 29). He who sent Him was with Him. He who sends us has also promised to be with us.

2. He is Loved by the Father (John 5, 20). This love is manifested in the Father showing Him all things. Is not Christ's love to us exhibited in a like fashion ?

3. He had the Authority of the Father (John 5, 22). Those who honour not Him honour not the

Father. The Father's authority is despised when Christ is despised.

4. HE POSSESSED LIFE LIKE THE FATHER (John 5, 26). The life of Christ, like the Father's, is a life-imparting life. He is the author of life.

5. HE WAS INDWELT BY THE FATHER (John 14, 10). The Father's works were wrought out in Him. " It is God who worketh in us."

6. HE WAS SUBMISSIVE TO THE FATHER (Matt. 26, 29). The evidence of an indwelling Christ is a will entirely yielded to Him.

7. HE ALWAYS PLEASED THE FATHER (John 8, 29). He pleased not Himself. If we can truly say, " I seek not mine own glory," we may please Him too.

8. HE MANIFESTED THE NAME OF THE FATHER (John 17, 6). " Ye are the epistle of Christ."

9. HE FINISHED THE WORK GIVEN HIM BY THE FATHER (John 18, 4). The finishing of the work is to us as it was to Him, the gaining of a victory.

10. HE YIELDED HIS SPIRIT TO THE FATHER (Luke 23, 46). Home is sweet when the will of the Father has been done, and His name glorified. Surely now those longings expressed by the loving, suffering Son will be fully satisfied (John 17, 1).

III. REVEAL THE NATURE OF HIS OWN MISSION.—

1. HE CAME NOT TO BE MINISTERED UNTO (Matt. 20, 28). The great ones of the earth love to be lionised

and feasted. He came to give what the world needed—
" His life."

2   HE CAME TO GLORIFY THE FATHER (John 17, 4).
The goodness of God is made to pass before us in Christ
His Son. He magnified the Father's name in the
presence of the people.

3.   HE CAME TO SHOW US A LIFE OF FAITH (John 5,
30). He could say, " The words that I speak, I speak
not of Myself." His faith was in His Father, and so
the Father acted through Him. May Christ so dwell in
our hearts by faith.

4.   HE CAME TO REVEAL A LIFE OF SELF-DENIAL
(John 8, 50). So truly human was Jesus Christ that he
might have sought His own glory, but He did not. He
came to seek and to save that which was lost.

5.   HE CAME TO MANIFEST PATIENCE IN POVERTY
(Matt. 8, 20). Godliness, with contentment, is great
gain. Gain won through faith.

6.   HE CAME TO SUFFER AND TO DIE (Mark 8, 31).
This was a necessity laid upon Him, because of the love
He had for us. " He bore our sins in His own body."

7.   HE CAME TO OPEN A NEW WAY (John 10, 9).
The Good Shepherd gave His life for the sheep, that He
might become the Door into the pastures that are ever
green.

8.   HE CAME THAT HE MIGHT BECOME THE HEAD
OF THE CORNER (Matt. 21, 42). Despised and rejected
of men, God hath highly exalted Him. Among the
ten thousand stones in the building He is the chiefest.

9. HE CAME, AND HE WILL COME AGAIN (Matt. 25, 31). His promise is, " I will come again" (John 14, 3). It will be a personal appearing. "This same Jesus " (Acts 1, 11). He comes in His glory to raise the dead, to change the living, to take vengeance on them who obey not the Gospel, to destroy Antichrist, to restore His people Israel, to rule the nations, to reward the faithful, and to bring in everlasting righteousness. " Even so, come, Lord Jesus."

THE HOLY GHOST OUR TEACHER.

There are two great personalities which are much forgotten in these days—the devil, the father of lies; and the Holy Ghost, the Spirit of truth.

I. A DIVINE TEACHER IS NEEDED.—Every sinner needs a Divine Saviour ; every saint needs a Divine Teacher. " He shall teach " (John 14, 26) ought to be as real to us as " He shall save " (Matt. 1, 21). This great Teacher is needed because—

1. THE THINGS OF GOD KNOWETH NO MAN (1 Cor. 2, 11). Every unregenerate man is ignorant of the things of God. Man cannot find out God by *searching ;* only by *revelation.* This revelation is by the Holy Spirit (1 Cor. 2, 11).

2. THE NATURAL MAN CANNOT RECEIVE THE THINGS OF GOD (1 Cor. 2, 14). Not only has the Holy Spirit to *reveal* the things of God, but He must also change the heart, and give the *nature to receive* them.

3. HOLY MEN OF OLD WERE TAUGHT BY THE SPIRIT (2 Peter 1, 21). Holy men to-day must have the same Teacher. He shall guide you into all truth (John 16, 13).

II. A DIVINE TEACHER HAS COME.—

1. HE WAS SENT BY THE FATHER IN THE NAME OF THE SON (John 14, 26). Both Father and Son are deeply interested in the education of His children. This gift implies that there is much more for Christians in this life than mere salvation from wrath.

2. HE HAS COME TO INSTRUCT (Neh. 9, 30). Two things every Christian ought to be—clean and wise. Ignorance of the things of God is an evidence of a grieved Spirit.

3. HE SEARCHETH ALL THINGS (1 Cor. 2, 10). This Teacher is all-sufficient ; the deep mysteries of God are known to Him and revealed by Him.

4. HE ABIDETH IN YOU (John 14, 17). " Your body is the temple of the Holy Ghost " (1 Cor. 6, 19). He is always at hand, so that " Ye need not that any man teach you " (1 John 2, 27).

5. HE SPEAKETH IN YOU (Matt. 10, 12). He must speak through us before He can speak to us. It is not ye that speak, for ye are dead, and your life is hid with Christ in God.

III. THE CHARACTER OF HIS TEACHING.—

He is the Spirit of wisdom, counsel, and knowledge (Isa. 11, 2). This text will be best understood by read· ing it backwards.

1. HE SHALL NOT SPEAK OF HIMSELF (John 16, 13). Like Christ, He makes Himself of no reputation. Does this feature of our Teacher characterise us ? Not I, but Christ.

2. HE AWAKENETH THE EAR (Isa. 1, 4, R.V.). Lord, give us the hearing ear. Ears some have, but they hear not. Why ? Asleep.

3. HE USES THE WORD (Eph. 6, 17). Being the Spirit of truth He delights in the word of truth and seeks to guide us into the truth.

4. HE RECEIVES THE THINGS OF GOD FOR US (John 16, 14). All the fulness is in Christ ; the Spirit receives and takes of the things of Christ that He might show them unto us.

5. HE SHOWS THINGS TO COME (John 16, 13). Now, since Christians are beginning to honour the Holy Spirit, they are beginning to understand " things to come."

6. HE BRINGS TO REMEMBRANCE (John 14, 26). He writes the truth in the heart and recalls it to our minds when needed. His memory never fails Him. Filled with the Spirit is the cure for a bad memory.

7. HE DIVIDES HIS GIFTS (1 Cor. 12, 8). " He divideth to every man severally as He will." (1 Cor. 12, 11). Covet earnestly the best gifts. Who teacheth like Him ? (Job 36, 22).

IV. THE PRIVILEGES OF THE TAUGHT.—

1. THEY KNOW HIM (Eph. 1, 17), not only as

their Saviour, but as their daily sufficiency and coming King.

2. THEY KNOW WHAT IS FREELY GIVEN THEM (1 Cor. 2, 12). They have, by faith, laid hold on the unsearchable riches of Christ. To such the promises are precious.

3. THEY ARE QUICK TO UNDERSTAND (Isa. 11, 3). Being taught of God they have the mind of God, and so quickly apprehend His will.

4. THEY SPEAK IN WISDOM (1 Cor. 2, 13). The Spirit of the Lord spake by me, and His word was in my tongue.

5. THEY HAVE AN HOLY UNCTION (1 John 2, 20). The heavenly breath is felt where the Spirit is. Paul judged not by the speech but by the *power* (1 Cor. 4, 19-20).

6. THEY NEED NO OTHER TEACHER (1 John 2, 27). Whether we read or hear the Word of God, let us sit at His feet. Learn of Me.

7. THEY ARE HELPFUL TO OTHERS (Isa. 1, 4, R.V.). This is the secret of a useful life—God working in you, both to will and to do of His good pleasure.

THE MISSION FIELD.

I. LOOK AT THE FIELD.—

1. THE FIELD IS THE WORLD (Matt. 13, 30). The Church is in the world, that it might be a blessing to

the world. The seed of the kingdom is sufficient for, and suitable to, every part of the field.

2. A WORLD IN BONDAGE (John 5, 19, R.V.). Possessed and polluted by the evil one. The thorns and briars of sin are the natural fruits of the soil.

3. A WORLD UNDER CONDEMNATION (Rom. 5, 12). All have sinned ; all are guilty ; all under death, that He might have mercy upon all.

4. A WORLD LOVED BY GOD (John 3, 16). That God does love the world is abundantly manifest in the gift of His Son. Why He did love such a world is a mystery to man and an eternal praise to God.

5. A WORLD ATONED FOR BY CHRIST. He is the propitiation for our sins, and not for ours only, but also for the sins of the whole world (1 John 2, 2). He is the mercy-seat, where the broken law is covered, and where all may meet with God.

6. A WORLD IN IGNORANCE OF GOD (1 Cor. 1, 21). It is sad to think of the millions still in ignorance of God's love and of Christ's atoning death. The soil cannot but be fruitless for good while it is yet destitute of the good seed.

7. A WORLD READY FOR HARVEST (John 6, 35-36). Christ saw the field already white in His day, because He saw already the grace and power by which this great work could be done. Alas ! that so little should be yet gathered in. " Oh, where are the reapers ? "

II. LOOK AT THE WORK.

It is said that when the Duke of Wellington was asked if it was worth while sending missionaries to a certain people, he said : " What are your standing orders ? " Well, here they are—

1. GO INTO ALL THE WORLD (Mark 16, 15). The great Redeemer had His eye and heart on every part of the field when He gave His life a ransom for all.

2. BE WITNESSES UNTO ME (Acts 1, 8). This implies more than mere testimony. We cannot be true witnesses of Christ's transforming, cleansing, keeping power, unless we have in heart been renewed, possessed, and transformed.

3. TEACH ALL NATIONS (Matt. 28, 19). All nations need the knowledge of Christ. Christ is sufficient for the needs of all nations.

4. PREACH THE GOSPEL (2 Cor. 10, 16). The tidings of the Father's love ; of the Saviour's sufferings and triumph ; of the Spirit's presence and power ; of the coming of the King.

5. DECLARE HIS GLORY (1 Chron. 16, 24). Declare the glory of His character ; the glory of His resurrection ; the glory of His future kingdom.

6. BID TO THE MARRIAGE (Matt. 22, 9). Don't forget to give each and all a hearty invitation. God is no respecter of persons. Whosoever will may come.

7. PRAY THE LORD OF THE HARVEST (Matt. 9, 28). Pray HIM to thrust out labourers into His harvest. Pray Him to thrust out those who are waiting on money

to send them. The Church is waiting on the *means* to send them. " Pray *Him* to send," and the means will be sent with them.

III. LOOK AT THE WORKERS.—

1. THEY ARE POSSESSED (John 17, 23). The vessel needs filling before it can be a blessing. Paul had the Son revealed in him before he was called to preach Him. Moses had the vision before he received his commission (Ex. 3, 1-10).

2. THEY ARE SENT (John 17, 28). Sent as the Father has sent the Son. What does that mean ? Think of where Christ came from, what He came to do, and how He did the will of His Father.

3. THEY ARE FAITHFUL (Acts 8, 4). Though scattered abroad by persecution they preached the Word everywhere. Faithful to Him who called them. Ye serve the Lord Christ.

4. THEY ARE TAUGHT (Jer. 1, 7). He who dwells within teaches how and what to speak. Out of your hearts shall flow rivers of living water. This spake He of the Spirit.

5. THEY ARE DEBTORS (Rom. 1, 14-15). We are debtors to all classes, inasmuch as we have that committed to us (the Gospel) which all need. We owe the unsaved the Gospel. The Lord give us grace to pay our debt.

6. THEY ARE COURAGEOUS (2 Cor. 10, 16). They went into the regions beyond, where the Gospel was as

yet unknown, not boasting in the fruit of other men's labours. Dare to be a Daniel.

7. THEY ARE SUCCESSFUL (Acts 17, 6). The world needs to be turned upside down, for just now it is wrong side up. Its feet, instead of its face, are turned to God. Who is sufficient for these things? Greater is He that is in you.

IV. LOOK AT THE ENCOURAGEMENTS.—

1. THINK OF THE WILL OF GOD (1 Tim. 2, 3-4). It is His will that all be saved. He willeth not the death of any. In seeking the salvation of men we seek the fulfilment of His will.

2. THINK OF THE SUFFERINGS OF CHRIST (Gal. 1, 4). How precious is that shed blood in the eyes of God the Father ; how powerful is that blood to cleanse.

3. THINK OF THE GIFT OF THE SPIRIT (Acts 1, 8), which proves a resurrected Saviour and an accepted Advocate. By the Spirit's presence the living Saviour, in all His love and power, abides within us.

4. THINK OF THE POWER OF THE GOSPEL (Rom. 1, 16). The message we have to proclaim is the divine complement to human need. It is God's panacea for the woes of the world.

5. THINK OF THE PROMISE (Matt. 28, 19-20). "Certainly I will be with you." This was God's answer to Moses. "Who am I?" The question is not, "Who am I?" but, "Who is He that is with me?"

6. THINK OF THE REWARDS (Mark 10, 29-30). "Ye

shall receive wages." What a fee! Heaven's coin paid in grace by the hand of the King.

7. THINK OF THE DIVINE PURPOSE. All the ends of the earth shall see the salvation of God. All kings and nations shall yet serve Him. The kingdoms of this world shall yet become the kingdom of our Lord and of His Christ. Be not weary in well-doing.

REWARDS.

What manner of love is this? that God should so love us as to give up His Son to die for us, and then reward us for every little thing done for Him. Oh, the grace of God—it is grace upon grace. Look at—

I. THE REWARDER.—Rewards are usually given according to the dignity of the rewarder.

1. THINK OF HIS GREATNESS (Col. 3, 24). The Lord Himself is the rewarder. The world was made by Him and for Him. He inhabiteth eternity. He speaks and it is done.

2. THINK OF HIS RICHES (Gen. 15, 1). Is it earthly blessing? The earth is the Lord's and the fulness thereof. Is it spiritual gifts? The fulness of the Godhead dwelleth in Him. He who *was rich* became poor, that we, through His poverty, might be made rich.

3. THINK OF HIS GOODNESS (Matt. 6, 4). How sweet are these words: "Thy Father Himself." The Father who gave His Son, how will He not, *with Him*, freely give us all things. O how great is Thy goodness!

4. THINK OF HIS FAITHFULNESS (Phil 2, 8-10).
The One who, for God, became a worm and no man, is
exalted by God with a name above every name. We
see Him enduring the cross, and we see Him crowned
with glory and honour (Heb. 2, 9). Having been
faithful to His only Son, He will be faithful to His every
son.

II. THE REWARDED.—Not every one will
have their works rewarded. The wood, hay, and
stubble will be burned. If any man's work *abide*, he
shall receive a reward (1 Cor. 3, 12-15). Rewards are
given to—

1. THE EARNEST SEEKER (Heb. 11, 6). Not
those who seek rewards merely, but *Him*—" My soul
thirsteth for the living God."

2. THE CAREFUL WORKER (1 Cor. 3, 13-14).
Take heed how and what ye build. Remember the
testing fire. Be diligent in this business ; be fervent
in spirit—red hot.

3. THE CHEERFUL GIVER (Matt. 10, 42). The Lord
loveth a cheerful giver. Whatsoever ye do, do it
heartily. The least thing done in Christ's Name will
be rewarded.

4. THE RIGHTEOUS SOWER (Prov. 11, 18). Jesus
Christ was the righteous Sower. What a reward
He has received ! (Heb. 2, 9). Let us follow His
example (Ps. 126, 6).

5. THE UPRIGHT DEALER (2 Sam. 22, 21). The

Christian ought to do his business as in the sight of God, with an equal balance and with clean hands.

6. THE HUMBLE WALKER (Prov. 22, 4). The reward of humility is riches and honour. Christ humbled Himself, wherefore God highly axalted Him (v. 29).

7. THE STEADFAST BELIEVER (Heb. 10, 25). Whatever hinders your confidence in God is robbing you of a great recompense of reward. Listen not to the tempting devil. This is the victory—even our faith.

8. THE GODLY SUFFERER (Matt. 5, 11-12). Jesus Himself, as our Captain, was consecrated through suffering. We suffer with Him that we may be also glorified together.

9. THE FAITHFUL WARRIOR (2 Tim. 4, 8). On God's side the battle is the Lord's ; on our side it is the fight of faith. Be faithful unto death and gain the crown of life.

III. THE REWARDS.—

1. THEY ARE GREAT (Gen. 15, 1). Will be according to the greatness of the Giver. To have Himself is to have an exceeding great reward. " If He is mine, then all is mine."

2. THEY ARE SURE (Col. 3, 24). Because they are of the Lord. He is faithful that hath promised.

3. THEY ARE VARIED. Every man shall receive according to his own labour (1 Cor. 3, 8). In this case it will not be " every man his *penny*." The penitent thief cannot expect the reward of the laborious Paul

T VIII

4. THEY ARE SUFFICIENT (Matt. 25, 21). Doubtless everyone will be abundantly satisfied with their own reward. His " well done " will be enough for this. But what is meant by " the joy of the Lord ? "

5. THEY ARE ETERNAL (2 Cor. 4, 17). These are laurels which never wither ; blessings which perish not with the using. Who can count the value of " an eternal weight of glory ? "

6. THEY ARE TO BE COVETED (2 John 8). Men will beguile us of our reward if they succeed in beguiling us away from lovingly serving the Lord. Press on toward the mark for the prize.

IV. THE REWARDING.—

1. WILL BE ACCORDING TO OUR WORKS (1 Cor. 3, 13). He shall reward every man according to his *works* (Matt. 16, 27), not according to his profession.

2. WILL BE OPENLY (Matt. 6, 4). Secret acts for Christ are not to be *only* secretly rewarded, although the faithful worker gets many a secret reward.

3. WILL BE IN THIS PRESENT TIME (Luke 18, 29-30). The rewards are not all reserved for us in heaven. Daniel's self-denial was rewarded with heavenly wisdom (chap. 1).

4. WILL BE IN THE LIFE TO COME (Rev. 22, 12). When clothed upon with our house which is from heaven, we will be the more able to receive and enjoy heavenly blessings.

5. WILL BE WHEN HE COMES (Matt. 16, 27) The great rewards are bestowed when the Rewarder Him

self appears. When He comes *for* His saints they shall receive the new body—the eternal fitness. When He comes with His saints they shall be rewarded with honours.

6. WILL BE DURING HIS REIGN (Rev. 20, 4). Know ye not that the saints shall judge the world?

7. WILL BE THROUGH ALL ETERNITY (2 Cor. 4, 17). Where I am there shall ye be also—" For ever with the Lord." Hallelujah.

APOSTOLIC CHRISTIANITY: AS SEEN IN THE ACTS.

I.—APOSTOLIC FAITH.

The history of the Prodigal in Luke 15 is pretty much the history of the Church. Now that she " begins to be in want," she must needs " Arise and go back " to her original sphere of power and prestige. What did those early saints believe?

1 They believed in the DIVINITY of Jesus Christ 3, 16
2 They believed in the ATONING work of Christ, 20, 28
3 They believed in the WORD of Christ 27, 25
4 They believed in the GOSPEL of Christ 8, 5
5 They believed in the NAME of Christ 3, 16
6 They believed in the PRESENCE of Christ .. 18, 9-10
7 They believed in the POWER OF THE HOLY SPIRIT, 1, 8: 2, 38: 8, 15: 10, 44-45: 11, 16: 15, 8

II.—APOSTOLIC PRAYER.

1 They Prayed at stated times 3, 1
2 They Prayed, believing in Much Prayer 6, 4

III.—APOSTOLIC COURAGE.

They had courage—

IV.—APOSTOLIC POWER.

I.—The Nature of this Power.

II.—The Manifestations of this Power.

By the Power of the Holy Ghost—

6 The Servant is Separated and Sent 13, 2-4
7 The Enemy is Fearlessly Denounced 13, 9-10

V.—APOSTOLIC TESTIMONY.

There is no uncertain sound here. They testified—

1 That Jesus was *the Christ, the Son of God*...2, 36 : 9, 20
2 That God raised *Him from the dead* ...... 3, 15 : 4, 33
3 That His Name has power to heal *through Faith* 3, 16
4 That Salvation is *Only in His Name* 4, 12
5 That Christ is the *God-Ordained Judge* of all, 10, 42
6 That all believers are *Justified from all things*, 13, 39
7 That all believers should *receive the Gift of the Holy Ghost* ... .2, 39 : 19, 2

VI.—APOSTOLIC SUCCESS.

They succeeded—

1 In Receiving the Promise of the Father, 1, 4 : 2, 4
2 In Converting sinners unto God .... 2, 41 : 4, 4
3 In Working Miracles of Grace .... 3, 7 : 16, 18
4 In bringing Answers to their Prayers, 4, 31 : 12, 5 : 16, 26
5 In Spreading their doctrine abroad ...... 5, 28 : 42
6 In Getting immediate result through preaching Christ ....8, 5-8 : 9, 20-21
7 In Raising persecution because of their faithfulness .... 4, 21   13, 50-52   14, 2 : 17, 32
8 In doing the work given them to do 26, 18

THE BLESSED HOPE.

TITUS 2, 13-14.

We don't hope for what we already possess. Every Christian has Forgiveness of Sins, Peace with God, and Eternal Life.

This blessed hope is characterised as—

1 A Good Hope .... 2 Thess. 2, 16
2 A Sure Hope .... Heb. 6, 18
3 A Living Hope .... Peter 1, 3
4 A Saving Hope .... Rom. 8, 24
5 A Purifying Hope .... 1 John 3, 3
6 A Comforting Hope .... 1 Thess. 4, 18

It is the blessed hope of—

1 The Individual .... Acts 1, 11
2 The Church .... John 14, 1-3
3 The Servant .... Luke 19, 13
4 Of Israel ....Rom. 11, 26
5 Of Creation ...., Rom. 8, 22-23

THE ARM OF THE LORD.

As revealed in Isaiah.

The *Arm* of the Lord is symbolic of Christ, as His *hand* is of the Holy Spirit.

1 His Character, as Jehovah's representative, Isa. 40, 10
2 Salvation through Him .... Isa. 40, 11
3 Condition of Salvation, "Trust" .... Isa. 51, 5
4 The Call .... Isa. 51, 9-10
5 The Unvailing .... Isa. 52, 10
6 The Appeal .... Isa. 53, 1

7 The Testimony .... Isa. 59, 16
8 The Final Victory .... Isa. 63, 12
Cursed be he that maketh *flesh* his arm (Jer. 17, 5).

APOSTOLIC EXAMPLE.
ACTS 20, 19-28.

" Be ye followers of me," said the apostle, " Even as I also am of Christ " (1 Cor. 11, 1).

He is an example for us—

1 In Humble Service for God .... v. 19
2 In Faithfulness to the Word of God .... v. 20
3 In Shewing the right attitude toward God ... v. 21
4 In being Taught by the Spirit of God ...... vv. 22-23
5 In Patiently suffering the will of God .... v. 24
6 In Preaching the Kingdom of God .... v. 25
7 In boldly Declaring the whole Counsel of God, v. 27
8 In Caring for the Church of God .... v. 28

PETER.

The Biography of Peter is singularly instructive for every follower of Christ.

1 His Call. The *first* of the Twelve .... Matt. 10, 2
2 His Courage .... Matt. 14, 28
3 His Confession .... Matt. 16, 15-16
4 His Impulsiveness .... Matt. 17, 4 ; John 18, 10
5 His Self-Confidence .... Mark 14, 29-31
6 His Indifference .... Mark 14, 37
7 His Cowardliness .... Mark 14, 54
8 His Denial .... Mark 14, 68-71
9 His Repentance .... Mark 14, 72

10 His Forgiveness .... Mark 16, 7
11 His Faith .... John 20, 2-4
12 His Love .... John 21, 7
13 His Devotion ....John 21, 15
14 His Boldness .... Acts 2, 14 ; 4, 19-20
15 His Power .... Acts 3, 6 : 5, 3

He was a man of like passions as we are : *Be of good cheer.*

WORK FOR CHRIST.
Acts 9, 6.

1 The Field is Large .... Matt. 13, 38
2 The Need is Great .... John 4, 35
3 The Time is Now .... Gal. 6, 10
4 The Call is Urgent .... Matt. 20, 6
5 The Work is Varied .... Matt. 13, 34
6 The Partner is Almighty .... 2 Cor. 6, 1
7 The Means are Provided .... Luke 19, 13
8 The Reward is Sure .... Dan. 12, 3

SPIRITUAL GROWTH.
Matt. 6, 27-28.

1 Growth implies *life.* Life is a Mystery ...... John 3, 3
2 Growth implies *favourable Conditions.*
3 Growth is *natural*, where there is life.
4 Growth is *gradual.* " First the blade."
5 Growth is not the result of *Effort* " Consider the lilies " (v. 27).
6 Growth implies healthy *activity at the roots.* Receiving much.
7 Growth is needful to *perfection of character.*

THE SHEPHERD AND THE SHEEP.

I.—" THE LORD IS MY SHEPHERD " (v. 1).

1. WHO IS THIS SHEPHERD ? " Jehovah." Who *was*, and *is*, and is *to come*   The title occurs 7,600 times. Jehovah Rohi. " The Lord my Shepherd."

2. HOW HE HAS BECOME A SHEPHERD. " All have gone astray " (Isa. 53, 6). He came to seek and save the *lost*.

3. WHAT HE HAS DONE FOR THE SHEEP.
He has entered the door of the fold .... John 10, 2
He has given His life *for* the sheep .... John 10, 11
He has given His sheep *eternal life* .... John 10, 28
He has given them the proof of eternal security,

John 10, 29

4. WHO ARE HIS SHEEP ? It is characteristic of them that—
They *hear* His Voice .... v. 27
They *knew* Him .... v. 14
They *follow* Him .... v. 27

II.—" I SHALL NOT WANT " (v. 1).

1. WHO SHALL NOT WANT ? He who can truly say, " The Lord is *my* Shepherd."

2. WHY HE SHALL NOT WANT.—Because the Lord *is* his Shepherd, and HE is rich in possessions, wise in administration, strong to defend, and gracious to give.

3. WHAT IS IT TO BE IN WANT?

It is to be like Belshazzar when weighed in the
balance .... Dan. 5, 27

It is to be like the Prodigal in the far country,
Luke 15, 14

It is to be like the Foolish Virgins without oil,
Matt. 25, 8

It is to be like the rich man in hell .... Luke 16, 24

III.—" HE MAKETH ME TO LIE DOWN " (v. 2).
These words imply—

1. PLEASANT FEEDING. " Green pastures." The
pastures of God's Word are always fresh, tender, satisfying.

2. PEACEFUL RESTING. He maketh me to *lie
down*. Resting implies not only satisfaction, but a
conscious feeling of perfect security.

3. GENTLE CONSTRAINING. " He *maketh me* to lie
down." What gracious compulsion His is.

4. PLEASANT WALKING. " Beside the still waters."
(" Waters of quietness," marg.). The Scriptures of
truth, the Lord's day of rest, the sweet hour of
prayer, etc.

5. FAITHFUL LEADING. " *He* leadeth me." He
leads into the fulness of blessing. " My soul followeth
hard after Thee" (Ps. 63, 8).

IV.—" HE RESTORETH MY SOUL " (v. 3).

1. WHEN IS RESTORATION NEEDED?

When in a Weak and Fainting condition.

When in a Sinful and Backsliding state.

2. WHAT ARE THE SIGNS OF BACKSLIDING ?

Following afar off, through fear or shame.

Discontent and Restlessness with the leading of God

Growing disregard for the fellowship of saints.

Secret neglect of His " green pastures " and preference
for the thoughts of men.

3. HOW IS RESTORATION EFFECTED ? " He restoreth."

By the Shepherd's look .... Luke 22, 61

By the Shepherd's crook .... Ps. 119, 67

V.—" HE LEADETH ME, FOR HIS OWN NAME'S SAKE (v. 3).

1. THE LEADER. " *He* leadeth "—

By the Word of His mouth.

By the Example of His Life.

By the Promptings of His Spirit.

2. THE LED. " He leadeth *Me.*"

Because my eye is on Him.

Because I believe in Him.

Because I yield to Him.

3. THE PATHS. " Paths of Righteousness (Rightness).

Into the path of Peace.

Into the path of Prayer.

Into the path of Power.

4. THE PURPOSE OF HIS LEADING. " For His
own Name's sake."

For the Sake of His Word.

For the Sake of His Work.
For the Sake of His Will.

VI.—" I WILL FEAR NO EVIL " (v. 4).

1. TESTING EXPERIENCE. " The valley of the shadow of death."
The valley of temporal Adversity.
The valley of severe bodily or family Affliction.
The valley of bitter persecution.

2. BLESSED ASSURANCE. " I will fear no evil."
I will fear no evil place .... World
I will fear no evil thing .... Flesh
I will fear no evil one .... Devil

3. JOYFUL TESTIMONY. " Thou art with Me."
Thou art with me as the Way.
Thou art with me as the Truth.
Thou art with me as the Life.

VII.—" THEY COMFORT ME " (v. 4).

The " Rod and Staff" comfort because they are *His* and they are His *all the way*.

1. THE COMFORT OF HIS ROD (club).
It was their *Weapon of defence* against the enemy.
It was the *Breaker up of their way* among thorns and briars.

2. THE COMFORT OF HIS STAFF (Crook).
With it they were *rescued* from danger.
Under it they were *numbered* for safety.

The rod and the staff are emblems of the Power of the Spirit, and the assuring character of His Word.

VIII.—" THOU PREPAREST A TABLE BE-
FORE ME " (v. 5).

1. WHAT ? " Thou preparest a *table*." A table
tells of forethought and fellowship.

2. WHO ? " *Thou* preparest." This preparation is
perfectly consistent with His character.

3. WHERE ? " In the presence of mine enemies."
Shepherds sometimes cut *down* branches to feed the
flock.

4. FOR WHOM ? " Before *me*." Personal experience of His special care.

IX.—" THOU ANOINTEST MY HEAD, MY
CUP RUNNETH OVER " (v. 5).

There is a vital connection between the anointed
head and the overflowing cup.

1. THE ANOINTED HEAD. (Oil a symbol of the
Holy Spirit)—
Is a sign of man's separation unto God.
It is the Seal of God's Consecration (filling) of man,
for His Service.

2. THE OVERFLOWING CUP. The overflowing Cup
is the result of the overflowing oil.
It means a life of abounding satisfaction, "running over."
It means of Life of Blessing for others. The overflow
is not waste, but for the salvation of others.
It means a Life of Joyful Testimony. " *My* cup runneth over." No wonder when " the Lord is the
portion of my cup."

X. — " SURELY GOODNESS AND MERCY SHALL FOLLOW ME " (v. 6).

When we can say, " He *leadeth* me," we may confidently say, " Goodness and Mercy shall *follow* me."

I. THE PILGRIM'S ATTENDANTS.

" Goodness " to gather up the *precious* results of our lives.

" Mercy " to cleanse and forgive the faults and its failings.

2. THE PILGRIM'S CONSOLATION. " All the days of my life."
All the dark and stormy days.
All the bright and fruitful days.

3. THE PILGRIM'S HOME. " The House of the Lord."
The house that has been prepared by the Lord.
The house where the Lord Himself dwells.
Time is but the dressing-room of Eternity.

4. THE PILGRIM'S CONFIDENCE. " *I will* dwell in the House of the Lord for ever."
He knows Him in whom he has believed.
He believes and expects what He has promised.

THE REVELATIONS OF THE HOLY SPIRIT.
JOHN 16, 12-14.

1 He Reveals the Pierced Saviour .... Zech. 12, 10
2 He Reveals the Way into Truth .... John 16, 13
3 He Reveals the Love of God .... Rom. 5, 5
4 He Reveals the Things of Christ .... John 16, 14

5 He Reveals the Things God hath Prepared, 1 Cor. **2, 10**
6 He Reveals the Valley of Need .... Ezek. 37, 1
7 He Reveals the Path of Service .... Acts 8 29

ALL ONE IN CHRIST.
HEBREWS 2, 11.

1 In Christ we are Possessed by one Life ... John 15, 5
2 In Christ we belong to One Body ... 1 Cor. 12, 12-14
3 In Christ we are joined by One Spirit ...... 1 Cor. 6, 17
4 In Christ we are Secure on One Standing, John 17, 21
5 In Christ we are Stones of One Building ... Eph. 2, 22
6 In Christ we are Membersof One Family, Eph.3,14-15
7 In Christ we are Parts of One Temple ... Eph. 2, 21-22

"LET US GO FORTH."
HEBREWS 13, 13.

1. WHAT FROM ?
From the Formality of a Powerless Religion.
From the Pleasures of a Sinful World.
From the Deceptions of a Self-centred Life.

2. WHAT TO ? " Unto Him."
Unto Him as those who believe in Him.
Unto Him as those who are separated to Him.
Unto Him as those who are prepared to Suffer with Him.
Unto Him as those who will Testify for Him.

QUALIFICATIONS FOR SERVICE.

1 Come to Christ .... Matt. 11, 28-29
2 Go for Christ .... Matt. 28, 19

3 Trust in Christ .... Matt. 28, 20
4 Act like Christ .... John 13, 14-15

THE PLEASURE OF THE LORD.

1 With regard to His Enemies .... Ezek. 33, 11
2 With regard to His Son .... Isa. 53,10
3 With regard to His Word .... Isa. 55, 11
4 With regard to His Gospel .... 1 Cor. 1, 21
5 With regard to His Service .... Gal. 1, 15-16
6 With regard to His people .... 1 Sam. 12, 22
7 With regard to His Purpose .... Luke 12, 32

THE PRECIOUS CHRIST.
1 PETER 2, 7.

1. THE CHARACTER OF CHRIST. "He is Precious." In Him is Costliness, Rarity, Adaptability.

2. TO WHOM CHRIST IS PRECIOUS. "Unto you.... which believe." His sweetness must be tasted to be known.

3. WHY CHRIST IS PRECIOUS TO THE BELIEVER.
Because He is their Life .... Col. 3, 4
Because He is their Sustenance .... John 6, 55
Because He is their Peace .... Eph. 2, 14
Because He is their Character .... 1 Cor. 1, 30
Because He is their Example .... 1 Peter 2, 21
Because He is their All-sufficiency .... 2 Cor. 8, 9

PAUL'S THREEFOLD TESTIMONY.
ACTS 27, 23-25.

1 As to His Life. "Whose I am."
2 As to his Work. "Whom I serve."
3 As to his Creed. "I believe God."

A SATISFYING SIGHT.

1 JOHN 3, 2.

1 Who shall we see ? See *Him*.
2 Who shall see *Him ?* " *We* shall."
3 How shall we see Him ? " As He is."
4 What will be the effect of seeing Him ? " We shall be like Him."
5 Is this quite certain ? " We *shall*."

SEVEN PRAYERS IN MATTHEW 8.

1 The Cry of Misery. " If Thou wilt Thou canst make me clean " .... v. 2
2 The Cry of Compassion. " Lord, my servant lieth at home sick," etc. .... vv. 5-6
3 The Cry of Faith. " Lord speak the word only " v. 8
4 The Cry of Procrastination. " Suffer me first " v. 21
5 The Cry of Fear. " Lord save us, we perish " ... v. 25
6 The Cry of Opposition... " What have we to do with Thee ? " .... v. 29
7 The Cry of Rejection. " They besought Him that He would depart " ....v. 34

BACKSLIDING.

JER. 8, 5. REV. 2, 4-5.

I. SOME OF ITS CAUSES.

1 The fear of man. Ashamed to confess.
2 Worldly associations in business or companionship.
3 Unequally yoked with unbelievers in marriage.
IJ VIII

4 Yielding to the desire for what is *new* rather than profitable.

5 Maintaining an unforgiving spirit toward another (Mark 11, 25-26).

6 Harbouring unclean thoughts and feelings.

7 Refusing to make confession to God when conscious of having sinned.

II. Some of its Evidences.

1 Neglecting the Word of God as the bread of life.

2 Little desire for secret prayer and communion with God.

3 Growing fondness for worldly pleasures.

4 Satisfied with present attainments in spiritual things.

5 Trifling excuses for neglecting Christian fellowship.

6 Tendency to discontent and fault-finding.

7 Decreasing anxiety for the salvation of others.

III. The Remedy.

Return. Repent. Confess. Renounce. Perform. Jer. 8, 5 ; Rev. 2, 4-5.

THE CHRISTIAN'S RELATIONSHIP.

As believers in the Lord Jesus Christ we are related—

1 To the Father as CHILDREN,
            John 20, 17 ; Matt. 6, 9 ; Rom. 9, 26

2 To the Son as SERVANTS, Matt. 23, 8-10 ; John 13, 13

3 To the Spirit as TEMPLES, 1 Cor. 6, 19-20, and as
            CHANNELS, John 7, 38

4 To the World as WITNESSES, Acts 1, 8 ; John 17, 18

5 To one another as BRETHREN, Matt. 23, 8 ; Heb. 2, 11

MEMBERS OF HIS BODY.
EPH. 5, 30.

The Church, as His Body, is all that is *visible* of Christ to the world.   *In* one Spirit are we all baptised into one body.

1 As Members we enjoy one Gracious Privilege
John 15, 5
2 As Members we have one Unquestionable Security
Col. 3, 3 (" in Christ")
3 As Members we obey one Sovereign Will ... Eph. 5, 23
4 As Members we are energised by One Mighty Spirit ....1 Cor. 12, 7-11
5 As Members we are united in working out One Great Purpose .... 2 Cor. 6, 1
6 As Members we have a special care one for another .... 1 John 3, 16
7 As Members we are specially cared for by the One to whom we belong .... Eph. 5, 29

OUR PRIVILEGES.
JUDE 20-25.

But ye beloved—

1 Building on the Faith of God.
2 Praying in the Spirit of God.
3 Keeping in the Love of God.
4 Looking for the Mercy of God.
5 Manifesting the Compassion of God.
6 Active in the Work of God (v. 23).
7 Hating garments that are unlike God.
8 Kept by the Power of God.
9 Faultless in the Presence of God.

Gospel Outlines.

CHRIST AND THE COMMON PEOPLE.

MARK 12, 37.

Three times over in this chapter the enemies of Christ try to "catch Him in His words" (vv. 14, 23, 28). The result in each case is, as it always has been, utter defeat. " The common people heard Him gladly." This is Mark's interjection, right between the " Sayings of Jesus " (vv. 37-38), and there is a world of revelation in it.

I.—THE COMMON PEOPLE. Who are they ? They were in Christ's day, as they are largely now, " Sheep without a Shepherd." Society is composed of three classes. The intellectual, the monied, and the labouring poor—Wit, Wealth, and Work. The heart of humanity is somewhere near the centre of the " common people " who take things at their surface value.

II.—THEY HEARD HIM GLADLY. Why ? There is no specific reason given, but much is implied. To the poor the Gospel is preached. The Gospel of Christ, like the Sabbath, was made for man, and is specially suitable for the masses. It was the learned who sought to entangle Him in His talk (v. 13). Some of our modern scholars are very active in the same vain business. They heard Him gladly—

1. BECAUSE HE TREATED THEM FAIRLY. He shewed no respect of persons. He did not talk of them as the " dregs " or " scum " of Society, or as those belonging to the " vulgar throng," or as members of the " many headed beast." He dealt with them as "men " because in His eyes " All souls are precious."

2. BECAUSE HE SPOKE TO THEM PLAINLY. He talked like one of themselves. The philosophers of Greece and Rome kept the common people in brutish ignorance. Jesus Christ had the " tongue of the learned," not that He might speak great swelling words of man's wisdom, far beyond the reach of the ignorant multitude, but that He might " know how to speak a word in season to *him that is weary* " (Isa. 50, 4). He was wiser than the wisest, yet His language was child-like in its simplicity.

3. BECAUSE OF HIS SYMPATHY. He could not look upon the hungry multitude without having " compassion on them " (chap. 8, 2). His heart was in all that He said. Love is ever more powerful than logic.

4. BECAUSE OF HIS TEACHING. He knew what was in man, and His words were abundantly fitted to meet man's need. He knew that there was sin in man, and also much weary restlessness, and inexpressible thirst. So He said, " If any man thirst let him come unto Me " (John 7, 37). The burdened and heavy laden were lovingly offered His rest (Matt. 11, 28). Our poet Burns once told a friend that " the gift of grace in Christ was far too good news to be true." But this Gospel of Christ *is* absolutely true.

5. BECAUSE HE SPOKE WITH AUTHORITY. There was no note of uncertainty in His teaching. He did not speculate. He declared the truth. He had a message from God to men, and He knew it, and fearlessly delivered it. So must His servants speak, if they would honour Him and win men for God. " We know in whom we have believed."

But note that " *hearing* Him gladly " is not enough. It is possible to hear Him gladly, and ultimately treat Him madly. " The glow of a warm impression is one thing, the sturdiness of an enduring principle is another." The " common people " can cry " Hosanna " to-day and " Crucify " to-morrow. The stony-ground hearers receive the Word with gladness, yet bring forth no fruit (Mark 4, 16-17). It is not He that heareth gladly shall be saved, but " He that heareth and believeth " (John 5, 24).

COUNT THE COST.
LUKE 14, 28.

Man is not a mere creature of circumstances, like a plant. Christ expects us to act as reasonable men, and to sit down and count the cost before starting any very serious undertaking. This " tower " referred to stands for beauty, safety and prospect, and is applicable to all " character builders " (v. 27). We cannot count the cost until we have first the vision of some great possibility before us. No wise man desires his life to end like the tower of Babel, in shame and confusion. To live the Christian life is indeed a great and solemn undertaking. Many begin this tower and seem not able to finish, bringing themselves into ridicule, and the tower into a laughing stock. Count the cost.

I.—THE COST OF BEING A CHRISTIAN. It is costly. It costs some more than others. Natural temperament, early training and environment may influence greatly. Whatever the price, it must be paid. We must count on—

1. GIVING UP ALL SIN. Christ gave Himself for us that He might "redeem us from all iniquity" (Titus 2, 14). Sin is the worst of all investments. Every scheme in which it has a place is rotten. The wicked must forsake his ways.

2. SURRENDERING THE WILL. "What *wilt Thou* have me to do?" must be the attitude of the soul. We must count what it will cost the self life to put Christ *first* in everything, and to seek first His Kingdom.

3. SEPARATION FROM THE WORLD. We are to go after Him bearing His cross (v. 27). By His cross the world is to be crucified unto us, and we to the world (Gal. 6, 14). When we find our all in Christ it is easy to give up all for Him. If any man love the world, the love of the Father is not in him.

4. OPPOSITION BY THE WORLD. The world that hated Him will hate you also. Noah by his work of faith condemned the world (Heb. 11, 7), and no doubt the world condemned him. Abel had to suffer because his works were righteous. In the world ye shall have tribulation, but be of good cheer, I have overcome the world.

5. TEMPTATION BY THE DEVIL. The ungodly are not tempted as the Christians are. Through the lust of the eye and the pride of life he still offers his subtle illusions. But Christ is able to deliver and succour the tempted.

6. SELF-DENIAL. "If any man would come after Me, let him deny himself." The Christian life is a life of faith in the Son of God, and so must be a life of *self-*denial. " Not I, but Christ." Christ counted the cost when He came forth to live the life of the Father among sinful men. As the Father sent Me, so have I sent you." But consider also—

II.—THE COST OF *NOT* BEING A CHRISTIAN. If the soul's wealth of capacity and power is invested in the things of this world, utter and eternal bankruptcy will surely follow. Can you afford this ? The business of a Christless life is an awfully expensive one. He shall suffer loss. What a loss ! The loss of—

1 The Forgiving Love of God the Father.
2 The Saving Power of Christ the Son.
3 The Comforting Presence of the Holy Spirit.
4 The Assuring Promises of His Holy Word.
5 The Joy of Service in His prevailing Name.
6 The Blessed Hope of seeing Him, and being like Him.

7 The Glories and Rewards of His Everlasting Kingdom and Presence.

COUNT THE COST. What did it cost the prodigal to come ? His rags and his wretchedness

THY WORD IS A LAMP.

PSALM 119, 105.

An unquestionable light is in it, adapted and suitable for every age. No modern light can equal it. It is as Pollock says, " This lamp from off the everlasting Throne." It is—

I.—A READING Lamp. A lamp for reading the mind and thoughts of God, and also for reading our own hearts.

II.—A HEATING Lamp. An incandescent glow that burns like a fire in the bones (Jer. 20, 9).

III.—A TRAVELLER'S Lamp. A lamp for my feet, and a light for my path. It is equally useful in every country and clime.

IV.—A MINER'S Lamp, suitable for the deepest pit of sin, and the darkest places of work and service. Proof against the black damp of the evil heart.

V.—A SAFETY Lamp. Sir Humphrey Davy's discovery has in no sense lessened its value. Can be used in the most dangerous places. C.H. 4 gas of the world has no damaging effect on it. It is not only a Safety, but a *Saving* lamp.

VI.—A LIGHTHOUSE Lamp. It stands aloft and its beams shine out over the dark waters of a needy world. To neglect its warnings is to suffer shipwreck. It is a divine *Search-light* flashing out in the darkness of this sin-shadowed earth.

VII.—A NIGHT Lamp. Gentle enough to shine with its mellow flame in the sick-chamber, bringing heaven's light into the weary heart, and brightening the pale face, with the eternal hope that is in Christ Jesus our Lord (Ps. 23).

SON, REMEMBER.
LUKE 16, 25.

On the authority of Christ this " *certain* rich man " must be taken as a real historical person. This startling appeal is made to his memory.

I.—MEMORY IS A MARVELLOUS GIFT. Loss of memory means loss of all usefulness, of all dignity and responsibility ; it is the loss of our identity. The brain itself is a mere pulp, it is the *mind* that remembers, now and in eternity.

II.—MEMORY IS THE STOREHOUSE OF THE SOUL. " Son, remember." Its capacity for storage is tremendous. Be careful what you put into it, as such goods may be required again. It may be a palace of precious keepsakes, or a chamber of horrors. It is a museum of records of events, the reference book for a coming judgment. It is the seed plot of this life, and of that which is to come.

III.—MEMORY IS AFFECTED BY THE STATE OF THE HEART. " Son, remember." What we are choosing now is determined by what we *love*. If we love the world then our hearts will be set on it. We remember most clearly what we have loved most dearly. Our youthful impressions, because of their intensity, usually abide longest with us. Some set their hearts on " things above," while others " mind earthly things."

IV.—MEMORY IS THE REPRODUCTIVE FACULTY. "Son, remember." It supplies the evidence for the final judgment, and may be one of " the books which will be opened in that great day." When a Christless man dies he has " nothing left but a majestic memory." We never speak of a *sinful* memory ; it may be weak or strong, but it is not in itself sinful, as it is but a mirror that reflects back what has been set before it. "Son, remember that thou in thy *lifetime* receivedst," etc. Here "Remembrance wakes with all her busy train, swells at the heart, and turns the past to pain." Peter wept when he thought thereon. Soul, remember that this is thy lifetime, and that the best of all "good things "—the Gospel of Christ— is within your reach. Receive Him, and then your sins and iniquities will be remembered no more.

REVIVAL.

"Wilt Thou not revive us again ?" Ps. 85, 6.

1. THE NEED OF REVIVAL. The need is apparent wherever there is Coldness, Languidness, and Fruitlessness.

2. THE SOURCE OF REVIVAL. "Thou." It is God, the Spirit, that quickeneth. No artificial appliances will bring a revival in Nature.

3. THE MEANS OF REVIVAL. "*Wilt* Thou not ?" The fervent prayer of the righteous availeth much. James 5, 17 ; Ps. 65, 9 ; Isa. 40, 28.

4. THE SUBJECTS OF REVIVAL. " Us." It is a personal need.

5. THE EFFECT OF REVIVAL. '' That Thy people may rejoice in Thee.''

ATTENTION.
HEBREWS 2, I.

We are called upon here to give heed to—

1. *Our Privilege.* " Things which we have *heard.*" Precious things revealed to us by the Gospel.

2. *Our Duty.* "We *ought* to give earnest heed." Hear, and your soul shall live. Strive to enter in.

3. *Our Danger.* " Lest at any time we should let them run out as leaking vessels " (margin). In at the one ear and out at the other. Hold fast that which thou hast.

GLORYING IN THE CROSS.
GAL. 6, 14.

We glory in the Cross because in it we see—

1 The Fulfilment of Prophecy. Gen. 3, 15. Isa. 55. Dan. 9, 24-26.

2 The Love of God Exhibited ....1 John 3, 16

3 The Love of Christ Declared... John 15, 13; Gal. 2, 20

4 The Removal of that which was against us, Col. 2, 14

5 The Redemption price for our souls ...... Gal. 3, 13

6 The Way of Escape from our sins ... 1 Peter 2, 24

7 The Foundation of our Peace established,

Col. 1, 20 ; Eph. 2, 16

Apt Illustrations.

SECRET SINS.

There is an insect that has a very close resemblance
to the "bumble bee," but which is a terrible enemy to it.
Because of its likeness, it sometimes finds its way in a
fraudulent manner into the bees' nest, and there deposits
eggs. But when these eggs are hatched the larvæ
devour the larvæ of the bees. It comes in as a friend
and helper, but turns out to be a devouring enemy.
Such is that secret sin harboured in the heart. It eats
away the vitals of the spiritual life, and effectually
destroys the power of growth and usefulness. It is all
the more dangerous when it comes in the likeness of a
friend and helper in the work.

SPIRITUAL BLINDNESS.

"Men tell us sometimes," says Drummond, "there is
no such thing as an atheist. There must be. There
are some men to whom it is true there is no God. They
cannot see God, because they have no eye." When the
fool says *in his heart*, there is no God, it would appear
that in his foolish heart he believes what he says, because
he has actually no capacity for seeing God, because of
the blindness of his heart. That *purity* of heart which
sees God, is a God-given eye to see Himself.

FORMALITY.

There is a variety of apple called "Apple-John," which is considered to be in *perfection* when it is shrivelled and withered. There are also those who believe in an apple-John religion, which to them is perfect only when it is thoroughly dried up of all spiritual power and utterly destitute of the sap of life and growth. The trees of the Lord are full of sap.

SPIRITUAL EDUCATION.

True education is not the cramming of the mind with different ideas, but the developing of our capacities, so that their real character may be brought out to the best advantage, and the highest purposes of our lives accomplished. In the caterpillar all the rudiments of the butterfly may be seen, but a great change is needful to liberate the higher faculties, and make the caterpillar that new creature it seeks to be. Jesus Christ said, "Learn of Me." He educates by regenerating the character and opening the way for the full development of all the capacities of the new man. To learn of Christ, then, is to be conformed into His likeness, and so be able to fulfil all the purposes of God in the new life.

TENACIOUS SELF.

Perhaps the most ferocious animal in creation is the "hamster rat." When it takes a grip, rather than yield it will allow itself to be beaten in pieces with a stick. If it seizes a man's hand, it must be killed before it will quit its hold. How like this "hamster rat" is our own proud, unyielding, sinful self. That selfish spirit, that would cling to and suck the life out of the new heaven-born nature, will not quit its hold until it has been put to death.

LIFE-GIVING BREATH.

In South America the wind from the marshes comes charged with the germs of intermittent fever, and often the most deadly cholera accompanies *stillness* in the atmosphere. A storm is the best purifier of the air, and the inhabitants long eagerly for it. From the marshy places of our lower nature the fever of lust and unsanctified passion comes. The stillness of inactivity and do-nothingness is always favourable to the cholera of doubt and unbelief. The great preventive is the soul-stirring breath of the Holy Ghost. When He comes as a mighty, rushing wind, the whole atmosphere of the life is purified.

THE TREASURE HUNT.

What a flutter was created in the minds of many by the £20 prize offered by the proprietor of a Scottish paper to the one who finds the hidden medallion. With what eagerness have many been searching night and day, heedless of who sees them, or of what others may think. They are seeking for treasure which they believe is within their reach. Although only one can possibly get the prize, yet hundreds will search. The treasure of "eternal life" lies hidden in the open field of God's Word, and although *every* searcher may find this prize, how few there be that seek it.

HANDFULS ON PURPOSE

SERIES IX

Preface.

IT is with deep thankfulness to the Giver of every good gift that we send forth this NINTH SERIES of "Handfuls on Purpose." It is very gratifying to us that the interest taken in them has been steadily growing from the first; and as they have been the means of leading many Christian workers into a closer study of the Word for themselves, we rejoice, as this was one of the chief objects of their publication.

In preparing these "Handfuls" we have sought to get at the heart-thoughts of the Word of God, so that weary workers and busy men might find food for the strengthening of their faith, and assisting in their work for the Master.

Without making any claim of literary or critical value, we have sought to give *original* matter, very little if any in the whole series having been copied.

We purpose, if the Lord will, adding one more Volume to the Series, and thus in measure encompassing the task on our heart, of going through the entire Book.

We esteem it a great privilege to have the opportunity of ministering in any small degree, to the encouragement and usefulness of the lowliest of Christ's servants, believing that "inasmuch as ye did it unto one of the least of these My brethren, ye have done it unto Me" (Matt. 25. 40). In this volume, which we trust will also be found helpful in "the quiet hour," we have once more humbly attempted to fulfil the Apostle's injunction, "Let him that is taught in the Word *communicate* unto him that teacheth in all good things" (Gal. 6. 6). What we have prayerfully received, we herewith prayerfully give.

JAMES SMITH.

Index of Subjects.

SEED THOUGHTS.

INDEX OF TEXTS.

Handfuls on Purpose

THE GREAT INVITATION.
Isaiah 1. 1-20.

Israel had fallen into degenerate times: and just as "Moses was born" in the time of national darkness and despair (Acts 7. 19, 20), so did the "Vision" come to Isaiah, the Son of Amos (v. 1). God has His own time and way of unveiling human guilt, and Divine mercy. These two pictures are exhibited before us here in this chapter.

I. Their Guilty Condition. They are charged with rebellion. "I have nourished and brought up sons and they have rebelled against Me." He nourished them and brought them up out of Egypt, and through the wilderness, into a land of privilege and plenty. Yet they rebelled against Him. Have we not also, as a people, been nourished and brought up in a land of Gospel light and privilege? Are we still rebelling against Him? This wretched condition was the result of a certain moral process. There was—

1. Inconsiderateness. "My people doth not consider." They became more thoughtless and thankless toward their Owner and Provider than the ox, or the ass. When we cease to *regard* the work of the Lord, and to *consider* the operations of His hands in our behalf, we have already entered the path of the backslider.

2. PRESUMPTION. "They have forsaken the Lord, they have provoked the Holy One of Israel" (v. 4). Their thoughtlessness has resulted in a wilful and deliberate departure from the Living God. When the backslider has determined to have his own will and way there will be a breaking of the Lord's bands, and a casting away of His cords (Psa. 2. 3).

3. PERVERSITY. "Why should ye be stricken?...ye will revolt more and more" (v. 5). God could not deal with them as sons in chastisement. So far gone were they that they would not "endure" it, but only harden their neck in more bitter revolt (Heb. 12. 5-8). It is pitiful in the extreme when God has to say, "In vain have I smitten your children: they receive no correction" (Jer. 2. 30).

4. CORRUPTION. "Whole head sick...whole heart faint ...no soundness...putrifying sores," etc. (vv. 5, 6). This sickness, and faintness, these wounds, and sores, can never be healed, bound up, and mollified, apart from Him whom they have despised and rejected. *Corruption* is the result of being separated from the Source of Life— the Living One. To forsake the Lord is to prefer corruption and death to health and life (Matt. 5. 13).

II. **His Merciful Offer.** "Come now let us reason together, saith the Lord," etc. (vv. 18-20). These words contain—

1. A REVELATION. They reveal the infinite mercifulness of the God whom they had rejected and offended. Why should *He* make the first offer to His rebel creatures? "Oh, 'twas love, wondrous love." While we were yet sinners Christ died for us.

2. AN INVITATION. "Come now, let us reason together." God recognises and declares man's kinship with Himself. "Come, let *us reason.*" He does not "reason" with the

brute creation. How gracious this invitation is. God might have driven out the whole nation from His presence as He drove out the man from the garden. "Come now," for where sin did abound grace hath much more abounded (Rom. 5. 20). "Come now," and let us reason together, for sin has been atoned at Calvary's Cross.

3. A Promise. "Though your sins be as scarlet, they shall be as white as snow." It has been said that "any man can dye his soul with sin, but only God can bleach it." God's power is in and behind His promise to turn the scarlet-dyed clothes of a harlot-soul into the white robes of a blood-washed saint. "Come *now*," for neither the number nor the depths of your sins need be any hindrance, salvation is of the Lord. "The blood of Jesus Christ, His Son, cleanseth us from all sin" (1 John 1. 7).

4. A Warning. "But if ye refuse and rebel, ye shall be devoured with the sword" (v. 20). This is the Divine ultimatum. If men refuse, and rebel against His free offer of mercy and forgiveness, if they will not yield to the Divine *reasonableness*, then their end is destruction. God is merciful, but God cannot lie (Titus 1. 2). If His promises are despised, His judgments will not slumber. Come now, for behold now is the day of salvation.

FAILURE IN THE MIDST OF PRIVILEGE.
Isaiah 5. 1-7.

This song of the prophet is a parable in honour of Jehovah, recalling His marvellous goodness to His people, and their failure and ingratitude to Him.

I. The Work Done. (vv. 1, 2). These two verses contain a brief, but perfect outline of Israel's history. The "fruitful hill"—Canaan. "Fenced" with promises. "Planted with the choicest vine"—His chosen people.

"Gathered out of the stones"—idols, etc. "Built a tower"—Temple. "Made a winepress"—Altar of Sacrifice. "He looked for grapes, and it brought forth wild grapes." Utter failure. All this is typical of what God in mercy hath done for us individually, and as a nation. We also have been brought out of the bondage of paganism and spiritual darkness, and planted beside the "fruitful hill" called Calvary.

II. **The Result Shown.** "He looked for grapes, and *it brought forth wild grapes.*" There was the semblance of the fruit desired, but they were *wild*, utterly inconsistent with their profession, and entirely unfit for His use. There was nothing to satisfy the soul of the great Planter and Protector. Fleshly works by professing Christians are but wild grapes. They that are in the flesh cannot please God. Our God is quick to discern the real character of the fruit of His planting. The *wild* grape is the outcome of the old, wild, carnal nature that has not yet been completely subdued by the new life. Be not deceived, God is not mocked.

III. **The Challenge Made.** "And now...judge, I pray you, betwixt Me and My vineyard, what could have been done more to My vineyard that I have not done in it" (vv. 3, 4). He had poured out His favours on His vineyard, but they had stained it with the blood of His Son. Could He have shown more love, more considerateness, more longsuffering mercy for His people than He did? Think of His dealings with them from Egypt to Canaan. Think also of His dealings with us, in the gift and sufferings of His Son, and in His merciful providence, that He might have us a people for the honour of His Name. Now, judge. What could He do more? (Matt. 23. 37).

IV. **The Doom Incurred.** "And now...I will tell you what I will do...I will take away the hedge...and break down the wall...I will also command the clouds that they rain no rain upon it" (vv. 5, 6). Desolation comes upon them because His *protection* is removed, and His *gifts* withheld. The darkness of doom is the absence of the light of Grace. When Christ was compelled to turn His back on the temple, He had to say, "Behold your house is *left unto you* desolate." To be left to ourselves is to be desolate. My Spirit will not always strive with man. Repent. Return. Believe. Submit.

FITNESS FOR SERVICE.
Isaiah 6. 1-8.

"In the year that King Uzziah died I saw." Uzziah had reigned fifty-two years in Jerusalem. During all that time "he was marvellously helped till he was strong." But when he became strong, in his own eyes, his heart was lifted up to his destruction. He died a leper, for the Lord had smitten him (2 Chron. 26). At such a mournful time, and in such distressing circumstances, the Vision of the thrice Holy One came to Isaiah. What a change from the vision of a defeated, leprous king to that of the exalted Throne of the Eternal One. Our day of shame and sorrow may be the day of a new revelation of hope.

I. A Glorious Vision. "I saw also the Lord sitting upon a throne, high and lifted up," etc. He had seen the downfall of Uzziah, but he saw *also* the glory of the unfailing God. This vision is the reality of that which was seen by the high priest in type, when he passed through the Veil into the "Holiest of All." The Lord enthroned, and His glory filling the house. The landscape was there all the time, with its riches and beauty, although we did not see it till the Veil of mist was rolled away. The pure in heart see God. We, like the prophet, must have

this vision if we would become meet for the service of
God. We must needs see Jesus, our Lord, who humbled
Himself to the death for us. "High and lifted up,"
exalted and enthroned, and the glory of His person and
work filling the temple. Satisfying to the full every
heavenly and Divine requirement (Heb. 2. 9).

II. **A Humbling Confession.** "Then said I, woe is
me! for I am undone (cut off)...I am a man of unclean
lips," etc. A vision of the highness and holiness of God
is a *self*-humbling sight. "Unclean lips" are but the
weapons of an unclean heart. It was when Job saw the
Lord that he abhorred himself (Job 42. 5, 6). It is in
His light that we see light clearly. This is God's method.
First, revelation, then self-discovery, self-abhorrence,
and self-abandonment. The vision of Bethlehem, Calvary
and Olivet, first smites with conviction then inspires
with hope. Having "seen the King, the Lord of Hosts,"
he has seen *his own* need, and the need of *the people*, for
they also have "unclean lips" (v. 5). There will be hope
for the people when the servants of God have had a clear
vision of God, and of their own condition and need.

III. **A Great Salvation.** "Then flew one of the
Seraphim unto me, having a live coal in his hand" (v. 6).
The vision, the confession, *"then"* the live coal. The
Seraphim fitly represents the personal work of the Holy
Spirit in taking the things of the "Altar" (the substitutionary
work of Christ), and applying them to the troubled and
unclean soul. The lips were touched with fire because
the sin was purged, and the iniquity taken away. ·This
salvation is threefold—

1. PARDON. "Thy sin is covered" *(margin)*. Covered
by the atoning blood of God's Lamb. Such a covering
as only God can cast over the guilt and heinousness of
sin (Heb. 1. 3).

2. PURITY. "Thine iniquity is taken away." Not only is sin covered, but the cause of sinning is dealt with. The iniquity, or lack of equity in the nature, toward God and man is taken away. *Renewed* in your mind, morally straightened.

3. POWER. "Lo, this hath touched thy lips." The touch of the living coal was as the sealing of the Holy Spirit (Eph. 1. 13). It was power from on high putting his *lips* into touch and perfect accord with the holy *Altar*. Only the fire-touched lips can speak out the real significance of the Cross of Christ. Pentecost was needed to emphasise Calvary.

IV. A Definite Commission. The call of God was distinctly heard. "I heard the voice of the Lord, saying, whom shall I send" (v. 8). It was not a voice commanding him to go, but a voice revealing to him, in a new fashion, God's longing desire to declare His mind and will to the people through His willing servants. Who will go for us? The man with the fire-touched lips is now ready to say, "Here am I, send me." He who has been cleansed, and claimed by the Altar fire, yields himself at once unto God as an instrument of righteousness. Now that his uncleanness and unwillingness have been taken away, the Lord says, "Go" (v. 9).

THE ALMIGHTY SANCTUARY.
ISAIAH 8. 11-14.

THIS message from the Lord to the prophet in times of distress and perplexity, contains a message of guidance and comfort to all who are in similar circumstances.

I. The Danger. Judah was in distress, because Syria and Israel had formed a confederacy against them. Many also in Judah were disaffected to the house of David, and in secret sympathy with the enemies of their country. They were "refusing the waters of Shiloah, which go softly" and rejoicing in the glory of a heathen king (v. 6). To which party should the prophet, the man of God, ally himself? This problem is with the Church to-day. There is a confederacy against it; organised parties of practical atheists. Within the Church herself there are also those who are "refusing the waters of Shiloah (Gospel), which go softly." Too softly for those who are the secret enemies to the Kingdom of God, and of His Christ, and who prefer the broad, turbulent waters of worldly pleasures and politics.

II. The Remedy. It consisted of—

1. A REVELATION. "The Lord spake to me...and instructed me that I should not walk in the way of this people" (v. 11). Judah had lost sight of God, and of their relationship to Him, and, as a result, were seeking to "associate themselves" with a prosperous, heathen kingdom. But God's Word to the prophet was, "thou shalt *not walk in the way of this people.*" The Church must choose whether she will separate herself unto God, or form a league with the aggressive forces of infidelity.

2. A REBUKE. "Say ye not, a confederacy...neither fear ye their fear, nor be afraid" (v. 12). God's Word warns us against glibly using the language of the ungodly. "Say ye not." Don't you fall into their snare, or into their manner or spirit of working. Don't you be terrified at their numbers and organisation. Neither be afraid of their proposals, or propaganda. They shall be "broken in pieces...their counsel shall come to naught" (vv. 9, 10). Those of Judah who were crying out for a confederacy with Assyria as a protection against the combined forces of Syria and Ephraim, were but showing their fatal weakness, as those who dwelt in the land of

"Immanuel" (v. 8). Such compromising on the part of God's people needs to be sternly rebuked. Whatever tends to lessen faith in God is dishonouring to Him.

3. A COUNSEL. "Sanctify the Lord of Hosts Himself, and let Him be your fear, and let Him be your dread" (v. 13). To "Sanctify the Lord of Hosts" is to *set Him apart* from all else as the sole object of our confidence. When our Lord said, "For their sakes I sanctify Myself" (John 17. 19), He shows the position He Himself hath chosen for His people's good. The dangers may seem great, the united forces in opposition to us may be formidable and fearful, but as the greater always overshadows the less, so, when the Lord of Hosts is sanctified by us and becomes our "fear and dread," we will not fear what man can do unto us. Fear Him. The dreaded mystery of holiness and power is with Him.

4. AN ASSURANCE. "And He shall be for a sanctuary," etc. (v. 14). He shall become an holy place of refuge and of rest for your soul. Hide thyself in God, and all the confederacies of men shall never prevail against thee. "God is our refuge and strength...*therefore* will not we fear." This hiding place is indeed a "dreadful place." But the more dreadful the place is the more secure are they who hide in it. He will become "a stone of stumbling and a rock of offence" to those who are opposed to His work and will. "They shall stumble and fall, and be broken, and be snared, and taken" that take counsel together against the Lord and His anointed ones. "Say ye not a confederacy," but say, God is my Sanctuary.

THE GREAT FEAST.
ISAIAH 25. 6-9.

THIS is another vision given to the prophet. He sees Mount Zion as a table spread with rich and abundant

provisions for "All people." It is the Millennial time
of fullness and victory for His ancient people, when
Jerusalem shall become a "praise in the earth," and when
all nations shall "Call Him Blessed," who is their God
and King. While the dispensational aspect must not be
overlooked, we should like to read these verses, for our
personal profit, more in the light of the Gospel of the
Grace of God.

I. **The Place.** "In this mountain." God not only
appoints the event, but also the place where it shall be
accomplished. He hath appointed Zion as the place
of His revealed glory. He also appointed "the place
called Calvary" for the revelation of His grace. Here the
Lord of Hosts hath made a feast for all people.

II. **The Provision.** It implies ample sufficiency for
the whole need of man. There is—

1. PERFECT SATISFACTION. "Fat things full of marrow
...wines on the lees well refined." Blessings that
strengthen, and that cheer and inspire. There is no leanness
of soul, for those who feed in the work and fullness
of Jesus Christ. Every promise of His is full of marrow
and fatness. The wine of His Word is always on the lees
of eternal verities. It is old and good. "Wherefore
spend money for that which...satisfieth not? Hearken
diligently unto Me, and eat that which is good, and let
your soul delight itself in fatness" (Isa. 55. 1, 2).

2. FULL SALVATION. (1) The *"Covering" of Darkness*
has been destroyed. "He will destroy the face of the
covering cast over the people" (v. 7). The darkened
understanding has been enlightened (Eph. 4. 18). The
true light now shineth. (2) The *"Veil" of unbelief* has
been taken away. This veil that is "Spread over the
nations" is taken away by *turning* to the Lord (2 Cor.
3. 15-18).

3. The POWER OF DEATH has been destroyed. "He will swallow up death in victory" (v. 8). Christ, in dying, hath destroyed death, and him that hath the power of death (Heb. 2. 14). The power of death, in itself, is a tremendous power, it is truly the "terrors of death."

4. The ASSURANCE OF COMFORT has been given. "The Lord God will wipe away tears from off all faces." The proofs of sorrow and suffering are visible in many faces. The day of His salvation is the day of peace and rest for the soul. A French writer has asked, "Where are now the calm, peaceful faces that were seen long ago?" Christ is our peace, "My peace I give unto you."

5. The "REBUKE" OF FAILURE is taken away (v. 8). The Salvation of God includes deliverance from a life of stumbling and failure. Oh, what reproach lies upon the servants of God to-day, because this full Salvation is not realised. God means all this for His people. "For the Lord hath *spoken* it."

III. **The Testimony.** "It shall be said in that day, Lo, this is our God" (v. 9). When God's Salvation is experienced there is no doubt at all as to its God-likeness. This is the expression of a saved and satisfied soul. The word God is in the plural here, and has reference to the Trinity. To know Him, and Jesus Christ whom He hath sent by the Holy Spirit, is Eternal Life. Those who can say *"This* is our God," can confidently add, "And He will save us," for, "We have waited for Him, we will be glad and rejoice in His Salvation" (v. 9). We speak that we do know. In a fuller sense, this will be the testimony of God's people, when the Lord Himself shall descend from Heaven with a shout" (1 Thess. 4. 16, 17). Meanwhile His Salvation is offered unto "All people" (Luke 2. 10). "Look unto Me, and be ye saved, all the ends of the earth; for I am God" (Isa. 45. 22).

REBELLIOUS CHILDREN.
ISAIAH 30. 1-3.

OH, how sad it is when the "woe" of the rebellious has to be pronounced by the Lord on His own children.

I. **The Nature of It.** It is seen in their *counsellors.* "They take counsel, but not of ME." Worldly wisdom is preferred to heavenly. It is seen in their *covering.* "They cover with a covering, but not of *My Spirit.*" They clothe themselves with pride, and fleshly energy, instead of the power of the Holy Spirit. It is seen in their *walk.* "That walk to go down into Egypt." Their faces are toward the world, and their desire is to get into its ways. It is seen in their *Motives.* "To strengthen themselves in the strength of Pharaoh, and to trust in the shadow of Egypt." They seek worldly strength, and worldly protection, to advance their cause. The heart that is in rebellion against God, and His Christ, is certain to seek the help of the ungodly.

II. **The Result of It.** The result is *"Shame."* "Therefore shall the strength of Pharaoh be your shame." The strength of Pharaoh may do for a Pharaoh, but it will be *your* shame as a professed child of God. The strength of Pharaoh lay in the arm of flesh, and there is a curse upon the man "that maketh flesh his arm, and whose *heart departeth from the Lord"* (Jer. 17. 5). Trust in the shadow of Egypt will be your *confession* (v. 3). Nothing but shame and confusion will come upon the Church of God, if, for the sake of popularity and prestige, she allies with the godless forces of to-day.

OUR REFUGE AND OUR REMEDY.
ISAIAH 32. 1-5.

MAN'S character needs a "double cure." A place of refuge from danger, and a remedy from the disease of sin.

When "A King shall reign in righteousness" within, then the princes of that Kingdom "Shall rule in justice" (v. 1). Note the—

I. **Need Suggested.** We are exposed to the "wind" and the "tempest." These are the ordinary, and extraordinary trials and dangers that all have to face. The "wind," the common current of popular error: the "tempest," the crushing influence of temptation and lust. Then there is the "dry place." The experience of disappointment and helplessness, finding the world's cisterns empty in the time of deepest need. Then comes the "weary land" experience. A fainting of the heart at the discovery that the world provides no resting place for the weary feet of an anxious pilgrim.

II. **Refuge Appointed.** "A MAN shall be an hiding place." Who is this Man? Jehovah says, this is "The Man that is My Fellow" (Zech. 13. 7). The One Mediator between God and men, the *Man* Christ Jesus (1 Tim. 2. 5). He is—

1. A HIDING PLACE. That is the feature of His character as Redeemer and Lord. The wind that drives away the chaff cannot move those who hide in Him. "I flee to Thee to hide me."

2. A COVERT from the tempest. A place of secrecy where the most powerful forces outside cannot find the hidden one.

3. The SHADOW of a great rock. The strength of this protection is here indicated, and especially the blessed fact that this shadow can be enjoyed by those who are presently in "a weary land." "Behold the *Man.*"

III. **Blessings Enjoyed.** All who sit under His shadow have great delight. Here are several things which characterise those saved by the Lord, and who are abiding under the court of His wings enjoying His fellowship.

1. Their EYES are clear. "The eyes of them that see shall not be dim" (v. 3). They have seen their need, they have seen their opportunity, now they see God.

2. Their EARS are opened. "The ears of them that hear shall hearken." They have heard His invitation, they have obeyed His call, now they eagerly listen to His Word.

3. Their HEART is taught. "The heart also of the hasty shall understand knowledge" (v. 4). Yes, those who rest in Him as their "hiding place" shall be taught of the Lord (Isa. 54. 13). The hasty heart shall be righted there.

4. Their TONGUE is loosed. "The tongue of the stammerers shall be ready to speak plainly." There is nothing like the power of the truth of the Gospel for taking the stammer out of a man's tongue, and making him *ready* to speak plainly." Plain speaking, on the part of the saved ones, is expected by the Saviour.

5. Their LIFE is purified. "The vile person shall no more be called liberal, nor the crafty said to be bountiful" (v. 5, R.V., *margin*). A purified life means purified morals. Righteousness with God means practical righteousness with our fellow men. The man whose eyes are opened, and whose tongue has been loosed to "speak plainly," will not laud the immoral and the crafty because of their big subscriptions, or high social position. He is no respecter of persons, and must call things by their right names.

THE EXCELLENCY OF OUR GOD.
ISAIAH 35. 1-6.

IN the light of New Testament teaching, this portion is most inspiring. There is a—

I. **Vision of Hope.** "They shall see the glory of the Lord, the excellency of our God." How is this glory, or excellency, to be seen? Here, as in the Gospels, it is seen in the transforming power of His grace. The "wilderness," the "solitary place," and the "desert," are made glad and beautiful because of it. The excellency of our God is seen in imparting to the barren waste the majesty of Lebanon, the beauty of Carmel, and the fruitfulness of Sharon (v. 2). Israel, as a nation, is that "wilderness, and solitary place," which shall yet "be glad...and blossom abundantly" at the revelation of the Lord: but *now* we may see the excellency of our God in the face of Jesus Christ (2 Cor. 4. 6). What transformations He hath wrought in the "wilderness and solitary places" of the souls of men, and of social life!

II. Condition of Need. The people of God are here reminded of three sources of weakness that are hindering their life and work. They have *"weak hands."* Hands that hang down (Heb. 12. 12). The hands represent the instruments of work. What could even Hercules do with a hammer of soap? How can a servant work, or a soldier fight, with weak hands? They are powerless for service. Then there is the *"feeble knees."* They cannot walk straight and steady. They are easily upset. A little opposition, or the wind of some new doctrine, is enough to impede their progress, or turn them aside. Their knees are feeble, through the lack of the practice of prayer. Another weakness is seen in the *"fearful heart."* This is the worst of all, and the cause of all. When the heart is pure and strong, the hands and the knees will soon be strong and steady. Fearfulness is the result of the lack of faith.

III. Message of Cheer. The servant of God is commissioned to *strengthen* the weak hands, to *confirm* the feeble knees, and *encourage* the fearful in heart (v. 4). But how is this to be done? Never were many of God's people so much in need of this, as now. With the work, comes the message of power, "Behold *your God* will come." The excellency of your God consists in this, that He delights to make the desert blossom as the rose, and to make the weak, the feeble, and the fearful, to triumph in His strength. Your God who will come with vengeance on your enemies, and a recompense to His own, He will save you. Let not your heart be troubled because of the signs of the times. Ye believe in God. Behold, He cometh with clouds (Titus 2. 13; Rev. 1. 7). Say to them that are feeble and fearful, Be strong; Behold your God.

IV. Work of Grace. The excellency of our God is seen in making—

1. The EYES of the blind to see (v. 5). The eyes are the windows of the soul. In spiritual blindness, it is the *spirit* that is blind; to such, sight is a new faculty (Acts 26. 18; Eph. 1. 18).

2. The EARS of the deaf to hear. As with sight, so with hearing; the ear is but the instrument, it is the spirit within that is made to hear Him.

3. The FEET of the lame to leap (v. 6). The morally helpless, and crippled, by sin and iniquity, are made to leap like an hart. Salvation means renewal (Acts 3. 2-10).

4. The TONGUE of the dumb to sing. Tongues that were silent for God, will, at His touch, break forth into praise (Psa. 15. 15). For in the wilderness of the unrenewed and wasted life, the waters of grace shall break out as streams in the desert. Ye shall see the glory, and the excellency of our God.

THE POWER OF PRAYER.

ISAIAH 37. 14-20.

THE historical setting should be closely studied. A great trouble had come to Hezekiah, the king, because of the

Assyrian invasion, and the imperious attitude of Rabshakeh the captain. "Trouble" has been said to be "A Divine diet for the new man." It is often more profitable than it is palatable.

I. The Cause of His Trouble. It was A letter." Only a letter, but a veritable "Messenger of Satan" to buffet him. For some the postman's bag may contain moral and social torpedoes. Who knows what the next post may bring? This was an attempt to *destroy his faith* in God (v. 10), to *dispossess* him of his inheritance, and to bring him into *bondage*. The enemies of our souls are always active toward the same end. Their letters may be beautifully written, but they are terribly bitter.

II. What He Did With It. "He spread it before the Lord" (v. 14). This solemn act revealed his *faith in God*. He did not spread it before the "face of Heaven," but before the face of an Almighty Personality. "He that cometh to God must believe that He is" (Heb. 11. 6). This also shows his *thoroughness*. He *spread* it. He laid the whole matter, from beginning to end, right before Him. Be definite in your dealings with God. Be as honest and confidential as He wishes you to be. Keep back nothing. Whatever is a trouble to you is interesting to your God and Father.

III. How He Succeeded. "The angel of the Lord" became his defence (v. 36). His argument was simple, but irresistible. "Now therefore, O Lord our God, save us from his hand, that all the kingdoms of the earth may know that Thou art the Lord" (v. 20). "When the angel of death spreads his wings in the blast," woe be to those who fight against the Kingdom of God. By the blast of God they perish (Job. 4. 9). Is there any sorrow too great, or circumstance too perplexing, that the

prayer of faith cannot bring comfort and deliverance?
"If ye have faith as a grain of mustard seed...nothing
shall be impossible unto you" (Matt. 17. 20).

POWER FOR THE FAINT.
ISAIAH 40. 28-31.

"HAST thou not known?" There is, oh! so much of the
goodness of God revealed to us in His Word that we have,
as yet, failed to understand or to profit by, that we
greatly need a question like this to arrest afresh our
attention to our real need, and His Almighty fullness.
We are reminded here of the—

I. **Need of Power.** "He giveth power to the faint."
He speaks of *power* because he knows we need it. It is
for lack of power that we "faint," and have "no might,"
and are "weary," and the "young men utterly fall" (v. 30).
There is to-day much fainting and weariness because of a
conscious inability to overcome the power of current
evils. An unhealthy moral atmosphere makes it difficult
for a spiritual man to breathe. Even "young men"
destitute of this power are an utter failure.

II. **Source of Power.** "Hast thou not heard that the
Everlasting God...fainteth not, neither is weary?" (v. 28).
"Hast thou not known *Me*?" (John 14. 9). All power
is given unto Him. All creative and sustaining power is
His. All fullness dwells in Him. If we are workers
together with Him who fainteth not, why should we
faint? Why this weariness in us if He who never is
weary is working in us to will and to do of His good
pleasure?

III. **Nature of Power.** Power is not something we
put on, it is something that puts on us. Something that
enters into our being, bringing increased capacity and
responsibility. Power, like love, dwells in the life of

God. To have more of His life means more of His power. The spirit of life is the spirit of power (Acts 1. 8). This power is not that of a new resolve, or of youthful vigour, or natural enthusiasm, it is the "power of God," because God has come in mightier measure into the life. Abundance of life means abundance of power.

IV. **Condition of Power.** "They that wait upon the Lord" (v. 31). This *waiting* upon the Lord must be interpreted as an honest confession, that there has been fainting and failure in the past. Because the promise is to the "faint, and to them that have no might" (v. 29). *His* strength can only be made perfect in weakness (2 Cor. 12. 9; Heb. 11. 34). Wait on the Lord, and change your weakness into His strength (v. 31, *margin*).

V. **Evidence of Power.** "They shall mount up...run, and not be weary...walk, and not faint." They mount up, like eagles, into a higher and purer atmosphere of life where they can run, and not be weary, walk and not faint. The enduement of power implies an ascension of the life into a higher and more mysterious plane of living, far above all the principalities and powers of earth and Hell that would discourage and destroy. He *giveth* power to the faint.

_____

FEAR THOU NOT.

ISAIAH 41. 9-16.

WHAT is here said of Israel? The seed of Abraham is also true of those who are His spiritual seed, the children of God by faith. These promises are made to "My servant whom I have chosen" (vv. 8, 9). If you are a servant chosen of God, then these promises are virtually for you. Each promise is a reason why you should "Fear not." He says, "Fear thou not, for—

I. **I am with thee.** "With you as your shield and great reward" (Gen. 15. 1).

II. I am **thy God.** Thy God is good, and thy God is almighty.

III. I will **strengthen** thee. If He is the strength of your life of whom should *you* be afraid? (Psa. 27. 1).

IV. I will **help** thee (v. 10). This implies co-operation. There is no help like His.

V. I will **uphold** thee. The right hand of His righteousness will stay you up.

VI. I will **defend** thee. "They that war against thee shall be as nothing, and as a thing of naught" (v. 12).

VII. I will **use** thee. "I will make *thee* a new, sharp, thrashing instrument" (v. 15). Every redeemed and consecrated soul will be a *new* instrument in His hand.

VIII. I will be **glorified** in thee. "Thou shalt rejoice in the Lord, and shalt glory in the Holy One of Israel" (v. 16; see Jer. 9. 24).

HOPE FOR THE NEEDY.
Isaiah 41. 17-20.

The "needy," who are they? In every city and country their name is legion. But the "needy" here are the most hopeless of all mortals. Look at this picture of—

I. **Lamentable Failure.** "The poor and needy seek water, and there is none. They are keenly conscious of their need, they are "poor," they seek a common mercy— "water"—they seek it where it cannot be found—"there is none." And they have been seeking until "their tongue faileth for thirst." What a picture of disappointment and desolation. While "the common salvation" is as plentiful and as cheap as water, yet, how many poor and needy souls are seeking it where "there is none," in their own hearts, prayers, and works.

II. **Inspiring Promises.** Israel was not asked to dig

wells in the wilderness, they were to drink from the smitten rock. Salvation is of the Lord. To the "poor and needy" three precious promises are given.

1. I will ANSWER them (R.V.). There is no answer to this thirst anywhere else but in God Himself. God is the only answer to the cry of humanity. He so loved the world that He gave His Son. Look unto Me, and be ye saved. God's answer is near when our absolute failure is recognised and confessed.

2. "I will OPEN RIVERS in the bare heights" (v. 18, R.V.) God's fullness of blessing often comes from unexpected sources, "bare heights." "My ways *are not* your ways saith the Lord." A tongue failing for thirst is "a bare height out of which He is able to bring rivers of water" (John 7. 37-39).

3. "I will PLANT in the wilderness the cedar...in the desert the fir tree and the pine" (v. 19). This is part of God's answer to the poor and needy wilderness of man's soul. It needs not only the cleansing and refreshing rivers, but the imparting of new principles for the beautifying of the life-like trees in the desert.

III. God-honouring Results. "That they may *see*, and *know*, and *consider*, and *understand* together that the hand of the Lord hath done this" (v. 20). All His works praise Him. Our transfigured lives are a testimony to others of the good hand of our God upon us. When, instead of the thorn and the brier, there comes up the fir, and the myrtle, it shall be to the Lord for a name, and an everlasting sign (Isa. 55. 13). It is a poor testimony for God when the tongue faileth for thirst. But He delighteth to answer our need, even for His Own Name's sake. It is when the new song is put into our mouth that, "Many shall see and fear, and shall trust in the Lord" (Psa. 40. 3).

SPIRITUAL ISRAEL

OR, WITNESSES FOR GOD. ISAIAH 43. 1-10.

IT is not meet to take the children's bread, and cast it to dogs; neither is it meet to take the Jewish bread, and give it all to the Gentiles. The great and precious promises made in the chapter are for Israel, and much important truth is lost by applying them only to the Church. Israel, like the Church of God, has a glorious and triumphant future before it. Still, all that is here said of the Jew is perfectly true of the Church, and may be forcibly applied to all Christians who are the spiritual seed of Abraham.

I. They are Purchased. "Fear not, I have redeemed thee, I have called thee by thy name, thou art Mine." As Israel was redeemed out of Egyptian bondage and darkness, called into a separate life, and claimed by God as His own, so have we been redeemed from the bondage of sin and Satan, separated from the world, and claimed by our Redeemer as His own purchased possession. Ye are not your own, for ye are *bought* with a price, redeemed by the precious blood of Christ.

II. They are Preserved. "When thou passest through the waters I will be with thee...When thou walkest through the fire thou shalt not be burned" (v. 2). No nation has ever passed through such deep and troublous waters as the Jewish. No other people have had to walk through such fire of suffering and persecution as they. Yet Jacob has not been overthrown, nor has the flame destroyed him. The reason is, "I am with thee." As it is with Israel, so is it with the Church. Only, the sufferings of Israel have been for her own sins, while the sufferings of the Church have been for Christ's sake. Through the fire and the waters of testing and trial must every redeemed one pass. But "Fear not" is the Saviour's word of cheer, for, "I will be with thee" (Psa. 66. 12; see Psa. 23. 4).

III. They are Precious. "Thou wast precious in My sight...and I have loved thee" (v. 4). How a wayward, backsliding people can become precious to God is one of the mysteries of His grace. This fact is a proof that whom God loves He loves intensely (Dan. 7. 6). God can do nothing superficially. If He saves, He saves to the uttermost. When He gives life, it is life in abundance. Their preciousness to God is a guarantee of their protection and security. We are precious in His sight, not only because of what He has given for us, but because of what we are now, as members of the body of Christ, His Son.

IV. They are Privileged. "I have created Him for My glory" (v. 7). The *creation* of Israel as a nation is for the glory of God, and He shall yet be glorified in His people in this present world (Hosea 1. 10). We, like them, are His workmanship, created unto good works, which God hath before ordained, that we should walk in them. It is to the praise of the glory of His grace that He hath made us accepted in the beloved (Eph. 1. 5, 6). The Church of God is a new creation in Christ Jesus for His own glory, and this glory will yet be manifested in the ages to come (Eph. 2. 7).

V. They are Powerful. "Ye are My witnesses, saith the Lord" (v. 10). A witness is one who has sufficient knowledge to constitute a *proof*. Knowledge, like steam, is a power that cannot be ignored. The Jew is a witness to Christ crucified, the Christian is a witness to Christ risen. Judah and the Church are both witnesses for God. The Jews had committed to them the oracles of God (Rom. 3. 1, 2), which gave them power for God. The Church has committed unto it the Holy Spirit of God that it might have witnessing power for God (Acts 1. 8). Every Jew is a witness, so is every member of the body of Christ. Our witness-bearing depends on what we are, not what we say. If we are monuments of His grace we shall be witnesses for Him. What was said of Christ is true also of every man in Him, "Behold I have given him for a witness to the people."

———

GOD'S APPEAL TO THE BACKSLIDING.
ISAIAH 44. 21, 22.

THE goodness and longsuffering mercy of our God nowhere shines out more impressively than in His pitiful appeal to His backsliding people. "O Jacob," may remind them of their past pride and failure. "O Israel," of what His transforming grace had made them. Jacob, the wrestler, was turned into Israel the prince.

I. **An Urgent Call.** "O Jacob...O Israel...return unto Me." This clearly implies that they had turned away from Him, and that, for His own, and their own sakes, He longed for their return. All backsliding is a turning away of the affections from God to some other person or thing.

II. **A Powerful Argument.** He gives ample reasons why they should return.

1. I have FORMED thee. Israel, as a nation, would have had no existence but for the electing grace of God. They were chosen, not because they were better than others, but because it pleased Him to call them. Backsliders, think of that! God requireth that which is past.

2. I have FORGIVEN thee. "I have blotted out as a thick cloud...thy sins." Have you forgotten the time when He caused the sweet sense of His forgiving love to float into your soul? (Psa. 32. 1, 2).

3. I have NOT FORGOTTEN thee. "Thou shalt not be forgotten of Me." In your wilful wandering you have, like the prodigal, forgotten Him, but He has not forgotten you. "Return."

4. I have REDEEMED thee. The fact that He hath purchased you with His own blood that you might be His own peculiar treasure, is another strong reason why you should return unto Him (1 Cor. 6. 20).

5. I have CLAIMED thee. Return, for, "Thou art My servant." He has not only a claim upon your person, but also upon your *service.* Think of His infinite goodness in still acknowledging you—even in your present, sinful, and profitless condition—as His servant. "I will arise and go to my father." _____

GOD'S RELATIONSHIP TO HIS PEOPLE.

Isaiah 48. 16-18.

"COME ye near unto Me, hear ye this." Here is something God is specially desirous that we should give heed to. Let us draw near unto Him, and hear it as fresh from His own lips. "Oh, hear it again." That Christ is the eternal Son of God who was with Him "from the beginning" and who was sent by "the Lord God, and His Spirit," and who hath declared Him who is—

I. Thy Redeemer. "Thy Redeemer, the Holy One of Israel." Who gave Himself for our sins that He might redeem us from all iniquity. Jehovah is our Redeemer in the person of His Son.

II. Thy Teacher. "I am the Lord thy God which teacheth thee to profit." His teaching is not only instruction for the mind, but the impartation of life and light, of ability to receive and to act. He worketh in us both to will and to do (Psa. 25. 8-10).

III. Thy Leader. "I am the Lord thy God...which leadeth thee by the way that thou shouldest go." As He led Israel about and instructed him (Deut. 32), so, by His Spirit, doth He still lead His redeemed people. The Church never was in greater need of being "Led by the Lord" than now.

IV. **Thy Keeper**. "O that thou hadst hearkened...then had thy peace been as a river." They are kept in perfect peace whose mind is *stayed* on Him. Great peace have they which love Thy law (Psa. 119. 165). Hearken to the voice of Him whose blood preacheth peace, and whose life is the pledge that thy peace may be as full and constant as "a river."

DIVINE QUESTIONS FOR THE BACKSLIDING.

Isaiah 50. 1-3.

The Jews were captives in Babylon. The sin of idolatry which, in God's sight, was the sin of spiritual adultery, had broken their marriage covenant with the Lord, and separated them from Him. It would seem that while they were in Babylon they murmured and complained against God, and the severity of their condition. Backsliders are slow to blame themselves for their present bondage and misery. But the Lord demands that they face the cause of their separation from Him by asking them five pointed questions, which appeal to any backslider.

I. **"Where is the Bill of Your Mother's Divorcement?"** Under the law, and because of the hardness of their hearts (Matt. 19. 8), Moses allowed a man to divorce—cut off—his wife if found unfaithful, by giving her a "bill of divorcement." This bill was the *evidence* that she had been put away by her husband (Deut. 24. 1). The Lord demands of those grumbling sons, born in Babylon of backsliding parents, to produce the bill of their divorcement on the evidence that *He* had cut them off. Where is the proof that God is to blame for the backslider's failure and misery? Your iniquities have separated between you and your God (Isa. 59. 2).

II. **"To Which of My Creditors Have I Sold You?"**

Another permission allowable under the law was, that a father had a right, if oppressed with debt, to sell his children (Exod. 21. 7: Neh. 5. 5). The Divine argument is, did I sell you because of My poverty? Have I had to part with you because I was not rich enough to keep you? If I have sold you, then, name the creditor to whom I have sold you. Backslider, what have you to say to this? Have you separated yourself from God because He had not enough to supply all your need? The truth must be out, and here it is, "Behold, for your iniquities have ye sold yourselves" (v. 1, *l.c.*)

III. "Wherefore...When I called was there None to Answer?" Another charge brought against them was that they had refused to respond to the call of His servants, the prophets. They gave Him no answer, but remained deaf to His entreaties. How is it that while you are so dissatisfied with your position and condition, you still refuse to obey His call to repentance as the way out of bondage into liberty and restoration? He is still calling through His Son, and by His Spirit, to the self-oppressed backsliders. How is it that so few answer Him?

IV. "Is My Hand Shortened at All that it Cannot Redeem?" You may have gone far away, but have you gone beyond His redemption point? Have you gone beyond the length of His arm to reach you? Backsliders, answer this question. Is His hand too short for your rescue? Is His blood too weak for your redemption? You think of your distance from God, will you also think of the length of His arm of mercy? He is able to save to the uttermost. If we confess our sins He is faithful and just to forgive us.

V. "Have I no Power to Deliver?" Your miserable, Babylonian bondage seems to indicate that your God hath no power to deliver you. As long as you remain in your backsliding state you are dragging the Name and Character of God into public dishonour (chap. 52. 5). As a proof of His saving power He reminds them of what He had done. At His rebuke the Red Sea was made dry, and the river of Jordan made as a wilderness for them. He had power also to "Clothe the heavens with blackness, and make sackcloth their covering" (v. 3). This He did when He delivered them out of Egypt (Exod. 10. 21). This He did when He gave His Son to die for us on the Cross (Luke 23. 44). Has He no power to save thee? Then why art thou not saved?

LET US STAND TOGETHER—SUBSTITUTION.

ISAIAH 50. 4-9.

THESE words are mighty with solemn significance, coming as they do—prophetically—from the lips of the suffering Son of God. Although spoken 700 years before the birth of Christ they are becoming, only, on His lips.

I. His Wisdom. "The Lord God hath given me the tongue of them that are taught that I should know how to sustain with words him that is weary" (v. 4, R.V.). He had the tongue of the taught even when twelve years of age (Luke 2. 46, 47). Never man spake like this Man. He was taught of God (John 8. 28. 38). He is the "Wisdom of God." His words hath sustained the weary in all generations. Let them dwell in you richly (Col. 3. 16).

II. His Obedience. "The Lord God hath opened mine ear, and I was not rebellious" (v. 5). Having heard the Word of God, and learned all that it meant for Him, He turned not back, but said, "Lo, I come...I delight to do Thy will O My God, yea Thy law is within My heart" (Psa. 40. 6-8). How often, on our part, hath the open ear been followed with a rebellious will! We see, but do not delightfully obey the vision in a whole-hearted consecration, but often "turn away backward."

III. His Sufferings. "I gave my back to the smiters ...I hid not My face from shame and spitting" (v. 6). He *"gave,"* and He *"hid not."* Assuring us that His sufferings were purely voluntary. They would be of no value otherwise. The *smiting* and the *spitting* suggest the twofold character of our Lord's humiliation and agony. The physical and the moral suffering and derision. The scattering of the flock of Israel over the face of the earth is an evidence that the Shepherd has been smitten (Matt. 26. 31).

IV. His Confidence. "The Lord God will help Me, therefore shall I not be confounded...I know that I shall not be ashamed" (v. 7). He was helped, and not confounded, in the hour of His extreme sorrow, for an angel from Heaven strengthened Him (Luke 22. 43). No one ever needed help more than He did, and no one was ever so confident of getting it. He knew that He was doing the will of the Lord God, and so doubted not. His face was set "like a flint," because there was no wavering in his heart.

V. His Testimony. "He is near that justifieth Me" (v. 8). God was near to Him, and He knew that God was justifying Him in all that He said and suffered. Justified in the Spirit He could truly say, "I am not alone." The sufferings of Christ were also the sufferings of the Father. God was in Christ reconciling the world unto Himself.

VI. His Invitation. "Let us stand together." Might we not take this as our Lord's appeal to His own. He has identified Himself with us, now we are invited to identify ourselves with Him. It is absolutely true that with Christ we fall or stand *together*. Hear Him say, "Let us stand together"—

1. In the PLACE OF CONDEMNATION. He bore *our* sins

in His own body. He suffered *for us* the Just for the unjust. Let us stand with Him at that Cross bearing together the terrible shame of it. We are condemned already. Let us acknowledge it.

2. In the LIBERTY OF JUSTIFICATION. If we were judged in Christ we shall also be justified in Him (v. 8, *f.c.*) He was justified in that He was raised again from the dead; herein is our justification (Rom. 4. 25). Let us stand together on resurrection ground (2 Cor. 5. 12, R.V.).

3. In the LIFE OF CONSECRATION. We are workers together with Him. The life of service is a life of holy fellowship and activity in the Lord. Your enemy is mighty, and your strength is but weakness, therefore, says He, "Let us stand together." In standing together with Him we shall also be found standing together with one another. Then, finally, we shall "stand together" in the presence of His glory, being "glorified together."

THE GREAT REPORT.

ISAIAH 53. 1.

THE Prophet, as he was moved by the Holy Ghost, passes in vision down through 700 years into the very midst of the days of Christ's humiliation and suffering, and speaks as an eyewitness. Infidelity has no reasonable explanation of this record so absolutely true to fact. "Who hath believed our report?" Notice the—

I. **Nature of the Report**. See chapter 52. 7-15. It contains "Good tidings of Good." It was the publication of "peace" and "salvation" (v. 7). It refers to the prudence and exalted character of Christ the Servant (v. 13). It reveals the *astonishing* fact that His sufferings would be unique among the sons of men (v. 14). It also sounds the note of final victory (v. 15). It is a true report.

II. **Character of the Publishers.** "Who hath believed *our* report." To Him gave all the prophets witness (Acts 10. 43). The prophets, moved by the Holy Spirit, were God's witnesses. They were workers together with Him. The report was His through them. There is no exaggeration or false colouring about it. These reporters are in real sympathy with God and His work. So they ask Him, "Who hath believed *our* report?" Paul beseeched men in Christ's stead (2 Cor. 5. 20).

III. **Responsibility of the Hearers.** "Who hath *believed*?" The message is the most wonderful and timely that ears have ever heard. The reporters are the most trustworthy that have ever spoken. The demand is the most reasonable that was ever made—faith. Who hath *believed* our report. Faith cometh by hearing, and hearing by the Word of God. Here, then, is God's Word of grace and salvation. Where is your faith? It is not enough to believe in the Teacher like Nicodemus. We must show our faith like Rebekah who heard, believed, and followed (Gen. 24). Without faith it is impossible to please Him.

_____

THE ARM OF THE LORD.

Isaiah 53. 1.

The "arm" is here used as a figure of the true Christ as the Head of the Church. He is also the "Arm of the Lord." This metaphor is deeply suggestive. The—

I. **Significance of It.** "The arm of the Lord" (Jehovah). It is the symbol of almighty power. Christ is the power of God. This power is a *living* power, an arm that is vitally connected with the Personal and Eternal God. It is no dead force like hydraulic pressure, but a power that worketh by love. His arm is also the symbol of mercy. Though His arm be strong to smite, 'tis also strong to save. His arm hath brought salvation (Isa. 59. 16).

II. Baring of It. "The Lord hath made bare His holy arm" (chap. 62. 10). In making bare His arm (Christ) the Lord has revealed His great power both to smite and to save. What mighty spiritual muscle there is unveiled in the life and death of Jesus Christ. It is the work of the Holy Spirit, and of every preacher of the Gospel, to make manifest the naked and almighty saving arm of God.

THE MAN OF SORROWS.

Isaiah 53. 3-6.

THE world in every age has had many a sorrowful man, but there has been only one "Man of Sorrows." The sorrows of the Son of Man were entirely unique and unparalleled. His was the sorrow of a unique—

I. Humiliation. Many a man, nurtured in the lap of opulence, has, through accident or failure, been reduced to poverty and shame, but no one ever had so much to give up as Christ had when He "emptied Himself, and took upon Him the form of a servant...becoming obedient unto death" (Phil. 2. 7, 8, R.V.). He who was rich—how rich!—for our sakes became poor, and, Oh, how poor!

II. Opposition. The contradiction that He suffered at the hands of sinners against Himself was also unique. Although "A Man of Sorrows" He was despised and rejected of men. Handel was found weeping while setting these words to music. The common sympathy bestowed on ordinary, suffering mortals was denied Him. The opposition of Satan to the "Death of the Cross" was another bitter element in the sorrows of the Saviour. Note the temptation in the wilderness. The *rebuking* of the wind; the same word used when dealing with "unclean spirits." The rebuking of Peter, and the "get thee behind Me. Satan," when he said "far be it from Thee, Lord" (referring to His suffering death). Even when He was on the Cross they cried, "Come down," and we will believe in Thee.

III. **Anticipation.** Many a time have we been constrained to say, "It is good for us that we do not know what is before us" when some sudden and dire calamity has befallen us. These things are mercifully hidden from us. But Christ foresaw all that was before Him. He came, not to be ministered unto, but to minister, and to give His life a ransom for many. "I, if I be lifted up from the earth...This He said signifying what death He should die" (John 12. 32, 33). His was also the sorrow of a unique—

IV. **Separation.** He trod the winepress *alone*. He was perfectly at home in Heaven, but He was awfully alone on earth. His very nature, as Holy and Divine, made Him "Separate from sinners," although, He was made in the "likeness of sinful flesh." Circumstances, disposition, and choice, often bring upon men the sorrow of a separated life. No one could feel this so intensely as the Son of Man who was also the Son of God.

V. **Relationship.** His was emphatically the sorrow of a unique relationship. "Surely He hath borne *our* griefs, and carried *our* sorrows" (v. 4). He alone could do this as a fond, devoted mother carries the griefs and sorrows of a beloved, suffering child. So intense was His love and sympathy for us as sinful men that He could not refrain from bearing our griefs and our sorrows. It was in this wholly, devoted One that Jehovah was pleased to lay "the iniquity of us all" (v. 6). It was for us that He poured out His holy, sorrowful soul unto death (v. 12). Behold and see if there be any sorrow like unto *My* sorrow. Is it nothing to you, all ye that pass by? (Lam. 1. 12).

"FEAR NOT,"

OR, THE HERITAGE OF THE LORD'S SERVANTS.
ISAIAH 54.

"FEAR NOT" (v. 4). Then follows several powerful reasons why God's people should not fear. Closing with these words, "This is the heritage of the servants of the Lord" (v. 17). "Fear not,—

I. **"For Thou Shalt Not be Ashamed"** (v. 4). Having believed in Him who is the chief corner-stone, elect, precious, thou shalt not be confounded (1 Peter 2. 6).

II. **"For Thou Shalt Forget the Shame of Thy Youth"** (v. 4). In the forgiving love of God ye shall find forgetfulness of the sins of your youthful ignorance and folly.

III. **"For Thy Maker is Thy Husband...and Thy Redeemer"** (v. 5). A threefold relationship. Thine by creation, Thine by redemption, Thine by a mutual choice—"Husband" (Eph. 5. 25).

IV. **"For the Lord hath Called Thee...forsaken and grieved in spirit"** (v. 6). If the Lord called us when we were forsaken and grieved because of our sins and failure, how much more may we depend on Him to bless us now.

V. **"For with Great Mercies will I Gather Thee"** (v. 7). By His mercy hath He saved us, and by His mercies will He, as with Israel, gather us as His jewels.

VI. **"For with Everlasting Kindness will I Have Mercy on Thee"** (vv. 8, 10). He who loved us with an "everlasting love" hath obtained "eternal redemption for us" (Heb. 9. 12).

VII. **"For I have Sworn...that I would not be Wroth with Thee"** (vv. 9, 10). The rainbow of promise is now round about the throne (Rev. 4. 3; see Heb. 6. 18).

VIII. For "**I will Lay Thy Stones with Fair Colours**" (vv. 11, 12). Your character as a building shall be strong, beautiful, and precious.

IX. "**For All Thy Children shall be Taught of the Lord**" (v. 13). The promise is unto you and to your children (Acts 2. 39). Words whereby thou and all thy house shall be saved (Acts 11. 14).

X. For "**No Weapon that is Formed Against Thee shall Prosper**" (v. 17). The gates (powers) of Hell shall not prevail against the purpose of God. See the weapons mentioned in Romans 8. 35-39. This is the heritage of the servants of the Lord. Fear not!

THE GOSPEL OF GOD.

ISAIAH 55. 1-3.

THE great verities, and the deep mysteries that are in nature, in no wise hinder us from simply appropriating the things needful for our physical life. Why should the mysteries of the Bible hinder any one from satisfying their spiritual and eternal need? A man does not need to be a philosopher to know how to eat when he is hungry. There is infinite grace in these opening verses.

I. **The Provision**. "Waters,...wine, milk" (v. 1). This is, of course, figurative language, but profoundly significant as coming from the lips of the Eternal God. "Waters" sugge t the abundance of the grace and mercy offered in His Word. Wine refers to their quickening and reviving influence in the soul. "Milk" indicates their strengthening and satisfying nature as a food. It is well known that milk contains all the essentials of life. These are emblems of the promises of God, without which man cannot truly live (Luke 4. 4).

II. The Rebuke.

1. About FOOLISH SPENDING.   "Wherefore do ye spend money for that which is not bread." The money of time, of talent, and opportunity, that's being spent for things that do not bring bread to the real hunger of the soul. Money that might be put to a much better use.   If men would only spend half as much time and thought on their souls as they do on the pleasures of the world, they would find some *"bread"* for their more real, yet starved, inner man.   Spending money for that which does not meet the true need of the man is a poor and foolish investment.

2. FRUITLESS LABOUR is rebuked.   "Wherefore do ye...labour for that which satisfieth not?"   A poor woman at our door one day, on being asked what hopes she had for Heaven, said: "I expect to do penance."   Working *for* salvation is labour which satisfieth not.   What has not satisfied you in the past will not satisfy you in the future.   This "labour" may take many a different form. but there is no satisfaction in *it* as a purchasing price.

III. **The Invitation.**   Three words are used to express the yielding of the will, and the appropriation of God's gifts.   "Come...Buy...Eat."   The urgency of this call appears in this threefold "Come."   "Ho, every one that thirsteth.   Come...Come...Come."

1. Come TO THE WATERS, the Scriptures of truth, pure and clear, from the throne of God.

2. Come and BUY.   Buy wine and milk without money—without a price.

3. Come and TAKE His offered blessing of eternal life as freely as if you had bought it.   Claim it with as much confidence as you would claim an article that you had duly paid for.

4. Come and EAT (v. 2). This blessing is not to be pocketed, but assimilated. It is not something we merely hold, but something, the influence of which, possesses and transforms us. He that eateth of this bread shall live for ever. "The Bread of God...giveth life unto the world" (John 6. 33-35, 53).

IV. **The Promise.** Certain results are assured by God to those who Hear, Come, Buy, and Eat.

1. There is LIFE. "Thy soul shall live" (v. 3). What a life this is. A life righted with God, and for God.

2. There is DELIGHT. "Thy soul shall delight itself in fatness" (fullness). This is not the delight of fancy, but of fact. There is never any famine in the Kingdom of God. All the fullness of the Godhead, in Christ, is the source of our supply.

3. There is CONTINUANCE. You ask, will it last? Hear what He says. "I will make an everlasting covenant with you, even the sure mercies of David" (v. 3). It is not to those who criticise, but to those who obey the promise is made.

V. **The Appeal.** "Ho, *every one* that thirsteth, Come." "If any man thirst let Him come unto *Me* and drink" (John 7. 37). He who made the eye shall He not see? He who made the ear shall He not hear? He who made the spirit of man shall He not understand the deepest needs of that Spirit? What light is to the eye, and music is to the ear, God's precious Word is to the soul. Come ye to the waters.

_____

UNFAITHFUL WATCHMEN.
ISAIAH 56. 10-12.

A WATCHMAN is one whose duty is literally to "look about" (1 Sam. 14. 16). The Lord's watchmen are to look about for the aggressive movements of the enemy, and for any signs of backsliding among His people. What shall become of the people when the Lord has to charge His watchmen with—

I. Blindness? "His watchmen are blind" (v. 10). They see not the danger of the wicked, and so fail to warn him that he may "save his life," and his blood is required at the watchman's hands (Ezek. 3. 18). The old note of warning seems to have almost died out of the present day ministry.

II. Ignorance? "They are all ignorant." "Without knowledge" (R.V.). They literally "do not know" the mind of God. Modern watchmen are in danger of being so engrossed with the critical opinions of men as to get into darkness with regard to the real purpose of God in their lives. To be ignorant of God's revealed will is to be a failure (Matt. 15. 14), and a stumbling block.

III. Cowardliness? "They are dumb dogs, they cannot bark." Why are they dumb? Because they mistake enemies for friends. Because of the fear of man, and their love of the world. Being blind to men's danger, and ignorant of God's will, they have no deep conviction, and so they go on sinning the sin of a guilty silence. "Beware of dogs," the dumb ones are more dangerous than the noisy ones.

IV. Laziness? "Dreaming, lying down, loving to slumber" (R.V.). "Talking in their sleep" (*margin*). They are too lazy to find out what the mind of the Lord is, and go on talking like men in a dream: and the worst of it is, that they love this sort of thing. They have visions, but they are not the visions of God, but those of their own, blind fancy. They have no message from God to the people, but still they go on dreaming dreams.

V. Selfishness? "Greedy dogs which can never have enough...they look to their own way" (v. 11). They seek their own good, and they go their own way. While this is a feature of unrenewed, human nature, it is to be an emphatic characteristic of the perilous times of the last days when "Men shall be lovers of their own selves, covetous" (2 Tim. 3. 1, 2). The covetous man hath no inheritance in the Kingdom of Christ and of God (Eph. 5. 5). In a self-centred life there is no testimony for God and His Gospel.

VI. **Recklessness?** "Come ye, say they, I will fetch wine, and we will fill ourselves with strong drink, and to-morrow shall be as to-day, and much more abundant" (v. 12). Such traitors must have an inspiration of some sort. If they have not the Spirit of God, then they will have the spirit of the world. Being out of harmony with the revealed purposes of God, they fall in line with the baser passions and delusions of the people, saying, "to-morrow...shall be much more abundant" (2 Peter 3. 3, 4). While the Holy Ghost saith, "To-day." All this is being enacted just now before our eyes. Lack of spirituality leads to laxity in morals. Because of the unfaithfulness of the watchmen many to-day are filling themselves with the "strong drink" of a delusive and destructive theology. Every Christian should be a watchman. "What I say unto you, I say unto all, Watch."

_____

PRACTICAL CHRISTIANITY

OR, HINDRANCE, TO PRAYER, ISAIAH 58. 1-9.

THE prophets were not only predictors, they were "instruments of righteousness unto God." They were not only "Seers," they were doers of the Word. God's servants must be *faithful*. "Cry aloud and spare not." Their attitude must be *unmistakable*. "Lift up thy voice like a trumpet." Their message must be *practical*. "Shew my people their transgressions" (v. 1).

I. Their Sinful Condition. They had drifted into a formal observance of religion, but at heart it was practical ungodliness. They took pleasure in knowing His ways, and forsook not His ordinances (v. 2), yet they were practising self-deception and delusion. They seem to think that by appointing a periodical fast, and afflicting their souls, that this would atone for their gluttony and insincerity (vv. 3, 4). God is ʀot mocked (v. 5). "Bearing the head like a bulrush, and spreading sackcloth and ashes under him," doth not touch the *sin* of the soul. See Matthew 15. 8; James 1. 22.

II. The Divine Remedy. "Is not this the fast that I have chosen?" (vv. 6, 7). Here is God's interpretation of "a fast." His fasts are soul-saving facts. His remedy is exactly suited to the disease. He says the fast *you* need is to—

1. "Loose the Bonds of wickedness" (ʀ.v.). Wickedness, or lawlessness, is spiritual bondage. Every unrighteous thought is a fetter for the soul.

2. "Undo the Heavy Burdens." Many are carrying burdens that are too heavy for them, burdens that you could help to undo by your sympathy and co-operation. James says, "I will shew you my faith by my works."

3. Break every Yoke." "Let the oppressed go free." The yoke of every oppressor is to be broken. Break the yoke of evil habit, fear of man, love of the world, pride of life, self-will, covetousness, etc.

4. Care for the Poor (v. 7). Give "bread to the hungry." Shelter to the outcast. Covering to the naked. The man who shutteth up the bowels of his compassion from the destitute cannot know the indwelling love of God (1 John 3. 17).

III. The Assured Result. *"Then."* This word is emphasised in the Hebrew.

1. "Then shall thy LIGHT break forth" (v. 8). Obedience to God's will is the clearing of the window through which the light of His favour will shine as the morning.

2. "Then shall thy HEALING spring forth." Unto the upright there ariseth light in the darkness. This light has healing in its beams. The moral diseases within cannot stand the dawn of the light of His truth.

3. "Then thy RIGHTEOUSNESS shall go before thee." Thy rightness with God, and with men, will go before thee like the prayers of Cornelius, as a memorial before God (Acts 10. 4).

4. "Then THE GLORY OF THE LORD shall be thy reward." Righteousness before thee, and the glory of the Lord behind thee. What a testimony this is. Leaving behind the sweet savour of His presence and glory. The Shepherd's care before thee, and His goodness and mercy following thee all the days of thy life. What a rearguard!

5. "Then shalt thou call, and the Lord SHALL ANSWER" (v. 9). Then shall your fellowship with Him be sweet, and your prayers answered. When iniquity is cleared out of the heart, then the way is clear for the Lord to show favour (Psa. 66. 18). If we would receive of Him, "whatsoever we ask," it will be "because we keep His commandments, and do those things that are pleasing in His sight" (1 John 3. 22).

INTERCESSORS WANTED.
ISAIAH 59. 1-16.

"BEHOLD, the Lord's hand is not shortened, that it cannot save; neither His ear heavy, that it cannot hear" (v. 1). So He "*wondered* that there was no intercessor" (v. 16). The language is human, but the feeling expressed is mysteriously Divine. Talking after the manner of men, he wondered that there was no intercessor.

I. **Because there was Great Need for Such.** The iniquities of the people had separated them from God (v. 2). They were waiting for light, yet walking in darkness (v. 9). They groped like the blind, and stumbled at noon-day (v. 10). Their sins testified against them (v. 12), and truth had fallen in the street (v. 14). Yet no one sufficiently felt the sorrow and sin of the whole situation as to give themselves to intercessory prayer unto God. It was very different with Moses (Exod. 32. 32), and with Paul (Rom. 10. 1). Does the present condition of Church work, and of Church life, not constitute a like demand for intercessors? May the Lord not wonder also—

II. **Because of the Encouragement Given to Intercessors.** "Behold, the Lord's hand is not shortened that it cannot save; neither His ear heavy that it cannot hear" (v. 1). He who hath delivered us, will He not yet deliver? (2 Cor. 1. 10). Hath He not set before every intercessor an "open door?" Every intercessor hath the encouragement of the Son of God who "ever liveth to make intercession for us" (Heb. 7. 25), and also of the Spirit of God who "likewise maketh intercession for us with groanings which cannot be uttered" (Rom. 8. 26). Now, "Ye that make mention of the Lord keep not silence" (Isa. 62. 6). He is the Rewarder of them that diligently seek Him (Heb. 11. 6).

III. **Because of the Possibilities within the Reach of an Intercessor.** If the Lord could then have found an intercessor, what a victory might have been His. Aaron became a passionate pleader when he ran, and "stood between the dead and the living, and the plague was stayed" (Num. 16. 48). Prayer was made without ceasing for Peter, and he was delivered out of the prison (Acts 12. 5). You remember how the widow got her victory over the injustice of a judge, "and shall not God avenge His own which cry day and night unto Him...I tell you that *He will*" (Luke 18. 1-8). We who are a kingdom and priests unto God (Rev. 5. 10, R.V.), let us offer this continual sacrifice unto Him, for the honour of His Name, the salvation of the sinner, and the sanctification of the saint. ———

THE GOSPEL OF CHRIST.

ISAIAH 61. 1-3.

IN these verses we have a brief outline of three dispensations. Grace, judgment, righteousness. The year of liberty, the day of vengeance, and the time of Judah's restoration. This is a great subject for a great preacher.

I. **The Preacher.** "The Spirit of the Lord is upon *Me*, because the Lord hath anointed *Me* to preach." In writing these words the prophet *must* have been moved by the Holy Spirit, for our Lord personally applies them to Himself in Luke 4. 16. The Spirit came upon Him (Luke 3. 22; Acts 10. 38), as the anointing of Jehovah for the work of this ministry. How great must the work be when it took such a person, and such an enduement, to accomplish it.

II. **The Message.** "Good tidings unto the meek" (poor and lowly ones, R.V., *margin*). How could there be "Good tidings" if there had not been something wrong, or awanting, somewhere? And why should the Holy Son of God need the anointing of the Spirit, by the Father, for the declaration of such tidings? Surely the tidings must be "good" and of eternal import to all who hear them when Father, Son and Holy Spirit, are so deeply interested in their proclamation, and when the power of the Triune God is needed to give them effect. What is the news?

1. HEALING FOR THE BROKENHEARTED. "He hath sent *Me* to bind up the brokenhearted." They that be whole need not a physician. How are hearts so easily broken? Why are so many disheartened? There must be many, and powerful, adverse influences at work. Yes, the world, the flesh, and the Devil. The result is defeat and failure. But He says, in *Me* is thine help. He hath sent *M*e. All that I am, and have, and do, is for thy heart's good. His Word and His work can heal the broken in heart, and bind up their wounds (Psa. 147. 3).

2. LIBERTY FOR THE CAPTIVES. "He hath sent *Me* to proclaim liberty to the captives." He only has the right and power to make such a proclamation. Who are the captives? Those who are enthralled by influences that delude and destroy. Souls who are fettered by sin and Satan. Christ can proclaim liberty because He hath been anointed by Jehovah to burst the prison gates. By His death and resurrection He hath broken every barrier down, and conquered every foe.

3. VISION FOR THE BLIND. "Opening of the eyes to them that are bound" (R.V., *margin*). There is not only healing and freedom offered, but also a new vision of spiritual things. Spiritual darkness is the bondage of many. Christ hath been sent to give light. He is the light of life, and of the world.

4. GRACE FOR ALL. "To proclaim the acceptable year of the Lord." The jubilee of freedom, and restoration to an afflicted world. Christ alone by the anointing of the Spirit was able to make such an announcement as this. Who else would dare to fix the time and conditions of man's acceptance with God. This is now the day of salvation by grace, the time when the Lord holds His gracious reception (2 Cor. 6. 2).

When the Anointed One read these words at Nazareth

(Luke 4. 18-20), He, contrary to all custom, "closed the book" without finishing the sentence, because "the day of vengeance of our God" had *not* yet come: but it will certainly follow at the close of this jubilee year of grace, when the Church shall be "caught up" (2 Thess. 1. 7-9).

_____

LONGING FOR GOD OR REVIVAL.
Isaiah 64. 1-3.

The previous chapter closes with these ominous words, "We are become as they over whom Thou never bearest rule" (R.V.). When God's people become like those over whom He has never had control, it is an awful proof of ingratitude and lawlessness, and a powerful argument for revival.

I. **The Need Felt.** "Oh, that Thou wouldest rend the heavens, that *Thou* wouldest come down." This is, of course, figurative language, expressive of a real spiritual experience. There is need for a "rending" of the heavens when the sin of backsliding has closed them, so that communion with God has been cut off. Even heavenly things may hide the Heavenly One. The veil of the Temple had to be rent, ere liberty of access could be enjoyed. "Oh, that Thou wouldest come down." The remedy for every need is in Him. A new manifestation of His power and glory would put to shame the sins of His people, and the false confidence of the ungodly. The soul's everlasting need is God, the world's dying need is God.

II. **The Work to be Done.** Mighty things are needing to be done. There is need for—

1. A Melting Work. "That the mountains may flow down at Thy presence." Mountains of difficulties, created by man's sin and vain imaginations. Mountains of selfishness, that dishonour God and hinder Him from

working. Mountains of indifference, that block the
channel of blessing.

2. A BURNING-UP WORK. "As when fire kindleth
the brushwood" (R.V.). The brushwood of vain thoughts,
self-confidence, and fleshly energy, needs burning up,
to make room for a more healthy growth. Brushwood
is a poor substitute for the golden grain. "Our God is a
consuming fire."

3. A WARMING WORK. "Oh, that Thou wouldest come
down...as fire that causeth the waters to boil." When
the heart is made to boil like a pot, because of the power
of His holy presence, then the *affections* will be hot.
Lukewarmness cannot exist where this fire is. Then the
prayers will be hot. Out of a burning heart will come
burning desires, clothed in burning words. Then the
testimony will be hot. When the heart is made to burn
within us, while He talks to us, the tongue will become
a flame of holy fire to speak forth the glories of His Name.
"He maketh His ministers a flame of fire."

III. **The Result Sought.** "To make Thy Name
known to Thine adversaries, that the nations may tremble
at Thy presence." We may long for the manifestation
of the power of God for our own personal deliverance, but
the mightier argument is, "That *Thy Name* may be
known." He seeks to be sanctified in His people, that
the heathen may know that He is God. His Name is
His glorious character. They that know His Name will
put their trust in Him. When God the Spirit comes in
power, it is to glorify the Name of the Eternal Son (John
16. 13, 14). Be filled with the Spirit, then for you the
heavens will be opened, thy mountains shall flow down,
thy brushwood burned up, and the waters of thy affections
and heart's desire made to boil. So shall His Name be
known, and others made to tremble at His presence.

THE NEW CREATION.

ISAIAH 65. 17-25.

THE closing chapters of this book are largely devoted to the coming glories of God's ancient people, and to the world-wide blessing that will flow out through them at the appearing of His Kingdom and glory. Note here some of the features of this new era.

I. There will be a Renewal of Natural Environments. "Behold, I create new heavens and a new earth" (v. 17). The glory of this new creation will be such that "the former shall not be remembered, nor come into mind." The "prince of the power of the air" will have no place in these heavens. Nor shall the fruit of the curse of sin ever appear in the new earth. Righteousness shall dwell there (2 Peter 3. 13). Creation shall then cease her groaning (Rom. 8. 22).

II. There will be a Regenerated People. "Behold, I create Jerusalem a rejoicing, and her people a joy, and I will...joy in My people, and the voice of weeping shall be no more heard" (vv. 18, 19). The people who have been a byword among the nations shall then become a joy and a praise on the earth. The well-known "weeping place" at Jerusalem will then be deserted for ever. In this day shall this nation be born again into a new life of fellowship with their crucified King. Then their sorrow and sighing shall flee away (Isa. 35. 10).

III. There will be Lengthened Lives. "There shall be no more thence an infant of days, nor an old man who hath not filled his days, for a child shall die an hundred years old." With the new creation will come all the blessings of great longevity. Not only long life, but also the assurance that the days will be *filled up* with fruitful and joyful service. This is the gift of God to them, as *eternal* life is the gift of God to us through Jesus Christ our Lord. If one should die at an hundred years old, he would be reckoned as a child. The blessings of God's grace means the enlargement of all that is deepest and best in the human soul.

IV. There will be New Social Conditions. "They shall build houses and inhabit them; they shall plant vineyards, and eat the fruit of them...My chosen ones shall long enjoy the work of their hands" (vv. 21, 22). They shall not build and another inhabit. They are assured of life, and of success in their labour. Bank failures, industrial strikes, and blighted crops, will be unknown and unthought of. Sickness and poverty will then have fled away, their disciplinary influences will no more be needed when the King Himself appears.

V. There will be a New Enjoyment of God. "It shall come to pass, that before they call I will answer; and while they are yet speaking, I will hear" (v. 24). What a change this will be compared with the present condition of the Jewish nation, and what a happy prospect for a desolate world. God's ear is never heavy that it cannot hear, but man's lust for self-glory hinders the operation of His grace. When God can "joy in His people" (v. 19), He will speedily answer their call.

VI. There will be an End of all Strife. "The wolf and the lamb shall feed together," etc. Then surely shall "man to man a brother be." The wolves and lambs of social and political life have been long at deadly variance, then they shall "feed together" in the bountiful mercies of their God and Saviour. The serpent alone receives no advantage in the new Kingdom. "Dust shall be the serpent's meat." It will not fatten much on that fare. Then shall the angelic song be fulfilled, "Glory to God in the highest, peace on earth, goodwill among men." For nothing shall hurt or destroy in all My holy mountain. saith the Lord" (v. 25).

CALLED AND EQUIPPED.

JEREMIAH 1. 1-10.

THE prophets of old knew nothing of human ordination, and instead of rushing hurriedly into the Lord's work, they frequently shrank from it. Moses said, "I am not eloquent." Isaiah said, "I am a man of unclean lips." Jonah fled in fear. Jeremiah exclaimed, "Oh! Lord God, I cannot speak." But out of weakness He ordains strength.

I. **The Call.** "Before I formed thee...I knew thee...I sanctified thee, and ordained thee" (v. 5). He was called before he was created, and set apart before he was born. The prophet could neither explain it nor deny it. His call, like all others, was the result of Sovereign grace. My sheep, He says, know My voice. Whom He did foreknow He also did predestinate, etc. (Rom. 8. 29).

II. **The Excuse.** "Ah, Lord God! behold, I cannot speak: for I am a child" (v. 6). A *child* is not expected to be an eloquent speaker, it is expected to be obedient, and trustful. The "Kingdom of God" must be received as a little child. Our sufficiency is not in ourselves, but of God (2 Cor. 3. 5). It is not to the wise and prudent that the great things of the Kingdom are revealed, but "unto babes" (Luke 10. 21).

III. **The Commission.** "Say not, I am a child: for thou shalt go to all that I shall send thee, and whatsoever I command thee thou shalt speak" (v. 7). The prophet has but one Master, and one purpose in his life, to go where he is sent, speaking the Word at His commandment. One is your Master, even Christ. The Lord may ask, "*Who* will go?" but He never asks His servant, "*Where* will ye go?" It is expected of God's called ones that His own message be faithfully spoken.

IV. **The Encouragement.** "Be not afraid of their faces: for I am with thee to deliver thee" (v. 8). In

declaring God's will there will be many "faces" that will
frown with rage, but be not afraid of *them* when you
have the smiling face of God's approval with you.   To
obey God is to oppose the course of this world.   Darkness
cannot overtake you while the true light of His presence
is abiding in you (Heb. 13. 6).

V. The Equipment.   "The Lord put forth His hand
and *touched* my mouth...Behold, I have put My *words*
in thy mouth" (v. 9). This Divine touch corresponds
with the touch of the tongue of fire in the upper room.
His "touch" and His "words" are beautifully and vitally
associated. With the Divine commanding there goes
the Divine enabling (Isa. 6. 6, 7). The touch is the
evidence of a personal contact. The hand of the Holy
Ghost makes the Word to burn like a fire.

VI. The Work.   "See, I have set thee...to root out,
and to pull down...to build and to plant" (v. 10).   A
distructive work is to be done before the constructive
work is begun. The garden must be cleaned of weeds
before the good seed is planted. That tottering wall
must be pulled down before a proper defence can be built
up. Sin must be put away, and the soul put right with
God, before a powerful character can be built up. It is
the "good and honest heart" that brings forth much fruit.
Sow not among thorns. The instrument to be used, in
this work of regeneration, is the *Word* of God, which is
quick and powerful to the casting down of imaginations,
and every high thing that exalteth itself against the
knowledge of God (2 Cor. 10. 4, 5).

WHY IS HE SPOILED?
JEREMIAH 2. 1-24.

ISRAEL a servant? A home-born slave? Why is he
spoiled? (v. 14). ("Why is he become a prey?" R.V.)
Sin spoils all that it touches. How sad to think of lives

full of glorious possibilities being deliberately spoiled for God by becoming the prey of an alien power. Even a dead fly may spoil the ointment. See—

I. **What He Was.** His past condition is characterised as one of great privilege and opportunity.

1. There was FELLOWSHIP. "I remember thee, the kindness of thy youth, the love of thine espousals" (v. 2). A delightful walking with God because there was agreement, the holy bliss of a new and first love.

2. There was OBEDIENCE. "Thou wentest after me in the wilderness." Following Him with willing and triumphant feet, even through a waste and howling desert.

3. There was SEPARATION. "Israel was holiness unto the Lord" (v. 3). Separated from Egypt unto God, and a witness for Him. What a high and holy position! How are the mighty fallen? Such were some of you, but,—where are you now?

II. **What He Did.** Israel has gone astray. "My people have committed two evils" (v. 13).

1. They have FORSAKEN ME, the fountain of living waters." In forsaking God they turned their back on the source of all good. To forsake any one is just to treat that one as if you knew him not. He began to act as if the Lord had no claim on him, and as if he had no more need of Him.

2. "They have HEWED OUT cisterns, broken cisterns that can hold no water." In turning away from the "fountain of living waters Israel discovers the need of trying to invent for themselves some substitute, and their best imitation of God's fountain is a "broken cistern" that can hold *no water*. The "living waters" represent soul-satisfying grace and truth. To forsake these for the man-made cisterns, of this world's honour, wealth, pleasure, and philosophy, is to let go the substance, and

vainly hunt the shadow. They can hold no spirit-refreshing water (Isa. 55. 1, 2).

III. What He Became. "Spoiled" (v. 14). Why? Because he forsook Him who is the Fountain, and sought by his own works to find satisfaction without God. This is the delusion of a sin-blinded soul. Anything is spoiled when it becomes unfit for the purpose for which it was intended. Israel is spoiled for God because he has "become a prey" to others (R.V.). Other lords have got control over him. Selfwill and love of the world have so possessed him that he has become their spoil.

1. He is spoiled like a DEGENERATE PLANT (v. 21). "I planted thee a right seed: how then art thou turned into a degenerate plant?" The damage is not in appearance only, but deep down in the heart, the *character* is changed. There is virtually a reversion to type.

2. He is spoiled like a STAINED GARMENT. "Though thou wash thee with nitre, and take thee much soap, thine iniquity is marked before Me" (v. 22). The nitre (mineral), and soap (vegetable), of man's invention, like the "broken cisterns," can do nothing to atone for the evil of departing from God.

3. He is spoiled like a WILD ASS (v. 24). An ass is a very useful animal, but a *wild* ass represents only wasted energy, uncontrolled and fruitless efforts. Such is the backsliding in heart in the sight of God. Though thou hast been a prey to the enemies of God, thou mayest yet be a praise by returning to God.

BACKSLIDING.

OR, MODERN DANGERS. JEREMIAH 8. 5-9.

BACKSLIDING is not a crisis, it is a process: a gradual sliding down the hill of "Holiness unto the Lord," into the low valley of the old self-life. Declension usually begins in unwatchfulness, and neglect of secret fellowship and trustfulness in God. "Why, then, is this people slidden back?" (v. 5). The reference here is to Judah and Jerusalem: but there are some salutary lessons for us in this present age. The causes of their backsliding and the evils incurred find their antitype in modern times. There was—

I. **Perverted Belief.** "They hold fast deceit" (v. 5). A perverted heart soons leads to a perverted faith. When the fountain of truth is forsaken, it is easy to believe any lie that may seem to favour such a condition (2 Thess. 2. 11, 12). He feedeth on ashes because a deceitful heart hath turned him aside (Isa. 44. 20).

II. **Misleading Testimony.** "They spake not aright" (v. 6). How could they *speak* aright, when they were not able to *think* aright? The Lord "hearkened and heard," but in this case no "book of remembrance was written," because they feared not the Lord, neither thought upon His Name (Mal. 3. 16). Their words were dishonouring to Him, and hurtful to others.

III. **Self-complacency.** "No man repented of his wickedness, saying, What have I done?" (v. 6). Their condition was one of "wickedness" in the sight of God, but so deluded were they that they had no thought that repentance was needed. When a backslider, who has lapsed in conduct, is conscious of his guilt, there is some hope of immediate confession; but those who lapse through a perverted mind, and have settled down in self-satisfaction, having come under the spell of some moral delusion, their case is indeed hard and pitiful (see 2 Cor. 4. 4).

IV. **Fleshly Enthusiasm.** "Every one turned to his course, as a horse rusheth headlong in battle" (v. 6, R.V.). There is no lack of self-confidence; they pride themselves in what they can do. They are more energetic in going their own way, than the servants of God often are in His way.

V. Ignorance of the Signs of the Times. "The stork...the swallow and the crane knoweth their appointed times, but My people knoweth not the ordinance of the Lord" (v. 7, R.V.). These birds, true to their natural instinct, observe their times, and yield to the call; but Israel, with their "fatal gift of freedom," refuses to obey. This is solemnly and sadly true of many of God's people in these present times, which are ominous with indications of coming events. But there are those who, true to the Spirit's teaching, discern the signs of the times, and who look for the new Heaven and the new earth promised. When God's people "know not the appointed times," they are in great danger of being deluded and deceived by the god of this world.

VI. Vain Confidence. They say, "We are wise, and the law of the Lord is with us. But behold the false pen of the scribes hath made it (the law) falsehood" (v. 8, R.V.). When false teachers pervert the Word of God and turn it into a lie, then blinded souls believe the lie, and say, "We are wise." They swallow the poison, and boast that the law of the Lord is with them. "Lo, they have *rejected* the word of the Lord; and what manner of wisdom is in them?" (v. 9, R.V.). The wisdom that is in them when God's Word is rejected, is that which is "foolishness with God" (1 Cor. 3. 19).

A SOLEMN DIALOGUE.
JEREMIAH 8. 19-22.

THE prophet's manner in dealing with these future events is somewhat dramatic. There are differences of opinions as to how they may be interpreted. We shall note—

I. **The Divine Question.** "Why have they provoked Me to anger with their images and vanities?" (v. 19). "Is not the *Lord* in Zion?" Then why seek help in the work of your own hands, and the "strange vanities" of your own imaginations? A picture of guilt and depravity of man's natural enmity to God, and spiritual stupidity. A man nowhere plays the fool so perfectly as in his professed religious life.

II. **The Mournful Reply.** "The harvest is past, the summer is ended, and we are not saved" (v. 20). In answer to God's question this is a confession of disappointment, and a cry of despair. Their cisterns of hope have turned out broken ones that can hold no water. They are like those who were depending on a plentiful harvest to save their lives, but nothing but famine stares them in the face. Like the foolish virgins, they have found the "door shut." The evil heart of unbelief leads to a dungeon of darkness.

III. **The Message of Sympathy.** "For the hurt of the daughter of My people am I hurt" (v. 21). This may be taken as the voice of the Lord through the prophet. It is true of both. God feels the terrible hurt that has come upon His people. He was wounded for our transgressions. The tears of Jesus Christ, shed over the great hurt of Jerusalem, were proof enough of how deeply He felt the hurt in His own soul. If His people are "dear to Him as the apple of His eye," it shows how tender the heart of God is toward them. In all their afflictions He was afflicted.

IV. **The Frank Confession.** "I am black; astonishment hath taken hold on Me" (v. 21). Yes, that is the word, "black." Black with shame and guilt because of unbelief and pride. "Astonishment!" Yes, that is the other word. Astonished at your own sinfulness and folly in provoking the Lord, and astonished at His great pity and compassion for you even in your well merited misery. What is more astonishing than the grace of God as seen in the face of Jesus Christ? If we confess our sins He is faithful and just to forgive us.

V. The Gospel of Hope. "Is there no balm in Gilead: is there no physician there?" (v. 22). Is there no provision in Gilead, is there no one there mighty enough to heal your wounds, and restore your souls to true spiritual health and hope? It is said that the balm of Gilead was used for healing the bites of serpents. The bite of the old serpent, the Devil, can only be healed by the balm of Christ's Cross, and the Physician that is found there. You say, "I am black." Yes, but is there no healing balm in Calvary?

VI. The Searching Rebuke. "Why then is not the health of My people recovered?" (v. 22). The balm and the Physician are there. Why then are ye not healed? Free and effectual provision has been made in Christ for your salvation. Why then are ye not saved? Is there no wisdom to direct, and power to overcome, in the Holy Ghost? Why then is not the *health* of His people, in these days, recovered? Has Calvary lost its power? Has the Great Physician vacated His place of mercy? Why then not prove the all-sufficiency of His grace by living a healthy, God-honouring life.

SOMETHING WORTH GLORYING IN.
JEREMIAH 9. 23, 24.

THREE times in this chapter is the Divine "ME" emphasised in the Hebrew (vv. 3, 6, and 24). God, Himself, is the source and centre of all good, and ought to be the undivided Object of all man's glorying.

I. What Some Glory In. There are three phases of

worldly glory. Wisdom, might, and wealth. Each has its votaries.

1. The WISE are tempted to glory in their wisdom. Worldly wisdom is the principle thing sought for by the worldly man, and he may glory in it just as another man may glory in his shame, as something that belongs to himself, as the fruit of his work (Isa. 5. 21).

2. The MIGHTY are tempted to glory in their might. It is all the same, whether that might is physical, intellectual, or social. Whatever distinguishes one man from his fellows is apt to become a cause for selfish glorying.

3. The RICH are tempted to glory in their riches. To them there is a sort of divinity in their wealth, and they glory in their golden god.

Thus saith the Lord, "Let not the wise glory in his wisdom," etc. All this glorying is in vain, for the wisdom of the wise will He bring to nothing...for God hath chosen the *foolish things of the world* to confound the wise...that no flesh should glory in His presence (1 Cor. 1. 27-29). The things that are foolish to the world are the "things that are freely given us of God" through Christ Jesus.

II. **What We Should Glory In**. "Let Him that glorieth glory in this, that he understandeth and knoweth ME." A modern philosopher spoke of Him as the "Great Unknowable." But it is possible, in a limited sense, of course, to understand and know Him. And this knowledge is the only thing worth glorying in. "He that glorieth, let him glory in the Lord" (1 Cor. 1. 31). All other glorying will finally be put to shame. It is life eternal to *know* Him and Jesus Christ whom He hath sent (John 17. 3). How is God known? Through the revelation of His Word, and more fully by His Son (John

1. 14-18). There are three reasons given us here why we should glory in Him—

1. Because of His LOVINGKINDNESS. "I am the Lord which exercise lovingkindness" (v. 24). Because of the excellency of His lovingkindness the children of men put their trust in Him (Psa. 36. 7). This great lovingkindness is seen at its flood-tide in the gift of His Son (John 3. 16; see 2 Cor. 4. 6). He that loveth not knoweth not God, for God is Love.

2. Because of His JUDGMENT. "Righteousness and judgment are the foundation of His throne" (Psa. 97. 2, R.V.). The judgments of God in the past have all been against wickedness and for righteousness. Witness the flood, Sodom, God's dealings with the nations, especially His ancient people Israel. We glory in God's judgment of sin, and also of the sinner, at the Cross of His crucified Son.

3. Because of His RIGHTEOUSNESS. Righteousness, crowned with lovingkindness, is the character of our God. Our Lord, His Son, gloried in this when He prayed, "O *righteous* Father" (John 17. 25). Our Advocate now is "Jesus-Christ the Righteous." "He is the Lord, the Righteous Judge, who will give the crown of righteousness to all who have loved His appearing" (2 Tim. 4. 8, R.V.). Let us then show our glorying by seeking first the Kingdom of God, and His righteousness. "For in these things I delight, saith the Lord" (v. 24). "Let him that glorieth glory in this."

CONCERNING THE DEARTH.
JEREMIAH 14. 1-9.

TIMES of dearth are testing times. Surely God hath a perfect right to withhold His gifts when, and, as He may. A dearth of water, or a dearth of spiritual power and fruitfulness, may be intended to have a salutary influence on the sufferers. "My ways are not your ways," saith the Lord. Notice the—

I. Evidence of the Dearth.

1. There was SORROWFUL PERPLEXITY. "Judah mourneth, and the gates thereof languish" (v. 2). The nation is distressed in soul, so that the gates—the market place—are deserted.

2. There were EMPTY VESSELS. "Their little ones (servants) returned with their vessels empty." All this is solemnly suggestive of the time of a spiritual drought when God's refreshing and reviving Spirit is withheld, and when there is a languishing of the work of God in the gates (Churches), and when the servants present only "empty vessels" to a thirsty household. No wonder that—

3. "SHAME AND CONFUSION covered their heads" (v. 3, l.c.). When the well of God's Word becomes dry and personal experience chapt, then empty vessels and dissatisfied souls will be plentiful. The dearth of conversions means the dearth of power.

II. Cause of the Dearth.
"O Lord, our iniquities testify against us...our backslidings are many; we have sinned against Thee" (v. 7). If the Heaven that is over us be brass, and the earth under us iron, it is because of our iniquities and backslidings. The iniquity that separates from God separates from the Fountain of Living Waters. The dew of His refreshing Spirit does not fall upon the barren desert. Shame and empty vessels are the consequences of backsliding hearts.

III. Remedy.
But can there be a remedy for a drought? Yes, when man's moral condition has become the cause of Heaven's rebellion. The remedy lies in our *attitude* toward the Lord Himself as a mighty Saviour. "O the Hope of Israel, the Saviour thereof in time of

trouble...Why shouldest Thou be...as a mighty man that cannot save?" (vv. 9, 10). This is a confession and an appeal. "Do Thou for Thy Name's sake" (v. 7). We need to waken up to the fact of our God's almightiness to deliver, and to the infinite depth of His compassion for His people. "Why shouldest Thou be...as a wayfaring man that turneth aside to tarry for a night?" (v. 8). Why should His behaviour toward us, as our personal Redeemer and Friend, be more like a wayfaring man than our abiding Companion and Helper? The reason is we have become, through our worldliness and unbelief, unfit for His fellowship. Still His desires are after His own to bless them with "abundance of life" (Luke 24. 29). There is no use of us saying, "Yet Thou, O Lord, art in the midst of us, and we are called by Thy Name" (v. 9), if we refrain not our feet from the paths of error and unbelief (v. 10). The remedy for spiritual drought is confession, restoration, and resignation (v. 22; John 15).

A CONFESSION AND A PLEA.
JEREMIAH 14. 17-22.

I. **The Need.** The condition described in verses 17-19 is that of desolation and hopelessness—"A great breach" (v. 17). "A famine" (v. 18). A sense of rejection and despair. "We looked for peace, but no good came; for healing, and behold dismay" (v. 18, R.V.). What a picture of the soul's condition without God.

II. **The Confession.** "We acknowledge, O Lord, our wickedness," etc. (v. 20). There is no other honest way of dealing with our sin. As God loves a cheerful giver, He also desires an honest confessor (see Psa. 32. 5; 1 John 1. 7).

III. **The Plea.** It is based on the *honour* of His Name. "Do not abhor us for Thy Name's sake" (v. 21). It also appeals to the *dignity* of His throne. "Do not disgrace the throne of Thy glory." The throne of His glory was the "Mercy Seat" in the Temple. It was the "Throne of Grace." This throne will never be disgraced by sending the humble, needy ones empty away. It had also reference to the *truthfulness* of His Word. "Remember, break not Thy covenant with us." He is faithful that hath promised. The exceeding riches of His grace has ever an open channel toward us through Christ Jesus (Eph. 2. 7).

IV. **The Resolve.** "Art not Thou He, O Lord" (who can cause rain and give showers) "therefore we will wait upon Thee" (v. 22). The God that answered Elijah, by both fire and rain, is well worth waiting on. For all the moral diseases and troubles that are sure to follow a spiritual dearth there is no remedy but in the outpouring of the Holy Spirit of God. His promise is, "I will pour water upon him that is thirsty, and floods upon the dry ground." Wait upon the Lord.

The language here used is truly that which befits penitent lips, but it may be used, as Judah did, in an impenitent spirit (chap. 15. 1).   ———

THE EXPERIENCES OF A WITNESS.
JEREMIAH 15. 16-20.

As witnesses for God we may learn much from the ex-periences of the "Holy men of old." Their dangers and temptations, as well as their privileges and responsibilities, were very much akin to our own. Note his—

I. **Joy in God's Word.** "Thy words were found, and I did eat them: and Thy Word was unto me the joy and rejoicing of mine heart" (v. 16). This may refer to God's first message spoken to him, as recorded in chapter 1. 7. This *joy* in God's Word implies two things—

1. That we are perfectly sure that it is the Word of God, and—

2. That we have really received it into the heart—*eaten*
it—so that it has become the hope and inspiration of our
lives. The Word of God is sweet to the taste of the
believer, but it must needs often produce bitter effects
in the heart when it begins its cleansing operations
(Rev. 10. 9).

II. **Identification with God's Name.** "For I am
called by Thy Name, O Lord God of Hosts." When
God's Word gets into the heart God's *Name* or character
must be stamped on the life. Likeness to God is the
mightiest testimony for God. To receive Christ Jesus as
"The Word of God" is to be conformed to the image of
God.

III. **Separation from God's Enemies.** "I sat not
in the assembly of the mockers," or them that made
merry (R.V.) in their sins and over sacred things. "I
sat alone because of Thy hand." Those whose delight
is in the Word of the Lord will not be found walking in
the counsel of the ungodly, or standing in the way of
sinners (Psa. 1. 1, 2). How can we witness against "All
ungodliness" if we are in any way identified with it?
(see 2 Cor. 6. 17, 18).

IV. **Perplexity at God's Dealings.** "Why is my
pain perpetual, and my wound incurable...Wilt Thou be
altogether unto me as a deceitful brook?" (v. 18, R.V.).
The deceitful brook is the one that fails and dries up at
the very time when its refreshing waters are most needed.
Will God so prove a failure to His servant in the time of
need? A feeling of disappointment has crept over his
spirit because God's purpose does not seem to run parallel
with his expectations. The prophet had yet something
more to learn. In the time of perplexity and seeming
defeat, wait.

V. **Assurance from God.** God speaks. The fountain

of living waters again break forth. The brook of Divine faithfulness has not proved deceitful (vv. 19-21). Look at—

1. THE PROMISES. "Thou shalt be as My mouth...I will make thee a fenced brazen wall (stability)...They shall not prevail against thee...I am with thee...I will deliver thee...I will redeem thee out of the hand of the terrible." They that wait on the Lord shall renew their strength by receiving fresh assurances from His Word, of His grace and goodness, His presence and power.

2. THE CONDITIONS. "If thou return." Get back to thy first love, into real, unclouded fellowship with God, and unquestioning obedience. "If thou...stand before Me." Abide with Him, and act as before His face. "If thou take forth the precious from the vile." Call things by their true name, and give to Caesar the things that are Caesar's, and to God the things that *are* God's. Then the God of Peace shall bruise Satan under your feet, and make you more than conquerors through "Him with whom we have to do."

THE CURSED AND THE BLESSED.

JEREMIAH 17. 5-8.

Two classes are contrasted here, in most simple, but emphatic terms, being prefaced by a "Thus saith the Lord." There are certain spiritual and unalterable laws that must come into operation according to our moral attitude to God and to His Word. His blight must come upon the godless as surely as His blessing comes on the godly. The curse means blessing withheld.

I. **Who are the Cursed?** "Cursed be the man that *trusteth in man*, and maketh flesh his arm, *whose heart*

departeth from the Lord." To trust in man, and make
flesh the arm of our confidence, is heart departure from the
Lord. Neither Judah's salvation, nor ours, can come
through the wisdom of man, or the power of any of earth's
princes (Psa. 118. 8, 9). Salvation is of the Lord. It is
the evil heart of unbelief that departs from the living
God (Heb. 3. 12). There is a faith in humanity which is
but a denial of God.

II. What is the Curse? "He shall be like the heath
in the desert" (v. 6). The heath in the desert is deserted
by the refreshing showers of Heaven. "He shall not see
when good cometh." He shall be like a blind man
incapable of seeing, or profiting by those mercies that are
within his reach. "He shall inhabit the parched places
in the wilderness." He shall live in a state and condition
that is barren of the promises of God. The godless often
seem to prosper greatly with regard to earthly possessions,
but as in God's sight they are destitute and miserable
(Rev. 3. 17). Their soul doth truly "inhabit parched
places" (see Job. 8. 11-13).

III. Who are the Blessed? "Blessed is the man that
trusteth in the Lord, and whose hope the Lord is" (v. 7).
To cease from man whose breath is in his nostrils, and
to give the Lord the undivided confidence of the heart,
is the secret of full and eternal blessedness. Blessed are
all they that put their trust in Him (Psa. 2. 12). Note
these two words, "trust" and "hope." The trust is but a
counterfeit if hope does not spring out of it. When
we truly trust the Lord we will certainly expect much
from Him. "Thou wilt keep him in perfect peace whose
mind is *stayed on Thee*: because he trusteth in Thee"
(Isa. 26. 3, 4).

IV. What is the Blessedness? The blessedness is
very great. This blessed man has—

1. A Good Position. "He is like a tree planted by the waters" (v. 8). Planted for a purpose, not like the heath in the desert growing wild—without grace. The believer is planted in Christ, a position of security, and infinite favour.

2. A Plentiful Supply. "That spreadeth out her roots by the river." All the resources of the continuous flow of the river of God's grace are at the disposal of this blessed man whose hope the Lord is. "Spread out all the roots" of your affections and desires into the river of His Word and will, for "My God is able to supply all your need according to the riches of His grace."

3. A Happy Ignorance. "He shall not see when heat cometh." The drought has no effect upon the tree that's planted by the waters of an unfailing river. What are "wild alarms" to others do not disturb his soul.

4. An Ever Fresh Experience. "His leaf shall be green." Abiding freshness belongs to all who abide in Christ, and in the current of His gracious purposes. The leaf of his testimony will be ever green.

5. A Blessed Freedom. "He shall not be careful in the year of drought." Freedom from care when *appearances* are all against him. Living on the promises of God saves from all fearfulness in the day of trial.

6. Continual Fruitfulness. "Neither shall cease from yielding fruit." The never-failing river of life produces in those who receive of its fullness a never-failing fruitfulness unto God (Rev. 22. 2; John 15. 5, 6; 16). This blessedness cometh by faith.

THE MARRED VESSEL.
Jeremiah 18. 1-6.

The prophet of the Lord is sent to the house of a potter that he might get an object lesson on the work and will

of God.   God can put a new meaning into the common
affairs of life.   Even the ants, and the lilies, can teach
the sluggard and the overly anxious.   The prophet is
humble enough to obey the call, and willing enough to
learn the mind of the Lord, even through the actions of
an illiterate potter.

I. The Clay.   This represents the "house of Israel"
(v. 6).   Dug out of Egypt, and brought into Canaan, the
great Potter's house where He desired to work in His
people.   Like Israel, we have been taken out of the clay
pit of darkness and slavery, and brought into the Kingdom
of His dear Son, that He might fashion us after His own
image.   The clay is the raw material.

II. The Wheels.   "Behold, he wrought a work on the
wheels."   The wheels of God's promises, purposes, and
providences, were all working together for their good
(Rom. 8. 28).   Being in the Kingdom of God we are in the
special sphere of His favour and grace.   All our circumstances are but the wheels in which our spiritual character
is being formed.   The lives of all the Bible saints are
witnesses to this.   We should not shirk our tribulations
knowing that "tribulations worketh patience, and patience
experience."

III. The Potter.   "Behold, as the clay is in the
potter's hand, so are ye in Mine hand, O house of Israel."
The Lord Himself is the Potter.   Oh, what possibilities
there are for us, as for Israel, being *in* "His hand."   Think
of your position, and of His purpose with you in placing
His mighty hand upon you.   See what Nehemiah was
able to accomplish because of the hand of God upon him
(Neh. 2. 8).   The Potter's purpose is to make the best
possible use of the material that is in His hand.   "The
Giver of all grace, who has called you to share His eternal
glory, through Christ...will Himself make you perfect"

(1 Peter 5. 10, *Weymouth*). The wonder-working hand of God is the Holy Spirit who worketh in us both to will and to do of His good pleasure.

IV. **The Vessel.** "The vessel that he made was marred in the hand of the potter, so he made it again another vessel." Even in the hand of the Divine Potter the vessel (Israel) was marred. Through disobedience they became another dishonoured vessel. Because of unbelief they have been cut off, and are still, as a nation, a marred vessel. Take heed lest there be in any of you an evil heart of unbelief. If the Holy Spirit, as the hand of God, is to fashion us into a vessel meet for the Master's use, there must be no unyielding part in our nature. The hard grit of a perverse will, or the sand of self seeking, will hinder and mar the work of the Heavenly Potter, whose gentle hands are so sensible to the least resistance. Every backslider is a marred vessel. Many like Saul, are marred because they have disobeyed the Word of the Lord. What might we not have been if the Divine Potter had had His will all the time with us?

V. **The Application.** "Cannot I do with you as this potter? saith the Lord." Thank God, although the vessel has been marred, "He can *make it again* another vessel." The regenerating Spirit is able to restore the marred vessel into something like the image of Him who worketh in you mightily. The vessel may have been dishonoured by resistance, but it has not been disowned. Can God do with *you* as this potter? Can He? Are you as clay, soft, pliable, and refined, in His hand? If so, the Potter's purpose may yet be fulfilled in you. He still needs vessels to bear His Name (character) among the nations of the earth (Acts 9. 15). Every vessel made meet for His use will be a vessel used in His service.

TONGUE SMITERS.

JEREMIAH 18. 18-20.

THE man of God will never be understood by the man of the world. We see the—

I. **Purpose of the Persecutors.** "Come, let us devise devices against Jeremiah." The devices devised by the ungodly against the servants of God are many. They have nothing against him, but must, in their enmity, devise something. Yet they confess that "the law shall not perish...nor the word from the prophet." They are convinced that the "law" cannot be broken, and that the testimony of God's man will not fail. Yet they say, "Come, let us smite him with the tongue, and let us *not* give heed to any of his words." They know he speaks the truth in God's Name, yet they smite him with the tongue of scorn and of calumny, and determine not to give heed to his message. This is surely a most humbling evidence of the enmity of the carnal mind against God.

II. **Appeal of the Prophet.** He appeals—

1. To the LORD HIMSELF. "Give heed to me, O Lord," etc. The tongue of the slanderer is as a poisoned arrow, but there is refuge in God from the strife of tongues. When others give no heed to our message it is good to realise that God gives heed to our cry.

2. To DIVINE RIGHTEOUSNESS. "Shall evil be recompensed for good?" No, God is not unrighteous to reward faithfulness with shame and defeat. The devices of the wicked shall never block the channel of Divine mercy and power to His own people. If we ask a fish will He give us a stone? He appeals also—

3. To HIS OWN FAITHFULNESS. "Remember that I stood before Thee to speak good for them, and to turn away Thy wrath from them." While they were devising devices against him, he was pleading with God for them.

While they were speaking evil of him, he was speaking "good for them." Like the Greatest of all prophets, he prayed for his enemies, and like Him also, he was hated without a cause (John 15. 25). The servant of God is clear of the blood of the lawless and the unbelieving when he can say, as he looks up into the face of the Eternal Father, "Remember that I stood before Thee...for them," as Abraham did (Gen. 18. 22). Pray for them that despitefully use you, remember that ye are the salt of the earth.

The terrible imprecations which follow in verses 21-23, show the awful judgments from which he sought to save them. Now, as it were, he steps aside from his pleadings, and allows the merited wrath of God to fall upon them. This the child of grace dare not do.

PASHUR.

Jeremiah 20. 1-6.

THIS short biography is full of warning to those honoured with authority, but who, in their pride of social position, despise and reject the testimony of the Word of God at the mouth of His servant.

I. **His Position.** "The son of a priest, and chief governor in the house of the Lord." From his connection, and official position, you would expect that he would be in real sympathy with the Lord's prophet. But, No! While he superintended the house of the Lord he was at enmity with the purpose of the Lord. A religious position does not always mean a religious condition.

II. **His Enmity to God's Word.** "He heard Jeremiah ...and smote him, and put him in the stocks" (vv. 1, 2). God's message was opposed to his thoughts and desires (19. 14, 15), so he insulted and imprisoned the messenger. As a straw may show which way the wind blows, so a word or a look may reveal the enmity of the heart against the truth of God.

III. His Sudden Exposure. "The Lord hath not called thy name Pashur ("most noble," or, "joy round about") but Magor-missabib"—*fear* round about (v. 3). Men may call themselves what they may, but God will name them according to what they are. Men may call themselves believers when God calls them unbelievers. A man is what God sees him to be. He is not mocked.

IV. His Deceitful Life. "Thou hast prophesied lies" (v. 6). His lies were manufactured to discredit the Word of God at the mouth of Jeremiah the prophet. Like Elymas the sorcerer, he sought to *pervert* the right way of the Lord. But the perverted and the perverters shall all be put to shame.

V. His Doom. "Behold, I will make thee a terror to thyself" (v. 4). What could be more terrible than this; a man a terror to himself? A sinner carrying his own brimstone in his own bosom as the product of his own deeds. Who shall deliver him from this body of death?

A CHEQUERED EXPERIENCE.
JEREMIAH 20. 7-11.

THE prophet here gives us a little bit of personal testimony. Within the compass of these few verses there is such a variety of experiences as makes one feel that he was a man of like passions with ourselves.

I. He was Enticed of the Lord. "O Lord, Thou hast enticed me, and I was enticed" (v. 7, *margin*) Another reading is, "Thou hast overcome" me, or, "Laid hold on me, and I was overcome." He was overcome by the enticing influence of the Word of God, it was "Stronger than I, and prevailed" (v. 7). This is the initial experience of a true prophet, a preacher, or a Christian. He himself must be "laid hold on," and "overcome" by the power of God's truth if he is to speak it in power.

II. **He was Mocked by Men.** "I am in derision daily, every one mocketh me." The man who has been "overcome" by God is derided by men. The godly man is still "Made a spectacle unto the world" (1 Cor. 4. 9). Marvel not if the world hate you.

III. **He was Indignant at the Treatment.** "Since I spake, I cried out" (v. 8). He complained against the violence done to the truth. Reproach for the Word of the Lord was hard to bear. Moses behaved differently (Heb. 11. 26).

IV. **He was Discouraged at Results.** "Then I said, I will not make mention of Him, nor speak any more in His Name" (v. 9). Faithful testimony had brought but reproach. Why should he persevere? Oh, this is so very human. We would be more faithful to God if we were getting more personal profit and pleasure by it. Shame!

V. **He was Inspired by the Word.** "But His Word was in my heart as a burning fire shut up in my bones... and I could not stay" (v. 9). This is how God "overcomes" by His Word in the lives of His people. We cannot but speak when the truth becomes like liquid fire in the heart (Acts 4. 20). Is it possible to have heard and believed the Gospel of God without feeling the woe of not preaching it? (1 Cor. 9. 16).

VI. **He was Misunderstood by His Friends.** "All my familiars (every man of my peace) watched for my halting." Even his choice acquaintances were ready to catch any seeming slip of the tongue, and to report it to his enemies. The unfavourable, gossiping of pretended friends is one of the sore trials of the servant of Christ.

Personal friends who understand not your spiritual character and mission.

VII. **He was Encouraged by the Lord**. "But the Lord is with me as a mighty, terrible One" (v. 11). The prophet's Saviour is more mighty and terrible than his oppressors. If God be for us who shall prevail against us? (Rom. 8. 31). When His Word burns like a fire in the bones the mighty and terrible One is at hand. Be not dismayed, for I am thy God.

THE FALSE AND THE TRUE.
JEREMIAH 23. 24-32.

THERE are two classes of prophets, or preachers, referred to here, whose successors are still with us: those who dream dreams, and proclaim them as the Word of the Lord, and those who have received God's message into their own hearts, that they might preach it.

I. **The Dreamers**. They say, "I have dreamed, I have dreamed" (v. 25). *They* have dreamed, so all the world should listen to them. Dreams may at times be very interesting, but they are destitute of authority. The dreamer is to tell his dream *as a dream*, but he is a "prophet of the deceit of his own heart," if he dares to substitute the imaginings of his own sleepy brains as the "Word of the Lord." These dreamers, like their modern followers, "prophesy lies," and "think to cause My people to forget My Name by their dreams" (v. 27). Such teachers as devise their own message, and declare it in God's Name, were never sent by Him. "Behold, I am against them that prophesy false dreams...I sent them not, nor commanded them, therefore, they shall not profit this people at all, saith the Lord" (v. 32). God's people would profit much more to-day if His servants would dream less, and trust more to His revealed will, and fearlessly proclaim it. These filthy dreamers are always exposed to "seducing spirits, and doctrines of devils," and those who will not endure sound doctrine, as in these latter days, will readily heap to themselves such man-pleasing teachers (2 Tim. 4. 3).

II. **The Receivers.** "He that hath My Word" (v. 28). He hath the Word, because he received it from the Lord. There is a vast difference between knowing the truth, and theorising, or dreaming about it. The apostles could say, "We speak that we do know." "What is the chaff to the wheat? saith the Lord" (v. 28). Just what a dream is to the revelation of God. The imaginations of the unrenewed mind are but as chaff in the reckoning of the Omniscient One. God's Word is not a fancy, nor a phantom, it is "A fire, and a hammer" (v. 29). Something that can make itself felt when in operation. God's Word is wheat to feed, fire to burn, and a hammer to break. "He that hath My Word," He says, "let him speak My Word faithfully." Worldly wisdom, as exhibited in the dreamer's dreams, is but the savour of death unto death. The wisdom of God, as revealed in His Word, is the savour of life unto life.

FAITHFULNESS AND FOOLISHNESS.
JEREMIAH 26. 1-16.

DRYDEN has said, "To take up half on trust, and half on try, name it not faith, but bungling bigotry." There was no "bungling bigotry" in the mind of Jeremiah, his attitude to God and to the people was one of fearless integrity.

I. **The Commission.** "Stand in the court of the Lord's house, and speak...all the words that I command thee to speak unto them; diminish not a word" (v. 2). In the Lord's house there must be no diminishing of the

Lord's Word. Those who attempt to modify the force
of God's Word lest the princes of the people should be
offended, are in danger of the curse pronounced in
Revelation 22. 19. What the "worshippers" in our
cities need, as well as those in the "cities of Judah," is
a faithful declaration of the whole truth as it is in Jesus
Christ, that they may "turn every man from his evil way"
(v. 3).

II. **The Message.** "Say unto them, Thus saith the
Lord; If ye will not hearken to Me, to walk in My law...
then I will make this house...and this city a curse"
(vv. 4-6). When the blight of God comes upon His
house because of unbelief and disobedience, then the
curse comes upon the *city*, and to *"all the nations* of the
earth." A backsliding Church is a social and national
curse. How can the house of the Lord maintain its
dignity and power as a witness for Him if the light of
Divine truth has grown dim?

III. **The Opposition** (vv. 8-11). "The priests, the
prophets, and all the people, said...Thou shalt surely die
...Why hast thou prophesied in the Name of the Lord,
saying, This house...and this city shall be desolate,"
etc.? The same charge was made against the Lord Jesus
Christ (Matt. 21. 23). God's Word, by the mouth of the
prophet, cut at the root of their pride, the *"house,"* and
the *"city,"* both dishonoured, and degraded, by their
sins. What is the Lord's house, or the Lord's city to
Him, when His people have backslidden in heart from
Him? To kill God's prophet would not kill God's
purpose. Every preacher of righteousness will surely
become a "pestilent fellow" to hypocritical professors.

IV. **The Call to Repentance.** "Then spake Jeremiah
...The Lord sent me to prophesy against this house...
Therefore now amend your ways...and obey the voice

of the Lord" (vv. 12, 13). The messenger can take back nothing, the responsibility of saving the "house and the city" lies in *their* repentance and obedience (Hos. 14. 2-4). If churches and cities are to be delivered from desolation and oppression, then let the "Voice of the Lord be obeyed."

V. The Personal Testimony. "As for me, behold, I am in your hand...but know...for a truth the Lord hath sent me unto you to speak all these words" (vv. 14, 15). The same language is found in Joshua 9. 25; 2 Samuel 15. 26. Every true servant of the Lord is more concerned about the faithful delivery of His message, than the deliverance of himself out of the hands of the enemies of God. When a man knows that he has the unerring Word of God in him and with him his soul is anchored.

VI. The Voice of Reason. "Then said the princes... This man is not worthy to die, for he hath spoken to us in the Name of the Lord *our* God" (v. 16). The princes and the people were more amenable to reason than the priests and the prophets. Religious pride and bigotry is often the bitterest enemy to the truth of God. The common people heard Christ gladly. Raw heathenism is not such an obstacle in the way of the Gospel as a Christianised paganism. "My sheep hear My voice, and they follow Me."

CLAIMING THE PROMISES.
JEREMIAH 29. 10-14.

THESE words form part of the letter which Jeremiah sent to those who were captives in Babylon (v. 1). This letter like the Gospel of God, is a revelation of His mind and will to those who, because of their sins, and iniquities, have become the slaves of an alien power.

I. The Thoughts of God. "I know the thoughts that I think" (v. 11). If great men have great thoughts,

what shall we say of the thoughts of God. What might
this world not give to know what God's thoughts are.

1. They are PERSONAL thoughts. "Thoughts that I
think *toward you.*" Neither science nor philosophy can
tell what God thinks of *us.* The heavens may declare
His glory, but His own lips must tell me what He thinks
of me. This He does in Christ, who loved me and gave
Himself for me.

2. They are PEACEFUL thoughts. "Thoughts of peace
and not of evil." Guilty man naturally imagines that
God's thoughts toward him are thoughts of war and
destruction. But, "God was in Christ reconciling the
world to Himself, not imputing their trespasses unto
them." "My thoughts are not your thoughts, saith the
Lord" (Isa. 55. 8). The Cross of Christ is God's thought
of peace toward a warring world. He hath made peace
by the blood of His Cross.

3. They are PROSPECTIVE thoughts. "To give you
hope in your end" (R.V.). Or, to secure for you a blessed
future. God's purposes with Judah are not yet fulfilled
(Zech. 12. 9, 10; 14. 20, 21). There is also a glorious
future for the Church of God (Eph. 2. 7). The thoughts
of God, revealed to us, and believed by us, inspires with
a new and blessed hope, not only for this life, but also
for the life which is to come (see Psalm 139. 17).

II. **The Expectation of God.** When God reveals
His thoughts to His people, He expects that they will
receive them, and act accordingly. He says—

1. "Ye shall CALL upon Me" (v. 12). How shall we
call on Him of whom we have not heard? But now that
we have heard, faith and prayer are expected to be
exercised. God looks for His promises to be claimed.

2. "Ye shall SEEK Me, and find Me, when ye shall

search for Me with all your heart." It is not enough to cry for deliverance, we must seek for the Deliverer. When His thoughts are so good and gracious towards us, why should we not seek the embrace of His Person? Those who see Him with all their heart make a whole-hearted discovery, for, when there is the purity of heart, there is the vision of God (Matt. 5. 8). "Seek, and ye shall find" (Luke 11. 9, 10).

III. **The Promises of God** (v. 14). These promises are the proofs of His exceeding great and precious thoughts to usward who believe. He promises—

1. To HEARKEN. "Ye shall pray unto Me, and I will hearken unto you" (v. 12). His ear is not heavy that it cannot hear, neither is it too far away, or too much occupied with others, to hearken unto *you.*

2. To ANSWER. "I will be found of you" (v. 14). God promises to reveal and surrender Himself to the seeking soul, and, oh, what a find! Infinite goodness and fullness for the soul's eternal need.

3. To DELIVER. "I will turn away your captivity." The bondage of sin He turns away by the revelation of His power; the bondage of darkness He turns away by the dawning of His light; the bondage of the world, the flesh, and the Devil, by the revelation of His Cross, His Word, and His Spirit.

4. To RESTORE. "I will gather you...and bring you again into the place." Their sin drove them away, but God's grace would bring them back. Christ suffered, the Just for the unjust, that He might *bring us to God.* As every Jew will yet be gathered out "from all the nations," so every child of God will yet be gathered out as members of the Body of Christ (Acts 15. 14).

RUIN AND REMEDY.

JEREMIAH 30. 11-22.

ISRAEL is a helpless captive in Babylon. All other nations have forsaken them in their time of need. A picture of a soul's ruin, and the world's indifference to its condition.

I. The Ruin. They are described as being—

1. GUILTY. "Because thy sins were increased, I have done these things unto thee" (v. 15). Sin leads to bondage, to suffering, and disappointment.

2. BRUISED. "Thy bruise (hurt, R.V.) is incurable." Sin has crushed man's soul out of its original shape. Man has absolutely no cure for it.

3. WOUNDED. "Thy wound is grievous." Heart rebellion against God is an awful gash in a man's, or a nation's, moral being. It is very grievous in its results, as they reach into Eternity.

4. FRIENDLESS. "There is none to plead thy cause" (v. 13). While in the "far country" the prodigal found no one to plead his cause. No man can redeem his brother. But *we* thank God for 1 John 2. 1.

5. HELPLESS. "Thou hast no healing medicines" (v. 13). Man's wisdom and ingenuity has invented many medicines, but there is no *healing* in them.

6. DESTITUTE. "All thy lovers have forgotten thee" (v. 14). The hewn-out cisterns have proved broken and worthless. Their lovers have proved mockers.

7. MISERABLE. "Why criest thou" (v. 15). It is the cry of hopeless despair. "Out of the depths have I cried." The discovery of our infinite poverty and need makes such a cry irresistible.

II. The Remedy. The cure for a sinner's woes is found in God alone, in His Presence, and His Promise. "I am with thee, saith the Lord, to save thee" (v. 11). Emmanuel, our Hope (Matt. 1. 21-23). In His sevenfold promise there is a perfect salvation. He promises—

1. HEALTH. "I will restore health unto thee" (v. 17). Restoration to Himself means health. "He is the health of my countenance" (Psa. 23. 3).

2. HEALING. "I will heal thee of thy wounds." Saved, not only from sickness, but also from unsoundness. The wounds may be deep, but not too deep for His healing power.

3. FREEDOM. "I will bring again the captivity" (v. 18). There is, not only healing, but emancipation from the power of the enemy.

4. FRUITFULNESS. "I will multiply them, and they shall not be few" (v. 19). An increase of numbers as the result of a better testimony for God.

5. HONOUR. "I will also glorify them." Despised and rejected of men they may be, but accepted and honoured of God they will be. Those who suffer for Christ shall also reign with Him. On the other side of the flood they sang the Song of Moses.

6. PROTECTION. "I will punish all that oppress them" (v. 20). The overthrowing of the Egyptians in the Red Sea is a warning to all who follow God's people with the intent of their hurt. His redeemed are His peculiar treasure.

7. ALL-SUFFICIENCY. "I will be your God" (v. 22). No greater promise could God give. No fuller blessing could He offer than this. "Lo, I am with you all the days." See Hebrews 13. 5, 6, Revised Version. Observe God's "I wills" in this provision.

THE RESTORATION.
JEREMIAH 32. 37-41.

HERE again, as in chapter 30, God's promise to deliver consists of seven "I wills."

  I. I will gather them out—**Separation** (Eph. 2. 3-5).

  II. I will bring them in—**Safety** (John 10. 27).

  III. I will be their God—**Assurance** (1 John 3. 1).

  IV. I will give them one heart—**Unity** (John 17. 20, 21).

  V. I will make a covenant with them—**Satisfaction** (2 Cor. 6. 17, 18).

  VI. I will put My fear in their hearts—**Worship** (Acts 9. 31).

  VII. I will rejoice over them—**Praise** (Phil. 3. 1).

GREAT, HIDDEN THINGS.
JEREMIAH 33. 1-9.

THE reference is to Jerusalem desolated by war. A picture of a ruined life through sin and unbelief.

  I. **The Condition of Blessing.** "Call upon Me" (v. 3).

  II. **The Mighty Promises.** "Great and hidden things."

  1. RENEWAL of health (v. 6).

  2. REVELATION of abundance of peace and truth (v. 6).

  3. DELIVERANCE from bondage (v. 7).

  4. RESTORATION of ruined things (v. 7).

  5. CLEANSING from all iniquity (v. 8).

  6. GOD-HONOURING testimony (v. 9).

THE RECHABITES.
JEREMIAH 35.

JONADAB, the son of Rechab, was a strong, wise man. His life and testimony was a protest, Elijah-like, against the sins of the age, Baal-worship, and intemperance. The Rechabites were a separate family living in patriarchal fashion—dwelling in tents (v. 6), and observing the vow of the Nazarite (Num. 6. 2-4). As they were used as a rebuke to Judah, so may we learn much from them.

I. They were the Sons of a Good Father. Jonadab was a man zealous for the cause of God (2 Kings 10. 15, 16). A righteous, courageous, and consistent example on the part of a parent goes a very long way in the formation of the character of the son. The good, as well as the evil, that men do live after them in their children.

II. They were Severely Tested. "Bring them into the house of the Lord...and give them wine to drink" (v. 2). They had come into the city for safety when the King of Babylon and his forces came into the land (v. 11). Now they are tempted by the prophet, in God's own house, to break their vow of abstinence. Truly, they might have been excused in the circumstances. City temptations are strong for young men in every age, especially now. How many are still tempted to take the intoxicating wine in the house of God, by God's own servants at "Communion Seasons," when the house of prayer smells like a saloon.

III. They were Faithful to their Convictions. "They said, We will drink no wine, as our father commanded us" (v. 6). Although their father was dead long years ago, and although no one might have reproached them for taking it on such an occasion, yet they remained true to their father's wish and their own consciences. Of course, Jeremiah knew well that they would not touch it, if they had his purpose and God's message would have been thwarted. The proverb, "When in Rome do as the Romans do," is often cowardly and immoral. This lax, accommodating principle has been the ruin of multitudes.

IV. They became an Example to Others. Their faith in their father, their obedience, and devotion, to his word and will, were used by God to rebuke His people's unbelief and disobedience. "They obeyed their father's commandment:...I have spoken unto you...but ye hearkened not unto Me" (v. 14). They were faithful to their father's words spoken three hundred years ago, but God's professed sons had disregarded and forgotten His words. How true is it still that, in our human and temporal relationships we show far more fidelity, than in our spiritual and eternal. The Rechabites had received but one command, and they obeyed. God's people had servants and prophets sent again and again (v. 15), repeating His Words to them, yet they hearkened not. How slow men are to believe God.

V. They were Rewarded. "Because ye have obeyed your father, and kept all his precepts...Jonadab shall not want a man to stand before Me for ever" (vv. 18, 19). Their obedience to their parent was well pleasing unto the Lord (Col. 3. 20). As a family they *lived long* on the earth. This is the special blessing attached to the "Honouring of thy father and mother" (Eph. 6. 1-3; Exod. 20. 12). Obedience to God's Word is rewarded with *everlasting* life (John 3. 34-36). All who honour His Word shall stand before Him for ever.

BURNING THE BOOK.
JEREMIAH 36.

THE Book of God, like the people of God, has, in every age, suffered persecution. It has been tortured and ruptured, pierced and ridiculed, burned and buried, but it has quenched the violence of fire, escaped the edge of the sword, stopped the mouths of lions, and turned to flight the armies of the aliens. Here we see Jehoiachin burning it, but God gave it a resurrection in a mightier form.

I. The Message Given. (1) It was from the Lord. "Take thee a roll of a book, and write therein all the words that I have spoken unto thee" (v. 2). Like the Gospel of Christ, it was a revelation from Heaven. (2) It was a message of solemn warning. "Against Israel, and against Judah, and against all the nations" (v. 2). Like the Gospel, it was of universal import. (3) It was sent in mercy. "It may be that Israel will hear...and return every man from his evil way, that I may forgive their sin" (v. 3). Like the Gospel, it was a manifestation of God's love for them, and His desire after their salvation.

II. The Message Heard. "So the king sent Jehudi to fetch the roll...and he read it in the ears of the king" (vv. 20, 21). What a privilege to hear such words of faithful warning mingled with Divine forbearance and mercy. The importance and responsibility of hearing His Word, and giving heed to it, is powerfully evidenced here. It was the most critical moment in the life of the king. Hear, and your soul shall live.

III. The Message Rejected. "He cut it with the penknife, and cast it into the fire" (v. 23). Any fool could do that. There are some people's tongues like penknives, they cut to pieces the Gospel of God. There is a penknife called "higher criticism" that has done its own share of destructive work, but the most common and persistent weapon used by the ungodly against the Word of God is "an evil heart of unbelief." It was not with the "roll of a book" that the king had to do, but with the God of the book. The paper, or the preacher, may be easily cut to pieces, but not so the message, the Word of God endureth for ever. There are many who would not burn the book, but who are *not afraid*, nor rend their garments when its words are read (v. 24).

IV. **The Message Renewed.** Another roll was taken and "all the words of the book which the king had burned in the fire" were written, "and there were *added* besides unto them *many like words*" (v. 32). The force of the message was augmented by resistance. God will never lower His demands because of the opposition and hatred of men (Acts 5. 40-42). No man is done with God's Word when he has rejected and destroyed it. That same Word will yet judge him. A man might as well expect to improve the weather by breaking the barometer, as to relieve his soul by rejecting God's message. The unbelief of some will never make the Word of God of none effect. Remember that He who is "The Word of God" was resurrected from the dead.

THE VOICE OF THE LORD.
JEREMIAH 38.

"OBEY, I beseech thee, the voice of the Lord...so it shall be well with thee" (v. 20). The "voice" here stands for the Word of the Lord. It is—

　I. A **Warning** voice (vv. 3, 4).

　II. A **Humbling** voice (v. 2).

　III. A **Hated** voice (vv. 4-6).

　IV. A **Convicting** voice (secret concern, v. 14).

　V. An **Assuring** voice (v. 20).

　VI. An **Infallible** voice (chap. 39. 2-7).

JEHOIACHIN'S DELIVERANCE.
JEREMIAH 52. 31-34.

"She sat and wept; with her untressed hair
She wiped the feet she was so blessed to touch;
And He wiped off the soiling of despair.—*Coleridge*.

THE Divine threatenings in Leviticus 26 find their terrible fulfilment in the reign of Jehoiachin. "Be not deceived,

God is not mocked." Sin brings to ruin every nation and individual that yields to its dark and foulsome dominion. The king of Babylon was Jehovah's sword of vengeance in the punishment of Judah for their rebellion against Him. Jehoiachin was taken captive and thrown into a Babylonian prison, where he remained for the long period of thirty-seven years. But Babylon's new king, Evil-merodach, had mercy on him, and in grace wrought a marvellous change for him, giving us an illustration of the wonder-working grace of God.

I. **Delivered.** "He did lift up Jehoiachin out of prison" (v. 27). This was his first necessity. He could in no wise lift himself up. The grace of God which bringeth salvation has a mighty uplifting power. "He brought me up out of an horrible pit, out of the miry clay" (Psa. 40. 2); and from the darkness and thraldom of Satan into the Kingdom of God's dear Son. As with the king of Judah so with us; there is no uplifting into liberty without the exercise of Royal Authority.

II. **Comforted.** "He spake kindly to him." The law has no kind word of comfort to speak, but grace has. By grace are ye saved. All those ransomed by the power of Christ are comforted by the ministry of the Holy Spirit. The religion of man attempts to speak comfortably to men in the prison of sin; the religion of God first saves, then comforts. The blood of His victory goes before the water of His consolation. He knows how to speak a word to the weary. In all the coming ages God's people will show forth His kindness towards them through Christ Jesus (Eph. 2. 7).

III. **Exalted.** "He set his throne above the throne of the kings that were with him in Babylon." Jehoiachin had the pre-eminence among the other kings who were as captives in Babylon. The whole incident may be prophetic of Judah's future exaltation and glory, as it is suggestive of the spiritual uplifting enjoyed by those who are risen and exalted into heavenly places in Christ Jesus. Abounding sin and failure is conquered and overcome by the much more abounding grace of God. If man's fall through sin has been great, his uplifting through grace has been greater. He can make the homeless beggar of the dunghill meet to sit among the princes of Heaven. "Oh, to grace how great a debtor!"

IV. **Clothed.** "He changed his prison garments." The prison garments speak of guilt, defeat, shame, and bondage; but now they are gone, and garments of beauty take their place. So it is with those whom grace hath saved. The old things which spoke of failure, degradation and imprisonment, are put off, and those things have been put on which tell of glory, honour, immortality, and eternal life. A change will soon be evident when once a soul has been emancipated from the law of sin and death— the filthy rags of self-righteousness give place to the righteousness of God, which is unto all and upon all them that believe (Zech. 3. 3).

V. **Honoured.** "He did eat bread continually before him." He had the daily privilege of having fellowship with him who had delivered him from the house of bondage. The prisoner was now the constant companion of his Saviour. The grace of God not only saves and transforms, but brings into abiding fellowship with Himself. The kindness of David wrought the same gracious work for Mephibosheth (2 Sam. 9. 7). The door of our King's banqueting-house is always open for His own specially invited guests. Eat, O friends!

VI. **Supplied.** "His allowance was a continual allowance given him of the king, a daily rate for every day, all the days of his life."

1. It was an ALLOWANCE. It was not a reward, or something given as wages. It was something placed at the disposal of him whom the king delighted to honour. It was the provision of grace. How much has God placed at the disposal of those who have been saved by His grace? All the unsearchable riches of Christ.

2. It was a DAILY allowance. "A daily rate for every day." Take no thought for your life. "My grace is sufficient for thee." To-morrow's allowance will come with to-morrow's need.

3. It was given him OF THE KING; out of the king's fullness, and from his own gracious hand were all his wants supplied. "My God shall supply all your need" (Phil. 4. 19).

4. It was an allowance FOR LIFE. "All the days of his life." The royal promise covered his every need. All is yours, for ye are Christ's.

THE LIVING CREATURES.
EZEKIEL 1.

IT was when the prophet was "among the captives" that the "heavens were opened, and he saw visions of God" (v. 1). John was in the Isle of Patmos when the revelation came to him. These "visions of God" which came to Ezekiel the priest, whatever be their import to Israel, are strikingly symbolic of the Church of God as seen in Revelation 4 (read R.V.). These living creatures resemble the Church in—

I. Their Origin. They came "out of the midst of... a whirlwind...a great cloud, and a fire" (vv. 4, 5). A fire that was "infolding (taking hold of) itself." The fire, cloud, and whirlwind, are suggestive of God of Mystery and of Judgment, all of which appear in the sufferings and death of Jesus Christ. The Church is born of God in the mystery of godliness, and delivered from the judgment of sin (Acts 2. 2).

II. **Their Character.** They are "Living creatures," literally "living ones." They are not dying ones. Not of the earth earthy, but from Heaven. They are living ones whose life is akin to God's, partakers of the Divine nature. Heirs of eternal life.

III. **Their Appearance.** "They had the likeness of a MAN" (v. 5). Created after the image of Him who is the Son of God, in righteousness and true holiness. The Church is in the likeness of the Man Christ Jesus. Having—

1. The face of a MAN for wisdom, and reverence in worship (v. 10).

2. The face of a LION for courage and strength in battle.

3. The face of an OX for patience and perseverance in service.

4. The face of an EAGLE for clear vision, and heavenly power in testimony.

Each had four wings, power to obey the Divine commission, and to keep themselves out of sight. With two they "covered their bodies" (v. 11).

IV. **Their Movements.** "They went every one straight forward" (v. 12). This method of action proves that they were of one mind, and dominated by one great purpose. How could it be otherwise when, "whither the Spirit was to go they went?" That the Church of God might go straight forward in one Spirit, doing His will, was partly the burden of Christ's great prayer in John 17 (Rom. 8. 14; John 17. 22).

V. **Their Influence.** "Their appearance was like burning coals of fire...like lamps...the fire was bright, and out of the fire went forth lightning" (v. 13). He maketh His ministers a flaming fire (Psa. 104. 4). The early Church was endued with "Cloven tongues like as of fire" (Acts 2. 3). "Burning coals," "lamps," and "lightning," are self-assertive, they are not to be hid. Be filled with the Spirit, and the coals of thought will burn, then the lamp of life will shine, and the lightning of conviction and revelation go forth (v. 14).

VI. **Their Accompaniments.** "And when the living creatures went the wheels went with them" (vv. 15-21). The rings of the wheels were so high that they were dreadful...and full of eyes...and the Spirit of the living creatures was in the wheels. Symbolic of the Providence of God in relation to His redeemed people. "All things work together for good to them that love God,...called according to His purpose" (Rom. 8. 28. See 2 Chronicles 16. 9). They were mysterious ("dreadful"), unerring ("full of eyes"), and in perfect accord with the living ones—the same Spirit was in them. What a comfort to the Church of God.

VII. **Their Translation.** "The living ones were lifted up from the earth" (v. 19. See chapter 10. 19). When they are lifted up the wheels are also lifted up. This is a solemn thought for an ungodly and Christ-rejecting world. The Church shall be lifted from the earth (1 Thess. 4. 17). But when the wheels of Almighty grace cease to move in the world, the flaming fire of retribution will be kindled (2 Thess. 1. 7-10). Life *from* God is the guarantee of life *with* God.

EQUIPMENT FOR SERVICE.
Ezekiel 2, 3.

THE first great essential in service is a "vision of God" (chap. 1. 1). A vision of His greatness, His holiness, and unfailing mercy. Saul, who became Paul, was not "disobedient to the heavenly vision." The vision comes

through the revelation of His Son in the Scriptures of truth
(John 1. 18).   Here are some characteristics, which,
without fail, belong to the true servant of God—

I. **They are Spirit-possessed.**   "The Spirit entered
into me" (chap. 2. 2).   The revelation of God prepares
for the entering of His Holy Spirit into the heart.   Be
filled with the Spirit.   He is always ready to possess
every consecrated life.

II. **They are God-sent.**   "He said unto me, I send
thee" (chap. 2. 3).   Those who are Spirit-taught, will
be Spirit-sent.   "As Thou has sent me into the world,"
said our Lord; *"even so* have I also sent them into the
world" (John 17. 18).   The vision of Calvary preceded
the Pentecostal enduement and witness-bearing.

III. **They are Willing Recipients of His Word**.
"He said, Son of Man...eat this roll, so I opened my
mouth" (chap. 3. 1-3).   His words are spirit and life
(John 6. 61-63), so the Spirit-taught soul receives them
gladly.   He receives the roll of the book, just as a little
child receives its food.   He opened his mouth, and the
Lord filled it, "and it was in his mouth as honey for
sweetness."   If the Word of God was more simply and
fully received, there would be more delight in it, and
more power through it.

IV. **They are Courageous.**   "Behold, I have made
thy face strong," etc. (chap. 3. 8).   A "strong face," is
an evidence of great force of character.   Leaders of men
have usually a strong facial expression.   God can make
your character to be strong and powerful.   The fear of
man is foreign to the man of God.

V. **They are Obedient.**   "The Spirit took me up...
and I wept in bitterness, in the heat of my spirit" (v. 14).
The Word of the Lord was sweet in his mouth, but somewhat bitter in its practical operation.   But although

there was bitterness to his soul in following the guidance of the Spirit, he obeyed. Paul gloried in tribulation *also*.

VI. **They are Humble.** "Then I came to them of the captivity...and I sat where they sat" (v. 15). This was how he reached the lapsed mass. He obeyed the Spirit of God, and went and sat down among them. Those who labour for Christ, must act like Him, humbling themselves for the sake of others.

VII. **They are Faithful.** "I have made thee a watchman" (chap. 3. 16-21). The watchman must "warn the wicked from his wicked way, to save his life." The wicked need warning, and the man who has seen "visions of God" is alone able sufficiently to give that warning. Paul was a faithful watchman, and could say, "I am pure from the blood of all men" (Acts 20. 26-31). Study to show thyself approved of God, a *watchman* that needeth not to be ashamed (2 Tim. 2. 15).

THE TIME OF LOVE.
EZEKIEL 16. 1-20.

ALL Scripture is given by inspiration of God, and is profitable for doctrine. In this chapter we have a revelation of the marvellous love and grace of God. Judah is here represented as a helpless, forsaken infant, perishing in the open field. The time of Divine love came when He, passing by, pitied, and saved with a great salvation. The need of a ruined Jerusalem is the need of every ruined soul.

I. **A Picture of Destitution.** Could any figures of speech be more expressive than this?

1. HELPLESSNESS. "I saw thee weltering in thy blood" (v. 6, R.V.). Jerusalem did not see herself in this sorrowful plight. God's judgment of sin is quite a different thing from man's (Rom. 3. 19; 5. 6).

2. HOPELESSNESS. "None eye pitied thee...to have compassion upon thee" (v. 5). No one is capable of pitying the *sinner* who knows not the holiness of God. Men can understand the sadness of poverty, shame and crime committed against himself or his fellow men, but not *sin* as against God. In this sense "No man can redeem his brother." In humanity there is absolutely no hope for man as guilty before God.

II. **A Picture of Salvation.** "Behold thy time, the time of love" (v. 8). The time of love was when "He passed by, and looked upon thee." Our time of love is now, while God in mercy and grace is passing by in the Gospel of His Son, beholding in pity and compassion our sin and misery. The proof and power of that love is seen in what He did.

1. HE SPARED. "I said unto thee, Live" (v. 6). He only could speak the Word of Life to this blood-stained outcast. He who "spared not" His own Son spared this sinning soul. The salvation of God is the sparing of the soul in unmerited mercy from guilt and death. Saved by grace alone.

2. HE CLEANSED. "Then I washed thee with water." Blood, the figure of pollution and sin, was washed away. Every spared one is a washed one (Gal. 1. 4). The life He gives is a clean life.

3. HE COVERED. "I spread My skirt over thee, and covered thy nakedness" (v. 8). He acts the part of a near kinsman (Ruth 3. 9). The skirt of His righteousness is unto all, and upon all them that believe.

4. HE CLAIMED. "And thou becamest Mine" (v. 8). Oh, what a change! From the "open field" of sin and shame, into the bosom of the family of God. From self-degradation and hopelessness, into the Kingdom of grace and of glory.

5. He Anointed. "And I anointed thee with oil" (v. 9). It is God's will that all His claimed, cleansed, and covered ones should be anointed with the Holy Spirit (Acts 1. 8; 19. 2).

6. He Crowned. "And I put...a beautiful crown upon thine head" (v. 12). He who began the good work of saving grace, carried it on to completion, so that we become "perfect through His comeliness" (v. 14). The crown is the emblem of dignity and power. The crowning day is coming, and now is.

7. He Used. "Thy renown went forth among the heathen for thy beauty" (v. 14). "Perfect through My majesty which I had put upon thee" (R.V.). "The glory which Thou gavest Me I have given them" (John 17. 22). Let your light so shine before men.

III. A Picture of Desecration (vv. 15-20). In every age God has had occasion to make the same sorrowful complaint against His ungrateful people. Blessed with all spiritual blessings in Christ Jesus, yet backsliding in heart, and using their God-given prestige for selfish and worldly ends. This picture is a very sad one, and all the more so that the sin shown in it is so common. It is the desecration of their—

1. Beauty. "Thou didst trust in thine own beauty, and playedst the harlot because of thy renown" (v. 15). This is what we sometimes term "religious pride," using the influence God in grace hath given us for base, selfish purposes.

2. Garments. "Thy garments thou didst take, and deckedst thy high places" (v. 16). The garments given her for glory and beauty (vv. 10, 11) desecrated to the adorning of a false and God-dishonouring religion. The teaching of Christ is now being used by some preachers for the building up of a new and unscriptural system.

3. TREASURES. "Thou hast also taken My gold and My silver...and madest to thyself images of men" (v. 17). Devoting the gifts of God to the honour and praise of men. The gold and silver of Divine truth debased, as if it were only the message of men.

4. CHILDREN. "Morover thou hast taken thy sons and thy daughters, whom thou hast borne unto Me, and these hast thou sacrificed...thou hast slain My children" (vv. 20, 21). What an awful charge! A backsliding Church is a murderer of its children. Those born of the Gospel of God, in the day of His power and grace, are often sacrificed and "devoured" by false teaching. All this has come about by having a "weak heart" toward the Lord God (v. 30). Let us take heed lest there be in any of us an evil heart of unbelief in departing from the living God.

SIN AND DEATH.
EZEKIEL 18. 1-23.

GOD charges the people with misrepresenting facts. He says, "What mean ye that ye use this proverb...saying, The fathers have eaten sour grapes, and the children's teeth are set on edge" (v. 2). Hereditary influence may be great, but that will not absolve from personal responsibility. "Behold, all souls are mine...the soul that sinneth, *it* shall die" (v. 4). There is no escape from this. Some searching and encouraging lessons are taught in this chapter. Notice that—

I. **All Souls Belong to God** (v. 4). He is the Author and Bestower of life. He is the Father of spirits. Souls in the deepest sense are spirits, and should glorify God as the chief end of their existence.

II. **Each Soul is Individually Responsible to God** "The soul that sinneth, it shall die" (vv. 4, 20). No man here is to die for his father's sin. The sinning son of the just man shall die in his sins (vv. 5-13), and the righteous son of a sinning father shall not die for his sins, but live (vv. 14-17). Every man must give an account of himself unto God. No man is condemned because of Adam's sin, but because "All have sinned."

III. **Righteousness is the Condition of Life.** "If a man be just...he shall surely live" (vv. 5, 9). A just man is literally a *lawful* man, a law-abiding man. A man whose life is in harmony with, and guided by, the holy law, or Word of God. Through Christ, the righteousness of God is now unto all and upon all that believe. All that believe are justified from all things (Acts 13. 38, 39). Apart from grace there is "None righteous, no, not one."

IV. **Wickedness is the Condition of Death** (v. 20). Wickedness here is literally *lawlessness*, the opposite of the *just* who are *lawful*. A lawless soul is a soul living in the sphere of death. Enmity to God's Word and will is the evidence of it. Those who are a law unto themselves are the murderers of their own souls. Repent and believe.

V. **Sin and Death are Inseparable.** "The soul that sinneth, it shall die" (v. 20). The wages of sin is death (Rom. 6. 23). "Wages" are something duly earned, and that must be justly paid. The soul that sinneth shall die, because, in sinning, the soul is choosing death rather than life. The presence of sin means death, as the absence of light means darkness.

VI. **God has no Pleasure in the Death of the Lawless.** "Have I any pleasure at all that the lawless should die? saith the Lord God" (v. 23). God's character, His Word, and His work in the Person of His Son, all emphatically declare His displeasure at the death of the sinning soul. Could any protest be louder than the cry of the Christ of

God upon the awful tree, "Father, forgive them, for they know not what they do." His will is that all men should be saved by coming into the knowledge of the truth (1 Tim. 2. 4).

VII. **Conversion is the Way into Life.** "He should return from His ways and live" (v. 23). The Lord is no respecter of persons, His "way is equal" (v. 25). "Him that cometh unto Me I will in no wise cast out." Except ye be converted—turned to the Lord—ye cannot enter the Kingdom of life. I am come that ye might have life. Come unto Me. Turn ye, turn ye from your evil ways, for why will ye die.

WARN THEM FROM ME.
Ezekiel 33. 7-11.

THE prophet is here reminded that he has been set apart as a "watchman unto the house of Israel" (v. 7; see chap. 3. 17-21). If there were no *danger* there would be no need of the watchman. The enemy is ever seeking whom he may devour. What He said to Ezekiel He now says unto all, "Watch" (Mark 13. 37). Notice the—

I. **Responsibilities of the Watchman.** They are twofold.

1. "To HEAR the word at His mouth" (v. 7). The watchman must not only have eyes to see and a mouth to speak, but ears to hear the Word of God as from His own mouth. The first necessity is to hear Him, and to enter intelligently and sympathetically into His mind and purposes.

2. To "WARN them from Me." Warn them, because there is impending danger; and warn them from Him, as one who is wholly devoted to His will. The watchman's responsibility lies in making men feel their responsibility to God.

II. **Responsibility of the Warned.** The "wicked" here are literally the *lawless.* Observe their—

1. CONDITION. "O lawless man, thou shalt surely die" (v. 8). Sin is lawlessness, and lawlessness is death. Death is the result of alienation from God.

2. OPPORTUNITY. "Warn them from Me." Through the prophet they were distinctly "warned of God." It is sad to be deluded and deceived, but it is surely a mercy to be faithfully warned of our danger. "Except ye repent ye shall likewise perish" was not spoken in anger, but in love. The warning comes *from* God just as directly as the invitation of His mercy (John 3. 36).

3. RESPONSIBILITY. "If he do not *turn from his way,* he shall die in his iniquity" (v. 9). The warning is "to turn." If he turns not he shall die in his sins, his blood shall be upon his own soul. Regeneration is the work of the Spirit of God; but conversion—*turning about*—at His bidding is an act of our own will. The trumpet warning of the law may be despised, and the trumpet blower may be reckoned behind the times, but turning from sin and faith in the Lord Jesus Christ is the only way into the Kingdom of God, which is righteousness, peace, and joy in the Holy Ghost.

III. **Attestation and Appeal of the Wronged One.** "As I live, saith the Lord God, I have no pleasure in the death of the wicked (lawless); ...turn ye, turn ye from your evil ways, for why will ye die" (v. 11). This is the agony of Divine love that found its fuller expression in the dying cry of His beloved Son on the atoning tree: "Father, forgive them, for they know not what they do." "The Lord is...longsuffering to usward, not willing that any should perish" (2 Peter 3. 9). "He that taketh warning shall deliver his soul" (v. 5).

HYPOCRITICAL PROFESSORS.

EZEKIEL 33. 30-33.

HYPOCRISY is literally the acting of a part on a stage, assuming a character that is unreal. A "saint abroad and a devil at home" is how Bunyan puts it. Those who "steal the livery of the court of Heaven" to serve themselves on earth are hypocrites of the most ardent type. Take a look at their behaviour as here depictured. See them in—

I. **Connection with God's Servant**. "Talking against thee by the walls and in the doors of their houses." This manner of tale-bearing, behind the wall and in the home, is most reprehensible. This secret, God-grieving tittle-tattle against His servants is not overlooked by Him. All closet work, whether it be good or bad, is open to His eyes.

II. **Connection with God's People**. They say, "Come, let us hear what is the Word from the Lord...and they sit before thee as My people sit, and hear thy words." They put on the form of Godliness so long as it helps their own personal interests. They assume the habits of God's people, while they secretly sneer at the real work of God. The only time they are among God's people is when they are hearing His Word.

III. **Connection with God's Message**.

1. THEY HAVE PLEASURE IN HEARING IT. "They hear Thy words...and lo, Thou art unto them as a very lovely song, as one that...can play well on an instrument." Ezekiel must have been an attractive preacher, with "a pleasant voice," and playing well, as on an instrument; and his message was, even to those hypocrites, "a very lovely song." That is just exactly what the message of God to sinful man is, "A *very* lovely song." But woe be to those who only hear it as a song for the ear, instead

of a message for the heart.   How much preaching there is to-day that "tickle the palate, but do not make men feel the bitterness of sin."   Good and entertaining preaching, that is to Godless hearers like a tune well played on an instrument, or a lively song sung with a pleasant voice. But in this case, as in very many others, the preacher was not to blame.

2. THEY IN HEART REJECT IT.   "They hear thy words, but they will not do them; for with their mouth they shew much love, but their heart goeth after their covetousness." They love in a measure to hear God's message, but they will not receive it.   "With their mouth and with their lips they honour Him, but have removed their heart far from Him" (Isa. 29. 13).   Such base and deceitful conduct brings upon such the "woe" pronounced upon all religious hypocrites, who are "like unto whited sepulchres" (Matt. 23. 27, 28).   It is awfully possible to flatter Him with the mouth, while lying to Him with the heart; but as a man thinketh in his heart, so is he before God.   With the heart man believeth unto righteousness, and with the heart man deceiveth unto everlasting condemnation.

FAITHLESS SHEPHERDS.
EZEKIEL 34. 1-10.

HERE are six conditions of need mentioned as expressive of sin and soul destitution, making clear the great need of faithful shepherds.

I. **Their Work.**

1. To feed the HUNGRY (v. 3).

2. To strengthen the WEAK (v. 4).   Weak through disease.

3. To heal the SICK (v. 4).

4. To bind up the BROKEN (v. 4).

5. To bring in the DRIVEN AWAY (v. 4). Backsliding.

6. To seek the LOST (v. 4).

II. Their Faithfulness.

1. They were SELFISH. They fed themselves and starved the flock (v. 3).

2. They were PROUD. They ruled with force, self-will, and not with love (v. 4, *l.c.*).

3. They were RUINOUS. The flock were scattered (v. 5). They became a prey to the beasts of the field (to false doctrine and lax example). "They wandered through all the mountains (false philosophies) and upon every high hill" (pride of intellect) (v. 6). The sheep became like distracted souls, seeking light and help in other godless religions.

4. They were DISOWNED of God (v. 10). Take heed to thyself. "Feed the flock of God which is among you, taking the oversight thereof, not by constraint, but willingly; not for filthy lucre, but of a ready mind; neither as being lords over God's heritage, but being ensamples to the flock" (1 Peter 5. 2, 3).

WHAT GOD WILL DO FOR HIS SHEEP.
EZEKIEL 34. 11-30.

As the unbelief of some cannot make the faith of God without effect (Rom. 3. 3), neither can the unfaithfulness of God's shepherds make the faithfulness of God to fail. With regard to His sheep—

I. He will **search** and seek them (v. 11). They shall hear His voice (John 10. 27).

II. He will **deliver** them (v. 12). The power of the enemy shall not hold them.

III. He will **bring** them (v. 13). Separate **them for** Himself.

IV. He will **feed** them (v. 14). Bring them into good pastures (Psa. 23).

V. He will **rest** them (v. 15). Cause them to lie down.

VI. He will **bind** up the broken (v. 16). Broken and useless members.

VII. He will **strengthen** the weak (v. 16). Weak through sickness and weariness.

VIII. He will **judge** their cause (vv. 17-22). When tempted, annoyed, and persecuted.

IX. He will **watch** over them (vv. 23-25; Heb. 13. 20).

X. He will **bless them** and make them a blessing (v. 26).

XI. He will **abundantly satisfy** them with good (vv. 29-31). _____

THE GREAT CHANGE.
Ezekiel 36. 25-32.

These wonderful words refer primarily to Israel's restoration. Under the law the heart of His people had become like a stone, but through His infinite grace a new heart would be given them, so that by the constraint of love they would walk in His ways. God's method in dealing with a sinful heart is revolutionary, it is a regeneration.

I. **The Disease.** "A stony heart" (v. 26). A heart that is "stony" is—

1. Cold. It has become insensible—past feeling. All warmth of affection for God and His Word has died away.

2. Hard. Not easily impressed. Unyielding as a rock. Indifferent to all the gracious influences of light and the force of spiritual truth. Callous.

3. Dead. Incapable of spiritual motion. No vitality toward God. Deaf to His call and dumb for His Name.

II. **The Remedy**. "A new heart will I give you...an heart of flesh." The only cure for a stony heart is a *new* heart. Polishing or carving a stone into an altered and improved form will not make it a "living stone." A heart of flesh is—

1. A NEW HEART. It is the gift of God, and takes the place of the stony heart, and so renewing the whole man. It is not only *new* to the man who gets it, but its manifestations are new to all who see them.

2. A SOFT HEART. Sensitive and childlike, easily impressed by the things of God. The stony nature has disappeared.

3. A WARM HEART. The love of God has found a home in it, and is shed abroad through it. It glows with compassion for the perishing, and burns with indignation against sin and iniquity.

4. A LIVING HEART. Once dead, but now alive unto God. A heart fitted to have communion with the living God. When Sir W. Raleigh was asked to adjust his head on the block he said, "It matters little how the head lies if *the heart is right*." Is thine heart right with God?

III. **The Results**. The new heart opens the way for the fullness of the new life. The new character reveals itself by—

1. POSSESSING HIS SPIRIT. "I will put My Spirit within you" (v. 27). His Spirit is the new motive power in the life. This new moral machinery requires a new power (Rom. 8. 9).

2. WALKING IN HIS STATUTES. "I will cause you to walk in My statutes." The daily life is made to become pleasing unto the Lord. To walk in His way is to walk with God.

3. DWELLING IN HIS LAND. "Ye shall dwell in the land that I gave to your fathers," etc. (v. 28). The good

land of His providence is the inheritance of all who have been made "new creatures in Christ Jesus. "

4. RESTING ON HIS PROMISES (vv. 29-32). They are exceeding great and precious, so that we might delight ourselves in the Lord, because for His own Name's sake hath He done all this for us (v. 32).

THE BONES AND THE BREATH.
EZEKIEL 37. 1-10.

THESE bones refer to "the whole house of Israel" (v. 11). As a nation, they are scattered over the open valley of the whole world, separated bone from his bone, and *very dry.* But the time will come when the breath of God's Spirit shall come upon them, and they shall "stand upon their feet an exceeding great army" of witnesses for God and for His Christ. But surely there is a present-day application of all Scripture, divinely breathed. Observe—

I. **How the Vision Came.** "The hand of the Lord was upon me, and carried me out in the Spirit" (v. 1). We must be "in the Spirit" to see things as they really are as God sees them. This is where revival begins.

II. **What the Vision Was.** "A valley full of bones. " A picture of utter desolation. A wrecked and ruined people. "Very many" and "very dry. " Through their backsliding and indifference to God's Word they had become like bleached bones; no evidence whatever of spiritual sap or life in them; dried up through pride, worldliness, and self-dependence. The same principles produce the same results to-day, but how few see it.

III. **A Testing Question.** "Son of man, can these bones live?" (v. 3). This question can only come home to those whose eyes have been opened to see the awful need of spiritual life. The blind man would answer, "What bones? I don't see any bones. Things are quiet and peaceful, and the valley is lovely and attractive." Think of the responsibility that rests with a Spirit-taught man! The opened eye is a new opening for work. If God hath given us to see the need of others, does He not mean to use us for their deliverance?

IV. A Thoughtful Answer. "I answered, O Lord God, Thou knowest." He only could know, for He alone could make them live. Science, art, and all the philosophies of men have no remedy for a soul dead in sin and dried up with iniquity. "THOU knowest." Salvation is of the Lord. It is good in a crisis like this to cast ourselves on the wisdom and power of God.

V. The Remedy. The Divine remedy is revealed when the need has been seen and painfully felt. It is two-fold. He is commanded to speak to the bones on God's behalf (v. 4), and to speak to God on their behalf (v. 9). Preach the Word of the Lord (v. 4) and pray for the power of the Holy Ghost. The preaching is to be in the faith of His promises. "Behold I will cause breath to enter into you, and ye shall live" (v. 5). It is the Spirit that quickeneth. The results were according as he had said (v. 10). An army of men raised from the dead stood upon their feet, ready to breathe out their God-given life in His service. "Likewise reckon ye also yourselves to be... alive unto God through Jesus Christ our Lord" (Rom 6. 11).

WATERS TO SWIM IN.
EZEKIEL 47. 1-12.

THIS mystical river is full of prophetic significance. In the time of Millennial blessing rivers of living water shall flow forth from the sanctuary of the Holy City into the desert and waste places of the earth (Zech. 14. 8), and "everything shall live whither the river cometh" (v. 9).

But this river may also be regarded as a beautiful emblem of the fullness of the blessing of the Gospel of Christ, or of the Pentecostal outpouring of the Holy Spirit.

I. **The River.** A free, spontaneous outburst.

1. Its SOURCE. "Out from under the threshold of the house" (temple) (v. 1). Out from the holy place, the place of the "Mercy seat," the throne of God. Like the Holy Spirit, it proceeded from the Father (John 15. 26).

2. Its COURSE. "The waters came down...at the south side of the altar" (v. 1). Yes, the only way these life-giving waters can reach a perishing world is by way of the altar—the Cross of Christ. The Holy Spirit was not given till after Christ had suffered and was glorified (see Rev. 22. 1).

3. Its FORCE. It grew in power and plenitude, although it had no tributary. The streams of earth can add nothing to the river of God. It became a river that could not be passed over. It had power to heal (v. 8), to revive (v. 9), and to bring forth fruit and abiding freshness (v. 12). Such is the power of the Holy Spirit working in those who believe in Him as the Scripture hath said (John 7. 38, 39). It is a symbol of the unsearchable riches of Christ and the boundless love of God.

II. **A Growing Experience of the River's Depth and Power.** Being obedient to the Divine Leader, he was brought in vision into a progressive experience of this fullness of blessing. Three times over we are told that "He brought me *through*," indicating that these were not final conditions, but the way to something deeper and better—a passing experience. Note the order—

1. ANKLE DEEP. "He brought me through; the waters were to the ankles" (v. 3). It was but a shallow acquaintance with the river of life, but still, he was in it. This

stage represents the "Spirit of *Faith*," the definite act of stepping into the current of the Divine will, although that will as yet is but little known.

2. KNEE DEEP. "Again He brought me...the waters were to the knees." The only way the waters can rise upon us is by our getting deeper down. Knee deep represents the "Spirit of *Prayer*." When the knees are captured for God there will be delight in His fellowship. It is possible to be a believer and yet have no liberty in prayer. Although this is but the second stage of the Christian life, how many fail to attain unto it, because they refuse to be *led* (v. 2).

3. LOIN DEEP. "Again...the waters were to the loins" (v. 4). The loins stand for the secret of the strength of a man. The river has laid hold of his strength. This represents the "Spirit of *Power*." The praying Christian will soon become a witnessing Christian. His loins are now girded with the power of God. When a man is loin deep there is less of the man seen, and the depth of the river is in greater evidence. Those only ankle deep make a big show of themselves, and misrepresent the fullness of the waters.

4. SWIMMING. "Afterward...the waters were risen, waters to swim in, a river that could not be passed over" (v. 5). The swimming Christian has got beyond his depth, and is now being borne up by the river of God. This last stage represents the "*Fullness* of the Spirit." Instead of wading through, he is now resting on the waters. This is an experience that cannot be passed over. There is nothing better than this in earth or in Heaven. The perfection is not in us, but in the abounding fullness of His provision for us. "Waters to swim in." "Launch out into the deep."

THE MAN OF PURPOSE.
DANIEL 1.

THE book of Daniel has been cast into the critics' den, but, like Daniel, it shall yet escape from the mouths of the lions. Rationalists are rejecting it because of its miracles and prophetic utterances. The Lord Jesus Christ approved of it, for it formed part of the canonical Scriptures in His time. Sir Isaac Newton said that "Christianity itself may be said to be founded on the prophecies of Daniel."

After the siege of Jerusalem (v. 1), Daniel had been taken captive to Babylon, a distance of about eight hundred miles. He was probably about fourteen years of age at that time.

I. **His Character.** We know nothing of his parents, but judging from his character as a lad, he must have been nurtured in a God-fearing home, for the soundest principles of life had been early formed. One has said: "There is nothing rarer than *personality*, for there are so many causes that hinder both interior and exterior, so many hostile forces to crush, so many illusions to lead astray." Blessed is that young man who can truly say, "I know in whom I have believed," etc. A personal knowledge of God is the mightiest of all safeguards for city life.

II. **His Temptations** (vv. 5, 6). Testing times will come. These are needed for our moral and spiritual development. The king's command was to select blameless youths, skilful and wise, to take the honoured place of students at the Royal College, and to "stand in the king's palace." It was to be a three years' course, to learn the tongue of the Chaldeans. The Chaldeans were the politicians, philosophers, theologians, and teachers of the nation. What an opportunity for a young, bright, hopeful man! But how could *he* eat that meat and drink

that wine which had been consecrated to idols, and defile
his conscience? The worldly man sees no difficulty, but
rather a grand chance to attain honour and earthly glory;
but it is very different with the man who is abiding in the
fellowship of God.

III. **His Purpose.** "He purposed in his heart that he
would not defile himself" (v. 8). This in our days would
be called "narrow-mindedness and puritanical bigotry."
In this connection see Paul's advice (Rom. 14. 21). That
man is of little value for God who is not able to stand
against popular opinion. The Talmud says: "A myrtle
tree remains a myrtle even in the desert." A *man of God*
should act as such in any circumstance. God is not
influenced by man-made conditions. A lad of fifteen
years was following the plough near the Carse of Gowrie,
the horses stopped in the middle of the furrow. At that
moment this question came to his mind: "Might I not
make more of my life than I am doing?" and straightening
himself up, he said, "God helping me, I will be a
missionary." That lad was Dr. James Stewart, of
Lovedale. Keep a conscience void of offence.

IV. **His Reward.** "God made Daniel to find favour"
(v. 9, R.V.). This was a great crisis in the life of Daniel.
He was found faithful, and God promoted him. Henceforth he is marked as a leader of the people. Faith in
God, and plain fare (v. 15), got the victory for both body
and soul. "Their countenances were fairer and fatter than
all who did eat the king's meat." Godliness is profitable.
Why? Because it is the highest type of character and the
best possible relationship to God and men. The wisdom
that profited Daniel was not found in the schools of the
learned, but in the closet of communion with the God of
Heaven. *Determine* to know nothing among men save
Jesus Christ and Him crucified, and the wisdom of God
will be in you.

THE MAN OF FAITH.

DANIEL 2. 16-28.

THE pleasures of the ungodly are easily spoiled. Because of a dream, the king's spirit is greatly troubled. The vision had vanished from his mind, and he demanded of his wise men that they should make it known (v. 5). A thing with them impossible (v. 10), but a new opportunity for the God of Daniel to manifest His wisdom and power.

I. **Faith Exercised.** It would seem as if the executioners were on their way to carry out the king's mad decree (v. 5), when Daniel "went in and desired of the king that he would give him time and he would show him the interpretation" (v. 16). How did he know that he would succeed in this? He believed that His God knew all about it, and that by coming into closer touch with Him the wisdom of God would be given him. All things are possible to them that believe. Paul could say: "Be of good cheer for I believe God" (Acts 27. 25).

II. **Prayer Answered.** "*Then* was the secret revealed unto Daniel in a night vision" (v. 19). Daniel invited his three companions to a night of prayer. They spread the matter before the God of Heaven, and *then* was the thing revealed. Prayer does not bring God down to our thoughts and actions, it brings our thoughts and actions up into His. Contact with God means being made like God.

III. **Thanks Given.** Daniel said, "Blessed be the Name of God for ever...He changeth the times...He giveth wisdom...He revealeth the deep and secret things" (vv. 20-23). If we would pray more, we would praise more. The secrets of the Lord are with them that fear Him. Draw near to Him and He will draw near to you.

IV. **Testimony Borne.** "There is a God in Heaven that revealeth secrets...as for me, this secret is not revealed to me for any wisdom that I have" (vv. 28-30). What a consolation this is. The door into this favour is open to all. The Holy Spirit has been given to guide into truth. He searcheth all things, yea, the deep things of God.

THE ALMIGHTY STONE.

DANIEL 2. 31-45.

DANIEL, by living in the fellowship of God, became a man of visions, and the interpreter of the Divine mind. The vision of the "Great Image" came to the king in a dream, perhaps that Daniel may have the opportunity of revealing the purposes of God in the ages to come. The different parts of the image represent successive kingdoms (vv. 38-40). The Stone is the symbol of Christ, who shall yet dash the nations to pieces like a potter's vessel, when there shall be "no place found for them" (vv. 34, 35, 44). Seven times in Scripture is our Lord Jesus Christ called a Stone, the symbol of strength and durability. We shall note four instances that refer to Israel, the Church, the Nations, and to the World.

I. **As a Stone, Israel Stumbled over Christ.** He was to them "a Stone of stumbling" because He came in the form of a Servant. As a Stone He was rejected by the Jewish builders (Matt. 21. 42), although He had been laid in Zion as the Foundation by Jehovah (Isa. 28. 16). Christ warned them that "Whosoever shall fall upon this Stone shall be broken" (Matt. 21. 44). They fell on it, and as a nation were broken, and are yet scattered abroad, dashed to pieces like a broken vessel.

II. **As a Stone, the Church was built on Christ.** When Peter confessed Him as "The Christ, the Son of the Living God," Jesus said, "Upon this rock I will build My church" (Matt. 16. 16-18). After Pentecost when Peter declared that the lame man had been healed through faith in the Name of Jesus, he also added, "This is the Stone which is set at nought of you builders, which is become the *head corner*" (Acts 4 .10, 11). We still come to Him as unto a "*Living* Stone" (1 Peter 2. 4). He is the Author of eternal life. Other foundation can no man lay. There is none other Name.

III. **As a Stone, Gentile power shall be broken by Christ.** "A Stone, cut out without hands, smote the image" (v. 34). In our days "hands" count for much, but this revolution shall be brought about "without hands." The image represents Gentile authority, "the kingdoms of this world." Their end shall come suddenly, like the falling of a stone from Heaven, and upon whom it shall fall it shall grind to powder (Matt. 21. 44). The whole image was "broken to pieces." His coming will be like a thief in the night, unexpected by those who are asleep, it will be like "lightning" (Matt. 24. 17), unmistakable. No need saying, To here, or To there, when the lightning flash comes, it is self-evident to all. Then the Babel tower of this world's Godless principles will be a heap of ruins, for like them they have brick for *stone*. This appearing of Christ cannot possibly refer to His *first* advent. Then the Roman kingdom was not divided like the ten toes. Gentile power was not destroyed at His first appearing. He then came as a Babe, not with the crushing force of a falling stone, taking vengeance on them that knew not God.

IV. **As a Stone, the World will yet be filled with the Glory of Christ.** His coming is not the end of the world, but the beginning of a new world. The Stone becomes a great Mountain, and *fills the whole earth* (v. 35). A mountain is the symbol of the Kingdom's strength and stability. When He comes in great power and glory, He who is strong to *smite* will also be strong to *save*. To understand this chapter read Psalm 72. "He shall put down all rule and all authority and power, for He must reign till He hath put all enemies under His feet" (1 Cor. 15. 24, 25). "Then the kingdoms of this world shall become the Kingdom of our God, and of His Christ." His Name is, and for ever will be, above every name. All nations shall yet call Him blessed.

THE NONCONFORMISTS.

Daniel 3.

These two images in chapters 2 and 3 represent man's rule and man's worship. This "image of gold" to be set up in the plain of Dura was the visible expression of Nebuchadnezzar's "new theology." It was to be a great affair. But true godly living is a very simple thing. A *Revelation* is needed. This new popular religion brings a new trial to the servants of God. There was—

I. **Their Temptation.** A new national idol had been set up (vv. 3-5). Man's unenlightened ingenuity is always setting up some new thing as an object of worship. It is all the more delusive with its grand musical attractions (v. 7). On the king's part it was but another exhibition of despotism and religious intolerance, another form of "man's inhumanity to man." The temptation at this time to Daniel and his three fellow-believers was to—

1. Save their Situation. They had been "set over the affairs of the province of Babylon" (chap. 2. 49). As government officials they held a high social position, and perhaps received a good salary. Demas forsook Paul when worldly advantage was to be gained (2 Tim. 4. 10). It was also a temptation to—

2. Sacrifice their Conscience. It affected their relationship with God. Of course all that the king demanded was *conformity*, what all sham religions are satisfied with. James Renwick, the last of the Scottish

martyrs, was offered freedom if he would "but let a drop of ink fall on the paper." But, no, when it was to be the sign of the denial of Christ.

II. **Their Testimony**. "Our God, whom *we serve*, is able to deliver us...We will not serve thy gods" (vv. 17, 18). This showed their—

1. FAITH IN THE POWER OF GOD. "If so be our God is able." Those who are serving God daily are not likely to be cast down suddenly. True hearted service gives stability of character in the time of trial.

2. SUBMISSION TO THE WILL OF GOD. "But if not...we will not" (v. 18). They would rather burn than turn. Like Job, they could say, "Though He slay me, yet will I trust" (see Acts 4. 19, 20). They were in Babylon, but they were not of it.

III. **Their Triumph**. They were cast into the furnace because of non-conformity, but "the fire had no power" (vv. 26, 27). The wrath of man is a poor, impotent thing in presence of the power of God. Their sufferings brought them—

1. A NEW SENSE OF FREEDOM. "Lo, I see four men loose walking in the midst of the fire" (v. 25). Liberty to walk in a furnace was a new experience for them. They could truly "glory in their affliction." They were not saved *from* the fiery furnace, but they were saved *in* it, which was a much greater deliverance. The peace of God in the heart is an indestructible principle, beyond the reach of any fiery trial. The world cannot take it away.

2. A NEW SOURCE OF FELLOWSHIP. There was a *fourth* in the fire, "like the Son of God." In being cast out by men, they were brought into sweeter communion with the Son of God. It was so with Paul and Silas (Acts 16). Bunyan, Rutherford, Madam Guyon, and multitudes of others who suffered for Christ.

3. A NEW OPPORTUNITY FOR SERVICE. "The king promoted them" (v. 30). Their sphere of usefulness was enlarged after their deeper experience of the power of God. What a testimony they had to give, as men who had passed from death into life; who were dead, but are now living in the power of a resurrection. Every severe trial borne for Christ's sake will bring a new revelation of Divine possibilities, that we may go back to live with a new force in our being. The Captain of our salvation was made perfect through suffering, and the servant is not greater than his Master. By refusing to bow to the image of gold man had set up, the image of God was more firmly set up in their own hearts.

NEBUCHADNEZZAR—RUIN AND REMEDY.
DANIEL 4. 29-37.

"ALL Scripture...is profitable for doctrine, reproof, correction, and instruction in righteousness." In the experiences recorded in this chapter there is something that might reprove our selfishness, correct our actions, and instruct in the righteousness of God. This personal testimony of Nebuchadnezzar was given as a Royal Edict (v. 1). One may know much about the ways of God and yet be an utter stranger experimentally to His saving grace. Think of—

I. **His Privileges.** He had been favoured with special opportunities. In chapter 2 we see God revealing to him in that "Great Image" the character and history of Gentile rule. He heard Daniel, the man of God, interpreting that vision. He had seen the mighty power and grace of God in saving the three Hebrews from the fiery furnace. He had also publicly confessed that there was no other god like the God of the Hebrews (chap. 3. 29). More than that, he had been solemnly warned of God by this vision of the great tree *hewn down* (v. 14), and of his heart being changed into a "beast's heart" (v. 16). He was moreover counselled to "break off his sins by righteousness, and his iniquities by shewing mercy" (v. 27). How many there are in this day of grace who likewise have been as mercifully dealt with by visions, warnings, and encouragements. Their need, like this king's, is *repentance* toward God.

II. His Pride. "At the end of twelve months he walked upon the palace of Babylon...and said, Is not this great Babylon that I have built?" etc. (vv. 29, 30). These *twelve* months were days of grace, but as "all things" seemed to "continue as they were," the warning of God was neglected and forgotten. On the royal palace, about four hundred feet high, he had a full view of "Great Babylon" lying around him, four-square, with a circumference of about sixty miles. There were twenty-five streets intersecting each other—150 feet wide and about 15 miles long. The city had a hundred brazen gates, and was walled about with a massive structure three hundred feet high and eighty feet broad, so that two chariots with four horses abreast could pass easily on the top. This wall was also ornamented with two hundred and fifty towers. The river Euphrates ran slowly through the midst of the city. The great bridge built by the king, and the royal palaces on each side, with the gorgeous temple and the magnificent "hanging gardens," might all be before his eyes when he said, "Is not this great Babylon that I have built...by the might of my power, and for the honour of my majesty?" (v. 30). When the Pharisee said, "I thank God that I am not as other men," he was also glorying in his great Babylon of self-righteousness. Cardinal Wolsey gloried in his Babylon of "worldly honour." All glorifying that is not in the Lord will come to naught.

III. **His Downfall.** "While the word was in the king's mouth, there fell a voice from Heaven saying, The kingdom is departed from thee," etc. (vv. 31, 32). Pride goeth before a fall. He who was glorying in the grandeur of his own works is now driven out from the presence of men as a raving maniac. The root cause of it was rebellion against the *Word of God*. Sin, like lunacy, separates and unfits for the fellowship of God.

IV. **His Recovery.** "At the end...I lifted up mine eyes to Heaven, and mine understanding returned unto me" (v. 34). What an awakening! To find himself living the life of a beast! The beast life is that of eating and drinking, with no knowledge of God. There are multitudes which need just such an awakening. What he wanted was understanding. To cut his hair, clip his nails, and to cast a royal robe over him was not the restoration that he needed. Outward reformation can never stand for an inward apprehension. The eyes of the understanding must be enlightened. It is not a new faculty, but a new vision of guilt and of God. The prodigal made this discovery "when he came to himself." The evidence of his sound conversion was, "Now I *praise* the King of Heaven" and *confess* that "those that walk in pride He is able to abase" (v. 37).

BELSHAZZAR'S DOOM;
OR, SINNING AGAINST LIGHT.
DANIEL 5. 22-31.

A HEATHEN genius once made a beautiful goblet, with a serpent coiled up at the bottom, with a pair of gleaming eyes, open mouth, and fang ready to sting, so that when the drinker emptied the cup the fearful thing suddenly appeared. Such are the pleasures of sin. At last they bite like a serpent. Such was the experience of Belshazzar at the end of his great godless feast (v. 1). Inflamed with wine, he demands that the holy vessels of the Lord be brought (v. 2), but in the same hour the hand of judgment appears (v. 5), and terror pierces his proud heart. Belshazzar is a solemn warning to those who are *sinning against the light*. Look at—

I. **His Opportunity.** "O Belshazzar...thou knewest all this" (v. 22). All what? See chapter 4. 27-34. He knew all about his father's (or grandfather's) *pride* and downfall, how he was humbled by God to the degrading life of a beast, and how when he looked up to Heaven his understanding returned again to him. He knew all this, yet went on in his life of sin and godlessness. Many sin in ignorance, but how many to-day are sinning against the "knowledge of the truth," like the Scribes and Pharisees of old; living the darkness of sinful pleasure, rather than the light of God's salvation.

II. **His Guilt.** "He lifted *himself* up against the Lord of Heaven" (v. 23). It is easily seen how this was done. He simply ignored the light and warnings of God, and put material and sinful things in the place of the "Lord of Heaven." The gods of silver, gold, brass, and iron had more influence over him than the "God of Heaven." The present-day form of this is following certain popular opinions and ignoring the revelation of God's will as declared in His Word. Lifting *"himself* up" by his own thoughts and works, and denying the Lord that bought him.

III. **His Failure.** "Thou art weighed in the balances and found wanting" (v. 27). The weighing process may have occupied several years. The Lord is slow to wrath. Character is formed through a course of actions. By Him actions are weighed. Job once uttered this request, "Oh that I were weighed in an even balance." God's balances are always just. While the sinner is thoughtlessly going on in his evil course, God is silently weighing him in His unerring balance. He was found *wanting*. Wanting in faith, in love, and in submission to His will. Belshazzar was uninfluenced by all God's providential dealings with him. Without any heart response, he "passed on and was punished." Judas, and all like him, will ultimately find "their own place," a place of their own preparing.

IV. His Doom. "That night was Belshazzar...slain" (v. 30). In the night of his greatest glory—the night of his great delusion. While he feasted, the Medes and Persians stealthily entered the city, and an unexpected end suddenly came. Lust, unbelief, and indifference are no protection against the overwhelming power of rejected truth. Those weighed and found wanting by God are destitute of all power of resistance. The thunder cloud of God's judgment may *gather* slowly, but when the lightning flash comes it will be sudden, irresistible, and fatal. How shall we escape if we neglect so great salvation?

DANIEL—STEADFAST IN THE FAITH.

Daniel 6.

DANIEL has now been probably sixty-eight years in the city of Babylon. He had lived under the reign of three kings, and was about eighty-five years old. He had had many severe trials and temptations, but he remained faithful to his God, his conscience, and his fellow-men. Notice his—

I. Integrity. "We shall not find any occasion against this Daniel, except we find it concerning the law of his God" (v. 5). His enemies themselves are witnesses to the purity of his life, His character was invulnerable. As a man of prayer and of faith he was faultless, even in the details of his arduous business life. The undercurrent of his nature was as pure as the upper. This was the secret of his moral strength. The *daily* life is perhaps the severest test of the Christian character, but the pure in heart shall see God, and seeing Him they shall endure.

II. **Steadfastness**. "When Daniel knew that the writing was signed he went...and prayed, and gave thanks before God, *as he did aforetime*" (v. 10). Their plot was to get the law of the Medes (unalterable) to clash with the law of Daniel and his God. Although he knew that they had succeeded in making and setting a trap for his feet, he trusted in God and went on as aforetime. Circumstances, adverse as they were, had no effect in changing his holy purpose to be true to God, and his own conscience. General Gordon, when in the Sudan, used to lay his handkerchief at the door of his tent each morning while he prayed, and no one dared to enter till the signal was removed. Courage, brother, do not stumble in your prayer life. Be steadfast in your faith and practice.

III. **Sufferings**. He was doubtless persecuted through envy (v. 3). Their dastardly scheme seemed to succeed. Daniel is condemned to the lions. This was the Persians' mode of capital punishment, as the fiery furnace was that of the Babylonians. This is one strong proof of the authenticity of the book. This was a great crisis in the experience of the prophet. Must all be sacrificed to appease the wrath of these haters of godliness? Every sacrifice we make for God brings for us a fuller enjoyment of the salvation of God.

IV. **Deliverance**. "My God hath shut the lions' mouths," etc. (vv. 20-22). This was a new experience of the power of God. While his enemies are rejoicing over his supposed destruction, Daniel is rejoicing in a new salvation. God will vindicate the faith of His own true servant. He is able to do exceedingly above all that we think.

V. Faith. "Because he believed in his God" (v. 23, *l.c.*). God will not deny Himself. To trust Him is to put Him on His honour. The secret of victory in the Christian life lies deep down in our oneness of life and purpose with Him.

VI. Doom of Enemies. "They were cast into the den and their bones broken in pieces" (v. 24). The triumph of the wicked is short. They digged a pit for the servant of God, and they themselves fell into it, as Haman was hanged on his own gallows. As these enemies of Daniel had to do with Daniel's God, so the enemies of the Gospel of Christ have to do with the Christ of the Gospel. To reject the Word of God is to reject the God of the Word. The wrath of God must abide on the unbeliever (John 3. 36). Blessed are all they that put their trust in Him.

THE END OF THE MATTER.
DANIEL 7.

"HITHERTO is the end of the matter" (v. 28). What has been here referred to is prophetic of the final condition of things in this world. This book is divided into two parts. Chapters 1-7 give the narrative portion unbroken. Chapters 7-12 give the prophetic references unbroken. Chronological order is not adhered to. Daniel, as a man of vision, was a man of action. The visions of God and His truth ought ever to have practical results.

I. The Vision. This revelation and the interpretation are a repetition of the vision of the image in chapter 2. The four parts of the image correspond perfectly with the four "beasts" seen here. As the Stone broke in pieces the image of the Gentile kingdoms, so here the "Son of Man" takes the dominion from the beasts (vv. 12-14). The world-kingdoms are all as "beasts" rising up out of the great sea of humanity. The "beasts" referred to, note, are all beasts of prey—savage, oppressive, ferocious. Not like the ox or the sheep. These powers, represented as strong, unreasonable, brute forces, contain a sorrowful reflection on our boasted civilisation. They have been permitted by God to rise up into power and authority for some wise purpose. Even nations may need surgical operations as well as individuals. Part of the vision has been already fulfilled in the downfall of the Babylonian, Persian, Grecian, and Roman kingdoms. The rest will as certainly follow.

II. **The Blessed End** (v. 28). A new monarchy is coming. The history of the "Beast" kingdoms has been written in tears and blood. The new Kingdom will be the Kingdom of God and of His Christ. What notable events!

1. THE COMING OF THE SON OF MAN. "Behold the Son of Man came with the clouds of Heaven" (v. 13). He is the new Head of humanity. The "beasts" are from the earth. He is the Lord from Heaven. Study the parable of the "Nobleman" in Luke 19. See Matthew 24. 27 as to the suddenness of His appearing.

2. THE DESTRUCTION OF THE BEASTS' POWER. "They had their dominion taken away" (v. 12). They have had a long rule, but the world hath not learned to know God, and never will through *beastly* government. 'Tis the Man Christ Jesus, now crowned Lord of all, whose right it is to reign. He shall reign, and the uttermost parts of the earth shall become His possession.

3. THE ESTABLISHMENT OF A NEW KINGDOM. "And there was given Him dominion and glory, and a kingdom,... and all nations shall serve Him" (v. 14). This kingdom will be *universal*—"All people, nations, and languages." It will be *everlasting*—"An everlasting dominion which shall not pass away." Every tongue shall confess Him Lord, to the glory of God the Father.

4. THE VICTORY OF THE SAINTS. "And the time came that the saints possessed the kingdom" (v. 22). So the promise will be fulfilled: "The saints of the Most High shall take the kingdom" (v. 18). Blessed "end of the matter" this! It is the *saints* that shall rule, not the *sects*. Know you not that the saints shall judge the world? (1 Cor. 6. 2). Fear not, little flock, it is your Father's good pleasure to give you the Kingdom. Yes, there is a good time coming for the trusting, toiling, suffering servants of God. "If *children*, then heirs." We must first possess the Divine *nature* before we can enter into the Divine inheritance. A criminal has no place or say in the state, he is always treated as an alien. Neither can a sin-loving soul have any place in the Kingdom of God, which is righteousness and peace, and joy in the Holy Ghost. "My hope," said a dying saint, "is in the justice of God—the justice of God to Jesus Christ." Ye are complete in Him. _____

DIVINE LEADING.
Psalm 107. 7.

1. He leads like a **Saviour**, out of the desert of sin (Deut. 32. 10).

2. He leads like a **teacher**, into the knowledge of self and of God (John 16. 13).

3. He leads like **an eagle**, above the things of earth (Deut. 32. 11, 12).

4. He leads like a **shepherd** into pastures of greenness and paths that are right (Psa. 23. 2, 3).

5. He leads like a **guide** who is faithful to the end (Isa. 58. 11).

6. He leads like a **father** dealing with a weary child (Deut. 1. 31).

7. He leads as a **lamb** unto the living fountains of eternal delight (Rev. 7. 17).

EXPOSITORY OUTLINES.
New Testament.

JUSTIFICATION.
ROMANS 3-5.

IN the book of Job (chap. 25. 4) this great question is asked: "How can a man be justified with God?" And in these chapters before us we have a clear and decided answer. The importance of the question *demands* a plain heart-satisfying answer. The question is often asked: "How can a man get on best in the world?" How can a man be healthy? How gain the favour and patronage of men? How can a man be happy? etc. But when a man discovers himself a guilty sinner before God his question is: "How can a man be *justified*?" We shall try and answer this question by asking a few others.

I. **Do all Men Alike Need to be Justified?** In Romans 3 we read, "All are under sin" (v. 9); "All the world guilty" (v. 19); "All have come short" (v. 23). The portrait of both Jew and Gentile under the law is distinctly drawn in verses 10 to 18. And the result sought is "*every mouth stopped,*" every conscience smitten, every soul guilty before God. Each one believing and becoming subject to the judgment of God (see *margin*). All must be justified alike, for all are condemned alike, "for there is no difference" (v. 22).

II. **What is it to be Justified?** In these chapters we notice a sevenfold blessing possessed by the justified. Taking the facts as we find them, they are these—

1. To be justified is to be FORGIVEN (chap. 4. 7, 8).

2. To be justified is to be SAVED FROM WRATH (chap. 5. 9).

3. To be justified is to be RECKONED RIGHTEOUS (chap. 4. 9).

4. To be justified is to have PEACE WITH GOD (chap. 5. 1).

5. To be justified is to REJOICE IN HOPE (chap. 5. 2).

6. To be justified is to POSSESS THE LOVE OF GOD (chap. 5. 5).

7. To be justified is to be RECONCILED TO GOD (chap. 5. 10).

In view of these precious blessings, what is it *not* to be justified? The difference is as far apart as light and darkness, Heaven and Hell.

III. Who is it that God Justifieth? "Oh," says the wisdom of man, "I believe God justifies the good and the godly." But what saith the Scriptures? "He justifieth the *un*godly" (chap. 4. 5). "For Christ died for the ungodly" (chap. 5. 6). "He came to save *sinners*." So "while we were *sinners* Christ died for us (chap. 5. 8). He came not to call the righteous, therefore how could God justify them, whom Christ had not called? Man must take his place in the ranks of the ungodly before he can be justified in God's sight. It is very humbling, but it is the "bowed down" He raiseth up.

IV. How can God Justify the Guilty? Jesus was delivered for our *offences*, and raised for our justification (chap. 4. 25). God hath set Jesus forth to be a propitiation that He might be just and the Justifier of him which believeth on Jesus (chap. 25, 26). God can justify the guilty, because atonement has been made for them (chap. 5. 11). The propitiation was God's own appointment. He Himself paid the price of atonement (Exod. 30. 15); and that price having been fully paid, He is just in justifying the believers in Jesus. Man's guilt is first forgiven, then God can righteously justify. He cannot justify men in an ungodly state, it is the *believers in Jesus* He justifies, for when we believe in Him we are forgiven and so fit to be justified.

V. Will a Man not be Justified by his Good Works? "By the deeds of the law shall *no flesh* be justified *in His sight*" (chap. 3. 20). If a man does as well as he can (and who does that?) will he not be justified? Yes, in the sight of men (James 2. 21), but not in the sight of God. "If Abraham were justified by works, he hath whereof to glory (in the sight of men), but not *before God*" (chap. 4. 2). There can be no good works in God's sight unless they come from a good heart. And the fact that a man trusts his own goodness instead of God's proves that his heart is still at enmity against Him.

VI. In what Way does God Justify a Man? He justifies him judicially, as by His own righteous act as Judge, the moment he believes in Jesus as his atoning Substitute. But there are three words that occur ten times in this fourth chapter that clearly express the nature and manner of this justification. These words are, "counted," "reckoned," "imputed." Thus the righteousness of God is counted, reckoned, imputed to the believer. In the same sense as our sins were *laid on* or imputed to Christ. It is wholly a *Divine* reckoning. This righteousness is *"upon all* that believe" (chap. 3. 22) just as surely as He bore our sins in His own body. Where is feeling then? It is excluded. The question is: What hath the Lord done?

VII. Can a Man be Justified by simply Believing? Yes, completely, at once, and for ever—and in no other way. God justifies the *believer in* Jesus (chap. 3. 26). Therefore we conclude that a man is justified by faith (chap. 3. 28). Therefore being justified by *faith*, we have peace with God (chap. 5. 1). Abraham *believed* God, and it was counted for righteousness (chaps. 4. 3-16; 3. 22; Acts 13. 39). The *believing* is ours, the *counting* is God's. By faith we count on God's Word being true, and act accordingly. He that does not reckon on this is an unbeliever; and he that believeth not is condemned already (John 3. 18).

JOY IN GOD.
ROMANS 5. 11.

"JOY" has been defined as the "smile of happiness, and the flower of glory." This joy is—

I. **Needed**. There is room for a broader "smile of happiness" on the countenance of our life and work. But the smile may be on the face while an aching sorrow is in the heart. This joy comes through the experience of God's salvation, but how possible it is to know God, and yet, like David, to lose the "joy of His salvation" (Psa. 51. 12). Where there is spiritual bondage there can only be a joyless testimony. It is when the captivity of the soul is turned back that the joy becomes so great; then we are like men that dream (Psa. 126. 1).

II. **Possible**. It is the will of Christ that His joy should be in us (John 15. 11). Christ's joy was the joy of conscious fellowship with the Father. This "oil of joy" is a blessed substitute for the spirit of heaviness. No Christian worker should be without it. Even when he goes forth weeping, bearing precious seed, he knows that he will doubtless come back rejoicing, bringing sheaves with him (Psa. 126. 5, 6). Peter and John found this joy possible even while suffering shame for the Name and cause of Jesus Christ (Acts 5. 41; see Acts 16. 25).

III. **Conditional**. It is joy "in the Lord" (Isa. 61. 10). It is not joy in ourselves, in anything *we* have or are. It is joy in God through our Lord Jesus Christ, through whom **we** have obtained reconciliation (Rom. 5. 11).

This holy gladness can come from no other source, and from no other condition. There is a joy that is like beauty in a face, it is attractive, but only skin deep: this joy is as deep as the heart of the Eternal God; it is joy unspeakable and full of glory (1 Peter 1. 8). To rejoice in the Lord is to be joyful—

1. In His NAME. His Name stands for all that He is in His essential character (Psa. 20. 5).

2. In His WORK. The *redeemed* of the Lord shall come with singing, and everlasting joy upon their head (Isa. 51. 11).

3. In His WORD. When His words are believed the soul must rejoice, as one who has found great treasure (Neh. 8. 12).

IV. **Effectual**. It is "your strength" or "stronghold" (R.V., *margin*). Joy is strength, in the same sense in which despair is weakness. Joy in the Lord is one of the most aggressive of all spiritual forces. It was D. L. Moody who said that "God never uses a discouraged man." This joy is a power, because it is the evidence of a life happily adjusted to the perfect will of God. This strength is needed to overcome the manifold temptations that are ever at hand (James 1. 1-3), and to uphold when we are made partakers of the sufferings of Christ (1 Peter 4. 13). If joy in the Lord is to make us strong, then let us rejoice in the Lord alway, and again I say, rejoice. The Lord Himself fulfil His joy in us for His own Name's sake (John 17. 15).

THE BELIEVER'S RELATIONSHIPS.
ROMANS 6.

THIS chapter explains the "death and life" character of the Christian. The beginning, the cause, and effect of both are clearly stated. To the unspiritual this statement is full of inexplicable riddles. And even to many who know

Christ it is full of mysteries. To those who are taught of
the Spirit it is an exact portrait of the birth and life of the
new inner man. It teaches—

I. **The Believer's Relationship to Christ.** This
connection is of the closest possible kind. It implies—

1. DEATH WITH CHRIST. "Crucified with Him" (v. 6).
"Baptised into His death" (v. 3). "By one Spirit are we
all baptised into one body" (1 Cor. 12. 13). Our first
connection with Christ is with His death. Our first
dealings with God must be as a sinner. Life for God
implies the death of self. "I am crucified with Christ,
nevertheless I live." The question of sin must be settled
first. It is settled for us in our identity with His death.

2. BURIAL WITH CHRIST. *"Therefore* we are buried
with Him" (v. 4). When a man is buried he is supposed
to be out of sight, and on the fair way soon to be beyond
all possibility of identification. If the death has not been
real the burial will not take place. We don't bury as long
as there is a spark of life remaining. So the old man will
not be put out of sight as long as he lives. You might try
to hide him and conceal his working, but if he is not *dead*
he will be seen or heard somehow.

3. RESURRECTION WITH CHRIST. "Like as Christ was
raised from the dead so we also" (v. 4). Resurrection can
only follow where death has taken place. The power of
the old life must go before the new can come; and this new
life is wholly *from God*. It is a being born from above, a
new creation. "You hath He quickened who were dead."
As surely as we have been dead and buried, so surely are
we risen. "Passed from death into life" (John 5. 24).

4. LIKENESS TO CHRIST. "We shall be also in the likeness of His resurrection" (v. 5). This resurrection likeness
is the result of being planted in the *likeness* of His death.
If we have not felt the pangs of crucifixion we cannot have

the resurrection image, any more than we can have day without night. This is the Divine likeness, the likeness of a conqueror, one endued with power.

II. The Believer's Relation to Sin. It is—

1. THE RELATIONSHIP THAT LIFE HAS TO DEATH. "Reckon yourselves dead indeed unto sin, but alive unto God" (v. 11). Sin is not dead, but the believer is to be dead to it. Death puts an end to fellowship in this life. There is a great gulf fixed between the living and the dead. No passing from one to another. So ought it to be with the Christian and sin.

2. THE RELATIONSHIP THE ACQUITTED HAVE TO THE BROKEN LAW. "He that is dead is freed (justified) from sin" (v. 7). When a man has been acquitted before the Court, the law has no more claim on him. So the believer has been liberated from the claims of sin. The claims of the law end in death. Having therefore died in Christ, we are justified from sin. It will still make demands, but, remember, ye are *free* (v. 18).

3. THE RELATIONSHIP THE VICTOR HAS TO THE VANQUISHED. "Sin shall not have dominion over you" (v. 14). It is a foe disarmed, a king dethroned; as one whose power and authority are destroyed, but whose nature remains unchanged and unchangeable. A frozen serpent (that is powerless until warmed), over which we have the mastery and can easily destroy. Sin was once our master, but we must no longer "*obey* it" (v. 12).

III. The Believer's Relationship to Service. It is—

1. ONE OF PERSONAL SURRENDER. "Yield *yourselves* unto God" (v. 13). They first gave themselves unto the Lord. The whole man, with his affections and desires, must be consecrated to God. Some are prepared to yield time and money, but still reserve *themselves* for themselves.

Your members are to be yielded as His servants to righteousness (v. 19).

2. ONE OF HEARTY OBEDIENCE. "Ye have obeyed *from the heart*" (v. 17). There can be no true service without hearty obedience. There is much service done to please man. God looketh upon the heart. If a man has not obeyed the *doctrine* of Christ he cannot be a *servant* of Christ. His *truth* and *work* go together.

3. ONE OF SINGLENESS OF PURPOSE. "Become servants to God" (v. 22). "Whatsoever ye do, do it heartily as unto the Lord." Call no man master in this matter. If a believer has got the single eye, where is man-pleasing? There is often a wide difference between men-pleasers and God-pleasers. "Ye are not your own, for ye are bought with a price."

NO CONDEMNATION.

ROMANS 8. 1.

I. **What?** "No condemnation!" What a happy privilege! What a blessed hope! All the black dread past blotted out. Blessed are the people that are in such a case.

II. **When?** "Now." "There is therefore *now* no condemnation." Then this great blessing may be enjoyed in this present life. We may walk through this world of sin and sadness with the assurance in our hearts that we are forgiven, and that our sins have already been judged, and that the night of guilt is passed and the day of peace hath dawned in the soul.

III. **Why?** Because "In Christ Jesus." *He* is the Refuge of the soul. *God* is our refuge and strength. Here the soul is as secure as Noah was in the ark. To be "in Christ" is to be cleansed from all sin, and wrapt up in the centre of God's eternal purposes. To be in Him is to be a branch in the True Vine, fitted to bear fruit. In Christ, we are complete, for He is made of God unto us, wisdom, righteousness, sanctification, and redemption (1 Cor. 1. 30). In Him, we are *not* found with our own righteousness, but clothed upon with the beauty of the Lord. If any man be in Christ he is a *new creation*, therefore there is now no condemnation to them which are in Christ Jesus.

THE LAW OF THE SPIRIT.

ROMANS 8. 2.

THE *law* of the Spirit is as certain as the law of gravitation. He has His fixed method of operation, although, like the wind, He goeth where He listeth.

I. **Its Nature.** "It is the law of *life*." "The law of the Spirit of life." The law of the living One. It is the Spirit that quickeneth. The letter killeth, but the Spirit giveth life. The moral law cannot give life, its force is only felt in making sin exceeding sinful. "I through the law am dead" (Gal. 2. 19).

II. **Its Sphere of Action.** "The law of the Spirit of life *in Christ Jesus*." This law of life can only operate through the Prince of Life. The living truth of God comes to us through Him who is the Word of God (John 3. 34). The Spirit of the Lord was upon Him to preach good tidings to the meek. The last Adam was made a life-giving Spirit (1 Cor. 15. 45).

III. **Its Power.** "Hath made me *free* from the law of sin and death." The law of the Spirit of life in Christ Jesus is mightier than the law of sin and death, bringing deliverance and freedom. Where the Spirit of the Lord is there is liberty. "Stand fast therefore in the liberty

wherewith Christ hath made us free" (Gal. 5. 1). Having
been made free from sin, it is that we might become
servants to God (Rom. 6. 18-23). The sting of death is
sin, but thanks be to God which giveth us the victory
through our Lord Jesus Christ (1 Cor. 15. 56, 57).

THE CONDEMNATION OF SIN.
ROMANS 8. 3.

I. **The Weakness of the Law.** "What the law could
not do." The law can do much for it is "holy, just, and
good," but it cannot forgive sin. It is utterly weak to
justify a sinner. "By the deeds of the law shall no flesh
be justified." The law made nothing perfect (Heb. 7. 18).

II. **The Love of God.** "God sending His own Son."
In this was manifested the love of God toward us (1 John
4. 9). Who can measure the depths of this love in allowing
His "Only Beloved" to be identified with human sin and
guilt (John 3. 16).

III. **The Grace of Christ.** "His own Son in the
likeness of sinful flesh." What grace is this on the part of
the Son! "The Word was made flesh and dwelt among us...
full of grace and truth. Although in the form of God,
and equal with God, He made Himself of no reputation...
and became obedient unto death, even the death of the
cross" (Phil. 2. 6-8). By grace are ye saved.

IV. **The End of Sin.** "And condemned sin in the
flesh." By the offering of His body as a sacrifice, He hath
finished transgression and made an end of sin as an obstacle
in man's way to God. "He was made sin for us...that
we might be made the righteousness of God *in Him*"
(2 Cor. 5. 21). We are sanctified through the offering
of the body of Jesus Christ once for all (Heb. 10. 10).
Sin was condemned in Him that we might be justified
in Him.

THE RIGHTEOUSNESS OF THE LAW.
ROMANS 8. 4, 5.

I. Its Character. The law is righteous, and demands righteousness. It is "Holy, just, and good." It is an expression of the righteousness of God. By the law is the *knowledge* of sin. They are ignorant of God's righteousness who seek to establish their own.

II. Its Fulfilment. "The law might be fulfilled in us." Fulfilled by our submitting to the righteousness of God in Christ, for He is the end of the law for righteousness to every one that believeth. *Love* is the fulfilling of the law. For with the *heart* man believeth unto righteousness. We can only be made the righteousness of God *in Him*, who was made sin for us (1 Cor. 5. 21).

III. The Condition. "Who walk not after the flesh, but after the Spirit." They who would rejoice in Christ Jesus can have no confidence in the flesh (Phil. 3. 3). To walk after the Spirit is to walk in the mind of Jesus Christ. Walk in the Spirit and ye shall not fulfil the lusts of the flesh. Those led by the Spirit are not under the law. Walk in the Spirit and the righteousness of the law will be abundantly fulfilled in you, for the fruit of the Spirit which is "love, joy, peace, longsuffering, gentleness, goodness, faith, meekness, self-control," will be manifested. Surely the law could not have a better fulfilment than this. These are not *works*, but the *fruit* of the indwelling Spirit (Gal. 5. 16-25). Those created after the Spirit will mind the things of the Spirit (v. 5).

THE CARNAL AND SPIRITUAL MINDS.
ROMANS 8. 6, 7.

I. The Carnal Mind. "The carnal (or fleshly) mind is *death*." There is absolutely nothing in it that is pleasing to God. He that soweth to this fleshly mind shall reap corruption, the proof of death. They that are in the flesh cannot please God. The carnal mind is not death in a passive sense, for it is even worse than that, it is "enmity against God," and so very bitter that *it* cannot possibly be *subject* to the law of God (v. 7). A corrupt tree cannot bring forth good fruit. The only cure for the carnal mind is crucifixion. Saul was delivered from his fleshly mind when he said, "What wilt Thou have me to do?" "I am crucified with Christ."

II. **The Spiritual Mind**. "To be spiritually minded is life and peace." It is the evidence of a great change. Life and peace are the results of this new Spirit-creation. The enmity has been slain by the Cross. They now sow to the Spirit and reap life everlasting. The spiritual mind is a mind illumined by the Spirit of truth, enjoying the love of God, and seeking the carrying out of His purposes. They are alive unto God, and thus members are yielded to Him as instruments of righteousness (Rom. 6. 11-13). It is the good tree that cannot bring forth evil fruit (Matt. 7. 18). It is a condition of life in Christ and peace with God.

————

IN THE SPIRIT.

ROMANS 8. 8, 9.

I **Not in the Flesh**. "Ye are not in the flesh," although still in the body. They that are *in* the flesh (carnal mind) cannot please God, for they are in a state of death (v. 6). Ye are not in that condition, for ye have passed from death into life, being born of God.

II. **In the Spirit**. Not in the fleshly mind is to be in the spiritual mind. Not to have the Spirit of Christ is to be none of His. The *flesh* stands for sinful, helpless man the Spirit is the holy, mighty, life-giving One. To be in the Spirit is to be in God, bound up in the bundle of the living ones.

III. **The Spirit in You.** "If so be that the Spirit of God dwell in you." "Know ye not that ye are the temple of God, and that the Spirit of God dwelleth in you?" (1 Cor. 3. 16). After that ye believed ye were sealed with the Holy Spirit of promise. Because ye are sons, God hath sent forth the Spirit of His Son into your hearts (Gal. 4. 6). The indwelling Spirit is the secret of Divine wisdom and power. He is able to work the good will of God in the heart and through the life. If the Spirit of God who leads into all truth, is in you, then you need not that any man teach you (John 2. 27).

THE RESURRECTING SPIRIT.

Romans 8. 10, 11.

I. **The Cause of Death.** "Sin." "The body is dead because of sin." Sin was the death of the soul, it is also the death of the body. In Christ Jesus both soul and *body* will yet be delivered from its power (John 11. 25, 26).

II. **The Secret of Life.** "The Spirit is life because of righteousness." The Spirit brings life because it brings the soul of the believer into *rightness* of relationship with God. "He that is joined unto the Lord is one Spirit" (1 Cor. 6. 17).

III. **The Abode of the Spirit.** "The Spirit that raised up Jesus *dwell in you*." When Christ was restored to the home of His Father's bosom, the Holy Spirit came to seek a home in the hearts of those redeemed by His blood. "He shall abide with you for ever."

IV. **The Relationship Between the Spirit and Christ.** "If Christ be in you...His Spirit dwelleth in you." The indwelling or abiding of Christ in the Spirit is often spoken of as synonymous. "Strengthened by *His Spirit in the inner man*, that *Christ* may *dwell in your hearts* by faith" (Eph. 3. 16, 17). The precious truth is this, that Christ's presence and power is realised by us in our hearts by the Holy Ghost which is given to us. Hear what the Spirit saith.

V. The Power of the Spirit. We are taught here that—

1. HE RAISED UP CHRIST FROM THE DEAD. He was put to death in the flesh, but quickened by the Spirit (1 Peter 3. 18). This same mighty Spirit who hath quickened us into newness of life quickened Him.

2. HE SHALL ALSO QUICKEN YOUR MORTAL BODIES. He who raised up the Lord Jesus shall raise us up also (2 Cor. 4. 14). This corruptible must put on incorruption. The Holy Spirit, who hath begun the good work *in* us, will perfect that which concerneth us, even our mortal bodies. By the same Spirit shall they be changed like unto His own glorious body (2 Cor. 5. 4, 5).

THE NEW LIFE.
ROMANS 8. 12-14.

I. This is a Life not After the Flesh. "We are debtors not to live after the flesh." Fleshly wisdom or energy could never produce such a life. It is a life which ye have from God. Born of God.

II. This Life Owes Nothing to the Flesh. "We are debtors *not to the flesh.*" It received nothing from the flesh, gave nothing to it. The new man owes the old man nothing. Let the time past suffice for the will of the flesh.

III. This is a Life Opposed to the Flesh. "Mortify the deeds of the body." The salvation brought to us by the grace of God teaches us to deny *all* ungodliness. Paul kept his body under lest he should be cast aside as a useless weapon (1 Cor. 9. 2-7).

IV. This Life should be in the Power of the Spirit. "If ye *through* the Spirit." In yielding to the Spirit we shall obey the truth, thereby our souls shall be purified

(1 Peter 1. 22). This is God's great purpose concerning us (2 Thess. 2. 13).

V. This Life is to be Under the Control of the Spirit. "Led by the Spirit." When the Spirit comes within us it is that we might "walk in His ways" (Ezek. 36. 27). He will guide you into all truth.

VI. This is to be a Life of Fellowship. "Sons of God." Beloved now are we the sons of God. Our fellowship is with the Father, and with His Son Jesus Christ, and in the *Communion* of the Holy Ghost.

THE PRIVILEGES OF SONSHIP.

ROMANS 8. 15-17.

IN our present condition we are very slow to apprehend all that is meant by being "Sons of God."

I. Sons are Delivered from Bondage. "They have not received the spirit of bondage." The fear of the law has been taken away (Exod. 20. 18, 19). As many as are of the works of the law are under the curse. Perfect love casteth out fear.

II. Sons have the Spirit of Adoption. "We have received the Spirit of adoption." They are not only *adopted*, but they have the true *Spirit* of children born of God.

III. Sons Acknowledge the Father. "We cry Abba Father." I will arise and go to my father, and will say unto him, *Father*, the Maker and Lord of all is my Father.

IV. As Sons they have the Witness of the Spirit. "The Spirit beareth witness with our spirit that *we are* the children of God" (1 John 5. 10).

V. As Sons they are Heirs of God. "If children, then heirs." Having been joined to Christ they become joint-

heirs with Christ, and He is "Heir of all things." All
things are yours, for ye are Christ's, and Christ is God's.

VI. As Sons they Suffer with Him. "If so be that we
suffer with Him." The disciple is not greater than his
Lord. If ye be reproached for the Name of Christ, happy
are ye.

VII. As Sons they shall be Glorified with Him.
"Glorified *together*." The Head and the members are not
separated in suffering, nor in glory. The *will* of Christ the
Son has made this sure (John 17. 24). Having been made
partakers of the divine nature they shall also be made
partakers of His heavenly glory.

THE FUTURE MANIFESTATION.
Romans 8. 18-25.

I. It is a Great Reality (vv. 18, 19). "It doth not yet
appear what we shall be." Just now the world knoweth us
not as it knew Him not. When He shall appear then shall
we *appear* with Him.

**II. It will be the Deliverance of Creation from
Bondage** (v. 21). When Adam sinned the ground was
cursed for his sake. At the appearing of the Second Adam,
the Lord from Heaven, the curse will be rolled away.

III. It will have an Effect in every Creature (v. 22,
margin). The glorious *manifestation* of the sons of God will
herald the Gospel of the Kingdom of God to every creature.

IV. It will be the Redemption of the Body (v. 23).
The sealing of the Holy Spirit is *until* the day of Redemption, when we shall have a body like unto His own glorious
body (Phil. 3. 20, 21).

V. It is a Time Earnestly Longed for (v. 23). We
look for the Saviour, the Lord Jesus Christ. The Spirit
and the Bride say, Come, and let him that heareth of the

Coming Saviour *say Come.* Come, Lord Jesus—Come quickly.

VI. The Prospect of it gives Joy in Suffering (v. 18). Our present affliction is *light,* knowing that it worketh for us an eternal weight of glory *while we look* at the things which are *unseen.* Like Moses let us have respect unto the recompense of reward, and endure *as seeing Him* who is invisible. The sufferings of this present time are not worthy to be compared with the glory which shall be revealed in us. _____

THE PLEADING SPIRIT.

ROMANS 8. 26, 27.

I. The Spirit is Needed. "We know not what we should pray for as we ought." Without the guiding Spirit the Lord would need to be saying to us continually what He said to the mother of Zebedee's children, "Ye know not what ye ask."

II. The Spirit Helpeth our Infirmities. He imparts the needed wisdom whereby we may know *our* need and Christ's fullness.

III. The Spirit Maketh Intercession for the Saints. It is not ye that speak, but the Spirit of your Father which speaketh in you. The indwelling Spirit pleads for the *saint* before both God and men. Being filled with the Spirit is the sure way to prevail, both in prayer and testimony.

IV. The Spirit Maketh Intercession with Groanings. The groanings of the Spirit are often realised by a soul *thirsting* for God in silently waiting before Him in the unspeakable solemnity of holy adoration.

V. The Spirit Maketh Intercession According to the Will of God. What was true of the Son is also true of the Spirit. Him God *heareth* at all times, because He delights to do His will. If we are "praying always in the Spirit" we are praying always according to the will of God. If we ask anything according to His will He heareth us. Believe in the Holy Ghost.

VI. **The Searcher of Hearts Knoweth what is the Mind of the Spirit.** Solomon says: "The prayer of the *upright* is the Lord's delight." How will He delight, then, in the prayer of the Holy Spirit! The great Heart-Searcher looks for the mind of the Spirit in us. Let our wills to Him be given. _____

THE ALL-SUFFICIENT PROMISE.

ROMANS 8. 28.

I. **To Whom it is given.**

1. TO THE LOVING ONES. "To them that love God." We love Him because He first loved us. He seeks first, not the work of our hands, but the love of our hearts.

2. TO THE CALLED ONES. "To them who are the called according to His purpose." "Beloved of God called to be saints." Make your calling sure (2 Tim. 1. 9).

II. **The Nature of It.** It is—

1. GREAT. "All things." All things that pertain to life and godliness are included here. "All things are yours."

2. ACTIVE. "All things *work*." In the kingdom of grace everything is constantly on the move for the believer's good. As in the material world, there is no standing still here.

3. HARMONIOUS. "All things work *together*." There is no jarring or irregularities where all is working according to *His purpose*. All is right for the called of God, even when it seems most wrong. "Believe ye that I am able to do this?"

4. PRECIOUS. "All things work together *for good*."

Jacob said, "All these things are against me," but they were all for good (Gen. 50. 20). Have faith in God.

5. SURE. "We know." We know, because we know the faithfulness of the God in whom we trust. Faithful is He that hath promised. And because *we know*, our hearts are kept in perfect peace with regard to things present and things to come. "My grace is sufficient for you."

_____

THE ETERNAL PURPOSE.
ROMANS 8. 29, 30.

I. The Great Purpose of God.

1. THAT HIS SON SHOULD BE THE FIRSTBORN among many brethren. He humbled Himself, but God hath highly exalted Him. In all things He must have the pre-eminence.

2. THAT BELIEVERS SHOULD BE CONFORMED to the image of His Son. As His workmanship, we are created *in Christ Jesus*, who is the image of the invisible God. Be not conformed to the world.

II. The Footsteps of Grace.
It is profoundly interesting to notice the workings of infinite love on the way out to seek and save the lost.

1. FOREKNOWN. "Whom He did foreknow." "I knew thee before thou camest forth" (Jer. 1. 5). Written in the book of life, before the foundation of the world (Eph. 1. 4).

2. PREDESTINATED. Appointed according to the will of God. In Acts 4. 28 the same word is translated *determined*. Whom He foreknew, them He hath appointed.

3. CALLED. There is no room for cavilling at these things. Let us say with Paul, "*It pleased God*, who called me by His grace." Called through the Holy Ghost to be a separate people unto Himself.

4. JUSTIFIED. "Whom He called, them He also justi-

fied." It is God that justifieth. Who shall lay anything to the charge of God's elect? Justified freely by His Grace.

5. GLORIFIED. "Whom He justified, them He also glorified." The glory which thou hast given Me, I have given them." If we suffer with Him, we shall also be glorified together by having a body like unto His *glorious* body.

THE GREAT CHALLENGE.
ROMANS 8. 31-35.

I. Who can be Against us if God be for us? (v. 31). "The Lord is on my side, I will not fear what man can do unto me" (Psa. 118. 6). Greater is He that is *in you* than he that is in the world. All the resources of God are for those who are for Him.

II. Who can Condemn when Christ has Died for us and is risen again? (v. 34). Having died with Him, we are now risen with Him. Free from the law. To them who are in Christ Jesus there is therefore now no condemnation, neither by God, man, angel, nor Devil.

III. Who can Lay Anything to our Charge when God has Justified? (v. 33). The heritage of the servants of the Lord is, "No weapon that is formed against them shall prosper" (Isa. 54. 17). When Satan attempted to bring a charge against Joshua, the Lord rebuked him (Zech. 3. 1, 2).

IV. Who shall Separate us from the Love of Him who Gave Himself for us? (v. 35). "I have given unto them eternal life, they shall never perish, neither shall any *pluck them out* of my hand." The Lord's people purchased by His own blood, are too precious to be easily parted with. The Father having *loved* His own which were in the world, He loved them unto the end.

V. Who can Hinder God from Giving us all Things when He Spared not His Son? (v. 32). Being reconciled, we shall be *saved in His life* (Rom. 5. 10, R.V., *margin*). In Him every need will be met. Ye are Christ's, and all things are yours. How will He not *with Him* freely give us all things?

MORE THAN CONQUERORS.

ROMANS 8. 35-37.

I. **We are to be Conquerors.** Not slaves to the fashions and pleasures of the world, but victors for God. Having been born of God, we belong to the *upper* class, and overcome the world through faith.

II. **We are Conquerors in the Midst of Suffering.** Tribulation, distress, persecution, famine, nakedness, peril, and sword. All these are still with us, but faith gives the victory. We are always delivered unto death for Jesus' sake. This present world always keeps in the place of death those who have the life of Jesus in them, but they conquer still, and press on to know Him.

III. **We are More than Conquerors.** Enemies are not only conquered and subdued, but brought as willing servants into the work of the Lord. Saul was *more* than conquered when he became a preacher of the Gospel he so much hated. Take note of this. To be more than conquerors we must be *more than conquered*. It is not enough that we be overcome, there must be the willing and entire surrender of ourselves into the hands of God, to say, to be, and to do all that He may appoint.

IV. **We are More than Conquerors through Him.** The power of conquest and aggressive work for God is not in ourselves, nor in our plans and organisations, but in the God who worketh in us. Thanks be unto God who giveth us the victory through our Lord Jesus Christ. They overcame by the blood of the Lamb. The blood of the Lamb is the sharp edge of the sword of the Word, the Spirit's holy weapon. Cling to it, use it.

THE LOVE OF GOD.

ROMANS 8. 38, 39.

I. Nature of It. "The love of God." God is love, so that in manifesting His love He manifests Himself. Herein is love. Yes, herein is God. Not that we loved Him, but that He loved us. Behold, what love!

II. Channel of It. "Which is in Christ Jesus." He is the Mediator *between* God and men, the Ladder that reaches from earth to Heaven. In Him was manifested the love of God toward us that we might live *through* Him. "I am the Way."

III. Objects of It. "Us." He loved us and gave Himself for us (John 3. 16). Herein is love, not that we loved God, but that He loved us, and sent His Son to be the propitiation for our sins. Us, even when we were dead in trespasses and sin.

IV. Power of It. "Neither death," etc., "shall be able *to separate* us from the love of God." "I have loved thee with an everlasting love." The trifling things of this world may be allowed at times to separate our love from Him, but, bless His Holy Name, nothing can separate from His love. His love is stronger than death.

V. Assurance of It. "I am persuaded." It is a great testimony when we can say in truth, "We have *known* and *believed* the love that God hath to us" (1 John 4. 16). Having the love of God shed abroad in our hearts, and going on living day by day as those who believe in the infinite and everlasting love of God, this is the secret of a restful, joyful, contented life. "I am persuaded that nothing shall separate me from the love of God, which is in Christ Jesus our Lord."

* * * * * * * *

SELF-DEDICATION.

ROMANS 12. 1, 2.

IN the foregoing chapters Paul has been dealing with fundamental doctrines. Now he comes to the application, for he is no mere theorist. Christianity is intensely practical, and the *beseeching* of the apostle proves how keenly he feels it. The Christianity of some is like a certain fish that is almost nothing but head. Whole-heartedness for God ought to characterise every Christian, and this is evidenced by our presenting our bodies a living sacrifice unto God.

I. **The Sacrifice to be Offered.** "Present your *bodies.*" We are so apt to be content with committing our *souls* unto Him, and to give the body as a sacrifice to the soul. We seem to think that our *bodies* are all our own, and that our *souls* belong to God. Now the body is the temple of soul and spirit, and the medium through which these act, and by which they manifest themselves. The inner man thus acts through the outer man. Then the *medium* ought to be in the hands of God as well as the individual actor. In fact, unless God has full charge of the whole being, the Divine power will be withheld. He does not *give us* power so much as He desires to manifest His power *through us.* Each one must *present his own body*, as the Jew presented his lamb, and *left it* in the hands of the priest.

II. **The Nature of this Sacrifice.** It is to be—

1. A LIVING Sacrifice. The death of Christ has swept for ever all dead sacrifices from the altar. Now He seeks *living* ones. That is, we are, as it were, to *live on the altar.* The old sacrifices were on the altar only for a few moments. Ours is a CONSECRATED LIFE. "To me to live is Christ."

2. A HOLY Sacrifice. "Know ye not that your bodies

are the temple of the Holy Ghost?" This temple must be holy, for God dwelleth in you, and in offering the body a sacrifice we offer Him what He has already claimed and sanctified for Himself.

3. An ACCEPTABLE Sacrifice. In the margin of the Revised Version it is *"wellpleasing* unto God." Not only acceptable, but in reality satisfying to God. God is not fully pleased with regard to our salvation until we offer ourselves a willing, holy, sacrifice unto Him. We are saved to serve.

III. The Motives Urged. These are twofold.

1. THE MERCIES OF GOD. "I beseech you by the mercies of God." "Great are Thy mercies, O Lord" (Psa. 119. 156). What are His mercies toward us? Think of His love in Christ, His forgiveness, His peace, His joy, His Holy Spirit, His promises (chap. 8). These should constrain us to yield ourselves entirely up to Him. The *goodness* of God ought to lead us to repentance in this matter of withholding from Him what is His due, nay, what is His own by right of purchase (1 Cor. 6. 20).

2. THE REASONABLENESS OF THE SERVICE. "Which is your reasonable service." It is but rational that we should yield ourselves to God if He has redeemed us to Himself. It is but reasonable that He should have *all.* Then it is most unreasonable to withhold what is His.

IV. The Consequences of this Sacrifice.

1. A NONCONFORMING TO THE WORLD. "And be not conformed to the world." This is the remedy for worldly conformity. A definite yielding of ourselves unto God and a *constant* acknowledgment of the same. There is no likelihood of the dead following the fashion of this world. "Reckon ye yourselves dead." "He gave Himself for us that He might deliver us from this present evil world" (Gal. 1. 4) Those who are wholly in God's hands are not

much troubled as to whether this or the other thing is consistent with the Christian life. *He* decides.

2. A TRANSFORMING OF THE CHARACTER. "Be ye transformed by the *renewing* of your mind." The transforming of the outward life will just be in proportion to the renewing of the inner man. When Christ was transfigured it was but the visible manifestation of the glory within. "As a man thinketh in his heart so is he." Many long for the renewed life who wish not the renewed *mind*. The yielding is ours, the transforming is God's.

3. A NEW EXPERIENCE OF THE GOOD WILL OF GOD. "That ye may prove what is that good...will of God." Many have never proved the goodness and perfection of the will of God, because they have not given themselves wholly to God. And so the will of God to them is irksome. They dread it, instead of delight in it. The will of God is *perfect*, and only in His will are our lives perfect before Him. When the acceptable sacrifice is presented the acceptable will will be proved. He is able to work in us both *to will* and to do of His good pleasure.

OUR REASONABLE SERVICE.
ROMANS 12. 1.

THE thought of sacrifice runs through the books of the Bible like the crimson thread in the ropes and cords of government. Sacrifice has two general aspects: (1) As a *gift*, handed over for the good of another, as in Mark 7. 11; (2) As an object of "burning" to be utterly *used up*, as in Leviticus 1. 9. Cain's offering belonged to the one class, and was incomplete. Abel's belonged to the other, and was acceptable. Both were voluntary acts, and so became a revelation of character. Here are three reasons why sacrifice on our part is most reasonable: Because—

I. **Sacrifice was Made for Us.** "Christ loved us and

gave Himself for us" (Eph. 5. 2). *"Himself* for our *sins"* (Gal. 1. 4). What a costly sacrifice for such a purpose. By the sacrifice of Himself He hath put away sin for ever, as an obstacle in the sinner's way of approach unto God (Heb. 9. 26). In giving Himself, He gave all that He was and had: not an impoverished self, for He who was rich for our sakes became poor, that we, through His self-emptying, might become rich (2 Cor. 8. 9). He, as the "corn of wheat," willingly died, that He might bring forth fruit in the lives of those for whom He died. If He gave Himself for us, surely we should give ourselves for Him.

II. Sacrifice is Asked of Us. "I beseech you therefore by the mercies of God, that ye present your bodies a living sacrifice unto God" (Rom. 12. 1). Why the *body*? Because the body is the instrument, or weapon, of the Holy Spirit, which dwelleth in you. The possibilities of the body, for good or evil, are tremendous (Rom. 6. 13). How often backsliding and failure may be traced to the unconsecrated members of the body. To be a "living sacrifice" is to be continually and completely at God's disposal. This is "holy and acceptable to God." And also because of its *acceptability* to Him, it is most reasonable that it should be given. The yielding of ourselves unto God is the root and branch of self-denial, without which there can be no true discipleship (Matt. 16. 14). It is true in the deepest possible sense, that "Ye are not your own, for ye have been bought with a price: *therefore* we should glorify God in our bodies and our spirits which are His" (1 Cor. 6. 20). Is it not reasonable that God should have His own, that which He hath bought with His own blood? We are robbing God when we are keeping back this part (bodies) of His purchased possession.

III. Sacrifice Ensures Greater Blessing for Us. In presenting ourselves "a living sacrifice" to God, we are saving ourselves from being "conformed to this age," and also putting ourselves into that position in which we can "prove the good and acceptable and perfect will of God" (Rom. 12. 1, 2). The goodness and beautiful perfectness of the will of God we shall never prove in our own personal experience until we are completely abandoned to it; just as we cannot prove the power of water to sustain our own bodies until we have made an entire committal. A life wholly surrendered to God is the only reasonable life which a Christian can live. It is the secret of usefulness, because it means the proper adjustment of the faculties and functions of our being to the perfect will and purposes of God. Every gift laid on the altar is sanctified by the altar.

SEALED WITH THE HOLY SPIRIT.

EPHESIANS 1. 13.

HERE is *Weymouth's* translation of Ephesians 1. 13: "In Him you Gentiles also, after listening to the Message of the truth, the Good News of your salvation—having believed in Him—were sealed with the promised Holy Spirit."

I. **The Seal** is the Holy Spirit, which was promised, and is now given. His presence in our hearts is the evidence of our approval in the sight of God (2 Cor. 1. 22, R.V.). As a seal may be marred and broken, so the Holy Spirit may be "grieved" and "quenched."

II. **The Sealer** is God, who gives the Spirit to them that believe. "Him hath God the Father sealed" (John 6. 27). He that wrought us for this very thing is God, who gave unto us the earnest of the Spirit (2 Cor. 5. 5).

III. **The Sealed** are they "who have heard the Gospel of salvation, and have trusted in Christ" (Eph. 1. 12, 13). It is "because ye are sons, God hath sent forth the Spirit of His Sons into your hearts" (Gal. 4. 6).

IV. **The Significance** of the Sealing. It is usually

given as the closing act of a bargain. Mohammed is called by the Moslems, "the seal of the prophets," because they believe him to be the last of that order. The sealing of the Holy Spirit speaks of—

1. SECURITY. The stone laid at the mouth of the den where Daniel was imprisoned was "sealed with the king's signet" (Dan. 6. 17) that the purpose *might not be changed*. The sealing of the stone at the sepulchre of Jesus was also with the same intent. Those who are chosen of God, "according to His purpose," are built upon that foundation of God, which standeth sure having this seal. "The Lord knoweth them that are His." None shall pluck them out of His hand.

2. OWNERSHIP. When the Holy Spirit descended upon the Son of God there came also the voice saying, "This is My beloved Son." Those sealed by the Spirit are owned of God. All who are *established* by God in Christ are also anointed and sealed (2 Cor. 1. 21, 22). The blood of Christ redeems *to* God. The Holy Spirit possesses *for* God. God's marked men are those whom the pleasure-loving world would avoid, those who "sigh and cry" (Ezek. 9. 4).

3. AUTHORITY. The seal is the sign of authority. Joseph and Mordecai were both clothed with royal authority when they received the seal of the king (Gen. 41. 41, 42; Esther 8. 8). Possessed of the king's seal, they acted in the king's name; so we possessed of the Holy Spirit are to act "in Christ's stead" (2 Cor. 5. 20). They are witnesses unto Him in whom the power of the Holy Ghost has come (Acts 1. 8).

4. LIKENESS. A seal imparts its own image to the object sealed; that is, if the object is in a condition to receive and retain the image. Not even the Holy Spirit can imprint the image of Christ on a hard and stony heart. The humble and contrite heart will have God the Holy Ghost dwelling with them (Isa. 57. 15). Those sealed by the Spirit will have

the mind of the Spirit, which is "the mind of Christ."
The work of the Spirit with us produces the character of
Christ in us. Yield yourselves unto God. He is able to
work in you both to will and to do of His good pleasure.

THE POWER OF FAITH.

1 JOHN 5. 4.

AN old writer says, "Faith is the *foot* of the soul; so it
comes to Christ. Faith is the *hand* of the soul; so it
receives Christ. Faith is the *arm* of the soul; so it embraces
Christ. Faith is the *eye* of the soul; so it looks upon Christ.
Faith is the *mouth* of the soul; so it feeds on Christ. Faith
is the *lips* of the soul; so it kisses Christ."

I. **Faith is Precious**. It is infinitely precious, because
of its own infinite possibilities. With it, nothing needful
is impossible. It is the hand that takes with firm, unfailing grip the faithful promises of the God of salvation.
The fruits of faith are precious. By it we are justified
(Rom. 5. 1), sanctified (Acts 26. 18). It is by faith we
"live" (Rom. 1. 17), "stand" (Rom. 11. 20), "walk"
(2 Cor. 5. 7), "wait" (Gal. 5. 5, R.V.). It is a soul-
revolutionising grace, because it involves the surrender
of the will to the living, transforming Word of God.
"To take up half on trust, and half on try, is not faith, but
bungling bigotry." God glorifies faith, because faith
glorifies God. Without faith it is impossible to please
Him.

II. **Faith should be Progressive**. Paul commended
the Thessalonians because their "faith grew exceedingly."
Faith cannot but grow when there is a growing knowledge
of God, and of the fullness and faithfulness of His Word.
Faith, like love, will not be driven or forced, it must needs
be fed and inspired. The manner of its growth is "from
faith to faith" (Rom. 1. 17). Not from one confession of

faith to another, but it may be from little faith to great faith, from great faith to greater faith, from the greater human faith into the absolute and perfect "faith of God" (Mark 9. 22, *margin*). The "faith of God" is God's faith in His own Word and work. He shall not be discouraged, His Word shall not return to Him as having missed the mark. Lord, increase our faith, and let it grow up and out, into the faith that Thou Thyself hast in Thine own Spirit-breathed Word and blood-sprinkled work.

III. Faith shall be Triumphant. Faith lays hold of the mightiest of all weapons, when it grips the Word of God, which is the Sword of the Spirit. The victories mentioned in Hebrews 11 were all achieved by the weapon of faith. The world's truly mighty ones have all been men of faith. The hands of Christ were omnipotent, because they were the hands of faith. This is the victory that overcometh the world even our faith (1 John 5. 4). By faith we overcome the world—

1. Like ENOCH, by being translated out of it into the Kingdom of God's dear Son (Heb. 11. 4).

2. Like NOAH, by accepting God's warning, and entering the ark of God's salvation (Heb. 11. 7).

3. Like ABRAHAM, by obeying God's call, and stepping out into the unknown (Heb. 11. 8).

4. Like MOSES, by refusing to be called the son of the world; choosing rather to suffer affliction with the people of God (Heb. 11. 24-27).

5. Like JOSHUA, by marching round the walls, and expecting their downfall (Heb. 11. 30).

6. Like GIDEON and DAVID, by subduing kingdoms... and obtaining promises (Heb. 11. 32, 33). These all obtained a good report through faith. "Said I not unto thee, that if thou wouldest believe, thou shouldest see the glory of God."

LOVEST THOU ME?

JOHN 21. 15.

"LOVEST *thou* ME?" Let this tender but heart-searching question of our Lord come home to our own hearts. It is not enough for Him that we love His words and works if Himself be not the chief object of our affections. If "'Tis what I love determines how I love," then love for Christ, the "altogether lovely," should determine the manner and intensity of our love for others.

I. **Love Desired**. "Lovest thou Me?" Three times with varying emphasis did Christ put this question to Peter (John 21. 15-17). Zeal for truth without a personal devotion to the Son of God, as the embodiment of Divine love, is not true piety, but an exhibition of "mildewed theology." In uttering these words to Peter, the Son of Man was but seeking that fruit which could alone satisfy His own gracious heart. In degree, our love cannot be equal to His, but it ought in kind to resemble it.

II. **Love Acknowledged**. Where there is love to Christ, He is always quick to recognise and confess it. The woman in Simon's house who had washed, wiped, kissed, and anointed His feet because "She loved much," was not only noticed and commended, but used by the Lord as a powerful rebuke to the frozen-hearted Pharisee (Luke 7. 44-47). It is only love alone that can understand love, and make an adequate response. Perfect love casteth out fear.

III. **Love Manifested**. Love must reveal itself, it cannot be hid. If God loved the world, that love is seen in the gift of His Son. If Christ loved the Church, then He gave Himself for it. If we love God, then we shall love our brother also. Love to Christ will show itself—

1. By SEEKING Him. It was Mary's love for Him that

constrained her so passionately to seek Him (John 20. 15). The love of Christ constraineth us.   Whom seek ye?

2. By CONFESSING **Him.**   Peter said, "Yea, Lord, Thou knowest that I love Thee" (John 21. 15).   With the waning of our first love comes a waning of our desire for testimony.   If we love Him with all our heart, then we shall confess Him with all our strength and might.

3. By SERVING **Him.**   After Peter's threefold confession of love for Him, came the Lord's threefold injunction to serve Him.   "Feed."   *Feeding* His sheep and His lambs— not thrashing or amusing them—is the evidence of love for the Lord Jesus Christ.   "Love, which is the essence of God, is not for levity, but for the total good of man," is how Emerson puts it.   Jacob's seven years' service for Rachel seemed but a few days, because of the love he had for her.   Love lightens labour.

4. By SACRIFICING **for Him.**   The love that cannot sacrifice is shallow and hypocritical.   The sinner in Simon's house, because of her "much love," sacrificed her "hair" and her "precious ointment" to Him (Luke 7. 38; see also John 12. 3).   The apostle who could say, "He loved me and gave Himself for me," did also say, "I am ready not to be bound only, but also to die for the Name of the Lord Jesus" (Acts 21. 13).   "Love can be bought with nothing but with itself."   Just as the highest act of God's love was the sacrifice of His Son, the express image of Himself, so the highest act of human love is the sacrifice of self for the glory of God.

THE PRIESTHOOD OF BELIEVERS.
REVELATION 5. 9, 10.

IT is well for us to keep in mind the difference between priesthood and apostleship.   The priest represented the people before God, the apostle represents God before the people. Jesus Christ was both Apostle and High Priest. God's purpose in grace was to manifest Himself to man; this He might have done without any human medium, but it pleased Him to call Aaron and his sons, that they might, through sacrifice, act as mediators between Him and the people, thus shadowing forth Him who was to be the great High Priest and only Mediator between God and man. Christ was a Priest after the order of Melchisedec—royal priesthood—having no predecessor and no successor. By His birth He set aside the Aaronic priesthood, by His death the veil of the temple was rent in twain. He offered Himself a sacrifice, and entered "by His own blood." Now we who believe have been redeemed to God by His blood and made unto God kings and priests.

I. Our Calling. No man taketh this honour unto himself but he that, is called of God, as was Aaron (Heb. 5. 4). Aaron was chosen of God, and his sons were chosen with him (Lev. 8. 2). We are chosen in Christ—and what a mystery—before the foundation of the world. The sons of Aaron were priests by birth. There is no other way of getting into the priesthood that God accepts and owns but by being "born from above." Neither a priestly robe nor a priestly profession constituted a priest; the sons of Aaron were priests independently of these. In these days it is to be feared that many are substituting the robe and the profession for the call of God.

II. Our Character.

1. WE ARE CLEANSED. "Aaron and his sons were washed with water" (Lev. 8. 6). Whom He calls, them He also justifies. The call of God implies cleansing from all sin. Called to be holy. There can be no fitness for service till the question of sin has been settled and guilt put away. "Except I wash thee thou hast no part with Me."

2. WE ARE CLOTHED. "And Moses brought Aaron's

sons, and put coats upon them" (v. 12). Aaron, as a type
of our great High Priest, wears the "breastplate," and is
clothed with robes of "glory and beauty;" the sons, as
representing believers, put on the "pure linen," which
speaks of the righteousness of the saints, which is the
righteousness of God unto all, and upon all them that
believe.

3. WE ARE CLAIMED. "The blood was put upon their
ear, hand, and foot" (Lev. 8. 24). The blood speaks of
redemption, redeemed to God, and claimed by God—
"priests unto God" (Rev. 5. 10). The blood-sprinkled
foot, hand, and ear may remind us of a blood-purchased
body, soul, and spirit. Ye are not your own, ye are bought
with a price, therefore glorify God in your bodies and
spirits, which are His.

4. WE ARE SANCTIFIED. The anointing oil was sprinkled
upon them and upon their garments (v. 30). This holy
anointing shadows forth the blessing of Pentecost. The
precious ointment flowed from the head of Aaron, the high
priest, down to the skirts of his garments. This was
fulfilled at Pentecost, when the Holy Spirit, typified by
the oil, was poured out over the head of Him who is our
great High Priest, down to "your sons and daughters"
(Acts 2. 17), who are as the skirts of His garments. No
priest was allowed to officiate without this anointing;
before we can be "priests unto God" we must be anointed
with this heavenly oil. For what is called "Divine service"
there must needs be a Divine fitness.

III. Our Privilege.

1. WE ARE PRIESTS UNTO GOD. As ambassadors, we
are sent forth for God. It is to be lamented that these
offices are so largely confounded among men in their
Christian practice. Before God, we should ever come with
solemn, sacred, humble, heart-felt awe. As priests, there

must be no frivolity, no pretence nor unreality. Before men, as witnesses, there must be no flinching, no wavering, or cowardliness; the whole truth, and nothing but the truth, must be told out. Alas, when men invert this order, and bring the brazen face to God and the velvet tongue to the ungodly.

2. As PRIESTS, WE HAVE LIBERTY OF ACCESS. Only the priest was allowed to pass through the veil into the presence of God. Oh, what grace to be permitted to stand before God! By Him—who was sacrificed for us—we also have access by faith into this grace wherein we stand, and rejoice in hope of the glory of God (Rom. 5. 2). Liberty of access surely implies liberty of success.

3. As PRIESTS, WE OFFER SPIRITUAL SACRIFICES (1 Peter 2. 5). The world sets little value on a humble "broken spirit," but it is a sacrifice of sweet savour unto God (Psa. 51. 17). May we so be saved from all pride and self-will, that the incense of a "broken spirit" may ever ascend. If this is our character and condition we shall be well fitted to offer the sacrifice of praise which shall glorify God.

4. As PRIESTS, WE MAKE INTERCESSION. Abraham acted the priest when he pleaded for Sodom; Moses, when he interceded for the people; Paul, when he prayed for Israel. What a privilege and power prayer is! And it is within the reach of every Christian. Many may not be able to sing or preach, but all can "make intercession." If as priests we were more frequently in the secret place of the closet, we would prevail more as princes with God and with man. The people of Israel were blessed after the priest had been in the presence of God. So our Father will not reward us openly as witnesses unless we have been much with Him secretly as priests (Matt. 6. 6). Believer, are you using this privilege as you ought?

OUR GOD A CONSUMING FIRE

HEBREWS 12. 29.

HERE are a few striking words used in Scripture to describe the essential character of God. (1) God is Spirit (R.V., *margin*). Herein is seen His indivisibility and greatness. (2) God is Love. This reveals His unfathomable and unchangeable goodness. What a privilege to dwell in such an abode (1 John 4. 16). (3) God is Light. And this, because He is Love. In Him is no darkness at all. No uncertainty. No unrighteousness. (4) God is Fire. Not in figure, but in reality—a *consuming* fire. This solemn, dreadful, aspect of God's nature is frequently overlooked. Herein is the death of sin and self; herein is the life of holiness. This is the God with which we as Christians have to do. It was as fire God first appeared to His servant Moses; this made the place holy ground, and although the bush was not consumed, we may be assured that everything unclean *within* the bush would be burned up. We carry about with us daily the mystery of the burning bush "Know ye not that God dwelleth *in* you?" Yet the frail bush of our bodies is not consumed. We have this treasure in *earthen* vessels that the excellency of the power may be of God.

I. **As a Fire our God Consumes.** On the altar, the fire, as a symbol of God's presence, was ever burning. On the altar of our heart, as on the throne of our being, there still dwells the Spirit of burning. This holy fire cannot suffer the approach of that which is unclean. The Nadabs and Abihus of pride and self-conceit are instantly devoured (Num. 10). It was a self-crucifying revelation Paul received, when it pleased God to reveal His Son *in* him (Gal. 1. 15, 16; 2. 20). The Holy of Holies was such, because the pillar of fire abode there. Hence there was no way of entrance without blood. May the Blood of Jesus so guard the way of access into our inmost soul, where the Holy Spirit dwells, and may this holy fire consume all that would approach *without* the blood.

II. **As a Fire our God Purifies.** The presence of God was the purifying and the sanctifying of the Temple. It is true now, that when the Lord the Spirit suddenly comes into the temple of our body He is like a refiner's fire. "Who shall stand *when He appeareth*?" (Mal. 1. 3). There must be no other authority when He appeareth; every power of our being must become subject to Him, and in the submitting they are purified. As every vessel of the Tabernacle was given to God, and claimed and used by Him, so the members of our body are to be yielded to Him as instruments of righteousness (Rom. 6. 13).

III. **As a Fire our God Empowers.** What a real power fire is. Think of the fire-driven engines that push the mighty ironclads like ploughshares through the deep. Wherever fire is, its power is felt. "Our God is a consuming fire." Can He be in us without a Divine power being seen and felt? When the disciples were baptised with the Holy Ghost and with fire it could not be hid. "These men," they said, "are full of new wine." When the *live* coal touched the lips of the prophet, how quickly the power was seen in him. "Here am I, send me" (Isa. 6). The indwelling fire is the remedy for all formality and coldness in the Lord's service. It is the eternal enemy of the chilly, freezing breath of unbelief. "He shall baptise you with fire." Are you willing to be baptised with this baptism?

CHRIST IN ME.

GALATIANS 2. 20.

PAUL had two distinct revelations of Jesus. While on the way to Damascus Jesus was revealed to him. This revelation slew the enmity of his heart and converted him to

God. Then he writes to the Galatians that "It pleased God to reveal His Son *in* me" (Gal. 1. 16). This second revelation proved his sanctification and fitness for service, for he adds, "That I might preach Him among the heathen." How barren and fruitless our testimony for God is until Christ in all His power and sufficiency is revealed—not only in Heaven—but *in us*. Then, like him, we can triumphantly say, "I live, yet not I, but *Christ liveth in me.*" If Christ is in me, then I must be—

I. **A New Creature.** When the "Living One" enters, then the reign of death ceases, "I am come that ye might have life." Regeneration is the incoming of the "Life of God" into the soul by the Holy Spirit. Which were born, not of blood—it is not hereditary; nor of the will of the flesh—it is not by carnal energy; nor of the will of man—it is not by intellectual power, *but of God*. How will evolutionists explain this? Until Christ is trusted and received there can only be death and degeneration; but when He enters into the heart and life of man how completely His Word is fulfilled: "Behold, I make all things new."

II. **A Temple of God.** Solemn thought. Shall God in very deed dwell with men? "Know ye not that ye are the temple of God?" (1 Cor. 3. 16). As God came down and dwelt in the temple of Solomon, so God the Holy Ghost has come to dwell in the body of each believer, to show forth the glory of His grace and power (1 Cor. 6. 19, 20). The indwelling of the Spirit implies the all-cleansing of the blood. Cleansed, possessed, used. Spirit, soul, and body.

III. **Governed by His Will.** "Not My will, but Thine be done," was a gleam of Heaven's glory from Jesus as the temple of God. The house cannot stand that has two opposing wills within. If I recognise "Christ in me,"

then all my ways and purposes will be heartily submitted
to Him. The earth is His footstool, but He sitteth not
on a footstool, but on a throne, the centre of power and
authority. The *reign of Christ* within is the divine remedy
for unruly passions, ungovernable tempers, fruitless
testimony, and the spirit-grieving life of selfishness. Thy
Kingdom come, Thy will be done *in us*, as it is in Heaven.

IV. **In Possession of all Sufficiency.** The continual
needs of the spiritual life are very great, but all fullness
dwells in Him; and if He dwells in us, then we may be
filled with all the fullness of God. Surely the "unsearchable riches of Christ" are sufficient to meet the daily and
hourly demands of our new and God-given natures. "Christ
in me." What a reservoir to draw from. Christ in me,
to fill up every crevice in my being, as the waters cover the
deep. Christ in me, to impel and constrain, as the steam
in the engine. "God is able to make all grace abound
toward you, that ye always may have all sufficiency in all
things" (2 Cor. 9. 8).

V. **Sinful Pleasures will have no Attraction for Me.**
"If any man love the world, the love of the Father is not
in him." What fellowship can light have with darkness?
If Christ fully satisfies the desires of the heart there will
be no cravings for things contrary to His will. When
Christians hanker after doubtful things, it is an evidence
that Christ is not fully trusted. She that is satisfied with
her lover does not seek another. The cabbage leaf cannot
have the attraction for the butterfly that it had for the
caterpillar. Those whose lives are hid with Christ in God
will set their affections on all things above.

VI. **Willing to Sacrifice for Others.** If Christ is
in me, then the Christ-like life will be manifested.
"He came not to be ministered unto, but to minister"
(Matt. 20. 28). He glorified God by a life of self-sacrifice

for the good of man. He did not seek popularity by striving and crying in the street (Matt. 12. 19). If Christ is in us there will be no striving for the chief seats of honour; no courting the praise of man. Since Christ hath loved us, and given himself for us, ought we not, through love to the perishing, give ourselves to God for their salvation?

VII. **More than Conqueror.** The Christ-possessed soul will come into contact with principalities and powers, with rulers of the darkness, and with wicked spirits, in a way that others cannot understand; but "greater is He that is *in you* than he that is in the world" (1 John 4. 4). Let us never forget while fighting against unbelief, unrighteousness, and all the powers of darkness, that the battle is the Lord's. God, who dwelleth in you, He doeth the works. "God working in you, both to will and to do of His good pleasure" (Phil. 2. 13). How the apostle must have realised the power of the indwelling Saviour when he exclaimed, "I can do all things through Christ which strengtheneth me." By faith we, too, must reckon on His almighty power, so great things will be done in His Name. Doubting or ignoring "Christ in us" is the source of weakness, fruitlessness, and discouragement in the service of God. Believe God, that Christ by the Spirit dwells in you; reckon always in His presence, power, and fullness, and soon you will sing, "Thanks be to God, which giveth us the victory, through our Lord Jesus Christ!" ———

THE RESURRECTION.
1 Corinthians 15. 20-22; 35-58.

There were some in the Corinthian Church who taught that "there is no resurrection of the dead" (v. 12). To combat this fatal error, and to establish the doctrine more firmly in the minds of the saints, Paul wrote this magnificent compendium of the subject. There is nothing like it anywhere; no, not in all the world, for the great apostle here delivers that which he had *received* from the risen Christ Himself (vv. 3, 4). The great truths of this resurrection chapter are—

I. The Resurrection of Christ. "But now is Christ risen from the dead" (v. 20). The Christ of the *Scriptures* must die, be buried, and rise again (vv. 3, 4). That Jesus was the Christ was proved by His rising from the dead, and appearing to Cephas, and to "five hundred brethren at once" (vv. 5, 6). To *deceive* five hundred *brethren* at once would have been about as great a wonder as rising from the dead, especially when these brethren were at first very sceptical. This is no myth, but a fact established by many infallible proofs (Acts 1. 3).

II. The Resurrection Hope. "If Christ be not raised, your *faith* is vain; ye are *yet in your sins*, and they who have died in this faith are *perished*" (vv. 17, 18). Upon this foundation—the resurrection of Christ—this Spirit-taught apostle builds the whole structure of the Christian faith. The death of Christ will avail us nothing if *He is not risen* and accepted of God in our behalf. He died for our sins, but He must be raised and exalted with God's right hand ere forgiveness could be preached in His Name (Acts 5. 31). If Christ be not raised, there is no hope for man (Rom. 5. 10).

III. The Resurrection of the Dead. Nothing but confusion and error can come to those who think that Paul is here speaking of a general resurrection at the last day. The *dead* referred to in this chapter are those who have "fallen asleep *in Christ*" (v. 18). "Even so *in Christ* shall all be made alive" (v. 22). All are *in* Adam, but all are *not in* Christ. "They that *are Christ's* at His coming" (v. 23). The wicked dead shall have no part in the first resurrection (Rev. 20. 5). How could he speak of *them* as "sown in dishonour, and raised in *glory*?" (v. 43).

IV. The Resurrection Body. Paul now raises this great double question, and proceeds to answer it. "How are the dead *raised up*? and with *what body* do they come?" (vv. 35-49).

1. It will NOT be the SAME BODY that is sown in the grave (v. 37). Thank God, there will be no cripples in Heaven; no deformed bodies there.

2. It will be a GOD-GIVEN BODY (v. 38). A body in everything pleasing to Him, and worthy of a redeemed spirit (2 Cor. 5. 1).

3. It will be a body in every way SUITED TO THE INDIVIDUAL SPIRIT. "To every *seed* his own body (v. 38). One body may differ from another body in glory, as "one star differeth from another" (vv. 41, 42).

4. It will be an INCORRUPTIBLE BODY (v. 42). Incapable of death, disease, or decay.

5. It will be a BODY OF GLORY (v. 43). Like unto His own glorious body (Matt. 17. 2).

6. It will be a body of POWER (v. 43). Not subject to the laws of earth. Every material fetter broken.

7. It will be a SPIRITUAL BODY (v. 44). Entirely subject to the volitions of the blood-washed spirit (1 John 3. 2). Then shall we be in the *image* of the heavenly (v. 49).

V. The Resurrection Mystery. "Behold I show you a mystery," etc. (vv. 51-54). Here the apostle reveals a truth that had hitherto been veiled, and, strange to say, a truth that is still veiled to many, although revealed, viz., that *all* the children of God shall *not die*, but that all must be changed (v. 51). The Lord Himself will come, and those who are alive and remain at that time shall be caught up *together* with those who have fallen asleep in Christ, but

who shall then be raised from the dead (Thess. 4. 15-17).
In a moment, in the twinkling of an eye, the dead shall be
raised, and *we* (those living at that time) shall be changed
(v. 52). It is appointed unto *men*—not *all* men—once to
die (Heb. 9. 27).

VI. The Resurrection Song. This song is entitled,
"Death swallowed up in victory" (v. 54). It is a victory
over the *power* of sin, and sin, too, that was *strengthened*
by a holy law (v. 56). It is a perfect victory over all the
effects of sin. "O death, where is thy sting?" Where is
not the effect of thy poison in these new bodies of ours?
"O grave, where is thy victory?" Once thou didst claim
our bodies as thy spoil, but thou hast been eternally defeated in this new incorruptible body. But this is a song
of *praise* as well as of triumph. "Thanks be to God, who
giveth us the victory *through our Lord Jesus Christ*"
(v. 57). He alone could "swallow up death in victory"
(Isa. 25. 8). This will be the complete fulfilment of
Hosea 13. 14. Notice there His "*I wills.*"

VII. The Resurrection Incentive. Paul now closes
his great argument with an exhortation which is full of
motive power. "*Therefore,* my beloved brethren, be ye
stedfast" (v. 58). Seeing that such glorious prospects are
before us, what manner of persons ought we *now* to be?

1. There should be STABILITY OF CHARACTER. "Be ye
stedfast, immoveable." Let not the unbelief of others
turn you aside from the faith of this Gospel.

2. There should be CONSTANCY OF SERVICE. "Always
abounding in the work of the Lord," knowing that it is
not in vain; for in the resurrection state, and at the
Judgment-Seat of Christ, the reward will be given (Rev.
22. 12). Every man's work shall be tried of what sort it
is (1 Cor. 3. 12-15).

THE ASCENDED LORD.

LUKE 24. 50-53; ACTS 1. 4-11.

"HE led them out as far as to Bethany." From Bethany He started on His journey to the Cross of shame; from there also He starts on His journey to the Crown of glory. Here the disciples witnessed their Lord slowly rising up before their eyes. While His body was gradually ascending into the Heavens, He "lifted His hands and blessed them," and as He blessed He slowly vanished into the cloud that carried Him into Heaven. Do we wonder that after He was gone they still stood "gazing up into Heaven?" They had scarcely awakened to the fact of His resurrection when they beheld another wonder equally momentous and glorious. "Truly, this was the Son of God." If our worldly hopes are crucified with Christ, we shall have new and brighter hopes in His resurrection and translation to the Father's throne. Associated with the Ascension, we have brought before us some of the "things which accompany salvation" (Heb. 6. 9). Let us give earnest heed to them.

I. **The Baptism of the Holy Ghost.** "Ye shall be baptised with the Holy Ghost" (Acts 1. 5-8). Jesus *died* for our sins, and *rose again* for our justification, and *ascended* for our enduement with the power of the Holy Ghost. The power of the Holy Spirit upon His disciples was the witness that Christ, the Crucified One, was now in the presence of the Father (John 16. 7). These early and true-hearted followers did not believe, as the great majority of modern Christians do, that the fruit of Christ's *death* was the sum of salvation; they waited, and received the fruit of His *Ascension*—the baptism of the Holy Spirit (Acts 2. 4). "Did ye receive the Holy Ghost when ye believed?" (Acts 19. 2, R.V.).

II. **Witnessing for Christ.** "Ye shall be witnesses

unto Me," etc. (Acts 1. 8). So faithful were these Spirit-filled disciples that in a short time they had "filled Jerusalem with the doctrine" (Acts 5. 28). The power of the Spirit was with them, so we read that "with great power gave the apostles witness of the resurrection of the Lord Jesus" (chap. 4. 33). We are unauthorised witnesses for Christ unless we have been "endued with power from on high." Our teaching and preaching will be but "sounding brass" unless we are "filled with the Holy Ghost"—just a sounding trumpet; no divine articulating voice. That we may be true witnesses for Him, let us receive the "promise of the Father" as well as the promise of the Son.

III. **The Hope of His Coming Again.** "This same Jesus shall so come in like manner as ye have seen Him go" (v. 11). To say, as some do, that the coming of the Holy Spirit was the coming of "this same Jesus" is not only a denial of the personality of the Spirit, and an insult to common sense, but also a wilful perversion of the Word of God. It looks, says the author of "The Coming Kingdom of God," as if some men so hated the thought of a returning personal Christ that they are prepared to believe any absurdity rather than accept it. "The Lord Himself shall descend from Heaven with a shout" (1 Thess 4. 16). This is the hope of the Church of God, which is being presently *called out* (*ekklesia*) as a witness to His Name. This is the Bride for which Christ has promised to come and "receive unto Himself" (John 14). As soon as the Lord was out of sight the disciples were taught to believe in and to *look for* His coming again. This is the hope that cheers in service and purifies the life (1 John 3. 3).

THE SECOND ADVENT.
1 Thessalonians 4. 13-18; 5. 1-6.

This is a subject full of vital interest for these latter days. Paul's teaching here is clear and urgent. In every chapter of this epistle he refers to the Lord's Coming. In the portion before us he states several facts that might be looked at separately.

I. That the Lord will Come Again. "The Lord Himself shall descend from Heaven" (v. 16). This is not the coming of death, neither is it the coming of the Holy Spirit. It is the coming of "the Lord Himself." It is as much a *personal* coming as when David anointed himself and *changed his apparel* and came into the house of the Lord (2 Sam. 12. 20).

II. That those who Sleep in Jesus will Come with Him (v. 14). All those who have died in the faith have been put to sleep in the grace and presence of Jesus. So when He comes He brings those redeemed spirits with Him, for they are His own peculiar treasure, bought by His own blood, and cannot be separated from Him.

III. That those who are Alive when He comes shall not go Before those who are Asleep (v. 15). Neither time nor circumstances can give any precedence on that day. Those who have died in the Lord shall lose nothing by it; those who remain alive at His coming shall be spared the pain of dying, but shall not have any advantage thereby in the way of pre-eminence before Him (2 Cor. 4. 14).

IV. That the Dead in Christ shall Rise First (v. 16). All those who have died trusting in the Lord Jesus Christ, having been saved by His grace, shall have a part in this *"first"* resurrection. It will only be "they that *are* Christ's at His coming" (1 Cor. 15. 23). Blessed and holy is he that hath part in this first resurrection; on such the second death hath no power. The rest of the dead, who have died in their sins, shall not be raised till one thousand years after (Rev. 20. 5, 6).

V. That all Shall be Caught up Together (v. 17).

When Christ comes those Christians who are living on the earth shall be "changed in a moment, in the twinkling of an eye," and *together* with those who have been raised from the dead will be "caught up" to meet the Lord in the air. They are all *one* in Christ Jesus. One shepherd, one flock.

VI. That we Shall be for Ever with Him (v. 17). To be *for ever* with Him, who is the Wisdom and Fullness of God, for whom all things were made, and by whom all things consist, implies more than tongue can tell or finite minds can grasp. They follow the Lamb whithersoever He goeth. Then shall Christ's own prayer be answered, "With Me where I am" (John 17. 24). Surely we may comfort one another with these words (v. 18).

VII. That this will be an Awful Day for the Unbelieving. While *they* are saying "Peace and safety." He shall come as a thief in the night, then "sudden destruction shall come upon them" (vv. 1-3). A thief does not give any warning as to the time he will break into the house. He will be careful to choose the most *unexpected* moment. Sudden and everlasting destruction from the *presence of the Lord* will be the doom of every Christ-rejecter at His coming (2 Thess. 1. 9). These are terrible words; their terror lies in the fact that they are true, and that this fulfilment may be at any moment. Are you prepared?

VIII. That the Christian should be Looking for His Coming. All who are Christ's are the "Children of light," having been saved from the darkness that is in this world through sin. They are "not of the night," sleeping the sleep of indifference or unbelief, but are those who are expected to "watch and be sober" (vv. 5, 6). It is high time to wake up, for now is your full and final salvation nearer than when ye believed (Rom. 13. 11)

SUFFERING FOR CHRIST.

2 CORINTHIANS 11. 24-33.

WHEN Paul was called as a *chosen vessel* to bear the Name of Jesus Christ before the Gentiles, and kings, and the children of Israel, the Lord uttered these significant words: "For I will shew him how great things he must suffer for My Name's sake" (Acts 9. 15, 16). He who would live godly, by receiving Christ's Word, occupying His place, acting only in His Name, and for His glory, must suffer; for the world still lieth with the wicked one, and the carnal mind is still at enmity against God. "Woe unto you when all men speak well of you." The sufferings of this servant of God were terrible. See the—

I. Reason why He Speaks of Them. Some "false apostles and deceitful workers" had been glorying in themselves, and seemingly doing all they could to belittle the name and character of Paul. He condescends (as a fool) to take them on their own ground by giving them a list of his sufferings and perils in the cause of Jesus Christ. Had the great apostle not played the fool for once, we never would have known the half of all that he endured in faithfulness to his Master. The fact that he felt ashamed to speak of his *sufferings* for the Christ who had died for him shows the nobleness of his true inward character.

II. Nature of Them. They are simply appalling. It is almost hard to believe that any one man could go through such an ordeal in the course of a single lifetime. Five times lashed, at the hands of the Jews, receiving 39 strokes each time. Three times beaten with rods by a Roman official. Three times shipwrecked and tossed in the deep, perhaps clinging to a spar for a whole "night and a day." Many long and wearisome journeys. Endured eight different kinds of *peril*, suffered eight kinds of bodily privations, and, beside all this, having the personal care of all the churches upon him. But all this tribulation, distress, persecution, famine, nakedness, and peril did not separate him from the love of God in Christ Jesus (Rom. 8. 35). How like his sufferings were to those "many sorrows" which marred the face of his Holy Master, and how truly did he thereby become a "partaker of the sufferings of Christ."

III. **Effect of Them.** He did not mourn over them, he *gloried in them* (vv. 30, 31). He did not look upon them as misfortunes, but as marks of his Master's favour. They were medals won in his battles for the Lord (2 Cor. 12. 9, 10). Glorying in tribulation was an article in Paul's creed (Rom. 5. 3). He knew that if "we suffer with Christ, we shall also reign with Him" (2 Tim. 2 .12). Perhaps this was one of the reasons why they could sing praises in the prison, with bleeding backs and aching limbs (Acts 16. 25). Only those who look at the things which are *unseen*, can possibly "esteem the reproach of Christ greater riches than the treasures of Egypt (Heb. 11. 26). "If men revile you and persecute you, and say all manner of evil against you *falsely* for *My sake*, rejoice and be exceedingly glad; for great is your reward in Heaven."

THE CHRISTIAN'S ARMOUR.
EPHESIANS 6. 10-20.

BUNYAN was wise in sending his Pilgrims into the armoury immediately after supper. As soon as we are brought into communion with God, we need to be fitted for the fight of faith. All who are in the Kingdom of God's dear Son have got the forces of the kingdom of Satan against them, so they need to be panoplied with the whole armour of God. Let us look at—

I. **The Enemy.** "Not flesh and blood, but principalities, powers, world rulers, spiritual hosts of wickedness"

(v. 12, R.V.). All the authorities of Hell and all the rulers of the darkness of this world, who are in league with the Devil, are opposed to the progress of the Kingdom of Jesus Christ. Not *flesh and blood*, but that wicked spirit that works in the children of disobedience, using flesh and blood as an instrumentality (Eph. 2. 2). Our warfare is not so much with mortal beings as with the immortal powers of evil that rule in their lives, and that come to us in the form of the *"wiles* of the Devil." These wiles are very varied, and are adapted to suit the different tendencies of the age or the individual. If he fails with his *wiles* he will surely try his "fiery darts" (v. 16). These may come as unclean thoughts shot into the mind like ignited arrows from the pit. Truly, in the face of such a mighty and invisible foe we need the whole armour of God.

II. **The Armour.** Our putting on of the armour of God simply means being fortified against all the powers of evil by those virtues or moral excellences by which the Son of God was able to withstand all the temptations of the Devil (Col. 2. 15). This armour consists of six parts—

1. THE GIRDLE OF TRUTH. The loins of the mind are to be girded with the truth as it is in Jesus Christ, and so made strong to think and act for Him. This *truth* is "light from Heaven," which scatters all the darkness of doubt and fear, and enables one to speak out what they *do know*, and not what they *don't know*, like those who don the girdle of doubt.

2. THE BREASTPLATE OF RIGHTEOUSNESS. A conscience void of offence toward God and men, is that *rightness* which is as a protecting breastplate for the peace and joy of the *heart*. This breastplate Christ constantly wore, because He always delighted to do the will of His Father.

3. THE SHOES OF PREPAREDNESS. The "Gospel of

peace" provides for our feet the shoes of preparedness, so that we should be always *ready* to do His will and to run in the way of His commandments. Those who have received the Gospel of peace should have swift feet to publish it (Isa. 52. 7).

4. THE SHIELD OF FAITH. The Roman shield was so large that the soldier could hide himself completely behind it, thus it was above or over all. This was the shield behind which David sheltered when he faced the terrible Goliath. This piece of armour signifies that unstaggered confidence in God which always overcomes (1 John 5. 4).

5. THE HELMET OF SALVATION. The assurance of salvation is a mighty protection for the *head* in these days when there is so much false teaching all about us. The strength of this helmet lies in the fact that God Himself is our Salvation. This piece, like the others, is the *gift* of God, so we are to *take* it.

6. THE SWORD OF THE SPIRIT. The sword of the Spirit is the *Word of God*, not the thoughts or opinions of men. Jesus Christ did not fail to use the *written* Word when assaulted by the arch-enemy of God and man (Matt. 4. 4). There be many in our days that seem at a loss to know where to find this sword now; the Devil has so blinded their minds that they imagine that the "Word of God" has been buried in a heap of ancient rubbish, and so they go on fighting with the rotten sticks of their own theories. Nothing but failure and shame can follow where the Word of God is not preached, because the Holy Spirit of God, the author of life and blessing, can use no other weapon. It is the sword of the Spirit.

III. **The Warfare.** The attitudes to be maintained in this conflict are—

1. STANDING. "That we may be able to *stand*." Having

been *justified* freely by His grace, and *accepted* in the Beloved, we have got a blessed standing, from which the great enemy of souls is ever seeking to drive us. The stratagem of the Devil is to get in between our souls and God, that the source of our spiritual supply may be cut off.

2. WRESTLING. "We wrestle against principalities," etc. In this warfare we cannot hide ourselves in the host. Wrestling is a *personal* conflict, an individual contact with the enemy. By putting on the whole armour of God every single Christian is to overcome by faith in Him who is able always to give the victory.

3. PRAYING AND WATCHING. This will not only keep the armour bright, but will keep it on. Polished armour hanging up in the hall of our creed will not save us in the day of battle. A praying heart and watchful eyes will never be taken unawares by the scouts of the kingdom of Satan. Daniel prayed three times a day, and, in spite of the trap carefully set by his enemies, he triumphed. This is the victory that overcometh the world, even our faith.

———

PAUL'S LAST LETTER.
2 TIMOTHY 4. 6-18.

THERE is always a special pathos about the last words of loved ones. Such are very frequently a revelation of the inner character and life. It is so with this final message from the pen of our beloved apostle. As we bow our ear to catch this message, as it were from his dying lips, we are not left to faintly guess what he means. There is a telling ring in his voice, his mind is clear, his words are emphatic, and speak out volumes of truth. They speak of—

I. **Perfect Resignation.** "I am now ready to be offered." He who had poured out his life in the service of the Lord Jesus Christ was now *ready* to have his blood poured out as a sacrifice for Him. At one time he was in a strait about this (Phil. 1. 23), but now he was ready. He was like one who had everything packed up in readiness to step on board that ship which was to take him to a better country. Be ye also ready.

II. **Assured Success.** "I have fought the good fight. I have finished the course. I have kept the faith" (R.V.). He was perfectly confident that his life and testimony as a servant of the Lord was no failure, but that the will of God in calling him to His work had been fulfilled in him. As a *warrior* he had *fought* and conquered; as a *racer* he had abode in the course and honourably finished the race; as a *custodian* he had firmly *kept* the faith delivered to him. He was faithful unto death (Rev. 2. 10).

III. **Joyful Hope.** "Henceforth there is laid up for me a crown," etc. The Lord, who was his *righteous* Judge, had this crown *laid up* for him, although Nero, the *un*-righteous judge, had laid up for him a sword. In view of his crowning day, Paul could joyfully sing: "O death, where is thy sting?" The Lord always *lays up* treasure and honour for those who faithfully serve Him now in the day of His rejection at the hands of men (James 1. 12).

IV. **Painful Experiences.** It was surely with a deeply grieved soul that the aged apostle told of "Demas," who had *forsaken* him, "having loved this present world," and of Alexander, the coppersmith, who had done him "much evil," and of how that "no man stood with him" while on his first trial, but "all forsook him." In all this Paul was a sharer of his Master's sorrows (Matt. 26. 56). *"Only Luke is with me."* Love of the world, back-biting, and cowardliness are still the sins that bring sorrow to many a faithful servant of God. In the world he had tribulation, but in Christ he had peace.

V. **Forgiving Love.** "I pray God that it may not be

laid to their charge." He is true to the Spirit of his Master
in praying for those who "despitefully used him and persecuted him" (Matt. 5. 44). This ought to be the desire
of all who have themselves experienced the forgiving grace
of God. To overcome the *evil* actions of others with your
good actions is to fight in the armour of God.

VI. **Divine Faithfulness.** "Notwithstanding the Lord
stood with me and strengthened me" (v. 17). While
giving his "first answer" before the unrighteous judge, he
doubtless experienced the fulfilment of the Lord's promise :
"It is not ye that speak, but the Spirit of your Father
which is in you" (Matt. 10. 19, 20). Paul's last testimony,
like that of Joshua, is to the unfailing faithfulness of his
God and Saviour (Joshua 23. 14). "Lo, I am with you
alway !"

VII. **Unfailing Confidence.** "The Lord *shall* deliver
me from every evil work, and *will* preserve me unto His
heavenly Kingdom" (v. 18). Come what may, there is no
shadow of doubt or tremor of fear in the heart of this noble
man as to his present safety from all *evil* and his future
reward and eternal satisfaction in the coming Kingdom of
His glory. He is assured that the sufferings of this present
life are not worthy to be compared with the glory that shall
be revealed in that day when "He shall appear." Look
up, for the day of your redemption draweth near.

REJOICE IN THE LORD.

WHY should Christians need to be exhorted to rejoice in
the Lord? Does the lack of joy in Christ not betray a lack
of faith. We shall observe the—

I. **Object of the Believer's Joy.** We are to rejoice—

1. IN THE LORD (Psa. 35. 9). Not only must we be
in Christ to rejoice in Him, but He Himself must be
to us our all.

2. In the Lord AS OUR GOD (Joel 2. 23). Jesus said, "I ascend unto My God, and your God." Do we know what is meant when we say, "My God, my Father?" A God for a Father.

3. In the Lord AS OUR KING (Psa. 149. 2). We may well be joyful in *our* King, for there is no king like Him.

4. In the Lord AS THE HOLY ONE (Isa. 41. 16). Only those who love holiness can taste of this joy. The pure in heart shall see God, and glory in Him, as the Holy One.

5. In the Lord AS THE SAVING ONE (Phil. 3. 3). When Christ is received by faith it is then that the Simeon song is sung: "I have seen Thy salvation."

6. In the Lord AS THE ALL-SUFFICIENT ONE (Hab. 3. 17). If our joy is in the blessing instead of in the Blesser it will soon wither.

II. **Ground of this Joy.** Every good gift is from above. "That *My joy* might remain in you." We rejoice in the Lord—

1. BECAUSE OF HIS SALVATION (Psa. 35. 9). Oh, the grace, which brought salvation, and delivered us from the fearful pit of guilt, and cleansed us from the miry clay of sin.

2. BECAUSE OF HIS COVERING (Isa. 61. 10). He clothed the first sinners with coats of skin—implying sacrifice. So we are covered (Rom. 3. 22).

3. BECAUSE OF HIS WORD (Psa. 119. 14). His faithful word, when believed, or eaten, becomes the joy and rejoicing of the heart.

4. BECAUSE OF HIS FAITHFULNESS (Psa. 5. 11). Those who put their trust in Him may rejoice, because they shall never be put to shame.

5. BECAUSE OF HIS PROTECTION (Psa. 28. 7). He is not only our Shield to defend, but our Strength to sustain.

This sense of safety ought to increase our joy. Fear is the flight of happiness.

6. BECAUSE OF HIS ASSISTANCE (Psa. 63. 7). How often, as a loving Father, has He stretched forth His helping hand in our time of need.

7. BECAUSE OF HIS REVIVING. If our spiritual life droops, so does our joy. Every revival of life is a revival of Joy.

8. BECAUSE OF HIS PRESENCE (Psa. 16. 11). There is fullness of joy in His presence *now* as well as hereafter. This joy might be ours always for has He not said, "Lo, I am with you alway?"

9. BECAUSE OF HIS JOY (Zeph. 3. 17). You may well rejoice in the Lord when He rejoices over thee with singing.

III. **Character of this Joy.** It is—

1. HOLY JOY (Lev. 23. 40). It is a rejoicing *before* the Lord; the joy the high-priest had in entering into the holiest of all; the joy that Jesus had.

2. A GREAT JOY (Isa. 61. 10). Great in the sense of being divine, Godlike, and signal.

3. A THANKFUL JOY (Joel 2. 23). The heart that is glad in the Lord delights to pour out its gratitude to the Lord.

4. A HOPEFUL JOY (Zech. 9. 9.) This Heaven-born joy anticipates the coming King, in whom, though now we see Him not, yet believing, we rejoice.

5. A CONTINUAL JOY (Phil. 4. 4). If we rejoice in His Name, and know that His Name shall endure *for ever*, then we may rejoice in the Lord *alway*.

6. A GOD-GLORIFYING JOY (Psa. 89. 16). Glorying, not in our own name, but in His. Oh, for more of this pure gladness which magnifies His precious Name!

7. A TRIUMPHANT JOY (Hab. 3. 18). It is not bound

up with the things of this world, but in the eternal God Himself.

8. UNSPEAKABLE JOY (1 Peter 1. 8). We call it joy, but the fullness of the delight, the ecstasy, the bliss, no language can tell. "God, my exceeding joy."

IV. Consequences of this Joy. Rejoicing in the Lord is the happy mood that makes our lives most fruitful. This joy—

1. GIVES FITNESS TO SACRIFICE (2 Chron. 23. 18). Our offerings must be made with rejoicing (Rom. 12. 1). The Lord loveth a cheerful giver.

2. GIVES POWER FOR TESTIMONY (Psa. 107. 22). His works are to be *declared* with rejoicing. If the joy of the Lord is not in our own hearts our declarations will be of little avail.

3. GIVES DELIVERANCE FROM SELF (Phil. 3. 3). If our joy is only in Christ Jesus our confidence will be also in Him.

4. GIVES STRENGTH FOR SERVICE (Neh. 8. 10). The joy of having God's promise ought to strengthen us in our work, as it did Nehemiah.

5. GIVES COURAGE FOR WITNESS-BEARING (Psa. 20. 5). If our joy in the Lord were measured by the height of our banners, how would it stand with us? Rejoice, again, I say, rejoice; rejoice in the Lord.

ASK AND YE SHALL RECEIVE.

MEN ought always to pray, and not to faint. Those who pray most have most encouragement to pray. Their testimony is: "I love the Lord because He hath heard my voice."

I. The Promises. They are—

1. SURE (John 16. 23). "Verily, *I* say unto you." Think of the Promiser. I, who made the Heavens and the

earth. I, who have all power; the faithful and true
Witness, the God who cannot lie, the Lord thy Redeemer.

2. SIMPLE (Matt. 7. 7). The statements here are such
as any child might understand. How gracious our God is
to put such great and mysterious truths in such child-like
language, so unlike the wisdom of this world.

3. SUFFICIENT. This *"whatsoever* ye shall ask"* is surely
a wide door and effectual. There is enough here for the
life that now is and for the life which is to come. His
"How much more" (Luke 11. 13) is surely sufficient to
assure His *willingness* to give. All the promises are "Yea
and amen" in Him.

II. **The Conditions.** Like the promises, they are
plain and simple. That we—

1. ASK (Matt. 7. 7). As children, we are to let our
requests be made known in a child-like fashion.

2. ASK OF THE FATHER (John 16. 23). Your Father
knoweth that ye have need of these things. We have
liberty of access. What a privilege!

3. ASK IN THE NAME OF JESUS. Let us ever remember
that this new way is through the rent veil of the Redeemer's
flesh, but let us come with boldness.

4. ASK ACCORDING TO HIS WILL (1 John 5. 14, 15).
If the Word of Christ is dwelling in us richly, then we will
ask those things which are pleasing to Him.

5. ASK IN FAITH (Mark 11. 24). He that cometh to
God must *believe.* "Elias was a man subject to like
passions as we are, and he prayed, and the Heaven gave
rain." Believe and thou shalt see.

6. ABIDE IN HIM (John 15. 7). The branch not abiding
in the vine need not pray to be filled with sap. Seeking
His glory, ye may ask what ye will, and it shall be done
unto you.

7. THAT OUR HEART DOES NOT CONDEMN US (1 John 3. 21, 22). It is possible—and, alas, so common—to ask with the lips what the heart never expects. He answers us not by the length and breadth of our petitions, but of our faith.

III. **The Hindrances.** We don't speak here of hindrances to praying, but of those things which hinder the answers.

1. INSINCERITY (1 John 3. 21). It is quite possible to keep up the form of prayer and to be asking great things from God, while the heart is condemning it all.

2. WILFULNESS (Psa. 66. 18). Conscious of iniquity in the heart, but unwilling to confess it. First get reconciled to God about this matter, then bring your petition.

3. SELFISHNESS (Jas. 4. 3). Oh, the pride and subtlety of self asking divine things to feed the fires of its lusts. We pray for success that *we* might be successful. He will not give His glory to another.

4. IMPATIENCE (Psa. 40. 1). David says: "I waited patiently and He heard my cry." Don't be a run-away knocker. Have the patience of God. If God can afford to wait so well might we.

5. UNBELIEF (Mark 11. 24). This closes the door of expectancy. All things are possible to them that believe. Have faith in God. Believe ye that I am able to do this?

IV. **The Examples.** In the above texts we have some soul-inspiring examples of how the Lord answers prayer, and from which we may learn—

1. THAT THE LORD IS INTERESTED IN ALL THAT CONCERNS HIS CHILDREN (1 Sam. 1. 27). What was a reproach to Hannah (barrenness) the Lord rolled away (2 Peter 1. 8).

2. THAT WE SHOULD BRING ALL OUR WANTS TO THE LORD (Exod. 17. 4-7). Be careful for nothing, be prayerful in everything (Phil. 4. 6).

3. THAT WE SHOULD EXPECT THE VERY THINGS WE ASK
(Ezra 8. 21). Hannah said, "For *this* child I prayed."
Although Paul did not get the thorn removed, yet from the
fact that he prayed *three* times we see that he had been
taught to expect what he asked (2 Cor. 12. 8).

4. THAT THERE IS NOTHING TOO HARD FOR THE LORD
(2 Kings 4. 23). Though he be dead, yet shall he live.
Look unto Me, for *I* am God.

5. THAT THE LORD OFTEN GIVES FAR ABOVE WHAT WE
ASK (1 Kings 3. 9-14). Elijah prayed that he might die
(1 Kings 19. 4), but the Lord translated him into Heaven.

6. THAT THE PRAYER OF FAITH IS THE MIGHTIEST
WEAPON ON EARTH (1 Kings 17. 30-39). Think of what it
has done in the past, is doing now, and might do in the
future through you—only believe.

THE FRUIT OF THE SPIRIT.

I. Source of the Fruit.

1. THE SOURCE IS NOT IN THE BRANCH. The branch
cannot bear fruit of *itself* (John 15. 4, 5). In me, that is, in
my flesh, dwelleth no good thing. Might as well expect
figs from thistles as the fruit of the Spirit from the carnal
mind.

2. THE SOURCE IS IN CHRIST HIMSELF. All the fullness
of the Godhead dwelleth in Him. He, as the true and
living Vine, has His roots in the Eternal Father. He as
Man is the Bowl into which the oil flows from the living
trees, and from which all the lamps receive their supply
(Zech. 4. 2), and are filled with the fruits of righteousness.

3. THE SUPPLY IS BY THE HOLY SPIRIT (Rom. 5. 5).
The sap in the vine is a beautiful metaphor of the Holy
Spirit flowing through Christ into those who are abiding
in Him. The sap quickens into newness of life.

4. IT FILLS THE ABIDING BRANCH with the life of the

vine (John 6. 63). So by His Spirit are we made possessors of the Divine life. If any man have not the Spirit of Christ he is none of His.

II. Characteristics of the Fruit-Bearers. They are—

1. CHOSEN ONES (John 15. 16). As withered and worthless branches they have been chosen of God. While we were like the unwashed outcast in Ezekiel 16, He passed by and set His love upon us:

2. ADOPTED ONES (Rom. 8. 15). Not only chosen, but adopted into His family; planted into the Living Vine, and made partakers of the fullness therein. "All one in Christ."

3. ABIDING ONES (John 15. 5). Those who feel and know that their life and strength depend entirely upon their union with the Living One. When first planted into Christ they were as dry as the boards of the Tabernacle.

4. SANCTIFIED ONES (Rom. 15. 10). Having been chosen and adopted, they have been sanctified—set apart—for the Lord's use. When the Spirit possesses the Christian, as the sap does the engrafted branch, it is that God might be glorified in him.

5. RECEIVING ONES (Acts 1. 8). They have nothing to give until they have first received of His Holy Spirit. What can a branch give to a vine before it becomes a part of it? Well may the branches say, "What have we that we have not *received*?"

6. POSSESSED ONES (1 Cor. 3. 16). The branch not *possessed* by the sap is a withered one, and cannot show forth the character of the vine. "Abide in Me and I in you." It is God who dwelleth in you; He doeth the work.

7. FILLED ONES (Acts 2. 4). The branch must first be filled with sap before it can be fruitful. Fruit is the result of abundance of life. Be *filled* with the Spirit.

III. **Character of the Fruit.** Here we would observe, and let us put emphasis on the fact—

1. THAT THIS FRUIT IS THE FRUIT OF THE SPIRIT (Eph. 5. 9). It is not of the Christian—apart from the Spirit— but the outcome of the presence and power of the Holy Spirit abiding in the Christian. The branch does not *labour* to bring forth fruit, but the sap does, and so it is the fruit of the sap. "It is God who worketh in you."

2 THIS FRUIT MEANS THE CHARACTER OF CHRIST (Rom. 5. 5). If the Holy Ghost sheds abroad in our hearts the *love* of God, it is that this string of pearls, mentioned in 1 Corinthians 13, and worn by Jesus Christ, might be exhibited in us. If this love is begotten in us by the Spirit it will enable us to bring forth such fruit as that mentioned in Colossians 3. As the sap takes the things of the root and reveals them on the branch, so does the Spirit take the things of Christ and show them unto us, that they might be manifested through us.

3. THE FRUIT IS THE PROOF AND POWER OF THE CHRISTIAN. "By their fruit ye shall know them." The light of a Spirit filled life will lead others to glorify our Father in Heaven. If Christ dwells in our heart by faith the features of His character will be seen in our life.

IV. Preciousness of the Fruit.

1. IT BRINGS GLORY AND PRAISE TO GOD (Phil. 1. 11). Herein is my Father glorified that ye bear much fruit. Christ said, "I am the true Vine, My Father is the Husbandman." How much this Husbandman must have rejoiced over the fruit of this Vine.

2. IT BRINGS SATISFACTION TO THE HEART OF CHRIST (Cant. 4. 6). To see His own image in the lives of His people must be fruit sweet to His taste. The fruits that

bring praise to the Father are all His own. *"His* pleasant fruits."

3. IT IS A WITNESS TO THE GRACE AND POWER OF GOD (Acts 1. 8). A fruit-bearing Christian is a wonderful exhibition of Divine mercy. They are witnesses, through the Holy Spirit, to the mighty saving, satisfying power of Jesus Christ.

4. IT LEADS OTHERS TO BELIEVE IN GOD (Acts 2. 41). "They seeing your good works, may glorify your Father." When they saw the boldness of Peter and John they took knowledge of them that they had been with Jesus. If we abide in Christ we shall be like Joseph, "A fruitful bough by the well, whose branches run over the wall."

SPIRITUAL WEALTH.
Proverbs 10. 22.

1. It is Needed,   ..   "The Blessing."
2. It is Divine, ...   "The blessing of the Lord."
3. It is Abundant,   ..   "It maketh Rich."
4. It is Enduring,   ..   "He addeth no Sorrow."

WAKE UP.
1 Thessalonians 5. 6.

1. A melancholy fact—Others are asleep, because blind and insensible.

2. A timely warning—"Let us not sleep." Spiritually this is an age of drowsiness.

3. An urgent call—"Let us watch and be sober," because the Devil is busy, and Christ is coming.

GOSPEL OUTLINES.

THE GOSPEL TRUMPET.

JOEL 2. 15.

IT is surely most fitting, in the present religious condition, that at the opening of this year we should hear this urgent call to the Lord's trumpeters to "Sound an alarm." Spiritual slumber and apathy to soul-saving work seem to have settled down upon the modern Zion. "Minding earthly things" an attitude over which the apostle wept (Phil. 3. 19), appears to be the special tendency of the Church to-day. If the watchmen who *see this sword* are silent, who shall sound the alarm?

I. **The Trumpeters.** In Numbers 10. 8 they are the "*Sons* of Aaron," those who have come into the sacred privilege by *birth*. The trumpets were of silver that they might give a clear, sweet, distinct sound. The Gospel of God is no harsh, uncertain note, when sounded with loving, consecrated heart and lip. In Ezekiel 33. 6, the trumpeter is a watchman. The servant of God is not only a priest to worship, but also a watchman to warn. His eye is to be quick to discern the signs of the times, and His lip ready to sound forth the needful note.

II. **The Uses of the Trumpet**—may indicate the work of the preacher and the character of the Gospel.

1. It was blown OVER THE BURNT-OFFERINGS and sacrifices (Num. 10. 10). This was the joyful sound of atonement. Blessed are the people that know this trumpet sound (Psa. 89. 15, R.V., *margin*)—redemption and peace by the blood of His Cross.

2. It was blown AT THE ANOINTING OF A KING (2 Kings

9. 13). Sound out the tidings that the Crucified One is now crowned with glory and honour. This is what Peter did (see Acts 10. 38-40).

3. It was blown BEFORE THE ARK OF GOD (1 Chron. 15. 24). The coming of this symbol of His presence was heralded by the watchful, joyful trumpeter. "Behold, He cometh!" Sound out this blessed note, ye watchmen of the Lord.

4. It was BLOWN TO WARN (Ezek. 33. 4). The day of battle is ever with us. The power of sin and the hosts of Hell offer no truce. If there is no warning given, who shall prepare himself for the battle?

5. It was blown TO SOUND AN ALARM (Joel 2. 1). This prophet sees the mustering of the nations. "A day of darkness and of gloominess, a day of clouds and of thick darkness," for the "day of the Lord cometh." Sound an alarm, for the awful day is approaching when upon all "faces shall gather blackness" (v. 6). This note of "alarm" is not wanted in these days, but it never was more needed. Awake! Awake!

III. **The Responsibility of the Trumpeters.** Some of the trumpeters may be so blind that they do not *see* the danger; but if they see...and blow not the trumpet...the blood of those who perish, through their cowardly neglect, will God require at their hands (Ezek. 33. 6). The Lord's watchmen should be the first to see, and the first to sound the note or warning. A faithful witness delivereth souls. We should be instant in season, for the time will come when "the voice of...trumpeters shall be heard no more" (Rev. 18. 22).

————

THE LADDER OF GRACE.
COLOSSIANS 1. 9-14.

PAUL's letters are as much alive to-day as when they were first read in the Churches 1800 years ago. Why do they still live and thrive increasingly amid the fires of adverse criticism? Because the living breath of Christ is in them. Who could preach like Paul? Only those who could pray like him. The pulpit is weak to-day because the closet is cold. We have here one of Paul's wonderful prayers for his brethren. This passage seems like a ladder of grace, making a way from darkness to light, from emptiness to fullness, from death to life. Paul, standing on the heights of grace, counts the steps from the top downward; but we shall understand it better by beginning at the bottom. The first step, then, of this ladder of life is—

I. **Forgiveness.** Forgiveness of sins is the first blessing God offers man, although many think, in their ignorance, that this is the last benefit man can get from God. There is a good deal of Protestant Popery abroad—a kind of belief that God only forgives our sins when we come to die. If this was so, surely Paul must have been very presumptuous when he said, as he does here, that "In Him we *have* the forgiveness of sins." Until we have received the forgiveness of our sins, we have not advanced one step heavenward. The first round on the ladder is forgiveness. The second is—

II. **Redemption.** "We have redemption through His blood." To redeem means to buy back. In these evil days the redemptive work of Christ is largely ignored in certain quarters. When an article is taken out of the pawn, it is said to be redeemed, and when redeemed it is out of the hands of the broker, and into the hands of the purchaser. The old pawnbroker to whom we had sold ourselves for naught is the Devil. But Christ, having redeemed us by His blood, claims us as His own. The next step upward is—

III. **Translation.** "He hath translated us into the Kingdom of His dear Son." Only redeemed ones can grow in this Kingdom. The process of translating is a mystery. There is nothing like it in nature as far as we know. No passing from one kingdom into another. The mineral never becomes vegetable, and the vegetable never becomes animal. But by the grace of God a sinner can be translated into a saint. This is evidenced by the changed lives of many round about us.

IV. **Deliverance.** The next step is "delivered from the powers of darkness." Sin, like a mighty vampire, has spread its darkening wings over the minds of men. With regard to spiritual things, we are, apart from God—stone blind. The power of darkness is a fearful power. How many are enveloped in its misery. God delivers us from it by opening the eyes of our understanding, and planting our feet upon the rock of His eternal truth. The next step lifts us into great hope.

V. **Partakers.** "Made partakers of the inheritance of the saints in light." Partakers, not purchasers. It is said that in England's palace one day, the King asked his nobles by what title they held their lands. Immediately hundreds of swords flashed in the light. They replied, "By these we won them, and by these we will keep them." It is not so with us. Christ, the sword of our excellence, has conquered for us. We reap because He hath sown. We win because He hath triumphed. We inherit because He hath died. The next step is—

VI. **Strengthened.** This word reminds us that we are still in the place of weakness, work, and warfare; and suggests sufficiency for all our need. "Strengthened with all might." As thy days so shall thy strength be. But notice that the strength here spoken of is to be manifested in patience and longsuffering. Restlessness and a short temper are sure signs of weakness.

VII. **Fruitful** in every good **work** is the next round in this ladder. The work of Christ has brought the possibility of a truly successful life, within the reach of every man. If a man plants rotten potatoes he cannot expect good ones. The redeemed life should be fruitful in every good work. Apart from Christ our lives are as barren as branches severed from the vine. The last and highest experience is—

VIII. **Filled** with the knowledge of His will, etc. This implies walking in the light and rejoicing in certainties. The higher we climb in spiritual experience the more clear the air becomes. Many never seem to get out of cloudland; they seem content to abide in the midst of doubts and fears. How many of us have started on this ladder of life? Here is a man who wants to climb with the world on his back. Here is another riding on his church with the confession of faith under his arm. Here is another so filled with pride that he is puffed up like a publican or rather like a Pharisee. But the first step implies forgiveness—so the first act on our part must be confession.

———

BACKSLIDING—ITS CAUSE, COURSE, AND CURE.

Jeremiah 2. 1-37.

THE prodigal did not arrive among the swine the first day he left his father. The course of the backslider is gradual. A little thing at the fountain head may alter the course of a river. A little sin "in" the heart may change the current of a life. We have here—

I. **A Happy Condition.** "When thou wentest *after* Me in the wilderness Israel was holiness unto the Lord" (v. 3). These words suggest two important truths.

1. That to please God we must follow Him.

2. That in *following Him* we are *holiness* unto the Lord. Holiness is the fruit of obedience and fellowship. This is

the root thought of consecration, and exceedingly practical. While Peter was rejoicing in the Lord, he could say, "To whom can we go?" but when doubt and fear arose in his heart he forsook Him and fled. The obedient followers of Christ will never be found mourning beside the broken cisterns.

II. **A Foolish Step.** "They have forsaken Me and hewed them out broken cisterns," etc. (v. 13). God is the Fountain of living waters; when He is forsaken men have to *hew* for themselves. And what do they get for all their labours? "Broken cisterns that can hold no water." Disappointment (Rom. 10. 4). *Labouring* for living waters is an evidence of God unknown or God forsaken. It is the gift of God (John 4. 10). How vain to seek the streams without the fountain; how foolish to seek the blessing without the Blesser! "All my springs are in Thee." All my blessings in Christ are but foretastes of His inexhaustible fullness. The *forsaking* is always followed with the *hewing*. When a man has lost his pleasure in the prayer meeting he will be likely to seek it in the dram shop; when the Bible becomes dry the novel will be sought. "Broken cisterns."

III. **A Sorrowful Contrast.** "I planted thee a noble vine; how art thou turned into the degenerate plant?" (v. 21). Oh, think of it! Forsaking God means degeneration in life and character. If you have begun to pray less you have begun to degenerate. If you have a growing dislike for the company of the godly, the process of degeneration is fast going on. If you are not bearing the rich fruits of former years it is because you are a *degenerate* plant. The vine cannot thrive in a barren land; no more can ye. If we would continue to be fruitful, let us *abide* where the Lord hath planted us (Rom. 6. 3; John 15. 4).

IV. **A Fruitless Attempt.** "Though thou wash thee...

yet thine iniquity is marked before Me, saith the Lord"
(v. 22). It is very common for the backslider in heart to
keep up the *form* of godliness when the power is gone, but
though they take the nitre of earnestness and the much
soap of profession, yet is their iniquity marked before
God. Solemn words! Be not deceived; God is not mocked.
A backslider can no more wash himself than an unbelieving
sinner.   He that *covereth* his sins shall not prosper.   No
amount of outward pretence will atone for secret sin in
sight of God.

V. **A Solemn Change**. "Thou hast taught the wicked
ones thy ways: also in thy skirts is found the blood of
souls" (vv. 33, 34). How guilty and responsible are those
Christians who have forsaken the Lord and gone back to
the world. They dishonour Christ by their lives, which
teach the wicked a *Godless* religion—a religion the world
loves. By forsaking the blood that cleanseth from all sin
the blood of souls is on their skirts. If the light that is in
thee be darkness, how great is that darkness!

VI. **A Presumptuous Plea**. "Yet thou sayest, I am
innocent, I have not sinned" (v. 35). A backslider has
arrived at about the last stage of degeneration when he
begins to justify himself; he has got into the painless state
of spiritual mortification.

VII. **A Dismal Prospect**. "The Lord hath rejected
thy confidences, and thou shalt not prosper in them"
(v. 37). The confidence that is not placed in the Lord
Himself is sheer presumption. Special meetings may be
got up, new methods may be invented, some excitement
may be awakened, but if thy *heart* is not right with God
thou shalt not prosper. "Man looketh on the outward
appearance, but the Lord looketh on the heart" (1 Sam.
16. 7). It is possible for a backslider, in reforming his
manner of life, to regain the confidence of his Christian

brethren, but unless there is cleansing and heart restoration to God he shall not prosper. He may be a branch among the other branches, but if he is not in fellowship with the life-giving Vine he is but a withered branch, and shall not prosper.

VIII. A Gracious Remedy. "Return thou backsliding Israel, for I am merciful, saith the Lord" (chap. 3. 12). Oh, how simple the condition, "Only acknowledge thine iniquity" (v. 13). Oh, how encouraging the offer, "I am *merciful.*" Oh, how gracious the promise, "I will heal" (v. 22). If we confess our sins, He is faithful and just to forgive. David acknowledged his transgression and was forgiven (Psa. 32. 5). The prodigal confessed and was restored (Luke 15). Return, confess, rejoice.

SOLOMON AND THE QUEEN OF SHEBA;
Or, Christ and His Servants.
1 Kings 10. 1-10.

A greater than Solomon is here (Matt. 12. 42). We have perhaps a picture here of the glory that shall yet characterise the "Greater Solomon" and His servants in the age to come (Isa. 60. 1-6). What brought the Queen of Sheba to behold the wisdom and glory of Solomon has brought many a humbler one to behold the greater glory of Jesus, viz., "the hearing of faith." We might consider—

I. **What She Heard.** "She heard of his fame."

1. The Fame of his Riches. "Silver was nothing accounted in his days" (v. 21). But what are the riches of Christ? (Eph. 3. 8; Col. 2. 9).

2. The Fame of his Wisdom. This was the wisdom that cometh from above (1 Kings 3. 12). Many seek after wisdom (v. 24) who reject Christ, the wisdom of God (1 Cor. 1. 24-30; James 1. 5).

3. THE FAME OF HIS POWER. Concerning the *Name of the Lord.* If Solomon's intimacy with God made him great, what must we say of Him who was "God manifest in the flesh?" (Phil. 2. 9).

II. What She Did. She did not make light of it, like those in Matthew 22. 5. Nor postpone it like Felix (Acts 24. 25).

1. SHE CAME TO HIM. This was much better than merely thinking *about* him. When the prodigal came to himself he came to his Father (John 6. 37).

2. SHE COMMUNED WITH HIM. "She told him all that was in her heart" (v. 2), and the king hid nothing from her (v. 3). A full confession brings fullness of blessing (Psa. 32. 5-7). Oh, the joy of telling Jesus! Cast thy burden on the Lord (Matt. 14. 12).

III. What She Saw.

1. SHE SAW HIS WISDOM. Having come to Christ, the wisdom of God in the scheme of redemption has greatly amazed us (Eph. 1. 4-8).

2. SHE SAW HIS HOUSE. The Church of Christ as an house fitly framed together is the next marvel (Eph. 2. 19-22).

3. SHE SAW HIS TABLE. The great and liberal provision God has made in Christ for His own (2 Cor. 9. 8).

4. SHE SAW HIS ASCENT. (Probably the arched viaduct that led from his house to the Temple.) The ascent of the "Greater than Solomon" was much more glorious (Acts 1. 9).

5. SHE SAW HIS SERVANTS. (*a*) Their *position*— "Sitting" (Luke 10. 39). (*b*) Their *privilege*—"Continually with thee *hearing thy wisdom*" (v. 8; John 6. 45). (*c*) Their *pleasure*—"Happy are these, thy servants" (v. 8; Psa. 100. 2; Rom. 5. 11).

IV. What Followed. The results were manifest—

1. SHE WAS HUMBLED. "There was no more spirit in her." Seeing the Lord means a downfall (Acts 9. 4; Rev. 1. 17).

2. SHE CONFESSED. "It was a true report." Those who come to Jesus will be forced to acknowledge the truth of the Gospel.

3. SHE PRAISED. "Blessed be the Lord." This is the result of a satisfied soul (Psa. 103. 1-5).

4. SHE GAVE. "She gave the king gold" (v. 10) "Yield *yourselves* unto God" (Rom. 12. 1, 2).

ELIJAH ON CARMEL;
OR, FAITH VINDICATED.
1 KINGS 18. 19-39.

THERE are only two religions: (1) The Religion of Man; (2) The Religion of God. Man's religion may have much that is attractive and pleasing to men, but it lacks *power* and *authority*. It is a lifeless body. The religion of God is attested as Divine by miraculous fire from Heaven in answer to believing prayer (v. 37; Acts 2. 3). We have here—

I. The Religion of Form and its Followers.

1. THEY ARE MANY. "Baal's prophets are four hundred and fifty" (v. 22). A depraved religion will always be popular with a depraved humanity (Matt. 27. 21). The proverb, *"Vox populi, vox Dei,"* is in spiritual matters untrue (Matt. 7. 13).

2. THEY ARE EARNEST. They cried aloud and cut themselves with knives," etc. (v. 28). Zeal, but not according to knowledge (Rom. 10. 3), is like a steam-engine on the wrong track. Good misdirected.

3. THEY ARE DECEIVED. "Neither was there voice, nor any to answer" (v. 29). The favour and power of God is not to be purchased with self-effort (Titus 3. 5; Acts

8. 20). The fire of the heavenly baptism will not come upon us by leaping upon the altar and *cutting ourselves* (1 Cor. 13. 3), it is by *faith* (Gal. 3. 14; John 7. 38, 39).

II. **The Religion of God and His Worshippers.** It cannot be said of Christians that they worship they know not what (1 John 5. 20).

1. THEY are COMPARATIVELY FEW. "I only remain" (v. 22). Here is but one against four hundred and fifty, but that one is not Elijah, but *God*, whom Elijah trusted. The battle is the Lord's (read 1 John 4. 4).

2. THEY ARE DELIBERATELY FAITHFUL. "Come near unto Me." See the calmness of Elijah. No "leaping and cutting" with him. He makes not haste, because he believes in God (Isa. 28. 16). Oh, for such faith (James 5. 17).

3. THEY ARE DIVINELY FAVOURED. "Then the fire of the Lord fell" (v. 38). Our God is a consuming fire. When He comes He consumes the stony heart, and licks up the dust of sin (Matt. 3. 11, 12).

III. **The Call of the Prophet for Decision.** "How long halt ye between two opinions?" (v. 21). Notice—

1. THAT THERE ARE TWO OPINIONS. God's and man's. "My thoughts are not your thoughts, saith the Lord." They are as wide apart as light and darkness. Which do you follow? (See Psalm 139. 17).

2. THAT THERE ARE MANY WHO HALT BETWEEN THEM. The choice is between the "wisdom of man" and the "wisdom of God" (1 Cor. 1. 19-30), between sin unto death and obedience unto righteousness (Rom. 6. 16).

3. THAT THEY ONLY ARE SAFE WHO DECIDE FOR GOD. When the *people* saw it they said, "The Lord, He is God," but the *prophets* were slain at the brook (v. 39). What are the results of seeing the "goodness and severity of God" at the Cross of Christ?

SOME FACTS ABOUT PRAYER, FOR MEN.
LUKE 18. 1.

"MEN ought always to pray, and not to faint." So said the Lord of men and of salvation. Then—

I. Prayer is a **real** thing. It is something of intrinsic value. "He that cometh to God must believe that He is" (Heb. 11. 6). A man once confessed that, "Before I was converted I prayed to nobody. Now I pray to God."

II. Prayer is a **simple** thing. Any child can pray. It is the offering up of our desires unto God. It is asking because we feel our need, and believe that we can receive. There is no mystery in this.

III. Prayer is a **desirable** thing. "Men *ought* to pray." They ought to pray, just as they ought to work and eat. Men ought to deal fairly with God, as they ought to deal fairly with their fellowmen. It is their duty and privilege.

IV. Prayer is a **manly** thing. "*Men* ought to pray." Man is the only animal that can naturally look up. Some men live the brutish life by never looking up. Lift up your face to God, and maintain your dignity as a man.

V. Prayer is a **constant** thing. "Men ought *always* to pray." He ought to keep on praying, just as he keeps on desiring. Men ought to exercise their bodies daily to be healthy and strong; so ought they to exercise their souls toward God. Continue in work if you wish to grow rich in the world's goods. Continue in prayer if you would grow rich in faith and grace.

VI. Prayer is a **testing** thing. "And not to faint." It is easy to grow weary in this well doing. Ye shall reap if ye faint not. Praying always and *not fainting* is the evidence of strong faith. The trial of your faith is precious.

VII. Prayer is a **profitable** thing. "Ask and ye shall receive." Our Lord would never have said that "Men ought always to pray" if He did not mean always to give. As a proof of this, see the little parable in verses 2-7.

THE FAITHFUL SAYING.

1 TIMOTHY 1. 15.

THIS is the Apostle's own testimony, a declaration of his own experience (vv. 12-15). The "saying" is not his own, he got it from others. It is of world-wide significance.

I. **It Reveals the Love of God.** Nature may seem "red, tooth and claw." God is love.

II. **It Reveals the Grace of Christ.** "Christ Jesus came into the world." Where from? What to do? (1 Cor. 8. 9).

III. **It Reveals the Need of Man.** "Came into the world to *save sinners.*" He came not as a capitalist to assist in case of failure, but as a Saviour to save.

IV. **It is a Faithful Saying.** It is in perfect accord with the character of God and the condition of men. It has come from the lips of Him who is the Truth (John 7. 17).

V. **It is Worthy of all Acceptation.** Worthy of being accepted by all, and worthy of being altogether accepted by all classes and conditions of men.

EBENEZER.

1 SAMUEL 7. 12.

THE circumstances connected with this "stone of help" are suggestive of the way into spiritual victory. There was—

1. **Conscious Need.** "All . . . lamented after the Lord" (v. 2).

2. **Confession Made.** "We have sinned" (v. 6).

3. **Separation Demanded.** "Put away strange gods... serve Him only" (v. 3).

4. **Substitution Acknowledged.** "Samuel took a sucking lamb" (v. 9).

5. **Deliverance Wrought.** "The Lord thundered... and discomfited" (v. 10).

6. **Testimony Given.** "Hitherto hath the Lord helped us" (v. 12).

_____

THE RULE OF CHRIST'S PEACE.
COLOSSIANS 3. 15.

1. **A Wonderful Theme.** "The peace of Christ" (R.V.). Nothing could disturb it (John 14. 27).

2. **A Blessed Possession.** "The peace of Christ in your hearts." In Me ye have peace (John 16. 33).

3. **A Happy Government.** "The peace of Christ *rule* in your hearts" (arbitrate, R.V., *margin*).

4. **A Gracious Calling.** "To the which also ye were called." We don't climb into it, we are called into it.

5. **A Mystical Union.** "In one body."

6. **A God-honouring Result.** "Be ye thankful" (Eph. 5. 20).

_____

"CERTAINLY I WILL BE WITH THEE."
EXODUS 3. 12.

THINK of—

1. The **Character** of His Presence.

2. The **Purpose** of His Presence. Guide, defend, comfort.

3. The **Power** of His Presence. Purity, plenty, progress, praise.

_____

LESSONS FROM THE HARVESTFIELD.
SONG OF SOLOMON 7. 11.

"LET us go forth into the field" and learn—

1. That a **harvest time will come.** Seed sown shall not always remain a *hidden* thing.

2. That **much comes from little.** Some an hundredfold. They who sow wind, reap whirlwind.

3. That **a fruitful life comes through death.** "Except a corn of wheat die, it abideth alone."

4. That **like comes from like.** "Whatsoever a man soweth, *that* shall he reap."

5. That **when we cease to grow we begin to die.**

6. That **grain is most valued when ripe.**

7. That **the chaff and the wheat grow together.**

8. That **the harvesting does not alter its character.**

9. That **the harvest is followed with a sifting.**

FEAR NOT.
ISAIAH 43. 1-10.

FEAR not, for—

1. I have **redeemed thee** (v. 1). Purchase.

2. I have **called thee** (v. 1). Grace.

3. I will be **with thee** (v. 2). Fellowship.

4. I have **loved thee** (v. 4). Favour.

5. I will **gather thee** (v. 5). Hope.

6. I have **created thee** for My glory. Privilege.

7. Ye are **My witnesses** (v. 10). Responsibility.

THE BELIEVER'S JOY IN THE LORD.
HABAKKUK 3. 17-19.

1. The believer has **joy.** "I will rejoice" (v. 18).

2. It is joy **in the Lord.** "I will joy in...God."

3. It is the **joy of salvation.** "I will joy in the God of my salvation."

4. It s the **joy of satisfaction.** "My strength."

5. It is the **joy of anticipation.** "He will make me to walk upon high places."

6. It is a joy that **adversity cannot destroy.** "Although...yet" (vv. 17, 18).

WONDERFUL LOVE.
Ezekiel 16. 4-14.

I. The Condition of the Sinner.

1. UNWASHED. "Neither wast thou washed" (v. 4).
2. UNPITIED. "None eye pitied thee" (v. 5).
3. EXPOSED. "Cast out in the open field" (v. 5).
4. LOATHSOME. "To the loathing of thy person."
5. OPPRESSED. "Trodden underfoot" (v. 6, *margin*).

II. The Love of the Saviour. Seen in His—

1. COMING NEAR. "I passed thee by" (v. 6).
2. INFINITE COMPASSION. "I looked upon thee; behold thy time was a time of love" (v. 8).
3. WORD OF POWER. "I said unto thee, Live" (v. 6).

III. The Privileges of the Saved.

1. SHELTERED. "I spread My skirt over thee" (v. 8).
2. WASHED. "Then washed I thee" (v. 9).
3. CLOTHED. "I clothed thee" (v. 10).
4. ANOINTED. "I anointed thee" (v. 9).
5. GIRDED. "I girded thee" (service) (v. 10).
6. ADORNED. "I decked thee with ornaments" (v. 11). "Thy beauty perfect through *My* comeliness" (v. 14).
7. CROWNED. "I put a beautiful crown upon thy head" (v. 12). Saved by grace alone.

THE BLESSED MAN.
Psalm 112.

I. The Cause of his Blessedness.

1. He FEARS THE LORD (v. 1).
2. He has a fixed TRUST in the Lord (v. 7).
3. He has a CHARACTER like the Lord's (v. 4, *l.c.*).

II. The Nature of his Blessedness.

1. He has DELIGHT in the Word of God (v. 1).

2. His CHILDREN are honoured (v. 2).

3. His HOUSE is well furnished (v. 3).

4. His RIGHTEOUSNESS endureth for ever (v. 3 .

5. He has LIGHT in time of darkness (v. 4).

6. He is SAVED from all fear (vv. 7, 8).

7. He shall be EXALTED (v. 9, *l.c.*).

8. His ENEMIES shall be humbled (v. 10).

THE EXPERIENCES OF A SOUL.
PSALM 119.

1. Breaking (v. 20).

2. Cleaving (v. 25).

3. Melting (v. 28).

4. Fainting (v. 81).

5. Waiting (v. 109).

6. Trusting (v. 167).

7. Longing (v. 175).

THE DIVINE KEEPER.
PSALM 121.

THE word "keeper" occurs in this Psalm six times in the Revised Version.

I. His Ability to Keep.

1. ALMIGHTY. "Made the Heaven and the earth."

2. EVER AWAKE. "He slumbereth not."

II. The Manner of His Keeping.

1. He keeps the SOUL (v. 7, R.V.).

2. He keeps from OPPRESSION. "The Lord thy *Shade*" (vv. 5, 6).

3. He keeps from EVIL (v. 7).

4. He keeps while in the routine of DAILY BUSINESS. "Thy going out and thy coming in" (v. 8).

5. He keeps to the END. "Even for evermore."

CAPTIVITY TURNED INTO SINGING.
PSALM 126.

THERE was—

1. **Bondage**. "Captivity of Zion" (v. 1).

2. **Prayer**. "Turn again our captivity, O Lord" (v. 4).

3. **Answer**. "The Lord turned" (v. 1).

4. **Astonishment**. "We were like them that dream" (v. 1).

5. **Joyfulness**. "Our mouths filled with laughter and singing" (v. 2).

6. **Fruitfulness**. "Then said they," etc.

7. **Encouragement**. "They that sow in tears shall reap in joy" (vv. 5, 6).

———

HE IS ABLE.
PSALM 145. 14-21.

1. To **Uphold** the fallen (v. 14).

2. To **Raise** the bowed down (v. 14).

3. To **Give Meat** in due season (v. 15).

4. To **Satisfy** the living (v. 16).

5. To **Fulfil the** desires of them that fear Him (v. 19).

6. To **Save** them that cry (v. 19).

7. To **Preserve** them that love Him (v. 20).

———

EBENEZER.
1 SAMUEL 7. 12.

I. **The Way to it.**

1. CONFESSION. "We have sinned" (v. 6).

2. CONVERSION. "Return unto the Lord" (v. 3).

3. CONSECRATION. "Prepare your heart and serve Him only" (v. 3).

II. **The Manner of it.**   It was through—
  1. SACRIFICE. "A lamb for a burnt offering" (**v**. 10).
  2. INTERCESSION.   "Samuel cried unto the Lord."
  3. JUDGMENT.   "The Lord thundered" (v. 10).

III. **The Influence of it.**
  1. Look UP. "The Lord hath."
  2. Look BACK. "Hitherto."
  3. Look BEYOND.   "He hath" and He will.

CHRIST OUR LIFE.
COLOSSIANS 3. 4.

  1. He is the **Source** of it (John 10. 10).
  2. He is the **Confidence** of it (John 10. 28).
  3. He is the **Sustenance** of it (John 6. 50).
  4. He is the **Object** of it (Phil. 1. 21).
  5. He is the **Example** of it (1 Peter 2. 21).
  6. He is the **Security** of it (Col. 3. 3).
  7. He is the **Crown** of it (James 1. 12).

HAVE FAITH IN GOD.
MARK 11. 22.

THIS is a word of encouragement for the—
  1. **Seeking Sinner** (Acts 16. 31).
  2. **Trembling Believer** (Psalm 73. 23).
  3. **Tempted Follower** (Gen. 15. 1).
  4. **Bereaved Sufferer** (Gen. 45. 26).
  5. **Penitent Backslider** (Isaiah 55. 7).
  6. **Discouraged Worker** (Isaiah 59. 19).
  7. **Dying Christian** (Psalm 23. 4).

THE YOKE OF CHRIST.

MATTHEW 11. 28, 29.

1. What it Means. Fellowship *with Himself*, walking with Him. Gripped and fastened to the same divine purpose.

2. Who are to Take it? All who would follow Him, sharing His sufferings and glory.

3. What is Found in it? "Rest to the soul." Rest in His will, way, and work.

———

THE FACE OF JESUS.

To see His face is to get a vision of Jehovah Jesus. What is to be seen in that face?

1. Perfection. "The glory of God in the face of Jesus" (2 Cor. 4. 6).

2. Consecration. "Look upon the face of Thine anointed" (Psalm 84. 9).

3. Determination. "He stedfastly set His face to go up, etc." (Luke 9. 51).

4. Substitution. "His visage (face) was so marred more than any man" (Isa. 52. 14; Isa. 53. 2, 3).

5. Rejection. "They did spit on His face" (Matt. 26. 67).

6. Glorification. "His face like the sun" (Rev. 1. 16; Matt. 17. 2).

7. Consummation. "From whose face the earth and the Heaven fled away" (Rev. 20. 11).

8. Salvation. "Cause Thy face to shine and we shall be saved" (Psalm 80. 3). Seek His face (Psalm 27. 8).

PETER'S FALL.

MARK 14.

DOWNWARD steps—

1. **Self-confidence,** ..   ..   ..   verse 29.
2. **Proud Boasting,**   ..   ..   verse 31.
3. **Unwatchfulness,** ..   ..   ..   verse 37.
4. **Cowardliness,**   ..   ..   ..   verses 50-54.
5. **Ungodly Company,**   ..   ..   verse 54.
6. **Denying the Lord,**   ..   ..   verse 71.
7. **Weeping,** ..   ..   verse 72.

RARE YOUNG MEN.

1 JOHN 2. 14.

1. Their **character**. "Ye are strong."
2. The **evidence** of their strength. "Ye have overcome the wicked one."
3. The **source** of their strength. "The Word of God abideth in you." His Word is pure, peaceable, and powerful.

THE WORD OF GOD NO VAIN THING.

DEUTERONOMY 32. 47.

I. **What the Word of God is Not.** "It is not a vain thing."

1. Because its QUICKENING power is needed (Psa. 119. 5).
2. Because it has ILLUMINATING power (Psa. 119. 105).
3. Because of its IRRESISTIBLE power (Jer. 23. 29).

II. **To Whom it is No Vain Thing.** "It is no vain thing *for you*." For *you* who have heard and believed.

III. **Why it is No Vain Thing.** "Because it is *your life*."

1. It is the SOURCE of your life (1 Peter 1. 23-25).
2. It is the SUSTENANCE of your life (1 Peter 2. 2).
3. It is the STRENGTH of your life (Eph. 6. 17).

THE LADDER OF GRACE.

COLOSSIANS 9. 1-14.

THIS passage should be read in its reverse order to get progressive experience.

1. **Forgiveness** of sins (v. 14).
2. **Redemption** through blood (v. 14).
3. **Translated** into the Kingdom (v. 13).
4. **Delivered** from the power of darkness (v. 13).
5. **Partakers** of the inheritance (v. 12).
6. **Strengthened** with all might (v. 11).
7. **Fruitful** in every good work (v. 10).
8. **Filled** with the knowledge of His will (v. 9).

EMBLEMS OF THE CHURCH.

1. **As a pearl** it is costly (Matt. 13. 46).
2. **As an house** it is orderly (1 Peter 2. 5).
3. **As a pillar** it is a witness (1 Tim. 3. 5).
4. **As a flock** it is dependent (1 Peter 5. 2).
5. **As a family** it bears His image (Eph. 3. 15).
6. **As a wife** it is vitally connected (Rev. 19. 7).
7. **As a body** it is all of one (Eph. 1. 22, 23).
8. **As a candlestick** it is exalted (Rev. 1. 12).

SETTLED.

PSALM 119. 89.

I. **What is Settled?** "O Lord Thy Word is settled."

II. **Where is it Settled?** "Settled in Heaven."

III. **What is the Result of this Settlement?**

1. This is a ROCK OF REFUGE for the weary (Matt. 11. 28).

2. This is a STAFF OF STRENGTH for the Christian (John 10. 35).

3. This is a DART OF DEFIANCE for the Devil (Eph 6. 17).

4. This is a DISMAL DIRGE for the impenitent (Psa. 9. 17; John 3. 36).

ENOCH.
HEBREWS 11. 5, 6.

THIS is a short but most inspiring biography. **"Enoch"** means *dedicated.*

1. He **pleased God.** This proves that he had *faith* in God (v. 6).

2. He **knew** that he pleased God. "He had this testimony." This must have been to him a great source of *comfort* and *courage.*

3. **How** he pleased God. "He *walked* with God" (Gen. 5. 24).

4. The **result** of pleasing God. "He was translated." Death had no power over him. It is so with the life that is hid with Christ in God. "By *faith* he was translated."

THE POWER OF THE SPIRIT.
ACTS 1. 8.

To the believer the power of the Spirit is the power of an ever present Divine *Personality* (John 16. 7-14).

1. His is **convicting** power (John 16. 8, *margin*).

2. His is **life-giving** power (John 6. 63).

3. His is **teaching** power (John 16. 13).

4. His is **revealing** power (John 16. 14).

5. His is **witnessing** power (Acts 1. 8; Rom. **8. 16**).

6. His is **interceding** power (Rom. 8. 26).

7. His is **indwelling** power (1 Cor. 3. 16; 6. 19)

"BELIEVE AND THOU SHALT SEE."
John 11. 40.

This statement may be regarded as a word of—

1. **Rebuke** to the questioning unbeliever.
2. **Guidance** to the anxious seeker.
3. **Comfort** to the suffering believer.
4. **Cheer** to the discouraged worker.
5. **Hope** to the dying Christian.

————

HEART-TROUBLE AND ITS CURE.
John 14. 1.

I. **The Disease.** *Heart*-trouble. "Let not your heart be troubled." This disease is *common*. Its causes *varied*. Its cure humanly impossible.

II. **The Remedy.** "Ye believe in God, *believe also in Me.*" In Me—

1. As the Son of the Father (v. 2).
2. As the Provider for His own (v. 2).
3. As the Way to the Father (v. 6).
4. As the Image of the Father (v. 9).
5. As the Representative of the Father (vv. 10, 11).
6. As the Answerer of prayer (vv. 13, 14).
7. As the Giver of the Holy Spirit (v. 16).
8. As the Coming One (v. 3).

————

WHAT MEANETH THIS?
Acts 2. 12.

The gift of the Holy Spirit, which was a source of "amazement" to some and "mockery" to others, is full of precious meaning to us who believe.

1. It means that He who died for our sins is **now exalted** at the right hand of God (v. 33; John 7. 39).

2. It means the **fulfilment of prophecy** (v. 16).

3. It means that Christ has *power* to **fulfil His promises** (chap. 1. 5; 11. 4).

4. It means **power for testimony** (vv. 17, 18).

5. It means **fullness of blessing** for every believer' (vv. 38, 39).

6. It means that God can **mightily use weak things** (v. 7).

7. It means that God would have **all men to be saved** (v. 21).

_____

ASSURANCE OF VICTORY.
JOHN 16. 33.

1. The Christian's **Sphere of Service.** "In the world."

2. The Christian's **Source of Suffering.** "In the world ye shall have tribulation."

3. The Christian's **Secret of Comfort.** "In Me ye might have peace."

4. The Christian's **Source of Joy.** "Be of good cheer."

5. The Christian's **Assurance of Victory.** "I have overcome the world."

_____

HEART-SEARCHING.
1 SAMUEL 16. 7.

1. **Two Aspects of Man.** The "outward appearance" and the "heart." These are often contradictory.

2. **The Judgment of Men.** "Man looketh on the outward appearance."

3. **The Judgment of God.** "The Lord looketh on the heart." Man says, "Reform." God says, "Repent."

SEED THOUGHTS.

———

SEED AND BREAD.

"For as the rain cometh down from Heaven.. that it may give seed to the sower and bread to the eater, so shall My Word be that goeth forth out of My mouth" (Isa. 55. 10, 11).

THE seed is the word, and the Word of God is the incorruptible seed. As the rain comes down from Heaven to water the earth, so this Word comes forth from the mouth of God to revive the hearts of men.

Oh, ye pilgrim witnesses, that go over the broad field of this world as sowers for the Son of Man, see to it that the basket of your heart is filled with the good seed of the Kingdom.

The Word of God is God's own seed for the sower. Ye need no other. All else is chaff compared with this. But remember it is not merely Scriptural words you are to sow, it is the *Word of God*, or God's own message to men; and you will find that this seed will grow best when planted in its native shell of simple Scripture language. This seed is also to be the "bread of the eater." If the Word of God is not the food and strength of the preacher's own soul, he will sow it but sparingly indeed. All who live must eat. If we live by faith in the Son of God, His Word will be sweet unto our taste. ———

THE WORD AND THE HAND.

"Now Lord, grant unto Thy servants, that with all boldness they may speak Thy Word, by stretching forth Thine hand to heal" (Acts 4. 29, 30).

GREAT boldness is needed to preach God's Word. There

are so many who are ready to *threaten* when His Word is courageously spoken. But after all something more is needed if souls are to be wounded with a sense of sin, and healed by His mighty grace. Unless *His hand* is stretched forth with His Word, no healing power will be felt. The hand of God's Spirit is greatly hindered where there is doubting and fearfulness; but don't let us imagine that our boldness and faithfulness alone will suffice to bring souls to Christ. We must remember that it is the "Spirit that quickeneth." Along with our testimony there must be stretched forth that almighty and invisible hand that can lay hold on the hearts of ungodly men and turn them whithersoever He will. When this hand is stretched forth signs and wonders will be done. Have faith in God.

THE SHADOW OF PETER.

"They brought forth the sick into the streets, that at least the shadow of Peter passing by might overshadow them" (Acts 5. 15).

EVERY shadow was not the shadow of Peter. It took two things to make Peter's shadow—*light* and his own *presence.* Wherever Peter went walking in the light he carried with him the influence of his shadow. Every Christian, walking in the light of God, will have a shadow accompanying him. Those who walk in the darkness of doubt will carry no healing virtue with their presence. Alas for those who are aping at somebody else, and losing the power of their *own* presence. No sick ones will be helped by the shadow (influence) of such hollow pretenders.

THE FACE OF AN ANGEL.

"And looking stedfastly on Stephen, saw his face, as it had been the face of an angel" (Acts 6. 15).

THERE are but few angel faces to be seen in this selfish, sin-distorted world. The features of the soul not infrequently stamp themselves upon the countenance. If the angelic image of Jesus has been impressed upon the "inner man," some of the halo of His glory will be seen without. Observe it was when Stephen was charged with *blasphemy* that the sweet calmness of an angel rested upon his face, proving that in this holy man's heart there was no railing for railing, but *contrariwise*. When some Christians are being persecuted and maligned, the face of a fiend is more easily seen. Oh, love your enemies, and pray for them that despitefully use you (Acts 7. 60).

———

PRAYER AND HUNGER.

"*Peter went up to pray, and he became very hungry*" (Acts 10. 9, 10).

PRAYER is a healthy exercise. There are many who know nothing of real soul-hunger, because they spend so little time in prayer. Lack of prayer is one of the most fruitful causes of spiritual dyspepsia. Much prayer creates much hunger for the Word of God, which is the bread of life. If you have lost, or are losing, your appetite for spiritual things, arise and pray, and soon you will be glad to "Arise and eat."

———

BELIEVING AND TURNING.

"*A great number believed and turned unto the Lord*" (Acts 11. 21).

WHAT good will your so-called belief do you if it has not resulted in your *turning* to the Lord? Many profess to believe, but they continue in their sins. The faith that saves is the faith that turns our hearts and lives to Christ. It is not your believing that saves, but the Lord on whom alone your faith must rest. It is not, "Believe and be saved," but, "Believe *on the Lord Jesus Christ*, and thou shalt be saved."

SMITTEN.

"The angel of the Lord smote him, because he gave not God the glory" (Acts 12. 23).

THE cause of the sudden downfall of this proud ruler should be a warning to all, especially to the preacher. Public speakers are greatly tempted to seek the honours of man more than God. The worms of pride and self-conceit have already begun their destructive work when we cease to give God the glory. It is quite possible to make a great oration and preach very eloquently, and yet at the same time, as far as spiritual power is concerned, be smitten of God. In the eyes of men the appearance may be as fair and beautiful as Jonah's gourd, but if God is not honoured the deadly canker-worm is at the roots.

ALTARS OF BRICK.

"A people that provoked Me to My face, burning incense upon altars of brick" (Isa. 65. 3).

As the altar sanctifieth the gift, it must therefore be holy. God had expressly said that in making an altar of stone: "If thou lift thy tool upon it thou hast polluted it" (Exod. 20. 25). On the altar, the gifts of the worshippers are to be laid, therefore the *altar* itself must not in any way represent the *workmanship* of the offerer. Is it not to be feared that many still provoke the Lord to His face by offering incense on altars of brick. The altar of the Cross is ignored, and the mud-burned altar of human wisdom and self-righteousness is substituted, offering God any-thing, on the ground of our own worthiness is simply provoking Him to His face (Rom. 10. 1-4).

DO NOTHING RASHLY.

"Ye men of Ephesus, seeing that these things cannot be spoken against, ye ought to be quiet and do nothing rashly" (Acts 19. 36).

It was a wholesome advice the town clerk gave the uproarious multitude who crowded the theatre at Ephesus, and who had been yelling for two hours, "Great is Diana of the Ephesians!" He seemingly had great faith in the image which fell down from Jupiter, and so had no fear of men damaging the character of the divine goddess. Might Christians not now be the better of the town clerk's counsel amidst this uproar about the methods of so-called "Higher" and rationalistic critics of the Holy Scriptures? We believe the truth revealed in the Bible has come down from Heaven, and cannot be successfully spoken against. Therefore let us be quiet and do nothing rashly.

———

"I THANK MY GOD."

"I thank my God always on your behalf, for the grace of God which is given you" (1 Cor. 1. 4).

It is delightfully easy to thank God for the grace we ourselves have received, but it requires great grace to thank God *always* for the grace which is given to others. Even Christans are apt to be jealous and envious, thinking themselves better fitted to serve God than their neighbours. Such selfishness can never walk in the fellowship of the Spirit. "In honour preferring one another." We are unfit to be used of God as long as we are unwilling to acknowledge and thank God for the grace and gifts He has bestowed on others for the edifying of the Body, the Church. This readiness to thank God always for the grace given to others shows a spirit in full and sweetest fellowship with the mind and purposes of God.

SPEECH AND POWER.

"I will know not the speech of them which are puffed up, but the power" (1 Cor. 4. 19).

"THAT was a good speech." "He is a very eloquent speaker." Such language is common, but Paul has another way of judging such tongue deliverances. "I will know not the speech, but the *power*." Unspiritual minds can only judge the speech, the outward form—they know not the power. What power is this, by which the very heart-life of Christians is revealed? It is that holy, gracious, gentle, heart-melting, inscrutable something called "anointing," that makes eternal and spiritual things very real and precious and powerful to those who hear. The Holy Spirit acting through the heart and speech of the preacher. Without this power all preaching is but as sounding brass and tinkling cymbals. May our speech be always seasoned with such salt.

SUFFERINGS AND CONSOLATION.

"For as the sufferings of Christ abound in us, so our consolation also aboundeth by Christ" (2 Cor. 1. 5).

THE sufferings of Christ were peculiar. He suffered on account of His holiness. He was so like the Father—being "the image of the invisible God"—that all who loved not the Father hated Him. He suffered also because of His faithfulness. He spoke the truth, and because the world loved not the truth He was despised and rejected of men. If we, as Christians, have consecrated ourselves to God to do His will and to manifest His truth, as Christ did, we shall understand something of the sufferings of Christ. But it is here where we are misunderstood and hated by the world, that the "consolation also aboundeth by Christ." To drink deeply of the heavenly comfort, we must enter fully into the spirit and sympathies of Christ.

THE OPEN FACE.

*"But we all with open face, beholding as in a glass, the
glory of the Lord, are changed into the same image"*
(2 Cor. 3. 18).

THE open face is needed in approaching the mirror of God's
Holy Word, if we would see ourselves as we really are, and
be transfigured into the image of the Lord of glory. The
Word of God will have no transforming power in our hearts
if we look into it only with that blinking critical eye that
proudly sits in judgment upon the truth. The Lord give
us that frank, open, honest face that rejoices in the truth,
that our inner man may be changed into His image. If
the truth of God transforms not our hearts and lives, we
have not the open face.

WHAT SEEK YE?

*"Then Jesus turned and saw them following, and saith
unto them, What seek ye?"* (John 1. 38).

JESUS did not say, "Whom seek ye?" because He knew
they sought Himself; but, "What seek ye?" What is it
in Me that ye seek? Ah, this opens a wide door of entrance, there is so much in Jesus worth seeking. Some
only seek to look at Him, others seek His forgiving smile.
There are others who seek to know His dwelling-place,
that they might abide with Him. What seekest thou,
O my soul? Seek His wisdom to guide thee. Seek His
peace to possess thee, His power to keep thee, His Spirit
to abide in thee and transform thee into His Divine
image. Seek that His will may be done in thee as it is
done in Heaven, and that His presence may be an abiding
reality with thee. Seek, and ye shall find.

GOD AT HAND.

"Am I a God at hand, saith the Lord, and not a God afar off?" (Jer. 23. 23).

WHAT a comfort to the believer that God, even our God, has been pleased to reveal Himself as a God *at hand*. Always within reach, always at hand to answer the cry of need, and to bless the touch of faith. Oh, the fullness of love and power that dwells in Him, and all this at hand for every time of need. Why should we be fretful and discontented with such a Friend continually at hand? But, alas, how many deal with Him as if He were for ever afar off and beyond the grasp of their feeble faith. "Lo, I am with you alway." A God at hand! What strength this should give. What holy courage this Divine nearness should inspire.

————

THE BREAD OF GOD.

"For the Bread of God is He which cometh down from Heaven, and giveth life unto the world" (John 6. 33).

THE Bread of God is not only the bread of life, but the life-giving and life-sustaining bread from Heaven. God has in mercy reckoned up the real need of this poverty-stricken, starving-to-death world; and so gave His Son, as His gift of bread, for famished souls. The bread of fashion, of riches, or worldly preferment, soon becomes stale. There is no real soul-nutriment in the bread baked in the world's oven. The life-giving bread must come from the life-giving God. Jesus Christ, the Bread of God—the Bread that delights the heart of God—and, oh, what grace that this Bread has come from Heaven to give life unto the world. Have you received it? Are you feeding on it? He that eateth this Bread shall live for ever.

HIMSELF FOR OUR SINS.

"Our Lord Jesus Christ, who gave Himself for our sins"
(Gal. 1. 3, 4).

WHAT a contrast! Himself—our sins. He gave the law
to expose our sins. He gave Himself for our sins. The
law is a schoolmaster to bring us to Christ. How deep
must the love of Christ be for sinful man, when He *gave*
Himself as a price for the redemption of the guilty. How
helpless and hopeless man's condition must have been when
nothing less than HIMSELF could suffice to save. How
wide the door of salvation must now be, since Himself
hath opened it. He gave Himself—the well-beloved Son.
How willingly God the Father would accept this gift!
Having given Himself, men have now their choice between
Himself and their sins. Receive Him!

NOT AFTER MAN.

*"But I certify you, brethren, that the Gospel which was
preached of me is not after man* (Gal. 1. 11).

THE Gospel is not after man's wisdom, for it is foolishness
to the worldly-wise. It is not after man's affections; the
carnal mind is enmity against it. Seeing then that the
Gospel is contrary to the mind and will of man, it could
not be evolved out of the inner consciousness of man.
It is not of man, neither can it be of the Devil, who hates
it unto death. It is of God. This truth was burnt into the
very bones of Paul's moral nature, and should burn in
the bones of every Christian—born, not of the flesh, nor
of the will of man, but of God. The Gospel is supernatural and Divine, therefore doth the natural man
despise it. To them that believe it is the power of God.

THE PURCHASED POSSESSION.

"Until the redemption of the purchased possession, unto the praise of His glory" (Eph. 1. 14).

THIS is a truth, great, deep, and wonderful. This title embraces the whole Church of God, and suggests the mystery of God's gracious and eternal purpose. God has a possession—this possession is His people, redeemed by the blood of His Son (v. 7), and sealed with the Spirit of promise (v. 13). In this present time God, by the Spirit through the Gospel, is gathering out a people for Himself. Not yet has He got the full lot of His inheritance, but they shall be Mine, saith the Lord, when I make up my jewels. How marvellous that by His death and resurrection, Christ, in purchasing an inheritance for us in God, should at the same time and by the same means purchase an inheritance for God in us who are His people. By and by the kingdom shall be delivered up to the Father, and God shall be All in all.

ROOTED.

"Rooted and built up in Him" (Col. 2. 7).

YES, rooted and *built* up. Not stuck in and *tied* up. The tree that is well rooted does not need outward props to keep it right. Rooted in Christ. Every longing and desire centred on Him, and abiding in Him, will be fully supplied from Him.

From Christ must come the building material. In me, that is, in my flesh, dwelleth no good thing. We are built up in His likeness, just as His Spirit, as the life-giving sap, flows and abides in us. Out of Him there is no life, and consequently no growth, no building up.

We will be unhealthy Christians unless *all* the roots of our being are resting in Christ alone. Rooted in Him, barrenness will be impossible.

HIS SON IN ME.

"It pleased God to reveal His Son in me" (Gal. 1. 15, 16).

WHAT a revelation! Paul had Christ revealed *to* him on the way to Damascus. Now he speaks of Christ revealed *in* him. What a change! The image of the invisible God begotten in him! What a mystery! What a reality! His Son in me, in the gentleness and meekness of His gracious character. His Son in me in His love for perishing sinners. His Son in me in His patience in suffering. His Son in me in His faithfulness to the truth. His Son in me in His delight to do the will of God the Father. His Son in me! This is the death-warrant to pride, self-seeking, and every unhallowed lust; to all backbiting and every impure motive. His Son in me—this is the secret of consecration, and of a life of power and fruitfulness for God. "I am crucified with Christ, nevertheless I live, yet not I, but Christ liveth in me."

THE UNSEARCHABLE RICHES OF CHRIST.

"Unto me, who am less than the least of all saints, is this grace given, that I should preach the unsearchable riches of Christ" (Eph. 3. 9).

THIS may be regarded as the explanatory title of Christ's great atoning work. All the difficulties and mysteries of redemption are met and revealed in the "unsearchable riches of Christ." How can a sinner's guilt be put away and the sinner justified? How can a heart at enmity with God be changed and filled with the love of God? How can the righteous claims of a holy law be satisfied with regard to those who have no power and no desire to yield to its claims? How can God be just and yet justify the ungodly? How can the poor soul of man be possessed with the Spirit of God and brought into the fullness of Divinity, being conformed into His image? The answer to all this, and infinitely more, is found in these wonderful words: "The unsearchable riches of Christ."

FOLLOWERS OF GOD.

"Be ye therefore followers of God as dear children" (Eph. 5. 1).

THE root idea here is the *imitation* of God. We cannot imitate those we do not know. To imitate God we must know Him, and to know Him means eternal life, without which we can in no way resemble Him. Imitating God means the manifestation of a life which is Divine. Christ was the perfect *image* of His Father. He must so live in us that this Divine imitation may be begotten in our character and lives. He has left us an example, that we should follow His steps. It is so much easier imitating some eminent Christian than Christ, and in so doing become self-satisfied. Are we imitating God in His compassion for the perishing, in His jealousy for His own glory, in His mercy and longsuffering, in His self-sacrificing love?